Understanding Operating Systems

Seventh Edition

Ann McIver McHoes

Ida M. Flynn

CENGAGE
Learning·

Australia • Canada • Mexico • Singapore • Spain • United Kingdom • United States

CENGAGE
Learning®

**Understanding Operating Systems,
Seventh Edition**
Ann McIver McHoes
Ida M. Flynn

Senior Product Manager: Jim Gish

Product Director: Kathleen McMahon

Senior Content Developer: Alyssa Pratt

Product Assistant: Sarah Timm

Content Project Manager: Jennifer
Feltri-George

Senior Rights Acquisitions Specialist:
Christine Myaskovsky

Art Director: Cheryl Pearl, GEX

Manufacturing Planner: Julio Esperas

Cover Designer: Cheryl Pearl, GEX

Cover Photos: ©Dabarti CGI/Shuttershock

Compositor: Integra

> For product information and technology assistance, contact us at
> **Cengage Learning Customer & Sales Support,
> www.cengage.com/support**
> For permission to use material from this text or product,
> submit all requests online at **www.cengage.com/permissions**
> Further permissions questions can be emailed to
> **permissionrequest@cengage.com**

Library of Congress Control Number: 2013945460

ISBN-13: 978-1-285-09655-1

ISBN-10: 1-285-09655-X

Cengage Learning
20 Channel Center Street
Boston, MA 02210
USA

Some of the product names and company names used in this book have been used for identification purposes only and may be trademarks or registered trademarks of their respective manufacturers and sellers.

Any fictional data related to persons, or companies or URLs used throughout this book is intended for instructional purposes only. At the time this book was printed, any such data was fictional and not belonging to any real persons or companies.

Cengage Learning reserves the right to revise this publication and make changes from time to time in its content without notice.

Cengage Learning is a leading provider of customized learning solutions with office locations around the globe, including Singapore, the United Kingdom, Australia, Mexico, Brazil and Japan. Locate your local office at: **www.cengage.com/global**

Cengage Learning products are represented in Canada by Nelson Education, Ltd.

To learn more about Cengage Learning, visit **www.cengage.com**

Purchase any of our products at your local college store or at our preferred online store **www.cengagebrain.com**

Printed in the United States of America
2 3 4 5 6 7 19 18 17 16 15

Contents

Contents

Chapter 7   Device Management   209

Chapter 8   File Management   255

Part Two — Operating Systems in Practice — 405

Chapter 13 — UNIX Operating Systems — 407

Chapter 16   Android Operating Systems   497

Appendix

Glossary

Bibliography

Index

Preface

Is this book for you? In these pages, we explain a very technical subject in a not-so-technical manner, putting the concepts of operating systems into a format that many readers can quickly grasp.

For those who are new to the subject, this text demonstrates what operating systems are, what they do, how they do it, how their performance can be evaluated, and how they compare with each other. Throughout the text we describe the overall function and lead readers to additional resources where they can find more detailed information, if they so desire.

For those with more technical backgrounds, this text introduces the subject concisely, describing the complexities of operating systems without going into intricate detail. One might say this book leaves off where other operating system textbooks begin.

To do so, we've made some assumptions about our audiences. First, we assume the readers have some familiarity with computing systems. Second, we assume they have a working knowledge of an operating system and how it interacts with them. We recommend (although we don't require) that readers be familiar with at least one operating system. In the few places where, in previous editions, we used pseudocode to illustrate the inner workings of the operating systems, we have moved that code to the Appendix. In those places, we use a prose description that explains the events in familiar terms. The algorithms are still available but by moving them to the Appendix, we have simplified our explanations of some complex events.

Organization and Features

This book is structured to explain the functions of an operating system regardless of the hardware that houses it. The organization addresses a recurring problem with textbooks about technologies that continue to change—that is, the constant advances in evolving subject matter can make textbooks immediately outdated. To address this problem, we've divided the material into two parts: first, the concepts—which do not change quickly—and second, the specifics of operating systems—which change dramatically over the course of years and even months. Our goal is to give readers the ability to apply the topics intelligently, realizing that, although a command, or series of commands, used by one operating system may be different from another, their goals are the same and the functions of the operating systems are also the same.

Although it is more difficult to understand how operating systems work than to memorize the details of a single operating system, understanding general operating system concepts is a longer-lasting achievement. Such understanding also pays off in the long run because it allows one to adapt as technology changes—as, inevitably, it does. Therefore, the purpose of this book is to give computer users a solid background in the basics of operating systems, their functions and goals, and how they interact and interrelate.

Part One, the first 12 chapters, describes the theory of operating systems. It concentrates on each of the "managers" in turn and shows how they work together. Then it introduces network organization concepts, security, ethics, and management of network functions. Part Two examines actual operating systems—how they apply the theories presented in Part One and how they compare with each other.

Chapter 1 gives a brief introduction to the subject. The meat of the text begins in Chapters 2 and 3 with memory management because it is the simplest component of the operating system to explain and has historically been tied to the advances from one operating system to the next. We explain the role of the Processor Manager in Chapters 4, 5, and 6, first discussing simple systems and then expanding the discussion to include multiprocessing systems. By the time we reach device management in Chapter 7 and file management in Chapter 8, readers will have been introduced to the four main managers found in every operating system. Chapters 9 and 10 introduce basic concepts related to networking, and Chapters 11 and 12 discuss security, ethics, and some of the tradeoffs that designers consider when attempting to satisfy the needs of their user population.

Each chapter includes learning objectives, key terms, and research topics. For technically oriented readers, the exercises at the end of each chapter include problems for advanced students. Please note that some advanced exercises assume knowledge of matters not presented in the book, but they're good for those who enjoy a challenge. We expect some readers from a more general background will cheerfully pass them by.

In an attempt to bring the concepts closer to home, throughout the book we've added real-life examples to illustrate abstract concepts. However, let no one confuse our conversational style with our considerable respect for the subject matter. The subject of operating systems is a complex one and it cannot be covered completely in these few pages. Therefore, this textbook does not attempt to give an in-depth treatise of operating systems theory and applications. This is the overall view.

Part Two introduces four operating systems in the order of their first release: UNIX, Windows, Linux, and the most recent, Android. Here, each chapter discusses how one operating system applies the concepts discussed in Part One and how it compares with the others. Again, we must stress that this is a general discussion—an in-depth examination of an operating system would require details based on its current standard version, which can't be done here. We strongly suggest that readers use our discussion as a guide—a base to work from—when comparing the advantages and disadvantages of a specific operating system and supplement our work with current research that's readily available on the Internet.

The text concludes with several reference aids. Terms that are important within a chapter are listed at its conclusion as key terms. The extensive end-of-book Glossary includes brief reader-friendly definitions for hundreds of terms used in these pages. The Bibliography can guide the reader to basic research on the subject. Finally, the Appendix features pseudocode algorithms and the ACM Code of Ethics.

Not included in this text is a detailed discussion of databases and data structures, except as examples of process synchronization problems. This is because these structures only tangentially relate to operating systems and are frequently the subject of other courses. We suggest that readers begin by learning the basics as presented in the following pages before pursuing these complex subjects.

Changes to the Seventh Edition

This edition has been thoroughly updated and features many improvements over previous editions:

- A new chapter featuring the Android operating system
- New chapter spotlights on industry innovators; award-winning individuals who have propelled operating system technologies.
- Numerous new examples of operating system technology
- Updated references to the expanding influence of wireless technology
- New collection of memory and processor management pseudocode algorithms in the Appendix for those who want to understand them in greater detail.
- Enhanced discussion of patch management and system durability
- New discussions of Amdahl's law and Flynn's taxonomy
- More discussion describing the management of multiple processors
- Updated detail in the chapters that discuss UNIX, Windows, and Linux
- New homework exercises in every chapter

The MS-DOS chapter that appeared in previous editions has been retired. But, in response to faculty requests, it continues to be available in its entirety from the Cengage website so adopters can still allow students to learn the basics of this command-driven interface using a Windows emulator.

Numerous other changes throughout the text are editorial clarifications, expanded captions, and improved illustrations.

A Note for Instructors

The following supplements are available when this text is used in a classroom setting. All supplements can be downloaded from the Instructor Companion Site. Simply search for this text at sso.cengage.com. An instructor login is required.

Electronic Instructor's Manual. The Instructor's Manual that accompanies this textbook includes additional instructional material to assist in class preparation, including Sample Syllabi, Chapter Outlines, Technical Notes, Lecture Notes, Quick Quizzes, Teaching Tips, and Discussion Topics.

ExamView® Test Bank. This textbook is accompanied by ExamView, a powerful testing software package that allows instructors to create and administer printed, computer, and Internet exams. ExamView includes hundreds of questions that correspond to the topics covered in this text, enabling students to generate detailed study guides that include page references for future review.

PowerPoint Presentations. This book comes with Microsoft PowerPoint slides for each chapter. These are included as a teaching aid for classroom presentations, either to make available to students on the network for chapter review, or to be printed for classroom distribution. Instructors can add their own slides for additional topics that they introduce to the class.

Solutions. Selected solutions to Review Questions and Exercises are provided.

Order of Presentation

We have built this text with a modular construction to accommodate several presentation options, depending on the instructor's preference. For example, the syllabus can follow the chapters as listed in Chapter 1 through Chapter 12 to present the core concepts that all operating systems have in common. Using this path, students will learn about the management of memory, processors, devices, files, and networks, in that order. An alternative path might begin with Chapter 1, move next to processor management in Chapters 4 through 6, then to memory management in Chapters 2 and 3, touch on systems security and management in Chapters 11 and 12, and finally move to device and file management in Chapters 7 and 8. Because networking is often the subject of another course, instructors may choose to bypass Chapters 9 and 10, or include them for a more thorough treatment of operating systems.

We hope you find our discussion of ethics helpful in Chapter 11, which is included in response to requests by university adopters of the text who want to discuss this subject in their lectures.

In Part Two, we examine details about four specific operating systems in an attempt to show how the concepts in the first 12 chapters are applied by a specific operating system. In each case, the chapter is structured in a similar manner as the chapters in Part One. That is, they discuss the management of memory, processors, files, devices, networks, and systems. In addition, each includes an introduction to one or more user interfaces for that operating system. To illustrate the use of graphical user interfaces in UNIX systems, we include references to the Macintosh OS X operating system in the UNIX chapter.

With this edition, we have added a discussion of the Android operating system. By adding this software, specifically written for use in a mobile environment using phones and tablets, we are able to explore the challenges unique to these computing situations.

If you have suggestions for inclusion in this text, please send them along. Although we are squeezed for space, we are pleased to consider all possibilities.

Acknowledgments

Our gratitude goes to all of our friends and colleagues, who were so generous with their encouragement, advice, and support over the two decades of this publication. Special thanks go to Bob Kleinmann, Eleanor Irwin, and Roger Flynn for their assistance.

As always, thanks to those at Cengage, Brooks/Cole, and PWS Publishing who have made significant contributions to all seven editions of this text, especially Alyssa Pratt, Kallie Swanson, Mike Sugarman, and Mary Thomas Stone. In addition, the following individuals made key contributions to this edition: Jennifer Feltri-George, Content Project Manager, and Suwathiga Velayutham, Integra.

We deeply appreciate the comments of the reviewers who helped us refine this edition:

Larry Merkle, Computational Optimization Services; Michelle Parker, Indiana University—Purdue University Fort Wayne; and Kong-Cheng Wong, Governors State University.

And to the many students and instructors who have sent helpful comments and suggestions since publication of the first edition in 1991, we thank you. Please keep them coming.

Ann McIver McHoes, mchoesa@duq.edu

Ida M. Flynn

Part One

Operating Systems Concepts

"Dost thou not see ... the bees working together to put in order theirseveral parts of the universe?"

—Marcus Aurelius Antoninus (121–180)

Like honey bees, the core mechanisms of operating systems must work together to manage the operating system's memory, processing capability, devices and peripherals, files, and networks—and do so in an appropriate and secure fashion. Here in Part One, we present an overview of these operating systems essentials.

- Chapter 1 introduces the subject.
- Chapters 2 and 3 discuss main memory management.
- Chapters 4 through 6 cover processor management.
- Chapter 7 concentrates on device management.
- Chapter 8 is devoted to file management.
- Chapters 9 and 10 briefly review networks.
- Chapter 11 discusses system security.
- Chapter 12 explores system management.

In Part Two (Chapters 13 through 16), we look at four specific operating systems and how they apply the concepts presented here in Part One.

Throughout our discussion of this very technical subject, we try to include definitions of terms that might be unfamiliar to you, but it isn't always possible to describe a function and define the technical terms while keeping the explanation clear. Therefore, we've put the key terms with definitions at the end of each chapter and again in the glossary at the end of the text. Items listed in the Key Terms are shown in **boldface** the first time they are mentioned significantly.

Throughout the book we keep our descriptions and examples as simple as possible to introduce you to the system's complexities without getting bogged down in technical detail. Therefore, remember that for almost every topic explained in the following pages, there's much more information available for you to study. Our goal is to introduce you to the subject and to encourage you to pursue your personal interests using other sources. Enjoy.

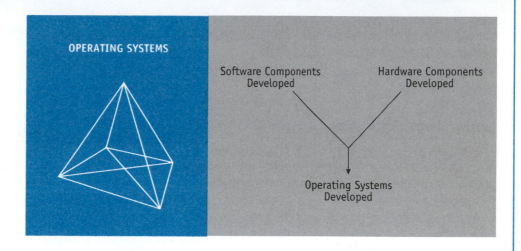

Chapter 1 | Introducing Operating Systems

OPERATING SYSTEMS

Software Components Developed → ← Hardware Components Developed

↓

Operating Systems Developed

❝*I think there is a world market for maybe five computers.*❞

—attributed to Thomas J. Watson (1874–1956; chairman of IBM 1949–1956)

Learning Objectives

After completing this chapter, you should be able to describe:

• Innovations in operating systems development

• The basic role of an operating system

• The major operating system software subsystem managers and their functions

• The types of machine hardware on which operating systems run

• The differences among batch, interactive, real-time, hybrid, and embedded operating systems

• Design considerations of operating systems designers

Introduction

To understand an operating system is to begin to understand the workings of an entire computer system, because the operating system software manages each and every piece of hardware and software. In the pages that follow, we explore what operating systems are, how they work, what they do, and why.

This chapter briefly describes the workings of operating systems on the simplest scale. The following chapters explore each component in more depth and show how its function relates to the other parts of the operating system. In other words, you see how the pieces work together harmoniously to keep the computer system working smoothly.

What Is an Operating System?

A computer system typically consists of software (programs) and hardware (the tangible machine and its electronic components). The operating system software is the chief piece of software, the portion of the computing system that manages all of the hardware and all of the other software. To be specific, it controls every file, every device, every section of main memory, and every moment of processing time. It controls who can use the system and how. In short, the operating system is the boss.

Therefore, each time the user sends a command, the operating system must make sure that the command is executed, or if it's not executed, it must arrange for the user to get a message explaining the error. Remember: this doesn't necessarily mean that the operating system executes the command or sends the error message—but it does control the parts of the system that do.

Operating System Software

The pyramid shown in Figure 1.1 is an abstract representation of the operating system in its simplest form and demonstrates how its major components typically work together.

At the base of the pyramid are the four essential managers of every major operating system: the **Memory Manager, Processor Manager, Device Manager,** and **File Manager.** These managers and their interactions are discussed in detail in Chapters 1 through 8 of this book. Each manager works closely with the other managers as each one performs its unique role. At the top of the pyramid is the User Interface, which allows the user to issue commands to the operating system. Because this component has specific elements, in both form and function, it is often very different from one operating system to the next—sometimes even between different versions of the same operating system.

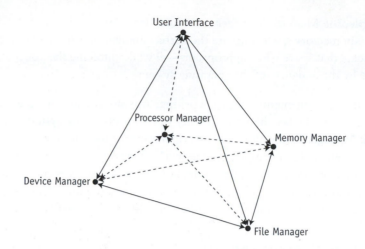

Regardless of the size or configuration of the system, the four managers illustrated in Figure 1.2 must, at a minimum, perform the following tasks while collectively keeping the system working smoothly:

• Monitor the system's resources

• Enforce the policies that determine what component gets what resources, when, and how much

• Allocate the resources when appropriate

• Deallocate the resources when appropriate

(figure 1.2)

Each manager at the base of the pyramid takes responsibility for its own tasks while working harmoniously with every other manager.

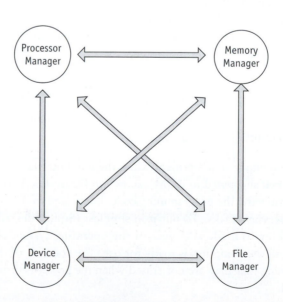

For example, the Memory Manager must keep track of the status of the computer system's main memory space, allocate the correct amount of it to incoming processes, and deallocate that space when appropriate—all while enforcing the policies that were established by the designers of the operating system.

An additional management task, networking, was not always an integral part of operating systems. Today the vast majority of major operating systems incorporate a **Network Manager** to coordinate the services required for multiple systems to work cohesively together. For example, the Network Manager must coordinate the workings of the networked resources, which might include shared access to memory space, processors, printers, databases, monitors, applications, and more. This can be a complex balancing act as the number of resources increases, as it often does.

Main Memory Management

The Memory Manager (the subject of Chapters 2 and 3) is in charge of main memory, widely known as **RAM** (short for random access memory). The Memory Manager checks the validity of each request for memory space, and if it is a legal request, allocates a portion of memory that isn't already in use. If the memory space becomes fragmented, this manager might use policies established by the operating systems designers to reallocate memory to make more useable space available for other jobs that are waiting. Finally, when the job or process is finished, the Memory Manager deallocates its allotted memory space.

A key feature of RAM chips—the hardware that comprises computer memory—is that they depend on the constant flow of electricity to hold data. When the power fails or is turned off, the contents of RAM is wiped clean. This is one reason why computer system designers attempt to build elegant shutdown procedures, so the contents of RAM can be stored on a nonvolatile device, such as a hard drive, before the main memory chips lose power during computer shutdown.

A critical responsibility of the Memory Manager is to protect all of the space in main memory, particularly that occupied by the operating system itself—it can't allow any part of the operating system to be accidentally or intentionally altered because that would lead to instability or a system crash.

Another kind of memory that's critical when the computer is powered on is **Read-Only Memory** (often shortened to **ROM**), shown in Figure 1.3. This ROM chip holds software called **firmware**, the programming code that is used to start the computer and perform other necessary tasks. To put it in simplest form, it describes in prescribed steps when and how to load each piece of the operating system after the power is turned on and until the computer is ready for use. The contents of the ROM chip are nonvolatile, meaning that they are not erased when the power is turned off, unlike the contents of RAM.

RAM is the computer's main memory and is sometimes called "primary storage" to distinguish it from "secondary storage," where data is stored on hard drives or other devices.

Processor Management

The Processor Manager (discussed in Chapters 4 through 6) decides how to allocate the central processing unit (CPU); an important function of the Processor Manager is to keep track of the status of each job, process, thread, and so on. We will discuss all of these in the chapters that follow, but for this overview, let's limit our discussion to **processes** and define them as a program's "instance of execution." A simple example could be a request to solve a mathematical equation: this would be a single job consisting of several processes, with each process performing a part of the overall equation.

The Processor Manager is required to monitor the computer's CPU to see if it's busy executing a process or sitting idle as it waits for some other command to finish execution. Generally, systems are more efficient when their CPUs are kept busy. The Processor Manager handles each process's transition, from one state of execution to another, as it moves from the starting queue, through the running state, and finally to the finish line (where it then tends to the next process). Therefore, this manager can be compared to a traffic controller. When the process is finished, or when the maximum amount of computation time has expired, the Processor Manager reclaims the CPU so it can allocate it to the next waiting process. If the computer has multiple CPUs, as in a multicore system, the Process Manager's responsibilities are greatly complicated.

Device Management

The Device Manager (the subject of Chapter 7) is responsible for connecting with every device that's available on the system and for choosing the most efficient way to allocate each of these printers, ports, disk drives, and more, based on the device scheduling policies selected by the designers of the operating system.

Good device management requires that this part of the operating system uniquely identify each device, start its operation when appropriate, monitor its progress, and finally deallocate the device to make the operating system available to the next waiting process. This isn't as easy as it sounds because of the exceptionally wide range of devices

A flash memory device is an example of secondary storage because it doesn't lose data when its power is turned off.

that can be attached to any system. For example, let's say you're adding a printer to your system. There are several kinds of printers commonly available (laser, inkjet, inkless thermal, etc.) and they're made by manufacturers that number in the hundreds or thousands. To complicate things, some devices can be shared, while some can be used by only one user or one job at a time. Designing an operating system to manage such a wide range of printers (as well as monitors, keyboards, pointing devices, disk drives, cameras, scanners, and so on) is a daunting task. To do so, each device has its own software, called a **device driver**, which contains the detailed instructions required by the operating system to start that device, allocate it to a job, use the device correctly, and deallocate it when it's appropriate.

File Management

The File Manager (described in Chapter 8), keeps track of every file in the system, including data files, program files, utilities, compilers, applications, and so on. By following the access policies determined by the system designers, the File Manager enforces restrictions on who has access to which files. Many operating systems allow authorized individuals to change those permissions and restrictions. The File Manager also controls the range of actions that each user is allowed to perform with files after they access them. For example, one user might have read-only access to a critical database, while the systems administrator might hold read-and-write access and the authority to create and delete files in the same database. Access control is a key part of good file management and is tightly coupled with system security software.

When the File Manager allocates space on a secondary storage device (such as a hard drive, flash drive, archival device, and so on), it must do so knowing the technical requirements of that device. For example, if it needs to store an archival copy of a large file, it needs to know if the device stores it more efficiently as one large block or in several smaller pieces that are linked through an index. This information is also necessary for the file to be retrieved correctly later. Later, if this large file must be modified after it has been stored, the File Manager must be capable of making those modifications accurately and as efficiently as possible.

Network Management

Operating systems with networking capability have a fifth essential manager called the Network Manager (the subject of Chapters 9 and 10) that provides a convenient way for authorized users to share resources. To do so, this manager must take overall responsibility for every aspect of network connectivity, including the requirements of the available devices as well as files, memory space, CPU capacity, transmission connections, and types of encryption (if necessary). Networks with many available resources require management of a vast range of alternative elements, which enormously complicates the tasks required to add network management capabilities.

Networks can range from a small wireless system that connects a game system to the Internet, to a private network for a small business, to one that connects multiple computer systems, devices, and mobile phones to the Internet. Regardless of the size and complexity of the network, these operating systems must be prepared to properly manage the available memory, CPUs, devices, and files.

User Interface

The user interface—the portion of the operating system that users interact with directly—is one of the most unique components of an operating system. Two primary types are the **graphical user interface** (GUI) shown in Figure 1.4 and the **command line interface.** The GUI relies on input from a pointing device such as a mouse or your finger. Specific menu options, desktops, and formats often vary widely from one operating system to another (and sometimes from one version to another).

The alternative to a GUI is a command line interface, which responds to specific commands typed on a keyboard and displayed on the monitor, as shown in Figure 1.5. These interfaces accept typed commands and offer skilled users powerful additional control because typically the commands can be linked together (concatenated) to perform complex tasks with a single multifunctional command that would require many mouse clicks to duplicate using a graphical interface.

While a command structure offers powerful functionality, it has strict requirements for every command: each must be typed accurately, each must be formed in correct syntax, and combinations of commands must be assembled correctly. In addition, users need to know how to recover gracefully from any errors they encounter. These command line interfaces were once standard for operating systems and are still favored by power users but have largely been supplemented with simple, forgiving graphical user interfaces.

(figure 1.4)

An example of the graphical user interface (GUI) for Ubuntu Linux.

(figure 1.5)

Using the Linux command line interface to show a partial list of valid commands.

Cooperation Issues

None of the elements of an operating system can perform its individual tasks in isolation—each must also work harmoniously with every other manager. To illustrate this using a very simplified example, let's follow the steps as someone chooses a menu option to open a program. The following series of major steps are typical of the discrete actions that would occur in fractions of a second as a result:

1. The Device Manager receives the electrical impulse caused by a click of the mouse, decodes the command by calculating the location of the cursor, and sends that information through the User Interface, which identifies the requested command. Immediately, it sends the command to the Processor Manager.

2. The Processor Manager then sends an acknowledgment message (such as "waiting" or "loading") to be displayed on the monitor so the user knows that the command has been sent successfully.

3. The Processor Manager determines whether the user request requires that a file (in this case a program file) be retrieved from storage or whether it is already in memory.

4. If the program is in secondary storage (perhaps on a disk), the File Manager calculates its exact location on the disk and passes this information to the Device Manager, which retrieves the program and sends it to the Memory Manager.

5. If necessary, the Memory Manager finds space for the program file in main memory and records its exact location. Once the program file is in memory, this manager keeps track of its location in memory.

6. When the CPU is ready to run it, the program begins execution by the Processor Manager. When the program has finished executing, the Processor Manager relays this information to the other managers.

7. The Processor Manager reassigns the CPU to the next program waiting in line. If the file was modified, the File Manager and Device Manager cooperate to

store the results in secondary storage. (If the file was not modified, there's no need to change the stored version of it.)

8. The Memory Manager releases the program's space in main memory and gets ready to make it available to the next program to require memory.

9. Finally, the User Interface displays the results and gets ready to take the next command.

Although this is a vastly oversimplified demonstration of a very fast and complex operation, it illustrates some of the incredible precision required for an operating system to work smoothly. The complications increase greatly when networking capability is added. Although we'll be discussing each manager in isolation for much of this text, remember that no single manager could perform its tasks without the active cooperation of every other manager.

Cloud Computing

One might wonder how **cloud computing** (in simplest terms, this is the practice of using Internet-connected resources to perform processing, storage, or other operations) changes the role of operating systems. Generally, cloud computing allows the operating systems to accommodate remote access to system resources and provide increased security for these transactions. However, at its roots, the operating system still maintains responsibility for managing all local resources and coordinating data transfer to and from the cloud. And the operating system that is managing the far-away resources is responsible for the allocation and deallocation of all its resources—this time on a massive scale. Companies, organizations, and individuals are moving a wide variety of resources to the cloud, including data management, file storage, applications, processing, printing, security, and so on, and one can expect this trend to continue. But regardless of where the resource is located—in the box, under the desk, or the cloud, the role of the operating system is the same—to access those resources and manage the system as efficiently as possible.

An Evolution of Computing Hardware

To appreciate the role of the operating system (which is software), it may help to understand the computer system's **hardware**, which is the physical machine and its electronic components, including memory chips, the central processing unit (CPU), the input/output devices, and the storage devices.

- **Main memory (RAM)** is where the data and instructions must reside to be processed.
- The **central processing unit (CPU)** is the "brains" of the computer. It has the circuitry to control the interpretation and execution of instructions. All storage

Platform	Operating System
Telephones, tablets	Android, iOS, Windows
Laptops, desktops	Linux, Mac OS X, UNIX, Windows
Workstations, servers	Linux, Mac OS X Server, UNIX, Windows Server
Mainframe computers	Linux, UNIX, Windows, IBM z/OS
Supercomputers	Linux, UNIX

(table 1.1)

A brief list of platforms and a few of the operating systems designed to run on them, listed in alphabetical order.

references, data manipulations, and input/output operations are initiated or performed by the CPU.

- Devices, sometimes called I/O devices for input/output devices, include every peripheral unit attached to the computer system, from printers and monitors to magnetic disk and optical disc drives, , flash memory, keyboards, and so on.

At one time, computers were classified by memory capacity, which is no longer the case. A few of the operating systems that can be used on a variety of platforms are shown in Table 1.1.

In 1965, Intel executive Gordon Moore observed that each new processor chip contained roughly twice as much capacity as its predecessor (number of components per integrated function), and that each chip was released within 18–24 months of the previous chip. His original paper included a graph (shown in Figure 1.6) predicting that the trend would cause computing power to rise exponentially over relatively brief periods of time, and it has. Now known as Moore's Law, the trend has continued and

Mac OS X, HP-UX, and Sun Solaris are only three of many operating systems that are based on UNIX.

(figure 1.6)

Gordon Moore's 1965 paper included the prediction that the number of transistors incorporated in a chip will approximately double every 24 months [Moore, 1965].

Courtesy of Intel Corporation.

Number of components per integrated function for minimum cost per component extrapolated vs time.

is still remarkably accurate. Moore's Law is often cited by industry observers when making their chip capacity forecasts.

Types of Operating Systems

Operating systems fall into several general categories distinguished by the speed of their response and the method used to enter data into the system. The five categories are batch, interactive, real-time, hybrid, and embedded systems.

Batch systems feature jobs that are entered as a whole and in sequence. That is, only one job can be entered at a time, and once a job begins processing, then no other job can start processing until the resident job is finished. These systems date from early computers, when each job consisted of a stack of cards—or reels of magnetic tape—for input and were entered into the system as a unit, called a batch. The efficiency of a batch system is measured in **throughput,** which is the number of jobs completed in a given amount of time (usually measured in minutes, hours, or days.)

Interactive systems allow multiple jobs to begin processing and return results to users with better response times than batch systems, but interactive systems are slower than the real-time systems we talk about next. Early versions of these operating systems allowed each user to interact directly with the computer system via commands entered from a typewriter-like terminal, and the operating system used complex algorithms to share processing power (often with a single processor) among the jobs awaiting processing. Interactive systems offered huge improvements in response over batch-only systems with **turnaround times** in seconds or minutes instead of hours or days.

Real-time systems are used in time-critical environments where reliability is critical and data must be processed within a strict time limit. This time limit need not be ultra-fast (though it often is), but system response time must meet the deadline because there are significant consequences of not doing so. They also need to provide contingencies to fail gracefully—that is, preserve as much of the system's capabilities and data as possible to facilitate recovery. Examples of real-time systems are those used for spacecraft, airport traffic control, fly-by-wire aircraft, critical industrial processes, and medical systems, to name a few. There are two types of real-time systems depending on the consequences of missing the deadline: hard and soft systems.

- Hard real-time systems risk total system failure if the predicted time deadline is missed.
- Soft real-time systems suffer performance degradation, but not total system failure, as a consequence of a missed deadline.

Although it's theoretically possible to convert a general-purpose operating system into a real-time system by merely establishing a deadline, the need to be extremely predictable is not part of the design criteria for most operating systems so they can't provide the guaranteed response times that real-time performance requires. Therefore, most embedded systems (described below) and real-time environments require operating systems that are specially designed to meet real-time needs.

Hybrid systems, widely used today, are a combination of batch and interactive. They appear to be interactive because individual users can enter multiple jobs or processes into the system and get fast responses, but these systems actually accept and run batch programs in the background when the interactive load is light. A hybrid system takes advantage of the free time between high-demand usage of the system and low-demand times.

Networks allow users to manipulate resources that may be located over a wide geographical area. Network operating systems were originally similar to single-processor operating systems in that each machine ran its own local operating system and served its own local user group. Now network operating systems make up a special class of software that allows users to perform their tasks using few, if any, local resources. One example of this phenomenon is cloud computing.

As shown in Figure 1.7, wireless networking capability is a standard feature in many computing devices: cell phones, tablets, and other handheld Web browsers.

Embedded systems are computers that are physically placed inside the products that they operate to add very specific features and capabilities. For example, embedded systems can be found in automobiles, digital music players, elevators, and pacemakers, to

✔ One example of software available to help developers build an embedded system is Windows Embedded Automotive.

(figure 1.7)

Example of a simple network. The server is connected by cable to the router and other devices connect wirelessly.

name a few. Computers embedded in automobiles facilitate engine performance, braking, navigation, entertainment systems, and engine diagnostic details.

Operating systems for embedded computers are very different from those for general computer systems. Each one is designed to perform a set of specific programs, which are not interchangeable among systems. This permits the designers to make the operating system more efficient and take advantage of the computer's limited resources (typically slower CPUs and smaller memory resources), to their maximum.

Before a general-purpose operating system, such as Linux, UNIX, or Windows, can be used in an embedded system, the system designers must select which operating system components are required in that particular environment and which are not. The final version of this operating system generally includes redundant safety features and only the necessary elements; any unneeded features or functions are dropped. Therefore, operating systems with a small kernel (the core portion of the software) and other functions that can be mixed and matched to meet the embedded system requirements have potential in this market.

Grace Murray Hopper (1906–1992)

Grace Hopper developed one of the world's first compilers (intermediate programs that translate human-readable instructions into zeros and ones that are the language of the target computer) and compiler-based programming languages. A mathematician, she joined the U.S. Navy Reserves in 1943. She was assigned to work on computer systems at Harvard, where she did her groundbreaking efforts which included her work developing the COBOL language, which

was widely adopted. In 1969, the annual Data Processing Management Association awarded her its "Man of the Year Award," and in 1973, she became the first woman of any nationality and the first person from the United States to be made a Distinguished Fellow of the British Computer Society.

For more information, see
www.computerhistory.org.

National Medal of Technology and Innovation (1991):
"For her pioneering accomplishments in the development of computer programming languages that simplified computer technology and opened the door to a significantly larger universe of users."

Brief History of Operating Systems Development

The evolution of operating system software parallels the evolution of the computer hardware it was designed to control.

1940s

Computers from this time were operated by the programmers presiding from the main console—this was a hands-on process. In fact, to fix an error in a program, the programmer would stop the processor, read the contents of each register, make the corrections in memory, and then resume operation. To run programs on these systems, the programmers would reserve the entire machine for the entire time they estimated it would take for the computer to execute their program, and the computer sat idle between reservations. As a result, the machine was poorly utilized because the processor, the CPU, was active for only a fraction of the time it was reserved and didn't work at all between reservations.

There were a lot of variables that could go wrong with these early computers. For example, when Harvard's Mark I computer stopped working one day in 1945, technicians investigating the cause for the interruption discovered that a moth had short-circuited Relay 70 in Panel F, giving its life in the process. The researcher, Grace Murray Hopper, duly placed the dead insect in the system log as shown in Figure 1.8 noting, "First actual case of bug being found." The incident spawned the industry-wide use of the word "bug" to indicate that a system is not working correctly, and the term is still commonly used today.

1950s

Two improvements were widely adopted during this decade: the task of running programs was assigned to professional computer operators (instead of individual programmers) who were assigned to maximize the computer's operation and schedule the incoming jobs as efficiently as possible. Job scheduling required that waiting jobs be put into groups with similar requirements (for example, by grouping all jobs running with a certain language compiler) so the entire batch of jobs could run faster. But even with these batching techniques, there were still extensive time lags between the CPUs that were fast and the I/O devices that ran much slower. Eventually, several factors helped improve the performance of the CPU and the system.

- The speeds of I/O devices, such as tape drives and disks, gradually increased.
- To use more of the available storage area in these devices, records were grouped into blocks before they were retrieved or stored. (This is called "blocking," meaning that several logical records are grouped within one physical record and is discussed in detail in Chapter 7.)

(figure 1.8)

Dr. Grace Hopper's
research journal included
the first computer bug,
the remains of a moth that
became trapped in the
computer's relays, caus-
ing the system to crash.
[Photo © 2002 IEEE]

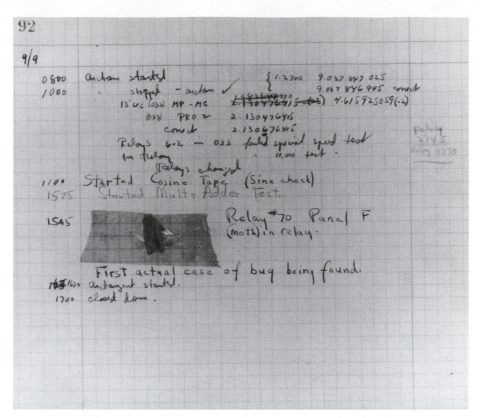

- To reduce the discrepancy in speed between the I/O and the CPU, an interface called the control unit was placed between them to act as a buffer. A buffer is an interim storage area that works as a temporary holding place. As the slow input device reads one record, the control unit places each character of the record into the buffer. When the buffer is full, the entire record is quickly transmitted to the CPU. The process is just the opposite for output devices: the CPU places the entire record into the buffer, which is then passed on by the control unit at the slower rate required by the output device.

The buffers of this generation were conceptually similar to those now used routinely by Web browsers to make video and audio playback smoother, as shown in Figure 1.9.

1:06

(figure 1.9)

Typical buffer indicator showing progress. About one third of this file has already been displayed and a few seconds more are ready in the buffer.

During the second generation, programs were still assigned to the processor one-at-a-time in sequence. The next step toward better use of the system's resources was the move to shared processing.

1960s

Computers in the mid-1960s were designed with faster CPUs, but they still had problems interacting directly with the relatively slow printers and other I/O devices. The solution was called multiprogramming, which introduced the concept of loading many programs at one time and allowing them to share the attention of the single CPU.

The most common mechanism for implementing multiprogramming was the introduction of the concept of the interrupt, whereby the CPU was notified of events needing operating systems services. For example, when a program issued a print command, called input/output (I/O) command, it generated an interrupt, which signaled the release of the CPU from one job so it could begin execution of the next job. This was called *passive multiprogramming* because the operating system didn't control the interrupts, but instead, it waited for each job to end on its own. This was less than ideal because if a job was CPU-bound (meaning that it performed a great deal of non-stop CPU processing before issuing an interrupt), it could monopolize the CPU for a long time while all other jobs waited, even if they were more important.

To counteract this effect, computer scientists designed *active multiprogramming,* allowing the operating system a more active role. Each program was initially allowed to use only a preset slice of CPU time. When time expired, the job was interrupted by the operating system so another job could begin its execution. The interrupted job then had to wait until it was allowed to resume execution at some later time. Soon, this idea, called time slicing, became common in many interactive systems.

1970s

During this decade, computers were built with faster CPUs, creating an even greater disparity between their rapid processing speed and slower I/O times. However, multiprogramming schemes to increase CPU use were limited by the physical capacity of the main memory, which was a limited resource and very expensive. For example, the first Cray supercomputer, shown in Figure 1.10, was installed at Los Alamos National Laboratory in 1976 and had only 8 megabytes (MB) of main memory, significantly less than many computing devices today.

A solution to this physical limitation was the development of virtual memory, which allowed portions of multiple programs to reside in memory at the same time. In other words, a virtual memory system could divide each program into parts and keep those parts in secondary storage, bringing each part into memory only as it was needed.

(figure 1.10)

The Cray I supercomputer boasted 8 megabytes of main memory and a world-record speed of 160 million floating-point operations per second. Its circular design allowed no cable to be more than 4 feet (1.2 meters) in length.

Virtual memory soon became standard in operating systems of all sizes and paved the way to much better use of the CPU.

1980s

Hardware during this time became more flexible, with logical functions that were built on easily replaceable circuit boards. And because it had become cheaper to create these circuit boards, more operating system functions were made part of the hardware itself, giving rise to a new concept—**firmware**, a word used to indicate that a program is permanently held in read only memory (ROM), as opposed to being held in secondary storage.

Eventually the industry moved to multiprocessing (having more than one processor), and more complex languages were designed to coordinate the activities of the multiple processors servicing a single job. As a result, it became possible to execute two programs at the same time (in parallel), and eventually operating systems for computers of every size were routinely expected to accommodate multiprocessing.

The evolution of personal computers and high-speed communications sparked the move to networked systems and distributed processing, enabling users in remote locations to share hardware and software resources. These systems required a new kind of operating system—one capable of managing multiple sets of subsystem managers, as well as hardware that might reside half a world away.

On the other hand, with distributed operating systems, users could think they were working with a system using one processor, when in fact they were connected to a cluster of many processors working closely together. With these systems, users didn't need to know which processor was running their applications or which devices were storing their files. These details were all handled transparently by the operating system—something that required more than just adding a few lines of code to a uniprocessor operating system. The disadvantage of such a complex operating system was the requirement for more complex processor-scheduling algorithms.

1990s

The overwhelming demand for Internet capability in the mid-1990s sparked the proliferation of networking capability. The World Wide Web was first described in a paper by Tim Berners-Lee; his original concept is shown in Figure 1.11. Based on this research, he designed the first Web server and browser, making it available to the general public in 1991. While his innovations sparked increased connectivity, it also increased demand for tighter security to protect system assets from Internet threats.

The decade also introduced a proliferation of multimedia applications demanding additional power, flexibility, and device compatibility for most operating systems, as well as large amounts of storage capability (in addition to longer battery life and cooler operation). These technological advances required commensurate advances by the operating system.

2000s

The new century emphasized the need for improved flexibility, reliability, and speed. The concept of virtual machines was expanded to allow computers to accommodate multiple operating systems that ran at the same time and shared resources. One example is shown in Figure 1.12.

Virtualization allowed separate partitions of a single server to support a different operating system. In other words, it turned a single physical server into multiple virtual servers, often with multiple operating systems. Virtualization required the operating system to have an intermediate manager, to oversee the access of each operating system to the server's physical resources.

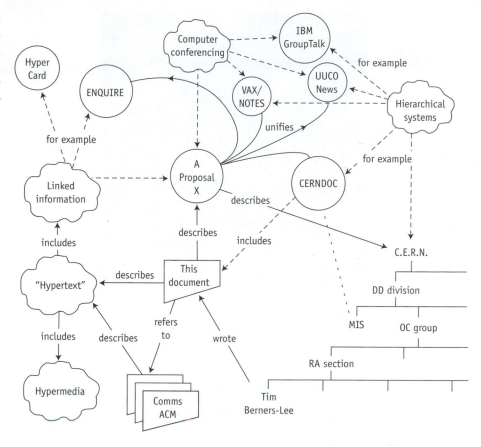

(figure 1.11)

Illustration from the 1989 proposal by Tim Berners-Lee describing his revolutionary "linked information system."

(figure 1.12)

With virtualization, different operating systems can run on a single computer.

Courtesy of Parallels, Inc.

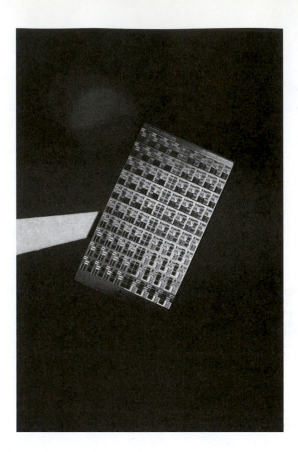

(Figure 1.13)

This single piece of silicon can hold 80 cores, which (to put it in simplest terms) can perform 80 calculations at one time.

(Courtesy of Intel Corporation)

Processing speed enjoyed a similar advancement with the commercialization of multi-core processors, which can contain from two to many cores. For example, a chip with two CPUs (sometimes called a dual-core chip) allows two sets of calculations to run at the same time, which sometimes leads to faster job completion. It's almost as if the user has two separate computers, and thus two processors, cooperating on a single task. Designers have created chips that have dozens of cores, as shown in Figure 1.13.

Does this hardware innovation affect the operating system software? Absolutely—because the operating system must now manage the work of each of these processors and be able to schedule and manage the processing of their multiple tasks.

2010s

Increased mobility and wireless connectivity spawned a proliferation of dual-core, quad-core, and other multicore CPUs with more than one processor (also called a core) on a computer chip. Multicore engineering was driven by the problems caused by nano-sized transistors and their ultra-close placement on a computer chip. Although chips with millions of transistors that were very close together helped increase system performance dramatically, the close proximity of these transistors also allowed current to "leak," which caused the buildup of heat, as well as other issues. With the development of multi-core technology, a single chip (one piece of silicon) was equipped with two or more processor cores. In other words, they replaced a single large processor with two half-sized processors (called dual core), four quarter-sized processors (quad core), and so on. This design allowed the same sized chip to produce less heat and offered the opportunity to permit multiple calculations to take place at the same time.

Design Considerations

The people who write operating systems are faced with many choices that can affect every part of the software and the resources it controls. Before beginning, designers typically start by asking key questions, using the answers to guide them in their work. The most common overall goal is to maximize use of the system's resources (memory, processing, devices, and files) and minimize downtime, though certain proprietary systems may have other priorities. Typically, designers include the following factors into their developmental efforts: the minimum and maximum RAM resources, the number and type of CPUs available, the variety of devices likely to be connected, the range of files, networking capability, security requirements, default user interfaces available, assumed user capabilities, and so on.

For example, a mobile operating system for a tablet might have a single CPU and need to manage that CPU to minimize the heat it generates. Likewise, if the operating system manages a real-time system, where deadlines are urgent, designers need to manage the memory, processor time, devices, and files so urgent deadlines will be met. For these reasons, operating systems are often complex pieces of software that juggle numerous applications, access to networked resources, several users, and multiple CPUs in an effort to keep the system running effectively.

As you might expect, no single operating system is perfect for every environment. Some systems can be best served with a UNIX system, others benefit from the structure of a Windows system, and still others work best using Linux, Mac OS, or Android, or even a custom-built operating system.

Conclusion

In this chapter, we looked at the overall function of operating systems and how they have evolved to run increasingly complex computers and computer systems. Like any complicated subject, there's much more detail to explore. As we'll see in the remainder of this text, there are many ways to perform every task, and it's up to the designer of the operating system to choose the policies that best match the system's environment.

In the following chapters, we'll explore in detail how each portion of the operating system works, as well as its features, functions, benefits, and costs. We'll begin with the part of the operating system that's the heart of every computer: the module that manages main memory.

Key Terms

batch system: a type of computing system that executes programs, each of which is submitted in its entirety, can be grouped into batches, and executed without external intervention.

central processing unit (CPU): a component with circuitry to control the interpretation and execution of instructions.

cloud computing: a multifaceted technology that allows computing, data storage and retrieval and other computer functions to take place over a large network, typically the Internet.

Device Manager: the section of the operating system responsible for controlling the use of devices. It monitors every device, channel, and control unit and chooses the most efficient way to allocate all of the system's devices.

embedded computer system: a dedicated computer system that often is part of a larger physical system, such as jet aircraft or automobiles. Often, it must be small, fast, and able to work with real-time constraints, fail-safe execution, and nonstandard I/O devices.

File Manager: the section of the operating system responsible for controlling the use of files.

firmware: software instructions or data that are stored in a fixed or "firm" way, usually implemented on some type of read only memory (ROM).

hardware: the tangible machine and its components, including main memory, I/O devices, I/O channels, direct access storage devices, and the central processing unit.

hybrid system: a computer system that supports both batch and interactive processes.

interactive system: a system that allows each user to interact directly with the operating system.

kernel: the primary part of the operating system that remains in random access memory (RAM) and is charged with performing the system's most essential tasks, such as managing main memory and disk access.

main memory: the memory unit that works directly with the CPU and in which the data and instructions must reside in order to be processed. Also called *primary storage*, *RAM*, or *internal memory*.

mainframe: the historical name given to a large computer system characterized by its large size, high cost, and relatively fast performance.

Memory Manager: the section of the operating system responsible for controlling the use of memory. It checks the validity of each request for memory space, and if it's a legal request, allocates the amount needed to execute the job.

multiprocessing: when two or more CPUs share the same main memory, most I/O devices, and the same control program routines. They service the same job stream and execute distinct processing programs concurrently.

multiprogramming: a technique that allows a single processor to process several programs residing simultaneously in main memory and interleaving their execution by overlapping I/O requests with CPU requests.

network: a system of interconnected computer systems and peripheral devices that exchange information with one another.

operating system: the primary software on a computing system that manages its resources, controls the execution of other programs, and manages communications and data storage.

Processor Manager: a composite of two submanagers, the Job Scheduler and the Process Scheduler, which decides how to allocate the CPU.

RAM: random access memory. See *main memory*.

real-time system: a computing system used in time-critical environments that require guaranteed response times, such as navigation systems, rapid transit systems, and industrial control systems.

server: a node that provides to clients various network services, such as file retrieval, printing, or database access services.

storage: the place where data is stored in the computer system. Primary storage is main memory. Secondary storage is nonvolatile media, such as disks and flash memory.

Interesting Searches

For more background on a few of the topics discussed in this chapter, begin a search with these terms.

- NASA - Computers Aboard the Space Shuttles
- IBM Computer History Archive
- History of the UNIX Operating System
- History of Microsoft Windows Products
- Computer History Museum

Exercises

Research Topics

Whenever you research computer technology, make sure your resources are timely. Note the date when the research was published, as this field changes quickly. Also be sure to validate the authenticity of your sources. Avoid any that may be questionable, such as blogs and publicly edited online sources.

A. New research on topics concerning operating systems and computer science are published by professional societies. Research the Internet or current literature to identify at least two prominent professional societies with peer-reviewed computer science journals, then list the advantages of becoming a member, the dues for students, and a one-sentence summary of a published paper concerning operating systems. Cite your sources.

B. Write a one-page review of an article about the subject of operating systems that appeared in a recent computing magazine or academic journal. Give a summary of the article, including the primary topic, your own summary of the information presented, and the author's conclusion. Give your personal evaluation of the article, including topics that made the article interesting to you (or not) and its relevance to your own experiences. Be sure to cite your source.

Exercises

1. Gordon Moore predicted the dramatic increase in transistors per chip in 1965 and his prediction has held for decades. Some industry analysts insist that Moore's Law has been a predictor of chip design, but others say it is a motivator for designers of new chips. In your opinion, who is correct? Explain your answer.

2. Give an example of an organization that might find batch-mode processing useful and explain why.

3. Name five current operating systems (other than those mentioned in Table 1.1) and identify the devices that each is designed to run on.

4. List three situations that might demand a real-time operating system and explain in detail the system characteristics that persuade you to do so.

5. Many people confuse main memory and secondary storage. Explain why this happens, and describe how you would explain the differences to classmates so they would no longer confuse the two.

6. Name the five key concepts about an operating system that you think a user needs to know and understand.

7. Explain the impact of the evolution of computer hardware and the accompanying evolution of operating systems software.

8. Give real-world examples of interactive, batch, real-time, and embedded systems and explain the fundamental differences among them.

9. Briefly compare active and passive multiprogramming and give examples of each.

10. Give at least two reasons why a regional bank might decide to buy six networked servers instead of one mainframe.

11. Select two of the following professionals: an insurance adjuster, a delivery person for a courier service, a newspaper reporter, a general practitioner doctor, or a manager in a supermarket. Suggest at least two ways that each person might use a mobile computer to work efficiently.

12. Compare the development of two operating systems described in Chapters 13-16 of this text, including design goals and evolution. Name the operating system each was based on, if any. Which one do you believe is more efficient for your needs? Explain why.

Advanced Exercises

Advanced Exercises are appropriate for readers with supplementary knowledge of operating systems.

13. In computing literature, the value represented by the prefixes kilo-, mega-, giga-, and so on can vary depending on whether they are describing many bytes of main memory or many bits of data transmission speed. Calculate the number of bytes in a megabyte (MB) and compare it to the number of bits in a megabit (Mb). If there is a difference, explain why that is the case. Cite your sources.

14. Draw a system flowchart illustrating the steps performed by an operating system as it executes the instruction to back up a disk on a single-user computer system. Begin with the user typing the command on the keyboard or choosing an option from a menu, and conclude with the result being displayed on the monitor.

15. In a multiprogramming and time-sharing environment, several users share a single system at the same time. This situation can result in various security problems. Name two such problems. Can we ensure the same degree of security in a time-share machine as we have in a dedicated machine? Explain your answer.

16. The boot sequence is the series of instructions that enable the operating system to get installed and running when you power on a computer. For an operating system of your choice, describe in your own words the role of firmware and the boot process.

17. A "dual boot" system gives users the opportunity to choose from among a list of operating systems when powering on a computer. Describe how this process works. Explain whether or not there is a risk that one operating system might intrude on the space reserved for another operating system.

Chapter 2

Memory Management: Simple Systems

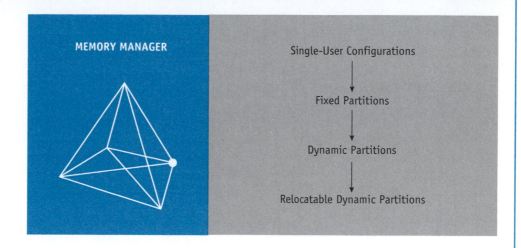

" Memory is the primary and fundamental power, without which there could be no other intellectual operation. "

—Samuel Johnson (1709–1784)

Learning Objectives

After completing this chapter, you should be able to describe:

- The basic functionality of the four memory allocation schemes presented in this chapter: single user, fixed partitions, dynamic partitions, and relocatable dynamic partitions
- Best-fit memory allocation as well as first-fit memory allocation
- How a memory list keeps track of available memory
- The importance of memory deallocation
- The importance of the bounds register in memory allocation schemes
- The role of compaction and how it can improve memory allocation efficiency

The management of **main memory** is critical. In fact, for many years, the performance of the *entire* system was directly dependent on two things: How much memory was available and how that memory was optimized while jobs were being processed.

This chapter introduces the role of main memory (also known as random access memory or **RAM**, core memory, or primary storage) and four types of memory allocation schemes: single-user systems, fixed partitions, dynamic partitions, and relocatable dynamic partitions. Let's begin with the simplest memory management scheme—the one used with the simplest computer systems.

Single-User Contiguous Scheme

This memory allocation scheme works like this: before execution can begin, each job or program is loaded in its entirety into memory and allocated as much contiguous space in memory as it needs, as shown in Figure 2.1. The key words here are *entirety* and *contiguous*. If the program is too large to fit into the available memory space, it cannot begin execution.

This scheme demonstrates a significant limiting factor of all computers—they have only a finite amount of memory. If a program doesn't fit, then either the size of the main memory must be increased, or the program must be modified to fit, often by revising it to be smaller.

A single-user scheme supports only one job at a time. It's not possible to share main memory.

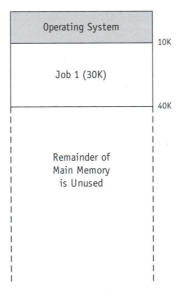

(figure 2.1)

Only one program can fit into memory at a time, even if there is room to accommodate other waiting jobs.

Single-user systems in a non-networked environment allocate, to each user, access to all available main memory for each job, and jobs are processed sequentially, one after the other. To allocate memory, the amount of work required from the operating system's Memory Manager is minimal, as described in these steps:

1. Evaluate the incoming process to see if it is small enough to fit into the available space. If it is, load it into memory; if not, reject it and evaluate the next incoming process,

2. Monitor the occupied memory space. When the resident process ends its execution and no longer needs to be in memory, make the entire amount of main memory space available and return to Step 1, evaluating the next incoming process.

An "Algorithm to Load a Job in a Single-User System" using pseudocode and demonstrating these steps can be found in Appendix A.

Once the program is entirely loaded into memory, it begins its execution and remains there until execution is complete, either by finishing its work or through the intervention of the operating system, such as when an error is detected.

One major problem with this type of memory allocation scheme is that it doesn't support multiprogramming (multiple jobs or processes occupying memory at the same time); it can handle only one at a time. When these single-user configurations were first made available commercially in the late 1940s and early 1950s, they were used in research institutions but proved unacceptable for the business community—it wasn't cost effective to spend almost $200,000 for a piece of equipment that could be used by only one person at a time. The next scheme introduced memory partitions.

Fixed Partitions

Each partition could be used by only one program. The size of each partition was set in advance by the computer operator, so sizes couldn't be changed without restarting the system.

The first attempt to allow for multiprogramming used **fixed partitions** (also known as static partitions) within main memory—each partition could be assigned to one job. A system with four partitions could hold four jobs in memory at the same time. One fact remained the same, however—these partitions were static, so the systems administrator had to turn off the entire system to reconfigure their sizes, and any job that couldn't fit into the largest partition could not be executed.

An important factor was introduced with this scheme: protection of the job's memory space. Once a partition was assigned to a job, the jobs in other memory partitions had to be prevented from invading its boundaries, either accidentally or intentionally. This problem of partition intrusion didn't exist in single-user contiguous allocation schemes because only one job was present in main memory at any given time—only the portion of main memory that held the operating system had to be protected. However, for the fixed partition allocation schemes, protection was mandatory for each partition in main memory. Typically this was the joint responsibility of the hardware of the computer and of the operating system.

The algorithm used to store jobs in memory requires a few more steps than the one used for a single-user system because the size of the job must be matched with the size of the available partitions to make sure it fits completely. ("An Algorithm to Load a Job in a Fixed Partition" is in Appendix A.) Remember, this scheme also required that the entire job be loaded into memory before execution could begin.

To do so, the Memory Manager could perform these steps in a two-partition system:

1. Check the incoming job's memory requirements. If it's greater than the size of the largest partition, reject the job and go to the next waiting job. If it's less than the largest partition, go to Step 2.

2. Check the job size against the size of the first available partition. If the job is small enough to fit, see if that partition is free. If it is available, load the job into that partition. If it's busy with another job, go to Step 3.

3. Check the job size against the size of the second available partition. If the job is small enough to fit, check to see if that partition is free. If it is available, load the incoming job into that partition. If not, go to Step 4.

4. Because neither partition is available now, place the incoming job in the waiting queue for loading at a later time. Return to Step 1 to evaluate the next incoming job.

This partition scheme is more flexible than the single-user scheme because it allows more than one program to be in memory at the same time. However, it still requires that the *entire* program be stored *contiguously* and *in memory* from the beginning to the end of its execution.

In order to allocate memory spaces to jobs, the Memory Manager must maintain a table which shows each memory partition's size, its **address**, its access restrictions, and its current status (free or busy). Table 2.1 shows a simplified version for the system illustrated in Figure 2.2. Note that Table 2.1 and the other tables in this chapter have been simplified. More detailed discussions of these tables and their contents are presented in Chapter 8, "File Management."

Partition Size	Memory Address	Access	Partition Status
100K	200K	Job 1	Busy
25K	300K	Job 4	Busy
25K	325K		Free
50K	350K	Job 2	Busy

(table 2.1)

A simplified fixed-partition memory table with the free partition shaded.

When each resident job terminates, the status of its memory partition is changed from busy to free to make it available to an incoming job.

(figure 2.2)

As the jobs listed in Table 2.1 are loaded into the four fixed partitions, Job 3 must wait even though Partition 1 has 70K of available memory. Jobs are allocated space on the basis of "first available partition of required size."

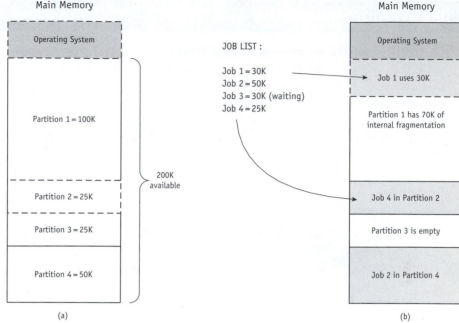

The fixed partition scheme works well if all of the jobs that run on the system are of similar size or if the sizes are known ahead of time and don't vary between reconfigurations. Ideally, that would require accurate, advance knowledge of all the jobs waiting to be run on the system in the coming hours, days, or weeks. However, under most circumstances, the operator chooses partition sizes in an arbitrary fashion, and thus not all incoming jobs fit in them.

There are significant consequences if the partition sizes are too small; large jobs will need to wait if the large partitions are already booked, and they will be rejected if they're too big to fit into the largest partition.

On the other hand, if the partition sizes are too big, memory is wasted. Any job that occupies less than the entire partition (the vast majority will do so) will cause unused memory in the partition to remain idle. Remember that each partition is an indivis- ible unit that can be allocated to only one job at a time. Figure 2.3 demonstrates one such circumstance: Job 3 is kept waiting because it's too big for Partition 3, even though there is more than enough unused space for it in Partition 1, which is claimed by Job 1.

This phenomenon of less-than-complete use of memory space in a fixed partition is called **internal fragmentation** (because it's inside a partition) and is a major drawback to this memory allocation scheme.

Jay W. Forrester (1918–)

Jay Forrester led the groundbreaking MIT Whirlwind computer project (1947-1953) that developed the first practical and reliable, high-speed random access memory for digital computers. At the time it was called "coincident current magnetic core storage." This invention became the standard memory device for digital computers and provided the foundation for main memory development through the 1970s. Forrester is the recipient of numerous awards, including the IEEE Computer Pioneer Award (1982), the U.S. National Medal of Technology and Innovation (1989), and induction into the Operational Research Hall of Fame (2006).

For more information:
http://www.computerhistory.org/fellowawards/hall/bios/Jay,Forrester/

Received the IEEE Computer Pioneer Award: "For exceptional advances in the digital computer through his invention and application of the magnetic-core random-access memory, employing coincident current addressing."

Dynamic Partitions

With the introduction of the **dynamic partition** allocation scheme, memory is allocated to an incoming job in one contiguous block, and each job is given only as much memory as it requests when it is loaded for processing. Although this is a significant improvement over fixed partitions because memory is no longer wasted inside each partition, it introduces another problem.

It works well when the first jobs are loaded. As shown in Figure 2.4, a dynamic partition scheme allocates memory efficiently as each of the first few jobs are loaded, but when those jobs finish and new jobs enter the system (which are not the same size as those that just vacated memory), the newer jobs are allocated space in the available partition spaces on a priority basis. Figure 2.4 demonstrates first-come, first-served priority—that is, each job is loaded into the first available partition. Therefore, the subsequent allocation of memory creates fragments of free memory *between* partitions of allocated memory. This problem is called **external fragmentation** and, like internal fragmentation, allows memory to be wasted.

In Figure 2.3, notice the difference between the first snapshot (a), where the entire amount of main memory is used efficiently, and the last snapshot, (e), where there are

> ✔ There are two types of fragmentation: internal and external. The type depends on the location of the wasted space.

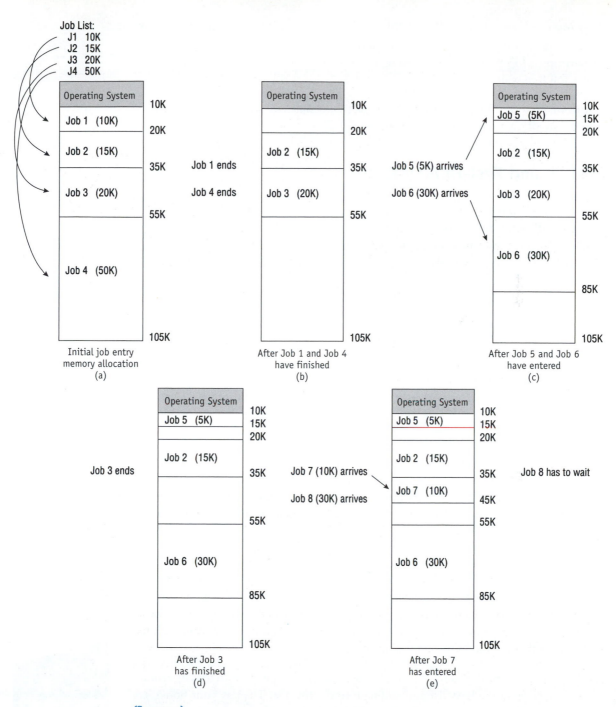

(figure 2.3)

Main memory use during dynamic partition allocation. Five snapshots (a-e) of main memory as eight jobs are submitted for processing and allocated space on the basis of "first come, first served." Job 8 has to wait (e) even though there's enough free memory between partitions to accommodate it.

three free partitions of 5K, 10K, and 20K—35K in all—enough to accommodate Job 8, which requires only 30K. However, because the three memory blocks are separated by partitions, Job 8 cannot be loaded in a contiguous manner. Therefore, this scheme forces Job 8 to wait.

Before we go to the next allocation scheme, let's examine two ways that an operating system can allocate free sections of memory.

Best-Fit and First-Fit Allocation

For both fixed and dynamic memory allocation schemes, the operating system must keep lists of each memory location, noting which are free and which are busy. Then, as new jobs come into the system, the free partitions must be allocated fairly, according to the policy adopted by the programmers who designed and wrote the operating system.

Memory partitions may be allocated on the basis of first-fit memory allocation or best-fit memory allocation. For both schemes, the Memory Manager keeps detailed lists of the free and busy sections of memory either by size or by location. The **best-fit allocation method keeps** the free/busy lists in order by size, from smallest to largest. The **first-fit allocation method** keeps the free/busy lists organized by memory locations, from low-order memory to high-order memory. Each has advantages depending on the needs of the particular allocation scheme. Best-fit usually makes the best use of memory space; first-fit is faster.

To understand the trade-offs, imagine that you are in charge of a small local library. You have books of all shapes and sizes, and there's a continuous stream of people taking books out and bringing them back—someone is always waiting. It's clear that your library is a popular place and you'll always be busy, without any time to rearrange the books on the shelves.

You need a system. Your shelves have fixed partitions with a few tall spaces for oversized books, several shelves for paperbacks and DVDs, and lots of room for textbooks. You'll need to keep track of which spaces on the shelves are full and where you have spaces for more. For the purposes of our example, we'll keep two lists: a free list showing all the available spaces, and a busy list showing all the occupied spaces. Each list will include the size and location of each space.

As each book is removed from its place on the shelf, you'll update both lists by removing the space from the busy list and adding it to the free list. Then as your books are returned and placed back on a shelf, the two lists will be updated again.

There are two ways to organize your lists: by size or by location. If they're organized by size, the spaces for the smallest books are at the top of the list and those for the

If you optimize speed, you may be wasting space. But if you optimize space, you may be wasting time.

largest are at the bottom, as shown in Figure 2.4. When they're organized by location, the spaces closest to your lending desk are at the top of the list and the areas farthest away are at the bottom. Which option is best? It depends on what you want to optimize: space or speed.

 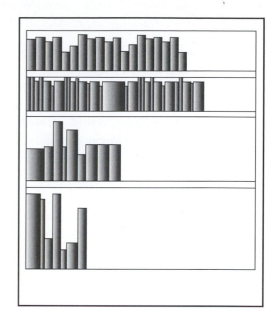

(figure 2.4)

The bookshelf on the left uses the best-fit allocation. The one on the right is first-fit allocation, where some small items occupy space that could hold larger ones.

If the lists are organized by size, you're optimizing your shelf space—as books arrive, you'll be able to put them in the spaces that fit them best. This is a best-fit scheme. If a paperback is returned, you'll place it on a shelf with the other paperbacks or at least with other small books. Similarly, oversized books will be shelved with other large books. Your lists make it easy to find the smallest available empty space where the book can fit. The disadvantage of this system is that you're wasting time looking for the best space. Your other customers have to wait for you to put each book away, so you won't be able to process as many customers as you could with the other kind of list.

In the second case, a list organized by shelf location, you're optimizing the time it takes you to put books back on the shelves by using a first-fit scheme. This system ignores the size of the book that you're trying to put away. If the same paperback book arrives, you can quickly find it an empty space. In fact, any nearby empty space will suffice if it's large enough—and if it's close to your desk. In this case you are optimizing the time it takes you to shelve the books.

This is a fast method of shelving books, and if speed is important, it's the better of the two alternatives. However, it isn't a good choice if your shelf space is limited or if many large books are returned, because large books must wait for the large spaces. If all of your large spaces are filled with small books, the customers returning large books must wait until a suitable space becomes available. (Eventually you'll need time to rearrange the books and compact your collection.)

Figure 2.5 shows how a large job can have problems with a first-fit memory allocation list. Jobs 1, 2, and 4 are able to enter the system and begin execution; Job 3 has to wait even though there would be more than enough room to accommodate it if all of the fragments of memory were added together. First-fit offers fast allocation, but it isn't always efficient. (On the other hand, the same job list using a best-fit scheme would use memory more efficiently, as shown in Figure 2.6. In this particular case, a best-fit scheme would yield better memory utilization.)

(figure 2.5)

Using a first-fit scheme, Job 1 claims the first available space. Job 2 then claims the first partition large enough to accommodate it, but by doing so it takes the last block large enough to accommodate Job 3. Therefore, Job 3 (indicated by the asterisk) must wait until a large block becomes available, even though there's 75K of unused memory space (internal fragmentation). Notice that the memory list is ordered according to memory location.

Job List:

Job number	Memory requested
J1	10K
J2	20K
J3	30K*
J4	10K

Memory List:

Memory location	Memory block size	Job number	Job size	Status	Internal fragmentation
10240	30K	J1	10K	Busy	20K
40960	15K	J4	10K	Busy	5K
56320	50K	J2	20K	Busy	30K
107520	20K			Free	
Total Available:	115K	Total Used:	40K		

Memory use has been increased, but the memory allocation process takes more time. What's more, while internal fragmentation has been diminished, it hasn't been completely eliminated.

The first-fit algorithm (included in Appendix A) assumes that the Memory Manager keeps two lists, one for free memory blocks and one for busy memory blocks. The operation consists of a simple loop that compares the size of each job to the size of each memory block until a block is found that's large enough to fit the job. Then the job is stored into that block of memory, and the Memory Manager fetches the next job from the entry queue. If the entire list is searched in vain, then the job is placed into a waiting queue. The Memory Manager then fetches the next job and repeats the process.

(figure 2.6)

Best-fit free scheme. Job 1 is allocated to the closestfitting free partition, as are Job 2 and Job 3. Job 4 is allocated to the only available partition although it isn't the best-fitting one. In this scheme, all four jobs are served without waiting. Notice that the memory list is ordered according to memory size. This scheme uses memory more efficiently but it's slower to implement.

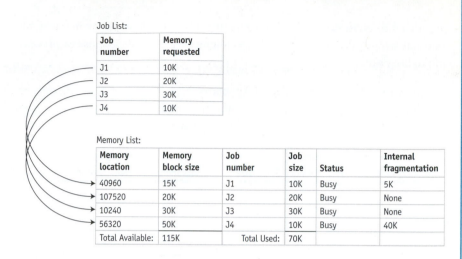

Job List:

Job number	Memory requested
J1	10K
J2	20K
J3	30K
J4	10K

Memory List:

Memory location	Memory block size	Job number	Job size	Status	Internal fragmentation
40960	15K	J1	10K	Busy	5K
107520	20K	J2	20K	Busy	None
10240	30K	J3	30K	Busy	None
56320	50K	J4	10K	Busy	40K
Total Available:	115K		Total Used:	70K	

In Table 2.2, a request for a block of 200 spaces has just been given to the Memory Manager. (The spaces may be words, bytes, or any other unit the system handles.) Using the first-fit scheme and starting from the top of the list, the Memory Manager locates the first block of memory large enough to accommodate the job, which is at location 6785. The job is then loaded, starting at location 6785 and occupying the next 200 spaces. The next step is to adjust the free list to indicate that the block of free memory now starts at location 6985 (not 6785 as before) and that it contains only 400 spaces (not 600 as before).

(table 2.2)

These two snapshots of memory show the status of each memory block before and after 200 spaces are allocated at address 6785, using the first-fit algorithm. (Note: All values are in decimal notation unless otherwise indicated.)

Status Before Request		Status After Request	
Beginning Address	Free Memory Block Size	Beginning Address	Free Memory Block Size
4075	105	4075	105
5225	5	5225	5
6785	600	*6985	400
7560	20	7560	20
7600	205	7600	205
10250	4050	10250	4050
15125	230	15125	230
24500	1000	24500	1000

The best-fit algorithm is slightly more complex because the goal is to find the smallest memory block into which the job will fit. One of the problems with it is that the entire table must be searched before an allocation can be made because the memory blocks are physically stored in sequence according to their location in memory (and not by memory block sizes as shown in Figure 2.6). The system could execute an algorithm to continuously rearrange the list in ascending order by memory block size, but that would add more overhead and might not be an efficient use of processing time in the long run.

The best-fit algorithm (included in Appendix A) is illustrated showing only the list of free memory blocks. Table 2.3 shows the free list before and after the best-fit block has been allocated to the same request presented in Table 2.2.

Status Before Request		Status After Request	
Beginning Address	Free Memory Block Size	Beginning Address	Free Memory Block Size
4075	105	4075	105
5225	5	5225	5
6785	600	6785	600
7560	20	7560	20
7600	205	*7800	5
10250	4050	10250	4050
15125	230	15125	230
24500	1000	24500	1000

(table 2.3)

These two snapshots of memory show the status of each memory block before and after 200 spaces are allocated at address 7600, using the best-fit algorithm.

In Table 2.3, a request for a block of 200 spaces has just been given to the Memory Manager. Using the best-fit algorithm and starting from the top of the list, the Memory Manager searches the entire list and locates a block of memory starting at location 7600, which is the block that's the smallest one that's also large enough to accommodate the job. The choice of this block minimizes the wasted space (only 5 spaces are wasted, which is less than in the four alternative blocks). The job is then stored, starting at location 7600 and occupying the next 200 spaces. Now the free list must be adjusted to show that the block of free memory starts at location 7800 (not 7600 as before) and that it contains only 5 spaces (not 205 as before). But it doesn't eliminate wasted space. Note that while the best-fit resulted in a better fit, it also resulted (as it does in the general case) in a smaller free space (5 spaces), which is known as a sliver.

Which is best—first-fit or best-fit? For many years there was no way to answer such a general question because performance depends on the job mix. In recent years, access times have become so fast that the scheme that saves the more valuable resource, memory space, may be the best. Research continues to focus on finding the optimum allocation scheme.

In the exercises at the end of this chapter, two other hypothetical allocation schemes are explored: next-fit, which starts searching from the last allocated block for the next available block when a new job arrives; and worst-fit (the opposite of best-fit), which allocates the largest free available block to the new job. Although it's a good way to explore the theory of memory allocation, it might not be the best choice for a real system.

Deallocation

Until now, we've considered only the problem of how memory blocks are allocated, but eventually there comes a time for the release of memory space, called **deallocation**.

For a fixed partition system, the process is quite straightforward. When the job is completed, the Memory Manager immediately deallocates it by resetting the status of the entire memory block from "busy" to "free." Any code—for example, binary values with 0 indicating free and 1 indicating busy—may be used, so the mechanical task of deallocating a block of memory is relatively simple.

A dynamic partition system uses a more complex algorithm (shown in Appendix A) because it tries to combine free areas of memory whenever possible. Therefore, the system must be prepared for three alternative situations:

• Case 1: When the block to be deallocated is adjacent to another free block
• Case 2: When the block to be deallocated is between two free blocks
• Case 3: When the block to be deallocated is isolated from other free blocks

Case 1: Joining Two Free Blocks

Table 2.4 shows how deallocation occurs in a dynamic memory allocation system when the job to be deallocated is next to one free memory block.

After deallocation, the free list looks like the one shown in Table 2.5.

> **(table 2.4)**
>
> *This is the original free list before deallocation for Case 1. The asterisk indicates the free memory block (of size 5) that's adjacent to the soon-to-be-free memory block (of size 200) that's shaded.*

Beginning Address	Memory Block Size	Status
4075	105	Free
5225	5	Free
6785	600	Free
7560	20	Free
(7600)	(200)	(Busy)[1]
*7800	5	Free
10250	4050	Free
15125	230	Free
24500	1000	Free

[1]Although the numbers in parentheses don't appear in the free list, they've been inserted here for clarity. The job size is 200 and its beginning location is 7600.

The text in the sidebar checkmark box reads:

> When memory is deallocated, it creates an opportunity for external fragmentation.

Beginning Address	Memory Block Size	Status
4075	105	Free
5225	5	Free
6785	600	Free
7560	20	Free
*7600	205	Free
10250	4050	Free
15125	230	Free
24500	1000	Free

(table 2.5)

Case 1. This is the free list after deallocation. The shading indicates the location where changes were made to indicate the free memory block (of size 205).

Using the deallocation algorithm, the system sees that the memory to be released is next to a free memory block, which starts at location 7800. Therefore, the list must be changed to reflect the starting address of the new free block, 7600, which was the address of the first instruction of the job that just released this block. In addition, the memory block size for this new free space must be changed to show its new size, which is the combined total of the two free partitions (200 + 5).

Case 2: Joining Three Free Blocks

When the deallocated memory space is between two free memory blocks, the process is similar, as shown in Table 2.6.

Using the deallocation algorithm, the system learns that the memory to be deallocated is between two free blocks of memory. Therefore, the sizes of the three free partitions (20 + 20 + 205) must be combined and the total stored with the smallest beginning address, 7560.

Beginning Address	Memory Block Size	Status
4075	105	Free
5225	5	Free
6785	600	Free
*7560	20	Free
(7580)	(20)	(Busy)[1]
*7600	205	Free
10250	4050	Free
15125	230	Free
24500	1000	Free

(table 2.6)

Case 2. This is the Free List before deallocation. The asterisks indicate the two free memory blocks that are adjacent to the soon-to-be-free memory block.

[1] Although the numbers in parentheses don't appear in the free list, they have been inserted here for clarity.

Because the entry at location 7600 has been combined with the previous entry, we must empty out this entry. We do that by changing the status to **null entry**, with no beginning address and no memory block size, as indicated by an asterisk in Table 2.7. This negates the need to rearrange the list at the expense of memory.

(table 2.7)

Case 2. The free list after a job has released memory. The revised entry is shaded.

Beginning Address	Memory Block Size	Status
4075	105	Free
5225	5	Free
6785	600	Free
7560	245	Free
*		(null entry)
10250	4050	Free
15125	230	Free
24500	1000	Free

Case 3: Deallocating an Isolated Block

The third alternative is when the space to be deallocated is isolated from all other free areas. For this example, we need to know more about how the busy memory list is configured. To simplify matters, let's look at the busy list for the memory area between locations 7560 and 10250. Remember that, starting at 7560, there's a free memory block of 245, so the busy memory area includes everything from location 7805 (7560 + 245) to 10250, which is the address of the next free block. The free list and busy list are shown in Table 2.8 and Table 2.9.

(table 2.8)

Case 3. Original free list before deallocation. The soon-to-be-free memory block (at location 8805) is not adjacent to any blocks that are already free.

Beginning Address	Memory Block Size	Status
4075	105	Free
5225	5	Free
6785	600	Free
7560	245	Free
		(null entry)
10250	4050	Free
15125	230	Free
24500	1000	Free

Beginning Address	Memory Block Size	Status
7805	1000	Busy
*8805	445	Busy
9250	1000	Busy

(table 2.9)

Case 3. Busy memory list before deallocation. The job to be deallocated is of size 445 and begins at location 8805. The asterisk indicates the soon-to-be-free memory block.

Using the deallocation algorithm, the system learns that the memory block to be released is not adjacent to any free blocks of memory; instead it is between two other busy areas. Therefore, the system must search the table for a null entry.

The scheme presented in this example creates null entries in both the busy and the free lists during the process of allocation or deallocation of memory. An example of a null entry occurring as a result of deallocation was presented in Case 2. A null entry in the busy list occurs when a memory block between two other busy memory blocks is returned to the free list, as shown in Table 2.10. This mechanism ensures that all blocks are entered in the lists according to the beginning address of their memory location from smallest to largest.

Beginning Address	Memory Block Size	Status
7805	1000	Busy
*		(null entry)
9250	1000	Busy

(table 2.10)

Case 3. This is the busy list after the job has released its memory. The asterisk indicates the new null entry in the busy list.

When the null entry is found, the beginning memory location of the terminating job is entered in the beginning address column, the job size is entered under the memory block size column, and the status is changed from "null entry" to free to indicate that a new block of memory is available, as shown in Table 2.11.

Beginning Address	Memory Block Size	Status
4075	105	Free
5225	5	Free
6785	600	Free
7560	245	Free
*8805	445	Free
10250	4050	Free
15125	230	Free
24500	1000	Free

(table 2.11)

Case 3. This is the free list after the job has released its memory. The asterisk indicates the new free block entry replacing the null entry.

Relocatable Dynamic Partitions

All of the memory allocation schemes described thus far shared some unacceptable fragmentation characteristics that had to be resolved as the number of waiting jobs became unwieldy and demand increased to use all the slivers of memory often left unused.

The solution to both problems was the development of **relocatable dynamic partitions**. With this memory allocation scheme, the Memory Manager relocates programs to gather together all of the empty blocks and compact them to make one block of memory large enough to accommodate some or all of the jobs waiting to get in.

When you use a defragmentation utility, you are causing memory to be compacted and file segments to be relocated so they can be retrieved faster.

The **compaction of memory**, sometimes referred to as memory defragmentation, is performed by the operating system to reclaim fragmented space. Remember our earlier example of the lending library? If you stopped lending books for a few moments and rearranged the books in the most effective order, you would be compacting your collection. But this demonstrates its disadvantage—this is an overhead process that can take place only while everything else waits.

Compaction isn't an easy task. Most or all programs in memory must be relocated so they're contiguous, and then every address, and every reference to an address, within each program must be adjusted to account for the program's new location in memory. However, all other values within the program (such as data values) must be left alone. In other words, the operating system must distinguish between addresses and data values, and these distinctions are not obvious after the program has been loaded into memory.

To appreciate the complexity of **relocation**, let's look at a typical program. Remember, all numbers are stored in memory as binary values (ones and zeros), and in any given program instruction it's not uncommon to find addresses as well as data values. For example, an assembly language program might include the instruction to add the integer 1 to I. The source code instruction looks like this:

```
ADDI I, 1
```

However, after it has been translated into actual code it could be represented like this (for readability purposes the values are represented here in octal code, not binary code):

```
000007 271 01 0 00 000001
```

Question: Which elements are addresses and which are instruction codes or data values? It's not obvious at first glance. In fact, the address is the number on the left (000007). The instruction code is next (271), and the data value is on the right (000001). Therefore, if this instruction is relocated 200 places, then the address would be adjusted (added to or subtracted) by 200, but the instruction code and data value would not be.

The operating system can tell the function of each group of digits by its location in the line and the operation code. However, if the program is to be moved to another place in memory, each address must be identified, or flagged. This becomes particularly important when the program includes loop sequences, decision sequences, and branching sequences, as well as data references. If, by chance, every address was not adjusted by the same value, the program would branch to the wrong section of the program or to a part of another program, or it would reference the wrong data.

The program shown in Figure 2.7 and Figure 2.8 shows how the operating system flags the addresses so that they can be adjusted if and when a program is relocated.

Internally, the addresses are marked with a special symbol (indicated in Figure 2.8 by apostrophes) so the Memory Manager will know to adjust them by the value stored in the relocation register. All of the other values (data values) are not marked and won't be changed after relocation. Other numbers in the program, those indicating instructions, registers, or constants used in the instruction, are also left alone.

Figure 2.9 illustrates what happens to a program in memory during compaction and relocation.

This discussion of compaction raises three questions:

1. What goes on behind the scenes when relocation and compaction take place?
2. What keeps track of how far each job has moved from its original storage area?
3. What lists have to be updated?

The last question is easiest to answer. After relocation and compaction, both the free list and the busy list are updated. The free list is changed to show the partition for

```
A          EXP 132, 144, 125, 110    ;the data values
BEGIN:     MOVEI              1,0     ;initialize register 1
           MOVEI              2,0     ;initialize register 2
LOOP:      ADD              2,A(1)    ;add (A + reg 1) to reg 2
           ADDI               1,1     ;add 1 to reg 1
           CAIG             1,4-1     ;is register 1 > 4-1?
           JUMPA             LOOP     ;if not, go to Loop
           MOVE               3,2     ;if so, move reg 2 to reg 3
           IDIVI              3,4     ;divide reg 3 by 4,
                                      ;remainder to register 4
           EXIT                       ;end
           END
```

(figure 2.7)

An assembly language program that performs a simple incremental operation. This is what the programmer submits to the assembler. The commands are shown on the left and the comments explaining each command are shown on the right after the semicolons.

(figure 2.8)

The original assembly language program after it has been processed by the assembler, shown on the right (a). To run the program, the assembler translates it into machine readable code (b) with all addresses marked by a special symbol (shown here as an apostrophe) to distinguish addresses from data values. All addresses (and no data values) must be adjusted after relocation.

(a) (b)

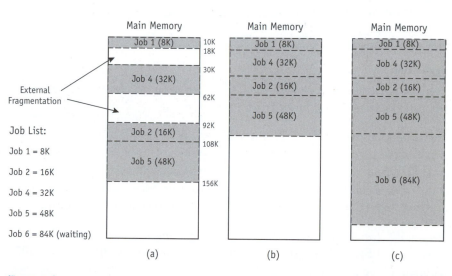

(a) (b) (c)

(figure 2.9)

Three snapshots of memory before and after compaction with the operating system occupying the first 10K of memory. When Job 6 arrives requiring 84K, the initial memory layout in (a) shows external fragmentation totaling 96K of space. Immediately after compaction (b), external fragmentation has been eliminated, making room for Job 6 which, after loading, is shown in (c).

the new block of free memory: the one formed as a result of compaction that will be located in memory starting after the last location used by the last job. The busy list is changed to show the new locations for all of the jobs already in progress that were relocated. Each job will have a new address except for those that were already residing at the lowest memory locations. For example, if the entry in the busy list starts at location 7805 (as shown in Table 2.9) and is relocated 762 spaces, then the location would be changed to 7043 (but the memory block size would not change—only its location).

To answer the other two questions we must learn more about the hardware components of a computer—specifically the registers. Special-purpose registers are used to help with the relocation. In some computers, two special registers are set aside for this purpose: the bounds register and the relocation register.

The **bounds register** is used to store the highest (or lowest, depending on the specific system) location in memory accessible by each program. This ensures that during execution, a program won't try to access memory locations that don't belong to it—that is, those that are out of bounds. The result of one such instance is reflected in the error message shown in Figure 2.10.

(figure 2.10)

This message indicates that a program attempted to access memory space that is out of bounds.
This was a fatal error resulting in the program's termination.

The **relocation register** contains the value that must be added to each address referenced in the program so that the system will be able to access the correct memory addresses after relocation. If a program isn't relocated, the value stored in the program's relocation register is zero. Figure 2.11 illustrates what happens during relocation by using the relocation register (all values are shown in decimal form).

Originally, Job 4 was loaded into memory starting at memory location 30K. (1K equals 1,024 bytes. Therefore, the exact starting address is: 30 * 1024 = 30720.) It required a block of memory of 32K (or 32 * 1024 = 32,768) addressable locations. Therefore, when it was originally loaded, the job occupied the space from memory location 30720 to memory location 63488-1.

Now, suppose that within the program, at memory location 31744, there's this instruction: LOAD 4, ANSWER. (This assembly language command asks that the data value

(figure 2.11)

Contents of the relocation register for Job 4 before the job's relocation and compaction (a) and after (b).

known as ANSWER be loaded into Register 4 for later computation. In this example, Register 4 is a working/computation register, which is distinct from either the relocation or the bounds registers mentioned earlier.) Similarly, the variable known as ANSWER, the value 37, is stored at memory location 53248 before compaction and relocation.

After relocation, Job 4 resides at a new starting memory address of 18K (to be exact, it is 18432, which is 18 * 1024). The job still has the same number of addressable locations, but those locations are in a different physical place in memory. Job 4 now occupies memory from location 18432 to location 51200-1 and, thanks to the relocation register, all of the addresses will be adjusted accordingly when the program is executed.

What does the relocation register contain? In this example, it contains the value –12288. As calculated previously, 12288 is the size of the free block that has been moved toward the high addressable end of memory where it can be combined with other free blocks of memory. The sign is negative because Job 4 has been moved back, closer to the low addressable end of memory, as shown at the top of Figure 2.10(b).

If the addresses were not adjusted by the value stored in the relocation register, then even though memory location 31744 is still part of Job 4's accessible set of memory locations, it would not contain the LOAD command. Not only that, but the other location, 53248, would be out of bounds. The instruction that was originally at 31744 has been moved to location 19456. That's because all of the instructions in this program have been moved back by 12K (12 * 1024 = 12,288), which is the size of the free block. Therefore, location 53248 has been displaced by –12288 and ANSWER, the data value 37, is now located at address 40960.

However, the precise LOAD instruction that was part of the original job has not been changed. The instructions inside the job are not revised in any way. And the original address where ANSWER had been stored, 53248, remains unchanged in the program no matter how many times Job 4 is relocated. Before the instruction is executed, the true address is computed by adding the value stored in the relocation register to the address found at that instruction. By changing only the value in the relocation register each time the job is moved in memory, this technique allows every job address to be properly adjusted.

In effect, by compacting and relocating, the Memory Manager optimizes the use of memory and thus improves throughput—an important measure of system performance. An unfortunate side effect is that this memory allocation scheme requires more overhead than with the previous schemes. The crucial factor here is the timing of the compaction—when and how often it should be done. There are three options.

- One approach is to perform compaction when a certain percentage of memory becomes busy—say 75 percent. The disadvantage of this approach is that the system would incur unnecessary overhead if no jobs were waiting to use the remaining 25 percent.

- A second approach is to compact memory only when there are jobs waiting to get in. This would entail constant checking of the entry queue, which might result in unnecessary overhead and thus slow down the processing of jobs already in the system.

- A third approach is to compact memory after a prescribed amount of time has elapsed. If the amount of time chosen is too small, however, then the system will spend more time on compaction than on processing. If it's too large, too many jobs will congregate in the waiting queue and the advantages of compaction are lost.

Each option has its good and bad points. The best choice for any system is decided by the operating system designers who, based on the job mix and other factors, try to optimize both processing time and memory use while keeping overhead as low as possible.

Conclusion

Four memory management techniques were presented in this chapter: single-user systems, fixed partitions, dynamic partitions, and relocatable dynamic partitions. Although they have differences, they all share the requirement that the entire program (1) be loaded into memory, (2) be stored contiguously, and (3) remain in memory until the entire job is completed. Consequently, each puts severe restrictions on the size of executable jobs because each one can be only as large as the biggest partition in memory. These schemes laid the groundwork for more complex memory management techniques that allowed users to interact more directly and more often with the system.

In the next chapter, we examine several memory allocation schemes that had two new things in common. First, they removed the requirement that jobs be loaded into contiguous memory locations. This allowed jobs to be subdivided so they could be loaded anywhere in memory (if space allowed) as long as the pieces were linked to each other in some way. The second requirement no longer needed was that the entire job reside in memory throughout its execution. By eliminating these mandates, programs were able to grow in size and complexity, opening the door to virtual memory.

Key Terms

address: a number that designates a particular memory location.

best-fit memory allocation: a main memory allocation scheme that considers all free blocks and selects for allocation the one that will result in the least amount of wasted space.

bounds register: a register used to store the highest location in memory legally accessible by each program.

compaction of memory: the process of collecting fragments of available memory space into contiguous blocks by relocating programs and data in a computer's memory.

deallocation: the process of freeing an allocated resource, whether memory space, a device, a file, or a CPU.

dynamic partitions: a memory allocation scheme in which jobs are given as much memory as they request when they are loaded for processing, thus creating their own partitions in main memory.

external fragmentation: a situation in which the dynamic allocation of memory creates unusable fragments of free memory between blocks of busy, or allocated, memory.

first-fit memory allocation: a main memory allocation scheme that searches from the beginning of the free block list and selects for allocation the first block of memory large enough to fulfill the request.

fixed partitions: a memory allocation scheme in which main memory is sectioned with one partition assigned to each job.

internal fragmentation: a situation in which a partition is only partially used by the program; the remaining space within the partition is unavailable to any other job and is therefore wasted.

main memory: the unit that works directly with the CPU and in which the data and instructions must reside in order to be processed. Also called *random access memory (RAM)*, *primary storage*, or *internal memory*.

null entry: an empty entry in a list.

RAM: another term for *main memory*.

relocatable dynamic partitions: a memory allocation scheme in which the system relocates programs in memory to gather together all empty blocks and compact them to make one block of memory that's large enough to accommodate some or all of the jobs waiting for memory.

relocation: (1) the process of moving a program from one area of memory to another; or (2) the process of adjusting address references in a program, by either software or hardware means, to allow the program to execute correctly when loaded in different sections of memory.

relocation register: a register that contains the value that must be added to each address referenced in the program so that the Memory Manager will be able to access the correct memory addresses.

Interesting Searches

For more background on a few of the topics discussed in this chapter, begin a search with these terms.

- Core Memory Technology
- technikum29 Museum of Computer and Communication Technology
- How RAM Works
- Static vs. Dynamic Partitions
- Internal vs. External Fragmentation

Exercises

Research Topics

A. Identify a computer (a desktop or laptop computer) that can accommodate an upgrade or addition of internal memory. Research the brand or type of memory chip that could be used in that system. Do not perform the installation. Instead, list the steps you would take to install the memory. Be sure to cite your sources.

B. For a platform of your choice, research the growth in the size of main memory from the time the platform was developed to the present day. Create a chart showing milestones in memory growth and the approximate date. Choose one from laptops, desktops, midrange computers, and mainframes. Be sure to mention the organization that performed the research and cite your sources.

Exercises

1. Describe a present-day computing environment that might use each of the memory allocation schemes (single user, fixed, dynamic, and relocatable dynamic) described in the chapter. Defend your answer by describing the advantages and disadvantages of the scheme in each case.

2. How often should memory compaction/relocation be performed? Describe the advantages and disadvantages of performing it even more often than recommended.

3. Using your own words, explain the role of the bounds register.

4. Describe in your own words the role of the relocation register.

5. Give an example of computing circumstances that would favor first-fit allocation over best-fit. Explain your answer.

6. Given the following information:

Job List:		Memory Block List:	
Job Number	Memory Requested	Memory Block	Memory Block Size
Job A	690K	Block 1	900K (low-order memory)
Job B	275K	Block 2	910K
Job C	760K	Block 3	300K (high-order memory)

   a. Use the first-fit algorithm to indicate which memory blocks are allocated to each of the three arriving jobs.

   b. Use the best-fit algorithm to indicate which memory blocks are allocated to each of the three arriving jobs.

7. Given the following information:

Job List:		Memory Block List:	
Job Number	Memory Requested	Memory Block	Memory Block Size
Job A	57K	Block 1	900K (low-order memory)
Job B	920K	Block 2	910K
Job C	50K	Block 3	200K
Job D	701K	Block 4	300K (high-order memory)

   a. Use the best-fit algorithm to indicate which memory blocks are allocated to each of the three arriving jobs.

   b. Use the first-fit algorithm to indicate which memory blocks are allocated to each of the three arriving jobs.

8. Next-fit is an allocation algorithm that starts by using the first-fit algorithm but keeps track of the partition that was last allocated. Instead of restarting the search with Block 1, it starts searching from the most

recently allocated block when a new job arrives. Using the following information:

Job List:		Memory Block List:	
Job Number	Memory Requested	Memory Block	Memory Block Size
Job A	590K	Block 1	100K (low-order memory)
Job B	50K	Block 2	900K
Job C	275K	Block 3	280K
Job D	460K	Block 4	600K (high-order memory)

Indicate which memory blocks are allocated to each of the three arriving jobs, and explain in your own words what advantages the next-fit algorithm could offer.

9. Worst-fit is an allocation algorithm that allocates the largest free block to a new job. It is the opposite of the best-fit algorithm. Compare it to next-fit conditions given in Exercise 8 and explain in your own words what advantages the worst-fit algorithm could offer.

10. Imagine an operating system that cannot perform memory deallocation. Name at least three effects on overall system performance that might result and explain your answer.

11. In a system using the relocatable dynamic partitions scheme, given the following situation (and using decimal form): Job Q is loaded into memory starting at memory location 42K.

   a. Calculate the exact starting address for Job Q in bytes.

   b. If the memory block has 3K in fragmentation, calculate the size of the memory block.

   c. Is the resulting fragmentation internal or external? Explain your reasoning.

12. In a system using the relocatable dynamic partitions scheme, given the following situation (and using decimal form): Job W is loaded into memory starting at memory location 5000K.

   a. Calculate the exact starting address for Job W in bytes.

   b. If the memory block has 3K in fragmentation, calculate the size of the memory block.

   c. Is the resulting fragmentation internal or external? Explain your reasoning.

13. If the relocation register holds the value -83968, was the relocated job moved toward the lower or higher addressable end of main memory? By how many kilobytes was it moved? Explain your conclusion.

14. In a system using the fixed partitions memory allocation scheme, given the following situation (and using decimal form): After Job J is loaded into a partition of size 50K, the resulting fragmentation is 7168 bytes. Perform the following:

   a. What is the size of Job J in bytes?

   b. What type of fragmentation is caused?

15. In a system using the dynamic partition memory allocation scheme, given the following situation (and using decimal form): After Job C of size 70K is loaded into a partition resulting in 7K of fragmentation, calculate the size (in bytes) of its partition and identify the type of fragmentation that is caused. Explain your answer.

Advanced Exercises

16. The relocation example presented in the chapter implies that compaction is done entirely in memory, without secondary storage. Can all free sections of memory be merged into one contiguous block using this approach? Why or why not?

17. In this chapter we described one way to compact memory. Some people suggest an alternate method: all jobs could be copied to a secondary storage device and then reloaded (and relocated) contiguously into main memory, thus creating one free block after all jobs have been recopied into memory. Is this viable? Could you devise a better way to compact memory? Write your algorithm and explain why it is better.

18. Given the memory configuration in Figure 2.12, answer the following questions. At this point, Job 4 arrives requesting a block of 100K.

    a. Can Job 4 be accommodated? Why or why not?

    b. If relocation is used, what are the contents of the relocation registers for Job 1, Job 2, and Job 3 after compaction?

    c. What are the contents of the relocation register for Job 4 after it has been loaded into memory?

    d. An instruction that is part of Job 1 was originally loaded into memory location 22K. What is its new location after compaction?

    e. An instruction that is part of Job 2 was originally loaded into memory location 55K. What is its new location after compaction?

    f. An instruction that is part of Job 3 was originally loaded into memory location 80K. What is its new location after compaction?

    g. If an instruction was originally loaded into memory location 110K, what is its new location after compaction?

(figure 2.12)

Memory configuration for Exercise 18.

Operating System	
	20K
Job 1 (10K)	30K
	50K
Job 2 (15K)	
	65K
	75K
Job 3 (45K)	
	120K
	200K

Programming Exercises

19. Here is a long-term programming project. Use the information that follows to complete this exercise.

Job List				Memory List	
Job Stream Number	**Time**	**Job Size**		**Memory Block**	**Size**
1	5	5760		1	9500
2	4	4190		2	7000
3	8	3290		3	4500
4	2	2030		4	8500
5	2	2550		5	3000
6	6	6990		6	9000
7	8	8940		7	1000
8	10	740		8	5500
9	7	3930		9	1500
10	6	6890		10	500
11	5	6580			
12	8	3820			
13	9	9140			
14	10	420			
15	10	220			
16	7	7540			
17	3	3210			
18	1	1380			
19	9	9850			
20	3	3610			
21	7	7540			
22	2	2710			
23	8	8390			
24	5	5950			
25	10	760			

At one large batch-processing computer installation, the management wants to decide what storage placement strategy will yield the best possible performance. The installation runs a large real storage computer (as opposed to "virtual" storage, which is covered in Chapter 3) under fixed partition multiprogramming. Each user program runs in a single group of contiguous storage locations. Users state their storage requirements and time units for CPU usage on their Job Control Card (it used to, and still does, work this way, although cards may not be used). The operating system allocates to each user the appropriate partition and starts up the user's job. The job remains in memory until completion. A total of 50,000 memory locations are available, divided into blocks as indicated in the previous table.

   a. Write (or calculate) an event-driven simulation to help you decide which storage placement strategy should be used at this installation. Your program would use the job stream and memory partitioning as indicated previously. Run the program until all jobs have been executed with the memory as is (in order by address). This will give you the first-fit type performance results.

   b. Sort the memory partitions by size and run the program a second time; this will give you the best-fit performance results. For both parts a. and b., you are investigating the performance of the system using a typical job stream by measuring:

      1. Throughput (how many jobs are processed per given time unit)
      2. Storage utilization (percentage of partitions never used, percentage of partitions heavily used, and so on)
      3. Waiting queue length
      4. Waiting time in queue
      5. Internal fragmentation

Given that jobs are served on a first-come, first-served basis:

   c. Explain how the system handles conflicts when jobs are put into a waiting queue and there are still jobs entering the system—which job goes first?

   d. Explain how the system handles the "job clocks," which keep track of the amount of time each job has run, and the "wait clocks," which keep track of how long each job in the waiting queue has to wait.

   e. Since this is an event-driven system, explain how you define "event" and what happens in your system when the event occurs.

   f. Look at the results from the best-fit run and compare them with the results from the first-fit run. Explain what the results indicate about the performance of the system for this job mix and memory organization. Is one method of partitioning better than the other? Why or why not? Could you recommend one method over the other given your sample run? Would this hold in all cases? Write some conclusions and recommendations.

20. Suppose your system (as explained in Exercise 19) now has a "spooler" (a storage area in which to temporarily hold jobs), and the job scheduler can choose which will be served from among 25 resident jobs. Suppose also that the first-come, first-served policy is replaced with a "faster-job, first-served" policy. This would require that a sort by time be performed on the job list before running the program. Does this make a difference in the results? Does it make a difference in your analysis? Does it make a difference in your conclusions and recommendations? The program should be run twice to test this new policy with both best-fit and first-fit.

21. Suppose your spooler (as described in Exercise 19) replaces the previous policy with one of "smallest-job, first-served." This would require that a sort by job size be performed on the job list before running the program. How do the results compare to the previous two sets of results? Will your analysis change? Will your conclusions change? The program should be run twice to test this new policy with both best-fit and first-fit.

Chapter 3

Memory Management: Virtual Memory Systems

"*Nothing is so much strengthened by practice, or weakened by neglect, as memory.*"

—Quintillian *(A.D. 35–100)*

Learning Objectives

After completing this chapter, you should be able to describe:

- The basic functionality of the memory allocation methods covered in this chapter: paged, demand paging, segmented, and segmented/demand paged memory allocation
- The influence that these page allocation methods have had on virtual memory
- The difference between a first-in first-out page replacement policy, a least-recently-used page replacement policy, and a clock page replacement policy
- The mechanics of paging and how a memory allocation scheme determines which pages should be swapped out of memory
- The concept of the working set and how it is used in memory allocation schemes
- Cache memory and its role in improving system response time

In this chapter we'll follow the evolution of memory management with four new memory allocation schemes. They remove the restriction of storing the programs contiguously, and most of them eliminate the requirement that the entire program reside in memory during its execution. Our concluding discussion of cache memory will show how its use improves the performance of the Memory Manager.

Paged Memory Allocation

Paged memory allocation is based on the concept of dividing jobs into units of equal size and each unit is called a **page**. Some operating systems choose a page size that is the exact same size as a section of main memory, which is called a **page frame**. Likewise, the sections of a magnetic disk are called **sectors** or blocks. The paged memory allocation scheme works quite efficiently when the pages, sectors, and page frames are all the same size. The exact size (the number of bytes that can be stored in each of them) is usually determined by the disk's sector size. Therefore, one sector will hold one page of job instructions (or data) and fit into one page frame of memory, but because this is the smallest addressable chunk of disk storage, it isn't subdivided even for very tiny jobs.

For many decades, the standard size of a page, page frame, and sector was identical at 512-bytes. Now the standard is moving to sectors of 4096-bytes (4K).

Before executing a program, a basic Memory Manager prepares it by:
1. Determining the number of pages in the program
2. Locating enough empty page frames in main memory
3. Loading all of the program's pages into those frames

When the program is initially prepared for loading, its pages are in logical sequence—the first pages contain the first instructions of the program and the last page has the last instructions. We refer to the program's instructions as "bytes" or "words."

The loading process is different from the schemes we studied in Chapter 2 because the pages do not have to be loaded in adjacent memory blocks. With the paged memory allocation, they can be loaded in noncontiguous page frames. In fact, each page can be stored in any available page frame anywhere in main memory.

The primary advantage of storing programs in noncontiguous page frames is that main memory is used more efficiently because an empty page frame can be used by any page of any job. In addition, the compaction scheme used for relocatable partitions is eliminated because there is no external fragmentation between page frames.

However, with every new solution comes a new problem. Because a job's pages can be located anywhere in main memory, the Memory Manager now needs a mechanism to keep track of them—and that means enlarging the size, complexity, and overhead of the operating system software.

The simplified example in Figure 3.1 shows how the Memory Manager keeps track of a program that is four pages long. To simplify the arithmetic, we've arbitrarily set the page size at 100 bytes. Job 1 is 350 bytes long and is being readied for execution. (The Page Map Table for the first job is shown later in Table 3.2.)

Notice in Figure 3.1 that the last page frame (Page Frame 11) is not fully utilized because Page 3 is less than 100 bytes—the last page uses only 50 of the 100 bytes available. In fact, very few jobs perfectly fill all of the pages, so internal fragmentation is still a problem, but only in the job's last page frame.

In Figure 3.1 (with seven free page frames), the operating system can accommodate an incoming job of up to 700 bytes because it can be stored in the seven empty page frames. But a job that is larger than 700 bytes cannot be accommodated until Job 1 ends its execution and releases the four page frames it occupies. And any job larger than 1100 bytes will never fit into the memory of this tiny system. Therefore, although paged memory allocation offers the advantage of noncontiguous storage, it still requires that the entire job be stored in memory during its execution.

(figure 3.1)

In this example, each page frame can hold 100 bytes. This job, at 350 bytes long, is divided among four page frames with internal fragmentation in the last page frame.

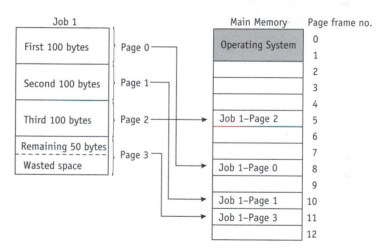

Figure 3.1 uses arrows and lines to show how a job's pages fit into page frames in memory, but the Memory Manager uses tables to keep track of them. There are essentially three tables that perform this function: the Job Table, the Page Map Table, and the Memory Map Table. Although different operating systems may have different names for them, the tables provide the same service regardless of the names they are given. All three tables reside in the part of main memory that is reserved for the operating system.

As shown in Table 3.1, the **Job Table (JT)** contains two values for each active job: the size of the job (shown on the left) and the memory location where its Page Map Table is stored (on the right). For example, the first job has a size of 400 and is at location 3096 in memory. The Job Table is a dynamic list that grows as jobs are loaded into the system and shrinks, as shown in (b) in Table 3.1, as they are later completed.

Job Table		Job Table		Job Table	
Job Size	PMT Location	Job Size	PMT Location	Job Size	PMT Location
400	3096	400	3096	400	3096
200	3100			700	3100
500	3150	500	3150	500	3150
(a)		(b)		(c)	

(table 3.1)

This section of the Job Table initially has one entry for each job (a). When the second job ends (b), its entry in the table is released and then replaced by the entry for the next job (c).

Each active job has its own **Page Map Table (PMT)**, which contains the vital information for each page—the page number and its corresponding memory address of the page frame. Actually, the PMT includes only one entry per page. The page numbers are sequential (Page 0, Page 1, Page 2, and so on), so it isn't necessary to list each page number in the PMT. The first entry in the PMT always lists the page frame memory address for Page 0, the second entry is the address for Page 1, and so on.

A simple **Memory Map Table (MMT)** has one entry for each page frame and shows its location and its free/busy status.

At compilation time, every job is divided into pages. Using Job 1 from Figure 3.1, we can see how this works:

- Page 0 contains the first hundred bytes.
- Page 1 contains the second hundred bytes.
- Page 2 contains the third hundred bytes.
- Page 3 contains the last 50 bytes.

As you can see, the program has 350 bytes; but when they are stored, the system numbers them starting from 0 through 349. Therefore, the system refers to them as Byte 0 through Byte 349.

How far away is a certain byte from the beginning of its page frame? This value is called the **displacement** (also called the offset) and it is a relative factor that's used to locate one certain byte within its page frame.

Here's how it works. In the simplified example shown in Figure 3.2, Bytes 0, 100, 200, and 300 are the first bytes for pages 0, 1, 2, and 3, respectively, so each has a displacement of zero. To state it another way, the distance from the beginning of the page frame to Byte 200 is zero bytes. Likewise, if the Memory Manager needs to access Byte 314, it can first go to the page frame containing Page 3 and then go to Byte 14 (the fifteenth) in that page frame.

Because the first byte of each page has a displacement of zero, and the last byte has a displacement of 99, the operating system can access the correct bytes by using its relative position from the beginning of its page frame.

While the computer hardware performs the calculations, the operating system is responsible for maintaining the tables that track the allocation and deallocation of storage.

(figure 3.2)

This job is 350 bytes long and is divided into four pages of 100 bytes each that are loaded into four page frames in memory.

In this example, it is easy for us to see intuitively that all bytes numbered less than 100 will be on Page 0, all bytes numbered greater than or equal to 100 but less than 200 will be on Page 1, and so on. (That is the advantage of choosing a convenient fixed page size, such as 100 bytes.) The operating system uses an algorithm to calculate the page and displacement using a simple arithmetic calculation:

BYTE_NUMBER_TO_BE_LOCATED / PAGE_SIZE = PAGE_NUMBER

To do the same calculation using long division, it would look like this:

$$
\begin{array}{r}
\text{page number} \\
\text{page size}\overline{)\text{byte number to be located}} \\
\underline{\text{xxx}} \\
\text{xxx} \\
\underline{\text{xxx}} \\
\text{displacement}
\end{array}
$$

For example, if we use 100 bytes as the page size, the page number and the displacement (the location within that page) of Byte 276 can be calculated as:

276 / 100 = 2 (with a remainder of 76)

The quotient (2) is the page number, and the remainder (76) is the displacement. Therefore, we know that the byte is located on Page 2, at Byte 76, which is exactly 77 bytes from the top of the page (remember that the first byte is located at zero).

Let's try another example with a more common page size of 4096 bytes. If we are seeking the location of Byte 6144, then we divide 6144 by 4096, and the result is 1.5 (which is 1 with a remainder of 2048). Therefore, the byte we are seeking is located midway on the second page (Page 1). To find the exact location, multiply the page size (4096) by the decimal (0.5) to discover that the byte we're seeking is located at Byte 2048 of Page 1 (which is exactly 2049 bytes from the start of the page).

Using the concepts just presented, and using the same parameters from the first example, answer these questions:

1. Could the operating system (or the hardware) get a page number that is greater than 3 if the program was searching for Byte 276?
2. If it did, what should the operating system do?
3. Could the operating system get a remainder/displacement of more than 99?
4. What is the smallest remainder/displacement possible?

Here are the answers:

1. No.
2. Send an error message and stop processing the program (because the page is out of bounds).
3. No.
4. Zero.

This procedure gives the location of an instruction with respect to the job's pages. However, these pages numbers are logical, not physical. Each page is actually stored in a page frame that can be located anywhere in available main memory. Therefore, the paged memory allocation algorithm needs to be expanded to find the exact location of the byte in main memory. To do so, we need to correlate each of the job's pages with its page frame number using the job's Page Map Table.

For example, if we look at the PMT for Job 1 from Figure 3.1, we see that it looks like the data in Table 3.2.

Page Number	Page Frame Number
0	8
1	10
2	5
3	11

(table 3.2)

Page Map Table for Job 1 in Figure 3.1.

In the first division example, we were looking for an instruction with a displacement of 76 on Page 2. To find its exact location in memory, the operating system (or the hardware) conceptually has to perform the following four steps.

STEP 1 Do the arithmetic computation just described to determine the page number and displacement of the requested byte: 276/100 = 2 with remainder of 76.

- Page number = the integer resulting from the division of the job space address by the page size = 2
- Displacement = the remainder from the page number division = 76

STEP 2 Refer to this job's PMT (shown in Table 3.2) and find out which page frame contains Page 2.

PAGE 2 is located in PAGE FRAME 5.

STEP 3 Get the address of the beginning of the page frame by multiplying the page frame number (5) by the page frame size (100).

```
ADDRESS_PAGE-FRAME = NUMBER_PAGE-FRAME * SIZE_PAGE-FRAME
ADDRESS_PAGE-FRAME = 5 * 100 = 500
```

STEP 4 Now add the displacement (calculated in Step 1) to the starting address of the page frame to compute the precise location in memory of the instruction:

```
INSTR_ADDRESS_IN_MEMORY = ADDRESS_PAGE-FRAME + DISPLACEMENT
INSTR_ADDRESS_IN_MEMORY = 500 + 76 = 576
```

The result of these calculations tells us exactly where (location 576) the requested byte (Byte 276) is located in main memory.

Here is another example. It follows the hardware and the operating system as an assembly language program is run with a LOAD instruction (the instruction LOAD R1, 518 tells the system to load into Register 1 the value found at Byte 518).

In Figure 3.3, the page frame size is set at 512 bytes each and the page size is also 512 bytes for this system. From the PMT we can see that this job has been divided into two pages. To find the exact location of Byte 518 (where the system will find the value to load into Register 1), the system will do the following:

1. Compute the page number and displacement—the page number is 1, and the displacement is 6: (518/512) = 1 with a remainder of 6.
2. Go to the job's Page Map Table and retrieve the appropriate page frame number for Page 1. (Page 1 can be found in Page Frame 3).
3. Compute the starting address of the page frame by multiplying the page frame number by the page frame size: (3 * 512 = 1536).

(figure 3.3)

This system has page frame and page sizes of 512 bytes each. The PMT shows where the job's two pages are loaded into available page frames in main memory.

4. Calculate the exact address of the instruction in main memory by adding the displacement to the starting address: (1536 + 6 = 1542). Therefore, memory address 1542 holds the value we are looking for that should be loaded into Register 1.

As you can see, this is not a simple operation. Every time an instruction is executed, or a data value is used, the operating system (or the hardware) must translate the job space address, which is logical, into its physical address, which is absolute. By doing so, we are resolving the address, called **address resolution** or address translation. All of this processing is overhead, which takes processing capability away from the running jobs and those waiting to run. (Technically, in most systems, the hardware does most of the address resolution, which reduces some of this overhead.)

A huge advantage of a paging scheme is that it allows jobs to be allocated in noncontiguous memory locations, allowing memory to be used more efficiently. (Recall that the simpler memory management systems described in Chapter 2 required all of a job's pages to be stored contiguously—one next to the other.) However, there are disadvantages— overhead is increased and internal fragmentation is still a problem, although it occurs only in the last page of each job. The key to the success of this scheme is the size of the page. A page size that is too small will generate very long PMTs (with a corresponding increase in overhead), while a page size that is too large will result in excessive internal fragmentation. Determining the best page size is an important policy decision— there are no hard and fast rules that will guarantee optimal use of resources, and it is a problem we'll see again as we examine other paging alternatives. The best size depends on the nature of the jobs being processed and on the constraints placed on the system.

Demand Paging Memory Allocation

Demand paging introduced the concept of loading only a part of the program into memory for processing. It was the first widely used scheme that removed the restriction of having the entire job in memory from the beginning to the end of its processing.

With demand paging, jobs are still divided into equally-sized pages that initially reside in secondary storage. When the job begins to run, its pages are brought into memory only as they are needed, and if they're never needed, they're never loaded.

Demand paging takes advantage of the fact that programs are written sequentially so that while one section, or module, is processed, other modules may be idle. Not all the pages are accessed at the same time, or even sequentially. For example:

With demand paging, the pages are loaded as each is requested. This requires high-speed access to the pages.

• Instructions to handle errors are processed only when a specific error is detected during execution. For instance, these instructions can indicate that input data was incorrect or that a computation resulted in an invalid answer. If no error occurs, and we hope this is generally the case, these instructions are never processed and never need to be loaded into memory.

• Many program modules are mutually exclusive. For example, while the program is being loaded (when the input module is active), then the processing module is inactive because it is generally not performing calculations during the input stage. Similarly, if the processing module is active, then the output module (such as printing) may be idle.

• Certain program options are either mutually exclusive or not always accessible. For example, when a program gives the user several menu choices, as shown in Figure 3.4, it allows the user to make only one selection at a time. If the user selects the first option (FILE), then the module with those program instructions is the only one that is being used, so that is the only module that needs to be in memory at this time. The other modules remain in secondary storage until they are "called." Many tables are assigned a large fixed amount of address space even though only a fraction of the table is actually used. For example, a symbol table might be prepared to handle 100 symbols. If only 10 symbols are used, then 90 percent of the table remains unused.

One of the most important innovations of demand paging was that it made virtual memory feasible. Virtual memory is discussed later in this chapter.

File   Edit   Object   Type   Select   Filter   Effect   View   Window   Help

(figure 3.4)

When you choose one option from the menu of an application program such as this one, the other modules that aren't currently required (such as Help) don't need to be moved into memory immediately.

The demand paging scheme allows the user to run jobs with less main memory than is required if the operating system is using the paged memory allocation scheme described earlier. In fact, a demand paging scheme can give the appearance of vast amounts of physical memory when, in reality, physical memory is significantly less than vast.

The key to the successful implementation of this scheme is the use of a high-speed direct access storage device (often shortened to DASD), which will be discussed in Chapter 7. (Examples of DASDs include hard drives or flash memory.) High speed access is vital because this scheme requires pages to be passed quickly from secondary storage to main memory and back again as they are needed.

How and when the pages are passed (also called swapped) between main memory and secondary storage depends on predefined policies that determine when to make room for needed pages and how to do so. The operating system relies on tables (such as the Job Table, the Page Map Tables, and the Memory Map Table) to implement the algorithm. These tables are basically the same as for paged memory allocation. With demand paging, there are three new fields for each page in each PMT: one to determine if the page being requested is already in memory, a second to determine if the page contents have been modified while in memory, and a third to determine if the page has been referenced most recently. The fourth field, which we discussed earlier in this chapter, shows the page frame number, as shown at the top of Figure 3.5.

The memory field tells the system where to find each page. If it is already in memory (shown here with a Y), the system will be spared the time required to bring it from secondary storage. As one can imagine, it's faster for the operating system to scan a table

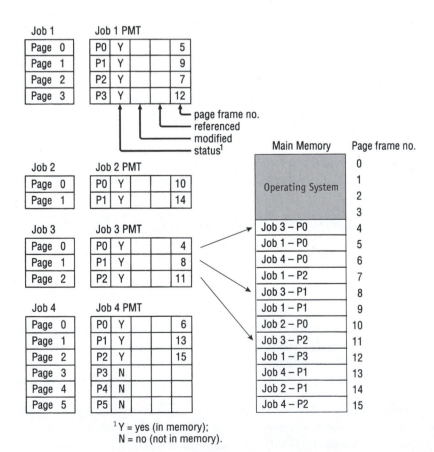

(figure 3.5)

Demand paging requires that the Page Map Table for each job keep track of each page as it is loaded or removed from main memory. Each PMT tracks the status of the page, whether it has been modified, whether it has been recently referenced, and the page frame number for each page currently in main memory. (Note: For this illustration, the Page Map Tables have been simplified. See Table 3.3 for more detail.)

[1] Y = yes (in memory);
N = no (not in memory).

located in main memory than it is to retrieve a page from a disk or other secondary storage device.

The modified field, noting whether or not the page has been changed, is used to save time when pages are removed from main memory and returned to secondary storage. If the contents of the page haven't been modified, then the page doesn't need to be rewritten to secondary storage. The original, the one that is already there, is correct.

The referenced field notes any recent activity and is used to determine which pages show the most processing activity and which are relatively inactive. This information is used by several page-swapping policy schemes to determine which pages should remain in main memory and which should be swapped out when the system needs to make room for other pages being requested.

The last field shows the page frame number for that page.

For example, in Figure 3.5 the number of total job pages is 15, and the number of total page frames available to jobs is 12. (The operating system occupies the first four of the 16 page frames in main memory.)

Assuming the processing status illustrated in Figure 3.5, what happens when Job 4 requests that Page 3 be brought into memory, given that there are no empty page frames available?

To move in a new page, one of the resident pages must be swapped back into secondary storage. Specifically, that includes copying the resident page to the disk (if it was modified) and writing the new page into the newly available page frame.

The hardware components generate the address of the required page, find the page number, and determine whether it is already in memory. Refer to the "Hardware Instruction Processing Algorithm" shown in Appendix A for more information.

If the Algorithm finds that the page is not in memory, then the operating system software takes over. The section of the operating system that resolves these problems is called the **page fault handler**, and an algorithm to perform that task is also described in Appendix A. The page fault handler determines whether there are empty page frames in memory so that the requested page can be immediately copied from secondary storage. If all page frames are busy, then the page fault handler must decide which page will be swapped out. (This decision is determined by the predefined policy for page removal.) Then the swap is made.

How many tables are changed because of this page swap? Immediately, three tables must be updated: the Page Map Tables for both jobs (the PMT with the page that was swapped out and the PMT with the page that was swapped in) as well as the Memory Map Table. Finally, the instruction that was interrupted is resumed, and processing continues.

A swap requires close interaction among hardware components, software algorithms, and policy schemes.

Although demand paging is a good solution to improve memory use, it is not free of problems. When there is an excessive amount of **page swapping** between main memory and secondary storage, the operation becomes inefficient. This phenomenon is called **thrashing**.

Thrashing is similar to the problem that students face when comparing explanations of a complex problem in two different textbooks. The amount of time you spend switching back and forth between the two books could cause you to spend more time figuring out where you left off in each book than you spend actually solving the issue at hand.

Caused when pages are frequently removed from memory but are called back shortly thereafter, thrashing uses a great deal of the computer's time and accomplishes very little. Thrashing can occur across jobs, when a large number of jobs are vying for a relatively low number of free pages (that is, the ratio of job pages to free memory page frames is high), or it can happen within a job—for example, in loops that cross page boundaries. We can demonstrate this with a simple example. Suppose that a loop to perform a certain sequence of steps begins at the bottom of one page and is completed at the top of the next page, as demonstrated in the C program in Figure 3.6. This requires that the command sequence go from Page 0 to Page 1 to Page 0 to Page 1 to Page 0, again and again, until the loop is finished.

```
for( j = 1; j < 100; ++j)        Page 0
    {
        k = j * j;

        m = a * j;
        printf("\n%d %d %d", j, k, m);   Page 1
    }
printf("\n");
```

(figure 3.6)

An example of demand paging that causes a page swap each time the loop is executed and results in thrashing. If only a single page frame is available, this program will have one page fault each time the loop is executed.

If there is only one empty page frame available, the first page is loaded into memory and execution begins. But, in this example, after executing the last instruction on Page 0, that page is swapped out to make room for Page 1. Now execution can continue with the first instruction on Page 1, but at the "}" symbol, Page 1 must be swapped out so Page 0 can be brought back in to continue the loop. Before this program is completed, swapping will have occurred 199 times (unless another page frame becomes free so both pages can reside in memory at the same time). A failure to find a page in memory is often called a **page fault**; this example would generate 199 page faults (and swaps).

Thrashing increases wear and tear on the hardware and slows data access.

In such extreme cases, the rate of useful computation could be degraded by at least a factor of 100. Ideally, a demand paging scheme is most efficient when programmers are aware of the page size used by their operating system and are careful to design their programs to keep page faults to a minimum; but in reality, this is not often feasible.

Page Replacement Policies and Concepts

As we just learned, the policy that selects the page to be removed, the **page replacement policy,** is crucial to the efficiency of the system, and the algorithm to do that must be carefully selected.

Several such algorithms exist, and it is a subject that enjoys a great deal of theoretical attention and research. Two of the most well-known algorithms are first-in first-out and least recently used. The **first-in first-out (FIFO) policy** is based on the assumption that the best page to remove is the one that has been in memory the longest. The **least recently used (LRU) policy** chooses the page least recently accessed to be swapped out.

To illustrate the difference between FIFO and LRU, let us imagine a dresser drawer filled with your favorite sweaters. The drawer is full, but that didn't stop you from buying a new sweater. Now you have to put it away. Obviously it won't fit in your sweater drawer unless you take something out—but which sweater should you move to the storage closet? Your decision will be based on a "sweater removal policy."

You could take out your oldest sweater (the one that was first in), figuring that you probably won't use it again—hoping you won't discover in the following days that it is your most used, most treasured possession. Or, you could remove the sweater that you haven't worn recently and has been idle for the longest amount of time (the one that was least recently used). It is readily identifiable because it is at the bottom of the drawer. But just because it hasn't been used recently doesn't mean that a once-a-year occasion won't demand its appearance soon!

What guarantee do you have that once you have made your choice you won't be trekking to the storage closet to retrieve the sweater you stored there yesterday? You could become a victim of thrashing, going back and forth to swap out sweaters.

Which is the best policy? It depends on the weather, the wearer, and the wardrobe. Of course, one option is to get another drawer. For an operating system (or a computer), this is the equivalent of adding more accessible memory. We explore that option after we discover how to more effectively use the memory we already have.

First-In First-Out

The first-in first-out (FIFO) page replacement policy will remove the pages that have been in memory the longest, that is, those that were "first in." The process of swapping pages is illustrated in Figure 3.7.

- Step 1: Page A is moved into the first available page frame.
- Step 2: Page B is moved into the second available page frame.
- Step 3: Page A is swapped into secondary storage.

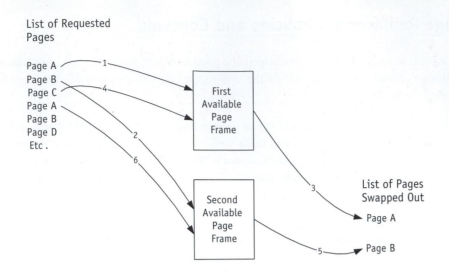

List of Requested
Pages

(figure 3.7)

First, Pages A and B are loaded into the two available page frames. When Page C is needed, the first page frame is emptied so C can be placed there. Then Page B is swapped out so Page A can be loaded there.

• Step 4: Page C is moved into the first available page frame.

• Step 5: Page B is swapped into secondary storage.

• Step 6: Page A is moved into the second available page frame.

Figure 3.8 demonstrates how the FIFO algorithm works by following a job with four pages (A, B, C, and D) as it is processed by a system with only two available page frames. The job needs to have its pages processed in the following order: A, B, A, C, A, B, D, B, A, C, D.

When both page frames are occupied, each new page brought into memory will cause an interrupt and a page swap into secondary storage. A page interrupt, which we identify with an asterisk (*), is generated anytime a page needs to be loaded into memory, whether a page is swapped out or not. Then we count the number of page interrupts and compute the failure rate and the success rate.

The efficiency of this configuration is dismal—due to the limited number of page frames available, there are 9 page interrupts out of 11 page requests. To calculate the failure rate, we divide the number of interrupts by the number of page requests:

$$Failure\text{-}Rate = Number\_of\_Interrupts / Page\_Requests\_Made$$

The failure rate of this system is 9/11, which is 82 percent. Stated another way, the success rate is 2/11, or 18 percent. A failure rate this high is usually unacceptable.

We are not saying FIFO is bad. We chose this example to show how FIFO works, not to diminish its appeal as a page replacement policy. The high failure rate here is caused by both the limited amount of memory available and the order in which pages are requested by the program. Because the job dictates the page order, that order can't be changed by

In Figure 3.8, using FIFO, Page A is swapped out when a newer page arrives, even though it is used the most often.

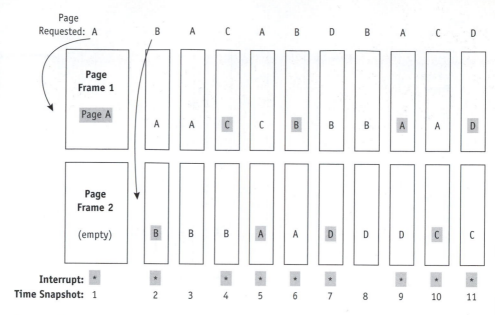

(figure 3.8)

Using a FIFO policy, this page trace analysis shows how each page requested is swapped into the two available page frames. When the program is ready to be processed, all four pages are in secondary storage. When the program calls a page that isn't already in memory, a page interrupt is issued, as shown by the gray boxes and asterisks. This program resulted in nine page interrupts.

the system, although the size of main memory can be changed. However, buying more memory may not always be the best solution—especially when you have many users and each one wants an unlimited amount of memory. As explained later in this chapter, there is no guarantee that buying more memory will always result in better performance.

Least Recently Used

The least recently used (LRU) page replacement policy swaps out the pages that show the least recent activity, figuring that these pages are the least likely to be used again in the immediate future. Conversely, if a page is used, it is likely to be used again soon; this is based on the theory of locality, explained later in this chapter.

To see how it works, let us follow the same job in Figure 3.8 but using the LRU policy. The results are shown in Figure 3.9. To implement this policy, a queue of requests is kept in FIFO order, a time stamp of when the page entered the system is saved, or a mark in the job's PMT is made periodically.

The efficiency of the configuration for this example is only slightly better than with FIFO. Here, there are 8 page interrupts out of 11 page requests, so the failure rate is 8/11, or 73 percent. In this example, an increase in main memory by one page frame

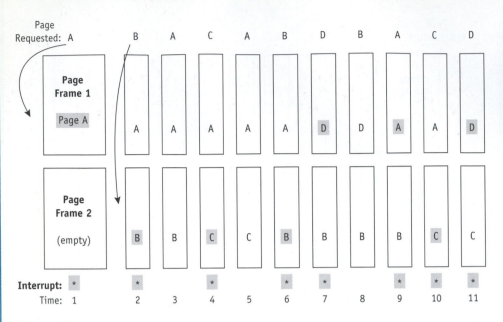

(figure 3.9)

Memory management using an LRU page removal policy for the program shown in Figure 3.8. Throughout the program, 11 page requests are issued, but they cause only 8 page interrupts.

would increase the success rate of both FIFO and LRU. However, we can't conclude on the basis of only one example that one policy is better than the other. In fact, LRU will never cause an increase in the number of page interrupts.

The same cannot be said about FIFO. It has been shown that *under certain circumstances* adding more memory can, *in rare cases,* actually cause an increase in page interrupts when using a FIFO policy. This was first demonstrated by Laszlo Belady in 1969 and is called the **FIFO Anomaly** or the **Belady Anomaly**. Although this is an unusual occurrence, the fact that it exists, coupled with the fact that pages are removed regardless of their activity (as was the case in Figure 3.8), has removed FIFO from the most favored policy position.

Clock Replacement Variation

A variation of the LRU page replacement algorithm is known as the **clock page replacement policy** because it is implemented with a circular queue and uses a pointer to step through the reference bits of the active pages, simulating a clockwise motion. The algorithm is paced according to the computer's **clock cycle**, which is the time span between two ticks in its system clock. The algorithm checks the reference bit for each page. If the bit is one (indicating that it was recently referenced), the bit is reset to zero and the bit for the next page is checked. However, if the reference bit is zero (indicating that the page has not recently been referenced), that page is targeted for removal. If all the reference bits are set to one, then the pointer must cycle through the entire circular queue again, giving each page a second and perhaps a third or fourth chance. Figure 3.10 shows a circular queue containing the reference bits for eight pages currently in memory. The pointer indicates the page that would be considered next for removal. Figure 3.10 shows what happens to the reference bits of the pages that have been given a second chance. When a new page, 146, has to be allocated to a page frame, it is assigned to the next space that has a reference bit of zero, the space previously occupied by Page 210.

Bit Shifting Variation

A second variation of LRU uses an 8-bit reference byte and a bit-shifting technique to track the usage of each page currently in memory. When the page is first copied into memory, the leftmost bit of its reference byte is set to 1, and all bits to the right of the one are set to zero. See Figure 3.11. At specific time intervals of the clock cycle, the Memory Manager shifts every page's reference bytes to the right by one bit, dropping their rightmost bit. Meanwhile, each time a page is referenced, the leftmost bit of its reference byte is set to 1.

This process of shifting bits to the right and resetting the leftmost bit to 1 when a page is referenced gives a history of each page's usage. For example, a page that has not been used for the last eight time intervals would have a reference byte of 00000000, while one that has been referenced once every time interval will have a reference byte of 11111111.

When a page fault occurs, the LRU policy selects the page with the smallest value in its reference byte because that would be the one least recently used. Figure 3.11 shows how the reference bytes for six active pages change during four snapshots of usage. In (a), the six pages have been initialized; this indicates that all of them have been referenced once. In (b), Pages 1, 3, 5, and 6 have been referenced again (marked with 1), but Pages 2 and 4 have not (now marked with 0 in the leftmost position). In (c), Pages 1, 2, and 4 have been referenced. In (d), Pages 1, 2, 4, and 6 have been referenced. In (e), Pages 1 and 4 have been referenced.

As shown in Figure 3.11, the values stored in the reference bytes are not unique: Page 3 and Page 5 have the same value. In this case, the LRU policy may opt to swap out all of the pages with the smallest value or may select one among them based on other criteria such as FIFO, priority, or whether the contents of the page have been modified.

Two other page removal algorithms, MRU (most recently used) and LFU (least frequently used), are discussed in exercises at the end of this chapter.

Page Number	Time Snapshot 0	Time Snapshot 1	Time Snapshot 2	Time Snapshot 3	Time Snapshot 4
1	10000000	11000000	11100000	11110000	11111000
2	10000000	01000000	10100000	11010000	01101000
3	10000000	11000000	01100000	00110000	00011000
4	10000000	01000000	10100000	11010000	11101000
5	10000000	11000000	01100000	00110000	00011000
6	10000000	11000000	01100000	10110000	01011000
	(a)	(b)	(c)	(d)	(e)

(figure 3.11)

Notice how the reference bit for each page is updated with every time tick. Arrows (a) through (e) show how the initial bit shifts to the right with every tick of the clock.

The Mechanics of Paging

Before the Memory Manager can determine which pages will be swapped out, it needs specific information about each page in memory—information included in the Page Map Tables.

For example, in Figure 3.5, the Page Map Table for Job 1 includes three bits: the status bit, the referenced bit, and the modified bit (these are the three middle columns: the two empty columns and the Y/N column represents "in memory"). But the representation of the table shown in Figure 3.5 is simplified for illustration purposes. It actually looks something like the one shown in Table 3.3.

✓ Each Page Map Table must track each page's status, modifications, and references. It does so with three bits, each of which can be either 0 or 1.

Page No.	Status Bit	Modified Bit	Referenced Bit	Page Frame No.
0	1	1	1	5
1	1	0	0	9
2	1	0	0	7
3	1	0	1	12

(table 3.3)

Page Map Table for Job 1 shown in Figure 3.5. A 1 = Yes and 0 = No.

As we said before, the status bit indicates whether the page is currently in memory. The referenced bit indicates whether the page has been called (referenced) recently. This bit is important because it is used by the LRU algorithm to determine which pages should be swapped out.

The modified bit indicates whether the contents of the page have been altered; if so, the page must be rewritten to secondary storage when it is swapped out before its page frame is released. (A page frame with contents that have not been modified can be overwritten directly, thereby saving a step.) That is because when a page is swapped into memory it isn't removed from secondary storage. The page is merely copied—the original remains intact in secondary storage. Therefore, if the page isn't altered while it is in main memory (in which case the modified bit remains unchanged at zero), the page needn't be copied back to secondary storage when it is swapped out of memory—the page that is already there is correct. However, if modifications were made to the page, the new version of the page must be written over the older version—and that takes time. Each bit can be either 0 or 1, as shown in Table 3.4.

Status Bit		Modified Bit		Referenced Bit	
Value	Meaning	Value	Meaning	Value	Meaning
0	*not* in memory	0	*not* modified	0	*not* called
1	*resides* in memory	1	*was* modified	1	*was* called

The status bit for all pages in memory is 1. A page must be in memory before it can be swapped out so all of the candidates for swapping have a 1 in this column. The other two bits can be either 0 or 1, making four possible combinations of the referenced and modified bits, as shown in Table 3.5.

	Modified?	Referenced?	What it Means
Case 1	0	0	Not modified AND not referenced
Case 2	0	1	Not modified BUT was referenced
Case 3	1	0	Was modified BUT not referenced [Impossible?]
Case 4	1	1	Was modified AND was referenced

The FIFO algorithm uses only the modified and status bits when swapping pages (because it doesn't matter to FIFO how recently they were referenced), but the LRU looks at all three before deciding which pages to swap out.

Which pages would the LRU policy choose first to swap? Of the four cases described in Table 3.5, it would choose pages in Case 1 as the ideal candidates for removal because they've been neither modified nor referenced. That means they wouldn't need to be rewritten to secondary storage, and they haven't been referenced recently. So the pages with zeros for these two bits would be the first to be swapped out.

What is the next most likely candidate? The LRU policy would choose Case 3 next because the other two, Case 2 and Case 4, were recently referenced. The bad news is that Case 3 pages have been modified; therefore, the new contents will be written to secondary storage, and that means it will take more time to swap them out. By process of elimination, then we can say that Case 2 pages would be the third choice and Case 4 pages would be those least likely to be removed.

You may have noticed that Case 3 presents an interesting situation: apparently these pages have been modified without being referenced. How is that possible? The key lies in how the referenced bit is manipulated by the operating system. When the pages are brought into memory, each is usually referenced at least once. That means that all of the pages soon have a referenced bit of 1. Of course the LRU algorithm would be defeated if every page indicated that it had been referenced. Therefore, to make sure the referenced bit actually indicates *recently* referenced, the operating system periodically resets it to 0. Then, as the pages are referenced during processing, the bit is changed from 0 to 1 and the LRU policy is able to identify which pages actually are frequently referenced. As you can imagine, there is one brief instant, just after the bits are reset, in which all of the pages (even the active pages) have reference bits of 0 and are vulnerable. But as processing continues, the most-referenced pages soon have their bits reset to 1, so the risk is minimized.

The Working Set

One innovation that improved the performance of demand paging schemes was the concept of the **working set**, which is the collection of pages residing in memory that can be accessed directly without incurring a page fault. Typically, a job's working set changes as the job moves through the system: one working set could be used to initialize the job, another could work through repeated calculations, another might interact with output devices, and a final set could close the job.

For example, when a user requests execution of a program, the first page is loaded into memory and execution continues as more pages are loaded: those containing variable declarations, others containing instructions, others containing data, and so on. After a while, most programs reach a fairly stable state, and processing continues smoothly with very few additional page faults. At this point, one of the job's working sets is in memory, and the program won't generate many page faults until it gets to another phase requiring a different set of pages to do the work—a different working set. An example of working sets in Windows is shown in Figure 3.12.

On the other hand, it is possible that a poorly structured program could require that every one of its pages be in memory before processing can begin.

(figure 3.12)

Using a Windows operating system, this user searched for and opened the Resource Monitor and clicked on the Memory tab to see the working set for each open application.

Captured from Windows operating system.

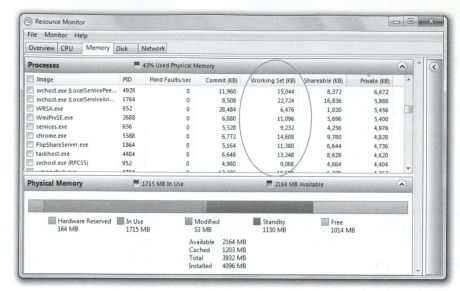

Fortunately, most programs are structured, and this leads to a **locality of reference** during the program's execution, meaning that during any phase of its execution, the program references only a small fraction of its pages. If a job is executing a loop, then the instructions within the loop are referenced extensively while those outside the loop may not be used at all until the loop is completed—that's locality of reference. The same concept applies to sequential instructions, subroutine calls (within the subroutine), stack implementations, access to variables acting as counters or sums, or multidimensional variables such as arrays and tables, where only a few of the pages are needed to handle the references.

It would be convenient if all of the pages in a job's working set were loaded into memory at one time to minimize the number of page faults and to speed up processing, but that is easier said than done. To do so, the system needs definitive answers to some difficult questions: How many pages comprise the working set? What is the maximum number of pages the operating system will allow for a working set?

The second question is particularly important in networked or time-sharing systems, which regularly swap jobs, or pages of jobs, into memory and back to secondary storage to accommodate the needs of many users. The problem is this: every time a job is reloaded back into memory (or has pages swapped), it has to generate several page faults until its working set is back in memory and processing can continue. It is a time-consuming task for the CPU, as shown in Figure 3.13.

One solution adopted by many paging systems is to begin by identifying each job's working set and then loading it into memory in its entirety before allowing execution to begin. In a time-sharing or networked system, this means the operating system must keep track of the size and identity of every working set, making sure that the

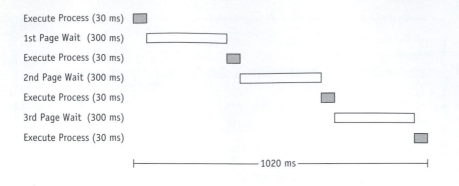

Execute Process (30 ms)
1st Page Wait (300 ms)
Execute Process (30 ms)
2nd Page Wait (300 ms)
Execute Process (30 ms)
3rd Page Wait (300 ms)
Execute Process (30 ms)

|← 1020 ms →|

(figure 3.13)

Time line showing the amount of time required to process page faults for a single program. The program in this example takes 120 milliseconds (ms) to execute but an additional 900 ms to load the necessary pages into memory. Therefore, job turnaround is 1020 ms.

jobs destined for processing at any one time won't exceed the available memory. Some operating systems use a variable working set size and either increase it when necessary (the job requires more processing) or decrease it when necessary. This may mean that the number of jobs in memory will need to be reduced if, by doing so, the system can ensure the completion of each job and the subsequent release of its memory space.

We have looked at several examples of demand paging memory allocation schemes. Demand paging had two advantages. It was the first scheme in which a job was no

Peter J. Denning (1942–)

Dr. Denning published his groundbreaking paper in 1967, in which he described the working set model for program behavior. He helped establish virtual memory as a permanent part of operating systems. Because of his work, the concepts of working sets, locality of reference, and thrashing became standard in the curriculum for operating systems. In the 1980s, he was one of the four founding principal investigators of the Computer Science Network, a precursor to today's Internet. Denning's honors include fellowships in three professional societies: the Institute of Electrical and Electronics Engineers (IEEE, 1982), American

Association for the Advancement of Science (AAAS, 1984), and Association of Computing Machinery (ACM, 1993).

For more information:
http://www.computerhistory.org/events/events .php?spkid=0&ssid=1173214027

Dr. Denning won the Association for Computing Machinery Special Interest Group Operating Systems Hall of Fame Award 2005: "The working set model became the ideal for designing the memory manager parts of operating systems. Virtual storage became a standard part of operating systems."

longer constrained by the size of physical memory (and it introduced the concept of virtual memory, discussed later in this chapter). The second advantage was that it utilized memory more efficiently than the previous schemes because the sections of a job that were used seldom or not at all (such as error routines) weren't loaded into memory unless they were specifically requested. Its disadvantage was the increased overhead caused by the tables and the page interrupts. The next allocation scheme built on the advantages of both paging and dynamic partitions.

Segmented Memory Allocation

The concept of segmentation is based on the common practice by programmers of structuring their programs in modules—logical groupings of code. With **segmented memory allocation**, each job is divided into several **segments** of different sizes, one for each module that contains pieces that perform related functions. A **subroutine** is an example of one such logical group. Segmented memory allocation was designed to reduce page faults that resulted from having a segment's loop split over two or more pages, for example. This is fundamentally different from a paging scheme, which divides the job into several pages all of the same size, each of which often contains pieces from more than one program module.

A second important difference with segmented memory allocation is that main memory is no longer divided into page frames, because the size of each segment is different ranging from quite small to large. Therefore, as with the dynamic partition allocation scheme discussed in Chapter 2, memory is allocated in a dynamic manner.

The Segment Map Table functions the same way as a Page Map Table but it manages segments instead of pages.

When a program is compiled or assembled, the segments are set up according to the program's structural modules. Each segment is numbered and a **Segment Map Table (SMT)** is generated for each job; it contains the segment numbers, their lengths, access rights, status, and (when each is loaded into memory) its location in memory. Figures 3.14 and 3.15 show the same job that's composed of a main program and two subroutines (for example, one subroutine calculates the normal pay rate, and a second one calculates

(figure 3.14)

Segmented memory allocation. Job 1 includes a main program and two subroutines. It is a single job that is structurally divided into three segments of different sizes.

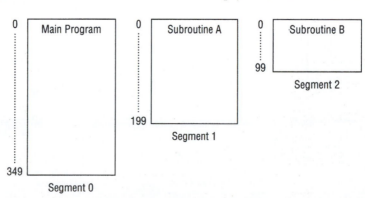

the overtime pay or commissions) with its Segment Map Table and main memory allocation. Notice that the segments need not be located adjacent or even near each other in main memory. (As in demand paging, the referenced and modified bits are used in segmentation and appear in the SMT even though they aren't included in Figure 3.15.)

The Memory Manager needs to keep track of the segments in memory. This is done with three tables, combining aspects of both dynamic partitions and demand paging memory management:

• The Job Table lists every job being processed (one for the whole system).

• The Segment Map Table lists details about each segment (one for each job).

• The Memory Map Table monitors the allocation of main memory (one for the whole system).

Like demand paging, the instructions within each segment are ordered sequentially, but the segments don't need to be stored contiguously in memory. We just need to know where each segment is stored. The contents of the segments themselves are contiguous in this scheme.

To access a specific location within a segment, we can perform an operation similar to the one used for paged memory management. The only difference is that we

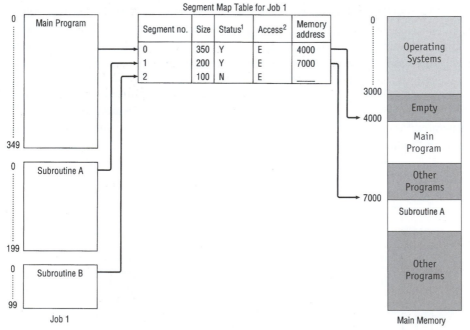

(figure 3.15)

The Segment Map Table tracks each segment for this job. Notice that Subroutine B has not yet been loaded into memory.

Segment Map Table for Job 1

Segment no.	Size	Status[1]	Access[2]	Memory address
0	350	Y	E	4000
1	200	Y	E	7000
2	100	N	E	____

[1] Y = in memory;
N = not in memory.

[2] E = Execute only.

work with segments instead of pages. The addressing scheme requires the segment number and the displacement within that segment; and because the segments are of different sizes, the displacement must be verified to make sure it isn't outside of the segment's range.

In Figure 3.16, Segment 1 includes all of Subroutine A, so the system finds the beginning address of Segment 1, 7000, and it begins there.

If the instruction requested that processing begin at byte 100 of Subroutine A (which is possible in languages that support multiple entries into subroutines) then, to locate that item in memory, the Memory Manager would need to add 100 (the displacement) to 7000 (the beginning address of Segment 1).

Can the displacement be larger than the size of the segment? No, not if the program is coded correctly; however, accidents and attempted exploits do happen, and

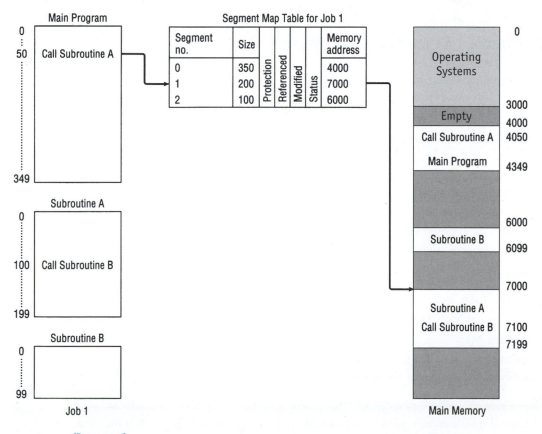

(figure 3.16)

During execution, the main program calls Subroutine A, which triggers the SMT to look up its location in memory.

the Memory Manager must always guard against this possibility by checking the displacement against the size of the segment, verifying that it is not out of bounds.

To access a location in memory, when using either paged or segmented memory management, the address is composed of two values: the page or segment number and the displacement. Therefore, it is a two-dimensional addressing scheme—that is, it has two elements: SEGMENT_NUMBER and DISPLACEMENT.

The disadvantage of any allocation scheme in which memory is partitioned dynamically is the return of external fragmentation. Therefore, if that schema is used, recompaction of available memory is necessary from time to time.

As you can see, there are many similarities between paging and segmentation, so they are often confused. The major difference is a conceptual one: pages are physical units that are invisible to the user's program and consist of fixed sizes; segments are logical units that are visible to the user's program and consist of variable sizes.

Segmented/Demand Paged Memory Allocation

The **segmented/demand paged memory allocation** scheme evolved from the two we have just discussed. It is a combination of segmentation and demand paging, and it offers the logical benefits of segmentation, as well as the physical benefits of paging. The logic isn't new. The algorithms used by the demand paging and segmented memory management schemes are applied here with only minor modifications.

This allocation scheme doesn't keep each segment as a single contiguous unit, but subdivides it into pages of equal size that are smaller than most segments and more easily manipulated than whole segments. Therefore, many of the problems of segmentation (compaction, external fragmentation, and secondary storage handling) are removed because the pages are of fixed length.

This scheme, illustrated in Figure 3.17, requires four types of tables:
• The Job Table lists every job in process (there's one JT for the whole system).
• The Segment Map Table lists details about each segment (one SMT for each job).
• The Page Map Table lists details about every page (one PMT for each segment).
• The Memory Map Table monitors the allocation of the page frames in main memory (there's one for the whole system).

Notice that the tables in Figure 3.17 have been simplified. The SMT actually includes additional information regarding protection (such as the authority to read, write, and execute parts of the file), and it also determines which specific users or processes are allowed to access that segment. In addition, the PMT includes indicators of the page's status, last modification, and last reference.

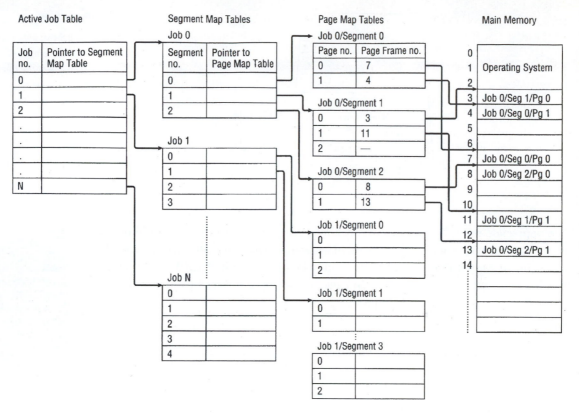

(figure 3.17)

How the Job Table, Segment Map Table, Page Map Table, and main memory interact in a segment/paging scheme.

Here's how it works: To access a certain location in memory, the system locates the address, which is composed of three entries: the segment number, the page number within that segment, and the displacement within that page. Therefore, it is a three-dimensional addressing scheme with the SEGMENT_NUMBER, the PAGE_NUMBER, and the DISPLACEMENT.

The major disadvantages of this memory allocation scheme are twofold: the overhead that is required to manage the tables (Segment Map Tables and the Page Map Tables), and the time required to reference them. To minimize the number of references, many systems take advantage of associative memory to speed up the process.

Associative memory is a name given to several registers that are allocated to each job that is active. See Figure 3.18. Their task is to associate several segment and page numbers belonging to the job being processed with their main memory addresses. These associative registers are hardware, and the exact number of registers varies from system to system.

(figure 3.18)

Hierarchy of data storage options, from most expensive at the top to cheapest at the bottom (adapted from Stuart, 2009).

To appreciate the role of associative memory, it is important to understand how the system works with segments and pages. In general, when a job is allocated to the CPU, its Segment Map Table is loaded into main memory, while its Page Map Tables are loaded only as they are needed. When pages are swapped between main memory and secondary storage, all tables are updated.

Here is a typical procedure:

1. When a page is first requested, the job's SMT is searched to locate its PMT.
2. The PMT is loaded (if necessary) and searched to determine the page's location in memory.
   a. If the page isn't in memory, then a page interrupt is issued, the page is brought into memory, and the table is updated. (As the example indicates, loading the PMT can cause a page interrupt, or fault, as well.) This process is just as tedious as it sounds, but it gets easier.
   b. Since this segment's PMT (or part of it) now resides in memory, any other requests for pages within this segment can be quickly accommodated because there is no need to bring the PMT into memory. However, accessing these tables (SMT and PMT) is time consuming.

Whenever a page request is issued, two searches can take place at the same time: one through associative memory and one through the SMT and its PMTs.

This illustrates the problem addressed by associative memory, which stores the information related to the most-recently-used pages. Then when a page request is issued, two searches begin at once—one through the segment and page map tables and one through the contents of the associative registers.

If the search of the associative registers is successful, then the search through the tables is abandoned and the address translation is performed using the information in the associative registers. However, if the search of associative memory fails, no time is lost because the search through the SMT and PMTs had already begun (in this schema). When this search is successful and the main memory address from the PMT has been determined, the address is used to continue execution of the program while the reference is also stored in one of the associative registers. If all of the associative registers are full, then an LRU (or other) algorithm is used and the least-recently-referenced associative register holds the information on this requested page.

For example, a system with eight associative registers per job will use them to store the SMT entries and PMT entries for the last eight pages referenced by that job. When an address needs to be translated from segment and page numbers to a memory location, the system will look first in the eight associative registers. If a match is found, the memory location is taken from the associative register; if there is no match, then the SMT and PMTs will continue to be searched and the new information will be stored in one of the eight registers as a result. It's worth noting that in some systems the searches do not run in parallel, but the search of the SMT and PMTs is performed after a search of the associative registers fails.

If a job is swapped out to secondary storage during its execution, then all of the information stored in its associative registers is saved, as well as the current PMT and SMT, so the displaced job can be resumed quickly when the CPU is reallocated to it. The primary advantage of a large associative memory is increased speed. The disadvantage is the high cost of the complex hardware required to perform the parallel searches.

Virtual Memory

With virtual memory, the amount of memory available for processing jobs can be much larger than available physical memory.

Virtual memory became possible with the capability of moving pages at will between main memory and secondary storage, and it effectively removed restrictions on maximum program size. With virtual memory, even though only a portion of each program is stored in memory at any given moment, by swapping pages into and out of memory, it gives users the appearance that their programs are completely loaded into main memory during their entire processing time—a feat that would require an incredibly large amount of main memory.

Virtual memory can be implemented with both paging and segmentation, as seen in Table 3.6.

(table 3.6)

Comparison of the advantages and disadvantages of virtual memory with paging and segmentation.

Virtual Memory with Paging	Virtual Memory with Segmentation
Allows internal fragmentation within page frames	Doesn't allow internal fragmentation
Doesn't allow external fragmentation	Allows external fragmentation
Programs are divided into equal-sized pages	Programs are divided into unequal-sized segments that contain logical groupings of code
The absolute address is calculated using page number and displacement	The absolute address is calculated using segment number and displacement
Requires Page Map Table (PMT)	Requires Segment Map Table (SMT)

Segmentation allows users to share program code. The shared segment contains: (1) an area where unchangeable code (called **reentrant code**) is stored, and (2) several data areas, one for each user. In this case, users share the code, which cannot be modified, but they can modify the information stored in their own data areas as needed without affecting the data stored in other users' data areas.

Before virtual memory, sharing meant that copies of files were stored in each user's account. This allowed them to load their own copy and work on it at any time. This kind of sharing created a great deal of unnecessary system cost—the I/O overhead in loading the copies and the extra secondary storage needed. With virtual memory, those costs are substantially reduced because shared programs and subroutines are loaded on demand, satisfactorily reducing the storage requirements of main memory (although this is accomplished at the expense of the Memory Map Table).

The use of virtual memory requires cooperation between the Memory Manager (which tracks each page or segment) and the processor hardware (which issues the interrupt and resolves the virtual address). For example, when a page that is not already in memory is needed, a page fault is issued and the Memory Manager chooses a page frame, loads the page, and updates entries in the Memory Map Table and the Page Map Tables.

Virtual memory works well in a multiprogramming environment because most programs spend a lot of time waiting—they wait for I/O to be performed; they wait for pages to be swapped in or out; and they wait when their turn to use the processor is expired. In a multiprogramming environment, the waiting time isn't wasted because the CPU simply moves to another job.

Virtual memory has increased the use of several programming techniques. For instance, it aids the development of large software systems, because individual pieces can be developed independently and linked later on.

Virtual memory management has several advantages:

• A job's size is no longer restricted to the size of main memory (or worse, to the free space available within main memory).

• Memory is used more efficiently because the only sections of a job stored in memory are those needed immediately, while those not needed remain in secondary storage.

• It allows an unlimited amount of multiprogramming, which can apply to many jobs, as in dynamic and static partitioning, or to many users.

• It allows the sharing of code and data.

• It facilitates dynamic linking of program segments.

The advantages far outweigh these disadvantages:

• Increased processor hardware costs.

• Increased overhead for handling paging interrupts.

• Increased software complexity to prevent thrashing.

Cache Memory

Cache memory is based on the concept of using a small, fast, and expensive memory to supplement the workings of main memory. Because the cache is usually small in capacity (compared to main memory), it can use more expensive memory chips. These are five to ten times faster than main memory and match the speed of the CPU. Therefore, if data or instructions that are frequently used are stored in cache memory, memory access time can be cut down significantly and the CPU can execute those instructions faster, thus raising the overall performance of the computer system. (It's similar to the role of a frequently called list of telephone numbers in a telephone. By keeping those numbers in an easy-to-reach place, they can be called much faster than those in a long contact list.)

(figure 3.19)

Comparison of (a) the traditional path used by early computers between main memory and the CPU and (b) the path used by modern computers to connect the main memory and the CPU via cache memory.

As shown in Figure 3.19(a), early computers were designed to have data and instructions transferred from secondary storage to main memory and then to special-purpose registers for processing—this path necessarily increased the amount of time needed to process those instructions. However, because the same instructions are used repeatedly in most programs, computer system designers thought it would be more efficient if the system would not use a complete memory cycle every time an instruction or data value is required. Designers found that this could be done if they placed repeatedly used data in general-purpose registers instead of in main memory.

Cache size is a significant contributor to overall response and is an important element in system design.

To solve this problem, computer systems automatically store frequently used data in an intermediate memory unit called **cache memory**. This adds a middle layer to the original hierarchy. Cache memory can be thought of as an intermediary between main memory and the special-purpose registers, which are the domain of the CPU, as shown in Figure 3.17(b).

A typical microprocessor has two or more levels of caches, such as Level 1 (L1), Level 2 (L2), and Level 3 (L3), as well as specialized caches.

In a simple configuration with only two cache levels, information enters the processor through the bus interface unit, which immediately sends one copy to the Level 2 cache, which is an integral part of the microprocessor and is directly connected to the CPU. A second copy is sent to one of two Level 1 caches, which are built directly into the chip. One of these Level 1 caches stores instructions, while the other stores data to be used by the instructions. If an instruction needs additional data, the instruction is put on hold while the processor looks for the missing data—first in the data Level 1 cache, and then in the larger Level 2 cache before searching main memory. Because the Level 2 cache is an integral part of the microprocessor, data moves two to four times faster between the CPU and the cache than between the CPU and main memory.

To understand the relationship between main memory and cache memory, consider the relationship between the size of the Web and the size of your private browser bookmark file. Your bookmark file is small and contains only a tiny fraction of all the available addresses on the Web; but the chance that you will soon visit a Web site that is in your bookmark file is high. Therefore, the purpose of your bookmark file is to keep your most frequently accessed addresses easy to reach so you can access them quickly. Similarly, the purpose of cache memory is to keep handy the most recently accessed data and instructions so that the CPU can access them repeatedly without wasting time.

The movement of data or instructions from main memory to cache memory uses a method similar to that used in paging algorithms. First, cache memory is divided into blocks of equal size called slots. Then, when the CPU first requests an instruction or data from a location in main memory, the requested instruction and several others around it are transferred from main memory to cache memory, where they are stored in one of the free slots. Moving a block at a time is based on the principle of locality of reference, which states that it is very likely that the next CPU request will be physically close to the one just requested. In addition to the block of data transferred, the slot also contains a label that indicates the main memory address from which the block was copied. When the CPU requests additional information from that location in main memory, cache memory is accessed first; and if the contents of one of the labels in a slot matches the address requested, then access to main memory is not required.

The algorithm to execute one of these "transfers from main memory" is simple to implement (a pseudocode algorithm can be found in Appendix A).

These steps become more complicated when there are no free cache slots, which can occur because the size of cache memory is smaller than that of main memory—in this case individual slots cannot be permanently allocated to blocks. To address this contingency, the system needs a policy for block replacement, which could be similar to those used in page replacement.

When designing cache memory, one must take into consideration the following four factors:

* *Cache size*. Studies have shown that having any cache, even a small one, can substantially improve the performance of the computer system.
* *Block size*. Because of the principle of locality of reference, as block size increases, the ratio of number of references found in the cache to the total number of references will tend to increase.
* *Block replacement algorithm*. When all the slots are busy and a new block has to be brought into the cache, a block that is least likely to be used in the near future should be selected for replacement. However, as we saw in paging, this is nearly impossible to predict. A reasonable course of action is to select a block that has not been used for a long time. Therefore, LRU is the algorithm that is often chosen for block replacement, which requires a hardware mechanism to determine the least recently used slot.
* *Rewrite policy*. When the contents of a block residing in cache are changed, it must be written back to main memory before it is replaced by another block. A rewrite policy must be in place to determine when this writing will take place. One alternative is to do this every time that a change occurs, which would increase the number of memory writes, possibly increasing overhead. A second alternative is to do this only when the block is replaced or the process is finished, which would minimize overhead but would leave the block in main memory in an inconsistent state. This would create problems in multiprocessor environments and in cases where I/O modules can access main memory directly.

The optimal selection of cache size and replacement algorithm can result in 80 to 90 percent of all requests being in the cache, making for a very efficient memory system. This measure of efficiency, called the cache hit ratio, is used to determine the performance of cache memory and, when shown as a percentage, represents the percentage of total memory requests that are found in the cache. One formula is this:

$$\text{HitRatio} = \frac{\text{number of requests found in the cache}}{\text{total number of requests}} * 100$$

For example, if the total number of requests is 10, and 6 of those are found in cache memory, then the hit ratio is 60 percent, which is reasonably good and suggests improved system performance.

$$HitRatio = (6/10) * 100 = 60\%$$

Likewise, if the total number of requests is 100, and 9 of those are found in cache memory, then the hit ratio is only 9 percent.

$$HitRatio = (9/100) * 100 = 9\%$$

Another way to measure the efficiency of a system with cache memory, assuming that the system always checks the cache first, is to compute the average memory access time (Avg_Mem_AccTime) using the following formula:

$$Avg\_Mem\_AccTime = Avg\_Cache\_AccessTime + (1-HitRatio)*Avg\_MainMem\_AccTime$$

For example, if we know that the average cache access time is 200 nanoseconds (nsec) and the average main memory access time is 1000 nsec, then a system with a hit ratio of 60 percent will have an average memory access time of 600 nsec:

$$AvgMemAccessTime = 200 + (1 - 0.60) * 1000 = 600\ nsec$$

A system with a hit ratio of 9 percent will show an average memory access time of 1110 nsec:

$$AvgMemAccessTime = 200 + (1 - 0.09) * 1000 = 1110\ nsec$$

Because of its role in improving system performance, cache is routinely added to a wide variety of main memory configurations as well as devices.

Conclusion

The memory management portion of the operating system assumes responsibility for allocating memory storage (in main memory, cache memory, and registers) and, equally important, for deallocating it when execution is completed.

The design of each scheme that we discuss in Chapters 2 and 3 addressed a different set of pressing problems. As we have seen, when some problems are solved, others were often created. Table 3.7 shows how these memory allocation schemes compare.

The Memory Manager is only one of several managers that make up the operating system. After the jobs are loaded into memory using a memory allocation scheme, the Processor Manager takes responsibility to allocate processor time to each job, and every process and thread in that job, in the most efficient manner possible. We will see how that is done in the next chapter.

(table 3.7)	Scheme	Problem Solved	Problem Created	Key Software Changes
The big picture. Comparison of the memory allocation schemes discussed in Chapters 2 and 3.	Single-user contiguous	Not applicable	Job size limited to physical memory size; CPU often idle	Not applicable
	Fixed partitions	Idle CPU time	Internal fragmentation; job size limited to partition size	Add Processor Scheduler; add protection handler
	Dynamic partitions	Internal fragmentation	External fragmentation	Algorithms to manage partitions
	Relocatable dynamic partitions	External fragmentation	Compaction overhead; job size limited to physical memory size	Algorithms for compaction
	Paged	Need for compaction	Memory needed for tables; Job size limited to physical memory size; internal fragmentation returns	Algorithms to manage tables
	Demand paged	Job size limited to memory size; inefficient memory use	Large number of tables; possibility of thrashing; overhead required by page interrupts; paging hardware added	Algorithm to replace pages; algorithm to search for pages in secondary storage
	Segmented	Internal fragmentation	Difficulty managing variable-length segments in secondary storage; external fragmentation	Dynamic linking package; two-dimensional addressing scheme
	Segmented/demand paged	Segments not loaded on demand	Table handling overhead; memory needed for page and segment tables	Three-dimensional addressing scheme

Key Terms

address resolution: the process of changing the address of an instruction or data item to the address in main memory at which it is to be loaded or relocated.

associative memory: the name given to several registers, allocated to each active process, whose contents associate several of the process segments and page numbers with their main memory addresses.

cache memory: a small, fast memory used to hold selected data and to provide faster access than would otherwise be possible.

clock cycle: the elapsed time between two ticks of the computer's system clock.

clock page replacement policy: a variation of the LRU policy that removes from main memory the pages that show the least amount of activity during recent clock cycles.

demand paging: a memory allocation scheme that loads a program's page into memory at the time it is needed for processing.

displacement: in a paged or segmented memory allocation environment, the difference between a page's relative address and the actual machine language address. Also called offset.

FIFO anomaly: an unusual circumstance through which adding more page frames causes an increase in page interrupts when using a FIFO page replacement policy.

first-in first-out (FIFO) policy: a page replacement policy that removes from main memory the pages that were brought in first.

Job Table (JT): a table in main memory that contains two values for each active job—the size of the job and the memory location where its page map table is stored.

least recently used (LRU) policy: a page-replacement policy that removes from main memory the pages that show the least amount of recent activity.

locality of reference: behavior observed in many executing programs in which memory locations recently referenced, and those near them, are likely to be referenced in the near future.

Memory Map Table (MMT): a table in main memory that contains an entry for each page frame that contains the location and free/busy status for each one.

page: a fixed-size section of a user's job that corresponds in size to page frames in main memory.

page fault: a type of hardware interrupt caused by a reference to a page not residing in memory. The effect is to move a page out of main memory and into secondary storage so another page can be moved into memory.

page fault handler: the part of the Memory Manager that determines if there are empty page frames in memory so that the requested page can be immediately copied from secondary storage, or determines which page must be swapped out if all page frames are busy. Also known as a *page interrupt handler*.

page frame: an individual section of main memory of uniform size into which a single page may be loaded without causing external fragmentation.

Page Map Table (PMT): a table in main memory with the vital information for each page including the page number and its corresponding page frame memory address.

page replacement policy: an algorithm used by virtual memory systems to decide which page or segment to remove from main memory when a page frame is needed and memory is full.

page swapping: the process of moving a page out of main memory and into secondary storage so another page can be moved into memory in its place.

paged memory allocation: a memory allocation scheme based on the concept of dividing a user's job into sections of equal size to allow for noncontiguous program storage during execution.

reentrant code: code that can be used by two or more processes at the same time; each shares the same copy of the executable code but has separate data areas.

sector: a division in a magnetic disk's track, sometimes called a "block." The tracks are divided into sectors during the formatting process.

segment: a variable-size section of a user's job that contains a logical grouping of code.

Segment Map Table (SMT): a table in main memory with the vital information for each segment including the segment number and its corresponding memory address.

segmented/demand paged memory allocation: a memory allocation scheme based on the concept of dividing a user's job into logical groupings of code and loading them into memory as needed to minimize fragmentation.

segmented memory allocation: a memory allocation scheme based on the concept of dividing a user's job into logical groupings of code to allow for noncontiguous program storage during execution.

subroutine: also called a "subprogram," a segment of a program that can perform a specific function. Subroutines can reduce programming time when a specific function is required at more than one point in a program.

thrashing: a phenomenon in a virtual memory system where an excessive amount of page swapping back and forth between main memory and secondary storage results in higher overhead and little useful work.

virtual memory: a technique that allows programs to be executed even though they are not stored entirely in memory.

working set: a collection of pages to be kept in main memory for each active process in a virtual memory environment.

Interesting Searches

For more background on a few of the topics discussed in this chapter, begin a search with these terms.

- Virtual Memory
- Working Set
- Cache Memory
- Belady's FIFO anomaly
- Thrashing

Exercises

Research Topics

A. The size of virtual memory can sometimes be adjusted by a computer user to improve system performance. Using an operating system of your choice, discover if you can change the size of virtual memory, how to do so, and the minimum and maximum recommended sizes of virtual memory. Cite your operating system and the steps required to retrieve the desired information. (*Important*! *Do not change* the size of your virtual memory settings. This exercise is for research purposes only.)

B. On the Internet or using academic sources, research the design of multicore memory and identify the roles played by cache memory. Does the implementation of cache memory on multicore chips vary from one manufacturer to another? Explain your research process and cite your sources.

Exercises

1. Compare and contrast internal fragmentation and external fragmentation. Explain the circumstances where one might be preferred over the other.

2. Explain the function of the Page Map Table in the memory allocation schemes described in this chapter. Explain your answer with examples from the schemes that use a PMT.

3. If a program has 471 bytes and will be loaded into page frames of 100 bytes each, and the instruction to be used is at byte 132, answer the following questions:

   a. How many pages are needed to store the entire job?

   b. Compute the page number and the exact displacement for each of the byte addresses where the data is stored. (Remember that page numbering starts at zero).

4. Assume a program has 510 bytes and will be loaded into page frames of 256 bytes each, and the instruction to be used is at byte 377. Answer the following questions:

   a. How many pages are needed to store the entire job?

   b. Compute the page number and exact displacement for each of the byte addresses where the data is stored.

5. Given that main memory is composed of only three page frames for public use and that a seven-page program (with Pages a, b, c, d, e, f, g) that requests pages in the following order:

   a, c, a, b, a, d, a, c, b, d, e, f

   a. Using the FIFO page removal algorithm, indicate the movement of the pages into and out of the available page frames (called a page trace analysis). Indicate each page fault with an asterisk (*). Then compute the failure and success ratios.

b. Increase the size of memory so it contains four page frames for public use. Using the same page requests as above and FIFO, do another page trace analysis and compute the failure and success ratios.

c. What general statement can you make from this example? Explain your answer.

6. Given that main memory is composed of only three page frames for public use and that a program requests pages in the following order:

   a, c, b, d, a, c, e, a, c, b, d, e

   a. Using the FIFO page removal algorithm, indicate the movement of the pages into and out of the available page frames (called a page trace analysis) indicating each page fault with an asterisk (*). Then compute the failure and success ratios.

   b. Increase the size of memory so it contains four page frames for public use. Using the same page requests as above and FIFO, do another page trace analysis and compute the failure and success ratios.

   c. What general statement can you make from this example? Explain your answer.

7. Given that main memory is composed of three page frames for public use and that a program requests pages in the following order:

   a, b, a, b, f, d, f, c, g, f, g, b, d, e

   a. Using the FIFO page removal algorithm, perform a page trace analysis and indicate page faults with asterisks (*). Then compute the failure and success ratios.

   b. Using the LRU page removal algorithm, perform a page trace analysis and compute the failure and success ratios.

   c. What conclusions do you draw from this comparison of FIFO and LRU performance? Could you make general statements from this example? Explain why or why not.

8. Let us define "most-recently-used" (MRU) as a page removal algorithm that removes from memory the most recently used page. Perform a page trace analysis using page requests from the previous exercise for a system with three available page frames, and again with six available page frames. Compute the failure and success ratios of each configuration, and explain why or why not MRU is a viable memory allocation system.

9. By examining the reference bits for the six pages shown in the table below, identify which of the eight pages was referenced most often as of the last time snapshot (Time 6). Which page was referenced least often? Explain your reasoning.

Page Number	Time 0	Time 1	Time 2	Time 3	Time 4	Time 5	Time 6
0	10000000	11000000	01100000	10110000	01011000	10101100	01010110
1	10000000	01000000	00100000	10010000	01001000	00100100	00010010
2	10000000	01000000	00100000	10010000	11001000	11100100	01110010
3	10000000	11000000	11100000	01110000	10111000	11011100	01101110
4	10000000	11000000	01100000	10110000	01011000	00101100	10010110
5	10000000	01000000	11100000	01110000	10111000	11011100	11101110
6	10000000	01000000	10100000	01010000	00101000	00010100	10001010
7	10000000	01000000	00100000	00010000	10001000	11000100	01100010

10. To implement LRU, each page uses a referenced bit. If we wanted to implement a least frequently used (LFU) page removal algorithm, in which the page that was used the least would be removed from memory, what would we need to add to the tables? What software modifications would have to be made to support this new algorithm?

11. Calculate the cache Hit Ratio using the formula presented in this chapter assuming that the total number of requests is 2056 and that 647 of those requests are found in the cache.

12. Calculate the cache Hit Ratio using the formula presented in this chapter assuming that the total number of requests is 78985 and that 4029 of those requests are found in the cache. Is this Hit Ration better or worse than the result of the previous exercise?

13. Given three subroutines of 550, 290, and 600 words each, if segmentation is used then the total memory needed is the sum of the three sizes (if all three routines are loaded). However, if paging is used, then some storage space is lost because subroutines rarely fill the last page completely, and that results in internal fragmentation. Determine the total amount of wasted memory due to internal fragmentation when the three subroutines are loaded into memory using each of the following page sizes:

   a. 100 words

   b. 600 words

   c. 700 words

   d. 900 words

14. Using a paged memory allocation system with a page size of 2,048 bytes and an identical page frame size, and assuming the incoming data file is 20,992, calculate how many pages will be created by the file. Calculate the size of any resulting fragmentation. Explain whether this situation will result in internal fragmentation, external fragmentation, or both.

Advanced Exercises

15. Describe the logic you would use to detect thrashing. Once thrashing was detected, explain the steps you would use so the operating system could stop it.

16 Given that main memory is composed of four page frames for public use, use the following table to answer all parts of this problem:

Page Frame	Time When Loaded	Time When Last Referenced	Referenced Bit	Modified Bit
0	9	307	0	1
1	17	362	1	0
2	10	294	0	0
3	160	369	1	1

a. The contents of which page frame would be swapped out by FIFO?

b. The contents of which page frame would be swapped out by LRU?

c. The contents of which page frame would be swapped out by MRU?

d. The contents of which page frame would be swapped out by LFU?

17. Explain how Page Frame 0 in the previous exercise can have a modified bit of 1 and a referenced bit of 0.

18. Given the following Segment Map Tables for two jobs:

SMT for Job 1

Segment Number	Memory Location
0	4096
1	6144
2	9216
3	2048
4	7168

SMT for Job 2

Segment number	Memory location
0	2048
1	6144
2	9216

a. Which segments, if any, are shared between the two jobs?

b. If the segment now located at 7168 is swapped out and later reloaded at 8192, and the segment now at 2048 is swapped out and reloaded at 1024, what would the new segment tables look like?

Programming Exercises

19. This problem studies the effect of changing page sizes in a demand paging system.

    The following sequence of requests for program words is taken from a 460-word program: 10, 11, 104, 170, 73, 309, 185, 245, 246, 434, 458, 364. Main memory can hold a total of 200 words for this program, and the page frame size will match the size of the pages into which the program has been divided.

    Calculate the page numbers according to the page size and divide by the page size to get the page number. The number of page frames in memory is the total number, 200, divided by the page size. For example, in problem (a) the page size is 100, which means that requests 10 and 11 are on Page 0, and requests 104 and 170 are on Page 1. The number of page frames is two.

    a. Find the success frequency for the request list using a FIFO replacement algorithm and a page size of 100 words (there are two page frames).

    b. Find the success frequency for the request list using a FIFO replacement algorithm and a page size of 20 words (10 pages, 0 through 9).

    c. Find the success frequency for the request list using a FIFO replacement algorithm and a page size of 200 words.

    d. What do your results indicate? Can you make any general statements about what happens when page sizes are halved or doubled?

    e. Are there any overriding advantages in using smaller pages? What are the offsetting factors? Remember that transferring 200 words of information takes less than twice as long as transferring 100 words because of the way secondary storage devices operate (the transfer rate is higher than the access [search/find] rate).

    f. Repeat (a) through (c) above, using a main memory of 400 words. The size of each page frame will again correspond to the size of the page.

    g. What happened when more memory was given to the program? Can you make some general statements about this occurrence? What changes might you expect to see if the request list was much longer, as it would be in real life?

    h. Could this request list happen during the execution of a real program? Explain.

    i. Would you expect the success rate of an actual program under similar conditions to be higher or lower than the one in this problem?

20. Given the following information for an assembly language program:

Job size = 3126 bytes

Page size = 1024 bytes

Instruction at memory location 532:	Load 1, 2098
Instruction at memory location 1156:	Add 1, 2087
Instruction at memory location 2086:	Sub 1, 1052
Data at memory location 1052:	015672
Data at memory location 2098:	114321
Data at memory location 2087:	077435

a. How many pages are needed to store the entire job?

b. Compute the page number and the displacement for each of the byte addresses where the data is stored.

c. Determine whether the page number and displacements are legal for this job.

d. Explain why the page number and/or displacements may not be legal for this job.

e. Indicate what action the operating system might take when a page number or displacement is not legal.

| # Processor Management

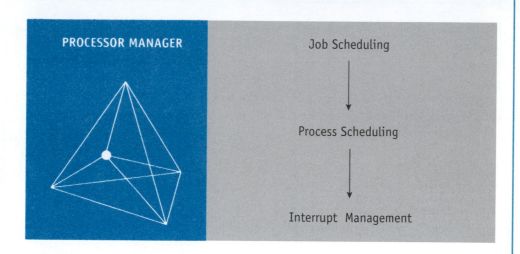

PROCESSOR MANAGER

Job Scheduling

↓

Process Scheduling

↓

Interrupt Management

"Nature acts by progress ... It goes and returns, then advances further, then twice as much backward, then more forward than ever."

—Blaise Pascal (1623–1662)

Learning Objectives

After completing this chapter, you should be able to describe:

• The relationship between job scheduling and process scheduling
• The advantages and disadvantages of several process scheduling algorithms
• The goals of process scheduling policies using a single-core CPU
• The similarities and differences between processes and threads
• The role of internal interrupts and of the interrupt handler

The Processor Manager is responsible for allocating the processor to execute the incoming jobs and to manage the tasks of those jobs. In this chapter, we'll see how a Processor Manager manages a system with a single CPU to do so.

Overview

In a simple system, one with a single user and one processor, the processor is busy only when it is executing the user's jobs or system software. However, when there are many users, such as in a multiprogramming environment, or when there are multiple processes competing to be run by a single CPU, the processor must be allocated to each job in a fair and efficient manner. This can be a complex task, as we show in this chapter, which is devoted to single processor systems. Those with multiple processors and multicore systems are discussed in Chapter 6.

Many operating systems use the idle time between user-specified jobs to process routine background tasks. So even if a user isn't running applications, the CPU may be busy executing other tasks.

Definitions

Before we begin, let's define some terms. The **processor**, the CPU, is the part of the hardware that performs calculations and executes programs.

A **program** is an inactive unit, such as a file stored on a disk. A program is not a process. For our discussion, a program or job is a unit of work that has been submitted by the user.

On the other hand, a **process** is an active entity that requires a set of resources, including a processor and special registers, to perform its function. A process, sometimes known as a **task,** is a single instance of a program in execution.

A **thread** is created by a process, and it can be scheduled and executed independently of its parent process. A process can consist of multiple threads. In a threaded environment, the process owns the resources that are allocated; it then becomes a more passive element, so its threads become the elements that use resources (such as the CPU). Manipulating threads is less time consuming than manipulating processes, which are more complex. Some operating systems support multiple threads with a single process, while others support multiple processes with multiple threads.

Multithreading allows applications to manage a separate process with several threads of control. Web browsers use multithreading routinely. For instance, one thread can retrieve images while another sends and retrieves e-mail. Multithreading can also increase responsiveness in a time-sharing system, increase resource sharing, and decrease overhead.

Here's a simplified example. If your single-core system allows its processes to have a single thread of control and you want to see a series of pictures on a friend's Web site, you can instruct the browser to establish one connection between the two sites and download one picture at a time. However, if your system allows processes to have multiple threads of control (a more common circumstance), then you can request several pictures at the same time, and the browser will set up multiple connections and download several pictures, seemingly at once.

Multiprogramming requires that the processor be allocated to each job or to each process for a period of time and deallocated at an appropriate moment. If the processor is deallocated during a program's execution, it must be done in such a way that it can be restarted later as easily as possible. It's a delicate procedure. To demonstrate, let's look at an everyday example.

Here you are, confident you can assemble a bicycle (perhaps despite the warning that some assembly is required). Armed with the instructions and lots of patience, you embark on your task—to read the directions, collect the necessary tools, follow each step in turn, and turn out the finished bike.

The first step is to join Part A to Part B with a 2-inch screw, and as you complete that task you check off Step 1. Inspired by your success, you move on to Step 2 and then Step 3. You've only just completed the third step when a neighbor is injured while working with a power tool and cries for help.

Quickly you check off Step 3 in the directions so you know where you left off, then you drop your tools and race to your neighbor's side. After all, someone's immediate need is more important than your eventual success with the bicycle. Now you find yourself engaged in a very different task: following the instructions in a first-aid kit and using antiseptic and bandages.

Once the injury has been successfully treated, you return to your previous job. As you pick up your tools, you refer to the instructions and see that you should begin with Step 4. You then continue with your bike project until it is finally completed.

In operating system terminology, you played the part of the *CPU* or *processor*. There were two *programs*, or *jobs*—one was the mission to assemble the bike and the second was to bandage the injury. Each step in assembling the bike (Job A) can be called a *process*. The call for help was an *interrupt*; when you left the bike to treat your wounded friend, you left for a *higher priority program*. When you were interrupted, you performed a *context switch* when you marked Step 3 as the last completed instruction and put down your tools. Attending to the neighbor's injury became Job B. While you were executing the first-aid instructions, each of the steps you executed was again a *process*. And when each job was completed, each was *finished* or terminated.

The Processor Manager would identify the series of events as follows:

`Get the input for Job A`	(find and read the instructions in the box)
`Identify the resources`	(collect the necessary tools)
`Execute the process`	(follow each step in turn)
`Receive the interrupt`	(receive call for help)
`Perform a context switch to Job B`	(mark your place in the assembly instructions)
`Get the input for Job B`	(find your first-aid kit)
`Identify the resources`	(identify the medical supplies)
`Execute the process`	(follow each first aid step)
`Terminate Job B`	(return home)
`Perform context switch to Job A`	(prepare to resume assembly)
`Resume executing the interrupted process`	(follow remaining steps in turn)
`Terminate Job A`	(turn out the finished bike)

As we've shown, a single processor can be shared by several jobs, or several processes—but if, and only if, the operating system has a scheduling policy, as well as a scheduling algorithm, to determine when to stop working on one job and proceed to another.

In this example, the scheduling algorithm was based on priority: you worked on the processes belonging to Job A (assembling the bicycle) until a higher priority job came along. Although this was a good algorithm in this case, a priority-based scheduling algorithm isn't always best, as we'll see in this chapter.

About Multi-Core Technologies

A dual-core, quad-core, or other multi-core CPU has more than one processing element (sometimes called a core) on the computer chip. Multi-core engineering was driven by the problems caused by nano-sized transistors and their ultra-close placement on a computer chip. Although such an arrangement helped increase system performance dramatically, the close proximity of these transistors also caused the unintended loss of electrical current and excessive heat that can result in circuit failure.

One solution was to create a single chip (one piece of silicon) that housed two or more processor cores. In other words, a single large processor was replaced with two smaller processors (dual core), or four even smaller processors (quad core). The combined multi-core chips are of approximately the same size as a single-processor chip but produce less current leakage and heat. They also permit multiple calculations to take place at the same time.

Fernando J. Corbato (1926–)

Fernando Corbato is widely recognized for his contributions to the design and development of two operating systems during the 1960s: the Compatible Time-Sharing System (CTSS) and the Multiplexed Information and Computing Service (Multics), both state-of-the-art, multi-user systems. (Years later, Multics became the basis of another operating system called UNIX.) Corbato has won many honors, including the IEEE Computer Society Computer Pioneer Award (1982). In 1976 he was elected to the National Academy of Engineering. In 1982 he became a Fellow of the American Association for the Advancement of Science.

For more information, see
http://amturing.acm.org/award_winners/ corbato_1009471.cfm

Corbato received the ACM 1990 A.M. Turing Award "for his pioneering work in organizing the concepts and leading the development of the general-purpose, large-scale, time-sharing and resource-sharing computer systems, CTSS and Multics."

Jason Dorfman MIT/CSAIL

Multiple core systems are more complex for the Processor Manager to manage than a single core. We discuss these challenges in Chapter 6.

Scheduling Submanagers

The Processor Manager is a composite of at least two submanagers: one in charge of job scheduling and the other in charge of process scheduling. They're known as the **Job Scheduler** and the **Process Scheduler**.

Typically a user views a job either as a series of global job steps—compilation, loading, and execution—or as one all-encompassing step—execution. However, the scheduling of jobs is actually handled on two levels by most operating systems. If we return to the example presented earlier, we can see that a hierarchy exists between the Job Scheduler and the Process Scheduler.

The scheduling of the two jobs, to assemble the bike and to bandage the injury, was on a priority basis. Each job was initiated by the Job Scheduler based on certain criteria. Once a job was selected for execution, the Process Scheduler determined when each step, or set of steps, was executed—a decision that was also based on certain criteria. When you started assembling the bike, each step in the assembly instructions was selected for execution by the Process Scheduler.

The same concepts apply to computer systems, where each job (or program) passes through a hierarchy of managers. Since the first one it encounters is the Job Scheduler, this is also called the **high-level scheduler**. It is concerned only with selecting jobs from a queue of incoming jobs and placing them in the process queue based on each job's characteristics. The Job Scheduler's goal is to put the jobs (as they still reside on the disk) in a sequence that best meets the designers or administrator's goals, such as using the system's resources as efficiently as possible.

This is an important function. For example, if the Job Scheduler selected several jobs to run consecutively and each had a lot of requests for input and output (often abbreviated as I/O), then the I/O devices would be kept very busy. The CPU might be busy handling the I/O requests (if an I/O controller were not used), resulting in the completion of very little computation. On the other hand, if the Job Scheduler selected several consecutive jobs with a great deal of computation requirements, then the CPU would be very busy doing that, forcing the I/O devices to remain idle waiting for requests. Therefore, a major goal of the Job Scheduler is to create an order for the incoming jobs that has a balanced mix of I/O interaction and computation requirements, thus balancing the system's resources. As you might expect, the Job Scheduler's goal is to keep most components of the computer system busy most of the time.

Process Scheduler

After a job has been accepted by the Job Scheduler to run, the Process Scheduler takes over that job (and if the operating systems support threads, the Process Scheduler takes responsibility for that function, too). The Process Scheduler determines which processes will get the CPU, when, and for how long. It also decides what to do when processing is interrupted; it determines which waiting lines (queues) the job should be moved to during its execution; and it recognizes when a job has concluded and should be terminated.

The Process Scheduler is a **low-level scheduler** that assigns the CPU to execute the individual actions for those jobs placed on the READY queue by the Job Scheduler. This becomes crucial when the processing of several jobs has to be orchestrated—just as when you had to set aside your assembly and rush to help your neighbor.

To schedule the CPU, the Process Scheduler takes advantage of a common trait among most computer programs: they alternate between CPU cycles and I/O cycles. Notice that the following job has one relatively long CPU cycle and two very brief I/O cycles:

Data input (often the first I/O cycle) and printing (often the last I/O cycle) are usually brief compared to the time it takes to do the calculations (the CPU cycle).

```
Ask Clerk for the first number
Retrieve the number that's entered (Input #1)
   on the keyboard                                    }  Brief I/O Cycle
Ask Clerk for the second number
Retrieve the second number entered (Input #2)
   on the keyboard


Add the two numbers (Input #1 + Input #2)
Divide the sum from the previous calculation
   and divide by 2 to get the average
   (Input #1 + Input #2) / 2                          }  CPU Cycle
Multiply the result of the previous calculation
   by 3 to get the average for the quarter
Multiply the result of the previous calculation
   by 4 to get the average for the year


Print the average for the quarter (Output #1)        }  Brief I/O Cycle
Print the average for the year (Output #2)

End
```

Although the duration and frequency of CPU cycles vary from program to program, there are some general tendencies that can be exploited when selecting a scheduling algorithm. Two of these are **I/O-bound** jobs (such as printing a series of documents) that have long I/O cycles and brief CPU cycles and **CPU-bound** jobs (such as finding the first 300,000 prime numbers) that have long CPU cycles and shorter I/O cycles. The total effect of all CPU cycles, from both I/O-bound and CPU-bound jobs, approximates a curve, as shown in Figure 4.1.

In a highly interactive environment, there's also a third layer of the Processor Manager called the **middle-level scheduler**. In some cases, especially when the system is overloaded, the middle-level scheduler finds it is advantageous to remove active jobs from

(figure 4.1)

Distribution of CPU cycle times. This distribution shows a greater number of jobs requesting short CPU cycles (the frequency peaks close to the low end of the CPU cycle axis), and fewer jobs requesting long CPU cycles.

memory to reduce the degree of multiprogramming, which allows other jobs to be completed faster. The jobs that are swapped out and eventually swapped back in are managed by the middle-level scheduler.

Job and Process States

As a job, a process, or a thread moves through the system, its status changes, often from HOLD, to READY, to RUNNING, to WAITING, and eventually to FINISHED, as shown in Figure 4.2. These are called the **job status**, **process status**, or **thread status**, respectively.

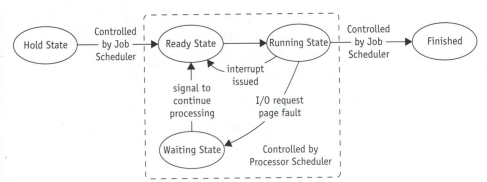

(figure 4.2)

A typical job (or process) changes status as it moves through the system from HOLD to FINISHED.

Here's how a job status can change when a user submits a job to the system. When the job is accepted by the system, it's put on HOLD and placed in a queue. In some systems, the job spooler (or disk controller) creates a table with the characteristics of each job in the queue and notes the important features of the job, such as an estimate of CPU time, priority, special I/O devices required, and maximum memory required. This table is used by the Job Scheduler to decide which job is to be run next.

The job moves to READY after the interrupts have been resolved. In some systems, the job (or process) might be placed on the READY list directly. RUNNING, of course, means that the job is being processed. In a single processor system, this is one "job" or process. WAITING means that the job can't continue until a specific resource is allocated or an I/O operation has finished, and then moves back to READY. Upon completion, the job is FINISHED and returned to the user.

In a multiprogramming system, the CPU is often be allocated to many jobs, each with numerous processes, making processor management quite complicated.

The transition from one job status, job state, to another is initiated by the Job Scheduler, and the transition from one process or thread state to another is initiated by the Process Scheduler. Here's a simple example:

- The job transition from HOLD to READY is initiated by the Job Scheduler (according to a policy that's predefined by the operating system designers). At this point, the availability of enough main memory and any requested devices is checked.
- The transition from READY to RUNNING is handled by the Process Scheduler according to a predefined algorithm (this is discussed shortly).

- The transition from RUNNING back to READY is handled by the Process Scheduler according to a predefined time limit or other criterion, such as a priority interrupt.
- The transition from RUNNING to WAITING is handled by the Process Scheduler and is initiated in response to an instruction in the job such as a command to READ, WRITE, or other I/O request.
- The transition from WAITING to READY is handled by the Process Scheduler and is initiated by a signal from the I/O device manager that the I/O request has been satisfied and the job can continue. In the case of a page fetch, the page fault handler will signal that the page is now in memory and the process can be placed back in the READY queue.
- Eventually, the transition from RUNNING to FINISHED is initiated by the Process Scheduler or the Job Scheduler when (1) the job is successfully completed and it ends execution, or (2) the operating system indicates that an error has occurred and the job must be terminated prematurely.

Thread States

As a thread moves through the system it is in one of five states, not counting its creation and finished states, as shown in Figure 4.3. When an application creates a thread, it is made ready by allocating to it the needed resources and placing it in the READY queue. The thread state changes from READY to RUNNING when the Process Scheduler assigns it to a processor. In this chapter we consider systems with only one processor. See Chapter 6 for systems with multiple processors.

(figure 4.3)

A typical thread changes states from READY to FINISHED as it moves through the system.

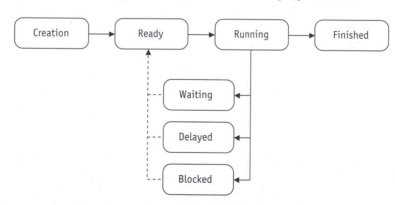

A thread transitions from RUNNING to WAITING when it has to wait for an event outside its control to occur. For example, a mouse click can be the trigger event for a thread to change states, causing a transition from WAITING to READY. Alternatively, another thread, having completed its task, can send a signal indicating that the waiting thread can continue to execute.

When an application has the capability of delaying the processing of a thread by a specified amount of time, it causes the thread to transition from RUNNING to DELAYED.

When the prescribed time has elapsed, the thread transitions from DELAYED to READY. For example, when using a word processor, the thread that periodically saves a current document can be delayed for a period of time after it has completed the save. After the time has expired, it performs the next save and then is delayed again. If the delay was not built into the application, this thread would be forced into a loop that would continuously test to see if it is time to do a save, wasting processor time and reducing system performance.

A thread transitions from RUNNING to BLOCKED when an I/O request is issued. After the I/O is completed, the thread returns to the READY state. When a thread transitions from RUNNING to FINISHED, all of its resources are released; it then exits the system or is terminated and ceases to exist.

As you can see, the same operations are performed on both traditional processes and threads. Therefore, the operating system must be able to support:

- Creating new threads
- Setting up a thread so it is ready to execute
- Delaying, or putting to sleep, threads for a specified amount of time
- Blocking, or suspending, threads that are waiting for I/O to be completed
- Setting threads to a WAIT state until a specific event has occurred
- Scheduling threads for execution
- Synchronizing thread execution using semaphores, events, or conditional variables
- Terminating a thread and releasing its resources

To do so, the operating system needs to track the critical information for each thread.

Control Blocks

Each process in the system is represented by a data structure called a **Process Control Block (PCB)** that performs the same function as a traveler's passport. Similarly, each thread is represented by a similar data structure called a **Thread Control Block** (TCB). Both kinds of control blocks (illustrated in Figure 4.4) contain the basic information that is detailed in Tables 4.1 and 4.2.

```
Thread identification
Thread state
CPU information:
        Program counter
        Register contents
Thread priority
Pointer to process that created this thread
Pointers to all other threads created by this thread
```

```
Process identification
Process status
Process state:
        Process status word
        Register contents
        Main memory
        Resources
        Process priority
Accounting
```

(figure 4.4)

Comparison of a typical Thread Control Block (TCB) vs. a Process Control Block (PCB).

Process Identification	Unique identification provided by the Job Scheduler when the job first enters the system and is placed on HOLD.
Process Status	Indicates the current status of the job—HOLD, READY, RUNNING, or WAITING—and the resources responsible for that status.
Process State	Contains all of the information needed to indicate the current state of the job such as: • *Process Status Word*—the current instruction counter and register contents when the job isn't running but is either on HOLD or is READY or WAITING. If the job is RUNNING, this information is left undefined. • *Register Contents*—the contents of the register if the job has been interrupted and is waiting to resume processing. • *Main Memory*—pertinent information, including the address where the job is stored and, in the case of virtual memory, the linking between virtual and physical memory locations. • *Resources*—information about all resources allocated to this job. Each resource has an identification field listing its type and a field describing details of its allocation, such as the sector address on a disk. These resources can be hardware units (disk drives or printers, for example) or files. • *Process Priority*—used by systems using a priority scheduling algorithm to select which job will be run next.
Accounting	This contains information used mainly for billing purposes and performance measurement. It indicates what kind of resources the job used and for how long. Typical charges include: • Amount of CPU time used from beginning to end of its execution. • Elapsed time the job was in the system until it exited. • Main storage occupancy—how long the job stayed in memory until it finished execution. This is usually a combination of time and space used; for example, in a paging system it may be recorded in units of page-seconds. • Secondary storage used during execution. This, too, is recorded as a combination of time and space used. • System programs used, such as compilers, editors, or utilities. • Number and type of I/O operations, including I/O transmission time, utilization of channels, control units, and devices. • Time spent waiting for I/O completion. • Amount of data read and the number of output records written.

(table 4.1)

Typical contents of a Process Control Block

(table 4.2)

Typical contents of a Thread Control Block

Thread Identification	Unique identification provided by the Process Scheduler when the when the thread is created.
Thread State	The current state of the thread (READY, RUNNING, and so on), which changes as the thread progresses through its execution.
CPU Information	Contains everything that the operating system needs to know about how far the thread has executed, which instruction is currently being performed, and what data is being used.
Thread Priority	Used to indicate the weight of this thread relative to other threads and used to determine which thread should be selected from the READY queue.
Process Pointer	This indicates the process that created the thread.
Sub-thread Pointers	This indicates other subthreads that were created by this thread.

Control Blocks and Queuing

The Process Control Block is created when the Job Scheduler accepts the job and is updated as the job progresses from the beginning to the end of its execution. Likewise, the Thread Control Block is created by the Process Scheduler to track the thread's progress from beginning to end.

Queues use these control blocks to track jobs the same way customs officials use passports to track international visitors. These control blocks contain all of the data needed by the operating system to manage the processing of the job. As the job moves through the system, its progress is noted in the control block.

It is the control block, and not the actual process or job, that is linked to other control blocks to form the queues as shown in Figure 4.5, which shows the path of a PCB through execution. Although each control block is not drawn in detail, the reader should imagine each queue as a linked list of PCBs.

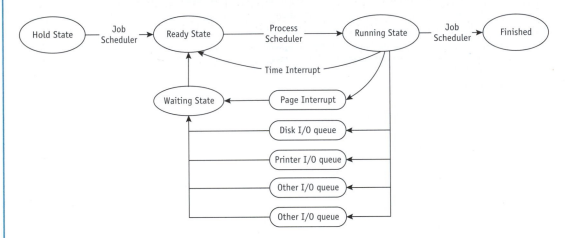

(figure 4.5)

Queuing paths from HOLD to FINISHED. The Job and Processor schedulers release the resources when the job leaves the RUNNING state.

For example, if we watch a PCB move through its queues, the PCB for each ready job is linked on the READY queue, and all of the PCBs for the jobs just entering the system are linked on the HOLD queue. The jobs that are WAITING, however, are linked together by "reason for waiting," so the PCBs for the jobs in this category are linked into several queues. Therefore, the PCBs for jobs that are waiting for I/O on a specific disk drive are linked together, while those waiting for the printer are linked in a different queue.

Whether they are linking PCBs or TCBs, these queues need to be managed in an orderly fashion, and that's determined by the process scheduling policies and algorithms.

Scheduling Policies

In a multiprogramming environment, there are usually more objects (jobs, processes, threads) to be executed than could possibly be run at one time. Before the operating system can schedule them, it needs to resolve three limitations of the system:

• There are a finite number of resources.

• Some resources, once they're allocated, can't be shared with another job.

• Some resources require operator intervention—that is, they can't be reassigned automatically from job to job.

What's a good **scheduling policy**? Several goals come to mind, but notice in the list below that some contradict each other:

• *Maximize throughput*. Run as many jobs as possible in a given amount of time. This could be accomplished easily by running only short jobs or by running jobs without interruptions.

• *Minimize response time*. Quickly turn around interactive requests. This could be done by running only interactive jobs and letting all other jobs wait until the interactive load ceases.

• *Minimize turnaround time*. Move entire jobs in and out of the system quickly. This could be done by running all batch jobs first (because batch jobs are put into groups so they run more efficiently than interactive jobs).

• *Minimize waiting time*. Move jobs out of the READY queue as quickly as possible. This could be done only by reducing the number of users allowed on the system so the CPU would be available immediately whenever a job entered the READY queue.

• *Maximize CPU efficiency*. Keep the CPU busy 100 percent of the time. This could be done by running only CPU-bound jobs (and not I/O-bound jobs).

• *Ensure fairness for all jobs*. Give everyone an equal amount of CPU and I/O time. This could be done by not giving special treatment to any job, regardless of its processing characteristics or priority.

As we can see from this list, if the system favors one type of user, then it hurts another, or it doesn't efficiently use its resources. The final decision rests with the system designer or administrator, who must determine which criteria are most important for that specific system. For example, you might want to "maximize CPU utilization while minimizing response time and balancing the use of all system components through a mix of I/O-bound and CPU-bound jobs." You would select the scheduling policy that most closely satisfies these goals.

Although the Job Scheduler selects jobs to ensure that the READY and I/O queues remain balanced, there are instances when a job claims the CPU for a very long time before issuing an I/O request. If I/O requests are being satisfied (this is done by an I/O controller and is discussed later), this extensive use of the CPU will build up the

READY queue while emptying out the I/O queues, which creates an unacceptable imbalance in the system.

To solve this problem, the Process Scheduler often uses a timing mechanism and periodically interrupts running processes when a predetermined slice of time has expired. When that happens, the scheduler suspends all activity on the job currently running and reschedules it into the READY queue; it will be continued later. The CPU is now allocated to another job that runs until one of three things happens: the timer goes off, the job issues an I/O command, or the job is finished. Then the job moves to the READY queue, the WAIT queue, or the FINISHED queue, respectively.

An I/O request is called a **natural wait** in multiprogramming environments (it allows the processor to be allocated to another job).

A scheduling strategy that interrupts the processing of a job and transfers the CPU to another job is called a **preemptive scheduling policy**; it is widely used in time-sharing environments. The alternative, of course, is a **nonpreemptive scheduling policy**, which functions without external interrupts (interrupts external to the job). Therefore, once a job captures the processor and begins execution, it remains in the RUNNING state uninterrupted until it issues an I/O request (natural wait) or until it is finished. In the case of an infinite loop, the process can be stopped and moved to the FINISHED queue whether the policy is preemptive or nonpreemptive.

Scheduling Algorithms

The Process Scheduler relies on a **scheduling algorithm**, based on a specific scheduling policy, to allocate the CPU in the best way to move jobs through the system efficiently. Most systems place an emphasis on fast user **response time**.

To keep this discussion simple, we refer to these algorithms as **process scheduling algorithms**, though they are also used to schedule threads. Here are several algorithms that have been used extensively for these purposes.

First-Come, First-Served

First-come, first-served (FCFS) is a nonpreemptive scheduling algorithm that handles all incoming objects according to their arrival time: the earlier they arrive, the sooner they're served. It's a very simple algorithm to implement because it uses a First In, First Out (FIFO) queue. This algorithm is fine for most batch systems, but it is unacceptable for interactive systems because interactive users expect quick response times.

With FCFS, as a new job enters the system, its PCB is linked to the end of the READY queue and it is removed from the front of the READY queue after the jobs before it runs to completion and the processor becomes available—that is, after all of the jobs before it in the queue have run to completion.

In a strictly FCFS system, there are no WAIT queues (each job is run to completion), although there may be systems in which control (context) is switched on a natural wait (I/O request) and then the job resumes on I/O completion.

The following examples presume a strictly FCFS environment (no multiprogramming). **Turnaround time** (the time required to execute a job and return the output to the user) is unpredictable with the FCFS policy. For example, consider the following three jobs:

• Job A has a CPU cycle of 15 milliseconds.

• Job B has a CPU cycle of 2 milliseconds.

• Job C has a CPU cycle of 1 millisecond.

For each job, the CPU cycle contains both the actual CPU usage and the I/O requests. That is, it is the total run time. The timeline shown in Figure 4.6 shows an FCFS algorithm with an arrival sequence of A, B, C.

(figure 4.6)

*Timeline for job sequence
A, B, C using the FCFS
algorithm.*

If all three jobs arrive almost simultaneously (at Time 0), we can calculate that the turnaround time (the job's finish time minus arrival time) for Job A is 15, for Job B is 17, and for Job C is 18. So the average turnaround time is:

$$\frac{(15 - 0) + (17 - 0) + (18 - 0)}{3} = 16.67$$

However, if the jobs arrived in a different order, say C, B, A, then the results using the same FCFS algorithm would be as shown in Figure 4.7.

(figure 4.7)

*Timeline for job sequence
C, B, A using the FCFS
algorithm.*

In this example, the turnaround time for Job A is 18, for Job B is 3, and for Job C is 1 and the average turnaround time (shown here in the order in which they finish: Job C, Job B, Job A) is:

$$\frac{(1 - 0) + (3 - 0) + (18 - 0)}{3} = 7.3$$

That's quite an improvement over the first sequence. Unfortunately, these two examples illustrate the primary disadvantage of using the FCFS concept—the average turnaround times vary widely and are seldom minimized. In fact, when there are three jobs in the READY queue, the system has only a 1 in 6 chance of running the jobs in the most advantageous sequence (C, B, A). With four jobs the odds fall to 1 in 24, and so on.

If one job monopolizes the system, the extent of its overall effect on system performance depends on the scheduling policy and whether the job is CPU-bound or I/O-bound. While a job with a long CPU cycle (in this example, Job A) is using the CPU, the other jobs in the system are waiting for processing or finishing their I/O requests (if an I/O controller is used) and joining the READY queue to wait for their turn to use the processor. If the I/O requests are not being serviced, the I/O queues remain stable while the READY list grows (with new arrivals). In extreme cases, the READY queue could fill to capacity while the I/O queues would be empty, or stable, and the I/O devices would sit idle.

On the other hand, if the job is processing a lengthy I/O cycle, the I/O queues quickly build to overflowing and the CPU could be sitting idle (if an I/O controller is used). This situation is eventually resolved when the I/O-bound job finishes its I/O cycle, the queues start moving again, and the system can recover from the bottleneck.

In a strictly FCFS algorithm, neither situation occurs. However, the turnaround time is variable (unpredictable). For this reason, FCFS is a less attractive algorithm than one that would serve the shortest job first, as the next scheduling algorithm does, even in an environment that doesn't support multiprogramming.

✔
FCFS is the only algorithm discussed in this chapter that includes a significant element of chance. The others do not.

Shortest Job Next

Shortest job next (SJN) is a nonpreemptive scheduling algorithm (also known as shortest job first, or SJF) that handles jobs based on the length of their CPU cycle time. It's possible to implement in batch environments where the estimated CPU time required to run the job is given in advance by each user at the start of each job. However, it doesn't work in most interactive systems because users don't estimate in advance the CPU time required to run their jobs.

For example, here are four jobs, all in the READY queue at Time 0. The CPU cycle, or run time, is estimated as follows:

Job:	A	B	C	D
CPU cycle:	5	2	6	4

The SJN algorithm would review the four jobs and schedule them for processing in this order: B, D, A, C. The timeline is shown in Figure 4.8.

(figure 4.8)

*Timeline for job sequence
B, D, A, C using the SJN
algorithm.*

The average turnaround time (shown here in the order in which they finish: Job B, Job D, Job A, Job C) is:

$$\frac{(2 - 0) + (6 - 0) + (11 - 0) + (17 - 0)}{4} = 9.0$$

Let's take a minute to see why this algorithm consistently gives the minimum average turnaround time. We use the previous example to derive a general formula.

We can see in Figure 4.7 that Job B finishes in its given time (2); Job D finishes in its given time plus the time it waited for B to run (4 + 2); Job A finishes in its given time plus D's time plus B's time (5 + 4 + 2); and Job C finishes in its given time plus that of the previous three (6 + 5 + 4 + 2). So when calculating the average, we have:

$$\frac{(2) + (4 + 2) + (5 + 4 + 2) + (6 + 5 + 4 + 2)}{4} = 9.0$$

As you can see, the time for the first job appears in the equation four times—once for each job. Similarly, the time for the second job appears three times (the number of jobs minus one). The time for the third job appears twice (number of jobs minus 2) and the time for the fourth job appears only once (number of jobs minus 3).

So the above equation can be rewritten as:

$$\frac{4*2 + 3*4 + 2*5 + 1*6}{4} = 9.0$$

Because the time for the first job appears in the equation four times, it has four times the effect on the average time than does the length of the fourth job, which appears only once. Therefore, if the first job requires the shortest computation time, followed in turn by the other jobs, ordered from shortest to longest, then the result will be the smallest possible average.

However, the SJN algorithm is optimal only when all of the jobs are available at the same time, and the CPU estimates must be available and accurate.

Priority Scheduling

Priority scheduling is one of the most common scheduling algorithms for batch systems and is a nonpreemptive algorithm (in a batch environment). This algorithm gives preferential treatment to important jobs. It allows the programs with the highest priority to be processed first, and they aren't interrupted until their CPU cycles (run times) are completed or a natural wait occurs. If two or more jobs with equal priority are present in the READY queue, the processor is allocated to the one that arrived first (first-come, first-served within priority).

Priorities can be assigned by a system administrator using characteristics extrinsic to the jobs. For example, they can be assigned based on the position of the user (researchers first, students last) or, in commercial environments, they can be purchased by the users who pay more for higher priority to guarantee the fastest possible processing of their jobs. With a priority algorithm, jobs are usually linked to one of several READY queues by the Job Scheduler based on their priority so the Process Scheduler manages multiple READY queues instead of just one. Details about multiple queues are presented later in this chapter.

Priorities can also be determined by the Processor Manager based on characteristics intrinsic to the jobs such as:

- *Memory requirements.* Jobs requiring large amounts of memory could be allocated lower priorities than those requesting small amounts of memory, or vice versa.
- *Number and type of peripheral devices.* Jobs requiring many peripheral devices would be allocated lower priorities than those requesting fewer devices.
- *Total CPU time.* Jobs having a long CPU cycle, or estimated run time, would be given lower priorities than those having a brief estimated run time.
- *Amount of time already spent in the system.* This is the total amount of elapsed time since the job was accepted for processing. Some systems increase the priority of jobs that have been in the system for an unusually long time to expedite their exit. This is known as **aging**.

These criteria are used to determine default priorities in many systems. The default priorities can be overruled by specific priorities named by users. There are also preemptive priority schemes. These are discussed later in this chapter in the section on multiple queues.

Shortest Remaining Time

Shortest remaining time (SRT) is a preemptive version of the SJN algorithm. The processor is allocated to the job closest to completion—but even this job can be interrupted if a newer job in the READY queue has a time to completion that's shorter.

This algorithm can't be implemented in an interactive system because it requires advance knowledge of the CPU time required to finish each job. It can work well in batch environments, because it can give preference to short jobs. A disadvantage is that SRT involves more overhead than SJN—it requires the operating system to frequently monitor the CPU time for all the jobs in the READY queue and it must perform context

When using SRT, if several jobs have the same amount of time remaining, the job that has been waiting the longest goes next. It uses the FCFS algorithm to break the tie.

switching for the jobs being swapped at preemption time (not necessarily swapped out to the disk, although this might occur as well).

The example in Figure 4.9 shows how the SRT algorithm works with four jobs that arrived in quick succession (one CPU cycle apart).

Arrival time:	0	1	2	3
Job:	A	B	C	D
CPU cycle:	6	3	1	4

The turnaround time for each job is its completion time minus its arrival time. The resulting turnaround time for each job is:

Job:	A	B	C	D
Completion Time minus Arrival Time	14-0	5-1	3-2	9-3
Turnaround	14	4	1	6

So the average turnaround time is:

$$\frac{(14 - 0) + (5 - 1) + (3 - 2) + (9 - 3)}{4} = 6.25$$

(figure 4.9)

Timeline for job sequence A, B, C, D using the preemptive SRT algorithm. Each job is interrupted after one CPU cycle if another job is waiting with less CPU time remaining.

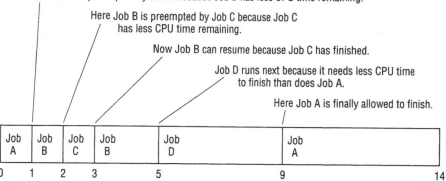

Here Job A is preempted by Job B because Job B has less CPU time remaining.

Here Job B is preempted by Job C because Job C has less CPU time remaining.

Now Job B can resume because Job C has finished.

Job D runs next because it needs less CPU time to finish than does Job A.

Here Job A is finally allowed to finish.

Job A	Job B	Job C	Job B	Job D	Job A

0   1   2   3   5   9   14

How does that compare to the same problem using the nonpreemptive SJN policy? Figure 4.10 shows the same situation with the same arrival times using SJN. In this case, the turnaround time is:

Job:	A	B	C	D
Completion Time minus Arrival Time	6-0	10-1	7-2	14-3
Turnaround:	6	9	5	11

So the average turnaround time is:

$$\frac{6 + 9 + 5 + 11}{4} = 7.75$$

(figure 4.10)

Timeline for the same job sequence A, B, C, D using the nonpreemptive SJN algorithm.

Note in Figure 4.10 that initially A is the only job in the READY queue so it runs first and continues until it's finished because SJN is a nonpreemptive algorithm. The next job to be run is C, because when Job A is finished (at time 6), all of the other jobs (B, C, and D) have arrived. Of those three, C has the shortest CPU cycle, so it is the next one run—then B, and finally D.

Therefore, in this example, SRT at 6.25 is faster than SJN at 7.75. However, we neglected to include the time required by the SRT algorithm to do the context switching. **Context switching** is the saving of a job's processing information in its PCB so the job can be swapped out of memory and of loading the processing information from the PCB of another job into the appropriate registers so the CPU can process it. Context switching is required by all preemptive algorithms so jobs can pick up later where they left off. When Job A is preempted, all of its processing information must be saved in its PCB for later, when Job A's execution is to be continued, and the contents of Job B's PCB are loaded into the appropriate registers so it can start running again; this is a context switch. Later, when Job A is once again assigned to the processor, another context switch is performed. This time the information from the preempted job is stored in its PCB, and the contents of Job A's PCB are loaded into the appropriate registers.

How the context switching is actually done depends on the architecture of the CPU; in many systems, there are special instructions that provide quick saving and restoring of information. The switching is designed to be performed efficiently but, no matter how fast it is, it still takes valuable CPU time and contributes to overhead. So although SRT appears to be faster, in a real operating environment, its advantages are diminished by the time spent in context switching. A precise comparison of SRT and SJN would have to include the time required to do the context switching.

Round Robin

Round Robin is a preemptive process scheduling algorithm that is used extensively in interactive systems. It's the computing version of two children taking turns using the television remote control. Round Robin is easy to implement. It isn't based on job characteristics but on a predetermined slice of time that's given to each job to ensure that the CPU is equally shared among all active processes and isn't monopolized by any one job.

This time slice is called a **time quantum**; its size is crucial to the performance of the system. It can vary from 100 milliseconds to 1 or 2 seconds.

Jobs are placed in the READY queue using a first-come, first-served scheme. The Process Scheduler selects the first job from the front of the queue, sets the timer to the time quantum, and allocates the CPU to this job. If processing isn't finished when time expires, the job is preempted and put at the end of the READY queue, and its information is saved in its PCB.

In the event that the job's CPU cycle is shorter than the time quantum, one of two actions will take place: (1) If this is the job's last CPU cycle and the job is finished, then all resources allocated to it are released and the completed job is returned to the user; (2) If the CPU cycle has been interrupted by an I/O request, then information about the job is saved in its PCB and it is linked at the end of the appropriate I/O queue. Later, when the I/O request has been satisfied, it is returned to the end of the READY queue to await allocation of the CPU.

The example in Figure 4.11 illustrates a Round Robin algorithm with a time slice of 4 milliseconds (I/O requests are ignored):

✔️ With Round Robin and a queue with numerous processes, each process gets its first access to the processor before the first process gets access a second time.

Arrival time:	0	1	2	3
Job:	A	B	C	D
CPU cycle:	8	4	9	5

(figure 4.11)

Timeline for job sequence A, B, C, D using the preemptive round robin algorithm with time slices of 4 ms.

Job A	Job B	Job C	Job D	Job A	Job C	Job D	Job C
0	4	8	12	16	20	24	25 26

The turnaround time is the completion time minus the arrival time:

Job:	A	B	C	D
Completion Time minus Arrival Time	20-0	8-1	26-2	25-3
Turnaround:	20	7	24	22

So the average turnaround time is:

$$\frac{20 + 7 + 24 + 22}{4} = 18.25$$

Note that in Figure 4.11, Job A was preempted once because it needed 8 milliseconds to complete its CPU cycle, while Job B terminated in one time quantum. Job C was preempted twice because it needed 9 milliseconds to complete its CPU cycle, and Job D was preempted once because it needed 5 milliseconds. In their last execution or swap into memory, both Jobs D and C used the CPU for only 1 millisecond and terminated before their last time quantum expired, releasing the CPU sooner.

The efficiency of Round Robin depends on the size of the time quantum in relation to the average CPU cycle. If the quantum is too large—that is, if it's larger than most CPU cycles—then the algorithm reduces to the FCFS scheme. If the quantum is too small, then the amount of context switching slows down the execution of the jobs and the amount of overhead is dramatically increased, as the three examples in Figure 4.12 demonstrate. Job A has a CPU cycle of 8 milliseconds. The amount of context switching increases as the time quantum decreases in size.

In Figure 4.12, the first case (a) has a time quantum of 10 milliseconds and there is no context switching (and no overhead). The CPU cycle ends shortly before the time quantum expires and the job runs to completion. For this job with this time quantum, there is no difference between the Round Robin algorithm and the FCFS algorithm.

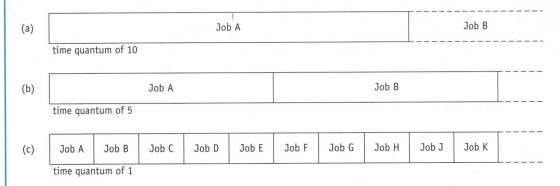

(figure 4.12)

Context switches for three different time quantums. In (a), Job A (which requires only 8 cycles to run to completion) finishes before the time quantum of 10 expires. In (b) and (c), the time quantum expires first, interrupting the jobs.

In the second case (b), with a time quantum of 5 milliseconds, there is one context switch. The job is preempted once when the time quantum expires, so there is some overhead for context switching and there would be a delayed turnaround based on the number of other jobs in the system.

In the third case (c), with a time quantum of 1 millisecond, there are 10 context switches because the job is preempted every time the time quantum expires; overhead becomes costly, and turnaround time suffers accordingly.

What's the best time quantum size? The answer should be predictable by now: it depends on the system. If it's a time-critical environment, the system is expected to respond immediately. If it's an archival system, turnaround time and overhead become critically important.

Here are two general rules of thumb for selecting the proper time quantum: (1) it should be long enough to allow 80 percent of the CPU cycles to run to completion, and (2) it should be at least 100 times longer than the time required to perform one context switch. These rules are used in some systems, but they are not inflexible.

Multiple-Level Queues

Multiple-level queues isn't really a separate scheduling algorithm, but works in conjunction with several of the schemes already discussed and is found in systems with jobs that can be grouped according to a common characteristic. We've already introduced at least one kind of multiple-level queue—that of a priority-based system with a different queue for each priority level.

Another kind of system might gather all of the CPU-bound jobs in one queue and all I/O-bound jobs in another. The Process Scheduler then alternately selects jobs from each queue to keep the system balanced.

A third common example can be used in a hybrid environment that supports both batch and interactive jobs. The batch jobs are put in one queue, called the background queue, while the interactive jobs are put in a foreground queue and are treated more favorably than those on the background queue.

All of these examples have one thing in common: The scheduling policy is based on some predetermined scheme that allocates special treatment to the jobs in each queue. With multiple-level queues, the system designers can choose to use different algorithms for different queues, allowing them to combine the advantages of several algorithms. For example, within each queue, the jobs are served in FCFS fashion or use some other scheme instead.

Multiple-level queues raise some interesting questions:

- Is the processor allocated to the jobs in the first queue until it is empty before moving to the next queue, or does it travel from queue to queue until the last job on the last queue has been served? And then go back to serve the first job on the first queue? Or something in between?
- Is this fair to those who have earned, or paid for, a higher priority?
- Is it fair to those in a low-priority queue?
- If the processor is allocated to the jobs on the first queue and it never empties out, when will the jobs in the last queues be served?
- Can the jobs in the last queues get "time off for good behavior" and eventually move to better queues?

The answers depend on the policy used by the system to service the queues. There are four primary methods to the movement: not allowing movement between queues, moving jobs from queue to queue, moving jobs from queue to queue and increasing the time quantums for lower queues, and giving special treatment to jobs that have been in the system for a long time (aging). We explore each of these methods with the following four cases.

Case 1: No Movement Between Queues

No movement between queues is a very simple policy that rewards those who have high-priority jobs. The processor is allocated to the jobs in the high-priority queue in FCFS fashion, and it is allocated to jobs in low-priority queues only when the high-priority queues are empty. This policy can be justified if there are relatively few users with high-priority jobs so the top queues quickly empty out, allowing the processor to spend a fair amount of time running the low-priority jobs.

Case 2: Movement Between Queues

Movement between queues is a policy that adjusts the priorities assigned to each job: High-priority jobs are treated like all the others once they are in the system. (Their initial priority may be favorable.) When a time quantum interrupt occurs, the job is preempted and moved to the end of the next lower queue. A job may also have its priority increased, such as when it issues an I/O request before its time quantum has expired.

This policy is fairest in a system in which the jobs are handled according to their computing cycle characteristics: CPU-bound or I/O-bound. This assumes that a job that exceeds its time quantum is CPU-bound and will require more CPU allocation than one that requests I/O before the time quantum expires. Therefore, the CPU-bound jobs are placed at the end of the next lower-level queue when they're preempted because of the expiration of the time quantum, while I/O-bound jobs are returned to the end of the next higher-level queue once their I/O request has finished. This facilitates I/O-bound jobs and is good in interactive systems.

Case 3: Variable Time Quantum Per Queue

Variable time quantum per queue is a variation of the movement between queues policy. It allows for faster turnaround of CPU-bound jobs.

In this scheme, each of the queues is given a time quantum twice as long as the previous queue. The highest queue might have a time quantum of 100 milliseconds. The second-highest queue would have a time quantum of 200 milliseconds, the third would have 400 milliseconds, and so on. If there are enough queues, the lowest one might have a relatively long time quantum of 3 seconds or more.

If a job doesn't finish its CPU cycle in the first time quantum, it is moved to the end of the next lower-level queue; and when the processor is next allocated to it, the job executes for twice as long as before. With this scheme, a CPU-bound job can execute for longer and longer periods of time, thus improving its chances of finishing faster.

Case 4: Aging

Aging is used to ensure that jobs in the lower-level queues will eventually complete their execution. The operating system keeps track of each job's waiting time, and when a job gets too old—that is, when it reaches a certain time limit—the system moves the job to the next highest queue, and so on, until it reaches the top queue. A more drastic aging policy is one that moves the old job directly from the lowest queue to the end of the top queue. Regardless of its actual implementation, an aging policy guards against the indefinite postponement of unwieldy jobs. As you might expect, **indefinite postponement** means that a job's execution is delayed for an undefined amount of time because it is repeatedly preempted so other jobs can be processed. (We all know examples of an unpleasant task that's been indefinitely postponed to make time for a more appealing pastime). Eventually the situation could lead to the old job's starvation causing it to never be processed. Indefinite postponement is a major problem when allocating resources and one that is discussed in detail in Chapter 5.

Earliest Deadline First

Earliest Deadline First (EDF), known as a dynamic priority algorithm, is a preemptive scheduling algorithm built to address the critical processing requirements of real-time systems and their pressing deadlines. Contrary to the fixed priority scheme explored earlier, where the priority of a job does not change after it enters the system, with EDF the priority can be adjusted as it moves through execution from START to FINISHED.

The primary goal of EDF is to process all jobs in the order that is most likely to allow each to run to completion before reaching their respective deadlines. Initially, the priority assigned to each job is based on the amount of time remaining until the job's impending deadline—and that priority is inversely proportional to its absolute deadline. So, in its simplest sense: the closer the deadline, the higher the priority. Sometime two or more jobs share the same deadline, in which case the tie is broken using any scheme such as first in, first out. Remember, the goal is to complete all jobs before each one reaches its deadline.

With this algorithm, a job's deadline can change and the algorithm can change its priority accordingly. For example, consider the following job stream and the timeline shown in Figure 4-13.

Job:	A	B	C	D	E	F
Arrival time:	0	1	2	3	3	5
Execution Time:	3	1	5	2	2	5
Deadline:	6	2	10	8	8	15
Time-before-deadline (at arrival time)	6	1	8	5	5	10

The tie between Jobs D and E (which both arrived at the same time) was broken arbitrarily with E going first. Notice that if we reorder the job stream by absolute deadline (regardless of the arrival time of each), we can see the order in which they might finish: Job B (at Time 2), Job A (Time 6), Job D and Job E (both at Time 8), Job C (Time 10), and Job F (Time 15).

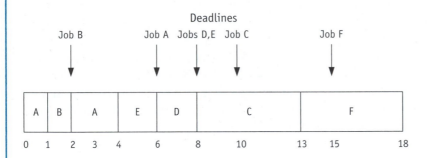

(figure 4-13)

EDF dynamic priority timeline showing processing order and deadlines, which were met by Jobs A-E.

Using this algorithm, the priority of each job can change as more important jobs enter the system for processing, and the job with the closest deadline immediately assumes highest priority. (Job A in Figure 4-13 assumed highest priority twice before it ran to completion.)

This example illustrates one of the difficulties with the EDF algorithm. By adding the total amount of computation/execution time, we can see that a total of 18 units will be required (if we ignore overhead operations), and yet the deadline for these six jobs is at Time 15. It's not possible to perform 18 units of execution in 15 units of time.

Additional problems can occur because of the algorithm's dynamic nature. For example, it is impossible to predict job throughput because the priority of a given job rises or falls depending on the mix of other jobs in the system. A job with a closer deadline will cause the other waiting jobs to be delayed. The EDF algorithm also has high overhead requirements because it constantly evaluates the deadlines of all the jobs awaiting execution.

Beware that while EDF is written to meet the needs of real-time environments, there is no guarantee that it is possible for it to succeed, and deadlines can still be missed when using this algorithm. Still, of the schemes discussed in this chapter, it is designed well to deal with the stringent requirements of dynamic real-time computing systems.

Managing Interrupts

We first encountered **interrupts** in Chapter 3, when the Memory Manager issued page interrupts to accommodate job requests. In this chapter, we examined another type of interrupt, such as the one that occurs when the time quantum expires and the processor is deallocated from the running job and allocated to another one.

There are other interrupts that are caused by events internal to the process. I/O interrupts are issued when a READ or WRITE command is issued (and we detail those in Chapter 7). Internal interrupts, or synchronous interrupts, also occur as a direct result of the arithmetic operation or other instruction currently being processed.

For example, interrupts can be generated by illegal arithmetic operations, including the following:
- Attempts to divide by zero (called an exception)
- Floating-point operations generating an overflow or underflow
- Fixed-point addition or subtraction that causes an arithmetic overflow

Illegal job instructions, such as the following, can also generate interrupts:
- Attempts to access protected or nonexistent storage locations, such as the one shown in Figure 4.14
- Attempts to use an undefined operation code
- Operating on invalid data
- Unauthorized attempts to make system changes, such as trying to change the size of the time quantum

(figure 4.14)

Sample Windows screen showing that the interrupt handler has stepped in after an invalid operation.

SearchFilterHost.exe - Application Error

The instruction at "0x0700609c" referenced memory at "0x00000014". The memory could not be "read".

Click on OK to terminate the program

OK

The control program that handles the interruption sequence of events is called the **interrupt handler**. When the operating system detects an error that is not recoverable, the interrupt handler typically follows this sequence:

1. The type of interrupt is described and stored—to be passed on to the user as an error message.
2. The state of the interrupted process is saved, including the value of the program counter, the mode specification, and the contents of all registers.
3. The interrupt is processed: The error message and the state of the interrupted process are sent to the user; program execution is halted; any resources allocated to the job are released; and the job exits the system.
4. The processor resumes normal operation.

If we're dealing with fatal, nonrecoverable interrupts, the job is terminated in Step 3. However, when the interrupt handler is working with an I/O interrupt, time quantum, or other recoverable interrupt, Step 3 simply suspends the job and moves it to the appropriate I/O device queue or READY queue (on time out). Later, when the I/O request is finished, the job is returned to the READY queue. If it was a time quantum interrupt, the job process or thread is already on the READY queue.

Conclusion

The Processor Manager must allocate the CPU among all the system's users and all of their jobs, processes, and threads. In this chapter we've made the distinction between job scheduling (the selection of incoming jobs based on their characteristics) and process and thread scheduling (the instant-by-instant allocation of the CPU). We've also described how interrupts are generated and resolved by the interrupt handler.

Each scheduling algorithm presented in this chapter has unique characteristics, objectives, and applications. A system designer can choose the best policy and algorithm only after carefully evaluating the strengths and weaknesses of each one that's available in the context of the system's requirements. Table 4.3 shows how the algorithms presented in this chapter compare.

In the next chapter we explore the demands placed on the Processor Manager as it attempts to synchronize execution of every job admitted to the system to avoid deadlocks, livelock, and starvation.

(table 4.3)

Comparison of the scheduling algorithms discussed in this chapter

Algorithm	Policy Type	Disadvantages	Advantages
First Come, First Served	Nonpreemptive	Unpredictable turnaround times; has an element of chance	Easy to implement
Shortest Job Next	Nonpreemptive	Indefinite postponement of some jobs; requires execution times in advance	Minimizes average waiting time
Priority Scheduling	Nonpreemptive	Indefinite postponement of some jobs	Ensures fast completion of important jobs
Shortest Remaining Time	Preemptive	Overhead incurred by context switching	Ensures fast completion of short jobs
Round Robin	Preemptive	Requires selection of good time quantum	Provides reasonable response times to interactive users; provides fair CPU allocation
Multiple-Level Queues	Preemptive/ Nonpreemptive	Overhead incurred by monitoring queues	Flexible scheme; allows aging or other queue movement to counteract indefinite postponement; is fair to CPU-bound jobs
Earliest Deadline First	Preemptive	Overhead required to monitor dynamic deadlines	Attempts timely completion of jobs

Key Terms

aging: a policy used to ensure that jobs that have been in the system for a long time in the lower-level queues will eventually complete their execution.

context switching: the acts of saving a job's processing information in its PCB so the job can be swapped out of memory and of loading the processing information from the PCB of another job into the appropriate registers so the CPU can process it. Context switching occurs in all preemptive policies.

CPU-bound: a job that will perform a great deal of nonstop computation before issuing an I/O request. It contrasts with *I/O-bound*.

earliest deadline first (EDF): a preemptive process scheduling policy (or algorithm) that selects processes based on the proximity of their deadlines (appropriate for real-time environments).

first-come, first-served (FCFS): a nonpreemptive process scheduling policy (or algorithm) that handles jobs according to their arrival time.

high-level scheduler: a synonym for the Job Scheduler.

I/O-bound: a job that requires a large number of input/output operations, resulting in substantial free time for the CPU. It contrasts with *CPU-bound*.

indefinite postponement: signifies that a job's execution is delayed indefinitely.

interrupt: a hardware signal that suspends execution of a program and activates the execution of a special program known as the interrupt handler.

interrupt handler: the program that controls what action should be taken by the operating system when a certain sequence of events is interrupted.

Job Scheduler: the high-level scheduler of the Processor Manager that selects jobs from a queue of incoming jobs based on each job's characteristics.

job status: the state of a job as it moves through the system from the beginning to the end of its execution.

low-level scheduler: a synonym for the Process Scheduler.

middle-level scheduler: a scheduler used by the Processor Manager when the system to remove active processes from memory becomes overloaded. The middle-level scheduler swaps these processes back into memory when the system overload has cleared.

multiple-level queues: a process scheduling scheme (used with other scheduling algorithms) that groups jobs according to a common characteristic.

multiprogramming: a technique that allows a single processor to process several programs residing simultaneously in main memory and interleaving their execution by overlapping I/O requests with CPU requests.

natural wait: an I/O request from a program in a multiprogramming environment that would cause a process to wait "naturally" before resuming execution.

nonpreemptive scheduling policy: a job scheduling strategy that functions without external interrupts so that once a job captures the processor and begins execution, it remains in the running state uninterrupted until it issues an I/O request or it's finished.

preemptive scheduling policy: any process scheduling strategy that, based on predetermined policies, interrupts the processing of a job and transfers the CPU to another job. It is widely used in time-sharing environments.

priority scheduling: a nonpreemptive process scheduling policy (or algorithm) that allows for the execution of high-priority jobs before low-priority jobs.

process: an instance of execution of a program that is identifiable and controllable by the operating system.

Process Control Block (PCB): a data structure that contains information about the current status and characteristics of a process.

Process Scheduler: a low-level scheduler that establishes the order in which processes in the READY queue will be served by the CPU.

process status: information stored in the job's PCB that indicates the current location in memory of the job and the resources responsible for that status.

processor: (1) a synonym for the CPU, or (2) any component in a computing system capable of performing a sequence of activities.

program: a unit of instructions.

queue: a linked list of PCBs that indicates the order in which jobs or processes will be serviced.

response time: one measure of the efficiency of an interactive system that tracks the time required for the system to respond to a user's command.

Round Robin: a preemptive process scheduling policy (or algorithm) that allocates to each job one unit of processing time per turn to ensure that the CPU is equally shared among all active processes and isn't monopolized by any one job.

scheduling algorithm: an algorithm used by the Job or Process Scheduler to allocate the CPU and move jobs or processes through the system.

scheduling policy: any policy used by the Processor Manager to select the order in which incoming jobs, processes, and threads will be executed.

shortest job next (SJN): a nonpreemptive process scheduling policy (or algorithm) that selects the waiting job with the shortest CPU cycle time.

shortest remaining time (SRT): a preemptive process scheduling policy (or algorithm) similar to the SJN algorithm that allocates the processor to the job closest to completion.

task: (1) the term used to describe a process, or (2) the basic unit of concurrent programming languages that defines a sequence of instructions that may be executed in parallel with other similar units.

thread: a portion of a process that can run independently. Multithreaded systems can have several threads running at one time with the same or different priorities.

Thread Control Block (TCB): a data structure that contains information about the current status and characteristics of a thread.

thread status: information stored in the thread control block that indicates the current position of the thread and the resources responsible for that status.

time quantum: a period of time assigned to a process for execution before it is preempted.

turnaround time: a measure of a system's efficiency that tracks the time required to execute a job and return output to the user.

Interesting Searches

For more background on a few of the topics discussed in this chapter, begin a search with these terms:

- Thread Scheduling Priorities
- CPU Cycle Time
- Processor Bottleneck
- Processor Queue Length
- I/O Interrupts

Exercises

Research Topics

A. Multi-core technology can often, but not always, make applications run faster. Research some real-life computing environments that are expected to benefit from multi-core chips and briefly explain why. Cite your academic sources.

B. Compare two processors currently being produced for laptop computers. Use standard industry benchmarks for your comparison and briefly list the advantages and disadvantages of each. You can compare different processors from the same manufacturer (such as two Intel processors) or different processors from different manufacturers (such as Intel and AMD).

Exercises

1. Compare and contrast a process and a thread.
2. Which scheduler is responsible for scheduling threads in a multithreading system?
3. Five jobs arrive nearly simultaneously for processing and their estimated CPU cycles are, respectively: Job A = 12, Job B = 2, Job C = 15, Job D = 7, and Job E = 3 ms.
   a. Using FCFS, and assuming the difference in arrival time is negligible, in what order would they be processed? What is the total time required to process all five jobs? What is the average turnaround time for all five jobs?

b. Using SJN, and assuming the difference in arrival time is negligible, in what order would they be processed? What is the total time required to process all five jobs? What is the average turnaround time for all five jobs?

4. Assume a multiple level queue system with a variable time quantum per queue, and that the incoming job needs 50 ms to run to completion. If the first queue has a time quantum of 5 ms and each queue thereafter has a time quantum that is twice as large as the previous one, how many times will the job be interrupted, and on which queue will it finish its execution? Explain how much time it spends in each queue.

5. Using the same multiple level queue system from the previous exercises, if a job needs 130 ms to run to completion, how many times will the job be interrupted and on which queue will it finish its execution? Does it matter if there are other jobs in the system?

6. Assume that your system has one queue for jobs waiting for printing and another queue for those waiting for access to a disk. Which queue would you expect to have the faster response? Explain your reasoning.

7. Using SJN, calculate the start time and finish time for each of these seven jobs:

Job	Arrival Time	CPU Cycle
A	0	2
B	1	11
C	2	4
D	4	1
E	5	9
F	7	4
G	8	2

8. Given the following information:

Job	Arrival Time	CPU Cycle
A	0	15
B	2	2
C	3	14
D	6	10
E	9	1

Calculate which jobs will have arrived ready for processing by the time the first job is finished or first interrupted using each of the following scheduling algorithms.

a. FCFS

b. SJN

c. SRT

d. Round Robin (use a time quantum of 5, but ignore the time required for context switching and natural wait)

9. Using the same information from the previous exercise, calculate the start time and finish time for each of the five jobs using each of the following scheduling algorithms. It may help to draw the timeline.

a. FCFS

b. SJN

c. SRT

d. Round Robin (use a time quantum of 5, but ignore the time required for context switching and natural wait)

10. Using the same information given for Exercise 8, compute the turnaround time for every job for each of the following scheduling algorithms (ignore context switching overhead times). It may help to draw the timeline.

a. FCFS

b. SJN

c. SRT

d. Round Robin (using a time quantum of 5)

11. Given the following information for a real-time system using EDF:

Job:	A	B	C	D	E	F
Arrival time:	0	0	1	1	3	6
Execution Time:	3	1	6	2	7	5
Deadline:	6	1	44	2	16	15
Time-before-deadline (at arrival time)						

Compute the time-before-deadline for each incoming job. Give the order in which the six jobs will finish, and identify any jobs that fail to meet their deadline. It may help to draw a timeline.

Advanced Exercises

12. Consider this variation of Round Robin. A process that has used its full time quantum is returned to the end of the READY queue, while one that has used half of its time quantum is returned to the middle of the queue. One that has

used one-fourth of its time quantum goes to a place one-fourth of the distance away from the beginning of the queue. Explain the advantages and disadvantages of this scheduling policy? Identify the user group that would find this most advantageous.

13. When using a personal computer, it can be easy to determine when a job is caught in an infinite loop or system-wide freeze. The typical solution to this problem is for the user to manually intervene and terminate the offending job, or in the worst case, all jobs. What mechanism would you implement in the Process Scheduler to automate the termination of a job that's in an infinite loop? Take into account jobs that legitimately use large amounts of CPU time, such as a task that is calculating the first 300,000 prime numbers.

14. Some guidelines for selecting the right time quantum were given in this chapter. As a system designer, which guidelines do you prefer? Which would the average user prefer? How would you know when you have chosen the best time quantum? What factors would make this time quantum best from the system's point of view?

15. Using the process state diagrams of Figure 4.2, explain why there's no transition:
    a. From the READY state to the WAITING state
    b. From the WAITING state to the RUNNING state

Programming Exercises

16. Write a program that will simulate FCFS, SJN, SRT, and Round Robin scheduling algorithms. For each algorithm, the program should compute waiting time and turnaround time of every job as well as the average waiting time and average turnaround time. The average values should be consolidated in a table for easy comparison. You may use the following data to test your program. The time quantum for Round Robin is 4 ms. (Assume that the context switching time is 0).

Job	Arrival Times	CPU Cycle (in milliseconds)
A	0	16
B	3	2
C	5	11
D	9	6
E	10	1
F	12	9
G	14	4

Job	Arrival Times	CPU Cycle (in milliseconds)
H	16	14
I	17	1
J	19	8

17. Modify your program from Exercise 16 to generate a random job stream and change the context switching time to 0.4 ms. Compare outputs from both runs and discuss which would be the better policy. Describe any drastic changes encountered (or a lack of changes), and explain why.

Chapter 5 | Process Management

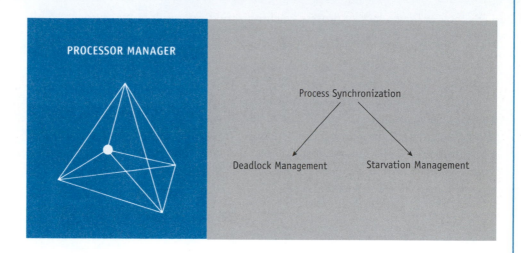

PROCESSOR MANAGER

Process Synchronization

Deadlock Management   Starvation Management

> ❝ *We have all heard the story of the animal standing in doubt between two stacks of hay and starving to death.* ❞
>
> —Abraham Lincoln *(1809–1865)*

Learning Objectives

After completing this chapter, you should be able to describe:

• The differences among deadlock, race, and starvation
• Several causes of system deadlock and livelock
• The difference between preventing and avoiding deadlocks
• How to detect and recover from deadlocks
• How to detect and recover from starvation
• The concept of a race and how to prevent it

We've already looked at resource sharing from two perspectives—that of sharing memory and sharing one processor—but the processor sharing described thus far was the best case scenario, free of conflicts and complications. In this chapter, we address the problems caused when many processes compete for relatively few resources, causing the system to stop responding as it should and rendering it unable to service all of the necessary processes.

Let's look at how a lack of **process synchronization** can result in two extreme conditions: deadlock or starvation.

System deadlock has been known through the years by many descriptive phrases, including "deadly embrace," "Catch 22," and "blue screen of death," to name a few. A simple example of a deadlock is illustrated in Figure 5.1. Let's say the ice cream store is closing and you just got the last available ice cream sundae—but the next person in line grabbed the only available spoon! If no additional ice cream sundaes AND no additional spoons become available, AND neither one of you decides to give up your resources, then a deadlock has occurred. Notice that it takes a combination of circumstances for a deadlock to occur.

(figure 5.1)

A very simple example of a deadlock: You hold the ice cream (a) but you need the only available spoon to eat it. Someone else holds the only spoon (b) but has no ice cream to eat.

(a) You   (b) Someone Else

In computer systems, a deadlock is a system-wide tangle of resource requests that begins when two or more jobs are put on hold, each waiting for a vital resource to become available. The problem builds when the resources needed by those jobs are the resources held by other jobs that are also waiting to run but cannot because they're waiting for other unavailable resources. The tangled jobs come to a standstill. The deadlock is complete if the remainder of the system comes to a standstill as well. When the situation can't be resolved by the operating system, then intervention is required.

Deadlock, Livelock, and Starvation

A **deadlock** is most easily described with an example that we return to throughout the chapter—a narrow staircase in a building. The staircase was built as a fire escape route, but people working in the building often take the stairs instead of waiting for the slow elevators. Traffic on the staircase moves well unless two people, traveling in opposite directions, need to pass on the stairs—there's room for only one person on each step. There's a landing at each floor that is wide enough for two people to share, but the stairs are not—they can be allocated to only one person at a time. In this example, the staircase is the system and the steps and landings are the resources. Problems occur when someone going up the stairs meets someone coming down, and each refuses to retreat to a wider place. This creates a deadlock, which is the subject of much of our discussion on process synchronization.

Similarly, if two people on a landing try to pass each other but cannot do so because as one steps to the right, the other steps to the left, and vice versa, then they will continue moving but neither will ever move forward. This is called **livelock**.

On the other hand, if a few patient people wait on the landing for a break in the opposing traffic, and that break never comes, they could wait there forever. That results in **starvation**, an extreme case of indefinite postponement, and is discussed at the end of this chapter.

Deadlock

Deadlock is more serious than indefinite postponement or starvation because it affects more than one job. Because resources are being tied up, the entire system (not just a few programs) is affected. There's no simple and immediate solution to a deadlock; no one can move forward until someone moves out of the way, but no one can move out of the way until either someone advances or everyone behind moves back. Obviously, it requires outside intervention. Only then can the deadlock be resolved.

Deadlocks became prevalent with the introduction of interactive systems, which generally improve the use of resources through dynamic resource sharing, but this capability also increases the possibility of deadlocks.

In some computer systems, deadlocks are regarded as a mere inconvenience that causes delays. But for real-time systems, deadlocks cause critical situations. For example, a deadlock in a hospital's life support system or in the guidance system aboard an aircraft could endanger lives. Regardless of the environment, the operating system must either prevent deadlocks or resolve them when they happen. (In Chapter 12, we learn how to calculate system reliability and availability, which can be affected by processor conflicts.)

Seven Cases of Deadlock or Livelock

A deadlock usually occurs when nonsharable, nonpreemptable resources, such as files, printers, or scanners, are allocated to jobs that eventually require other nonsharable, nonpreemptive resources—resources that have been locked by other jobs. However, deadlocks aren't restricted to files, printers, and scanners. They can also occur on sharable resources that are locked, such as disks and databases.

Directed graphs visually represent the system's resources and processes and show how they are deadlocked. Using a series of squares for resources, circles for processes, and connectors with arrows for requests, directed graphs can be manipulated to understand how deadlocks occur.

Case 1: Deadlocks on File Requests

If jobs are allowed to request and hold files for the duration of their execution, a deadlock can occur, as the simplified directed graph shown in Figure 5.2 illustrates.

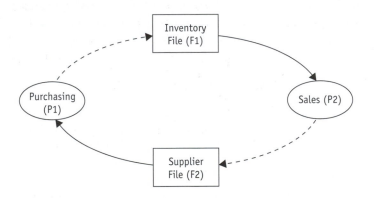

(figure 5.2)

Case 1. These two processes, shown as circles, are each waiting for a resource, shown as rectangles, that has already been allocated to the other process, thus creating a deadlock.

For example, consider the case of a home construction company with two application programs, Purchasing and Sales, which are active at the same time. Both need to access two separate files, called Inventory and Suppliers, to read and write transactions. One day the system deadlocks when the following sequence of events takes place:

1. The Purchasing process accesses the Suppliers file to place an order for more lumber.
2. The Sales process accesses the Inventory file to reserve the parts that will be required to build the home ordered that day.
3. The Purchasing process doesn't release the Suppliers file, but it requests the Inventory file so it can verify the quantity of lumber on hand before placing its order for more. However, Purchasing is blocked because the Inventory file is being held by Sales.

4. Meanwhile, the Sales process doesn't release the Inventory file (because it needs it), but requests the Suppliers file to check the schedule of a subcontractor. At this point, the Sales process is also blocked because the Suppliers file is already being held by the Purchasing process.

In the meantime, any other programs that require the Inventory or Suppliers files will be put on hold as long as this situation continues. This deadlock will remain until one of the two programs is closed or forcibly removed and its file is released. Only then can the other program continue and the system return to normal.

Case 2: Deadlocks in Databases

A deadlock can also occur if two processes access and lock records in a database.

To appreciate the following scenario, remember that database queries and transactions are often relatively brief processes that either search or modify parts of a database. Requests usually arrive at random and may be interleaved arbitrarily.

Database **locking** is a technique used to guarantee the integrity of the data through which the user locks out all other users while working with the database. Locking can be done at three different levels: the entire database can be locked for the duration of the request; a subsection of the database can be locked; or only the individual record can be locked. Locking the entire database (the most extreme and most successful solution) prevents a deadlock from occurring, but it restricts access to the database to one user at a time and, in a multiuser environment, response times are significantly slowed; this is normally an unacceptable solution. When the locking is performed on only one part of the database, access time is improved, but the possibility of a deadlock is increased because different processes sometimes need to work with several parts of the database at the same time.

Here's a system that locks each record in the database when it is accessed and keeps it locked until that process is completed. Let's assume there are two processes (The sales process and address process), each of which needs to update a different record (the final exam record and the current address record), and the following sequence leads to a deadlock:

1. The sales process accesses the first quarter record and locks it.
2. The address process accesses the current address record and locks it.
3. The sales process requests the current address record, which is locked by the address process.
4. The address process requests the first quarter record, which is locked by the sales process.

If locks are *not* used to preserve database integrity, the resulting records in the database might include only some of the data—and their contents would depend on the

Original Record

Jones
GPA = 2.5
ADDR: 5th Ave.

P1 Grades Process
reads data

P2 Address Process
reads data

work area

GPA updated

Jones
GPA = 3.0
ADDR: 5th Ave.

Jones
GPA = 2.5
ADDR: Main St.

address updated

P1 rewrites record to database with the new GPA

Jones
GPA = 3.0
ADDR: 5th Ave.

P2 rewrites record to database with the new address

Jones
GPA = 2.5
ADDR: Main St.

Final Record

(figure 5.3)

Case 2. P1 finishes first and wins the race but its version of the record will soon be overwritten by P2. Regardless of which process wins the race, the final version of the data will be incorrect.

order in which each process finishes its execution. Known as a **race** between processes, this is illustrated in the example shown in Figure 5.3. (Leaving all database records unlocked is an alternative, but that leads to other difficulties.)

Let's say you are a student of a university that maintains most of its files on a database that can be accessed by several different programs, including one for grades and another listing home addresses. You've just moved at the end of fall term, so you send the university a change of address form. It happens to be shortly after grades are submitted. One fateful day, both programs race to access a single record in the database:

1. The grades process (P1) is the first to access your college record (R1), and it copies the record to its own work area.
2. Almost simultaneously, the address process (P2) accesses the same record (R1) and copies it to its own work area. Now the same record is in three different places: the database, the work area for grade changes, and the work area for address changes.
3. The grades process changes your college record by entering your grades for the fall term and calculating your new grade average.
4. The address process changes your college record by updating the address field.
5. The grades process finishes its work first and writes its version of your college record back to the database. Now, your record has updated grades, but your address hasn't changed.

A race introduces the element of chance, an element that's totally unacceptable in database management. The integrity of the database must be upheld.

6. The address process finishes and rewrites its updated version of your record back to the database. This version has the new address, but it replaced the version that contains your grades! At this point, according to the database, you have no grade for this term.

If we reverse the order and say that the address process wins the race, your grades will be updated but not your address. Depending on your success in the classroom, you might prefer one mishap over the other. From the operating system's point of view, both alternatives are unacceptable, because both are incorrect and allow the database to become corrupted. A successful operating system can't allow the integrity of the database to depend on luck or a random sequence of events.

Case 3: Deadlocks in Dedicated Device Allocation

The use of a group of dedicated devices, such as two audio recorders, can also deadlock the system. Remember that dedicated devices cannot be shared.

Let's say two administrators, Chris and Jay, from the local board of education are each running education programs and each has a process (P1 and P2, respectively) that will eventually need to use both audio recorders (R1 and R2) together to copy a school board hearing. The two recorders are available at the time when both make the request; the system's allocation policy states that each recorder is to be allocated on an "as requested" basis. Soon the following sequence transpires:

1. Chris's process requests the recorder closest to the office, Recorder #1, and gets it.
2. Jay's process requests the recorder closest to the printer, Recorder #2, and gets it.
3. Chris's process then requests Recorder #2, but is blocked and has to wait.
4. Jay's process requests Recorder #1, but is blocked and the wait begins here, too.

Neither Chris's or Jay's job can continue because each is holding one recorder while waiting for the other process to finish and release its resource—an event that will never occur according to this allocation policy.

Case 4: Deadlocks in Multiple Device Allocation

Deadlocks aren't restricted to processes that are contending for the same type of device; they can happen when several processes request, and hold on to, several dedicated devices while other processes act in a similar manner, as shown in Figure 5.4.

(figure 5.4)

Case 4. Three processes, shown as circles, are each waiting for a device that has already been allocated to another process, thus creating a deadlock.

Consider the case of an engineering design firm with three programs (P1, P2, and P3) and three dedicated devices: scanner, printer, and plotter. The following sequence of events will result in deadlock:

1. Program 1 (P1) requests and gets the only scanner.
2. Program 2 requests and gets the only printer.
3. Program 3 requests and gets the only plotter.
4. Now, Program 1 requests the printer but is blocked.
5. Then, Program 2 requests the plotter but is blocked.
6. Finally, Program 3 requests the scanner but is blocked and the deadlock begins.

As was the case in the earlier examples, none of these programs can continue because each is waiting for a necessary resource that's already being held by another.

Case 5: Deadlocks in Spooling

Although in the previous example the printer was a dedicated device, printers can be sharable devices and join a category called "virtual devices" that uses high-speed storage to transfer data between it and the CPU. The spooler accepts output from several users and acts as a temporary storage area for all output until the printer is ready to accept it. This process is called **spooling**. However, if the printer needs all of a job's output before it will begin printing, but the spooling system fills the available space with only partially completed output, then a deadlock can occur. It happens like this.

Let's say it's one hour before the big project is due for a computer class. Twenty-six frantic programmers key in their final changes and, with only minutes to spare, all issue print commands. The spooler receives the pages one at a time from each of the students but the pages are received separately, several page ones, page twos, and so on. The printer is ready to print the first completed document it gets, but as the spooler canvasses its files, it has the first page for many programs but the last page for none of them. Alas, the spooler is full of partially completed output—so no other pages can be accepted—but none of the jobs can be printed (which would release their disk space) because the printer accepts only completed output files. It's an unfortunate state of affairs.

This scenario isn't limited to printers. Any part of the computing system that relies on spooling, such as one that handles incoming jobs or transfers files over a network, is vulnerable to such a deadlock.

Case 6: Deadlocks in a Network

A network that's congested or has filled a large percentage of its I/O buffer space can become deadlocked if it doesn't have protocols to control the flow of messages through the network, as illustrated in Figure 5.5.

(figure 5.5)

Case 6, deadlocked network flow. Notice that only two nodes, C1 and C2, have buffers. Each line represents a communication path. The arrows indicate the direction of data flow.

For example, a medium-sized hotel has seven computing devices on a network, each on different nodes, but only two of those nodes use a buffer to control the stream of incoming data. The front desk (C1) receives messages from the business office (C2) and from two tablets (C6 and C7), and it sends messages to only the business office. All of the communication paths and possible interactions are shown in Figure 5.5.

- Messages that are received by front desk from the two tablets and that are destined for the business office are buffered in its output queue until they can be sent.
- Likewise, messages received by the business office from the two scanners and destined for the front desk are buffered in its output queue.
- On a busy day, as data traffic increases, the length of each output queue increases until all of the available buffer space is filled.

- At this point, the front desk can't accept any more messages (from the business office or any other networked device) because there's no more buffer space available to store them.

- For the same reason, the business office can't accept any messages from the front desk or any other computer, not even a request to send data from the buffer, which could help alleviate the congestion.

- The communication path between the front desk and the business office has become deadlocked. Because the front desk can't send messages to any other computer except the one in the business office, and it can only receive (and not send) messages from the two tablets, those routes also become deadlocked.

At this point, the front desk can't alert the business office about the problem without having someone run there with a message (sometimes called a "sneaker net"). This deadlock can't be resolved without outside intervention.

Case 7: Deadlocks in Disk Sharing

Disks are designed to be shared, so it's not uncommon for two processes to access different areas of the same disk. This ability to share creates an active type of deadlock, known as livelock. Processes use a form of busy-waiting that's different from a natural wait. In this case, it's waiting to share a resource but never actually gains control of it. In Figure 5.6, two competing processes are sending conflicting commands, causing livelock (notice that neither process is blocked, which would cause a deadlock). Instead, each remains active but without achieving any progress and never reaching fulfillment.

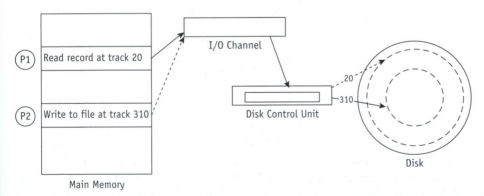

(figure 5.6)

Case 7. Two processes are each waiting for an I/O request to be filled: one at track 20 and one at track 310. But by the time the read/write arm reaches one track, a competing command for the other track has been issued, so neither command is satisfied and livelock occurs.

For example, at an insurance company the system performs many daily transactions. One day the following series of events ties up the system:

1. A process from Customer Service (P1) wishes to show a payment, so it issues a command to read the balance, which is stored on Track 20 of a disk.

2. While the control unit is moving the arm to Track 20, the Customer Service process is put on hold and the I/O channel is free to process the next I/O request.

3. While the arm is moving into position, Accounts Payable (P2) gains control of the I/O channel and issues a command to write someone else's payment to a record stored on Track 310. If the command is not "locked out," the Accounts Payable process is put on hold while the control unit moves the arm to Track 310.

4. Because the Accounts Payable process is "on hold" while the arm is moving, the channel can be captured again by the customer service process, which reconfirms its command to "read from Track 20."

5. Because the last command from the Accounts Payable process had forced the arm mechanism to Track 310, the disk control unit begins to reposition the arm to Track 20 to satisfy the customer service process. The I/O channel is released because the Customer Service process is once again put on hold, so it can be captured by the accounts payable process, which issues a WRITE command—only to discover that the arm mechanism needs to be repositioned again.

As a result, the arm is in a constant state of motion, moving back and forth between Tracks 20 and 310 as it tries to respond to the two competing commands, but it satisfies neither.

Necessary Conditions for Deadlock or Livelock

In each of these seven cases, the deadlock or livelock involved the interaction of several processes and resources, but each time, it was preceded by the simultaneous occurrence of four conditions that the operating system (or other systems) could have recognized: mutual exclusion, resource holding, no preemption, and circular wait. It's important to remember that each of these four conditions is necessary for the operating system to work smoothly. None of them can be removed easily without causing the system's overall functioning to suffer. Therefore, the system needs to recognize the combination of conditions before they occur.

To illustrate these four conditions, let's revisit the staircase example from the beginning of the chapter to identify the four conditions required for a locked system. (Note that deadlock and livelock share the same requirements, so the following discussion applies to both.)

When a deadlock occurs, all four conditions are present, though the opposite is not true—the presence of all four conditions does not always lead to deadlock.

1. When two people meet on the steps, between landings, they can't pass because the steps can hold only one person at a time. **Mutual exclusion**, the act of allowing only one person (or process) to have access to a step (or a dedicated resource), is the first condition for deadlock.

2. When two people meet on the stairs and each one holds ground and waits for the other to retreat, that is an example of **resource holding** (as opposed to resource sharing), the second condition for deadlock.

3. In this example, each step is dedicated to the climber (or the descender); it is allocated to the holder for as long as needed. This is called **no preemption**, the lack of temporary reallocation of resources, and is the third condition for deadlock.

4. These three lead to the fourth condition of **circular wait,** in which each person (or process) involved in the impasse is waiting for another to voluntarily release the step (or resource) so that at least one will be able to continue on and eventually arrive at the destination.

All four conditions are required for the deadlock to occur, and as long as all four conditions are present, the deadlock will continue. However, if one condition is removed, the deadlock will be resolved. In fact, if the four conditions can be prevented from ever occurring at the same time, deadlocks can be prevented. Although this concept may seem obvious, it isn't easy to implement.

Modeling Deadlocks

In 1972, Richard Holt published a visual tool to show how the four conditions can be modeled using **directed graphs.** (We used modified directed graphs in figures shown previously in this chapter.) These graphs use two kinds of symbols: processes represented by circles and resources represented by squares. A solid line with an arrow that runs from a *resource to a process,* as shown in Figure 5.7(a), means that that resource has already been allocated to that process (in other words, the process is holding that resource). A dashed line with an arrow going from a *process to a resource,* as shown in Figure 5.7(b), means that the process is waiting for that resource.

The directions of the arrows are critical because they indicate flow. If for any reason there is an interruption in the flow, then there is no deadlock. On the other hand, if cyclic flow is shown in the graph, (as illustrated in Figure 5.7(b), then there's a deadlock involving the processes and the resources shown in the cycle.

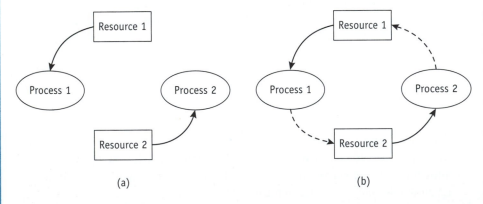

(a)   (b)

(figure 5.7)

In (a), Resource 1 is being held by Process 1 and Resource 2 is held by Process 2 in a system that is not deadlocked. In (b), Process 1 requests Resource 2 but doesn't release Resource 1, and Process 2 does the same — creating a deadlock. (If one process released its resource, the deadlock would be resolved.)

To practice modeling a system, the next three scenarios evaluate a system with three processes—P1, P2, and P3. The system also has three resources—R1, R2, and R3—each of a different type: printer, disk drive, and plotter. Because there is no specified order in which the requests are handled, we look at three different possible scenarios using graphs to help us detect any deadlocks.

Scenario 1: No Deadlock

The first scenario's sequence of events is shown in Table 5.1. The directed graph is shown in Figure 5.8.

Event	Action
1	Process 1 (P1) requests and is allocated the printer (R1).
2	Process 1 releases the printer.
3	Process 2 (P2) requests and is allocated the disk drive (R2).
4	Process 2 releases the disk drive.
5	Process 3 (P3) requests and is allocated the plotter (R3).
6	Process 3 releases the plotter.

Notice in the directed graph that no cycles were formed at any time. Therefore, we can safely conclude that a deadlock can't occur with this system at this time, even if each process requests each of the other resources because every resource is released before the next process requests it.

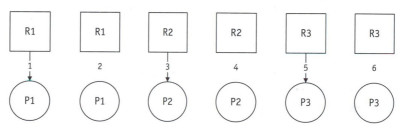

Scenario 2 – Resource Holding

Now, consider a second scenario's sequence of events shown in Table 5.2.

Event	Action
1	P1 requests and is allocated R1.
2	P2 requests and is allocated R2.
3	P3 requests and is allocated R3.
4	P1 requests R2.
5	P2 requests R3.
6	P3 requests R1.

The progression of the directed graph is shown in Figure 5.9. A deadlock occurs because every process is waiting for a resource that is being held by another process, but none will be released without intervention.

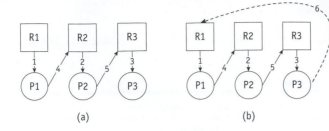

(figure 5.9)

Second scenario. The system (a) becomes deadlocked (b) when P3 requests R1. Notice the circular wait.

Scenario 3 – Deadlock Broken

The third scenario is shown in Table 5.3. As shown in Figure 5.10, the resources are released before deadlock can occur.

Event	Action
1	P1 requests and is allocated R1.
2	P1 requests and is allocated R2.
3	P2 requests R1.
4	P3 requests and is allocated R3.
5	P1 releases R1, which is allocated to P2.
6	P3 requests R2.
7	P1 releases R2, which is allocated to P3.

(table 5.3)

Scenario 3. This sequence of events is shown in the directed graph in Figure 5.10.

(c)

(figure 5.10)

The third scenario. After event 4, the directed graph looks like (a) and P2 is blocked because P1 is holding on to R1. However, event 5 breaks the deadlock and the graph soon looks like (b). Again there is a blocked process, P3, which must wait for the release of R2 in event 7 when the graph looks like (c).

Strategies for Handling Deadlocks

As these examples show, a system's requests and releases can be received in an unpredictable order, which makes it very difficult to design a foolproof preventive policy. In general, operating systems use some combination of several strategies to deal with deadlocks:

• Prevent one of the four conditions from occurring: **prevention**.

• Avoid the deadlock if it becomes probable: **avoidance**.

• Detect the deadlock when it occurs: **detection**.

• Recover from it gracefully: **recovery**.

Prevention

To prevent a deadlock, the operating system must eliminate one of the four necessary conditions discussed at the beginning of this chapter, a task complicated by the fact that the same condition can't be eliminated from every resource.

Mutual exclusion is necessary in any computer system because some resources, such as memory, CPU, and dedicated devices, must be exclusively allocated to one user at a time. In the case of I/O devices, such as printers, the mutual exclusion may be bypassed by spooling, which allows the output from many jobs to be stored in separate temporary spool files at the same time, and each complete output file is then selected for printing when the device is ready. However, we may be trading one type of deadlock (such as Case 3: Deadlocks in Dedicated Device Allocation) for another (Case 5: Deadlocks in Spooling).

Resource holding, where a job holds on to one resource while waiting for another one that's not yet available, could be sidestepped by forcing each job to request, at creation time, every resource it will need to run to completion. For example, if every job in a batch system is given as much memory as it needs, then the number of active jobs will be dictated by how many can fit in memory—a policy that would significantly decrease the degree of multiprogramming. In addition, peripheral devices would be idle because they would be allocated to a job even though they wouldn't be used all the time. As we've said before, this was used successfully in batch environments, although it did reduce the effective use of resources and restricted the amount of multiprogramming. But it doesn't work as well in interactive systems.

No preemption could be bypassed by allowing the operating system to deallocate resources from jobs. This can be done if the state of the job can be easily saved and restored, as when a job is preempted in a round robin environment or a page is swapped to secondary storage in a virtual memory system. On the other hand, preemption of a dedicated I/O device (printer, plotter, scanner, and so on), or of files during the modification process, can require some extremely unpleasant recovery tasks.

Circular wait can be bypassed if the operating system prevents the formation of a circle. One such solution proposed by Havender (1968) is based on a numbering system for the resources such as: printer = 1, disk = 2, scanner = 3, plotter = 4, and so on. The system forces each job to request its resources in ascending order: any "number one" devices required by the job would be requested first; any "number two" devices would be requested next; and so on. So if a job needed a printer and then a plotter, it would request them in this order: printer (1) first and then the plotter (4). If the job required the plotter first and then the printer, it would still request the printer first (which is a 1) even though it wouldn't be used right away. A job could request a printer (1) and then a disk (2) and then a scanner (3); but if it needed another printer (1) late in its processing, it would still have to anticipate that need when it requested the first one and before it requested the disk.

This scheme of "hierarchical ordering" removes the possibility of a circular wait and therefore guarantees the removal of deadlocks. It doesn't require that jobs state their maximum needs in advance, but it does require that the jobs anticipate the order in

Edsger W. Dijkstra (1930–2002)

Born in Rotterdam, The Netherlands, Edsger Dijkstra worked on many issues that became fundamental to computer science, including those involving recursion, real-time interrupts, the Minimum Spanning Tree Algorithm, and the Dining Philosophers Problem. He codeveloped the first compiler for Algol-60, a high-level programming language of that time. Dijkstra won numerous honors, including the IEEE Computer Society Computer Pioneer Award (1982). He was named a Distinguished Fellow of the British Computer Society (1971) and was one of the first recipients of the ACM Turning Award (1972).

For more information:
http://www.thocp.net/biographies/dijkstra_edsger.htm

Received the ACM 1972 A.M. Turing Award "for fundamental contributions to programming as a high, intellectual challenge; for eloquent insistence and practical demonstration that programs should be composed correctly, not just debugged into correctness; for illuminating perception of problems at the foundations of program design."

(Photo: Hamilton Richards)

which they will request resources. One of the difficulties of this scheme is discovering the best order for the resources so that the needs of the majority of the users are satisfied. Another difficulty is that of assigning a ranking to nonphysical resources such as files or locked database records where there is no basis for assigning a higher number to one over another.

Avoidance

Even if the operating system can't remove one of the conditions for deadlock, it can avoid one if the system knows ahead of time the sequence of requests associated with each of the active processes. As was illustrated in the graphs shown in Figure 5.7 through Figure 5.10, there exists at least one allocation of resources sequence that will allow jobs to continue without becoming deadlocked.

One such algorithm was proposed by Dijkstra in 1965 to regulate resource allocation to avoid deadlocks. The Banker's Algorithm is based on a bank with a fixed amount of capital that operates on the following principles:

- No customer will be granted a loan exceeding the bank's total capital.
- All customers will be given a maximum credit limit when opening an account.
- No customer will be allowed to borrow over the limit.
- The sum of all loans won't exceed the bank's total capital.

> ✔ **To remain in a safe state, the bank has to have sufficient funds to satisfy the needs of at least one customer.**

Under these conditions, the bank isn't required to have on hand the total of all maximum lending quotas before it can open up for business (we'll assume the bank will always have the same fixed total and we'll disregard interest charged on loans). For our example, the bank has a total capital fund of $10,000 and has three customers (#1, #2, and #3), who have maximum credit limits of $4,000, $5,000, and $8,000, respectively. Table 5.4 illustrates the state of affairs of the bank after some loans have been granted to customers #2 and #3. This is called a **safe state** because the bank still has enough money left to satisfy the maximum requests of all three customers.

(table 5.4)

The bank started with $10,000 and has remaining capital of $4,000 after these loans. Therefore, it's in a "safe state."

Customer	Loan Amount	Maximum Credit	Remaining Credit
Customer #1	0	4,000	4,000
Customer #2	2,000	5,000	3,000
Customer #3	4,000	8,000	4,000
Total loaned: $6,000			
Total capital fund: $10,000			

A few weeks later after more loans have been made, and some have been repaid, the bank is in the **unsafe state** represented in Table 5.5.

Customer	Loan Amount	Maximum Credit	Remaining Credit
Customer #1	2,000	4,000	2,000
Customer #2	3,000	5,000	2,000
Customer #3	4,000	8,000	4,000
Total loaned: $9,000			
Total capital fund: $10,000			

(table 5.5)

The bank only has remaining capital of $1,000 after these loans and therefore is in an "unsafe state."

This is an unsafe state because with only $1,000 left, the bank can't satisfy anyone's maximum request. Also, if the bank lent the $1,000 to anyone, it would be deadlocked (it wouldn't be able to make the loan). An unsafe state doesn't necessarily lead to deadlock, but it does indicate that the system is an excellent candidate for one. After all, none of the customers is required to request the maximum, but the bank doesn't know the exact amount that will eventually be requested; and as long as the bank's capital is less than the maximum amount available for individual loans, it can't guarantee that it will be able to fill every loan request.

If we substitute jobs for customers and dedicated devices for dollars, we can apply the same principles to an operating system. In the following example, the system has 10 devices. Table 5.6 shows our system in a safe state, and Table 5.7 depicts the same system in an unsafe state. As before, a safe state is one in which there are enough available resources to satisfy the maximum needs of at least one job. Then, using the resources released by the finished job, the maximum needs of another job can be filled and that job can be finished, and so on, until all jobs are done.

Job No.	Devices Allocated	Maximum Required	Remaining Needs
Job 1	0	4	4
Job 2	2	5	3
Job 3	4	8	4
Total number of devices allocated: 6			
Total number of devices in system: 10			

(table 5.6)

Resource assignments after initial allocations. This is a safe state: Six devices are allocated and four units are still available.

The operating system must be sure never to satisfy a request that moves it from a safe state to an unsafe one. Therefore, as users' requests are satisfied, the operating system must identify the job with the smallest number of remaining resources and

(table 5.7)

Resource assignments after later allocations. This is an unsafe state: Only one unit is available but every job requires at least two to complete its execution.

Job No.	Devices Allocated	Maximum Required	Remaining Needs
Job 1	2	4	2
Job 2	3	5	2
Job 3	4	8	4
Total number of devices allocated: 9			
Total number of devices in system: 10			

make sure that the number of available resources is always equal to, or greater than, the number needed for this job to run to completion. Requests that would place the safe state in jeopardy must be blocked by the operating system until they can be safely accommodated.

If this elegant solution is expanded to work with several classes of resources, the system sets up a "resource assignment table" for each type of resource and tracks each table to keep the system in a safe state.

> ✔
>
> **If the system is always kept in a safe state, all requests are eventually satisfied and a deadlock is avoided.**

Although the Banker's Algorithm has been used to avoid deadlocks in systems with a few resources, it isn't practical for most systems for several reasons:

- As they enter the system, jobs must predict the maximum number of resources needed. As we've said before, this isn't practical in interactive systems.
- The number of total resources for each class must remain constant. If a device breaks and becomes suddenly unavailable, the algorithm won't work (the system may already be in an unsafe state).
- The number of jobs must remain fixed, something that isn't possible in interactive systems where the number of active jobs is constantly changing.
- The overhead cost incurred by running the avoidance algorithm can be quite high when there are many active jobs and many devices, because the algorithm has to be invoked for every request.
- Resources aren't well utilized because the algorithm assumes the worst case and, as a result, keeps vital resources unavailable to guard against unsafe states.
- Scheduling suffers as a result of the poor utilization and jobs are kept waiting for resource allocation. A steady stream of jobs asking for a few resources can cause the indefinite postponement of a more complex job requiring many resources.

Detection

The directed graphs presented earlier in this chapter showed how the existence of a circular wait indicated a deadlock, so it's reasonable to conclude that deadlocks can be detected by building directed resource graphs and looking for cycles. Unlike the avoidance algorithm, which must be performed every time there is a request, the algorithm used to detect circularity can be executed whenever it is appropriate: every hour, once a day, when the operator notices that throughput has deteriorated, or when an angry user complains.

The detection algorithm can be explained by using directed resource graphs and "reducing" them. Begin with a system that is in use, as shown in Figure 5.11(a). The steps to reduce a graph are these:

1. Find a process that is currently using a resource and *not waiting* for one. This process can be removed from the graph by disconnecting the link tying the resource to the process, such as P3 in Figure 5.11(b). The resource can then be returned to the "available list." This is possible because the process would eventually finish and return the resource.

2. Find a process that's waiting only for resource classes that aren't fully allocated, such as P2 in Figure 5.11(c). This process isn't contributing to deadlock since it would eventually get the resource it's waiting for, finish its work, and return the resource to the "available list" as shown in Figure 5.11(c).

3. Go back to Step 1 and continue with Steps 1 and 2 until all lines connecting resources to processes have been removed, eventually reaching the stage shown in Figure 5.11(d).

If there are any lines left, this indicates that the request of the process in question can't be satisfied and that a deadlock exists. Figure 5.12 illustrates a system in which three processes—P1, P2, and P3—and three resources—R1, R2, and R3—aren't deadlocked.

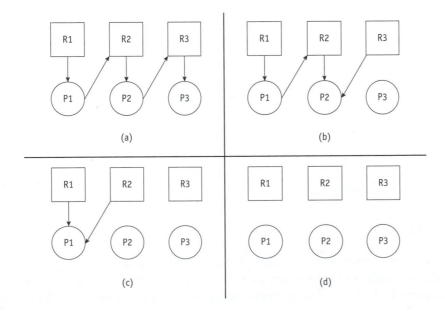

(a)

(b)

(c)

(d)

(figure 5.11)

This system is deadlock-free because the graph can be completely reduced, as shown in (d).

Figure 5.11 shows the stages of a graph reduction from (a), the original state. In (b), the link between P3 and R3 can be removed because P3 isn't waiting for any other resources to finish, so R3 is released and allocated to P2 (Step 1). In (c), the links between P2 and R3 and between P2 and R2 can be removed because P2 has all of its requested resources and can run to completion—and then R2 can be allocated to P1. Finally, in (d), the links between P1 and R2 and between P1 and R1 can be removed because P1 has all of its requested resources and can finish successfully. Therefore, the graph is completely resolved.

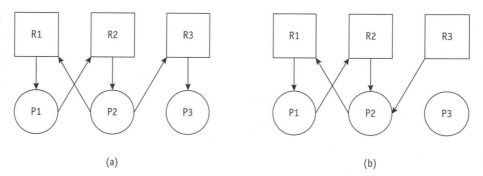

(a)   (b)

The deadlocked system in Figure 5.12 cannot be reduced because of a key element: P2 is linked to R1. In (a), the link between P3 and R3 can be removed because P3 isn't waiting for any other resource, so R3 is released and allocated to P2. But in (b), P2 has only two of the three resources it needs to finish and is waiting for R1. But R1 can't be released by P1, because P1 is waiting for R2, which is held by P2; moreover, P1 can't finish because it is waiting for P2 to finish (and release R2); and P2 can't finish because it's waiting for R1. This is a circular wait.

Recovery

Once a deadlock has been detected, it must be untangled and the system returned to normal as quickly as possible. There are several **recovery** algorithms, but they all have one feature in common: They all require at least one **victim**, an expendable job, which, when removed from the deadlock, will free the system. Unfortunately for the victim, removal generally requires that the job be restarted from the beginning or from a convenient midpoint.

The first and simplest recovery method, and the most drastic, is to terminate every job that's active in the system and restart them from the beginning.

The second method is to terminate only the jobs involved in the deadlock and ask their users to resubmit them.

The third method is to identify which jobs are involved in the deadlock and terminate them one at a time, checking to see if the deadlock is eliminated after each removal, until the deadlock has been resolved. Once the system is freed, the remaining jobs are allowed to complete their processing, and later, the halted jobs are started again from the beginning.

The fourth method can be put into effect only if the job keeps a record, a snapshot, of its progress so it can be interrupted and then continued without starting again from the beginning of its execution. The snapshot is like the landing in our staircase example: Instead of forcing the deadlocked stair climbers to return to the bottom of the stairs, they need to retreat only to the nearest landing and wait until the others have passed. Then the climb can be resumed. In general, this method is favored for long-running jobs to help them make a speedy recovery.

Until now we've offered solutions involving the jobs caught in the deadlock. The next two methods concentrate on the nondeadlocked jobs and the resources they hold. One of them, the fifth method in our list, selects a nondeadlocked job, preempts the resources it's holding, and allocates them to a deadlocked process so it can resume execution, thus breaking the deadlock. The sixth method stops new jobs from entering the system, which allows the nondeadlocked jobs to run to completion so they'll release their resources. Eventually, with fewer jobs in the system, competition for resources is curtailed so the deadlocked processes get the resources they need to run to completion. This method is the only one listed here that doesn't rely on a victim, and it's not guaranteed to work unless the number of available resources surpasses that needed by at least one of the deadlocked jobs to run (this is possible with multiple resources).

Several factors must be considered to select the victim that will have the least-negative effect on the system. The most common are:

- The priority of the job under consideration—high-priority jobs are usually untouched.
- CPU time used by the job—jobs close to completion are usually left alone.
- The number of other jobs that would be affected if this job were selected as the victim.

In addition, programs working with databases also deserve special treatment because a database that is only partially updated is only partially correct. Therefore, jobs that are modifying data shouldn't be selected for termination because the consistency and validity of the database would be jeopardized. Fortunately, designers of many database systems have included sophisticated recovery mechanisms so damage to the database is minimized if a transaction is interrupted or terminated before completion.

Starvation

So far in this chapter, we have concentrated on deadlocks and livelocks, both of which result from the liberal allocation of resources. At the opposite end is starvation, the result of conservative allocation of resources, where a single job is prevented from execution because it's kept waiting for resources that never become available. To illustrate this, the case of the Dining Philosophers Problem was introduced by Dijkstra in 1968.

Five philosophers are sitting at a round table, each deep in thought. In the center of the table, accessible to everyone, is a bowl of spaghetti. There are five forks on the table—one between each philosopher, as illustrated in Figure 5.13. Local custom dictates that each philosopher must use two forks, the forks on either side of the plate, to eat the spaghetti, but there are only five forks—not the 10 it would require for all five thinkers to eat at once—and that's unfortunate for Philosopher 2.

When they sit down to dinner, Philosopher 1 (P1) is the first to take the two forks (both F1 and F5) on either side of the plate and begins to eat. Inspired by this bold move, Philosopher 3 (P3) does likewise, acquiring both F2 and F3. Now Philosopher 2 (P2)

(figure 5.13)

The dining philosophers' table, before the meal begins.

decides to begin the meal, but is unable to begin because no forks are available: Fork #1 has been allocated to Philosopher 1, and Fork #2 has been allocated to Philosopher 3. In fact, by this time, four of the five forks have been allocated. The only remaining fork is situated between Philosopher 4 and Philosopher 5. So Philosopher 2 must wait.

Soon, Philosopher 3 finishes eating, puts down the two forks, and resumes pondering. Should the fork that's now free, Fork #2, be allocated to the hungry Philosopher 2, even though only that one fork is free? Although it's tempting, such a move would be a bad precedent, because if the philosophers are allowed to tie up resources with only the hope that the other required resource will become available, the dinner could easily slip into an unsafe state; it would be only a matter of time before each philosopher held a single fork, and nobody could eat. So the resources are allocated to the philosophers only when both forks are available at the same time. The status of the "system" is illustrated in Figure 5.14.

P4 and P5 are quietly thinking and Philosopher 1 is still eating. Philosopher 3 (who should be full) decides to eat some more and is able to take F2 and F3 once again. Soon thereafter, Philosopher 1 finishes and releases Fork #1 and Fork #5, but Philosopher 2

(figure 5.14)

Each philosopher must have both forks to begin eating, the one on the right and the one on the left. Unless the resources, the forks, are allocated fairly, some philosophers may starve.

162

is still not able to eat, because Fork #2is now allocated. This scenario could continue forever; as long as Philosopher 1 and Philosopher 3 alternate their use of the available resources, Philosopher 2 must wait. Philosophers 1 and 3 can eat any time they wish, while Philosopher 2 starves, only inches from nourishment.

In a computer environment, the resources are like forks and the competing processes are like dining philosophers. If the resource manager doesn't watch for starving processes and jobs and plan for their eventual completion, they could remain in the system forever waiting for the right combination of resources.

To address this problem, an algorithm designed to detect starving jobs can be implemented, which tracks how long each job has been waiting for resources (this is the same as aging, described in Chapter 4). Once starvation has been detected, the system can block new jobs until the starving jobs have been satisfied. This algorithm must be monitored closely: If monitoring is done too often, then new jobs will be blocked too frequently and throughput will be diminished. If it's not done often enough, then starving jobs will remain in the system for an unacceptably long period of time.

Conclusion

Every operating system must dynamically allocate a limited number of resources while avoiding the two extremes of deadlock and starvation.

In this chapter we discussed several methods of dealing with both livelock and deadlock: prevention, avoidance, detection, and recovery. Deadlocks can be prevented by not allowing the four conditions of a deadlock to occur in the system at the same time. By eliminating at least one of the four conditions (mutual exclusion, resource holding, no preemption, and circular wait), the system can be kept deadlock-free. As we've seen, the disadvantage of a preventive policy is that each of these conditions is vital to different parts of the system at least some of the time, so prevention algorithms are complex, and to routinely execute them requires significant overhead.

Deadlocks can be avoided by clearly identifying safe states and unsafe states and requiring the system to keep enough resources in reserve to guarantee that all jobs active in the system can run to completion. The disadvantage of an avoidance policy is that the system's resources aren't allocated to their fullest potential.

If a system doesn't support prevention or avoidance, then it must be prepared to detect and recover from the deadlocks that occur. Unfortunately, this option usually relies on the selection of at least one "victim"—a job that must be terminated before it finishes execution and then be restarted from the beginning.

In the next chapter, we look at problems related to the synchronization of processes in a multiprocessing environment.

Key Terms

avoidance: the dynamic strategy of deadlock avoidance that attempts to ensure that resources are never allocated in such a way as to place a system in an unsafe state.

circular wait: one of four conditions for deadlock through which each process involved is waiting for a resource being held by another; each process is blocked and can't continue, resulting in deadlock.

deadlock: a problem occurring when the resources needed by some jobs to finish execution are held by other jobs, which, in turn, are waiting for other resources to become available.

detection: the process of examining the state of an operating system to determine whether a deadlock exists.

directed graphs: a graphic model representing various states of resource allocations.

livelock: a locked system whereby two or more processes continually block the forward progress of the others without making any forward progress themselves. It is similar to a deadlock except that neither process is blocked or obviously waiting; both are in a continuous state of change.

locking: a technique used to guarantee the integrity of the data in a database through which the user locks out all other users while working with the database.

mutual exclusion: one of four conditions for deadlock in which only one process is allowed to have access to a resource.

no preemption: one of four conditions for deadlock in which a process is allowed to hold on to resources while it is waiting for other resources to finish execution.

prevention: a design strategy for an operating system where resources are managed in such a way that some of the necessary conditions for deadlock do not hold.

process synchronization: (1) the need for algorithms to resolve conflicts between processors in a multiprocessing environment; or (2) the need to ensure that events occur in the proper order even if they are carried out by several processes.

race: a synchronization problem between two processes vying for the same resource.

recovery: the steps that must be taken, when deadlock is detected, by breaking the circle of waiting processes.

resource holding: one of four conditions for deadlock in which each process refuses to relinquish the resources it holds until its execution is completed even though it isn't using them because it's waiting for other resources.

safe state: the situation in which the system has enough available resources to guarantee the completion of at least one job running on the system.

spooling: a technique developed to speed I/O by collecting in a disk file either input received from slow input devices or output going to slow output devices, such as printers.

starvation: the result of conservative allocation of resources in which a single job is prevented from execution because it's kept waiting for resources that never become available.

unsafe state: a situation in which the system has too few available resources to guarantee the completion of at least one job running on the system. It can lead to deadlock.

victim: an expendable job that is selected for removal from a deadlocked system to provide more resources to the waiting jobs and resolve the deadlock.

Interesting Searches

For more background on a few of the topics discussed in this chapter, begin a search with these terms:

- False Deadlock Detection
- Starvation and Livelock Detection
- Distributed Deadlock Detection
- Deadlock Resolution Algorithms
- Operating System Freeze

Exercises

Research Topics

A. In Chapter 3 we introduced the problem of thrashing. Research current literature to investigate the role of deadlock and any resulting thrashing. Discuss how you would begin to quantify the cost to the system (in terms of throughput and performance) of deadlock-caused thrashing. Cite your sources.

B. Research the problem of livelock in a networked environment. Describe how its consequences differ from those of deadlock, and give a real-life example of the problem that's not mentioned in this chapter. Identify at least two different methods the operating system could use to detect and resolve livelock. Cite your sources.

Exercises

1. For each of these conditions— deadlock, race, and starvation—give at least two "real life" examples (not related to a computer system environment) of each of these concepts. Then give your own opinion on how each of these six conditions can be resolved.

2. Given the ice cream sundae example from the beginning of this chapter, identify which elements of the deadlock represent the four necessary conditions for this deadlock.

3. Using the narrow staircase example from the beginning of this chapter, create a list of actions or tasks that could be implemented by the building manager that would allow people to use the staircase without risking a deadlock or starvation.

4. If a deadlock occurs at a combination of downtown intersections, as shown in the figure below, explain in detail how you would identify that a deadlock has occurred, how you would resolve it after it happens, and how you would act to prevent it from happening again.

A classic case of traffic deadlock on four one-way streets. This is "gridlock," where no vehicles can move forward to clear the traffic jam.

5. Regarding the role played by the "victim" in deadlock resolution, explain your answers to these questions.

   a. How is the victim chosen?

   b. What is the fate of the victim?

   c. Describe the actions required, if any, to complete the victim's tasks.

6. The figure below shows a tunnel going through a mountain and two streets parallel to each other—one at each end of the tunnel. Traffic lights are located at each end of the tunnel to control the cross flow of traffic through each intersection. Based on this figure, answer the following questions:

   a. How can deadlock occur, and under what circumstances?

   b. How can deadlock be detected?

   c. Give a solution to prevent deadlock and starvation.

Traffic flow diagram for Exercise 6.

7. Consider the directed graph shown below and answer the following questions:

   a. Is this system deadlocked?

   b. Which, if any, processes are blocked?

   c. What is the resulting graph after reduction?

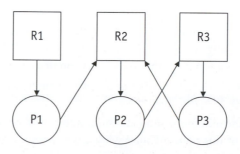

8. Consider the directed resource graph shown below and answer the following questions:

   a. Is this system deadlocked?

   b. Which, if any, processes are blocked?

   c. What is the resulting graph after reduction?

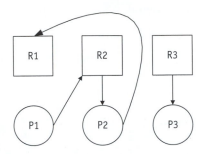

9. Consider a system with 13 dedicated devices of the same type. All jobs currently running on this system require a maximum of three devices to complete their execution. The jobs run for long periods of time with just two devices, requesting the remaining device only at the very end of the run. Assume that the job stream is endless and that your operating system's device allocation policy is a very conservative one: No job will be started unless all the required drives have been allocated to it for the entire duration of its run.

   a. What is the maximum number of jobs that can be in progress at once? Explain your answer.

   b. What are the minimum and maximum number of devices that may be idle as a result of this policy? Under what circumstances would an additional job be started?

10. Consider a system with 14 dedicated devices of the same type. All jobs currently running on this system require a maximum of five devices to complete their execution. The jobs run for long periods of time with just three devices, requesting the remaining two only at the very end of the run. Assume that the job stream is endless and that your operating system's device allocation policy is a very conservative one: No job will be started unless all the required drives have been allocated to it for the entire duration of its run.

    a. What is the maximum number of jobs that can be active at once? Explain your answer.

    b. What are the minimum and maximum number of devices that may be idle as a result of this policy? Under what circumstances would an additional job be started?

11. Suppose your system is identical to the one described in the previous exercise with 14 devices, but supports the Banker's Algorithm.

   a. What is the maximum number of jobs that can be in progress at once? Explain your answer.

   b. What are the minimum and maximum number of devices that may be idle as a result of this policy? Under what circumstances would an additional job be started?

12. Suppose your system is identical to the one described in the previous exercise, but has 16 devices and supports the Banker's Algorithm.

   a. What is the maximum number of jobs that can be in progress at once? Explain your answer.

   b. What are the minimum and maximum number of devices that may be idle as a result of this policy? Under what circumstances would an additional job be started?

13-16. For the systems described in Questions 13 through 16 below, given that all of the devices are of the same type, and using the definitions presented in the discussion of the Banker's Algorithm, answer these questions:

   a. Calculate the number of available devices.

   b. Determine the remaining needs for each job in each system.

   c. Determine whether each system is safe or unsafe.

   d. If the system is in a safe state, list the sequence of requests and releases that will make it possible for all processes to run to completion.

   e. If the system is in an unsafe state, show how it's possible for deadlock to occur.

13. This system has 16 devices.

Job No.	Devices Allocated	Maximum Required	Remaining Needs
Job 1	5	8	
Job 2	3	9	
Job 3	4	8	
Job 4	2	5	

14. This system has 12 devices.

Job No.	Devices Allocated	Maximum Required	Remaining Needs
Job 1	5	8	
Job 2	1	4	
Job 3	5	7	

15. This system has 14 devices.

Job No.	Devices Allocated	Maximum Required	Remaining Needs
Job 1	2	6	
Job 2	4	7	
Job 3	5	6	
Job 4	0	2	
Job 5	2	4	

16. This system has 32 devices.

Job No.	Devices Allocated	Maximum Required	Remaining Needs
Job 1	11	17	
Job 2	7	10	
Job 3	12	18	
Job 4	0	8	

Advanced Exercises

17. Explain how you would design and implement a mechanism to allow the operating system to detect which, if any, processes are starving.

18. As mentioned in this chapter, Havender proposed a hierarchical ordering of resources, such as disks, printers, files, ports, and so on. Explain in detail the limitations imposed on programs (and on systems) that have to follow such a hierarchical ordering system. Think of some circumstance for which would you recommend a hierarchical ordering system, and explain your answer.

17. Suppose you are an operating system designer and have been approached by the system administrator to help solve the recurring deadlock problem in your installation's spooling system. What features might you incorporate into the operating system so that deadlocks in the spooling system can be resolved without losing the work (the system processing) that was underway or already performed by the deadlocked processes?

19. Given the four primary types of resources—CPU, main memory, storage devices, and files—select for each one the most suitable technique described in this chapter to fight deadlock, and explain why that is your choice.

20. Consider a banking system with 10 accounts. Funds may be transferred between two of those accounts by following these steps:

lock A(i);   lock A(j);
update A(i);   update A(j);
unlock A(i);   unlock A(j);

  a. Can this system become deadlocked? If yes, show how. If no, explain why not.

  b. Could the numbering request policy (presented in the chapter discussion about detection) be implemented to prevent deadlock if the number of accounts is dynamic? Explain why or why not.

Chapter 6

Concurrent Processes

PROCESS MANAGER

Single-Processor Configurations

↓

Multiple-Process Synchronization

↓

Multiple-Processor Programming

> **"** *The measure of power is obstacles overcome.* **"**
>
> —Oliver Wendell Holmes, Jr. (1841–1935)

Learning Objectives

After completing this chapter, you should be able to describe:

- The critical difference between processes and processors and how they're connected
- The differences among common configurations of multiprocessing systems
- The basic concepts of multicore processor technology
- The significance of a critical region in process synchronization
- The essential ideas behind process synchronization software
- The need for process cooperation when several processors work together
- How processors cooperate when executing a job, process, or thread
- The significance of concurrent programming languages and their applications

In Chapters 4 and 5, we describe multiprogramming systems that use only one CPU, one processor, which is shared by several jobs or processes. This is called *multiprogramming*. In this chapter we look at another common situation, **multiprocessing** systems, which have several processors working together.

What Is Parallel Processing?

Parallel processing is a situation in which two or more processors operate in one system at the same time and may or may not work on related activities. In other words, two or more CPUs execute instructions simultaneously and the Processor Manager has to coordinate activities of each processor while synchronizing the cooperative interactions among all of them.

There are two primary benefits to parallel processing systems: increased reliability and faster processing.

The reliability stems from the availability of more than one CPU. Theoretically, if one processor fails, then the others can continue to operate and absorb the load. However, this capability must be designed into the system so that, first, the failing processor informs other processors to take over, and second, the operating system dynamically restructures its available resources and allocation strategies so that the remaining processors don't become overloaded.

The increased processing speed can be achieved when instructions or data manipulation can be processed in parallel, two or more at a time. Some systems allocate a CPU to each program or job. Others allocate a CPU to each working set or parts of it. Still others subdivide individual instructions so that each subdivision can be processed simultaneously (called concurrent programming). And others achieve parallel processing by allocating several CPUs to perform a set of instructions separately on vast amounts of data and combine all the results at the end of the job.

Increased flexibility brings increased complexity, however, and two major challenges remain: how to connect the processors into workable configurations and how to orchestrate their interaction to achieve efficiencies, which applies to multiple interacting processes as well. (It might help if you think of each process as being run on a separate processor.)

The complexities of the Processor Manager's multiprocessing tasks are easily illustrated with an example: You're late for an early afternoon appointment and you're in danger of missing lunch, so you get in line for the drive-through window of the local fast-food shop. When you place your order, the order clerk confirms your request, tells you how much it will cost, and asks you to drive to the pickup window; there, a cashier collects your money and hands over your order. All's well and once again you're on your way—driving and thriving. You just witnessed a well-synchronized multiprocessing system. Although you came in contact with just two processors (the order clerk and the cashier), there were at least two other processors behind the scenes who cooperated to make the system work—the cook and the bagger.

A fast food lunch spot is similar to the six-step information retrieval system below. It is described in a different way in Table 6.1.

a) Processor 1 (the order clerk) accepts the query, checks for errors, and passes the request on to Processor 2 (the bagger).

b) Processor 2 (the bagger) searches the database for the required information (the hamburger).

c) Processor 3 (the cook) retrieves the data from the database (the meat to cook for the hamburger) if it's kept off-line in secondary storage.

d) Once the data is gathered (the hamburger is cooked), it's placed where Processor 2 can get it (in the hamburger bin).

e) Processor 2 (the bagger) retrieves the data (the hamburger) and passes it on to Processor 4 (the cashier).

f) Processor 4 (the cashier) routes the response (your order) back to the originator of the request—you.

(table 6.1)

The six steps of the four-processor fast food lunch stop.

Originator	Action	Receiver
Processor 1 (the order clerk)	Accepts the query, checks for errors, and passes the request on to the receiver	Processor 2 (the bagger)
Processor 2 (the bagger)	Searches the database for the required information (the hamburger)	
Processor 3 (the cook)	Retrieves the data from the database (the meat to cook for the hamburger) if it's kept off-line in secondary storage	
Processor 3 (the cook)	Once the data is gathered (the hamburger is cooked), it's placed where the receiver can get it (in the hamburger bin)	Processor 2 (the bagger)
Processor 2 (the bagger)	Retrieves the data (the hamburger) and passes it on to the receiver	Processor 4 (the cashier)
Processor 4 (the cashier)	Routes the response (your order) back to the originator of the request	You

Synchronization is the key to any multiprocessing system's success because many things can go wrong. For example, what if the microphone broke down and you couldn't speak with the order clerk? What if the cook produced hamburgers at full speed all day, even during slow periods? What would happen to the extra hamburgers? What if the cook became badly burned and couldn't cook anymore? What would the bagger do if there were no hamburgers? What if the cashier took your money but didn't give you any food? Obviously, the system can't work properly unless every processor communicates and cooperates with every other processor.

Levels of Multiprocessing

Multiprocessing can take place at several different levels, each of which tends to require a different frequency of synchronization, as shown in Table 6.2. At the job level, multiprocessing is fairly benign. It's as if each job is running on its own workstation with shared system resources. On the other hand, when multiprocessing takes place at the thread level, a high degree of synchronization is required to disassemble each process, perform the thread's instructions, and then correctly reassemble the process. This may require additional work by the programmer, as we see later in this chapter.

Parallelism Level	Process Assignments	Synchronization Required
Job Level	Each job has its own processor, and all processes and threads are run by that same processor.	No explicit synchronization required after jobs are assigned to a processor.
Process Level	Unrelated processes, regardless of job, can be assigned to available processors.	Moderate amount of synchronization required.
Thread Level	Threads, regardless of job and process, can be assigned to available processors.	High degree of synchronization required to track each process and each thread.

(table 6.2)

Typical levels of parallelism and the required synchronization among processors

Introduction to Multi-Core Processors

Multi-core processors have several processors on a single chip. As processors became smaller in size (as predicted by Moore's Law) and faster in processing speed, CPU designers began to use nanometer-sized transistors (one nanometer is one billionth of a meter). Each transistor switches between two positions—0 and 1—as the computer conducts its binary arithmetic at increasingly fast speeds. However, as transistors reached nano-sized dimensions and the space between transistors became ever closer, the quantum physics of electrons got in the way.

In a nutshell, here's the problem. When transistors are placed extremely close together, electrons can spontaneously tunnel, at random, from one transistor to another, causing a tiny but measurable amount of current to leak. The smaller the transistor, the more significant the leak. (When an electron does this "tunneling," it seems to spontaneously disappear from one transistor and appear in another nearby transistor. It's as if a Star Trek voyager asked the electron to be "beamed aboard" the second transistor.)

Software that requires sequential calculations can run more slowly on a chip with dual cores than on a similar chip with one core because the calculations cannot be performed in parallel.

A second problem was the heat generated by the chip. As processors became faster, the heat also climbed and became increasingly difficult to disperse. These heat and tunneling issues threatened to limit the ability of chip designers to make processors ever smaller.

One solution was to create a single chip (one piece of silicon) with two "processor cores" in the same amount of space. With this arrangement, two sets of calculations can take place at the same time. The two cores on the chip generate less heat than a single core of the same size, and tunneling is reduced; however, the two cores each run more slowly than the single core chip. Therefore, to get improved performance from a dual-core chip, the software has to be structured to take advantage of the double calculation capability of the new chip design. Building on their success with two-core chips, designers have created multi-core processors with more than 80 cores on a single chip. An example is shown in Chapter 1.

Does this hardware innovation affect the operating system? Yes, because it must manage multiple processors, multiple units of cache and RAM, and the processing of many tasks at once. However, a dual-core chip is not always faster than a single-core chip. It depends on the tasks being performed and whether they're multi-threaded or sequential.

Typical Multiprocessing Configurations

Much depends on how the multiple processors are configured within the system. Three typical configurations are master/slave, loosely coupled, and symmetric.

Master/Slave Configuration

The **master/slave** configuration is an asymmetric multiprocessing system. Think of it as a single-processor system with additional slave processors, each of which is managed by the primary master processor as shown in Figure 6.1.

(figure 6.1)

In a master/slave multiprocessing configuration, slave processors can access main memory directly but they must send all I/O requests through the master processor.

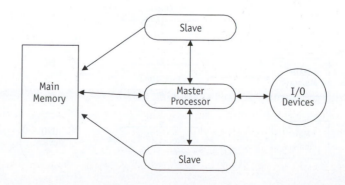

The master processor is responsible for managing the entire system—all files, devices, memory, and processors. Therefore, it maintains the status of all processes in the system, performs storage management activities, schedules the work for the other processors, and executes all control programs. This configuration is well suited for computing environments in which processing time is divided between front-end and back-end processors; in these cases, the front-end processor takes care of the interactive users and quick jobs, and the back-end processor takes care of those with long jobs using the batch mode.

The primary advantage of this configuration is its simplicity. However, it has three serious disadvantages:

- Its reliability is no higher than for a single-processor system because if the master processor fails, none of the slave processors can take over, and the entire system fails.

- It can lead to poor use of resources because if a slave processor should become free while the master processor is busy, the slave must wait until the master becomes free and can assign more work to it.

- It increases the number of interrupts because all slave processors must interrupt the master processor every time they need operating system intervention, such as for I/O requests. This creates long queues at the master processor level when there are many processors and many interrupts.

Loosely Coupled Configuration

The **loosely coupled configuration** features several complete computer systems, each with its own memory, I/O devices, CPU, and operating system, as shown in Figure 6.2. This configuration is called loosely coupled because each processor controls its own resources—its own files, access to memory, and its own I/O devices—and that means that each processor maintains its own commands and I/O management tables.

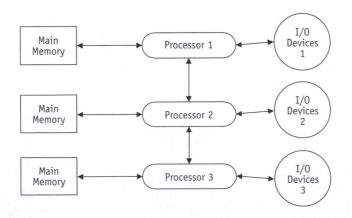

(figure 6.2)

In a loosely coupled multiprocessing configuration, each processor has its own dedicated resources.

The only difference between a loosely coupled multiprocessing system and a collection of independent single-processing systems is that each processor can communicate and cooperate with the others.

When a job arrives for the first time, it's assigned to one processor. Once allocated, the job remains with the same processor until it's finished. Therefore, each processor must have global tables that indicate where each job has been allocated.

To keep the system well balanced and to ensure the best use of resources, job scheduling is based on several requirements and policies. For example, new jobs might be assigned to the processor with the lightest load or the one with the best combination of output devices available.

This system isn't prone to catastrophic system failures because even when a single processor fails, the others can continue to work independently. However, it can be difficult to detect when a processor has failed.

Symmetric Configuration

A **symmetric configuration** (as depicted in Figure 6.3) features decentralized processor scheduling. That is, a single copy of the operating system and a global table listing each process and its status is stored in a common area of memory so every processor has access to it. Each processor uses the same scheduling algorithm to select which process it will run next.

(figure 6.3)

A symmetric multiprocessing configuration with homogeneous processors. Processes must be carefully synchronized to avoid deadlocks and starvation.

The symmetric configuration (sometimes called tightly coupled) has four advantages over loosely coupled configuration:

• It's more reliable.

• It uses resources effectively.

• It can balance loads well.

• It can degrade gracefully in the event of a failure.

The symmetric configuration is best implemented if all of the processors are of the same type.

However, it is the most difficult configuration to implement because the processes must be well synchronized to avoid the problems of races and deadlocks that we discuss in Chapter 5.

Whenever a process is interrupted, whether because of an I/O request or another type of interrupt, its processor updates the corresponding entry in the process list and finds another process to run. This means that the processors are kept quite busy. But it also means that any given job or task may be executed by several different processors during its run time. And because each processor has access to all I/O devices and can reference any storage unit, there are more conflicts as several processors try to access the same resource at the same time.

This presents the obvious need for algorithms to resolve conflicts among processors.

Process Synchronization Software

The success of **process synchronization** hinges on the capability of the operating system to make a resource unavailable to other processes while it is being used by one of them. These "resources" can include scanners and other I/O devices, a location in storage, or a data file, to name a few. In essence, the resource that's being used must be locked away from other processes until it is released. Only then is a waiting process allowed to use the resource. This is where synchronization is critical. A mistake could leave a job waiting indefinitely, causing starvation, or if it's a key resource, cause a deadlock. Both are described in Chapter 5.

It is the same thing that can happen in a crowded ice cream shop. Customers take a number to be served. The number machine on the wall shows the number of the person to be served next, and the clerks push a button to increment the displayed number when they begin attending to a new customer. But what happens when there is no synchronization between serving the customers and changing the number? Chaos. This is the case of the missed waiting customer.

Let's say your number is 75. Clerk 1 is waiting on Customer 73 and Clerk 2 is waiting on Customer 74. The sign on the wall says "Now Serving #74," and you're ready with your order. Clerk 2 finishes with Customer 74 and pushes the button so that the sign says "Now Serving #75." But just then, that clerk is called to the telephone and leaves the building due to an emergency, never to return (an interrupt). Meanwhile, Clerk 1 pushes the button and proceeds to wait on Customer 76—and you've missed your turn! If you speak up quickly, you can correct the mistake gracefully; but when it happens in a computer system, the outcome isn't as easily remedied.

Consider the scenario in which Processor 1 and Processor 2 finish with their current jobs at the same time. To run the next job, each processor must:

1. Consult the list of jobs to see which one should be run next.
2. Retrieve the job for execution.
3. Increment the READY list to the next job.
4. Execute it.

Both go to the READY list to select a job. Processor 1 sees that Job 74 is the next job to be run and goes to retrieve it. A moment later, Processor 2 also selects Job 74 and goes to retrieve it. Shortly thereafter, Processor 1, having retrieved Job 74, returns to the READY list and increments it, moving Job 75 to the top. A moment later Processor 2 returns; it has also retrieved Job 74 and is ready to process it, so it increments the READY list and now Job 76 is moved to the top and becomes the next job in line to be processed. Job 75 has become the missed waiting customer and will never be processed, while Job 74 is being processed twice—both represent an unacceptable state of affairs.

There are several other places where this problem can occur: memory and page allocation tables, I/O tables, application databases, and any shared resource.

Obviously, this situation calls for synchronization. Several synchronization mechanisms are available to provide cooperation and communication among processes. The common element in all synchronization schemes is to allow a process to finish work on a critical part of the program before other processes have access to it. This is applicable both to multiprocessors and to two or more processes in a single-processor (time-shared) system. It is called a **critical region** because it is a critical section and its execution must be handled as a unit. As we've seen, the processes within a critical region can't be interleaved without threatening the integrity of the operation.

The lock-and-key technique is conceptually the same one that's used to lock databases, as discussed in Chapter 5. It allows different users to access the same database without causing a deadlock.

Synchronization is sometimes implemented as a lock-and-key arrangement: Before a process can work on a critical region, it must get the key. And once it has the key, all other processes are locked out until it finishes, unlocks the entry to the critical region, and returns the key so that another process can get the key and begin work.

This sequence consists of two actions: (1) the process must first see if the key is available and (2) if it is available, the process must pick it up and put it in the lock to make it unavailable to all other processes. For this scheme to work, both actions must be performed in a single machine cycle; otherwise it is conceivable that while the first process is ready to pick up the key, another one would find the key available and prepare to pick up the key—and each could block the other from proceeding any further.

Several locking mechanisms have been developed, including test-and-set, WAIT and SIGNAL, and semaphores.

Test-and-Set

Test-and-set is a single, indivisible machine instruction known simply as **TS** and was introduced by IBM for its early multiprocessing computers. In a single machine cycle, it tests to see if the key is available and, if it is, sets it to unavailable.

The actual key is a single bit in a storage location that can contain a 0 (if it's free) or a 1 (if busy). We can consider TS to be a function subprogram that has one parameter (the storage location) and returns one value (the condition code: busy/free), with the notable feature that it takes only one machine cycle.

Therefore, a process (Process 1) tests the condition code using the TS instruction before entering a critical region. If no other process is in this critical region, then Process 1 is allowed to proceed and the condition code is changed from 0 to 1. Later, when Process 1 exits the critical region, the condition code is reset to 0 so another process is allowed to enter. On the other hand, if Process 1 finds a busy condition code when it arrives, then it's placed in a waiting loop where it continues to test the condition code—when it's free, it's allowed to enter.

Although it's a simple procedure to implement, and it works well for a small number of processes, test-and-set has two major drawbacks:

- First, when many processes are waiting to enter a critical region, starvation can occur because the processes gain access in an arbitrary fashion. Unless a first-come, first-served policy is set up, some processes could be favored over others.
- Second, the waiting processes remain in unproductive, resource-consuming wait loops, requiring context switching, because the processes repeatedly check for the key. This is known as **busy waiting**—which not only consumes valuable processor time, but also relies on the competing processes to test the key—something that is best handled by the operating system or the hardware.

WAIT and SIGNAL

WAIT and SIGNAL is a modification of test-and-set that's designed to remove busy waiting. Two new operations, WAIT and SIGNAL, are mutually exclusive and become part of the process scheduler's set of operations.

WAIT is activated when the process encounters a busy condition code. WAIT sets the process's process control block (PCB) to the blocked state and links it to the queue of processes waiting to enter this particular critical region. The Process Scheduler then selects another process for execution. SIGNAL is activated when a process exits the critical region and the condition code is set to "free." It checks the queue of processes waiting to enter this critical region and selects one, setting it to the READY state. Eventually the Process Scheduler will choose this process for running. The addition of the operations WAIT and SIGNAL frees the processes from the busy waiting dilemma and returns control to the operating system, which can then run other jobs while the waiting processes are idle (WAIT).

Semaphores

A **semaphore** is a non-negative integer variable that can be used as a binary signal, a flag. One of the most historically significant semaphores was the signaling device, shown in Figure 6.4, used by railroads to indicate whether a section of track was clear. When the arm of the semaphore was raised, the track was clear and the train was allowed to proceed. When the arm was lowered, the track was busy and the train had to wait until the arm was raised. It had only two positions: up or down (on or off).

(figure 6.4)

The semaphore used by railroads indicates whether your train can proceed. When it's lowered (a), another train is approaching and your train must stop to wait for it to pass. If it is raised (b), your train can continue.

(a) **Stop** (b) **All Clear**

In an operating system, a semaphore is set to either zero or one to perform a similar function: It signals if and when a resource is free and can be used by a process. Dutch computer scientist Edsger Dijkstra (1965) introduced two operations to overcome the process synchronization problem we've discussed. Dijkstra called them P and V, and that's how they're known today. The P stands for the Dutch word *proberen* (to test) and the V stands for *verhogen* (to increment). The P and V operations do just that: They test and increment.

Here's how semaphores work: If we let s be a semaphore variable, then the V operation on s is simply to increment s by 1. The action can be stated as:

$$V(s): s: = s + 1$$

This in turn necessitates a fetch (to get the current value of s), increment (to add one to s), and store sequence. Like the test-and-set operation, the increment operation must be performed as a single indivisible action to avoid race conditions. And that means that s cannot be accessed by any other process during the operation.

The operation P on s is to test the value of s, and if it's not 0, to decrement it by 1. The action can be stated as:

$$P(s): \text{If } s > 0 \text{ then } s: = s - 1$$

This involves a test, fetch, decrement, and store sequence. Again, this sequence must be performed as an indivisible action in a single machine cycle or be arranged so that the process cannot take action until the operation (test or increment) is finished.

The operations to test or increment are executed by the operating system in response to calls issued by any one process naming a semaphore as parameter (this alleviates the process from having control). If $s = 0$, it means that the critical region is busy and the process calling on the test operation must wait until the operation can be executed; that's not until $s > 0$.

In the example shown in Table 6.3, P3 is placed in the WAIT state (for the semaphore) on State 4. Also shown in Table 6.3, for States 6 and 8, when a process exits the critical region, the value of s is reset to 1, indicating that the critical region is free. This, in turn, triggers the awakening of one of the blocked processes, its entry into the critical region, and the resetting of s to 0. In State 7, P1 and P2 are not trying to do processing in that critical region, and P4 is still blocked.

State Number	Calling Process	Operation	Running in Critical Region	Results Blocked on s	Value of s
0					1
1	P1	test(s)	P1		0
2	P1	increment(s)			1
3	P2	test(s)	P2		0
4	P3	test(s)	P2	P3	0
5	P4	test(s)	P2	P3, P4	0
6	P2	increment(s)	P3	P4	0
7			P3	P4	0
8	P3	increment(s)	P4		0
9	P4	increment(s)			1

(table 6.3)

The sequence of states for four processes (P1, P2, P3, P4) calling test and increment (P and V) operations on the binary semaphore s. (Note: The value of the semaphore before the operation is shown on the line preceding the operation. The current value is on the same line.)

After State 5 of Table 6.3, the longest waiting process, P3, was the one selected to enter the critical region, but that isn't necessarily the case unless the system is using a first-in, first-out selection policy. In fact, the choice of which job will be processed next depends on the algorithm used by this portion of the Process Scheduler.

As you can see from Table 6.3, test and increment operations on semaphore s enforce the concept of mutual exclusion, which is necessary to avoid having two operations in a race condition. The name traditionally given to this semaphore in the literature is **mutex,** for MUTual EXclusion. So the operations become:

```
test(mutex):         if mutex > 0 then mutex: = mutex - 1
increment(mutex): mutex: = mutex + 1
```

In Chapter 5 we talk about the requirement for mutual exclusion when several jobs are trying to access the same shared physical resources. The concept is the same here, but we have several processes trying to access the same shared critical region. The procedure can generalize to semaphores having values greater than 0 and 1.

Thus far we've looked at the problem of mutual exclusion presented by interacting parallel processes using the same shared data at different rates of execution. This can apply to several processes on more than one processor, or interacting (codependent) processes on a single processor. In this case, the concept of a critical region becomes necessary because it ensures that parallel processes will modify shared data only while in the critical region.

In sequential computations mutual exclusion is achieved automatically because each operation is handled in order, one at a time. However, in parallel computations, the order of execution can change, so mutual exclusion must be explicitly stated and maintained. In fact, the entire premise of parallel processes hinges on the requirement that all operations on common variables consistently exclude one another over time.

Process Cooperation

There are occasions when several processes work directly together to complete a common task. Two famous examples are the problems of producers and consumers, and of readers and writers. Each case requires both mutual exclusion and synchronization, and each is implemented by using semaphores.

Producers and Consumers

The classic problem of **producers and consumers** concerns one or more processes that produce data that one or more process consumes later. They do so by using a single buffer. Let's begin with the case with one producer and one consumer, although current versions would almost certainly apply to systems with multiple producers and consumers, as shown in Figure 6.5.

Let's return for a moment to the fast-food framework at the beginning of this chapter because the synchronization between one producer process and one consumer process (the cook and the bagger) represents a significant issue when it's applied to operating systems. The cook *produces* hamburgers that are sent to the bagger, who *consumes* them. Both processors have access to one common area, the hamburger bin, which can hold only a finite number of hamburgers (the bin is essentially a buffer). The bin is a necessary storage area because the speed at which hamburgers are produced is rarely exactly the same speed at which they are consumed.

Problems arise at two extremes: when the producer attempts to add to a bin that's already full (as happens when the consumer stops all withdrawals from the bin), and

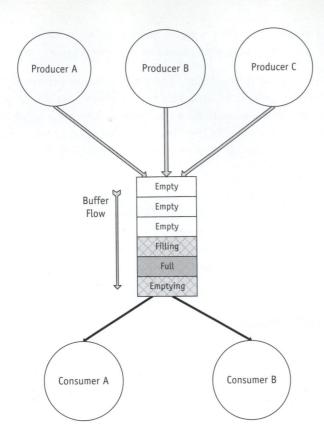

when the consumer attempts to make a withdrawal from a bin that's empty (such as when the bagger tries to take a hamburger that hasn't been deposited in the bin yet). In real life, the people watch the bin; if it's empty or too full, they quickly recognize and resolve the problem. However, in a computer system, such resolution is not so easy.

Consider the case of the prolific CPU that can generate output data much faster than a printer can print it. Therefore, to accommodate the two different speeds, we need a buffer where the producer can temporarily store data that can be retrieved by the consumer at a slower speed, freeing the CPU from having to wait unnecessarily. This buffer can be in many states, from empty to full, as shown in Figure 6.6.

The essence of the problem is that the system must make sure that the producer won't try to add data to a full buffer, and that the consumer won't try to make withdrawals from an empty buffer. Because the buffer can hold only a finite amount of data, the synchronization process must delay the producer from generating more data when the buffer is full. It must also be prepared to delay the consumer from retrieving data when the buffer is empty. This task can be implemented by two counting semaphores—one to indicate the number of *full* positions in the buffer and the other to indicate the

(figure 6.6)

Four snapshots of a single buffer in four states from completely empty (a) to almost full (d)

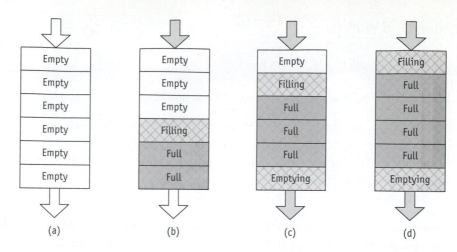

number of *empty* positions in the buffer. A third semaphore, mutex, ensures mutual exclusion between processes to prevent race conditions.

Notice that when there is only one producer and one consumer, this classic problem becomes a simple case of first in, first out (FIFO), as shown in Figure 6.7. However, when there are several producers and consumers, a deadlock can occur if they are all paused as they wait to be notified that they can resume their respective deposits and withdrawals.

(figure 6.7)

Typical system with one producer, one consumer, and a single buffer

Readers and Writers

The problem of **readers and writers** was first formulated by Courtois, Heymans, and Parnas (1971) and arises when two types of processes need to access a shared resource such as a file or database. The authors called these processes readers and writers.

An airline reservation system is a good example. The readers are those who want flight information. They're called readers because they only read the existing data; they don't modify it. And because none of them is changing the database, the system can allow many readers to be active at the same time—there's no need to enforce mutual exclusion among them.

The writers are those who are making reservations on a particular flight. Unlike the readers, the writers must be carefully accommodated for each flight because they are modifying existing data in the database. The system can't allow someone to be writing while someone else is reading or writing to the exact same file. Therefore, it must enforce mutual exclusion for any and all writers. Of course, the system must be fair when it enforces its policy to avoid indefinite postponement of readers or writers.

In the original paper, Courtois, Heymans, and Parnas offered two solutions using P and V operations.

- The first gives priority to readers over writers so readers are kept waiting only if a writer is actually modifying the data. However, if there is a continuous stream of readers, this policy results in writer starvation.
- The second policy gives priority to the writers. In this case, as soon as a writer arrives, any readers that are already active are allowed to finish processing, but all additional readers are put on hold until the writer is done. Obviously, if a continuous stream of writers is present, this policy results in reader starvation.
- Either scenario is unacceptable.

To prevent either type of starvation, Hoare (1974) proposed the following combination priority policy: When a writer is finished, any and all readers who are waiting or on hold are allowed to read. Then, when that group of readers is finished, the writer who is on hold can begin; any *new* readers who arrive in the meantime aren't allowed to start until the writer is finished.

The state of the system can be summarized by four counters initialized to 0:

- Number of readers who have *requested* a resource and haven't yet released it ($R1 = 0$)
- Number of readers who are *using* a resource and haven't yet released it ($R2 = 0$)
- Number of writers who have *requested* a resource and haven't yet released it ($W1 = 0$)
- Number of writers who are *using* a resource and haven't yet released it ($W2 = 0$)

This can be implemented using two semaphores to ensure mutual exclusion between readers and writers. A resource can be given to all readers, provided that no writers are processing (W2 = 0). A resource can be given to a writer, provided that no readers are reading (R2 = 0) and no writers are writing (W2 = 0).

Readers must always call two procedures: the first checks whether the resources can be immediately granted for reading; and then, when the resource is released, the second checks to see if there are any writers waiting. The same holds true for writers. The first procedure must determine if the resource can be immediately granted for writing, and then, upon releasing the resource, the second procedure will find out if any readers are waiting.

Concurrent Programming

Until now, we've looked at multiprocessing as several jobs executing at the same time on a single processor (which interacts with I/O processors, for example) or on multiprocessors. Multiprocessing can also refer to one job using several processors to execute sets of instructions in parallel. The concept isn't new, but it requires a programming language and a computer system that can support this type of construct. This type of system is referred to as a **concurrent processing** system, and it can generally perform data level parallelism and instruction (or task) level parallelism.

Frances E. Allen (1932–)

Fran Allen, mathematician and teacher, joined IBM intending only to pay off student loans; however, she stayed for 45 years as an innovator in sophisticated systems analysis, parallel processing, and code optimization. Her techniques are still reflected in programming language compilers. Allen's last big project for IBM was the Parallel Translator, where she applied her extensive experience with interprocedural flow analysis to produce new algorithms for extracting parallelism from sequential code. Allen was the first woman named an IBM Fellow (1989) and was the first female to win the ACM Turing Award (2006). As of this writing, she continues to

advise IBM on a number of projects, including its Blue Gene supercomputer.

For more information:
*http://amturing.acm.org/award_winners/allen_1012327
.cfm*

Won the Association for Computing Machinery Turing Award: "For pioneering contributions to the theory and practice of optimizing compiler techniques that laid the foundation for modern optimizing compilers and automatic parallel execution."

*Courtesy of International Business Machines Corporation,
© International Business Machines Corporation.*

In general, parallel systems can be put into two broad categories: **data level parallelism (DLP)**, which refers to systems that can perform on one or more streams or elements of data, and **instruction (or task) level parallelism (ILP)**, which refers to systems that can perform multiple instructions in parallel.

Michael Flynn (1972) published what's now known as Flynn's taxonomy, shown in Table 6.4, describing machine structures that fall into four main classifications of parallel construction with combinations of single/multiple instruction and single/multiple data. Each category presents different opportunities for parallelism.

	Number of Instructions	
	Single Instruction	**Multiple Instructions**
Single Data	SISD	MISD
Multiple Data	SIMD	MIMD

(table 6.4)

The four classifications of Flynn's Taxonomy for machine structures

Each category presents different opportunities for parallelism.

- The single instruction, single data (SISD) classification is represented by systems with a single processor and a single stream of data which presents few if any opportunities for parallelism.

- The multiple instructions, single data (MISD) classification includes systems with multiple processors (which might allow some level of parallelism) and a single stream of data. Configurations such as this might allow instruction level parallelism but little or no data level parallelism without additional software assistance.

- The single instruction, multiple data (SIMD) classification is represented by systems with a single processor and a multiple data streams.

- The multiple instructions, multiple data (MIMD) classification is represented by systems with a multiple processors and a multiple data streams. These systems may allow the most creative use of both instruction level parallelism and data level parallelism.

Amdahl's Law

Regardless of a system's physical configuration, the result of parallelism is more complex than initially thought. Gene Amdahl proposed in 1967 that the limits of parallel processors could be calculated, as shown in Figure 6.8.

In its simplest form, Amdahl's Law maintains that if a given program would take one hour to run to completion with one processor, but 80 percent of the program had to run sequentially (and therefore could not be sped up by applying additional processors to it), then the resulting program could run only a maximum of 20 percent faster. Interestingly, Amdahl used his work to promote the use of single processor systems even as parallel processors were becoming available.

(figure 6.8)

Amdahl's Law. Notice that all four graphs level off and there is no speed difference even though the number of processors increased from 2,048 to 65,536 (Amdahl, 1967).

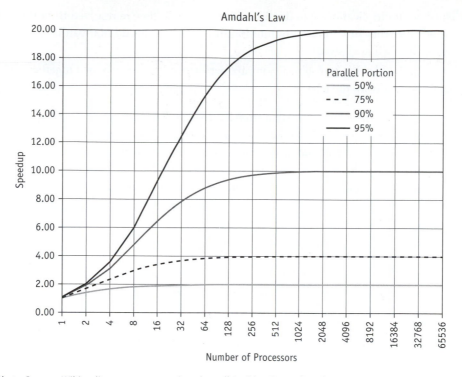

Amdahl's Law

Photo Source: Wikipedia among many others http://vi.wikipedia.org/wiki/T%E1%BA%ADp_tin: AmdahlsLaw.png.

Order of Operations

Before we delve more into parallelism, let's explore a fundamental concept that applies to all calculations. To understand the importance of this, try solving the following equation twice, once while resolving each calculation from the left, and then do the same thing from the right.

$$Z = 10 * 4 - 2$$

If we start from the left and do the multiplications first (10 * 4 = 40) and then the subtraction, we find that Z = 38. However, if we start from the right and do the subtraction first (4 – 2 = 2) and then do the multiplication, we find that Z = 20.

Therefore, to assure that every equation results in the exactly the same answer every time, mathematical convention states that each operation must be performed in a certain sequence or **order of operations** (also called precedence of operations or rules of precedence). These rules state that to solve an equation, all arithmetic calculations are performed *from the left* and in the following order:

• First, all calculations in parentheses are performed.

• Second, all exponents are calculated.

- Third, all multiplications and divisions are performed (they're resolved from the left whether they are divisions or multiplications—divisions do not wait until all multiplications are solved).

- Fourth, all additions and subtractions are performed (they're grouped together and then resolved from the left).

Each step in the equation is evaluated from left to right (because, if you were to perform the calculations in some other order, you would run the risk of finding the incorrect answer). In equations that contain a combination of multiplications and divisions, each is performed from the left whether they require division or multiplication. That is, we don't perform all multiplications first, followed by all divisions. Likewise, all subtractions and additions are performed from the left, even if subtractions are performed before any additions that appear to their right.

The order of operations is a mathematical convention, a universal agreement that dictates the sequence of calculations to solve any equation.

For example, if the equation is $Z = A / B + C * D$,

1. the division is performed first $(A / B = M)$,

2. the multiplication is performed second $(C * D = N)$, and

3. only then is the final sum performed $(Z = M + N)$.

On the other hand, if the equation includes one or more parentheses, such as $Z = A / (B + C) * D$, then

1. the parenthetical phrase is performed first $(B + C = M)$

2. the division is performed $(A / M = N)$ next.

3. Finally the multiplication is performed $(Z = N * D)$.

For many computational purposes and simple calculations, serial processing is sufficient; it's easy to implement and fast enough for most users. However, arithmetic expressions can be processed in a very different and more efficient way if we use a language that allows for concurrent processing.

Returning to our first equation, $Z = (A / B + C * D)$, notice that in this case the division $(A / B = M)$ can take place at the same time as the multiplication $(C * D = N)$. If the system had two available CPUs, each calculation could be performed simultaneously— each by a different CPU. Then (and only then) one CPU would add together the results of the two previous calculations $(Z = M + N)$.

Suppose the equation to be solved is more complex than our previous example. (Note the double asterisk indicates an exponent, and the two operations in parentheses need to be performed before all others so the exponential value can be found.)

$$Z = 10 - A / B + C (D + E) ** (F - G)$$

Table 6.5 shows the steps to compute it.

Step No.	Operation	Result

(table 6.5)

The sequential computation of the expression requires several steps. (In this example, there are six steps, but each step, such as the last one, may involve more than one machine operation.)

Step No.	Operation	Result
1	(D + E) = M	Store sum in M
2	(F − G) = N	Store difference in N
		Now the equation is $Z = 10 - A/B + C(M^N)$
3	(M) ** (N) = P	Store power in P
		Now the equation is $Z = 10 - A/B + C(P)$
4	A / B = Q	Store quotient in Q
		Now the equation is $Z = 10 - Q + C(P)$
5	C * P = R	Store product in R
		Now the equation is $Z = 10 - Q + R$
6	10 − Q + R = Z	Store result in Z

Applications of Concurrent Programming

Can we evaluate this equation faster if we use multiple processors? Let's introduce two terms—**COBEGIN** and **COEND**—that identify the instructions that can be processed concurrently (assuming that a sufficient number of CPUs are available). When we rewrite our expression to take advantage of concurrent processing, and place the results in three temporary storage locations (T1, T2, T3, and so on), it can look like this:

```
COBEGIN
     T1 = A / B
     T2 = (D + E)
     T3 = (F - G)
COEND

COBEGIN
     T4 = 10 - T1
     T5 = T2 ** T3
COEND

     Z = T4 + C(T5)
```

As shown in Table 6.5, to solve $Z = 10 - A / B + C (D + E)$ ** $(F - G)$, the first three operations can be done at the same time if our computer system has at least three processors. The next two operations are done at the same time, and the last expression is performed serially with the results of the first two steps, as shown in Figure 6.9.

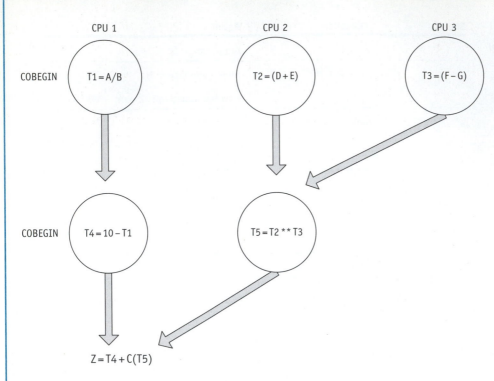

(figure 6.9)

Three CPUs can perform the six-step equation in three steps.

With this system, we've increased the computation speed, but we've also increased the complexity of the programming language and the hardware (both machinery and communication among machines). In fact, we've also placed a large burden on the programmer—to explicitly state which instructions can be executed in parallel. This is **explicit parallelism**.

When the **compiler** automatically detects the instructions that can be performed in parallel, it is called **implicit parallelism**, a field that benefited from the work of Turing Award winner Fran Allen.

It is the compiler that's used in multiprocessor systems (or even a massively multi-processing system such as the one shown in Figure 6.10), that translates the algebraic expression into separate instructions and decides which steps can be performed in parallel and which in serial mode.

For example, the equation $Y = A + B * C + D$ could be rearranged by the compiler as $A + D + B * C$ so that two operations $A + D$ and $B * C$ would be done in parallel, leaving the final addition to be calculated last.

As shown in the four cases that follow, concurrent processing can also dramatically reduce the complexity of working with array operations within loops, of performing

(figure 6.10)

The IBM Sequoia supercomputer, deemed the fastest on earth in 2012 by TOPS (http://www.top500.org), features 98,304 IBM 16-core processors, which equals more than 1.5 million processing cores. It has 1.6 petabytes of RAM and runs Linux. Courtesy of Lawrence Livermore National Laboratory

matrix multiplication, of conducting parallel searches in databases, and of sorting or merging files. Some of these systems use parallel processors that execute the same type of tasks.

Case 1: Array Operations

Let's say we need to perform an instruction on the objects in an array (an array is a collection of objects that have the same attributes so each object can be addressed individually). To do so, the code might say this:

```
for(j = 1; j <= 3; j++)
z(j) = a(j) + b(j);
```

These two instructions tell the Processor Manager to perform one identical operation $(a + b)$ on three different objects: $z(1) = a(1) + b(1)$, $z(2) = a(2) + b(2)$, $z(3) = a(3) + b(3)$.

Because the operation will be performed on three different objects, we can use three different processors to perform the instruction in one step as shown in Figure 6.11. Likewise, if the instruction is to be performed on 20 objects, and if there are 20 CPUs available, they can all be performed in one step, as well.

(figure 6.11)

Using CPUs and the COBEGIN command, three instructions in one array can be performed in a single step.

Case 2: Matrix Multiplication

Matrix multiplication requires many multiplication and addition operations that can take place concurrently, such as this equation: Matrix C = Matrix 1 * Matrix 2.

$$\text{Matrix C} = \text{Matrix 1} * \text{Matrix 2}$$

$$\begin{bmatrix} z & y & x \\ w & v & u \\ t & s & r \end{bmatrix} = \begin{bmatrix} A & B & C \\ D & E & F \end{bmatrix} * \begin{bmatrix} K & L \\ M & N \\ O & P \end{bmatrix}$$

To find z in Matrix C, you multiply each element from the first *column* of Matrix 1 by the corresponding element in the first *row* of Matrix 2, and then add the products. Therefore, one calculation is this: z = (A * K) + (D * L). Likewise, x = (C * K) + (F * L) and s = (B * O) + (E * P).

Using one processor, the answer to this equation can be computed in 27 steps. By multiplying several elements of the first row of Matrix 1 by corresponding elements in Matrix 2, three processors could cooperate to resolve this equation in fewer steps. The number of products that could be computed at the same time would depend on the number of processors available. With two processors, it takes only 18 steps to perform the calculations in parallel. With three, it would require even fewer. Notice that concurrent processing does not necessarily cut processing activity in direct proportion to the number of processors available. In this example, by doubling the number of processors from one to two, the number of steps was reduced by one-third—not by one-half.

Case 3: Searching Databases

Database searching is a common non-mathematical application for concurrent processing systems. For example, if a word is sought from a dictionary database or a part number from an inventory listing, the entire file can be split into discrete sections, with one processor allocated to each section. This results in a significant reduction in search time. Once the item is found, all processors can be deallocated and set to work on the next task. Even if the item sought is in the last record of the database, a concurrent search is faster than if a single processor were allocated to search the database.

Case 4: Sorting and Merging Files

The task of sorting a file or merging several sorted files can benefit from multiple processors. By dividing a large file into sections, each with its own processor, every section can be sorted at the same time. Then pairs of sections can be merged together until the entire file is whole again—and sorted. It's very similar to what you and a friend could do if you each held a portion of a deck of cards. Each of you (playing the part of a processor) could sort your own cards before you'd merge the two piles into one sorted deck.

Threads and Concurrent Programming

So far we have considered the cooperation and synchronization of traditional processes, also known as heavyweight processes, which have the following characteristics:

• They pass through several states from their initial entry into the computer system to their completion: ready, running, waiting, delayed, and blocked.
• They require space in main memory where they reside during their execution.
• From time to time they require other resources, such as data.

As we have seen in Chapters 3 and 4, these processes are often swapped between main memory and secondary storage during their execution to accommodate multiprogramming and to take advantage of virtual memory. Every time a swap occurs, overhead increases because of all the information that has to be saved.

To minimize this overhead time, most current operating systems support the implementation of threads, or lightweight processes, which have become part of numerous application packages. Threads are supported at both the kernel and at the user level; they can be managed by either the operating system or the application that created them.

A thread, discussed in Chapter 4, is a smaller unit within a process, which can be scheduled and executed. Threads share the same resources as the process that created them, which now becomes a more passive element because the thread is the unit that uses the CPU and is scheduled for execution. Processes might have from one to several active threads, which can be created, scheduled, and synchronized more efficiently because the amount of information needed is reduced. When running a process with multiple threads in a computer system with a single CPU, the processor switches very quickly from one thread to another, giving the impression that the threads are executing in parallel. However, it is only in systems with multiple CPUs that the multiple threads in a process are actually executed in parallel.

Each active thread in a process has its own processor registers, program counter, stack, and status, but each thread shares the data area and the resources allocated to its process. Each thread has its own program counter, which is used to store variables dynamically created by a process. For example, function calls in C might create variables that are local to the function. These variables are stored in the stack when the function is invoked and are destroyed when the function is exited. Since threads within a process share the same space and resources, they can communicate more efficiently, increasing processing performance.

Consider how a Web server can improve performance and interactivity by using threads. When a Web server receives requests for images or pages, it serves each request with a different thread. For example, the process that receives all the requests may have one thread that accepts these requests and creates a new separate thread for each request received. This new thread retrieves the required information and sends it to the remote client. While this thread is doing its task, the original thread is free to accept more requests. Web servers are multiprocessor systems that allow for the concurrent completion of several requests, thus improving throughput and response time. Instead of creating and destroying threads to serve incoming requests, which would increase the overhead, Web servers keep a pool of threads that can be assigned to those requests. After a thread has completed its task, instead of being destroyed, it is returned to the pool to be assigned to another request.

> As computer systems become more and more confined by heat and energy consumption considerations, system designers have been adding more processing cores per chip and more threads per processing core (Keckler, 2012).

Two Concurrent Programming Languages

Early programming languages did not support the creation of threads or the existence of concurrent processes. Typically, they gave programmers the possibility of creating a single process or thread of control. The Ada programming language was one of the first to do so in the late 1970s.

Ada

Ada 2012 is the International Standards Organization (ISO) standard and replaces Ada 2005. The scope of this revision is guided by a document issued to the committee charged with drafting the revised standard, the Ada Rapporteur Group (ARG). The essence is that the ARG was asked to pay particular attention to both object-oriented programming and to add real-time elements with a strong emphasis on real-time and high integrity features (Barnes, 2012). Specifically, ARGs charter was to:

1. Make improvements to maintain or improve Ada's advantages, especially in those user domains where safety and criticality are prime concerns, including improving the capabilities of Ada to take advantage of multicore and multithreaded architectures.

2. Make improvements to remedy shortcomings in Ada, such as the safety, use, and functionality of access types and dynamic storage management.

The U.S. Department of Defense (DoD) first commissioned the creation of the Ada programming language to support concurrent processing and the embedded computer systems found on jet aircraft, ship controls, and spacecraft, to name just a few. These types of systems must typically work with parallel processors, real-time constraints, fail-safe execution, and nonstandard input and output devices. It took ten years to complete; Ada was made available to the public in 1980.

It's named after Augusta Ada Byron, the Countess of Lovelace and a skilled mathematician who is regarded by some as the world's first programmer for her work on Charles Babbage's Analytical Engine in the 1830s. The Analytical Engine was an early prototype of a computer (Barnes, 1980). Notably, the mathematician was the daughter of renowned poet Lord Byron.

From the beginning, the new language was designed to be modular so several programmers can work on sections of a large project independently of one another. This allows several contracting organizations to compile their sections separately and have the finished product assembled together when its components are complete. From the beginning of the project, the DoD realized that their new language would prosper only if there was a global authority that could stifle the growth of mutually incompatible subsets and supersets of the language by creating unique, enhanced versions of the standard compiler with extra "bells and whistles," thus making them incompatible with each other. Toward that end, the DoD officially trademarked the name "Ada" and the language is now an ISO standard. Changes to it are currently made under the guidance of an ISO/IEC committee that has included national representatives of many nations, including Belgium, Canada, France, Germany, Italy, Japan, Sweden, Switzerland, the United Kingdom, and the U.S. (Barnes, 2012).

Specific details of all individual changes are integrated to form a new version of the official Annotated Ada Reference Manual scheduled for publication by the end of 2012. For the latest details and a copy of the manual, see *http://www.ada-auth.org/standards*.

Java

Java, developed by Sun Microsystems, Inc., was designed as a universal software platform for Internet applications and has been widely adopted. Java was released in 1995 as the first popular software platform that allowed programmers to code an application with the capability to run on any computer. This type of universal software platform was an attempt to solve several issues: first, the high cost of developing software applications for each of the many incompatible computer architectures available; second, the needs of distributed client-server environments; and third, the growth of the Internet and the Web, which added more complexity to program development.

Java uses both a compiler and an interpreter. The source code of a Java program is first compiled into an intermediate language called Java bytecodes, which are platform-independent. This means that one can compile a Java program on any computer that has a Java compiler, and the bytecodes can then be run on any computer that has a Java interpreter.

The interpreter is designed to fit in with the hardware and operating system specifications of the computer that will run the Java bytecodes. Its function is to parse and run each bytecode instruction on that computer.

This combination of compiler and interpreter makes it easy to distribute Java applications because they don't have to be rewritten to accommodate the characteristics of every computer system. Once the program has been compiled, it can be ported to, and run on, any system with a Java interpreter.

The Java Platform

Typically a computer platform contains the hardware and software where a program runs. The Java platform is a software-only platform that runs on top of other hardware-based platforms. It has two components: the Java Virtual Machine (Java VM), and the Java Application Programming Interface (Java API).

Java VM is the foundation for the Java platform and contains the Java interpreter, which runs the bytecodes provided by the compiler. Java VM sits on top of many different hardware-based platforms, as shown in Figure 6.12.

(figure 6.12)

A process used by the Java platform to shield a Java program from a computer's hardware.

The Java API is a collection of software modules that programmers can use in their applications. The Java API is grouped into libraries of related classes and interfaces. These libraries, also known as packages, provide well-tested objects ranging from basic data types to I/O functions, from network interfaces to graphical user interface kits.

The Java Language Environment

Java was designed to make it easy for experienced programmers to learn. Its syntax is familiar because it looks and feels like C++. It is object-oriented, which means it takes advantage of modern software development methodologies and fits well into distributed client-server applications.

One of Java's features is that memory allocation is done at run time, unlike C and C++, where memory allocation is done at compilation time. Java's compiled code references memory via symbolic "handles" that are translated into real memory addresses at run time by the Java interpreter. This means that the memory allocation and referencing models are not visible to programmers, but are controlled entirely by the underlying run-time platform.

Because Java applications run in distributed environments, security is a very important built-in feature of the language and of the run-time system. It provides compile-time checking and run-time checking, which helps programmers create very reliable software. For example, while a Java program is executing, it can request particular classes to be loaded from anywhere in the network. In this case, all incoming code is checked by a verifier, which ensures that the code is correct and can run safely without putting the Java interpreter at risk.

With its sophisticated synchronization capabilities, Java supports multithreading at the language level. The language library provides the Thread class, and the run-time system provides monitor and condition lock primitives. The Thread class is a collection of methods used to start, run, stop, and check the status of a thread. Java's threads are preemptive and, depending on the platform on which the Java interpreter executes, can also be time-sliced.

When a programmer declares some methods within a class to be synchronized, they are not run concurrently. These synchronized methods are under the control of software that makes sure that variables remain in a consistent state. When a synchronized method begins to run, it is given a monitor for the current object, which does not allow any other synchronized method in that object to execute. The monitor is released when a synchronized method exits, which allows other synchronized methods within the same object to run.

Java technology continues to be popular with programmers for several reasons:
- It offers the capability of running a single program on various platforms without having to make any changes.
- It offers a robust set of features, such as run-time memory allocation, security, and multithreading.
- It is used for many Web and Internet applications, and it integrates well with browsers that can run Java applets with audio, video, and animation directly in a Web page.

Conclusion

Multiprocessing can occur in several configurations: in a single-processor system where interacting processes obtain control of the processor at different times, or in systems with multiple processors, where the work of each processor communicates and cooperates with the others and is synchronized by the Processor Manager. Three multiprocessing hardware systems are described in this chapter: master/slave, loosely coupled, and symmetric.

The success of any multiprocessing system depends on the ability of the system to synchronize its processes with the system's other resources. The concept of mutual exclusion helps keep the processes with the allocated resources from becoming deadlocked. Mutual exclusion is maintained with a series of techniques, including test-and-set, WAIT and SIGNAL, and semaphores: P, V, and mutex.

Hardware and software mechanisms are used to synchronize the many processes, but care must be taken to avoid the typical problems of synchronization: missed waiting customers, the synchronization of producers and consumers, and the mutual exclusion of readers and writers. Continuing innovations in concurrent processing, including threads and multicore processors, are fundamentally changing how operating systems use these new technologies. Research in this area is expected to grow significantly over time.

In the next chapter, we look at the module of the operating system that manages the printers, disk drives, tape drives, and terminals—the Device Manager.

Key Terms

busy waiting: a method by which processes, waiting for an event to occur, continuously test to see if the condition has changed and remain in unproductive, resource-consuming wait loops.

COBEGIN: command used with COEND to indicate to a multiprocessing compiler the beginning of a section where instructions can be processed concurrently.

COEND: command used with COBEGIN to indicate to a multiprocessing compiler the end of a section where instructions can be processed concurrently.

compiler: a computer program that translates programs from a high-level programming language (such as C or Ada) into machine language.

concurrent processing: execution by a single processor of a set of processes in such a way that they appear to be happening at the same time.

critical region: a part of a program that must complete execution before other processes can begin.

explicit parallelism: a type of concurrent programming that requires that the programmer explicitly state which instructions can be executed in parallel.

implicit parallelism: a type of concurrent programming in which the compiler automatically detects which instructions can be performed in parallel.

loosely coupled configuration: a multiprocessing configuration in which each processor has a copy of the operating system and controls its own resources.

master/slave: an asymmetric multiprocessing configuration consisting of a single processor system connected to "slave" processors each of which is managed by the primary "master" processor, which provides the scheduling functions and jobs.

multicore processor: a computer chip that contains more than a single central processing unit (CPU).

multiprocessing: when two or more processors share system resources that may include some or all of the following: the same main memory, I/O devices, and control program routines.

mutex: a condition that specifies that only one process may update (modify) a shared resource at a time to ensure correct operation and results.

order of operations: the algebraic convention that dictates the order in which elements of a formula are calculated.

parallel processing: the process of operating two or more CPUs executing instructions simultaneously.

pointer: an address or other indicator of location.

process synchronization: (1) the need for algorithms to resolve conflicts between processors in a multiprocessing environment; or (2) the need to ensure that events occur in the proper order even if they are carried out by several processes.

producers and consumers: a classic problem in which a process produces data that will be consumed, or used, by another process.

readers and writers: a problem that arises when two types of processes need to access a shared resource such as a file or a database.

semaphore: a type of shared data item that may contain either binary or nonnegative integer values and is used to provide mutual exclusion.

symmetric configuration: a multiprocessing configuration in which processor scheduling is decentralized and each processor is of the same type.

test-and-set (TS): an indivisible machine instruction, which is executed in a single machine cycle to determine whether the processor is available.

WAIT and SIGNAL: a modification of the test-and-set synchronization mechanism that's designed to remove busy waiting.

Interesting Searches

For more background on a few of the topics discussed in this chapter, begin a search with these terms.

- Multicore CPU Speed
- Multithreaded Processing
- Real-time Processing
- Cluster Computing
- Ada Programming Language

Exercises

Research Topics

A. Research current literature to identify a computer model with exceptional parallel processing ability. Identify the manufacturer, the maximum number of processors the computer uses, how fast the machine can perform calculations, and typical applications for it. Cite your sources. If your answer includes terms not used in this chapter, be sure to define them.

B. Research current literature to identify a recent project that has combined the processing capacity of numerous small computers to address a problem. Identify the operating system used to coordinate the processors for this project and discuss the obstacles overcome to make the system work. If your answer includes terms not used in this chapter, be sure to define them. Cite your sources.

Exercises

1. One friend claims that a dual-core system runs at twice the speed as a single-core system; another friend disagrees by saying that it runs twice as many programs at the same time; a third friend says it runs twice as much data at the same time. Explain who is correct and why.

2. Describe the relationship between a process and a thread in a multicore system.

3. Compare the processors' access to printers and other I/O devices for the master/slave and the symmetric multiprocessing configurations. Give a true-to-life example where the master/slave configuration might be preferred.

4. Compare the processors' access to main memory for the loosely coupled configuration and the symmetric multiprocessing configurations. Give a true-to-life example where the symmetric configuration might be preferred.

5. Describe the programmer's role when implementing explicit versus implicit parallelism.

6. What steps does a well-designed multiprocessing system follow when it detects that a processor is failing? What is the central goal of most multiprocessing systems?

7. Give an example from real life of busy waiting.

8. In the last chapter, we discussed deadlocks. Describe in your own words why mutual exclusion is necessary for multiprogramming systems.

9. Describe the purpose of a buffer and give an example from your own experience where its use clearly benefits system response.

10. Consider this formula:

$$G = (A + C^2)*(E - 1)^3/D + B$$

a. Show the order that a processor would follow to calculate G. To do so, break down the equation into the correct order of operations, with one calculation per step. Show the formula for each step, assigning new letters to calculations as necessary.

b. Find the value of G: if A = 5, B = 10, C = 3, D = 8, and E = 5.

11. Consider this formula:

$$G = D + (A + C^2)*E/(D + B)^3$$

a. Show the order that a processor would follow to calculate G. To do so, break down the equation into the correct order of operations with one calculation per step. Show the formula for each step, assigning new letters to calculations as necessary.

b. Find the value of G: if A = 5, B = 10, C = 3, D = 8, and E = 5.

12. Rewrite each of the following arithmetic expressions to take advantage of concurrent processing and then code each. Use the terms COBEGIN and COEND to delimit the sections of concurrent code.

a. $A + B * R * Z - N * M + C^2$

b. $(X * (Y * Z * W * R) + M + N + P)$

c. $((J + K * L * M * N) * I)$

13. Rewrite each of the following expressions for concurrent processing and then code each one. Use the terms COBEGIN and COEND to delimit the sections of concurrent code. Identify which expressions, if any, might *not* run faster in a concurrent processing environment.

a. $H^2 * (O * (N + T))$

b. $X * (Y * Z * W * R)$

c. $M * T * R$

Advanced Exercises

14. Use the P and V semaphore operations to simulate the traffic flow at the intersection of two one-way streets. The following rules should be satisfied:

    - Only one car can cross at any given time.
    - A car should be allowed to cross the intersection only if there are no cars coming from the other street.
    - When cars are coming from both streets, they should take turns to prevent indefinite postponements in either street.

15. Explain the similarities and differences between the critical region and working set.

16. If a process terminates, will its threads also terminate, or will they continue to run? If all of its threads terminate, will the process also terminate, or will it continue to run? Explain your answers.

17. If a process is suspended (put into the "wait" state by an interrupt), will its threads also be suspended? Explain why the threads will or will not be suspended. Give an example to substantiate your answer.

18. Consider the following program segments for two different processes (P1, P2) executing concurrently and where B and A are not shared variables, but x starts at 0 and is a shared variable.

Processor #1	Processor #2
for(a = 1; a <= 3; a++)	for(b = 1; b <= 3; b++)
x = x + 1;	x = x + 1;

If the processes P1 and P2 execute only once at any speed, what are the possible resulting values of x? Explain your answers.

19. Examine one of the programs you have written recently and indicate which operations could be executed concurrently. How long did it take you to do this? When might it be a good idea to write your programs in such a way that they can be run concurrently? Are you inclined to do so? Explain why or why not.

20. Consider the following segment taken from a C program:

```
for(j = 1; j <= 12; j++)
{
    printf(" nEnter an integer value:");
    scanf("%d", &x);
    if(x == 0)
    y(j)=0;
    if(x != 0)
    y(j)=10;
}
```

a. Recode it so it will run more efficiently in a single-processor system.

b. Given that a multiprocessing environment with four symmetrical processors is available, recode the segment as an efficient concurrent program that performs the same function as the original C program.

c. Given that all processors have identical capabilities, compare the execution times of the original C segment with the execution times of your segments for parts (a) and (b).

Programming Exercises

21. Edsger Dijkstra introduced the Sleeping Barber Problem (Dijkstra, 1965): A barbershop is divided into two rooms. The waiting room has n chairs, and the work room only has the barber chair. When the waiting room is empty, the barber goes to sleep in the barber chair. If a customer comes in and the barber is asleep, he knows it's his turn to get his hair cut. So he wakes up the barber and takes his turn in the barber chair. But if the waiting room is not empty, the customer must take a seat in the waiting room and wait his turn. Write a program that will coordinate the barber and his customers.

22. Suhas Patil introduced the Cigarette Smokers Problem (Patil, 1971): Three smokers and a supplier make up this system. Each smoker wants to roll a cigarette and smoke it immediately. However, to smoke a cigarette the smoker needs three ingredients—paper, tobacco, and a match. To the great discomfort of everyone involved, each smoker has only one of the ingredients: Smoker 1 has lots of paper, Smoker 2 has lots of tobacco, and Smoker 3 has the matches. And, of course, the rules of the group don't allow hoarding, swapping, or sharing. The supplier, who doesn't smoke, provides all three ingredients and has an infinite amount of all three items. But the supplier provides only two of them at a time—and only when no one is smoking. Here's how it works. The supplier randomly selects and places two different items on the table (where they are accessible to all three smokers), and the smoker with the remaining ingredient immediately takes them, rolls, and smokes a cigarette. Once done smoking, the first smoker signals the supplier, who then places another two randomly selected items on the table, and so on.

Write a program that will synchronize the supplier with the smokers. Keep track of how many cigarettes each smoker consumes. Is this a fair supplier? Why or why not?

Chapter 7 | Device Management

> **"** *Nothing endures but change.* **"**
>
> —Heraclitus of Ephesus (*c. 540 B.C. – 480 B.C.*)

Learning Objectives

After completing this chapter, you should be able to describe:

• Features of dedicated, shared, and virtual devices

• Concepts of blocking and buffering, and how they improve I/O performance

• Roles of seek time, search time, and transfer time in calculating access time

• Differences in access times in several types of devices

• Strengths and weaknesses of common seek strategies and how they compare

• Levels of RAID and what sets each apart

Despite the multitude of input/output (I/O) devices that constantly appear (and disappear) in the marketplace and the swift rate of change in device technology, the Device Manager must manage every peripheral device of the system. To do so, it must maintain a delicate balance of supply and demand—balancing the system's finite supply of devices with users' almost-infinite demand for them.

Device management involves four basic functions:

- Monitoring the status of each device, such as storage hardware, monitors, USB tools, and other peripheral devices
- Enforcing preset policies to determine which process will get a device and for how long
- Allocating each device appropriately
- Deallocating each device at two levels—at the process (or task) level when an I/O command has been executed and temporarily released its device, and also at the job level when the job is finished and the device is permanently released

Types of Devices

The system's peripheral devices generally fall into one of three categories: dedicated, shared, and virtual. The differences are a function of the characteristics of the devices, as well as how they're managed by the Device Manager.

Dedicated devices are assigned to only one job at a time; they serve that job for the entire time it's active or until it releases them. Some devices, such as monitors, a mouse, and printers, often demand this kind of allocation scheme, because it would be awkward to let several users share them. A shared monitor, for example, might display half of one user's work and half of someone else's game. The disadvantage of having dedicated devices is that they must be allocated to a single user for the duration of a job's execution. This can be quite inefficient, especially in a situation such as an office printer that is exclusively allocated to one person, who is not using the device 100 percent of the time.

Shared devices can be allocated to several processes at the same time. For instance, a disk, or any other **direct access storage device** (often shortened to DASD), can be shared by several processes by interleaving their requests, but this interleaving must be carefully controlled by the Device Manager. All conflicts—such as when Process A and Process B need to read from the same disk—must be resolved based on predetermined policies to decide which request is handled first.

Virtual devices are a combination of the first two: They're dedicated devices that have been transformed into shared devices. For example, printers, which are dedicated devices, can be converted into sharable devices by using a spooling program that reroutes all print requests via a storage space on a disk. Only when all of a job's output is complete, and the printer is ready to print out the entire document, is the output sent to the printer for printing. (This procedure has to be managed carefully to prevent deadlock, as we explain in Chapter 5.) Because disks are sharable devices, this technique can convert one printer into several virtual printers, thus improving both its performance and use. Spooling is a technique that is often used to speed up slow dedicated I/O devices.

The **USB (universal serial bus) controller** acts as an interface between the operating system, device drivers, and applications and the devices that are attached via the USB host. One USB host controller (assisted by USB hubs) can accommodate as many as 127 different devices, including flash memory, phones, cameras, scanners, musical keyboards, and so on. Each device is uniquely identified by the USB host controller with an identification number, which allows many devices to exchange data with the computer using the same USB host connection.

The USB controller assigns bandwidth to each device depending on its priority:

• Highest priority is assigned to real-time exchanges where no interruption in the data flow is allowed, such as video or sound data.

• Medium priority is assigned to devices that can allow occasional interrupts without jeopardizing the use of the device, such as a keyboard or joystick.

• Lowest priority is assigned to bulk transfers or exchanges that can accommodate slower data flow such as a file update.

Management of I/O Requests

Although many users may think of an I/O request as an elementary machine action, the Device Manager actually divides the task into three parts, with each one handled by a specific software component of the device management subsystem. The I/O traffic controller watches the status of all devices, control units, and channels. The I/O scheduler implements the policies that determine the allocation of, and access to, the devices, control units, and channels. The I/O device handler performs the actual transfer of data and processes the device interrupts. Let's look at these in more detail.

The **I/O traffic controller** monitors the status of every device, control unit, and channel. It's a job that becomes more complex as the number of units in the I/O subsystem increases and as the number of paths between these units increases. The traffic controller has three main tasks to perform for each I/O request: (1) it must determine if there's at least one path to a device of the requested type available; (2) if there's more than one path available, it must determine which to select; and (3) if the paths are all busy, it must determine when one will become available. To do all this, the traffic controller maintains a database containing the status and connections for each unit in the I/O subsystem, grouped into Channel Control Blocks, Control Unit Control Blocks, and Device Control Blocks, illustrated in Figure 7.1.

Channel Control Block	Control Unit Control Block	Device Control Block
Channel ID Channel Status List Control Units Connected List Processes Waiting	Control Unit ID Control Unit Status List Channels Connected to it List of Devices Connected to it List Processes Waiting for it	Device ID Device Status List Control Units Connected List Processes Waiting

(figure 7.1)

Each control block contains the information it needs to manage the channels, control units, and devices in the I/O subsystem.

To choose a free path to satisfy an I/O request, the traffic controller traces backward from the control block of the requested device through the control units to the channels. If a path is not available, a common occurrence under heavy load conditions, the process (actually its Process Control Block, or PCB, as described in Chapter 4) is linked to the queues kept in the control blocks of the requested device, control unit, and channel. This creates multiple wait queues with one queue per path. Later, when a path becomes available, the traffic controller selects the first PCB from the queue for that path.

The **I/O scheduler** performs a job analogous to the one performed by the Process Scheduler described in Chapter 4 on processor management—that is, it allocates the devices, control units, and channels. Under heavy loads, when the number of requests is greater than the number of available paths, the I/O scheduler must decide which request to satisfy first. Many of the criteria and objectives discussed in Chapter 4 also apply here. In many systems, the major difference between I/O scheduling and process scheduling is that I/O requests are not preempted. Once the channel program has started, it's allowed to continue to completion even though I/O requests with higher priorities may have entered the queue. This is feasible because channel programs are relatively short—50 to 100 ms. Other systems subdivide an I/O request into several stages and allow preemption of the I/O request at any one of these stages.

Some systems allow the I/O scheduler to give preferential treatment to I/O requests from high-priority programs. In that case, if a process has high priority, then its I/O requests would also have high priority and would be satisfied before other I/O requests with lower priorities. The I/O scheduler must synchronize its work with the traffic controller to make sure that a path is available to satisfy the selected I/O requests.

The **I/O device handler** processes the I/O interrupts, handles error conditions, and provides detailed scheduling algorithms, which are extremely device dependent. Each type of I/O device has its own device handler algorithm. Later in this chapter, we explore several algorithms for hard disk drives.

I/O Devices in the Cloud

One might wonder how the development of cloud computing will affect device management in the long term. While we await the answer to that question, in the short term, the cloud does not greatly change the role of the local operating system with respect to accessing I/O devices in multiple far-flung locations.

That is, when a user sends a command from a laptop to access a high speed hard drive that's many miles away, the laptop's operating system still performs many of the steps outlined in this chapter and expects an appropriate response from the operating system for the hard drive. Therefore, the concepts explored in this chapter continue to apply even as the cloud allows access to many more devices.

Sequential Access Storage Media

The first secondary storage medium used for electronic digital computers was paper in the form of printouts, punch cards, and paper tape. Magnetic tape followed for routine **secondary storage** in early computer systems.

A good introduction to the details of storage management is to look at the simplest case: a **sequential access storage device**, which can easily be visualized as an archival magnetic tape that writes and reads records in sequence from the beginning of a reel of tape to the end.

The length of each sequential record is usually determined by the application program, and each record can be identified by its position on the tape. To appreciate just how long this takes, consider a hypothetical computer system that uses a reel of tape that is 2400 feet long. See Figure 7.2. Data is recorded on eight of the nine parallel tracks that run the length of the tape. (The ninth track, shown at the top of the figure, holds a **parity bit** that is used for routine error checking.)

The number of characters that can be recorded per inch is determined by the density of the tape, such as 1600 bytes per inch (bpi). For example, if you had records of

(figure 7.2)

Nine-track magnetic tape with three characters recorded using odd parity. A 1/2-inch wide reel of tape, typically used to back up a mainframe computer, can store thousands of characters, or bytes, per inch.

Parity Bits

Character Representation

Characters

160 characters each, and were storing them on a tape with a density of 1600 bpi, then theoretically you could store 10 records on one inch of tape. However, in actual practice, it would depend on how you decided to store the records: individually or grouped into blocks. If the records are stored individually, each record would need to be separated by a space to indicate its starting and ending places. If the records are stored in blocks, then each block is preceded by a space and followed by a space, with the individual records stored sequentially within the block.

To appreciate the difference between storing records individually or in blocks, let's look at the mechanics of reading data from a magnetic tape. The tape remains stopped until there's a request to access one or more records. Then the reel of tape starts to rotate and the tape passes under the read/write head. Magnetic tape moves under the read/write head only when there's a need to access a record; at all other times it's standing still.

Records are written in the same way (assuming that there's room on that reel of tape for the data to be written; otherwise a fresh reel of tape would need to be accessed). So the tape moves in jerks as it stops, reads, and moves on at high speed, or stops, writes, and starts again, and so on.

The tape needs time and space to stop, so a gap is inserted between each record. This **interrecord gap (IRG)** is about ½ inch long regardless of the sizes of the records it separates. Therefore, if 10 records are stored individually, there will be nine ½-inch IRGs between each record. In the Figure 7.3, we assume each record is only $\frac{1}{10}$ inch, so 5.5 inches of tape are required to store 1 inch of data—not a very efficient way to use the storage medium.

(figure 7.3)

IRGs in magnetic tape. Each record requires only 1/10 inch of tape. When 10 records are stored individually on magnetic tape, they are separated by IRGs, which adds up to 4.5 inches of tape. This totals 5.5 inches of tape.

An alternative is to group the records into blocks before recording them on tape. This is called **blocking** and it's performed when the file is created. (Later, when you retrieve them, you must be sure to unblock them accurately.)

The number of records in a block is usually determined by the application program, and it's often set to take advantage of the **transfer rate**, which is the density of the tape (measured in bpi), multiplied by the tape drive speed, called transport speed, which is measured in inches per second (ips):

$$\text{transfer rate (ips)} = \text{density} * \text{transport speed}$$

Let's say that in our hypothetical system the transport speed is 200 ips. Therefore, at 1600 bpi, a total of 320,000 bytes can be transferred in one second; so theoretically, the optimal size of a block (for this hypothetical system) is 320,000 bytes. But there's a catch: This technique requires that the *entire* block be read into a buffer, so the buffer must be at least as large as the block.

Notice in Figure 7.3 that the gap (now called an **interblock gap** or **IBG**) is still ½ inch long, but the data from each block of 10 records is now stored on only 1 inch of tape—so we've used only 1.5 inches of tape (instead of the 5.5 inches shown in Figure 7.4), and we've wasted only ½ inch of tape (instead of 4.5 inches).

(figure 7.4)

Two blocks of records stored on magnetic tape, each preceded by an IBG of 1/2 inch. Each block holds 10 records, each of which is still 1/10 inch. The block, however, is 1 inch, for a total of 1.5 inches.

Blocking has two distinct advantages:

- Fewer I/O operations are needed because a single READ command can move an entire block, the physical record that includes several logical records, into main memory.
- Less storage space is wasted because the size of the physical record exceeds the size of the gap.

The two disadvantages of blocking seem mild by comparison:

- Overhead and software routines are needed for blocking, deblocking, and recordkeeping.
- Buffer space may be wasted if you need only one logical record but must read an entire block to get it.

Another buffering concept is the circular buffer, which is the subject of a research topic at the end of this chapter.

How long does it take to access a block or record on magnetic tape? It depends on where the record is located, but we can make some general calculations. For example, our 2400-foot reel of tape with a tape transport speed of 200 ips can be read without stopping in 144 seconds (2.5 minutes). Therefore, it would take 2.5 minutes to access the last record on the tape. On the average, then, it would take 1.25 minutes to access a record. And to access one record after another sequentially would take as long as it takes to start and stop a tape.

As we can see in Table 7.1, **access times** can vary widely. That makes magnetic tape a poor medium for routine secondary storage except for files with very high sequential activity—that is, those requiring that 90 to 100 percent of the records be accessed sequentially during an application.

Benchmarks	Access Time
Maximum access	2.5 minutes
Average access	1.25 minutes
Sequential access	3 milliseconds

(table 7.1)

Access times for 2400-foot magnetic tape with a tape transport speed of 200 ips.

Direct Access Storage Devices

Direct access storage devices (DASDs), sometimes called random access storage devices, include all devices that can directly read or write to an arbitrary place in storage. DASDs can be grouped into three categories: magnetic disks, optical discs, and solid state (flash) memory. Although the variance in DASD access times isn't as wide as with magnetic tape, the location of the specific record can still have a direct effect on the amount of time required to access it. The remainder of this chapter is devoted to several popular forms of DASDs.

Magnetic Disk Storage

Magnetic disk drives, such as computer hard drives (and the floppy disk drives of yesteryear), usually feature one or more read/write heads that float over each surface of each disk. Disk drives can have a single platter, or a stack of magnetic platters, called a disk pack. Figure 7.5 shows a typical disk pack—several platters stacked on a common central spindle, separated by enough space to allow the read/write heads to move between each pair of disks.

(figure 7.5)

A disk pack is a stack of magnetic platters. The read/write heads move between each pair of surfaces, and all of the heads are moved in unison by the arm.

As shown in Figure 7.5, each platter has two surfaces for recording (top and bottom), and each surface is formatted with a specific number of concentric tracks where the data is recorded. The precise number of tracks can vary widely, but typically there are a thousand or more on a high-capacity hard disk. Each track on each surface is numbered with the outermost circle as Track 0 and the highest-numbered track in the center.

The arm, shown in Figure 7.6, moves two read/write heads between each pair of surfaces: one for the surface above it and one for the surface below, as well as one for the uppermost surface and another for the lowermost surface. The arm moves all of the heads in unison, so if one head is on Track 36, then all of the heads are on Track 36, even if there are many platters—in other words, they're all positioned on the same track but over their respective surfaces, thus creating a virtual cylinder.

(figure 7.6)

A typical hard drive from a PC showing the arm that floats over the surface of the disk.

© Courtesy Seagate Technology

This raises some interesting questions: Is it more efficient to write a series of records on surface one and, when that surface is full, to continue writing on surface two, and then on surface three, and so on? Or is it better to fill up every outside track of every surface before moving the heads inward to the next track position to continue writing?

It's slower to fill a disk pack surface-by-surface than it is to fill it up track-by-track—and that leads us to a valuable concept. If we fill Track 0 of all of the surfaces, we've got a virtual cylinder of data. There are as many cylinders as there are tracks, and the cylinders are as tall as the disk pack. You could visualize the cylinders as a series of smaller and smaller soup cans, each nested inside the larger ones.

To access any given record, the system needs three things: its cylinder number, so the arm can move the read/write heads to it; its surface number, so the proper read/write head is activated; and its sector number, as shown in Figure 7.7.

(figure 7.7)

On a magnetic disk, the sectors are of different sizes: bigger at the rim and smaller at the center. The disk spins at a constant angular velocity (CAV) to compensate for this difference. Some optical discs can read and write on multiple layers, greatly enhancing storage capacity.

One clarification: We've used the term *surface* in this discussion because it makes the concepts easier to understand. However, conventional literature generally uses the term *track* to identify both the surface and the concentric track. Therefore, our use of *surface/track* coincides with the term *track* or *head* used in some other texts.

Access Times

Depending on whether a disk has fixed or movable heads, there can be as many as three factors that contribute to the time required to access a file: seek time, search time, and transfer time.

To date, **seek time** has been the slowest of the three factors. This is the time required to position the read/write head on the proper track. **Search time**, also known as rotational delay, is the time it takes to rotate the disk until the requested record is moved under the read/write head. Data **transfer time** is the fastest of the three; that's when the data is actually transferred from secondary storage to main memory (primary storage).

Fixed-Head Magnetic Drives

Fixed-head disk drives are fast because each track has its own read/write head and seek time doesn't apply. The total amount of time required to access data depends on the rotational speed. Referred to as "search time," this varies from device to device, but is constant within each device. The total time also depends on the position of the record relative to the position of the read/write head. Therefore, total access time is the sum of search time plus transfer time.

$$\begin{array}{r} \text{search time (rotational delay)} \\ + \text{transfer time (data transfer)} \\ \hline \text{access time} \end{array}$$

Because the disk rotates continuously, there are three basic positions for the requested record in relation to the position of the read/write head. Figure 7.8(a) shows the best possible situation because the record is next to the read/write head when the I/O command is executed; this gives a rotational delay of zero. Figure 7.8(b) shows the average situation because the record is directly opposite the read/write head when the I/O command is executed; this gives a rotational delay of $t/2$ where t (time) is one full rotation. Figure 7.8(c) shows the worst situation because the record has just rotated past the read/write head when the I/O command is executed; this gives a rotational delay of t because it will take one full rotation for the record to reposition itself under the read/write head.

(figure 7.8)

As a disk rotates, Record 1 may be near the read/write head and ready to be scanned, as seen in (a); in the farthest position just past the head, (c); or somewhere in between, as in the average case, (b).

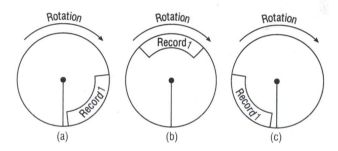

How long will it take to access a record? If one complete revolution takes 16.8 ms, then the average rotational delay, as shown in Figure 7.8(b), is 8.4 ms. The data-transfer time varies from device to device, but let's say the value is 0.00094 ms per byte—the size of the record dictates this value. (These are traditional values. The chapter exercises offer an opportunity to explore current rates.)

For example, Table 7.2 shows the resulting access times if it takes 0.094 ms (almost 0.1 ms) to transfer a record with 100 bytes.

(table 7.2)

Access times for a fixed-head disk drive at 16.8 ms/revolution.

Benchmarks	Access Time
Maximum access time	16.8 ms + 0.00094 ms/byte
Average access time	8.4 ms + 0.00094 ms/byte
Sequential access time	Depends on the length of the record (known as the transfer rate)

Data recorded on fixed head drives may or may not be blocked at the discretion of the application programmer. Blocking isn't used to save space because there are no IRGs between records. Instead, blocking is used to save time.

To illustrate the advantages of blocking the records, let's use the same values shown in Table 7.2 for a record containing 100 bytes and blocks containing 10 records. If we were to read 10 records individually, we would multiply the access time for a single record by 10:

$$
\begin{aligned}
\text{access time} \quad &= 8.4 + 0.094 = 8.494 \text{ for 1 record} \\
\text{total access time} \quad &= 10 * (8.4 + 0.094) = 84.940 \text{ for 10 unblocked records}
\end{aligned}
$$

On the other hand, to read one block of 10 records, we would make a single access, so we'd compute the access time only once, multiplying the transfer rate by 10:

$$
\begin{aligned}
\text{access time} \quad &= 8.4 + (0.094 * 10) \\
\text{total access time} \quad &= 8.4 + 0.94 \\
&= 9.34 \text{ for 10 records in 1 block}
\end{aligned}
$$

Once the block is in memory, the software that handles blocking and deblocking takes over. But, the amount of time used in deblocking must be less than what you saved in access time (75.6 ms) for this to be a productive move.

Movable-Head Magnetic Drives

Movable-head disk drives add the computation of seek time to the equation. Seek time is the time required to move the arm into position over the proper track. So now the formula for access time is:

$$
\begin{aligned}
&\text{seek time (arm movement)} \\
&\text{search time (rotational delay)} \\
+\;&\underline{\text{transfer time (data transfer)}} \\
&\text{access time}
\end{aligned}
$$

Of the three components of access time in this equation, seek time is the longest. We'll examine several seek strategies in a moment.

The calculations for search time (rotational delay) and transfer time are the same as those presented for fixed-head drives. The maximum seek time, which is the maximum time required to move the arm, can be 10 ms or less. Table 7.3 compares typical access times for movable-head drives.

Benchmarks	Access Time
Maximum access time	10 ms + 16.8 ms + 0.00094 ms/byte
Average access time	5 ms + 8.4 ms + 0.00094 ms/byte
Sequential access time	Depends on the length of the record, but generally less than 1 ms

(table 7.3)

Typical access times for a movable-head drive, such as a typical hard drive.

The variance in access time has increased in comparison to that of the fixed-head drive but it's relatively small—especially when compared to tape access, which varies from milliseconds to minutes. Again, blocking is a good way to minimize access time. If we use the same example as for fixed-head disks and consider the average case with 10 seeks followed by 10 searches, and assuming that the records are randomly distributed on the disk, we would get:

$$
\begin{aligned}
\text{access time} &= 5 + 8.4 + 0.094 = 13.494 \text{ ms for one record} \\
\text{total access time} &= 10 * 13.494 \\
&= 134.94 \text{ ms for 10 unblocked records}
\end{aligned}
$$

But when we put the 10 records into one block, the access time is significantly decreased:

$$
\begin{aligned}
\text{access time} &= 5 + 8.4 + (0.094 * 10) \\
\text{total access time} &= 13.4 + 0.94 \\
&= 14.34 \text{ ms for 10 records in 1 block}
\end{aligned}
$$

We stress that these figures wouldn't apply in an actual operating environment because we haven't taken into consideration what else is happening in the system while I/O is taking place. Therefore, although we can show the comparable performance of these components of the system, we're not seeing the whole picture until we explore how the components of the I/O subsystem work together.

Device Handler Seek Strategies

A **seek strategy** for the I/O device handler is the predetermined policy that the device handler uses to allocate access to the device among the many processes that may be waiting for it. It determines the order in which the processes get the device; the goal is to keep seek time to a minimum. We'll look at some of the most commonly used seek strategies—first-come, first-served (FCFS); shortest seek time first (SSTF); and SCAN with its variations (LOOK, N-Step SCAN, C-SCAN, and C-LOOK).

Every scheduling algorithm should do the following:
• Minimize arm movement
• Minimize mean response time
• Minimize the variance in response time

Because seek time is often the slowest element in most circumstances, access time is fastest if the entire data request can be fulfilled with a minimum of arm movement.

These goals are only a guide. In actual systems, the designer must choose the strategy that makes the system as fair as possible to the general user population, while using the system's resources as efficiently as possible.

First-come, first-served (FCFS) is the simplest device-scheduling algorithm; it is easy to program and essentially fair to users. However, on average, it doesn't meet any of the three goals of a seek strategy. To illustrate, consider a single-sided disk with one recordable surface where the tracks are numbered from 0 to 49. It takes 1 ms to travel from one track to the next adjacent one. For this example, let's say that while retrieving data from Track 15, the following list of requests has arrived: Tracks 4, 40, 11, 35, 7, and 14. Let's also assume that once a requested track has been reached, the entire track is read into main memory. The path of the read/write head looks like the graph shown in Figure 7.9.

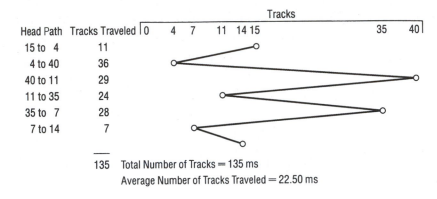

(figure 7.9)

The arm makes many time-consuming movements as it travels from track to track to satisfy all requests in FCFS order.

As demonstrated in Figure 7.9, it takes a long time, 135 ms, to satisfy the entire series of requests (rotating to the proper sector)—and that's before considering the work to be done when the arm is finally in place—search time and data transfer.

FCFS has an obvious disadvantage in that it allows extreme arm movement: from 15 to 4, up to 40, back to 11, up to 35, back to 7, and, finally, up to 14. Remember, seek time is the most time-consuming of the three functions performed here, so any algorithm that can minimize it is preferable to FCFS.

Shortest seek time first (SSTF) uses the same underlying philosophy as Shortest Job Next (described in Chapter 4), where the shortest jobs are processed first and longer jobs are made to wait. With SSTF, the request with the track closest to the one being served (that is, the one with the shortest distance to travel) is the next to be satisfied, thus tending to reduce seek time. Figure 7.10 shows what happens to the same track

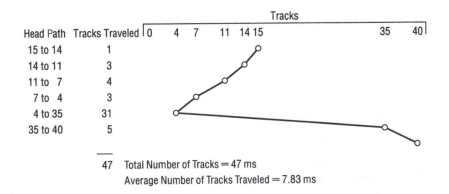

(figure 7.10)

Using the SSTF algorithm, with all track requests on the wait queue, arm movement is reduced by almost one third while satisfying the same requests shown in Figure 7.9 (using the FCFS algorithm).

requests that took 135 ms to service using FCFS; in this example, all track requests are present and on the wait queue.

Again, without considering search time and data transfer time, it took 47 ms to satisfy all requests—which is about one third of the time required by FCFS. That's a substantial improvement.

But SSTF has its disadvantages. Remember that the Shortest Job Next (SJN) process scheduling algorithm had a tendency to favor the short jobs and to postpone the long, unwieldy jobs. The same holds true for SSTF. It favors easy-to-reach requests and postpones traveling to those that are out of the way.

For example, let's say that in the previous example, the arm is at Track 11 and is preparing to go to Track 7 when the system suddenly gets a deluge of requests, including requests for Tracks 22, 13, 16, 29, 1, and 21. With SSTF, the system notes that Track 13 is closer to the arm's present position (only two tracks away) than the older request for Track 7 (five tracks away), so Track 13 is handled first. Of the requests now waiting, the next closest is Track 16, so off it goes—moving farther and farther away from Tracks 7 and 1. In fact, during periods of heavy loads, the arm stays in the center of the disk, where it can satisfy the majority of requests easily and it ignores (or indefinitely postpones) those on the outer edges of the disk. Therefore, this algorithm meets the first goal of seek strategies, but it fails to meet the other two.

SCAN uses a directional bit to indicate whether the arm is moving toward the innermost disk track or away from it. The algorithm moves the arm methodically from the outer to the inner track, servicing every request in its path. When it reaches the innermost track, it reverses direction and moves toward the outer tracks, again servicing every request in its path.

The most common variation of SCAN is **LOOK** (sometimes known as the elevator algorithm), in which the arm doesn't necessarily go all the way to either edge unless there are requests there. In effect, it "looks" ahead for a request before going to service it. In Figure 7.11, we assume that the arm is moving first toward the inner

(figure 7.11)

The LOOK algorithm makes the arm move systematically from the first requested track at one edge of the disk to the last requested track at the other edge. In this example, all track requests are on the wait queue.

Head Path	Tracks Traveled
15 to 35	20
35 to 40	5
40 to 14	26
14 to 11	3
11 to 7	4
7 to 4	3
	61

Tracks: 0 4 7 11 14 15 35 40

Total Number of Tracks = 61 ms
Average Number of Tracks Traveled = 10.16 ms

(higher-numbered) tracks before reversing direction. In this example, all track requests are present and on the wait queue.

Again, without adding search time and data transfer time, it took 61 ms to satisfy all requests, 14 ms more than with SSTF. Does this make SCAN a less attractive algorithm than SSTF? For this particular example, the answer is yes. But for the overall system, the answer is no. This is because it eliminates the possibility of indefinite postponement of requests in out-of-the-way places—at either edge of the disk.

Also, as requests arrive, each is incorporated in its proper place in the queue and is serviced when the arm reaches that track. Therefore, if Track 11 is being served when the request for Track 13 arrives, the arm continues on its way to Track 7 and then to Track 1. Track 13 must wait until the arm starts on its way back, as does the request for Track 16. This eliminates a great deal of arm movement and saves time in the end. In fact, SCAN meets all three goals for seek strategies.

N-Step SCAN, another variation of SCAN, holds all new requests until the arm starts on its way back. Any requests that arrive while the arm is in motion are grouped for the arm's next sweep (which will go all the way to the outermost track to the innermost track and back again).

With **C-SCAN** (an abbreviation for Circular SCAN), the arm picks up requests on its path during the inward sweep. When the innermost track has been reached, it immediately returns to the outermost track and starts servicing requests that arrived during its last inward sweep. With this modification, the system can provide quicker service to those requests that accumulated for the low-numbered tracks while the arm was moving inward. The theory here is that by the time the arm reaches the highest-numbered tracks, there are few requests immediately behind it. However, there are many requests at the far end of the disk and these have been waiting the longest. Therefore, C-SCAN is designed to provide a more uniform wait time.

C-LOOK is an optimization of C-SCAN, just as LOOK is an optimization of SCAN. In this algorithm, the sweep inward stops at the last high-numbered track request, so the arm doesn't move all the way to the last track unless it's required to do so. In addition, the arm doesn't necessarily return to the lowest-numbered track; it returns only to the lowest-numbered track that's requested.

Which strategy is best? It's up to the system designer to select the best algorithm for each environment. It's a job that's complicated because the day-to-day performance of any scheduling algorithm depends on the load it must handle; but some broad generalizations can be made based on simulation studies:

- FCFS works well with light loads, but as soon as the load grows, service time becomes unacceptably long.

What happens if two or more jobs or processes are tied? It depends on the policy, but the most common way ties are broken is to apply FCFS to break the tie. The oldest one is allowed to go next.

- SSTF is quite popular and intuitively appealing. It works well with moderate loads, but it has the problem of localization under heavy loads.
- SCAN works well with light to moderate loads, and it eliminates the problem of indefinite postponement. SCAN is similar to SSTF in throughput and mean service times.
- C-SCAN works well with moderate to heavy loads, and it has a very small variance in service times.

The best scheduling algorithm for a specific computing system may be a combination of more than one scheme. For instance, it might be a combination of two schemes: SCAN or LOOK during light to moderate loads, and C-SCAN or C-LOOK during heavy load times.

Search Strategies: Rotational Ordering

So far we've only tried to optimize seek times on hard disk drives. To complete the picture, we'll now look at a way to optimize search times by ordering the requests once the read/write heads have been positioned. This search strategy is called **rotational ordering**.

To help illustrate the abstract concept of rotational ordering, let's consider a virtual cylinder with a movable read/write head.

Figure 7.12 illustrates the list of requests arriving at this cylinder for different sectors on different tracks. For this example, we'll assume that the cylinder has only five tracks, numbered 0 through 4, and that each track contains five sectors, numbered 0 through 4. We'll take the requests in the order in which they arrive.

As shown in Figure 7.12, the cylinder takes 5 ms to move the read/write head from one track to the next. It takes 5 ms to rotate the cylinder from Sector 0 to Sector 4 and 1 ms

✔ As it transfers data from one sector to main memory, the read/write head moves from the beginning to the end of that sector. Therefore, when it is time to move to the next sector, it starts its journey from the end of that sector, not at its beginning.

(figure 7.12)

Example of a virtual cylinder with five sectors for each of its five tracks.

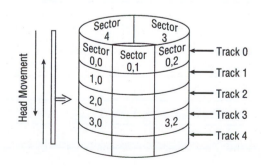

Request List	
Track	Sector
0	1
1	4
1	3
2	0
2	3
2	4
3	2
3	0

to transfer one sector from the cylinder to main memory. Here's how to calculate data retrieval time:

1. Note where the read/write head is starting from.
2. Multiply the number of tracks by the seek time.
3. Multiply the number of sectors by the search time.
4. Add the data transfer time for each sector.

Each request is satisfied as it comes in; the results are shown in Table 7.4.

Request	Track, Sector	Seek Time	Search Time	Data Transfer	Total Time
1.	0,1	0	1	1	2
2.	1,4	5	2	1	8
3.	1,3	0	3	1	4
4.	2,0	5	1	1	7
5.	2,3	0	2	1	3
6.	2,4	0	0	1	1
7.	3,2	5	2	1	8
8.	3,0	0	2	1	3
TOTALS		15 ms +	13 ms +	8 ms =	36 ms

(table 7.4)

It takes 36 ms to fill the eight requests on the movable-head cylinder shown in Figure 7.12. For this example, seek time is 5 ms/track, search time is 1 ms/sector, and data transfer is 1 ms.

Although nothing can be done to improve the time spent moving the read/write head (it's dependent on the hardware), the amount of time wasted due to rotational delay can be reduced. If the requests are ordered within each track so that the first sector requested on the second track is the next number higher than the one just served, rotational delay will be minimized, as shown in Table 7.5.

Request	Track, Sector	Seek Time	Search Time	Data Transfer	Total Time
1.	0,1	0	1	1	2
2.	1,3	5	1	1	7
3.	1,4	0	0	1	1
4.	2,0	5	0	1	6
5.	2,3	0	2	1	3
6.	2,4	0	0	1	1
7.	3,0	5	0	1	6
8.	3,2	0	1	1	2
TOTALS		15 ms +	5 ms +	8 ms =	28 ms

(table 7.5)

It takes 28 ms to fill the same eight requests shown in Table 7.5 after the requests are ordered to minimize search time, reducing it from 13 ms to 5 ms.

To properly implement this algorithm, the device controller must provide rotational sensing so the device driver can see which sector is currently under the read/write head. Under heavy I/O loads, this kind of ordering can significantly increase throughput, especially if the device has fixed read/write heads rather than movable heads.

Disk pack cylinders are an extension of the previous example. Once the heads are positioned on a cylinder, each surface has its own read/write head. So rotational ordering can be accomplished on a surface-by-surface basis, and the read/write heads can be activated in turn with no additional movement required.

Only one read/write head can be active at any one time, so the controller must be ready to handle mutually exclusive requests, such as Request 2 and Request 5 in Table 7.5. They're mutually exclusive because both are requesting Sector 3, one at Track 1 and the other at Track 2, but only one of the two read/write heads can be transmitting at any given time. One such policy could state that the tracks will be processed in a sweep from low-numbered to high-numbered tracks, followed by a sweep from high-numbered to low-numbered tracks (such as that used in SCAN). Therefore, to handle requests on a disk pack, there would be two orderings of requests: one to handle the position of the read/write heads making up the cylinder and the other to handle the processing of each cylinder.

Optical Disc Storage

The spelling convention for an optical storage device is *disc*, to differentiate it from a magnetic storage *disk*.

Advancements in laser technology made possible the advent of CD, DVD, and Blu-ray optical disc storage. There are many differences between an optical disc and a magnetic disk, including the design of the tracks and sectors.

A magnetic disk, which consists of concentric tracks of sectors, spins at a constant speed—this is called constant angular velocity (CAV). Because the sectors at the outside of the disk spin faster past the read/write head than the inner sectors, outside sectors are much larger than sectors located near the center of the disk. Although this format can waste storage space, it maximizes the speed with which data can be retrieved.

On the other hand, the most common optical disc consists of a single spiraling track of same-length sectors running from the center to the rim of the disc, as shown in Figure 7.13. Like the magnetic disk, this single track also has sectors, but all of them are the same length, regardless of their locations on the disc. That is, a sector close to the center is the same length as one near the outside rim. Because this design reduces wasted space, it allows many more sectors to fit on an optical disc compared to a magnetic disk of the same area. The disc drive adjusts the speed of the disc's spin to compensate for the sector's location on the disc—this is called constant linear velocity (CLV). Each sector contains the same amount of data, so the disc spins faster to read sectors located at the center of the disc and slower to read sectors near the outer edge. If you listen to an optical disc drive in action as it accesses different regions on a disc, you can hear it change speed—faster and slower—to retrieve data.

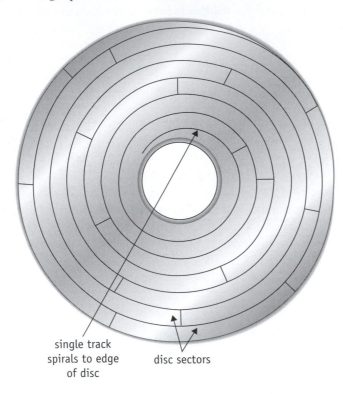

single track
spirals to edge
of disc

disc sectors

(figure 7.13)

On an optical disc, the sectors (not all sectors are shown here) are of the same size throughout the disc. The disc drive changes speed to compensate, but it spins at a constant linear velocity (CLV).

Some of the most important measures of optical disc drive performance are sustained data transfer rate and average access time. The data transfer rate is measured in megabytes per second and refers to the speed at which massive amounts of data can be read from the disc. This factor is crucial for applications requiring sequential access, such as for audio and video playback. For example, a DVD with a fast data transfer rate will drop fewer frames when playing back a recorded video segment than will a unit with a slower transfer rate. This creates an image that's much smoother.

However, to retrieve data that is not stored sequentially, the drive's access time may be more important. Access time indicates the average time required to move the head (with the laser) to a specific place on the disc. The fastest units have the smallest *average* access times, which is the most important factor when searching for information randomly, such as in a database. Therefore, a fast data transfer rate is most important for sequential disc access, such as for video playback, whereas fast access time is crucial when retrieving data that's widely dispersed on the disc.

A third important feature is cache size, which can have a substantial impact on perceived performance. A hardware cache acts as a buffer by transferring blocks of data to and from the disc, anticipating which data the user may want to retrieve next. Assuming the system anticipates correctly, data retrieval can be done much more quickly if the information remains in the cache. In some cases, the cache can also act as a read-ahead buffer, looking for the next block of information on the disc. Read-ahead caches might appear to be most useful for multimedia playback, where a continuous stream of data is flowing. However, because they fill up quickly, read-ahead caches actually become more useful when paging through a database or electronic book. In these cases, the cache has time to recover while the user is reading the current piece of information.

CD and DVD Technology

There are several types of optical disc systems, depending on the medium and the capacity of the discs: CDs, DVDs, and Blu-ray as shown in Figure 7.14.

(figure 7.14)

CD readable technology (left) uses a red laser to write on the bottom of the disc's substrate. DVDs (middle) use a smaller red laser to write on the disc's substrate so tracks can be layered, one on top of the other. Blu-ray (right) uses a finer blue laser to write on multiple layers with more tightly packed tracks. (from blu-raydisc.com)

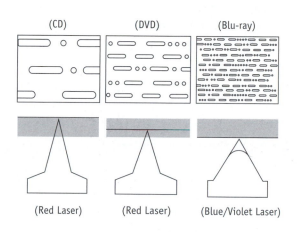

To put data on an optical disc, a high-intensity laser beam burns indentations on the disc that are called pits. These **pits** contrast with the unburned flat areas, called **lands.** The first sectors are located in the center of the disc; the laser moves outward, reading each sector in turn. Optical discs can have from one to multiple layers, allowing the laser to look through upper layers to read those below. For example, if a disc has two layers, the laser's course is reversed to read the second layer with the arm moving from the outer edge to the inner.

How does it work? Using a CD or DVD player, data is read back by focusing a low-powered red laser on it, which shines through the protective layer of the disc onto the track where data is recorded. Light striking a land is reflected into a photodetector, while light striking a pit is scattered and absorbed. The photodetector then converts the intensity of the light into a digital signal of ones and zeros.

✔ It's a common misperception that the pits and lands represent zeros and ones. Rather, it is the transition from one to the other that's interpreted as a zero or one.

If the CD or DVD disc drive allows writing (and not rewriting) to the disc, a more complex disc controller is required for this CD-R (compact disc recordable) and DVD-R technology. For example, a CD-R that has data on a single layer actually has several coatings, including one with a reflective coating and one with dye, which is used to record the data. The write head uses a high-powered laser beam to record data. A permanent mark is made on the dye when the energy from the laser beam is absorbed into it; it cannot be erased after it is recorded. When it is read, the existence of a mark on the dye causes the laser beam to scatter and light is not returned back to the read head. However, when there are no marks on the dye, the gold layer reflects the light right back to the read head. This is similar to the process of reading pits and lands. The software used to create recordable discs uses a standard format, such as ISO 9096, which automatically checks for errors and creates a table of contents to keep track of each file's location.

Similarly, rewritable discs (classified as CD-RW and DVD-RW) use a process called phase change technology to write, erase, and rewrite data. The disc's recording layer uses an alloy of silver, indium, antimony, and tellurium. The recording layer has two different phase states: amorphous and crystalline. In the amorphous state, light is not reflected as well as in the crystalline state.

To record data, a laser beam heats up the disc and changes the state from crystalline to amorphous. When data is read by means of a low-power laser beam, the amorphous state scatters the light that does not get picked up by the read head. This is interpreted as a 0 and is similar to what occurs when reading pits. On the other hand, when the light hits the crystalline areas, light is reflected back to the read head, and this is similar to what occurs when reading lands and is interpreted as a 1. To erase data, the optical disc drive uses a low-energy beam to heat up the pits just enough to loosen the alloy and return it to its original crystalline state.

Although DVDs use the same design and are the same size and shape as CDs, they can store much more data. Its red laser, with a shorter wavelength than the CD's infrared laser, makes smaller pits and allows the spiral of the disc's single track to be longer and wound tighter. Therefore, a dual-layer, single-sided DVD can hold the equivalent of 13 CDs.

When the advantages of compression technology (discussed in the next chapter) are added to the high capacity of a DVD, a single-sided, double-layer DVD can hold 8.6GB.

Blu-ray Disc Technology

A Blu-ray disc is the same physical size as a DVD or CD, but the laser technology used to read and write data is quite different. As shown in Figure 7.9, the pits on a Blu-ray disc are much smaller, and the tracks are wound much tighter than they are on a DVD or CD. Although Blu-ray products can be made backward compatible so they can accommodate the older CDs and DVDs, the Blu-ray's blue-violet laser has a shorter wavelength than the DVD's red laser. This allows data to be packed more tightly and stored in less space.

In addition, the blue-violet laser can write on a much thinner layer on the disc, allowing multiple layers to be written on top of each other and vastly increasing the amount of data that can be stored on a single disc. The disc's format was created to further the commercial prospects for high-definition video and to store large amounts of data, particularly for games and interactive applications.

Each Blu-ray disc can hold much more data than can a DVD of similar size. Like CDs and DVDs, Blu-ray discs are available in several formats: read-only (BD-ROM), recordable (BD-R), and rewritable (BD-RE).

Solid State Storage

Solid state storage technology uses a phenomenon known as Fowler-Nordheim tunneling to store electrons in a floating gate transistor, where they remain even after power is turned off.

Flash Memory Storage

Removable flash memory devices go by a variety of names: flash drives, memory cards, smart cards, thumb drives, camera cards, memory sticks, and more.

Flash memory is a type of electrically erasable, programmable, read-only memory (EEPROM) that's organized in a grid of cells in rows and columns. It's a nonvolatile storage medium that can emulate random access memory, but unlike RAM, it stores data reliably even when power is disrupted. Flash memory is the technology used as removable media for numerous devices, it can be used to expand virtual memory space for some operating systems, and it was the precursor for solid state drives, which are described next.

Flash memory gets its name from the technique used to erase its data. To write data, a relatively high voltage is sent through one transistor, called the floating gate, then through a metal oxide layer, and into a second transistor called the control gate, where the charge is stored in a cell until it's erased. To reset all values, a strong electrical field called a flash is applied to the entire card.

However, flash memory is not indestructible. It has two limitations: The bits can be erased only by applying the flash, and each flash erasure causes the storage area to become less stable. Over time (after a finite but very large number of uses, such as 10,000 to 1,000,000), a solid state memory device will no longer reliably store data.

Solid State Drives

Solid state drive (SSD) technology allows for fast but currently pricey storage devices. SSDs can rely on two types of data storage: that used in flash memory or that used in main memory (if some kind of battery is built in to guard against data loss when the power is cut abruptly).

A typical SSD, shown in Figure 7.15, can function in a smaller physical space than magnetic hard drives.

(figure 7.15)

An SSD (left) has no moving parts and is much smaller and faster than an equivalent hard disk drive (right) but the SSD cost per gigabyte can be substantially higher.

How do solid state drives compare to hard disk drives? Because solid state drives work electronically and have no moving parts, the concepts of seek time, search time, and rotational delay do not apply, suggesting that SSDs offer significantly better performance. Indeed, they require less power, they are silent, and they are relatively lightweight. However, there are some significant disadvantages to SSD technology. For example, when an SSD fails, it often does so without warning, without the messages or data errors that can forewarn a user of an impending HDD failure. With little opportunity to make last ditch efforts to recover valuable data, an SSD crash can be catastrophic.

Data transfer rates on a new, unboxed SSD are much faster than similar hard drives, but it begins slowing down and continues to do so as it is used, sometimes only a few weeks into its deployment. Once data is loaded on the SSD, it is often moved many times to achieve wear leveling, a practice that contributes to its overall performance degradation over time.

(table 7.6)

Typical comparison of two secondary storage devices. Advantageous features are shown with an asterisk (*).

Feature	Hard Disk Drive	Solid State Drive
Access Times	Slower	Faster *
Power consumption	Higher	Lower *
Weight	Heavier	Lighter *
Noise Production	Yes	No *
Contains moving parts	Yes	No *
Cost/GB	Lower *	Higher
Very High Capacity	Yes *	No
Lifetime of writes/rewrites	Longer *	Shorter

SSD and hard drive technology can be combined in one unit to create a hybrid drive. Alternatively, SSDs and hard drives can be combined within a system, called a hybrid system. Both techniques seek to maximize the benefits of each by storing fast-changing data or smaller sized files on the SSD and store the huge files or those accessed infrequently on the hard drives.

Components of the I/O Subsystem

Regardless of the hardware makeup of the system, every piece of the I/O subsystem must work harmoniously. The challenges are similar to those of the mythical "Flynn Taxicab Company," shown in Figure 7.16.

Let's say that many requests arrive from all over the city to the taxi company dispatcher. It's the dispatcher's job to handle the incoming calls as fast as they arrive to find out who needs transportation, where they are, where they're going, and when. Then the dispatcher organizes the calls into an order that will use the company's resources as efficiently as possible. That's not easy, because the cab company has a variety of vehicles at its disposal: ordinary taxicabs, station wagons, vans, limos, and a minibus. These are serviced by specialized mechanics. A mechanic handles only one type of vehicle, which is made available to many drivers. Once the order is set, the dispatcher calls the mechanic who, ideally, has the vehicle ready for the driver, who jumps into the appropriate vehicle, picks up the waiting passengers, and delivers them quickly to their respective destinations.

(figure 7.16)

The taxicab company works in a manner similar to an I/O subsystem. One mechanic can service several vehicles just as an I/O control unit can operate several devices, as shown in Figure 7.17.

That's the ideal—but problems sometimes occur—rainy days mean too many phone calls to fulfill every request, vehicles that are not mechanically sound, and a limo that is already busy when you call for a ride.

The **I/O subsystem**'s components perform similar functions. The channel plays the part of the dispatcher in this example. Its job is to keep up with the I/O requests from the CPU and pass them down the line to the appropriate control unit. The control units play the part of the mechanics. The I/O devices play the part of the vehicles.

I/O channels are programmable units placed between the CPU and the control units. Their job is to accommodate both the fast speed of the CPU and the slow speed of the I/O device, and they make it possible to overlap I/O operations with processor operations so the CPU and I/O can process concurrently. Channels use **I/O channel programs**, which can range in size from one to many instructions. Each channel program specifies the action to be performed by the devices and controls the transmission of data between main memory and the control units.

The channel sends one signal for each function, which might say "go to the top of the page" if the device is a printer, or "rewind" if the device is a tape drive. The **I/O control unit** interprets the signal. Although a control unit is sometimes part of the device, in most systems a single control unit is attached to several similar devices, so we distinguish between the control unit and the device.

Some systems also have a disk controller, or disk drive interface, which is a special-purpose device used to link the disk drives with the system bus. Disk drive interfaces control the transfer of information between the disk drives and the rest of the computer system. The operating system normally deals with the controller, not the device.

At the start of an I/O command, the information passed from the CPU to the channel is this:

- I/O command (READ, WRITE, CLOSE, etc.)
- Channel number
- Address of the physical record to be transferred (from or to secondary storage)
- Starting address of a memory buffer from which or into which the record is to be transferred

Because the channels are as fast as the CPU they work with, each channel can direct several control units by interleaving commands (just as we had several mechanics directed by a single dispatcher). In addition, each control unit can direct several devices (just as a single mechanic could repair several vehicles of the same type). A typical configuration might have one channel and up to eight control units, each of which communicates with up to eight I/O devices. Channels are often shared because they're the most expensive items in the entire I/O subsystem.

The system shown in Figure 7.17 requires that the entire path be available when an I/O command is initiated. However, there's some flexibility built into the system because each unit can work independently of the others, as explained in the next section. This figure also shows the hierarchical nature of the interconnection and the one-to-one correspondence between each device and its transmission path in this example.

(figure 7.17)

Typical I/O subsystem configuration.

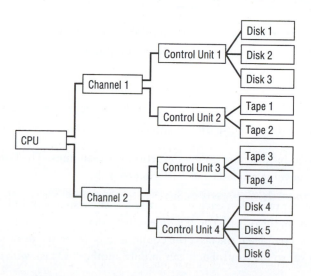

Additional flexibility can be built into the system by connecting more than one channel to a control unit or by connecting more than one control unit to a single device. That's the same as if the mechanics of the Flynn Taxicab Company could also make repairs for the ABC Taxicab Company, or if its vehicles could be used by ABC drivers (or if the drivers in the company could share vehicles).

These multiple paths increase the reliability of the I/O subsystem by keeping communication lines open even if a component malfunctions. Figure 7.18 shows the same system presented in Figure 7.17, but with one control unit connected to two channels and one device connected to two control units.

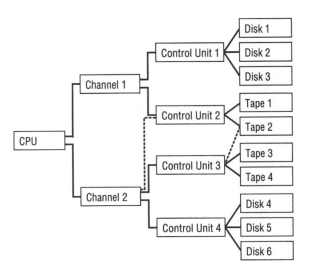

(figure 7.18)

I/O subsystem configuration with multiple paths, which increase both flexibility and reliability. With two additional paths, shown with dashed lines, if Control Unit 2 malfunctions, then Tape 2 can still be accessed via Control Unit 3.

Communication Among Devices

The Device Manager relies on several auxiliary features to keep running efficiently under the demanding conditions of a busy computer system, and there are three requirements it must fulfill:

• It needs to know which components are busy and which are free.
• It must be able to accommodate the requests that come in during heavy I/O traffic.
• It must accommodate the disparity of speeds between the CPU and the I/O devices.

The first is solved by structuring the interaction between units. The last two problems are handled by queuing requests and buffering records.

As we mentioned previously, each unit in the I/O subsystem can finish its operation independently from the others. For example, after a device has begun writing a record, and before it has completed the task, the connection between the device and its control unit can be cut off so the control unit can initiate another I/O task with another device.

Meanwhile, at the other end of the system, the CPU is free to process data while I/O is being performed, which allows for concurrent processing and I/O.

The success of the operation depends on the system's ability to know when a device has completed an operation. This is done with a hardware flag that must be tested by the CPU. Made up of three bits, the flag resides in the **Channel Status Word (CSW)**, which is in a predefined location in main memory that contains information indicating the status of the channel. Each bit represents one of the components of the I/O subsystem, one each for the channel, control unit, and device. Each bit is changed from 0 to 1 to indicate that the unit has changed from free to busy. Each component has access to the flag, which can be tested before proceeding with the next I/O operation to ensure that the entire path is free. There are two common ways to perform this test—polling and using interrupts.

Polling increases system overhead because the flag is tested in software. This overhead is similar to that caused by busy waiting, discussed in Chapter 5.

Polling uses a special machine instruction to test the flag. For example, the CPU periodically tests the channel status bit (in the CSW). If the channel is still busy, the CPU performs some other processing task until the test shows that the channel is free; then the channel performs the I/O operation. The major disadvantage with this scheme is determining how often the flag should be polled. If polling is done too frequently, the CPU wastes time testing the flag just to find out that the channel is still busy. On the other hand, if polling is done too seldom, the channel could sit idle for long periods of time.

The use of **interrupts** is a more efficient way to test the flag. Instead of CPU testing the flag, a hardware mechanism does the test as part of every machine instruction executed by the CPU. If the channel is busy, the flag is set so that execution of the current sequence of instructions is automatically interrupted and control is transferred to the interrupt handler. The interrupt handler is part of the operating system and resides in a predefined location in memory.

The interrupt handler's job is to determine the best course of action based on the current situation. Because it's not unusual for more than one unit to have caused the I/O interrupt, the interrupt handler must find out which unit sent the signal, analyze its status, restart it when appropriate with the next operation, and finally return control to the interrupted process.

Some sophisticated systems are equipped with hardware that can distinguish among several types of interrupts. These interrupts are ordered by priority, and each one can transfer control to a corresponding location in memory. The memory locations are ranked in order according to the same priorities as the interrupts. Therefore, if the CPU is executing the interrupt-handler routine associated with a given priority, the hardware automatically intercepts all interrupts at the same or at lower priorities. This multiple-priority interrupt system helps improve resource utilization because each interrupt is handled according to its relative importance.

Direct memory access (DMA) is an I/O technique that allows a control unit to directly access main memory. This means that once reading or writing has begun, the remainder of the data can be transferred to and from memory without CPU intervention. However, it is possible that the DMA control unit and the CPU will compete for the system bus if they happen to need it at the same time. To activate this process, the CPU sends enough information—such as the type of operation (read or write), the unit number of the I/O device needed, the location in memory where data is to be read from or written to, and the amount of data (bytes or words) to be transferred—to the DMA control unit to initiate the transfer of data; the CPU then can go on to another task while the control unit completes the transfer independently. The DMA controller sends an interrupt to the CPU to indicate that the operation is completed. This mode of data transfer is used for high-speed devices such as fast secondary storage devices.

Without DMA, the CPU is responsible for the movement of data between main memory and the device—a time-consuming task that results in significant overhead and decreased CPU utilization.

Buffers enable better handling of the movement of data between the relatively slow I/O devices and the very fast CPU. Buffers are temporary storage areas built into convenient locations throughout the system including: main memory, channels, and control units. They're used to store data read from an input device before it's needed by the processor as well as to store data that will be written to an output device. A typical use of buffers (mentioned earlier in this chapter) occurs when blocked records are either read from or written to an I/O device. In this case, one physical record contains several logical records and must reside in memory while the processing of each individual record takes place. For example, if a block contains five records, then a physical READ occurs with every six READ commands; all other READ requests are directed to retrieve information from the buffer (this buffer may be set by the application program).

To minimize the idle time for devices and, even more important, to maximize their throughput, the technique of double buffering is used, as shown in Figure 7.19. In this system, two buffers are present in the main memory, the channels, and the control units. The objective is to have a record ready to be transferred to or from memory at any time to avoid any possible delay that might be caused by waiting for a buffer to fill up with data. Thus, while one record is being processed by the CPU, another can be read or written by the channel.

When using blocked records, upon receipt of the command to "READ last logical record," the channel can start reading the next physical record, which results in overlapped I/O and processing. When the first READ command is received, two records are transferred from the device to immediately fill both buffers. Then, as the data from one buffer has been processed, the second buffer is ready. As the second is being read, the first buffer is being filled with data from a third record, and so on.

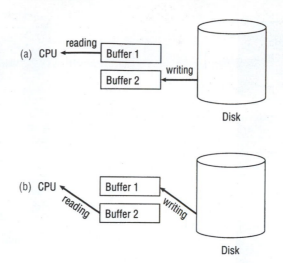

(figure 7.19)

Example of double buffering: (a) the CPU is reading from Buffer 1 as Buffer 2 is being filled; (b) once Buffer 2 is filled, it can be read quickly by the CPU while Buffer 1 is being filled again.

RAID

RAID consists of a set of physical disk drives that is viewed as a single logical unit by the operating system. RAID technology was proposed by researchers at the University of California at Berkeley, who created the acronym to stand for Redundant Array of Inexpensive Disks. The industry has since amended the acronym to mean Redundant Array of Independent Disks to emphasize the scheme's improved disk performance and reliability.

RAID begins with the assumption that several small-capacity disk drives are preferable to a few large-capacity disk drives, because by distributing the data among several smaller disks, the system can simultaneously access the requested data from the multiple drives. This results in faster I/O performance and improved data recovery in the event of disk failure.

A typical RAID array may have five disk drives connected to a specialized controller, which houses the software that coordinates the transfer of data to and from the disks in the array to a large-capacity disk connected to the I/O subsystem. Because this configuration can be managed by the operating system as a single large-capacity disk, no additional software changes are needed to accommodate it.

Here's how it works: Data is divided into segments called strips, which are distributed across the disks in the array. A set of consecutive strips across disks is called a **stripe**, and the whole process is called striping. Figure 7.20 shows how data strips are distributed in an array of four disks.

Data Transferred in Parallel

(figure 7.20)

Data being transferred in parallel from a Level 0 RAID configuration to a large-capacity disk. The software in the controller ensures that the strips are stored in correct order.

There are seven primary levels of RAID, numbered from Level 0 through Level 6. It should be noted that the levels do not indicate a hierarchy but rather denote different types of configurations and error correction capabilities. Table 7.7 provides a summary of these seven levels, including how error correction is implemented and the perceived effect on system performance.

RAID Level	Error Correction Method	I/O Request Rate	Data Transfer Rate
0	None	Excellent	Excellent
1	Mirroring	Read: Good Write: Fair	Read: Fair Write: Fair
2	Hamming code	Poor	Excellent
3	Word parity	Poor	Excellent
4	Strip parity	Read: Excellent Write: Fair	Read: Fair Write: Poor
5	Distributed strip parity	Read: Excellent Write: Fair	Read: Fair Write: Poor
6	Distributed strip parity and independent data check	Read: Excellent Write: Poor	Read: Fair Write: Poor

(table 7.7)

The seven standard levels of RAID provide various degrees of error correction. Cost, speed, and the system's applications are significant factors to consider when choosing a level.

However, these seven levels don't tell the whole story. When two levels are combined, as discussed in Nested Raid Levels, their strengths can complement each other and provide substantial benefits. Remember, though, that adopting a RAID configuration often requires the purchase of additional disk drives to implement them, which immediately increases hardware costs.

Level Zero

RAID Level 0 uses data striping without parity, without error correction. It is the only level that does not provide error correction, or redundancy, and so it is not considered a true form of RAID because it cannot recover from hardware failure. However, it does offer the same significant benefit of all RAID systems—that this group of devices appears to the operating system as a single logical unit.

David A. Patterson (1947–)

David Patterson was a leader of the 1987 team at the University of California, Berkeley that developed RAID as a way to divide and replicate computer data among multiple hard disk drives that can be managed by the operating system as a single disk. He is also known as the founding director of the Parallel Computing Laboratory (PAR Lab) on the Berkeley campus, which addresses the multicore challenge to software and hardware. He co-authored two books on computer architecture and organization with John Hennessy, President of Stanford University. In 2006, Patterson was elected to the American Academy of Arts and Sciences and the National Academy of Sciences. His many awards

include Japan's Computer & Communication Award (shared with Hennessy in 2007), the ACM Distinguished Service Award, and the ACM-IEEE Eckert-Mauchly Award (both in 2008).

For more information:
http://www.eecs.berkeley.edu/~pattrsn/

David Patterson shared the IEEE John von Neumann Medal in 2000 with John Hennessy for "creating a revolution in computer architecture through their exploration, popularization, and commercialization of architectural innovations."

Photo courtesy of David Patterson, University of California, Berkeley

Raid Level 0 is well suited to transfer large quantities of noncritical data. In the configuration shown in Figure 7.21, when the operating system issues a read command for the first four strips, all four strips can be transferred in parallel, improving system performance. Level 0 works well in combination with other configurations, as we'll see in our discussion about Nested RAID Levels.

RAID promotes the much-needed concept of data redundancy to help systems recover from hardware failure.

(figure 7.21)

RAID Level 0 with four disks in the array. Strips 1, 2, 3, and 4 make up a stripe. Strips 5, 6, 7, and 8 make up another stripe, and so on.

Level One

RAID Level 1 uses striping and is called a mirrored configuration because it provides redundancy by having a duplicate set of all data in a mirror array of disks, which acts as a backup system in the event of hardware failure. If one drive should fail, the system would immediately retrieve the data from its backup disk, making this a very reliable system. Figure 7.22 shows a RAID Level 1 configuration with three disks on each identical array: main and mirror.

(figure 7.22)

RAID Level 1 with three disks in the main array and three corresponding disks in the backup array, the mirrored array.

Using Level 1, read requests can be satisfied by either disk containing the requested data. The choice of disk could minimize seek time and rotational delay. The disadvantage is that write requests require twice as much *effort* because data must be written twice, once to each set of disks. However, this does not require twice the amount of *time* because both writes can be done in parallel.

Level 1 is an expensive system to construct because it requires twice the disk capacity of a Level 0 system, but its advantage of improved reliability makes it ideal for data-critical, real-time systems.

Level Two

RAID Level 2 uses very small strips (often the size of a byte or a word) and a Hamming code to provide error detection and correction, or redundancy. A **Hamming code** is a coding scheme that adds extra, redundant bits to the data and is therefore able to correct single-bit errors and detect double-bit errors.

Level 2 is an expensive and complex configuration to implement because the number of disks in the array depends on the size of the strip, and all drives must be highly synchronized in both rotational movement and arm positioning. For example, if each strip is 4 bits, then the Hamming code adds three parity bits in positions 1, 2, and 4 of the newly created 7-bit data item. In the example of RAID Level 2 shown in Figure 7.23, the array has seven disks, one for each bit. The advantage is that if a drive malfunctions, only one bit would be affected, and the data could be quickly corrected.

(figure 7.23)

RAID Level 2. Seven disks are needed in the array to store a 4-bit data item, one for each bit and three for the parity bits. Each disk stores either a bit or a parity bit based on the Hamming code used for redundancy.

RAID Level 2 - Hamming Code

Level Three

RAID Level 3 is a modification of Level 2; it requires only one disk for redundancy. Only one parity bit is computed for each strip, and it is stored in the designated redundant disk. Figure 7.24 shows a five-disk array that can store 4-bit strips and their parity bit.

If a drive malfunctions, the RAID controller considers all bits coming from that drive to be 0, and it notes the location of the damaged bit. Therefore, if a data item being

(figure 7.24)

RAID Level 3. A 4-bit data item is stored in the first four disks of the array. The fifth disk is used to store the parity for the stored data item.

read has a parity error, then the controller knows that the bit from the faulty drive should have been a 1 and corrects it. If data is written to an array that has a malfunctioning disk, the controller keeps the parity consistent so data can be regenerated when the array is restored. The system returns to normal when the failed disk is replaced and its contents are regenerated on the new disk.

Level Four

RAID Level 4 uses the same strip scheme found in Levels 0 and 1, but it computes a parity for each strip, and then it stores these parities in the corresponding strip in the designated parity disk. Figure 7.25 shows a Level 4 disk array with four disks; the first three hold data, while the fourth stores the parities for the corresponding strips on the first three disks.

(figure 7.25)

RAID Level 4. The array contains four disks: the first three are used to store data strips, and the fourth is used to store the parity of those strips.

The advantage of Level 4 is that if any one drive fails, data can be restored using the bits in the parity disk. Parity is computed every time a write command is executed. However, if data is rewritten, then the RAID controller must update both the data and parity strips. Therefore, the parity disk is accessed with every write (or rewrite) operation, sometimes causing a bottleneck in the system.

Level Five

RAID Level 5 is a modification of Level 4. Instead of designating one disk for storing parities, it distributes the parity strips across the disks, which avoids the bottleneck problem in Level 4. Its disadvantage is that regenerating data from a failed drive is more complicated. Figure 7.26 shows a Level 5 disk array with four disks.

(figure 7.26)

RAID Level 5 with four disks. Notice how the parity strips are distributed among the disks.

Level Six

RAID Level 6 was introduced by the Berkeley research team in a paper that followed its original outline of RAID levels. This system provides an extra degree of error detection and correction because it requires two different parity calculations. One calculation is the same as that used in Levels 4 and 5; the other is an independent data-check algorithm. Both parity calculations are distributed on separate disks across the array and are stored in the strip that corresponds to the data strips, as shown in Figure 7.27. The advantage here is that the double parity allows for data restoration even if two disks fail.

(figure 7.27)

RAID Level 6. Notice how parity strips and data check (DC) strips are distributed across the disks.

However, the redundancy increases the time needed to write data because each write operation affects two parity strips. In addition, Level 6 requires that two disks are dedicated to parity strips and not data, which therefore reduces the number of data disks in the array but increases the investment in hardware.

Nested RAID Levels

Nested levels, also called hybrid levels, are complex RAID configurations created by combining multiple standard levels. For example, a RAID Level 10 system consists of a Level 1 system mirrored to a second Level 1 system, both controlled by a single Level 0 system, as shown in Figure 7.28. Some RAID combinations are listed in Table 7.8.

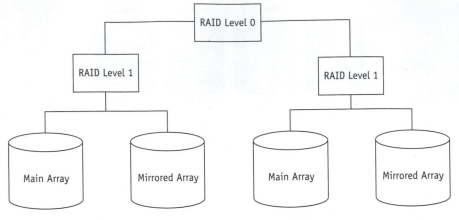

(figure 7.28)

A RAID Level 10 system.

Nested RAID Levels increase the complexity of disk management, but they also add protection against data loss—a benefit that for some system owners outweighs the increase in overhead.

Nested Level	Combinations
01 (or 0+1)	A Level 1 system consisting of multiple Level 0 systems
10 (or 1+0)	A Level 0 system consisting of multiple Level 1 systems
03 (or 0+3)	A Level 3 system consisting of multiple Level 0 systems
30 (or 3+0)	A Level 0 system consisting of multiple Level 3 systems
50 (or 5+0)	A Level 0 system consisting of multiple Level 5 systems
60 (or 6+0)	A Level 0 system consisting of multiple Level 6 systems

(table 7.8)

Some common nested RAID configurations, always indicated with two numbers that signify the combination of levels. For example, neither Level 01 nor Level 10 is the same as Level 1.

Conclusion

The Device Manager's job is to manage every system device as effectively as possible despite the unique characteristics of each. The devices can have varying speeds and degrees of sharability; some can handle direct access and some only sequential access. For magnetic media, they can have one or many read/write heads, and the heads can be in a fixed position for optimum speed or able to move across the surface for optimum storage space. For optical media, the Device Manager tracks storage locations and adjusts the disc's speed so data is recorded and retrieved correctly. For flash memory, the Device Manager tracks every USB device and assures that data is sent and received correctly.

Balancing the demand for these devices is a complex task that's divided among several hardware components: channels, control units, and the devices themselves. The success of the I/O subsystem depends on the communications that link these parts.

In this chapter we reviewed several seek strategies, each with distinct advantages and disadvantages, as shown in Table 7.9.

Strategy	Advantages	Disadvantages
FCFS	• Easy to implement • Sufficient for light loads	• Doesn't provide best average service • Doesn't maximize throughput
SSTF	• Throughput better than FCFS • Tends to minimize arm movement • Tends to minimize response time	• May cause starvation of some requests • Localizes under heavy loads
SCAN/LOOK	• Eliminates starvation • Throughput similar to SSTF • Works well with light to moderate loads	• Needs directional bit • More complex algorithm to implement • Increased overhead
N-Step SCAN	• Easier to implement than SCAN	• The most recent requests wait longer than with SCAN
C-SCAN/C-LOOK	• Works well with moderate to heavy loads • No directional bit • Small variance in service time • C-LOOK doesn't travel to unused tracks	• May not be fair to recent requests for high-numbered tracks • More complex algorithm than N-Step SCAN, causing more overhead

(table 7.9)

Comparison of hard disk drive seek strategies discussed in this chapter.

Our discussion of RAID included a comparison of the considerable strengths and weaknesses of each level, and combinations of levels, as well as the potential boost to system reliability and error correction that each represents.

Thus far in this text, we've reviewed three of the operating system's managers: the Memory Manager, the Processor Manager, and the Device Manager. In the next chapter, we'll meet the fourth, the File Manager, which is responsible for the health and well-being of every file used by the system, including the system's files, those submitted by users, and those generated as output.

Key Terms

access time: the total time required to access data in secondary storage.

blocking: a storage-saving and I/O-saving technique that groups individual records into a block that's stored and retrieved as a unit.

C-LOOK: a scheduling strategy for direct access storage devices that's an optimization of C-SCAN.

C-SCAN: a scheduling strategy for direct access storage devices that's used to optimize seek time. It's an abbreviation for circular-SCAN.

Channel Status Word (CSW): a data structure that contains information indicating the condition of the I/O path, including three bits for the three components of the I/O subsystem—one each for the channel, control unit, and device.

dedicated device: a device that can be assigned to only one job at a time; it serves that job for the entire time the job is active.

direct access storage device (DASD): any secondary storage device that can directly read or write to a specific place. Sometimes called a random access storage device.

direct memory access (DMA): an I/O technique that allows a control unit to access main memory directly and transfer data without the intervention of the CPU.

first-come, first-served (FCFS): the simplest scheduling algorithm for direct access storage devices that satisfies track requests in the order in which they are received.

flash memory: a type of nonvolatile memory used as a secondary storage device that can be erased and reprogrammed in blocks of data.

Hamming code: an error-detecting and error-correcting code that greatly improves the reliability of data, named after mathematician Richard Hamming, its inventor.

I/O channel: a specialized programmable unit placed between the CPU and the control units, which synchronizes the fast speed of the CPU with the slow speed of the I/O device and vice versa, making it possible to overlap I/O operations with CPU operations.

I/O channel program: the program that controls the input/output channels.

I/O control unit: the hardware unit containing the electronic components common to one type of I/O device, such as a disk drive.

I/O device handler: the module within the operating system that processes the I/O interrupts, handles error conditions, and provides detailed scheduling algorithms that are extremely device dependent.

I/O scheduler: one of the modules of the I/O subsystem that allocates the input/output devices, control units, and channels.

I/O subsystem: a collection of modules within the operating system that controls all I/O requests.

I/O traffic controller: one of the modules of the I/O subsystem that monitors the status of every device, control unit, and channel.

interblock gap (IBG): an unused space between blocks of records on a magnetic tape. It facilitates the tape's start/stop operations.

interrecord gap (IRG): an unused space between records on a magnetic tape. It facilitates the tape's start/stop operations.

interrupt: a hardware signal that suspends execution of a program and activates the execution of a special program known as the interrupt handler.

lands: flat surface areas on the reflective layer of an optical disc. Contrasts with pits.

LOOK: a scheduling strategy for direct access storage devices that's used to optimize seek time. Sometimes known as the elevator algorithm.

N-step SCAN: a variation of the SCAN scheduling strategy for direct access storage devices that's used to optimize seek times.

Parity bit: an extra bit added to a character, word, or other data unit and used for error checking.

pits: tiny depressions on the reflective layer of an optical disc. Contrasts with lands.

RAID: acronym for redundant array of independent disks; a group of hard disks controlled in such a way that they speed read access of data on secondary storage devices and aid data recovery.

rotational ordering: an algorithm used to reorder record requests within tracks to optimize search time.

SCAN: a scheduling strategy for direct access storage devices that's used to optimize seek time. The most common variations are N-step SCAN and C-SCAN.

search time: the time it takes to rotate the disk until the requested record is under the read/write head. Also known as rotational delay.

secondary storage: the place where data is stored in nonvolatile media, such as disks and flash memory. Contrasts with primary storage, a term for main memory.

seek strategy: a predetermined policy used by the I/O device handler to optimize seek times.

seek time: the time required to position the read/write head on the proper track from the time the I/O request is received by the device.

sequential access storage device: any medium that allows records to be accessed only in a sequential manner, one after the other.

shared device: a device that can be assigned to several active jobs at the same time.

shortest seek time first (SSTF): a scheduling strategy for direct access storage devices that's used to optimize seek time. The track requests are ordered so the one closest to the currently active track is satisfied first and the ones farthest away are made to wait.

stripe: a set of consecutive strips across RAID disks; the strips contain data bits and sometimes parity bits depending on the RAID level.

track: a path on a storage medium along which data is recorded.

transfer rate: the rate at which data is transferred to or from storage media.

transfer time: the time required for data to be transferred between secondary storage and main memory.

universal serial bus (USB) controller: the hardware interface between the operating system, device drivers, and applications that read and write to devices connected to the computer through a USB port.

virtual device: a dedicated device that has been transformed into a shared device through the use of spooling techniques.

Interesting Searches

For more background on a few of the topics discussed in this chapter, begin a search with these terms.

- Solid State Hard Drive
- Circular Buffers
- Universal Serial Bus (USB) Technology
- RAID Level Performance
- Blu-ray Storage Media

Exercises

Research Topics

A. To simplify our explanations about magnetic disk access speeds in this chapter, we use rotation speeds of 3600 rpm and sustained data transfer rates on the order of 1 megabyte per second. Current technology has pushed those numbers higher. Research current rotation speeds and data transfer rates for magnetic disks. Cite your sources, dates of the published research, and the type of computer (laptop, desktop, and so on) that uses that disk.

B. In this chapter, we describe liner recording on magnetic tape. Advances in tape development have been tremendous in recent years. Research the area of serpentine recording methods and compare the speed and space issues for both options. In your opinion, which would be preferable? Cite your sources.

Exercises

1. Briefly explain the differences between seek time and search time. In your opinion, why do some people confuse the two?

2. Given the following characteristics for a magnetic tape using linear recording as described in this chapter:

   Density = 1600 bpi

   Speed = 1500 inches/second

   Size = 2400 feet

   Start/stop time = 4 ms

   Number of records to be stored = 200,000 records

   Size of each record = 160 bytes

   Block size = 10 logical records

   IBG = 0.5 inch

Find the following:

a. Number of blocks needed

b. Size of the block in bytes

c. Time required to read one block

d. Time required to write all of the blocks

e. Amount of tape used for data only, in inches

f. Total amount of tape used (data + IBGs), in inches

3. Given the following characteristics for a magnetic disk pack with 10 platters yielding 18 recordable surfaces (not using the top and bottom surfaces):

Rotational speed = 13 ms

Transfer rate = 0.15 ms/track

Density per track = 19,000 bytes

Number of records to be stored = 200,000 records

Size of each record = 160 bytes

Block size = 10 logical records

Number of tracks per surface = 500

Find the following:

a. Number of blocks per track

b. Waste per track

c. Number of tracks required to store the entire file

d. Total waste to store the entire file

e. Time to write all of the blocks (Use rotational speed; ignore the time it takes to move to the next track.)

f. Time to write all of the records if they're not blocked. (Use rotational speed; ignore the time it takes to move to the next track.)

g. Optimal blocking factor to minimize wasted space

h. What would be the answer to (e) if the time it takes to move to the next track were 5 ms?

i. What would be the answer to (f) if the time it takes to move to the next track were 5 ms?

4. Given that it takes 1.75 ms to travel from one track to the next of a hard drive; that the arm is originally positioned at Track 15 moving toward the low-numbered tracks; and that you are using the LOOK scheduling policy: Compute the total seek time to satisfy the following requests—4, 40, 35, 11, 14, and 7. Assume all requests are initially present in the wait queue. (Ignore rotational time and transfer time; just consider seek time.)

5. Describe how secondary storage differs from primary storage and give an example of each.

6. Consider a virtual cylinder identical to the one shown in Figure 7.12 with the following characteristics: seek time is 4 ms/track, search time is 1.7 ms/sector, and data transfer time is 0.9 ms. Calculate the resulting seek time, search time, data transfer time, and total time for the following Request List, assuming that the read/write head begins at Track 0, Sector 0. Finally, calculate the total time required to meet all of these requests.

Track	Sector
1	0
1	4
1	0
3	1
2	4
3	0

7. Using an identical environment to the previous question, calculate the resulting seek time, search time, data transfer time, and total time for the following Request List, assuming that the read/write head begins at Track 3, Sector 0. Calculate the total time required.

Track	Sector
2	5
1	2
1	0
2	3
2	4
1	0

8. Minimizing the variance of system response time is an important goal, but it does not always prevent an occasional user from suffering indefinite postponement. If you were the system designer, what mechanism would you recommend for a disk scheduling policy to counteract this problem and still provide reasonable response time to the user population as a whole? What argument would you use with the system management to allow your changes?

9. Describe how implementation of a RAID Level 2 system would be beneficial to a university payroll system. In your own words, describe the disadvantages of such a system, if any, in that environment, and if appropriate, suggest an alternative RAID system and explain your reasoning.

Advanced Exercises

10. Explain in your own words the relationship between buffering and spooling. Suggest reasons why some people confuse the two.

11. Under light loading conditions, every disk scheduling policy discussed in this chapter tends to behave like one of the policies discussed in this chapter. Which one is it? Explain why light loading is different than heavy loading.

12. Assume you have a file of 10 records (identified as A, B, C, ... J) to be stored on a disk that holds 10 records per track. Once the file is stored, the records will be accessed sequentially: A, B, C, ... J. It takes 1 ms to transfer each record from the disk to main memory. It takes 2 ms to process each record once it has been transferred into memory and the next record is not accessed until the current one has been processed. It takes 10 ms for the disk to complete one rotation. Suppose you store the records in the order given: A, B, C, ... J. Compute how long it will take to process all 10 records. Break up your computation into (1) the time to transfer a record, (2) the time to process a record, and (3) the time to access the next record.

13. Given the same situation described in the previous exercise:

    a. Organize the records so that they're stored in non-alphabetical order (not A, B, C, ... J) to reduce the time it takes to process them sequentially in alphabetical order.

    b. Compute how long it will take to process all 10 records using this new order. Break up your computation into (1) the time to transfer a record, (2) the time to process a record, and (3) the time to access the next record.

14. Track requests are not usually equally or evenly distributed. For example, the tracks where the disk directory resides are accessed more often than those where the user's files reside. Suppose that you know that 50 percent of the requests are for a small, fixed number of cylinders.

    a. Which one of the scheduling policies presented in this chapter would be the best under these conditions?

    b. Can you design one that would be better?

15. Find evidence of the latest technology for optical disc storage and complete the following chart for three optical storage devices. Cite your sources and the dates of their publication.

Type	Transfer Rate (bytes per second)	Storage Capacity	Average Access Time	Cost in Dollars
CD-RW				
DVD-RW				
Blu-ray				

16. Give an example of an environment or application that best matches the characteristics of each of the following RAID levels:

    a. Level 0

    b. Level 1

    c. Level 3

    d. Level 5

    e. Level 6

Programming Exercise

17. Write a program that will simulate the FCFS, SSTF, LOOK, and C-LOOK seek optimization strategies. Assume that:

    a. The disk's outer track is the 0 track and the disk contains 200 tracks per surface. Each track holds eight sectors numbered 0 through 7.

    b. A seek takes $10 + 0.1 * T$ ms, where T is the number of tracks of motion from one request to the next, and 10 is a movement time constant.

    c. One full rotation takes 7 ms.

    d. Transfer time is 1.2 ms per sector.

    Use the following data to test your program:

Arrival Time	Track Requested	Sector Requested
0	45	0
23	132	6
25	20	2
29	23	1
35	198	7
45	170	5
57	180	3
83	78	4
88	73	5
95	150	7

For comparison purposes, compute the average, variance, and standard deviation of the time required to accommodate all requests under each of the strategies. Consolidate your results into a table.

Optional: Run your program again with randomly generated data and compare your results. Use a Poisson distribution for the arrival times and uniform distributions for the tracks and sectors. Use the same data for each strategy, and generate enough requests to obtain a 95% confidence interval for the mean access times. Recommend the best policy and explain why.

Chapter 8

File Management

DEVICE MANAGEMENT

Paper Storage Media ← - - - - Sequential Access

Magnetic Tape Storage Media

Magnetic Disk Storage Media ← - - - Direct Access

Optical Disc Storage

> *"Knowledge is of two kinds. We know a subject ourselves, or we know where we can find information upon it. "*
>
> —Samuel Johnson (1709–1784)

Learning Objectives

After completing this chapter, you should be able to describe:

• The fundamentals of file management

• File naming conventions, including the role of extensions

• The difference between fixed-length and variable-length record format

• The advantages and disadvantages of several file storage techniques

• Comparisons of sequential and direct file access

• Access control techniques and how they compare

• The role of data compression in file storage

The File Manager controls every file in the system. In this chapter we learn how files are organized logically, how they're stored physically, how they're accessed, and who is allowed to access them. We'll also study the interaction between the File Manager and the Device Manager.

There are a number of variables that directly affect the efficiency of the File Manager, notably these:

- how the system's files are organized (sequential, direct, or indexed sequential)
- how they're stored (contiguously, not contiguously, or indexed)
- how each file's records are structured (fixed-length or variable-length)
- how user access to all files is protected (controlled or not controlled)

The File Manager

The File Manager (the file management system) is the software responsible for creating, deleting, modifying, and controlling access to files—as well as for managing the resources used by the files. The File Manager provides support for libraries of programs and data, doing so in close collaboration with the Device Manager.

The File Manager has a complex job. It's in charge of the system's physical components, its information resources, and the policies used to store and distribute the files. To carry out its responsibilities, it must perform these four tasks:

1. Keep track of where each file is stored.

2. Use a policy that will determine where and how the files will be stored, making sure to efficiently use the available storage space and provide easy access to the files.

3. Allocate each file when a user has been cleared for access to it and then track its use.

4. Deallocate the file when the file is to be returned to storage and communicate its availability to others that may be waiting for it.

For example, the file system is like a library, with the File Manager playing the part of the librarian who performs the same four tasks:

1. A librarian uses the catalog to keep track of each item in the collection; each entry lists the call number and the details that help patrons find the books they want.

2. The library relies on a policy to store everything in the collection, including oversized books, journals, DVDs, and maps. And they must be physically arranged so people can find what they need.

3. When it's requested, the item is retrieved from its shelf and the borrower's name is noted in the circulation records.

4. When the item is returned, the librarian makes the appropriate notation in the circulation records and puts it back on the shelf.

In a computer system, the File Manager keeps track of its files with directories that contain the filename, its physical location in secondary storage, and important information about it.

The File Manager's policy determines where each file is stored and how the system and its users will be able to access them simply—via commands that are independent from device details. In addition, the policy must determine who will have access to what material, and this involves two factors: flexibility of access to the information and its subsequent protection. The File Manager does this by allowing access to shared files, providing distributed access, and allowing users to browse through public directories. Meanwhile, the operating system must protect its files against system malfunctions and provide security checks via account numbers and passwords to preserve the integrity of the data and safeguard against tampering. These protection techniques are explained later in this chapter.

The computer system *allocates* a file by activating the appropriate secondary storage device and loading the file into memory while updating its records of who is using what file.

Finally, the File Manager *deallocates* a file by updating the file tables and rewriting the file (if revised) to the secondary storage device. Any processes waiting to access the file are then notified of its availability.

Before we continue, let's take a minute to define some basic file elements, illustrated in Figure 8.1, that relate to our discussion of the File Manager.

(figure 8.1)

Files are made up of records. Records consist of fields.

	Field A	Field B	Field C	Field D
Record 19 →	Field A	Field B	Field C	Field D
Record 20 →	Field A	Field B	Field C	Field D
Record 21 →	Field A	Field B	Field C	Field D
Record 22 →	Field A	Field B	Field C	Field D

A **field** is a group of related bytes that can be identified by the user with a name, type, and size. A **record** is a group of related fields.

A **file** is a group of related records that contains information to be used by specific application programs to generate reports. This type of file contains data and is sometimes called a flat file because it has no connections to other files; unlike databases, it has no dimensionality.

A **database** is a group of related files that are connected at various levels to offer flexible access to the data stored in it. While databases can appear to the File Manager to be an ordinary type of file, in reality they can be quite complex. If the database requires a specific structure, the File Manager must be able to support it.

Program files contain instructions and data files contain data; however, as far as storage is concerned, the File Manager treats them both exactly the same way.

Directories (also known as folders) are special files that contain listings of filenames and their attributes.

C. Gordon Bell (1934–)

Gordon Bell, a pioneer in high-performance and parallel computing, was the architect for several mini-computers and timesharing computers and led development of the VAX computing environment. He is credited with formulating Bell's Law of Computer Classes, which describes how groups of computing systems evolve, from birth to possible extinction. Bell was the first recipient of the IEEE John von Neumann Medal in 1992 for "innovative contributions to computer architecture and design." He has been named a fellow of numerous organizations, including the IEEE, ACM, and National Academy of Sciences. As of 2012, he continues his work a principal researcher at Microsoft Research Silicon Valley Laboratory in San Francisco.

For more information:
http://research.microsoft.com/en-us/um/people/gbell/bio.htm

The Gordon Bell Prizes (administered jointly by the ACM and IEEE) are awarded each year to recognize outstanding achievement in high-performance computing, with particular emphasis on rewarding innovation in applying high-performance computing to applications in science. (For details, see http://awards.acm.org.)

Courtesy of Gordon Bell

Interacting with the File Manager

The File Manager responds to specific proprietary commands to perform necessary actions. As shown in Figure 8.2, some of the most common commands are OPEN, DELETE, RENAME, and COPY. In addition to these examples, the File Manager extrapolates other system-specific actions from the instructions it receives. For example, although there is no explicit command to create a new file; this is what happens the first time a user gives the command to "save" a new file—one that has not been saved previously. Therefore, this is interpreted as a CREATE command. In some operating systems, when a user issues the command NEW (to open a New file), this indicates to the File Manager that a file must be created.

(figure 8.2)

Typical menu of file options.

What's involved in creating a new file? That depends on how the writers of the operating system set things up. If the File Manager is required to provide detailed instructions for each system device (how to start it, get it to move to the correct place where the desired record is located, and when to stop), then the program is considered device dependent. More commonly, if that information is already available, usually in a **device driver** for each available device, then the program is considered **device independent**.

Therefore, to access a file, the user doesn't need to know its exact physical location on the disk pack (such as the cylinder, surface, and sector), the medium in which it's stored (archival tape, magnetic disk, optical disc, or flash storage), or the network specifics. That's fortunate because file access can be a complex process. Each logical command is broken down into a sequence of signals that trigger the step-by-step actions performed by the device and supervise the progress of the operation by testing the device's status. For example, when a program issues a command to read a record from a typical hard disk drive, the READ instruction can consist of the following steps:

1. Move the read/write heads to the cylinder or track where the record is to be found.
2. Wait for the rotational delay until the sector containing the desired record passes under the read/write head.
3. Activate the appropriate read/write head and read the record.
4. Transfer the record to main memory.
5. Set a flag to indicate that the device is now free to satisfy another request.

Meantime, while all of this is going on, the system must remain vigilant for error conditions that might occur.

Typical Volume Configuration

Normally the active files for a computer system reside on secondary storage units. Some systems use static storage, while others feature removable storage units—such as CDs, DVDs, USB devices, and other removable media—so files that aren't frequently used can be stored offline and mounted only when they are specifically requested.

Each storage unit, whether it's removable or not, is considered a **volume**, and each volume can contain several files, so they're called "multi-file volumes." However, some files are extremely large and are contained in several volumes; not surprisingly, these are called "multi-volume files."

Each volume in the system is given a name. The File Manager writes this name and other descriptive information, as shown in Figure 8.3, on an easy-to-access place—the innermost part of the CD or DVD or the first sector of the outermost track of the disk pack. Once the volume is identified, the operating system can begin interacting with the storage unit.

> ✔ Network resources are typically given a logical volume label for easy identification, such as z, x, w, etc.

(figure 8.3)

The volume descriptor, which is stored at the beginning of each volume, includes this vital information about the storage unit.

A **master file directory (MFD)** is stored immediately after the volume descriptor and lists the names and characteristics of every file contained in that volume. The filenames in the MFD can refer to program files, data files, and/or system files. And if the File Manager supports subdirectories, they're listed in the MFD as well. The remainder of the volume is used for file storage.

The first operating systems supported only a single directory per volume, which contained the names of files, usually organized in alphabetical, spatial, or chronological order. Although it was simple to implement and maintain, this scheme had some major disadvantages:

- It would take a long time to search for an individual file, especially if the MFD was organized in an arbitrary order.

- If the user had more than 256 files stored in the volume, the directory space (with a 256 filename limit) would fill up before the disk storage space filled up. The user would then receive a message of "disk full" when only the directory itself was full.

- Users couldn't create subdirectories to group the files that were related.

- For systems that accommodated more than one user, none of them could keep their files private because the entire directory was freely available to every user in the group on request.

- Each program in the entire directory needed a unique name, even those directories serving many users so, for example, only one person using that directory could have a program named PROGRAM1.

This could cause havoc. Consider, for example, an introductory computer science class. What if the first person named the first programming assignment PROGRAM1? Then the rest of the class would have interesting choices: write a new program and give it a different name; write a new program and name it PROGRAM1 (which would erase the original version); or simply open PROGRAM1, modify it, and then save it with changes. With the latter option, the entire class could end up with a single, though perhaps terrific, program.

Introducing Subdirectories

File Managers create an MFD for each volume that can contain entries for both files and subdirectories. A **subdirectory** is created when a user opens an account to access the computer system. Although this user directory is treated as a file, its entry in the MFD is flagged to indicate to the File Manager that this file is really a subdirectory and has unique properties—in fact, its records are filenames that point to files.

Although this was an improvement from the single directory scheme (now all of the students could name their first programs PROGRAM1), it didn't solve the problems encountered by prolific users who wanted to group their files in a logical order to improve the accessibility and efficiency of the system.

File Managers now routinely encourage users to create their own subdirectories. For some operating systems, these subdirectories are called folders or directories. This structure is an extension of the previous two-level directory organization, and it's implemented as an upside-down tree, as shown in Figure 8.4.

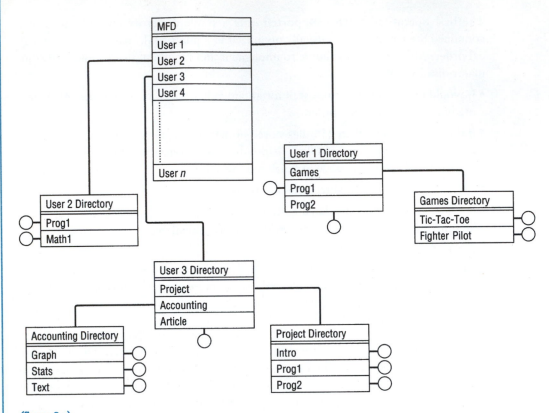

(figure 8.4)

File directory tree structure. The "root" is the MFD shown at the top, each node is a directory file, and each branch is a directory entry pointing to either another directory or to a real file. All program and data files subsequently added to the tree are the leaves, represented by circles.

Tree structures allow the system to efficiently search individual directories because there are fewer entries in each directory. However, the path to the requested file may lead through several directories. For every file request, the MFD is the point of entry, even though it is usually transparent to the user—it's accessible only by the operating system. When the user wants to access a specific file, the filename is sent to the File Manager. The File Manager first searches the MFD for the user's directory, and it then searches the user's directory and any subdirectories for the requested file and its location.

Regardless of the complexity of the directory structure, each file entry in every directory contains information describing the file; it's called the file descriptor. Information typically included in a file descriptor includes the following:

- Filename—within a single directory, filenames must be unique; in some operating systems, the filenames are case sensitive

- File type—the organization and usage that are dependent on the system (for example, files and directories)
- File size—although it could be computed from other information, the size is kept here for convenience
- File location—identification of the first physical block (or all blocks) where the file is stored
- Date and time of creation
- Owner
- Protection information—access restrictions, based on who is allowed to access the file and what type of access is allowed
- Max record size—its fixed size or its maximum size, depending on the type of record

File-Naming Conventions

A file's name can be much longer than it appears. Depending on the File Manager, it can have from two to many components. The two components common to many filenames are a **relative filename** and an **extension**.

To avoid confusion, in the following discussion we'll use the term "complete filename" to identify the file's **absolute filename** (that's the long name that includes all path information), and "relative filename" to indicate the name without **path** information that appears in directory listings and folders.

The filename character limit (256 characters for some Windows operating systems) can sometimes apply to the entire path and not just to the relative filename.

The relative filename is the name that differentiates it from other files *in the same directory*. Examples can include DEPARTMENT ADDRESSES, TAXES_PHOTOG, or AUTOEXEC (although we show these in upper case, most operating systems accommodate upper and lower case). Generally, the relative filename can vary in length from one to many characters and can include letters of the alphabet, as well as digits, and some can include special characters. However, every operating system has specific rules that affect the length of the relative name and the types of characters allowed.

For example, the MS-DOS operating system introduced in 1981 and very early versions of Windows required that all file names be a maximum of eight characters followed by a period and a mandatory three-letter extension. Examples of legal names were: BOOK-14.EXE, TIGER.DOC, EXAMPL_3.TXT. This was known as the "eight dot three" (8.3) filename convention and proved to be very limiting for users and administrators alike.

Most operating systems now allow names with dozens of characters, including spaces, exclamation marks, and certain other keyboard characters, as shown in Table 8.1. The exact requirements for your system should be verified.

Some operating systems (such as UNIX, Mac OS X, and Linux) do not require an extension, while other operating systems (including Windows) do require that an

Operating System	Case Sensitive	Any Special Characters Not Allowed	Extension Required	Maximum Character Length
UNIX	Yes	*, ?, $, &, [,], /, \	No	256
Mac OS X	Yes	Colon	No	255
Windows	No	Most special characters not allowed	Yes	255/256
Linux	Yes	*, ?, $, &, [,], /, \	No	256
MS-DOS	No	Only hyphen and underline allowed	Yes	8.3

(table 8.1)

File name parameters for several operating systems.

extension be appended to the relative filename. This is usually two, three, or four characters in length and is separated from the relative name by a period; its purpose is to identify the type of file required to open it. For example, in a Windows operating system, a typical relative filename for a music file might be BASIA_TUNE.AVI. AVI is an audio visual file. Similarly, TAKE OUT MENU.RTF and EAT IN MENU.DOC have different file extensions, but both indicate to the File Manager that they can be opened with a word processing application. What happens if an extension is incorrect or unknown? In that case most operating systems ask for guidance from the user.

Some extensions (such as EXE and DLL) are restricted by certain operating systems because they serve as a signal to the system to use a specific compiler or program to run these files. These operating systems strongly discourage users from choosing those extensions for their files.

There may be other components required for a file's complete name. Here's how a file named INVENTORY_COST.DOC is identified by different operating systems:

1. Using a Windows operating system, the file's complete name is composed of its relative name and extension, preceded by the drive label and directory name:

```
C:\IMFST\FLYNN\INVENTORY_COST.DOC
```

The DOC file extension indicates to the system that the file INVENTORY_COST.DOC can be opened with a word processing application program, and it can be found in the directory IMFST, subdirectory FLYNN, in the volume residing on drive C.

2. A UNIX or Linux system might identify the file as:

```
/usr/imfst/flynn/inventory_cost.doc
```

The first entry is a forward slash (/) representing the master directory, called the *root*. Next is the name of the first subdirectory, usr/imfst, followed by a sub-subdirectory, /flynn, in this multiple directory system. The final entry is the file's relative name, inventory_cost.doc. (UNIX and Linux filenames are case sensitive and are often expressed in lowercase.)

As you can see, the names tend to grow in length as the file manager grows in flexibility.

Why don't users see the complete file name when accessing a file? First, the File Manager selects a directory for the user when the interactive session begins, so all file operations requested by that user start from this "home" or "base" directory. Second, from this home directory, the user selects a subdirectory, which is called a **current directory** or **working directory**. Thereafter, the files are presumed to be located in this current directory. Whenever a file is accessed, the user types in the relative name, and the File Manager adds the proper prefix. As long as users refer to files in the working directory, they can access their files without entering the complete name.

The concept of a current directory is based on the underlying hierarchy of a tree structure, as shown in Figure 8.4. This allows programmers to retrieve a file by typing only its relative filename:

INVENTORY_COST.DOC

and not its complete filename:

C:\IMFST\FLYNN\INVENTORY_COST.DOC

Operating systems separate file elements with delimiters. For example, some use a forward slash (/) and others use a backward slash (\).

File Organization

When we discuss file organization, we are actually talking about the arrangement of records within a file, because all files are composed of records. When a user gives a command to modify the contents of a file, it's actually a command to access records within the file.

Record Format

All files are composed of records. When a user gives a command to modify the contents of a file, it's a command to access records within the file. Within each file, the records are all presumed to have the same format: they can be of fixed length or of variable length, as shown in Figure 8.5. These records, regardless of their format, can be accessible individually or grouped into blocks—although data stored in variable length fields takes longer to access.

(figure 8.5)

Data stored in fixed length fields (top) that extends beyond the field limit is truncated. Data stored in variable length fields (bottom) is not truncated.

| Dan | Whitesto | 1243 Elem | Harrisbur | PA | 412 683-1 | |

| Dan | Whitestone | 1243 Elementary Ave. | Harrisburg | PA | 412 683-1234 |

Fixed-length records are the easiest to access directly. The critical aspect of fixed-length records is the size. If it's too small to hold the entire record, then the data that is leftover is truncated, thereby corrupting the data. But if the record size is too large—larger than the size of the data to be stored—then storage space is wasted.

Variable-length records don't leave empty storage space and don't truncate any characters, thus eliminating the two disadvantages of fixed-length records. But while they can easily be read (one after the other sequentially), they're difficult to access directly because it's hard to calculate exactly where each record is located. That's why they're used most frequently in files that are likely to be accessed sequentially, such as text files and program files or files that use an index to access their records. The record format, how it's blocked, and other related information is kept in the file descriptor.

The amount of space that's actually used to store the supplementary information varies from system to system and conforms to the physical limitations of the storage medium, as we see later in this chapter.

Physical File Organization

The physical organization of a file has to do with the way records are arranged and the characteristics of the medium used to store it.

On magnetic disks (hard drives), files can be organized in one of several ways: sequential, direct, or indexed sequential. To select the best of these file organizations, the programmer or analyst usually considers these practical characteristics:

• Volatility of the data—the frequency with which additions and deletions are made
• Activity of the file—the percentage of records accessed during a given run
• Size of the file
• Response time—the amount of time the user is willing to wait before the requested operation is completed (especially crucial when doing time-sensitive searches)

Sequential record organization is by far the easiest to implement because records are stored and retrieved serially, one after the other. To find a specific record, the file is searched from its beginning until the requested record is found.

To speed the process, some optimization features may be built into the system. One is to select a key field from the record and then sort the records by that field before storing them. Later, when a user requests a specific record, the system searches only the key field of each record in the file. The search is ended when either an exact match is found or the key field for the requested record is smaller than the value of the record last compared. If this happens, the message "record not found" is sent to the user and the search is terminated.

Although this technique aids the search process, it complicates file maintenance because the original order must be preserved every time records are added or deleted. And to preserve the physical order, the file must be completely rewritten or maintained in a sorted fashion every time it's updated.

A **direct record organization** uses direct access files, which, of course, can be implemented only on DASDs—direct access storage devices (discussed in Chapter 7). These files give users the flexibility of accessing any record in any order without having to begin a search from the beginning of the file to do so. It's also known as "random organization," and its files are called "random access files."

Records are identified by their **relative addresses**—their addresses relative to the beginning of the file. These **logical addresses** are computed when the records are stored and then again when the records are retrieved.

The method used is quite straightforward. The user identifies a field (or combination of fields) in the record format and designates it as the **key field** because it uniquely identifies each record. The program used to store the data follows a set of instructions, called a **hashing algorithm**, which transforms each key into a number: the record's logical address. This is given to the File Manager, which takes the necessary steps to translate the logical address into a physical address (cylinder, surface, and record numbers), preserving the file organization. The same procedure is used to retrieve a record.

A direct access file can also be accessed sequentially, by starting at the first relative address and going to each record down the line.

Direct access files can be updated more quickly than sequential files because records can be quickly rewritten to their original addresses after modifications have been made. And there's no need to preserve the order of the records, so adding or deleting them takes very little time.

For example, data for a telephone mail-order firm must be accessed quickly so customer information can be retrieved quickly. To do so, they can use hashing algorithms to directly access their data. Let's say you're placing an order, and you're asked for your postal code and house number (let's say they are 15213 and 2737, respectively). The program that retrieves information from the data file uses that key in a hashing algorithm to calculate the logical address where your record is stored. So when the order clerk types 152132737, the screen soon shows a list of all current customers whose customer numbers generated the same logical address. If you're in the database, the clerk knows right away. If not, you will be soon.

Databases use a hash table to speed up access to data records. Using a hashing algorithm, each record is uniquely identified, and the hash table contains pointers to each record.

The problem with hashing algorithms is that several records with unique keys (such as customer numbers) may generate the same logical address—and then there's a collision, as shown in Figure 8.6. When that happens, the program must generate another logical address before presenting it to the File Manager for storage. Records that collide are stored in an overflow area that was set aside when the file was created. Although the program does all the work of linking the records from the overflow area to their corresponding logical address, the File Manager must handle the physical allocation of space.

Records
2737 Highland Ave.
15212

2737 Anderson Ave.
15213

2737 Boyd Rd.
15213

2737 Glen St.
15213

2737 Balsam Way
15214

Logical Addresses
152122737

152132737

152142737

(figure 8.6)

The hashing algorithm causes a collision. Using a combination of street address and postal code, it generates the same logical address (152132737) for three different records.

The maximum size of the file is established when it's created. If either the file fills to its maximum capacity or the number of records in the overflow area becomes too large, then retrieval efficiency is lost.

At that time, the file must be reorganized and rewritten, which requires intervention by the File Manager.

Indexed sequential record organization combines the best of sequential and direct access. It's created and maintained through an Indexed Sequential Access Method (ISAM) application, which removes the burden of handling overflows and preserves record order from the shoulders of the programmer.

This type of organization doesn't create collisions because it doesn't use the result of the hashing algorithm to generate a record's address. Instead, it uses this information to generate an index file, through which the records are retrieved. This organization divides an ordered sequential file into blocks of equal size. Their size is determined by the File Manager to take advantage of physical storage devices and to optimize retrieval strategies. Each entry in the index file contains the highest record key and the physical location of the data block where this record, and the records with smaller keys, are stored.

Therefore, to access any record in the file, the system begins by searching the index file and then goes to the physical location indicated at that entry. We can say, then, that the index file acts as a pointer to the data file. An indexed sequential file also has overflow areas, but they're spread throughout the file, perhaps every few records, so expansion of existing records can take place, and new records can be located in close physical sequence as well as in logical sequence. Another overflow area is located apart from the main data area, but is used only when the other overflow areas are completely filled. We call this the overflow of last resort.

This last-resort overflow area can store records added during the lifetime of the file. The records are kept in logical order by the software package without much effort on the part of the programmer. Of course, when too many records have been added here, the retrieval process slows down because the search for a record has to go from the index to the main data area and eventually to the overflow area.

When retrieval time becomes too slow, the file has to be reorganized. That's a job that, although it's not as tedious as reorganizing direct access files, is usually performed by maintenance software.

For most dynamic files, indexed sequential is the organization of choice because it allows both direct access to a few requested records and sequential access to many.

Physical Storage Allocation

The File Manager must work with files not just as whole units but also as logical units or records. By putting individual records into blocks, some efficiency can be gained. Records within a file must have the same format, but they can vary in length, as shown in Figure 8.7.

In turn, records are subdivided into fields. In most cases, their structure is managed by application programs and not by the operating system. An exception is made for those systems that are heavily oriented to database applications, where the File Manager handles field structure.

So when we talk about file storage, we're actually referring to record storage. How are the records within a file stored? Looked at this way, the File Manager and Device Manager have to cooperate to ensure successful storage and retrieval of records. In Chapter 7 on device management, we introduce the concept of logical versus physical records; this theme recurs here from the point of view of the File Manager.

(figure 8.7)

Every record in a file must have the same format but can be of different sizes, as shown in these five examples of the most common record formats. The supplementary information in (b), (c), (d), and (e) is provided by the File Manager, when the record is stored.

Contiguous Storage

When records use **contiguous storage**, they're stored one after the other. This was the scheme used in early operating systems. It's very simple to implement and manage. Any record can be found and read, once its starting address and size are known. This makes the directory very streamlined. Its second advantage is ease of direct access because every part of the file is stored in the same compact area.

The primary disadvantage is that a file can't be expanded unless there's empty space available immediately following it, as shown in Figure 8.8. Therefore, room for expansion must be provided when the file is created. If there's not enough room, the entire file must be recopied to a larger section of the disk every time records are added. The second disadvantage is fragmentation (slivers of unused storage space), which can be overcome by compacting and rearranging files. And, of course, the files can't be accessed while compaction is taking place.

Free Space	File A Record 1	File A Record 2	File A Record 3	File A Record 4	File A Record 5	File B Record 1	File B Record 2	File B Record 3	File B Record 4	Free Space	File C Record 1

(figure 8.8)

With contiguous file storage, File A can't be expanded without being rewritten to a larger storage area. File B can be expanded, by only one record replacing the free space preceding File C.

The File Manager keeps track of the empty storage areas by treating them as files—they're entered in the directory but are flagged to differentiate them from real files. Usually the directory is kept in order by sector number, so adjacent empty areas can be combined into one large free space.

Noncontiguous Storage

Noncontiguous storage allocation allows files to use any storage space available on the disk. A file's records are stored in a contiguous manner, only if there's enough empty space. Any remaining records and all other additions to the file are stored in other sections of the disk. In some systems, these are called the **extents** of the file and are linked together with pointers. The physical size of each extent is determined by the operating system and is usually 256—or some other power of two—bytes.

File extents are usually linked in one of two ways. Linking can take place at the storage level, where each extent points to the next one in the sequence, as shown in Figure 8.9. The directory entry consists of the filename, the storage location of the first extent, the location of the last extent, and the total number of extents not counting the first.

(figure 8.9)

Noncontiguous file storage with linking taking place at the storage level. File 1 starts in address 2 and continues in addresses 8, 20, and 18. The directory lists the file's starting address, ending address, and the number of extents it uses. Each block of storage includes its address and a pointer to the next block for the file, as well as the data itself.

Directory

File No.	Start	End	No. extents
1	②	18	3
2	3	11	2

271

The alternative is for the linking to take place at the directory level, as shown in Figure 8.10. Each extent is listed with its physical address, its size, and a pointer to the next extent. A null pointer, shown in Figure 8.10 as a hyphen (-), indicates that it's the last one.

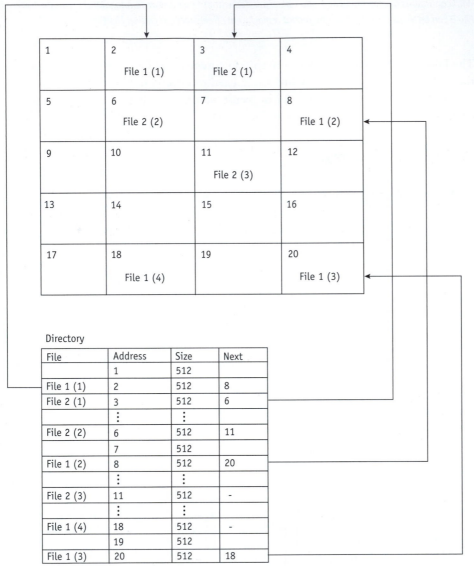

(figure 8.10)

Noncontiguous storage allocation with linking taking place at the directory level for the files shown in Figure 8.9.

Directory

File	Address	Size	Next
	1	512	
File 1 (1)	2	512	8
File 2 (1)	3	512	6
	⋮	⋮	
File 2 (2)	6	512	11
	7	512	
File 1 (2)	8	512	20
	⋮	⋮	
File 2 (3)	11	512	-
	⋮	⋮	
File 1 (4)	18	512	-
	19	512	
File 1 (3)	20	512	18

Although both noncontiguous allocation schemes eliminate external storage fragmentation and the need for compaction, they don't support direct access because there's no easy way to determine the exact location of a specific record.

Files are usually declared to be either sequential or direct when they're created, so the File Manager can select the most efficient method of storage allocation: contiguous for direct files and noncontiguous for sequential. Operating systems must have the capability to support both storage allocation schemes.

Files can then be converted from one type to another by creating a file of the desired type and copying the contents of the old file into the new file, using a program designed for that specific purpose.

Indexed Storage

Indexed storage allocation allows direct record access by bringing together the pointers linking every extent of that file into an index block. Every file has its own index block, which consists of the addresses of each disk sector that make up the file. The index lists each entry in the same order in which the sectors are linked, as shown in Figure 8.11. For example, the third entry in the index block corresponds to the third sector making up the file.

When a file is created, the pointers in the index block are all set to null. Then, as each sector is filled, the pointer is set to the appropriate sector address (to be precise, the

(figure 8.11)

Indexed storage allocation with a one-level index, allowing direct access to each record for the files shown in Figures 8.9 and 8.10.

273

address is removed from the empty space list and is copied into its position in the index block).

This scheme supports both sequential and direct access, but it doesn't necessarily improve the use of storage space, because each file must have an index block—usually the size of one disk sector. For larger files with more entries, several levels of indexes can be generated. In this case, to find a desired record, the File Manager accesses the first index (the highest level), which points to a second index (lower level), which points to an even lower-level index and eventually to the data record.

Access Methods

Access methods are dictated by a file's organization; the most flexibility is allowed with indexed sequential files and the least with sequential.

A file that has been organized in sequential fashion can support only sequential access to its records, and these records can be of either fixed or variable length, as shown in Figure 8.6. The File Manager uses the address of the last byte read to access the next sequential record. Therefore, the **current byte address (CBA)** must be updated every time a record is accessed, such as when the READ command is executed.

Figure 8.12 shows the difference between storage of fixed-length and of variable-length records.

Sequential Access

For *sequential access of fixed-length records*, the CBA is updated simply by incrementing it by the record length (RL), which is a constant:

$$CBA = CBA + RL$$

(figure 8.12)

Fixed- versus variable-length records. (a) Fixed-length records have the same number of bytes, so record length (RL) is the constant x. (b) With variable-length records, RL isn't a constant. Therefore, it's recorded on the sequential media immediately preceding each record.

For *sequential access of variable-length records*, the File Manager adds the length of the record (RL) plus the number of bytes used to hold the record length (N, which holds the value shown in Figure 8.13 as m, n, p, or q) to the CBA.

$$CBA = CBA + N + RL$$

Direct Access

Direct access is sometimes called "random access" because it allows data to be accessed in a random order. It contrasts with sequential access.

If a file is organized in direct fashion and if the records are of fixed length, it can be accessed in either direct or sequential order. In the case of *direct access with fixed-length records*, the CBA can be computed directly from the record length and the desired record number RN (information provided through the READ command) minus 1:

$$CBA = (RN - 1) * RL$$

For example, if we're looking for the beginning of the eleventh record and the fixed record length is 25 bytes, the CBA would be:

$$(11 - 1) * 25 = 250$$

However, if the file is organized for *direct access with variable-length records*, it's virtually impossible to access a record directly because the address of the desired record can't be easily computed. Therefore, to access a record, the File Manager must do a sequential search through the records. In fact, it becomes a half-sequential read through the file because the File Manager could save the address of the last record accessed, and when the next request arrives, it could search forward from the CBA— if the address of the desired record was between the CBA and the end of the file. Otherwise, the search would start from the beginning of the file. It could be said that this semi-sequential search is only semi-adequate.

An alternative is for the File Manager to keep a table of record numbers and their CBAs. Then, to fill a request, this table is searched for the exact storage location of the desired record, so the direct access reduces to a table lookup.

To avoid dealing with this problem, many systems force users to have their files organized for fixed-length records, if the records are to be accessed directly.

Records in an *indexed sequential file* can be accessed either sequentially or directly, so either of the procedures to compute the CBA presented in this section would apply, but with one extra step: the index file must be searched for the pointer to the block where the data is stored. Because the index file is smaller than the data file, it can be kept in main memory, and a quick search can be performed to locate the block where the desired record is located. Then, the block can be retrieved from secondary storage, and the beginning byte address of the record can be calculated. In systems that support

275

several levels of indexing to improve access to very large files, the index at each level must be searched before the computation of the CBA can be done. The entry point to this type of data file is usually through the index file.

As we've shown, a file's organization and the methods used to access its records are very closely intertwined; so when one talks about a specific type of organization, one is almost certainly implying a specific type of access.

Levels in a File Management System

The efficient management of files can't be separated from the efficient management of the devices that house them. This chapter and the previous one on device management present the wide range of functions that have to be organized for an I/O system to perform efficiently. In this section, we outline one of the many hierarchies used to perform those functions.

The highest level module is called the "basic file system," and it passes information through the access control verification module to the logical file system, which, in turn, notifies the physical file system, which works with the Device Manager. Figure 8.13 shows the hierarchy.

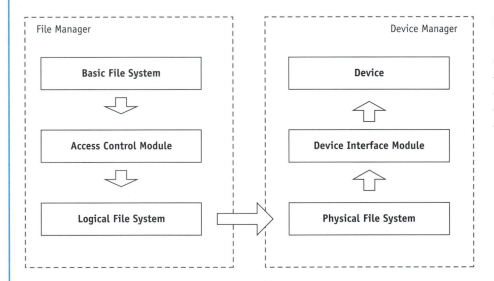

(figure 8.13)

Typical modules of a file management system showing how information is passed from the File Manager to the Device Manager.

Each level of the file management system is implemented using structured and modular programming techniques that also set up a hierarchy—that is, the higher positioned modules pass information to the lower modules, so that they, in turn, can perform the required service and continue the communication down the chain to the lowest module.

The lowest module communicates with the physical device and interacts with the Device Manager. Only then is the record made available to the user's program.

Each of the modules can be further subdivided into more specific tasks, as we can see when we follow this I/O instruction through the file management system:

READ RECORD NUMBER 7 FROM FILE CLASSES INTO STUDENT

CLASSES is the name of a direct access file previously opened for input, and STUDENT is a data record previously defined within the program and occupying specific memory locations.

Because the file has already been opened, the file directory has already been searched to verify the existence of CLASSES, and pertinent information about the file has been brought into the operating system's active file table. This information includes its record size, the address of its first physical record, its protection, and access control information, as shown in the UNIX directory listing in Table 8.2.

Access Control	No. of Links	Group	Owner	No. of Bytes	Date	Time	Filename
drwxrwxr-x	2	journal	comp	12820	Jan 10	19:32	ArtWarehouse
drwxrwxr-x	2	journal	comp	12844	Dec 15	09:59	bus_transport
-rwxr-xr-x	1	journal	comp	2705221	Mar 6	11:38	CLASSES
-rwxr--r--	1	journal	comp	12556	Feb 20	18:08	PAYroll
-rwx------	1	journal	comp	8721	Jan 17	07:32	supplier

(table 8.2)

A typical list of files on a UNIX system stored in the directory called journal. Notice that the file names can be in upper case, lower case, or a combination of both.

This information is used by the basic file system, which activates the access control verification module to verify that this user is permitted to perform this operation with this file. If access is allowed, information and control are passed along to the logical file system. If not, a message saying "access denied" is sent to the user.

Using the information passed down by the basic file system, the logical file system transforms the record number to its byte address using the familiar formula:

$$CBA = (RN - 1) * RL$$

This result, together with the address of the first physical record (and, in the case where records are blocked, the physical block size), is passed down to the physical file system, which computes the location where the desired record physically resides. If there's more than one record in that block, it computes the record's offset within that block using these formulas:

$$\text{block number} = \text{integers} \left[\frac{\text{byte address}}{\text{physical block size}} \right] + \text{address of the first physical record}$$

$$\text{offset} = \text{remainder} \left[\frac{\text{byte address}}{\text{physical block size}} \right]$$

This information is passed on to the device interface module, which, in turn, transforms the block number to the actual cylinder/surface/record combination needed to retrieve the information from the secondary storage device. Once retrieved, the device-scheduling algorithms come into play: the information is placed in a buffer and control returns to the physical file system, which copies the information into the desired memory location. Finally, when the operation is complete, the "all clear" message is passed on to all other modules.

Although we used a READ command for our example, a WRITE command is handled in the same way until the process reaches the device handler. At that point, the portion of the device interface module that handles allocation of free space, the allocation module, is called into play because it's responsible for keeping track of unused areas in each storage device.

We need to note here that verification, the process of making sure that a request is valid, occurs at every level of the file management system. The first verification occurs at the directory level when the file system checks to see if the requested file exists. The second occurs when the access control verification module determines whether access is allowed. The third occurs when the logical file system checks to see if the requested byte address is within the file's limits. Finally, the device interface module checks to see whether the storage device exists.

Therefore, the correct operation of this simple user command requires the coordinated effort of every part of the file management system.

Access Control Verification Module

The first operating systems couldn't support file sharing among users—if it had 10 users then it needed 10 copies of a compiler. Now systems require only a single copy to serve everyone, regardless of the number of active programs in the system. In fact, any file can be shared—from data files and user-owned program files to system files (if the licensing agreement allows). The advantages of file sharing are numerous. In addition to saving space, it allows for synchronization of data updates, as when two applications

Access control is a critical element of system security. It identifies who is allowed to access which files, as well as what operations that user is allowed to perform.

are updating the same data file. It also improves the efficiency of the system's resources, because if files are shared in main memory, then there's a reduction of I/O operations.

However, as often happens, progress brings problems. The disadvantage of file sharing is that the integrity of each file must be safeguarded, and that calls for control over who is allowed to access the file and what type of access is permitted. Let's explore five possible access levels that can be granted to a user for a file—the ability to READ only, WRITE only, EXECUTE only, DELETE only—or some combination of those four.

Access Control Matrix

The **access control matrix** uses a column to identify a user and a row to identify a file. Such an organization is intuitively appealing and easy to implement, but because it can grow to a huge size, it works well only for systems with few files and/or few users. The intersection of the row and column contains the access rights for that user to that file, as Table 8.3 illustrates. Notice that User 1 is allowed unlimited access to File 1, is allowed only to read and execute File 4, and is denied access to the other three files.

(table 8.3)

The access control matrix showing access rights for each user for each file.

	User 1	User 2	User 3	User 4	User 5
File 1	RWED	R-E-	----	RWE-	--E-
File 2	----	R-E-	R-E-	--E-	----
File 3	----	RWED	----	--E-	----
File 4	R-E-	----	----	----	RWED
File 5	----	----	----	----	RWED

(R = Read Access, W = Write Access, E = Execute Access, D = Delete Access, and a dash (-) = Access Not Allowed)

In the actual implementation, the letters RWED are represented not by letters but by bits 1 and 0: a 1 indicates that access is allowed, and a 0 indicates access is denied. Therefore, as shown in Table 8.4, the code for User 2 for File 1 would read "1010" and not "R-E-".

(table 8.4)

The five access codes for User 2 from Table 8.3. The resulting code for each file is created by assigning a 1 for each checkmark, and a 0 for each blank space.

Access	R	W	E	D	Resulting Code
R-E-	√	–	√	–	1010
R-E-	√	–	√	–	1010
RWED	√	√	√	√	1111
----	–	–	–	–	0000
----	–	–	–	–	0000

As you can see, the access control matrix is a simple method; but as the numbers of files and users increase, the matrix becomes extremely large—sometimes too large to store in main memory. Another disadvantage is that a lot of space is wasted because many of the entries are all null, such as in Table 8.3, where User 3 isn't allowed into most of the files, and where File 5 is restricted to all but one user. A scheme that conserved space would have only one entry for User 3 or one for File 5, but that's incompatible with the matrix format.

Access Control Lists

The **access control list** is a modification of the access control matrix. Each file is entered in the list and contains the names of the users who are allowed to access it and the type of access each is permitted. To shorten the list, only those who may use the file are named; those denied any access are grouped under a global heading such as WORLD, as shown in Table 8.5.

File	Access
File 1	USER1 (RWED), USER2 (R-E-), USER4 (RWE-), USER5 (--E-), WORLD (----)
File 2	USER2 (R-E-), USER3 (R-E-), USER4 (--E-), WORLD (----)
File 3	USER2 (RWED), USER4 (--E-), WORLD (----)
File 4	USER1 (R-E-), USER5 (RWED), WORLD (----)
File 5	USER5 (RWED), WORLD (----)

(table 8.5)

An access control list showing which users are allowed to access each of the five files. This method uses storage space more efficiently than an access control matrix.

Some systems shorten the access control list even more by establishing categories of users: system, owner, group, and world, as shown in Figure 8.14. The SYSTEM (sometimes called ADMIN) group is designated for system personnel who have unlimited access to all files in the system. The OWNER (sometimes called USER) controls all files in the owner's account. An owner assigns the GROUP designation to a file so

(figure 8.14)

A file's owner has the option to grant access to other users in the same group or to all owners (World, which is the largest group). By default, only administrators can access system files, the smallest group.

System   Owner   Group   World

that all users belonging to the owner's group have access to it. WORLD is composed of all other users in the system; that is, those who don't fall into any of the other three categories. In this system, the File Manager designates default types of access to all files at creation time, and it's the owner's responsibility to change them as needed.

Capability Lists

A **capability list** shows the access control information from a different perspective. It lists every user and the files to which each has access, as shown in Table 8.6. When users are added or deleted from the system, capability lists are easier to maintain than access control lists.

(table 8.6)

A capability list shows files for each user and requires less storage space than an access control matrix.

User	Access
User 1	File 1 (RWED), File 4 (R-E-)
User 2	File 1 (R-E-), File 2 (R-E-), File 3 (RWED)
User 3	File 2 (R-E-)
User 4	File 1 (RWE-), File 2 (--E-), File 3 (--E-)
User 5	File 1 (--E-), File 4 (RWED), File 5 (RWED)

Of the three schemes described so far, the one most commonly used is the access control list. However, capability lists are gaining in popularity because UNIX-like operating systems (including Linux and Android) control devices by treating them as files.

Although both methods seem the same, there are some subtle differences best explained with an analogy. A capability list may be equated to specific concert tickets that are made available to only individuals whose names appear on the list. On the other hand, an access control list can be equated to the reservation list in a restaurant that has limited seating, with each seat assigned to a certain individual.

Data Compression

Data compression algorithms consist of two types: lossless algorithms, which are typically used for text or arithmetic files and which retain all the data in the file throughout the compression-decompression process; and lossy algorithms, which are typically used for image and sound files and which remove data permanently without (we hope) compromising the quality of the file. At first glance, one would think that a loss of data would not be tolerable; but when the deleted data is unwanted noise, tones beyond a human's ability to hear, or light spectrum that we can't see, deleting this data can be undetectable and perhaps even desirable.

Text Compression

There are various methods to compress text in a database. We briefly describe three of them here: records with repeated characters, repeated terms, and front-end compression.

Records with repeated characters: Data in a fixed-length field might include a short name followed by many blank characters. This can be replaced with a variable-length field and a special code to indicate how many blanks were truncated.

For example, let's say the original string, ADAMS, looks like this when it's stored uncompressed in a field that's 15 characters wide (*b* stands for a blank character):

ADAMSbbbbbbbbbb

When it's encoded it would look like this:

ADAMSb10

Likewise, numbers with many zeros can be shortened with a code (in this case, the hash sign #) to indicate how many zeros must be added to recreate the original number. For instance, if the original entry is this number:

300000000

the encoded entry is this:

3#8

Repeated terms can be compressed by using symbols to represent each of the most commonly used words in the database. For example, in a university's student database, common words like *student, course, teacher, classroom, grade,* and *department* could each be represented with a single character that is unlikely to appear in the data. It's critical that the system be able to distinguish between compressed and uncompressed data.

Front-end compression builds on the previous data element. For example, the database that stores students' names in alphabetical order could be compressed, as shown in Table 8.7. The first data element in the list is not compressed. Each entry after that takes a given number of characters from the previous entry that they have in common, shown as an integer, and then adds the characters that make it unique. For example, "Smithbren, Ali" uses the first six characters from "Smithberger, Gino" and adds "ren, Ali." Therefore, the entry is "6ren, Ali."

(table 8.7)	Original List	Compressed List
	Smith, Betty	Smith, Betty
Front-end compression builds on the previous element in the list. The first element cannot be compressed.	Smith, Donald	7Donald
	Smith, Gino	7Gino
	Smithberger, Gino	5berger, Gino
	Smithbren, Ali	6ren, Ali
	Smithco, Rachel	5co, Rachel
	Smither, Kevin	5er, Kevin
	Smithers, Renny	7s, Renny
	Snyder, Katherine	1nyder, Katherine

There is a trade-off: storage space is gained, but overhead goes up and processing time is lost. Remember, for all data compression schemes, the system must be able to distinguish between compressed and uncompressed data.

Image and Sound Compression

Lossy compression allows a loss of data from the original image file to allow significant compression. This means the compression process is irreversible, as the original file cannot be reconstructed. The specifics of the compression algorithm are highly dependent on the type of file being compressed. JPEG is a popular option for still images and MPEG for video images. For video and music files, the International Organization for Standardization (ISO) has issued MPEG standards that "are international standards dealing with the compression, decompression, processing, and coded representation of moving pictures, audio, and their combination."

ISO is the world's leading developer of international standards. For more information about current compression standards and other industry standards, we encourage you to visit *www.iso.org*.

Conclusion

The File Manager controls every file in the system and processes user commands (read, write, modify, create, delete, and so on) to interact with available files on the system. It also manages the access control procedures to maintain the integrity and security of files under its control.

To achieve its goals, the File Manager must be able to accommodate a variety of file organizations, physical storage allocation schemes, record types, and access methods. And, as we've seen, this often requires complex file management software.

In this chapter we discussed:

- Sequential, direct, and indexed sequential file organization
- Contiguous, noncontiguous, and indexed file storage allocation
- Fixed-length versus variable-length records
- Three methods of access control
- Data compression techniques

To get the most from a File Manager, it's important to realize the strengths and weaknesses of its segments—which access methods are allowed on which devices and with which record structures—and the advantages and disadvantages of each.

Key Terms

absolute filename: a file's name, as given by the user, preceded by the directory (or directories) where the file is found and, when necessary, the specific device label.

access control list: an access control method that lists each file, the names of the users who are allowed to access it, and the type of access each is permitted.

access control matrix: an access control method that uses a matrix with every file, every user, and the type of access each user is permitted on each file.

capability list: an access control method that lists every user, the files to which each has access, and the type of access allowed to those files.

contiguous storage: a type of file storage in which all the information is stored in adjacent locations in a storage medium.

current byte address (CBA): the address of the last byte read. It is used by the File Manager to access records in secondary storage and must be updated every time a record is accessed.

current directory: the directory or subdirectory in which the user is working.

data compression: a procedure used to reduce the amount of space required to store data by reducing, encoding, or abbreviating repetitive terms or characters.

database: a group of related files that are interconnected at various levels to give users flexibility of access to the data stored.

device driver: a device-specific program module that handles the interrupts and controls a particular type of device.

device independent: a program or file that functions in the same correct way on different types of devices.

direct record organization: files stored in a direct access storage device and organized to give users the flexibility of accessing any record at random, regardless of its position in the file.

directory: a storage area in a secondary storage volume (disk, disk pack, etc.) containing information about files stored in that volume.

extension: in some operating systems, it's the part of the filename that indicates which compiler or software package is needed to run the files. In UNIX and Linux, it is called a *suffix*.

extents: any remaining records and all other additions to the file that are stored in other sections of the disk.

field: a group of related bytes that can be identified by the user with a name, type, and size. A record is made up of fields.

file: a group of related records that contains information to be used by specific application programs to generate reports.

file descriptor: information kept in the directory to describe a file or file extent.

fixed-length record: a record that always contains the same number of characters.

hashing algorithm: the set of instructions used to perform a key-to-address transformation in which a record's key field determines its location.

indexed sequential record organization: a way of organizing data in a direct access storage device. An index is created to show where the data records are stored. Any data record can be retrieved by consulting the index first.

key field: (1) a unique field or combination of fields in a record that uniquely identifies that record; or (2) the field that determines the position of a record in a sorted sequence.

logical address: the result of a key-to-address transformation.

master file directory (MFD): a file stored immediately after the volume descriptor. It lists the names and characteristics of every file contained in that volume.

noncontiguous storage: a type of file storage in which the information is stored in nonadjacent locations in a storage medium.

path: the sequence of directories and subdirectories the operating system must follow to find a specific file.

record: a group of related fields treated as a unit. A file is a group of related records.

relative address: in a direct organization environment, it indicates the position of a record relative to the beginning of the file.

relative filename: a file's name and extension that differentiates it from other files in the same directory.

sequential record organization: the organization of records in a specific sequence. Records in a sequential file must be processed one after another.

subdirectory: a directory created by the user within the boundaries of an existing directory. Some operating systems call this a folder.

variable-length record: a record that isn't of uniform length, doesn't leave empty storage space, and doesn't truncate any characters.

volume: any secondary storage unit, such as hard disks, disk packs, CDs, DVDs, removable disks, flash memory, or tapes.

working directory: the directory or subdirectory in which the user is currently working.

Interesting Searches

For more background on a few of the topics discussed in this chapter, begin a search with these terms.

- Cloud Computing File Storage
- File Backup Policies
- File Compression Techniques
- File Access Audits
- Filename Limitations
- Hash Function

Exercises

Research Topics

A. Research the size of operating system software by finding the amount of secondary storage (disk) space required to install different versions of the same operating system or different operating systems. If their sizes are substantially different, explain why that may be the case, such as platform issues, features, and so on. Cite your sources.

B. Consult current literature to research file-naming conventions for four different operating systems (not including UNIX, Windows, Linux, or Android, which are discussed in later chapters). Note the acceptable range of characters, maximum length, case sensitivity, and other details. Give examples of both acceptable and unacceptable filenames. For extra credit, explain how the File Managers for those operating systems shorten long filenames (if they do so) in their internal lists to make them easier to manipulate. Cite your sources.

Exercises

1. In your opinion, is file deallocation important? Explain your answer and describe how long you believe your own system would perform adequately if this service were no longer available. Discuss the consequences and any alternatives that users might have.

2. Do you think file retrieval is different on a menu-driven system than it is on a command-driven system? Explain your answer and describe any differences between the two. Give an example of when one would be preferred over the other.

3. On your own computer, find four files that are stored in four different directories. For each file, list both the relative filename and its complete filename.

4. Using your own computer, give the name of the operating system that runs it and give examples of five legal file names. Then give examples of five illegal file names, attempt to use them on your system to save a file, and describe what error message you received. Finally, explain how you could fix the filename so it would work on your system.

5. Imagine one real-life example of each: a multi-file volume and a multi-volume file. Include a description of the media used for storage and a general description of the data in the file.

6. Is device independence important to the File Manager? Why or why not? Describe the consequences if that were not the case.

7. As described in this chapter, files can be formatted with fixed-length fields or variable-length fields. In your opinion, would it be feasible to combine both formats in a single disk? Explain the reasons for your answer.

8. Describe in your own words why it's difficult to support direct access to files with variable-length records. Would it ever be necessary to access such a file directly? If so, suggest a method for handling this type of file if direct access should be required.

9. In your own words, describe the purpose of the working directory and how it can speed or slow file access. In your opinion, should there be more than one working directory? Explain.

10. The following is an access verification technique, listing several files and the access allowed for a single user. Identify the control technique used here, and for each, explain the type of access allowed.

    a. File_1   R-E-

    b. File_12   RWE-

    c. File_13   RW--

    d. File_14   --E-

11. The following is an access verification technique, listing several users and the access allowed for File_13. Identify the control technique used here, and for each, explain the type of access allowed. Finally, describe who is included in the WORLD category.

    a. User_10   --E-
    b. User_14   RWED
    c. User_17   RWE-
    d. WORLD   R---

12. The following is an access control matrix, listing three users and the access allowed for four files. For each entry in the matrix, show the resulting code in zeros and ones.

	User_10	User_17	WORLD
File_1	--E-	----	R---
File_12	R---	RWED	----
File_13	RWED	RWE-	----
File_14	RWED	--E-	R---

13. Devise a way to compress the following list of last names using a lossless technique similar to that shown in Table 8.6 for repeated terms. Describe your method and show the compressed list. Explain the characteristics that make your technique lossless (and not lossy).

    McConnor, Nelson
    McDavid, Nelson
    McDavid, Patricia
    McDonald, Mary
    McDonald, Marie
    McDonnell, Mike

14. Devise a way to compress the following list of city/town names from a travel database. Describe your method and show the compressed list. Explain if you would use a lossless or lossy technique and explain the advantages or disadvantages of using the other technique: Alban, Albany, Alma, Almon, Almond, Angelica, Angelo

Advanced Exercises

15. If you were asked to design the file access control system for a highly secure environment and were given a choice between the establishment of many access categories and just a few access categories, which would you select and why?

16. Compare and contrast dynamic memory allocation and the allocation of files in secondary storage.

17. When is compaction of secondary storage beneficial from the File Manager's perspective? Give several examples. List some problems that could be a result of compaction, and explain how they might be avoided.

18. While some File Managers implement file sharing by allowing several users to access a single copy of a file at the same time, others implement file sharing by providing a copy of the file to each user. List the advantages and disadvantages of each method.

19. Explain in your own words why it's important to defragment a hard drive regularly. Describe the critical steps performed by a defragmentation utility from the time it begins analysis of the disk through completion. Explain the consequence if a power failure occurred midway through this process, and what you would do to minimize subsequent resulting problems.

Chapter 9

Network Organization Concepts

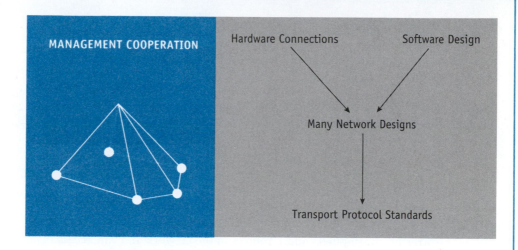

MANAGEMENT COOPERATION

Hardware Connections → Many Network Designs ← Software Design

Many Network Designs → Transport Protocol Standards

❝Knowledge of the universe would somehow be ... defective were no practical results to follow. **❞**

—Cicero (106–43 BC)

Learning Objectives

After completing this chapter, you should be able to describe:

• Several different network topologies—including the star, ring, bus, tree, and hybrid—and how they connect numerous hosts to the network

• Several types of networks: LAN, MAN, WAN, and wireless LAN

• The difference between circuit switching and packet switching, and examples of everyday use that favor each

• Conflict resolution procedures that allow a network to share common transmission hardware and software effectively

• The two transport protocol models (OSI and TCP/IP) and how the layers of each one compare

When computer facilities are connected together by data communication components, they form a network of resources to support the many functions of the organization. Networks provide an essential infrastructure for members of the information-based society to process, manipulate, and distribute data and information to each other. This chapter introduces the terminology and basic concepts of networks.

Basic Terminology

In general, a **network** is a collection of loosely coupled processors interconnected by communication links using cables, wireless technology, or a combination of both.

A common goal of all networked systems is to provide a convenient way to share resources while controlling users' access to them. These resources include both hardware (such as a CPU, memory, printers, USB ports, and disk drives) and software (such as application programs and data files).

There are two general configurations for operating systems for networks. The oldest added a networking capability to a single-user operating system. This is called a **network operating system (NOS)**. With this configuration, users are aware of the specific assortment of computers and resources in the network and can access them by logging on to the appropriate remote host or by transferring data from the remote computer to their own.

With the second configuration, users don't need to know where and how each machine is connected to the system; they can access remote resources as if they were local resources. A **distributed operating system** provides good control for distributed computing systems and allows their resources to be accessed in a unified way. A distributed operating system represents a total view across multiple computer systems for controlling and managing resources without local dependencies. Management is a cooperative process that encompasses every resource and involves every site.

A distributed operating system is composed of the same four managers discussed in Chapters 2 to 8, but with a wider scope. At a minimum, it must provide the following components: process or object management, memory management, file management, device management, and network management, as shown in Figure 9.1. A distributed operating system offers several important advantages over older operating systems and NOSs, including easy and reliable resource sharing, faster computation, adequate load balancing, good reliability, and dependable electronic communications among the network's users.

In a distributed system, each processor classifies the other processors and their resources as remote and considers its own resources local. The size, type, and identification of processors vary. Processors are referred to as sites, hosts, and nodes, depending on

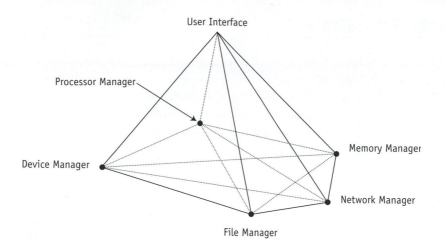

(figure 9.1)

This five-sided pyramid graphically illustrates how the five managers in a networked system work together and support the user interface.

the context in which they're mentioned. Usually, the term "site" indicates a specific location in a network containing one or more computer systems; the term "host" indicates a specific computer system found at a site whose services and resources can be used from remote locations; and "node" (or, more formally, "node name") refers to the name assigned to a computer system connected to a network to identify it to other computers in the network, shown in Figure 9.2.

Typically, a host at one site, called the server, has resources that a host at another site, called the client, wants to use. But the assignments aren't static. Hosts can alternate between being clients or servers depending on their requirements.

(figure 9.2)

Clients request data or services from the host server and wait for the response. If the client host has resources needed by the server host, the roles can be reversed.

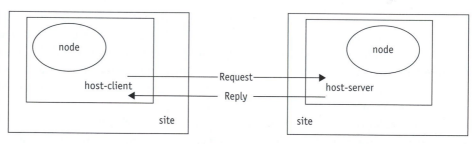

In this discussion, we've simplified the concept of client and server to represent static network software that's located at two different sites. That is, we've assumed that the host-client is a client all of the time, and that the host-server is always a server. However, the actual roles of client and server often alternate between two networked hosts, depending on the application and the network configuration. In this text, we use the simplest configuration to make our explanations of the concepts as clear as possible.

Network Topologies

Sites in any networked system can be physically or logically connected to one another in a certain **topology**, the geometric arrangement of connections (cables, wireless, or both) that link the nodes. The most common geometric arrangements are star, ring, bus, tree, and hybrid. In each topology, there are trade-offs among the need for fast communication among all sites, the tolerance of failure at a site or communication link, the cost of long communication lines, and the difficulty of connecting one site to a large number of other sites. It's important to note that the physical topology of a network may not reflect its logical topology. For example, a network that is wired in a star configuration can be logically arranged to operate as if it is a ring. That is, it can be made to manipulate a token in a ring-like fashion even though its cables are arranged in a star topology. To keep our explanations in this chapter as simple as possible, whenever we discuss topologies, we assume that the logical structure of the network is identical to the physical structure.

For the network designer, there are many alternatives available, all of which will probably solve the customer's requirements. When deciding which configuration to use, designers should keep in mind four criteria:

- Basic cost—the expense required to link the various sites in the system
- Communications cost—the time required to send a message from one site to another
- Reliability—the assurance that many sites can still communicate with each other even if a system link or site fails
- User environment—the critical parameters that the network must meet to be a successful business investment

It's quite possible that there are several possible solutions for each customer. The best choice would need to consider all four criteria. For example, an international data retrieval company might consider the fastest communications and the most flexible hardware configuration to be a cost-effective investment. But a neighborhood charity might put the most emphasis on having a low-cost networking solution. Over-engineering the neighborhood system could be just as big a mistake as under-engineering the international customer's network. The key to choosing the best design is to understand the available technology, as well as the customer's business requirements and budget.

Star

A **star topology**, sometimes called a hub or centralized topology, is a traditional approach to interconnecting devices in which all transmitted data must pass through a central controller when going from a sender to a receiver, as shown in Figure 9.3.

The labels of server and client are not necessarily permanent because they are relative to the transactions being performed. The same host can alternate between being a server and a client.

(figure 9.3)

*Star topology. Hosts
are connected to each
other through a central
controller, which assumes
all responsibility for
routing messages to the
appropriate host. Data
flow between the hosts
and the central controller
is represented by dotted
lines. Direct host-to-host
communication isn't
permitted.*

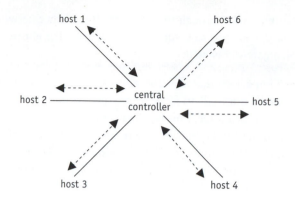

Star topology permits easy routing because the central station knows the path to all other sites. Also, because there is a central control point, access to the network can be controlled easily, and priority status can be given to selected sites. However, this centralization of control requires that the central site be extremely reliable and able to handle all network traffic, no matter how heavy.

Ring

In the **ring topology**, all sites are connected in a closed loop, with the first site connected to the last. See Figure 9.4.

A ring network can connect to other networks via the bridge or gateway, depending on the **protocol** used by each network. The protocol is the specific set of rules used to

(figure 9.4)

*Ring topology. Hosts are
connected to each other in
a circular fashion with data
flowing in one direction
only, shown here as
dotted lines. The network
can be connected to other
networks via a bridge or
gateway.*

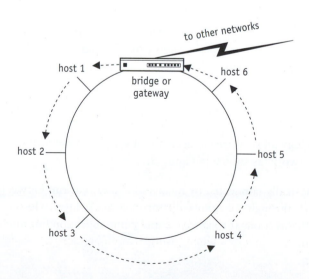

control the flow of messages through the network. If the other network has the same protocol, then a bridge is used to connect the networks. If the other network has a different protocol, a gateway is used.

Data is transmitted in packets that also contain source and destination address fields. Each packet is passed from node to node in one direction only, and the destination station copies the data into a local buffer. Typically, the packet continues to circulate until it returns to the source station, where it's removed from the ring. There are some variations to this basic topology that provide more flexibility—but at a cost. See the double loop network, shown in Figure 9.5, and a set of multiple rings bridged together, shown in Figure 9.6.

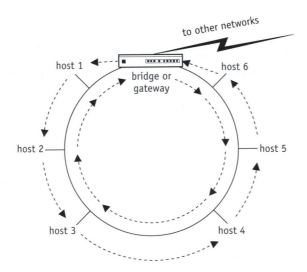

(figure 9.5)

Double loop computer network using a ring topology. Packets of data flow in both directions.

Although ring topologies share the disadvantage that every node must be functional for the network to perform properly, rings can be designed that allow failed nodes to be bypassed—a critical consideration for network stability.

Bus

In the **bus topology** all sites are connected to a single communication line running the length of the network, as shown in Figure 9.7.

Devices are physically connected by means of cables that run between them, but the cables don't pass through a centralized controller mechanism. Messages from any site circulate in both directions through the entire communication line and can be received by all other sites.

(figure 9.6)

Multiple rings bridged
together. Three rings
connected to each other
by two bridges. This
variation of ring topology
allows several networks
with the same protocol to
be linked together.

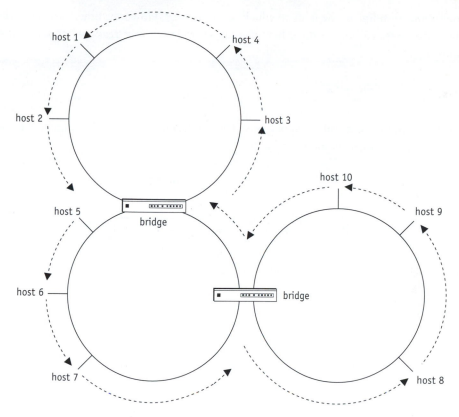

(figure 9.7)

Bus topology. Hosts are
connected to one another in
a linear fashion. Data flows
in both directions from
host to host and is turned
around when it reaches an
end point controller.

Because all sites share a common communication line, only one of them can success-fully send messages at any one time. Therefore, a control mechanism is needed to prevent collisions. In this environment, data may pass directly from one device to another, or it may be routed to an end point controller at the end of the line. In a bus, if the data reaches an end point controller without being accepted by a host, the end point controller turns it around and sends it back so the message can be accepted by the appropriate node on the way to the other end point controller. With some buses, each message must always go to the end of the line before going back down the communication line to the node to which it's addressed. However, other bus networks allow messages to be sent directly to the target node without reaching an end point controller.

Tree

The **tree topology** is a collection of buses. The communication line is a branching cable with no closed loops, as shown in Figure 9.8.

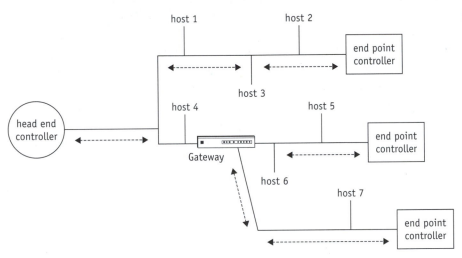

(figure 9.8)

Tree topology. Data flows up and down the branches of the trees and is absorbed by controllers at the end points. Gateways help minimize differences between the protocol used on one part of the network and the different protocol used on the branch with host 7.

The tree layout begins at the head end, where one or more cables start. Each cable may have branches that may, in turn, have additional branches, potentially resulting in quite complex arrangements. Using bridges as special fitters between buses of the same protocol and as translators to those with different protocols allows designers to create networks that can operate at speeds highly responsive to the hosts in the network. In a tree configuration, a message from any site circulates through the communication line and can be received by all other sites until it reaches the end points. If a message reaches an end point controller without being accepted by a host, the end point controller absorbs it—it isn't turned around as it is when using a bus topology. One advantage of bus and tree topologies is that even if a single node fails, message traffic can still flow through the network.

Hybrid

A hybrid topology is some combination of any of the four topologies discussed here. For example, a hybrid can be made by replacing a single host in a star configuration with a ring, as shown in Figure 9.9. Or a star configuration could have a bus topology as one of the communication lines feeding its hub, as shown in Figure 9.10.

(figure 9.9)

Hybrid topology, version 1. This network combines a star and a ring, connected by a bridge. Hosts 5, 6, 7, and 8 are located on the ring.

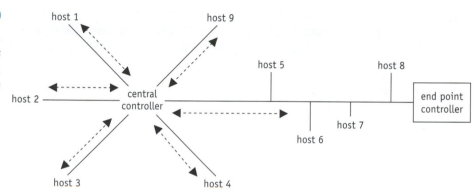

(figure 9.10)

Hybrid topology, version 2. This network combines star and bus topologies. Hosts 5, 6, 7, and 8 are located on the bus.

The objective of a hybrid configuration is to select among the strong points of each topology and combine them to meet that system's communications requirements most effectively.

Network Types

It's often useful to group networks according to the physical distances they cover. Networks are generally divided into local area networks, metropolitan area networks, and wide area networks. However, as communications technology advances, the characteristics that define each group are blurring. In recent years, the wireless local area network has become ubiquitous.

Personal Area Network

A personal area network (PAN) includes information technology that operates within a radius of approximately 10 meters of an individual and is centered around that one person. Also called body area networks (BANs), PANs include networks that include wearable technology (gloves, caps, monitors, and so on) that use the natural connectivity of the human body to communicate. Sometimes these small networks are connected to a bigger network such as a LAN.

Local Area Network

A **local area network (LAN)** defines a configuration including multiple users found within a single office building, warehouse, campus, or similar computing environment. Such a network is generally owned, used, and operated by a single organization and allows computers to communicate directly through a common communication line. Typically, it's a cluster of personal computers or workstations located in the same general area. Although a LAN is usually confined to a well-defined local area, its communications aren't limited to that area because the LAN can be a component of a larger communication network and can allow users to have easy access to other networks through a bridge or a gateway.

A **bridge** is a device and the software to operate it that connects two or more geographically distant local area networks that use the same protocols. For example, a simple bridge could be used to connect two local area networks that use the Ethernet networking technology (Ethernet is discussed later in this chapter.)

A **gateway,** on the other hand, is a more complex device and software used to connect two or more local area networks or systems that use different protocols. A gateway translates one network's protocol into another, resolving hardware and software incompatibilities. For example, the systems network architecture (commonly called SNA) gateway can connect a microcomputer network to a mainframe host.

High-speed LANs have a data rate that varies from 100 megabits per second to more than 40 gigabits per second. Because the sites are close to each other, bandwidths are available to support very high-speed transmission for fully animated, full-color graphics and video; digital voice transmission; and other high data-rate signals. The previously described topologies—star, ring, bus, tree, and hybrid—are normally used to construct local area networks. The transmission medium used may vary from one topology to another. Factors to be considered when selecting a transmission medium are cost, data rate, reliability, number of devices that can be supported, distance between units, and technical limitations.

Metropolitan Area Network

A **metropolitan area network (MAN)** defines a configuration spanning an area larger than a LAN, ranging from several blocks of buildings to an entire city, but not exceeding a circumference of 100 kilometers. In some instances MANs are owned and operated as public utilities, providing the means for internetworking several LANs.

A MAN is a high-speed network often configured as a logical ring. Depending on the protocol used, messages are either transmitted in one direction using only one ring, as illustrated in Figure 9.4, or in both directions using two counter-rotating rings, as illustrated in Figure 9.5. One ring always carries messages in one direction and the other always carries messages in the opposite direction.

Wide Area Network

The Internet is an example of a wide area network that's accessible from other networks.

A **wide area network (WAN)** defines a configuration that interconnects communication facilities in different parts of the world, or that's operated as part of a public utility. WANs use the communications lines of common carriers, which are government-regulated private companies, such as telephone companies that already provide the general public with communication facilities. WANs use a broad range of communication media, including satellite and microwaves; in some cases, the speed of transmission is limited by the capabilities of the communication line. WANs are generally slower than LANs.

The first WAN, called ARPANET, was developed in 1969 by the Advanced Research Projects Agency (ARPA). Its successor, the Internet, is the most widely recognized WAN, but there are other commercial WANs.

Wireless Local Area Network

A **wireless local area network (WLAN)** is a local area network that uses wireless technology to connect computers or workstations located within the range of the network. As shown in Table 9.1, the Institute of Electrical and Electronics Engineers (IEEE) has specified several standards for wireless networking, each with different ranges.

(table 9.1)

Comparison of IEEE standards for wireless networks.

IEEE Standard	Net Bit Rate	Frequency	Compatibility
802.11a	54 Mbps	5 GHz	First IEEE wireless standard
802.11b	11 Mbps	2.4 GHz	Not compatible with 802.11g
802.11g	54 Mbps	2.4 GHz	Fully compatible with 802.11b
			Not compatible with later standards
802.11n	600 Mbps	5 GHz	Fully compatible with 802.11g
			Not compatible with later standards
802.11ac	1.3+ Gbps	5 GHz	Fully compatible with 802.11n

For wireless nodes (workstations, laptops, and so on), a WLAN can provide easy access to a larger network or the Internet, as shown in Figure 9.11. Keep in mind that a WLAN typically poses security vulnerabilities because of its open architecture and the inherent difficulty of keeping out unauthorized intruders.

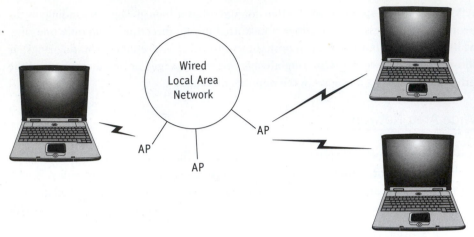

(figure 9.11)

In a WLAN, wirelessen-abled nodes connect to the cabled LAN via access points (APs) if they are located within the range of the device sending the signal.

The mobile WiMAX standard (802.16), approved in 2005 by the Institute of Electrical and Electronics Engineers, promises to deliver high-bandwidth data over much longer distances (up to 10 miles) than the current Wi-Fi standard (IEEE, 2007). This is a fast-changing subject, so we encourage you to research current literature for the latest developments.

Software Design Issues

So far we've examined the configurations of a network's hardware components. In this section we examine four software issues that must be addressed by network designers:

- How do sites use addresses to locate other sites?
- How are messages routed, and how are they sent?
- How do processes communicate with each other?
- How are conflicting demands for resources resolved?

Addressing Conventions

Network sites need to determine how to uniquely identify their users so they can communicate with each other and access each other's resources. Names, addresses, and routes are required because sites aren't directly connected to each other except over point-to-point links; therefore, addressing protocols are closely related to the network topology and geographic location of each site. In some cases, a distinction is made between "local name," which refers to the name by which a unit is known within its own system, and "global name," the name by which a unit is known outside its own system. This distinction is useful because it allows each site the freedom to identify its units according to their own standards without imposing uniform naming rules—something that would be difficult to implement at the local level. On the other hand, a global name must follow standard name lengths, formats, and other conventions.

Using an Internet address as a typical example, we can see that it follows a hierarchical organization, starting from left to right in the following sequence: from logical user to host machine, from host machine to net machine, from net machine to cluster, and from cluster to network. For example, in each Internet address—*someone@icarus.lis.pitt.edu* or *igss12@aber.ac.uk*—the periods and the @ sign separate each component. These electronic mail addresses, which are fairly easy to remember, must be translated (or "resolved," using a concept similar to that described in Chapter 3) to corresponding hardware addresses. This conversion is done by the networking section of the computer's operating system.

The examples given above follow the **Domain Name Service (DNS)** protocol, a general-purpose distributed data query service whose principal function is the resolution of Internet addresses. If we dissect *someone@icarus.lis.pitt.edu* into its components, we have the following:
- *someone* is the logical user,
- *icarus* is the host for the user called *someone*,
- *lis* is the net machine for *icarus*,
- *pitt* is the cluster for *lis*, and
- *edu* is the network for the University of Pittsburgh.

Not all components need to be present in all Internet addresses. Nevertheless, the DNS is able to resolve them by examining each one in reverse order.

Routing Strategies

A router is an internetworking device, primarily software driven, which directs traffic between two different types of LANs or between two network segments with different protocol addresses. It operates at the network layer, which is explained later in this chapter.

Routing allows data to get from one point on a network to another. To do so, each destination must be uniquely identified. Once the data is at the proper network, the router makes sure that the correct node in the network receives it. The role of routers changes as network designs change. Routers are used extensively for connecting sites to each other and to the Internet. They can be used for a variety of functions, including securing the information that is generated in predefined areas, choosing the fastest route from one point to another, and providing redundant network connections so that a problem in one area will not degrade network operations in other areas.

Routing protocols must consider addressing, address resolution, message format, and error reporting. Most routing protocols are based on an addressing format that uses a network and a node number to identify each node. When a network is powered on, each router records in a table the addresses of the networks that are directly connected. Because routing protocols permit interaction between routers, sharing network destinations that each router may have acquired as it performs its services becomes easy. At specified intervals, each router in the internetwork broadcasts a copy of its entire routing table. Eventually, all of the routers know how to get to each of the different destination networks.

Although the addresses allow routers to send data from one network to another, they can't be used to get from one point in a network to another point in the *same* network. This must be done through address resolution, which allows a router to map the original address to a hardware address and store the mapping in a table to be used for future transmissions.

A variety of message formats are defined by routing protocols. These messages are used to allow the protocol to perform its functions, such as finding new nodes on a network, testing to determine whether they're working, reporting error conditions, exchanging routing information, establishing connections, and transmitting data.

Data transmission does not always run smoothly. For example, conditions may arise that cause errors, such as a malfunctioning node or network. In cases such as these, routers and routing protocols would report the error condition, although they would not attempt to correct the error; error correction is left to protocols at other levels of the network's architecture.

Two of the most widely used routing protocols in the Internet are routing information protocol and open shortest path first.

Routing Information Protocol

In **routing information protocol (RIP)**, selection of a path to transfer data from one network to another is based on the number of intermediate nodes, or hops, between the source and the destination. The path with the smallest number of hops is always chosen. This distance vector algorithm is easy to implement. However, it may not be the best in today's networking environment because it does not take into consideration other important factors, such as bandwidth, data priority, or type of network. That is, it can exclude faster or more reliable paths from being selected just because they have more hops. Another limitation of RIP relates to routing tables. The entire table is updated and reissued every 30 seconds, whether or not changes have occurred; this increases internetwork traffic and negatively affects the delivery of messages. In addition, the tables propagate from one router to another. Thus, in the case of an internetwork with 15 hops, it would take more than seven minutes for a change to be known at the other end of the internetwork. Because not all routers necessarily have the same information about the internetwork, a failure at any one of the hops could create an unstable environment for all message traffic.

Open Shortest Path First

In **open shortest path first** (OSPF), selection of a transmission path is made only after the state of a network has been determined. This way, if an intermediate hop is malfunctioning, it's eliminated immediately from consideration until its services have been restored. Routing update messages are sent only when changes in the routing environment occur, thereby reducing the number of messages in the internetwork and reducing the size of the messages by not sending the entire routing table. However, memory usage is increased because OSPF keeps track of more information than RIP. In addition, the savings in bandwidth consumption are offset by the higher CPU usage needed for the calculation of the shortest path, which is based on Dijkstra's algorithm, simply stated as finding the shortest paths from a given source to all other destinations by proceeding in stages and developing the path in increasing path lengths.

When a router uses Dijkstra's algorithm, it computes all the different paths to get to each destination in the internetwork, creating what is known as a topological database. This data structure is maintained by OSPF and is updated whenever failures occur. Therefore, such a router simply checks its topological database to determine whether a path was available, and then uses Dijkstra's algorithm to generate a shortest-path tree to get around the failed link.

Connection Models

A communication network isn't concerned with the content of data being transmitted but with moving the data from one point to another. Because it would be prohibitive to connect each node in a network to all other nodes, the nodes are connected to a communication network designed to minimize transmission costs and to provide full connectivity among all attached devices. Data entering the network at one point is routed to its destination by being switched from node to node, whether by circuit switching or by packet switching.

Circuit Switching

Circuit switching is a communication model in which a dedicated communication path is established between two hosts. The path is a connected sequence of links; the connection between the two points exists until one of them is disconnected. The connection path must be set up before data transmission begins; therefore, if the entire path becomes unavailable, messages can't be transmitted because the circuit would not be complete. The telephone system is a good example of a circuit-switched network.

In terms of performance, there is a delay before signal transfer begins while the connection is set up. However, once the circuit is completed, the network is transparent to users and information is transmitted at a fixed rate of speed with insignificant delays at intermediate nodes.

Packet Switching

Packet switching is basically a store-and-forward technique in which a message is divided into multiple equal-sized units called packets, which are then sent through the network to their destination where they're reassembled into their original long format, as shown in Figure 9.12.

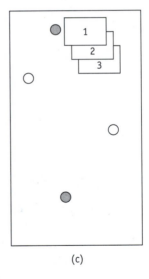

(a)　　　　　　(b)　　　　　　(c)

(figure 9.12)

A packet switching network does not require a dedicated connection. It sends packets using a three-step procedure: (a) divide the data into addressed packets; (b) send each packet toward its destination; (c) and, at the destination, confirm receipt of all packets, place them in order, reassemble the data, and deliver it to the recipient.

With packet switching, multiple copies of each message are sent along different routes. If one packet on one route becomes damaged or lost, an identical packet traveling another route can replace it.

Packet switching is an effective technology for long-distance data transmission. Because it permits data transmission between devices that receive or transmit data at different rates, it provides more flexibility than circuit switching. However, there is no guarantee that after a message has been divided into packets the packets will all travel along the same path to their destination or that they will arrive in their physical sequential order. In addition, packets from one message may be interspersed with those from other messages as they travel toward their destinations. To prevent these problems, a header containing pertinent information about the packet is attached to each packet before it's transmitted. The information contained in the packet header varies according to the routing method used by the network.

The idea is similar to sending a series of 30 reference books through a package delivery system. Six boxes contain five volumes each, and each box is labeled with its sequence number (e.g., box 2 of 6), as well as its ultimate destination. As space on passing delivery trucks becomes available, each box is forwarded to a central switching center, where it's stored until space becomes available to send it to the next switching center, getting closer to its destination each time. Eventually, when all six boxes arrive, they're put in their original order, the 30 volumes are unpacked, and the original sequence is restored.

As shown in Table 9.2, packet switching is fundamentally different from circuit switching, also a store-and-forward technique, in which an entire message is accepted by a central switching node and forwarded to its destination when one of two events occurs: all circuits are free to send the entire message at once, or the receiving node requests its stored messages.

Circuit Switching	Packet Switching
• Transmits in real time	• Transmits in batches
• Preferred in low-volume networks	• Preferred in high-volume networks
• Reduced line efficiency	• High line efficiency
• Dedicated to a single transmission	• Shared by many transmissions
• Preferred for voice communications	• Not good for voice communications
• Easily overloaded	• Accommodates varying priority among packets

(table 9.2)

Comparison of circuit and packet switching.

Packet switching provides greater line efficiency because a single node-to-node circuit can be shared by several packets and does not sit idle over long periods of time. Although delivery may be delayed as traffic increases, packets can still be accepted and transmitted.

That's also in contrast to circuit switching networks, which, when they become overloaded, refuse to accept new connections until the load decreases. Have you ever tried to buy tickets for a popular concert when they first go on sale? That problem is similar to a circuit switching network's overload response.

Packet switching allows users to allocate priorities to their messages so that a router with several packets queued for transmission can send the higher priority packets first. In addition, packet switching networks are more reliable than other types because most nodes are connected by more than one link, so that if one circuit should fail, a completely different path may be established between nodes.

There are two different methods of selecting the path: datagrams and virtual circuits. In the datagram approach, the destination and sequence number of the packet are added to the information uniquely identifying the message to which the packet belongs; each packet is then handled independently and a route is selected as each packet is accepted into the network. This is similar to the shipping label that's added to each package in the book shipment example. At their destination, all packets belonging to the same message are then reassembled by sequence number into one continuous message and, finally, are delivered to the addressee. Because the message can't be delivered until all packets have been accounted for, it's up to the receiving node to request retransmission of lost or damaged packets. This routing method has two distinct advantages: It helps diminish congestion by sending incoming packets through less heavily used paths, and it provides more reliability because alternate paths may be set up when one node fails.

In the virtual circuit approach, the destination and packet sequence number aren't added to the information identifying the packet's message, because a complete path from sender to receiver is established before transmission starts—all the packets belonging to that message use the same route. Although it's a similar concept, this is different from the dedicated path used in circuit switching because any node can have several virtual circuits to any other node. Its advantage over the datagram method is that its routing decision is made only once for all packets belonging to the same message—a feature that should speed up message transmission for long messages. On the other hand, it has a disadvantage in that if a node fails, all virtual circuits using that node become unavailable. In addition, when the circuit experiences heavy traffic, congestion is more difficult to resolve.

Conflict Resolution

Because a network consists of devices sharing a common transmission capability, some method to control usage of the medium is necessary to facilitate equal and fair access to this common resource. First we describe some medium access control techniques: round robin, reservation, and contention. Then we briefly examine three common medium access control protocols used to implement access to resources: carrier sense multiple access (CSMA); token passing; and distributed-queue, dual bus (DQDB).

Access Control Techniques

In networks, round robin allows each node on the network to use the communication medium. If the node has data to send, it's given a certain amount of time to complete the transmission. If the node has no data to send, or if it completes transmission before the time is up, then the next node begins its turn. Round robin is an efficient technique when there are many nodes transmitting over long periods of time. However, when there are few nodes transmitting over long periods of time, the overhead incurred in passing turns from node to node can be substantial, making other techniques preferable depending on whether transmissions are short and intermittent, as in interactive terminal-host sessions, or lengthy and continuous, as in massive file transfer sessions.

The round robin access control used here follows the same principles as round robin processor management, described in Chapter 4.

The reservation technique is well-suited for lengthy and continuous traffic. Access time on the medium is divided into slots, and a node can reserve future time slots for its use. The technique is similar to that found in synchronous time-division multiplexing, used for multiplexing digitized voice streams, where the time slots are fixed in length and preassigned to each node. This technique could be good for a configuration with several terminals connected to a host computer through a single I/O port.

The contention technique is better for short and intermittent traffic. No attempt is made to determine whose turn it is to transmit, so nodes compete for access to the medium. Therefore, it works well under light to moderate traffic, but performance tends to break down under heavy loads. This technique's major advantage is that it's easy to implement.

Access protocols currently in use are based on the previously mentioned techniques and are discussed here with regard to their role in LAN environments.

CSMA

Carrier sense multiple access (CSMA) is a contention-based protocol that's easy to implement. Carrier sense means that a node on the network will listen to or test the communication medium before transmitting any messages, thus preventing a collision with another node that's currently transmitting. Multiple access means that several nodes are connected to the same communication line as peers, on the same level, and with equal privileges.

Although a node will not transmit until the line is quiet, two or more nodes could come to that conclusion at the same instant. If more than one transmission is sent simultaneously, creating a collision, the data from all transmissions will be damaged and the line will remain unusable while the damaged messages are dissipated.

When the receiving nodes fail to acknowledge receipt of their transmissions, the sending nodes will know that the messages did not reach their destinations successfully and both will be retransmitted. The probability of this happening increases if the nodes are farther apart, making CSMA a less appealing access protocol for large or complex networks.

Therefore, the original algorithm was modified to include collision detection and was named carrier sense multiple access with collision detection (CSMA/CD). Ethernet is the most widely known CSMA/CD protocol. Collision detection does not eliminate collisions, but it does reduce them. When a collision occurs, a jamming signal is sent immediately to both sending nodes, which then wait a random period before trying again. With this protocol, the amount of wasted transmission capacity is reduced to the time it takes to detect the collision.

A different modification is CSMA with collision avoidance (CSMA/CA). Collision avoidance means that the access method prevents multiple nodes from colliding during transmission. However, opinion on its efficiency is divided. Some claim it's more efficient than collision detection, whereas others contend that it lowers a network's performance when there are a large number of nodes. The CSMA/CA protocol is implemented in LocalTalk, Apple's cabling system, which uses a protocol called LocalTalk link access protocol. A terminal connected to an Apple CSMA/CA network would send out a three-byte packet to indicate that it wants to start transmitting. This packet tells all other terminals to wait until the first is finished transmitting before they initiate transmissions. If collisions do occur, they involve only the three-byte packets, not the actual data. This protocol does not guarantee the data will reach its destination, but it ensures that any data that's delivered is error-free.

Token Passing

In a token passing network, a special electronic message, called a "token," is generated when the network is turned on. The token is then passed along from node to node. Only the node with the token is allowed to transmit, and after it has done so, it must pass the token on to another node. These networks typically have either a bus or ring topology and are popular because access is fast and collisions are nonexistent.

In a **token bus** network, the token is passed to each node in turn. Upon receipt of the token, a node attaches the data to it to be transmitted and sends the packet, containing both the token and the data, to its destination. The receiving node copies the data, adds the acknowledgment, and returns the packet to the sending node, which then passes the token on to the next node in logical sequence.

Initially, node order is determined by a cooperative decentralized algorithm. Once the network is up and running, turns are determined by priority based on node activity. A node requiring the token frequently will have a higher priority than one that seldom needs it. A table of node addresses is kept in priority order by the network. When a transmission is complete, the token passes from the node that just finished to the one having the next lower entry in the table. When the lowest priority node has been serviced, the token returns to the top of the table and the process is repeated.

This process is similar to a train engine pulling into the station. If the stationmaster has a delivery to send, those cars are attached to the engine and the train is dispatched to its destination with no intermediate stops. When it arrives, the cars are detached, and the engine is sent back to the point of origin with the message that the shipment was successfully received. After delivering that message to the shipment's originator, the engine proceeds to the next station to pick up a delivery.

Implementation of this protocol dictates higher overhead at each node than does CSMA/CD, and nodes may have long waits under certain conditions before receiving the token.

Token ring is the most widely used protocol for ring topology; it became better known than token bus when IBM made its Token Ring Network commercially available. It's based on the use of a token that moves between the nodes in turn and in one direction only. When it's not carrying a message, the token is called a "free" token. If a node wants to send a message, it must wait for the free token to come by. It then changes the token from free to busy and sends its message immediately following the busy token. Meanwhile, all other nodes must wait for the token to become free and come to them again before they're able to transmit a message.

The token ring network was developed by IBM in the 1970s.

The receiving node copies the message in the packet and sets the copied bit to indicate it was successfully received; the packet then continues on its way, making a complete round trip back to the sending node, which then releases the new free token on the network. At this point, the next node down the line with data to send can pick up the free token and repeat the process.

DQDB

The distributed-queue, dual bus (DQDB) protocol is intended for use with a dual-bus configuration, where each bus transports data in only one direction and has been standardized by one of the IEEE committees as part of its MAN standards. Transmission on each bus consists of a steady stream of fixed-size slots, as shown in Figure 9.13. Slots generated at one end of each bus are marked free and sent downstream, where they're marked busy and written to by nodes that are ready to transmit data. Nodes read and copy data from the slots, which then continue to travel toward the end of the bus, where they dissipate.

The distributed access protocol is based on a distributed reservation scheme. For example, if node C in Figure 9.13 wants to send data to node D, it would use Bus 1

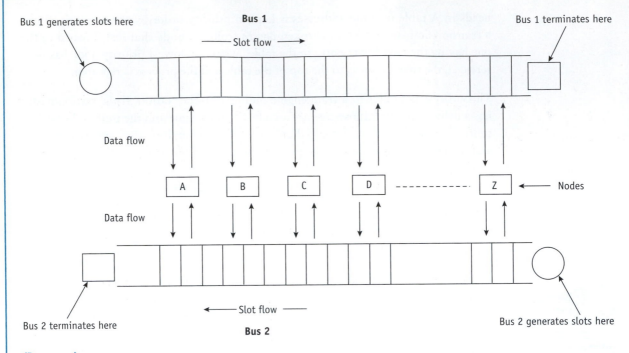

(figure 9.13)

Distributed-queue, dual bus protocol. Free slots are generated at one end of each bus and flow in only one direction. Using DQDB, if node C wants to send data to node D, it must wait for a free slot on Bus 1 because the slots are flowing toward node D on that bus.

because the slots are flowing toward D on that bus. However, if the nodes before C monopolize the slots, then C would not be able to transmit its data to D. To solve the problem, C can use Bus 2 to send a reservation to its upstream neighbors. The protocol states that a node will allow free slots to go by until outstanding reservations from downstream nodes have been satisfied. Therefore, the protocol must provide a mechanism by which each station can keep track of the requests of its downstream peers.

This mechanism is handled by a pair of first-in, first-out queues and a pair of counters, one for each bus, at each of the nodes in the network. This is a very effective protocol providing negligible delays under light loads and predictable queuing under heavy loads. This combination makes the DQDB protocol suitable for MANs that manage large file transfers and that are able to satisfy the needs of interactive users.

Transport Protocol Standards

During the 1980s, network usage began to grow at a fast pace, as did the need to integrate dissimilar network devices from different vendors—a task that became increasingly difficult as the number and complexity of network devices increased.

Soon the user community pressured the industry to create a single, universally adopted network architecture that would allow true multivendor interoperability. We compare two models here, OSI and TCP/IP.

OSI Reference Model

The **International Organization for Standardization (ISO)**, which makes technical recommendations about data communication interfaces, took on the task of creating a universal network architecture. Its efforts resulted in the **open systems interconnection (OSI) reference model,** which serves as a framework for defining the services that a network should provide to its users. This model provides the basis for connecting open systems for distributed applications processing. The word "open" means that any two systems that conform to the reference model and the related standards can be connected, regardless of the vendor.

Once the ISO identified all services, they collected similar functions together into seven logical clusters known as layers. One of the main reasons used to define the seven layers was to modularize easily localized functions so that each layer could be redesigned as necessary. This allowed its protocols to be changed in any way to take advantage of new advances in architecture, hardware, or software without changing the services expected from and provided to the adjacent layers. Boundaries between layers were selected at points that past experience had revealed to be effective. The resulting seven-layer OSI model handles data transmission from one terminal or application program to another. Figure 9.14 shows how data passes through the seven layers and how it's organized: from the application layer, the one closest to the user, to the physical layer, the one closest to the cables, modems, and circuits. A brief description of each layer's function follows.

Layer 1—Physical Layer

Layer 1 is at the bottom of the model. This is where the mechanical, electrical, and functional specifications for connecting a device to a particular network are described. Layer 1 is primarily concerned with transmitting bits over communication lines, so voltages of electricity and timing factors are important. This is the only layer concerned with hardware, and all data must be passed down to it for actual data transfer between units to occur. (Layers 2 through 7 all are concerned with software; so communication between units at these levels is only virtual.) Examples of physical layer specifications are 100Base-T, RS449, and CCITT V.35.

Layer 2—Data Link Layer

Because software is needed to implement Layer 2, this software must be stored in some type of programmable device, such as a front-end processor, network node, or

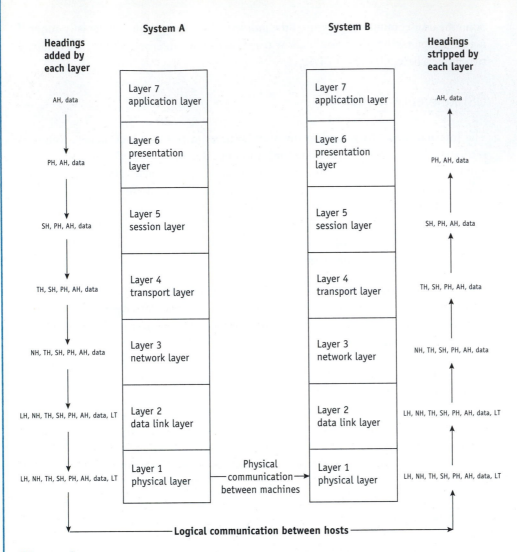

System A   System B

Headings
added by
each layer

Headings
stripped by
each layer

AH, data

| Layer 7 application layer | Layer 7 application layer |

AH, data

PH, AH, data

| Layer 6 presentation layer | Layer 6 presentation layer |

PH, AH, data

SH, PH, AH, data

| Layer 5 session layer | Layer 5 session layer |

SH, PH, AH, data

TH, SH, PH, AH, data

| Layer 4 transport layer | Layer 4 transport layer |

TH, SH, PH, AH, data

NH, TH, SH, PH, AH, data

| Layer 3 network layer | Layer 3 network layer |

NH, TH, SH, PH, AH, data

LH, NH, TH, SH, PH, AH, data, LT

| Layer 2 data link layer | Layer 2 data link layer |

LH, NH, TH, SH, PH, AH, data, LT

LH, NH, TH, SH, PH, AH, data, LT

| Layer 1 physical layer | Physical communication→ between machines | Layer 1 physical layer |

LH, NH, TH, SH, PH, AH, data, LT

← Logical communication between hosts →

(figure 9.14)

The OSI transport protocol model. At every layer of the sending unit, System A, a new header is attached to the previous packet before it's passed on to the next lower layer. Finally, at the data link layer, a link trailer (LT) is added, completing the frame, which is passed to the physical layer for transmission. Then the receiving unit removes each header or trailer until it delivers the data to the application program at Layer 7 on System B.

computer. Bridging between two homogeneous networks occurs at this layer. On one side, the data link layer establishes and controls the physical path of communications before sending data to the physical layer below it. It takes the data, which has been divided into packets by the layers above it, and physically assembles the packet for transmission by completing its frame. Frames contain data combined with control and error detection characters so that Layer 1 can transmit a continuous stream of bits without concern for their format or meaning. On the other side, it checks for transmission errors and resolves problems caused by damaged, lost, or duplicate message frames so that Layer 3 can work with error-free messages. Typical data link level protocols are High-Level Data Link Control (HDLC) and Synchronous Data Link Control (SDLC).

Layer 3—Network Layer

Layer 3 provides services such as addressing and routing that move data through the network to its destination. Basically, the software at this level accepts blocks of data from Layer 4, the transport layer, resizes them into shorter packets, and routes them to the proper destination. Addressing methods that allow a node and its network to be identified, as well as algorithms to handle address resolution, are specified in this layer. A database of routing tables keeps track of all possible routes a packet may take and determines how many different circuits exist between any two packet switching nodes. This database may be stored at this level to provide efficient packet routing and should be dynamically updated to include information about any failed circuit and the transmission volume present in the active circuits.

Layer 4—Transport Layer

Layer 4 is also known as the host-to-host or end-to-end layer because it maintains reliable data transmission between end users. A program at the source computer can send a virtual communication to a similar program at a destination machine by using message headers and control messages. However, the physical path still goes to Layer 1 and across to the destination computer. Software for this layer contains facilities that handle user addressing; it ensures that all the packets of data have been received and that none have been lost. This software may be stored in front-end processors, packet switching nodes, or host computers. In addition, this layer has a mechanism that regulates the flow of information so a fast host can't overrun a slower terminal or an overloaded host. A well-known transport layer protocol is Transmission Control Protocol (TCP).

Layer 5—Session Layer

Layer 5 is responsible for providing a user-oriented connection service and transferring data over the communication lines. While the transport layer is responsible for creating and maintaining a logical connection between end points, the session layer provides a user interface that adds value to the transport layer in the form of dialogue management and error recovery. Sometimes the session layer is known as the "data flow control" layer because it establishes the connection between two applications or two processes; it enforces the regulations for carrying on the session; it controls the flow of data; and it resets the connection if it fails. This layer might also perform some accounting functions to ensure that users receive their bills. The functions of the transport layer and session layer are very similar and, because the operating system of the host computer generally handles the session layer, it would be natural to combine both layers into one, as does TCP/IP.

Layer 6—Presentation Layer

Layer 6 is responsible for data manipulation functions common to many applications, such as formatting, compression, and encryption. Data conversion, syntax conversion, and protocol conversion are common tasks performed in this layer. Gateways connecting networks with different protocols are presentation layer devices; one of their functions is to accommodate totally different interfaces as seen by a terminal in one node and expected by the application program at the host computer. For example, IBM's Customer Information Control System (CICS) teleprocessing monitor is a presentation layer service located in a host mainframe, although it provides additional functions beyond the presentation layer.

Layer 7—Application Layer

At Layer 7, application programs, terminals, and computers access the network. This layer provides the interface to users and is responsible for formatting user data before passing it to the lower layers for transmission to a remote host. It contains network management functions and tools to support distributed applications. File transfer and e-mail are two of the most common application protocols and functions.

Once the OSI model is assembled, it allows nodes to communicate with each other. Each layer provides a completely different array of functions to the network, but all of the layers work in unison to ensure that the network provides reliable transparent service to the users.

TCP/IP Model

The **Transmission Control Protocol/Internet Protocol (TCP/IP) reference model** is probably the oldest transport protocol standard. It's the basis for Internet communications and is the most widely used network layer protocol today. It was developed for the U.S. Department of Defense's ARPANET and provides reasonably efficient and error-free transmission among different systems. Because it's a file-transfer protocol, large files can be sent across sometimes unreliable networks with a high probability that the data will arrive error free. Some differences between the TCP/IP model and

Vinton G. Cerf (1943–) & Robert E. Kahn (1938–)

TCP/IP was designed by two computer scientists, Vint Cerf and Bob Kahn. They first met in 1969 when Kahn came to Los Angeles looking for help testing the regional node of the newly born ARPANET. In 1974, the two authored a seminal paper describing a nonproprietary protocol for packet network communication. This protocol outlined an architecture for interconnecting networks, one that made minimal demands on other networks connecting to it. The work of Cerf and Kahn contributed to a seamless transition to global networking and improved the scalability of the Internet as it is known today. In 1991, looking to provide a neutral forum to facilitate the development of Internet standards, the two men founded the Internet Society, an international nonprofit organization and the home for the Internet Engineering Task Force, which sets technical standards for the Internet.

For more information see:

http://amturing.acm.org/ award_winners/

Cerf and Kahn jointly received the 2004 A.M. Turing Award for their "pioneering work on internetworking, including the design and implementation of the Internet's basic communications protocols, TCP/IP, and for inspired leadership in networking."

the OSI reference model are the significance that TCP/IP places on internetworking and providing connectionless services, and its management of certain functions, such as accounting for use of resources.

The TCP/IP model organizes a communication system with three main components: processes, hosts, and networks. Processes execute on hosts, which can often support multiple simultaneous processes that are defined as primary units that need to communicate. These processes communicate across the networks to which hosts are connected. Based on this hierarchy, the model can be roughly partitioned into two major tasks: one that manages the transfer of information to the host in which the process resides, and one that ensures it gets to the correct process within the host. Therefore, a network needs to be concerned only with routing data between hosts, as long as the hosts can then direct the data to the appropriate processes. With this in mind, the TCP/IP model can be arranged into four layers that roughly correlate to the OSI's seven layers, as shown in Figure 9.15. A brief description of the function of each follows.

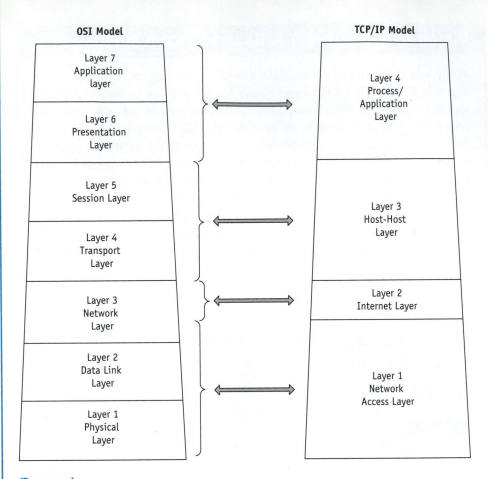

(figure 9.15)

Comparison of OSI and TCP/IP models and their corresponding functional layers.

Layer 1—Network Access Layer

The network access layer (sometimes called the data link layer) is equivalent to the physical, data link, and part of the network layers of the OSI model. Protocols at this layer provide access to a communication network. Some of the functions performed here are flow control, error control between hosts, security, and priority implementation.

Layer 2—Internet Layer

The Internet layer is equivalent to the portion of the network layer of the OSI model that isn't already included in the previous layer, specifically the mechanism that performs routing functions. Therefore, this protocol is usually implemented within gateways and hosts. An example of a standard set by the U.S. Department of Defense (DoD) is the Internet Protocol (IP), which provides connectionless service for end systems to communicate across one or more networks.

Layer 3—Host-Host Layer

The host-host layer (sometimes called the transport layer) is equivalent to the transport and session layers of the OSI model. As its name indicates, this layer supports mechanisms to transfer data between two processes on different host computers. Services provided in the host-host layer also include error checking, flow control, and manipulating connection control signals. An example of a standard set by the DoD is the Transmission Control Protocol (TCP), which provides a reliable end-to-end data transfer service.

Layer 4—Process/Application Layer

The process/application layer is equivalent to both the presentation and application layers of the OSI model. This layer includes protocols for computer-to-computer resource sharing.

Conclusion

Although operating systems for networks necessarily include the functions of the four managers discussed so far in this textbook—the Memory Manager, Processor Manager, Device Manager, and File Manager—they also need to coordinate all those functions among the network's many varied pieces of hardware and software, no matter where they're physically located.

There is no single gauge by which we can measure the success of a network's operating system, but at a minimum it must meet the reliability requirements of its owners. That is, when a node fails—and all networks experience node failure from time to time— the operating system must detect the failure, change routing instructions to avoid that node, and make sure every lost message is retransmitted until it's successfully received.

In this chapter, we've introduced the basic network organization concepts: common terminology, network topologies, types of networks, software design issues, and transport protocol standards. Bear in mind, however, that this is a complicated subject and we've only just touched the surface in these few pages.

Key Terms

bridge: a data-link layer device used to interconnect multiple networks using the same protocol.

bus topology: network architecture to connect elements together along a single line.

circuit switching: a communication model in which a dedicated communication path is established between two hosts and on which all messages travel.

distributed operating system: an operating system that provides control for a distributed computing system, allowing its resources to be accessed in a unified way.

Domain Name Service (DNS): a general-purpose, distributed, replicated data query service. Its principal function is the resolution of Internet addresses based on fully qualified domain names.

gateway: a communications device or program that passes data between networks having similar functions but different protocols.

International Organization for Standardization (ISO): a voluntary, nontreaty organization responsible for creating international standards in many areas, including computers and communications.

local area network (LAN): a data network intended to serve an area covering only a few square kilometers or less.

metropolitan area network (MAN): a data network intended to serve an area approximating that of a large city.

network: a collection of loosely coupled processors interconnected by communications links using cables, wireless technology, or a combination.

network operating system (NOS): the software that manages network resources for a node on a network and may provide security and access control.

open shortest path first (OSPF): a protocol designed for use in Internet Protocol (IP) networks, concerned with tracking the operational state of every network interface.

open systems interconnection (OSI) reference model: a seven-layer conceptual structure describing computer network architectures and the ways in which data passes through them.

packet switching: a communication model in which messages are individually routed between hosts, with no previously established communication path.

protocol: a set of rules to control the flow of messages through a network.

ring topology: a network topology; each node is connected to two adjacent nodes.

routing information protocol (RIP): a routing protocol used by IP, based on a distance-vector algorithm.

star topology: a network topology in which multiple network nodes are connected through a single, central node.

token bus: a type of local area network with nodes connected to a common cable using a CSMA/CA protocol.

token ring: a type of local area network with stations wired into a ring network.

topology: in a network, the geometric arrangement of connections (cables, wireless, or both) that link the nodes.

Transmission Control Protocol/Internet Protocol (TCP/IP) reference model: a common acronym for the suite of transport-layer and application-layer protocols that operate over the Internet Protocol.

tree topology: a network architecture in which elements are connected in a hierarchical structure.

wide area network (WAN): a network usually constructed with long-distance, point-to-point lines, covering a large geographic area.

wireless local area network (WLAN): a local area network with wireless nodes.

Interesting Searches

For more background on a few of the topics discussed in this chapter, begin a search with these terms.

- IEEE Wireless Standards
- WiMAX vs. Wi-Fi
- Voice Over Internet Protocol (VoIP)
- Network Topologies
- Routing Protocols

Exercises

Research Topics

A. Name several operating systems that run LANs today. Do not include different versions of a single operating system. For each operating system, list its name, the platform or network on which it operates, and its distributor or manufacturer. Cite your sources.

B. In this chapter, we discussed the WiMAX standard. Consult current literature to further explore the status of WiMAX technology. Describe any barriers to commercial use and the applications that show the most promise. Explain which countries expect to benefit the most and why. Be sure to cite your sources. If your discussion includes terms not used in the text, be sure to define them.

Exercises

1. Explain why network operating systems were phased out when distributed operating systems gained popularity.

2. In your own words, describe the functional differences between a bridge and a gateway. Give an example of each.

3. As mentioned in this chapter, sometimes clients and servers exchange roles, with clients becoming servers at times. Give an example where a client always remains the client and never becomes the server.

4. An early network topology was the token bus. Describe how the role of the token in the token bus network compares with the token ring network.

5. Explain the major advantages and disadvantages of a bus topology.

6. Explain the major advantages and disadvantages of a star topology.

7. Describe how a network with a star topology can be manipulated to act as if it uses a ring topology.

8. Using Figure 9.9, describe the flow of data from host to host as it moves from Host 1 to Host 6 including each controller or bridge.

9. Using Figure 9.10, describe the flow of data from host to host as it moves from Host 1 to Host 6 including each controller or bridge.

10. Describe a hybrid topology and draw graphic illustrations of two examples.

11. Discuss at least three advantages of a hard-wired LAN compared to a wireless LAN and describe one situation where the wired LAN would be preferred.

12. Discuss the primary difference between a bridge and a gateway, and give a real life example that uses each one.

13. Explain the role of routers when moving data from one host to another in the same network.

14. This chapter described packet routing. Give the two examples in which packets can be routed and explain how they differ.

15. Give two real life examples where packet switching is preferred over circuit switching and explain why.

16. Compare the virtual circuit approach to packet switching and describe its advantages.

17. Compare and contrast the two most widely used routing protocols: routing information protocol (RIP) and open shortest path first (OSFP).

18. Identify a network topology that would best suit each of the following environments and explain why:

    a. Dormitory floor

    b. University campus

    c. Airport

    d. State or province

Advanced Exercises

19. Although not explicitly discussed in the chapter, packet size would seem to have an impact on transmission time. Discuss whether or not this is true and explain why. Specifically compare the concept of the number of bits that constitute the *data* portion of the packet and the number of bits that constitute the *address* portion of the packet. Remember that the address is overhead and it has an impact on data transmission rates.

    Offer a comprehensive example comparing packet sizes and resulting transmission times. For example, look at some of your e-mail messages and compare the number of bytes that constitute the message with the number of bytes for the address. Compute the results for several e-mails and give your conclusions.

20. Discuss what is incorrect with the following logic: Packet switching requires control and address bits to be added to each packet, which causes considerable overhead in packet switching. In circuit switching, a dedicated circuit is set up and no extra bits are needed.

    a. Therefore, there is no overhead in circuit switching.

    b. Because there is no overhead in circuit switching, line utilization must be more efficient than in packet switching.

21. Describe the differences between CSMA/CD and CSMA/CA. Provide one real life example where CSMA/CD is used. Provide one real life example where CSMA/CA is used.

22. Explain the circumstances under which a token ring network is more effective than an Ethernet network.

23. Even though the OSI model of networking specifies seven layers of functionality, most computer systems use fewer layers to implement a network. Why do they use fewer layers? What problems could be caused by the use of fewer layers?

Chapter 10 | Management of Network Functions

INTERACTION AMONG MANAGERS

Single-User Operating Systems

Network Operating Systems

Distributed Operating Systems

"As knowledge increases, wonder deepens."

—Charles Morgan (1894–1958)

Learning Objectives

After completing this chapter, you should be able to describe:

• The complexities introduced to operating systems by network capabilities

• A network operating system (NOS) compared to a distributed operating system (DO/S)

• How a DO/S performs memory, process, device, and file management

• How a NOS performs memory, process, device, and file management

• Important features that differentiate a DO/S and a NOS

When organizations move toward completely decentralized systems, more and more computing devices are linked through complex networks of wireless communications, teleconferencing equipment, host computers, and other digital technologies. But there are two problems with this expansion. First, a tremendous demand is placed on data communication networks by the staggering number of hardware interconnections. Second, both the systems administrators and the user community place increasing pressure on these networks to operate with greater reliability, security, and speed.

In this chapter we explore the differences between network operating systems and distributed operating systems. We explain process-based and object-based operating system models and use them to define the roles of the Memory, Processor, Device, File, and Network Managers in network operating systems and in distributed operating systems.

History of Networks

Networks were created initially to share expensive hardware resources such as large mainframes, centralized high-speed printers, and sizable hard disks. These physical networks, with their network operating systems, allowed organizations to increase the availability of resources and spread the cost among many users. However, the focus of technology changed when system owners realized that a network's most prized resource wasn't the hardware—it was the information stored on it. Soon many operating systems were enhanced with network capabilities to give users throughout an organization easy access to centralized information resources.

Today, applications collectively known as computer-supported cooperative work (or groupware) use a set of technologies called **distributed processing** to allow even greater access to centralized information and to allow users to work together to complete common tasks.

Comparison of Two Networking Systems

The **network operating system (NOS)** was developed first. It evolved from the need to give users global access to resources, globally manage the network's processes, and make the network almost completely transparent for users and their sites' operating systems, known as local operating systems. A typical NOS is shown in Figure 10.1.

A network operating system gives local operating systems extended powers. That is, it gives the local system new ability to accept a request to perform processing or to access data that's not available locally. It starts by determining where the resources are located. Then it initiates the operation and returns the appropriate data or service to the requester.

An NOS relies on the node's local managers to perform tasks. The NOS does not have global control of network assets.

(figure 10.1)

In a NOS environment, each node, shown here as a circle, is managed by its own local operating system, shown here as triangles. Their respective network operating systems, shown here as squares, come into play only when one site's system needs to work with another site's system.

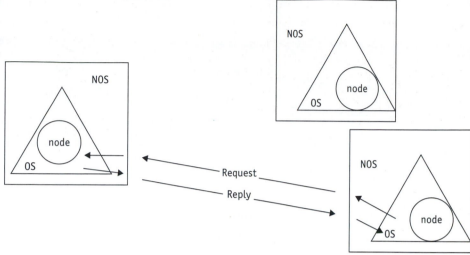

It's important that the NOS accomplish this transparently. The local operating system views the action as having been performed onsite. That's because the network operating system handles the interfacing details and coordinates the remote processing. It also coordinates communications among the local operating systems by tracking the status and location of all entities in the system.

The local operating systems are traditional operating systems designed to run a single computer. That means they can perform a task only if the process is part of their environment; otherwise, they must pass the request on to the network operating system to run it. To a local operating system, it appears that the NOS is the server performing the task, whereas in reality the NOS is only the facilitator.

The biggest limitation of an NOS is that it doesn't take global control over memory management, process management, device management, or file management. Rather, it sees these tasks as autonomous *local* functions that must interact with each other. This limited view is problematic because an operating system can't achieve true distributed computing or processing functions without *global* control of all assets, not only assets at the network communication level. This need for global control led to the development of the **distributed operating system (DO/S)**. Although they use a similar acronym, the DO/S described in this chapter must not be confused with the DOS (disk operating system) for microcomputers or MS-DOS, described in Chapter 14.

Distributed operating systems provide a unified environment designed to optimize operations for the network as a whole, not just for local sites, as illustrated in Figure 10.2.

The major difference between an NOS and a DO/S is how each views and manages the local and global resources. An NOS builds on capabilities provided by the local

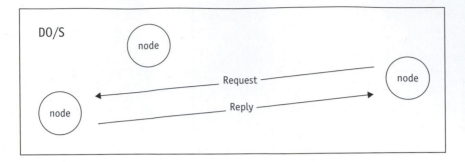

(figure 10.2)

In a DO/S environment, all nodes are part of a globally managed operating system designed to optimize all system resources. Requests between nodes are handled entirely by the DO/S as well as every operation at every node.

operating system and extends it to satisfy new needs. It accesses resources by using local mechanisms, and each system is controlled and managed locally based on that system's policy. Therefore, a system with seven nodes could have seven policies.

On the other hand, the DO/S considers system resources to be globally owned and manages them as such. It accesses resources using *global* mechanisms rather than *local* mechanisms, with system control and management based on a single system-wide policy. A comparison of the two types of systems is shown in Table 10.1.

Network Operating System (NOS)	Distributed Operating System (DO/S)
Local resources are owned by each local node.	Resources are owned by a global operating system.
Local resources are managed by local operating system.	Local resources are managed by a global operating system.
Access is allowed according to the policies of the local operating system.	Access is allowed according to the policy of the global operating system.
Requests are passed from one local operating system to another via the NOS.	Requests are passed directly from node to node via the operating system.

(table 10.1)

Comparison of an NOS and a DO/S, two types of operating systems used to manage networked resources.

For example, in a typical NOS environment, a user who wants to run a local process at a remote site must do the following:

(1) Log on to the local network.

(2) Instruct the local system to migrate the process or data to the remote site.

(3) Send a request to the remote site to schedule the process on its system.

Thereafter, the remote site views the process as a newly created process within its local operating system's environment and manages it without outside intervention. If the process needs to be synchronized with processes at remote sites, the process needs to have embedded calls to initiate action by the NOS. These calls are typically added on top of the local operating system to provide the communications link between the two

Before one node can communicate with another node on the network, the NOS of the first node must open communications with the NOS of the targeted network node.

processes on the different devices. This complicates the task of synchronization, which is the responsibility of the user and is only partially supported by the operating system.

On the other hand, a system managed by a DO/S handles the same example differently. If one site has a process that requires resources at another site, then the task is presented to the DO/S as just another process. The user acquires no additional responsibility. The DO/S examines the process control block to determine the specific requirements for this process. Then, using its process scheduler, the DO/S determines how to best execute the process based on the site's current knowledge of the state of the total system. The process scheduler then takes this process, along with all other processes ready to run on the network, and calculates their order of execution on each node while optimizing global run time and maintaining process priorities. The emphasis is on maintaining the operating system's global functionality, policies, and goals.

To globally manage the network's entire suite of resources, a DO/S is typically constructed with a replicated **kernel** operating system—low-level, hardware-control software (firmware) with system-level software for resource management. This software may be unique or duplicated throughout the system. Its purpose is to allocate and manage the system's resources so that global system policies, not local policies, are maximized. The DO/S also has a layer that hides the network and its

Tim Berners-Lee (1955–)

While working at CERN, the European Particle Physics Laboratory in Switzerland in 1989, Tim Berners-Lee invented what's now known as the Web, which he termed "an internet-based hypermedia initiative for global information sharing." He is the Director of the World Wide Web Consortium (W3C), a Web standards organization founded in 1994 which develops interoperable technologies

(specifications, guidelines, software, and tools) to lead the Web to its full potential. He has received many international honors, including a MacArthur Fellowship (1998); he was named a Foreign Associate of the National Academy of Sciences (2009); and he was knighted by H.M. Queen Elizabeth II in 2004 for services to the global development of the Internet.

For more information:

http://www.w3.org/People/Berners-Lee/

Recipient of the UNESCO Niels Bohr Gold Medal (2010) "For the development of hypertext, the World Wide Web and hence the foundation for the modern Internet."

intricacies from users so they can use the network as a single logical system and not as a collection of independent cooperating entities.

DO/S Development

Although the DO/S was developed after the NOS, its global management of network devices is the easier to understand, so we detail its fundamentals first. A similar discussion of NOS can be found toward the end of this chapter.

Because a DO/S manages the entire group of resources within the network in a global fashion, resources are allocated based on negotiation and on compromise among equally important peer sites in the distributed system. One advantage of this type of system is its ability to support file copying, electronic mail, and remote printing, without requiring the user to install special server software on local machines. Below, we discuss how operating system management functions are performed by a DO/S.

Memory Management

For each node, the Memory Manager uses a kernel with a paging algorithm to track the amount of memory that's available. The algorithm is based on the goals of the local system, but the policies and mechanisms that are used at the local sites are driven by the requirements of the global system. To accommodate both local and global needs, memory allocation and deallocation depend on scheduling and resource-sharing schemes that optimize the resources of the entire network.

The Memory Manager for a network works the same way as it does for a stand-alone operating system, but it's extended to accept requests for memory from both local and global sources. On a local level, the Memory Manager allocates pages based on the local policy. On a global level, it receives requests from the Process Manager to provide memory to new or expanding client or server processes. The Memory Manager also uses local resources to perform garbage collection in memory, perform compaction, decide which are the most and least active processes, and determine which processes to preempt to provide space for others.

To control the demand, the Memory Manager handles requests from the Process Manager to allocate and deallocate space based on the network's usage patterns. In a distributed environment, the combined memory for the entire network is made up of several subpools (one for each processor), and the Memory Manager has a subcomponent that exists on each processor.

When an application tries to access a page that's not in memory, a page fault occurs, and the Memory Manager automatically brings that page into memory. If the page is changed while in memory, the Memory Manager writes the changed page back to the file when it's time to swap the page out of memory.

Before allocating space, the Memory Manager examines the total free memory table. If the request can be filled, the memory is allocated and the table is modified to show the location of the allocated space.

The Memory Manager also manages virtual memory. Specifically, it allocates and deallocates virtual memory, reads and writes to virtual memory, swaps virtual pages to disk, gets information about virtual pages, locks virtual pages in memory, and protects the pages that need to be protected.

Pages are protected using hardware or low-level memory management software in each site's kernel. This protection is summoned as pages are loaded into memory. Several typical protection checks are performed on the pages, as shown in Table 10.2.

Type of Access Allowed	Levels of Protection Granted
Read and write	Allows users to have full access to the page's contents, giving them the ability to read and write.
Read-only	Allows users to read the page, but they're not allowed to modify it.
Execute-only	Allows users to use the page, but they're not allowed to read or modify it. This means that although a user's process can't read or write to the page, it can jump to an address within the page and start executing. This is appropriate for shared application software, editors, and compilers.
No access	Prevents users from gaining access to the page. This is typically used by debugging or virus protection software to prevent a process from reading from or writing to a particular page.

Process Management

In a network, the Processor Manager provides the policies and mechanisms to create, delete, abort, name, rename, find, schedule, block, run, and synchronize processes; it also provides real-time priority execution if required. The Processor Manager also manages the states of execution: READY, RUNNING, and WAIT, as described in Chapter 4. To do this, each CPU in the network is required to have its own run-time kernel that manages the hardware—the lowest-level operation on the physical device, as shown in Figure 10.3.

A kernel actually controls and operates the CPU and manages the queues used for states of execution, although upper-level system policies direct how process control

(figure 10.3)

Each kernel controls each piece of hardware, including the CPU. Each kernel is operated by the DO/S, which, in turn, is directed by the application software running on the host computer. In this way, the most cumbersome functions are hidden from the user.

blocks (PCBs) are stored in the queues and how they're selected to be run. Therefore, each kernel assumes the role of helping the system reach its operational goals.

The kernel's states are dependent on the global system's process scheduler and dispatcher, which organize the queues within the local CPU and choose the running policy that's used to execute the processes on those queues. Typically, the system's scheduling function has three parts: a decision mode, a priority function, and an arbitration rule.

Cooperation among managers is key to successful process management in a DO/S environment.

- The decision mode determines which policies are used when scheduling a resource. Options could include preemptive, nonpreemptive, Round Robin, and so on.

- The priority function gives the scheduling algorithm the policy that's used to assign an order to processes in the execution cycle. This priority is often determined using a calculation that's based on system characteristics, such as occurrence of events, task recurrence, system loading levels, or program run time characteristics. Examples of these run-time characteristics are most time remaining, least time remaining, and so on.

- The arbitration rule is a policy that's used to resolve conflicts between jobs of equal priority. That is, it typically dictates the order in which jobs of the same priority are to be executed. Two examples of arbitration rules are last-in first-out (LIFO) and first-in first-out (FIFO).

Most advances in job scheduling rely on one of three theories: queuing theory, statistical decision theory, or estimation theory. (These queuing and statistical decision theories are the same as those discussed in statistics courses.) An example of estimation theory is a scheduler based on process priorities and durations. It maximizes the system's throughput by using durations to compute and schedule the optimal way to interleave process chunks. Distributed scheduling is better achieved when migration of the scheduling function and policies considers all aspects of the system, including I/O, devices, processes, and communications.

Processes are created, located, synchronized, and deleted using specific procedures. To create a process, the process manager (which is part of the Processor Manager) creates a kind of process control block (PCB) with information similar to the PCBs discussed in Chapter 4. This PCB has additional information identifying the process's location in the network. To locate a process, the process manager uses a system directory or process that searches all kernel queue spaces—this requires system support for interprocess communications. To synchronize processes, the process manager uses message passing or remote procedure calls. To delete or terminate a process, the process manager finds the correct PCB and deletes it.

There are two ways to design a distributed operating system. The first is a **process-based DO/S**, in which network resources are managed as a large heterogeneous collection. The second and more recent is an **object-based DO/S**, which clumps each type of hardware with its necessary operational software into discrete objects that are manipulated as a unit. Of the two, a process-based DO/S most closely resembles the theory described in Chapter 4.

Process-Based DO/S

A process-based DO/S provides process management through the use of client/server processes synchronized and linked together through messages and ports (the ports are also known as channels or pipes). The major emphasis is on processes and messages and how they provide the basic features essential to process management, such as process creation, scheduling, pausing, communication, and identification, to name a few.

The issue of how to provide these features can be addressed in several ways. The processes can be managed from a single copy of the operating system, from multiple cooperating peers, or from some combination of the two. Operating systems for distributed computers are typically configured as a kernel on each site. All other services that are dependent on particular devices are typically found on the sites where the devices are located. As users enter the system, the scheduling manager gives them a unique process identifier and then assigns them to a site for processing.

In a distributed system, there is a high level of cooperation and sharing of actions and data maintained by the sites when determining which process should be loaded and where it should be run. This is done by exchanging messages among site operating systems. Once a process is scheduled for service, it must be initiated at the assigned site by a dispatcher. The dispatcher takes directions from the operating system's scheduler, allocates the device to the process, and initiates its execution. This procedure may necessitate one of the following: moving a process from memory in one site to memory at another site; reorganizing a site's memory allocation; reorganizing a site's READY, RUNNING, and WAIT queues; and initiating the scheduled process. The Processor Manager recognizes only processes and their demands for service. It responds to them based on the established scheduling policy, which determines what must be done to manage the processes. As mentioned in earlier chapters, policies for scheduling must consider issues such as load balancing, overhead minimization, memory loading minimization, first-come first-served, and least-time-remaining.

Synchronization is a key issue in network process management. For example, processes can coordinate their activities by passing messages to each other. In addition, to carry out the proper logistics to synchronize actions within a process, processes can use primitives to pass synchronization parameters from one port to another. **Primitives** are well-defined low-level operating system mechanisms such as "send and receive." For instance, when a process reaches a point at which it needs service from an external source, such as an I/O request, it sends a message searching for the service. While it waits for a response, the processor server puts the process in a WAIT state.

Interrupts, which cause a processor to be assigned to another process, also are represented as messages that are sent to the proper process for service. For example, an interrupt may cause the active process to be blocked and moved into a WAIT state. Later, when the cause for the interruption ends, the processor server unblocks the interrupted process and restores it to a READY state.

Object-Based DO/S

An object-based DO/S has a different way of looking at the computer system than a process-based DO/S. Instead of viewing the system as a collection of individual resources and processes, the system is viewed as a collection of **objects**. An object can represent a piece of hardware (such as a CPU or memory), software (such as files, programs, semaphores, and data), or a combination of the two (printers, scanners, USB ports, and disks—each bundled with the software required to operate it). Each object in the system has a unique identifier to differentiate it from all other objects in the system.

Objects are viewed by the operating system as abstract entities—data types that can go through a change of state, act according to set patterns, be manipulated, or exist in relation to other objects in a manner appropriate to the object's semantics in the system. This means that objects have a set of unchanging properties that defines them and their behavior within the context of their defined parameters. For example, a writable CD (CD-R) drive has unchanging properties that include the following: data can be written to a disc, data can be read from a disc, reading and writing can't take place concurrently, and the data's beginning and ending points can't be compromised. If we use these simple rules to construct a simulation of a CD-R drive, we have created an accurate representation of this object.

To determine an object's state, one must perform an appropriate (allowed) operation on it, such as reading or writing to a hard disk, because the object is identified by the set of operations one can send it. Typically, systems using this concept have a large number of objects but a small number of operations on the objects. For example, a printer might have three operations: one to advance a full page, one to advance one line, and one to advance one character.

Therefore, in an object-based DO/S, process management becomes object management, with processes acting as discrete objects. Process management, in this case, deals with the policies and mechanisms for controlling the operations and the creation and destruction of objects. Therefore, process management has two components: the kernel level and the process manager.

Kernel Level

The **kernel level** provides the basic mechanisms for building the operating system by creating, managing, scheduling, synchronizing, and deleting objects, and it does so dynamically. For example, when an object is created, it's assigned all the resources needed for its operation and is given control until the task is completed. Then the object returns control to the kernel, which selects the next object to be executed.

The kernel also has ultimate responsibility for the network's capability lists, discussed in Chapter 8. Each site has both a capability manager that maintains the capability list for its objects and a directory which lists the location for all capabilities in the system. This directory guides local requests for capabilities to the sites on which they're located.

For example, if a process requests access to a region in memory, the capability manager first determines whether the requesting process has been previously granted rights. If so, then it can proceed. If not, it processes the request for access rights. When the requester has access rights, the capability manager grants the requester access to the named object—in this case, the region in memory. If the named object is at a remote site, the local capability manager directs the requester, using a new address computation and message, to the remote capability manager.

The kernel is also responsible for process synchronization mechanisms and communication support. Typically, synchronization is implemented as some form of shared variable, such as the WAIT and SIGNAL codes discussed in Chapter 6. Communication among distributed objects can be in the form of shared data objects, message objects, or control interactions. Most systems provide different communications primitives to their objects, which are either synchronous (the sender and receiver are linked and ready to send and receive) or asynchronous (there is some shareable area such as a mailbox, queue, or stack to which the communicated information is sent). In some cases, the receiver periodically checks to see if anyone has sent anything. In other cases, the communicated information arrives at the receiver's workstation without any effort on the part of the receiver; it just waits. There can also be a combination of these. An example of this communication model might have a mechanism that signals the receiver whenever a communication arrives at the sharable area so the information can be fetched whenever it's convenient. The advantage of this system is that it eliminates unnecessary checking when no messages are waiting.

Finally, the kernel environment for distributed systems must have a scheduler with a consistent and robust mechanism for scheduling objects within the system according to its operation's goals.

If the kernel doesn't already have primitives (such as those we discussed in earlier chapters, test-and-set and P and V) to work with the hardware, then the process manager has to create its own primitives before going on with its job. The process manager has responsibility for the following tasks: creating objects, dispatching objects, scheduling objects, synchronizing operations on objects, communicating among objects, and deleting objects. To perform these tasks, the process manager uses the kernel environment, which provides the primitives it needs to capture the low-level hardware in the system.

For example, to run a database object, the process manager must perform the following steps in order:

1. Determine whether or not the object is in memory. If so, go to Step 3.
2. If the object is not in memory, find it on secondary storage, allocate space in memory for it, and log it into the proper locations.
3. Provide the proper scheduling information for the object.
4. Once the object has been scheduled, wait for the kernel dispatcher to pull it out and place it into the RUNNING state.

Thus far we've discussed the similarities between the object-based and process-based managers. The major difference between them is that objects contain all of their state information. That means that the information is stored *with* the object, not separately in another part of the system, such as in a PCB or other data structure separate from the object.

Device Management

In all distributed systems, devices must be opened, read from, written to, and closed. In addition, device parameters must be initialized and status bits must be set or cleared—just as in stand-alone systems. All of this can be done on a global, cluster, or localized basis.

Usually users prefer to choose devices by name and let the distributed operating system select and operate the best device from among those available. For example, if users need specific control of a device, then they should be able to call a device by name, such as DISK 12. When the choice is made, the DO/S takes control, allocating the unit when it's available, assigning it to the user when the OPEN command is issued, operating it, and then deallocating it when the job is finished.

The device can't be allocated until the Device Manager examines the device's status, determines that it's free, and sends the requesting process a unique device identifier—a name that's used for all communication between the process and the device. Later, when the process issues a CLOSE command, the device is released. That's when the DO/S resets the device's state information and returns its device control block to the device's READY queue. For example, when a user wants to print a file by executing a print command, the DO/S follows a process similar to this:

1. The user's File Manager places a copy of the file in the DO/S spooler directory.
2. The spooler selects the file from the spooler directory and initiates an OPEN request to the DO/S File Manager.
3. When the OPEN request is satisfied, the spooler initiates another OPEN request to a networked line printer's device driver.
4. When the second OPEN request is satisfied, the spooler sends the file to the printer's input buffer. This can be accomplished through a direct message transfer or through a packet transfer, as described in Chapter 9.
5. When printing is complete, the DO/S File Manager deletes the copy of the file from the spooler.
6. Finally, the device is reset and closed.

This system works only if the operating system keeps a global accounting of each network device and its availability, maintaining each device's status record and control block, and distributing this information to all sites. As shown in Figure 10.4, the DO/S

The details required to operate each disk drive are contained in device driver software.

(figure 10.4)

All devices are operated by their individual device managers or device drivers using specific status data that's controlled by the DO/S Device Manager. In this example, the network has three disk drives and three printers.

Device Manager is a collection of remote device drivers connected to and associated with the devices, but controlled by status data that's provided by the DO/S Device Manager.

Process-Based DO/S

All resources in the process-based DO/S are controlled by servers called guardians or administrators. These servers are responsible for accepting requests for service on the individual devices they control, processing each request fairly, providing service to the requestor, and returning to serve others, as shown in Figure 10.5.

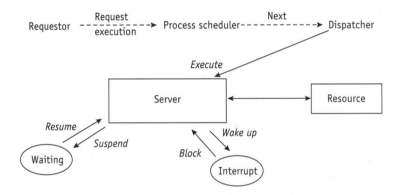

(figure 10.5)

In a process-based DO/S, requests move from the requestor to the process scheduler to the dispatcher to the server. Interrupt processing manages I/O or processing problems. The WAIT state is used to suspend and resume processing. It functions identically to the WAIT state described in Chapter 4.

However, not all systems have a simple collection of resources. Many have clusters of printers, disk drives, tapes, and so on. To control these clusters as a group, most process-based systems are configured around complex **server processes**, which manage multiple resources or divide the work among subordinate processes. The administrator process is configured as a Device Manager and includes the software needed to accept local and remote requests for service, decipher their meaning, and act on them. Typically a server process is made up of one or more device drivers, a Device Manager, and a network server component.

Object-Based DO/S

In an object-based DO/S, each device is managed the same way throughout the network. The physical device is considered an object, just like other network resources, and is surrounded by a layer of software that gives other objects a complete view of the object.

The physical device is manipulated by a set of operations—explicit commands that mobilize the device to perform its designated functions. For example, an object to control a tape unit requires operations to rewind, fast forward, and scan. To retrieve a certain record from an archival tape, a user issues an operation on a tape drive object such as this:

```
WITH TAPE 1 DO FAST FORWARD (N) RECORDS
```

This causes the tape drive to advance N records. This assumes, of course, that the operating system has already granted the user authorization to use the tape object.

A disk drive works the same way. Users access the drive by sending operations to the Device Manager to create a new file, destroy an old file, open or close an existing file, read information from a file, or write to it. Users don't need to know the underlying mechanisms that implement the operations—they just need to know which operations are enabled.

One advantage of an object-based DO/S is that several objects can be assembled to communicate and synchronize with each other to provide a distributed network of resources, with each object knowing the location of its distributed peers. So, if the local device manager can't satisfy a user's request, the request is sent to another device manager, a peer. Again, users don't need to know if the network's resources are centralized or distributed—only that their requests are satisfied.

For this system to be successful, the Device Manager object at each site needs to maintain a current directory of device objects at all sites. Then, when a requesting object needs to use a printer, for example, the request is presented to its local device manager. If the local manager has the means and opportunity to provide the proper service, it prints the request. If it can't meet the request locally, it sends the request to a peer Device Manager that has the appropriate resources. It's this remote Device Manager that processes the request and performs the operation.

File Management

Distributed file management gives users the illusion that the network is a single logical file system that's implemented on an assortment of devices and computers. Therefore, the main function of a DO/S File Manager is to provide transparent mechanisms to find, open, read, write, close, create, and delete files—no matter where they're located in the network, as shown in Table 10.3.

File management systems are a subset of database managers, which provide more capabilities to user processes than file systems and which are implemented as distributed database management systems as part of local area network systems.

Desired File Function	File Manager's Action
Find and Open	It uses a master directory with information about all files stored anywhere on the system and sets up a channel to the file.
Read	It sets up a channel to the file and attempts to read it using simple file access schemes. However, a read operation won't be immediately fulfilled if the file is currently being created or modified.
Write	It sets up a channel to the file and attempts to write to it using simple file access schemes. To write to a file, the requesting process must have exclusive access to it. This can be accomplished by locking the file, a technique frequently used in database systems. While a file is locked, all other requesting processes must wait until the file is unlocked before they can write to or read the file.
Close	It sends a command to the remote server to unlock that file. This is typically accomplished by changing the information in the directory at the file's storage site.
Create	It creates a unique file identifier in the network's master directory and assigns space for it on a storage device.
Delete	It erases the unique file identifier in the master directory and deallocates the space reserved for it on the storage device. Notice that the file is not necessarily erased; its space is just marked as available to write another file.

(table 10.3)

Typical file management functions and the necessary actions of the File Manager.

Therefore, the tasks required by a DO/S include those typically found in a distributed database environment. These involve a host of controls and mechanisms necessary to provide consistent, synchronized, and reliable management of system and user information assets, including the following:

- Concurrency control
- Data redundancy
- Location transparency and distributed directory
- Deadlock resolution or recovery
- Query processing

Concurrency Control

Concurrency control techniques give the system the ability to perform concurrent reads and writes, as long as the results of these actions don't jeopardize the contents of the database. That means that the results of all concurrent transactions are the same as if the transactions had been executed one at a time, in some arbitrary serial order, thereby providing the serial execution view on a database. The concurrency control mechanism keeps the database in a consistent state as the transactions are processed.

For example, let's say numerous airline passengers are making online plane reservations. By using concurrency control techniques, the File Manager allows each

Locking (such as at a database's field or record level) is one form of concurrency control.

person to read and write to a record on the airline's huge database if, and only if, each read and write doesn't interfere with another that's already taking place. These techniques provide a serial execution view on a database.

Data Redundancy

Data redundancy (the essence of RAID configurations discussed in Chapter 7) can make files much faster and easier to read. That's because the File Manager can allow a process to read the copy that's closest or easiest to access. Or, if the file is very large, the read request can be split into several different requests, each of which is fulfilled at a different file location. For example, if an airline reservation system received a request for information about passengers on a certain flight, and the entire database was stored in three different locations, then one read request could search the passengers with last names beginning with A–K, the second read request could search L–R, and the third read request could search S–Z. Then, the results of all three requests are combined before returning the results to the requester.

Data redundancy also has beneficial aspects from a disaster recovery standpoint because if one site fails, operations can be restarted at another site with the same resources. Later, the failed site can be reinstated by copying all files that were updated since the failure. The disadvantage of redundant data is the task of keeping multiple copies of the same file up-to-date at all times. Every time a file is updated, every other copy of the file must be updated in the identical way, and the update must be performed according to the system's reliability standards.

Based on the algorithm used and on the method of recovery, the system can require that updates be performed at all sites before any reads occur to a master site or to a majority of sites. Some typically used update algorithms are: unanimous agreement, primary site copy, moving primary site, and majority site agreement.

Location Transparency and Distributed Directory

Location transparency means that users don't need to be concerned with the physical location of their files. This is the essence of cloud computing. Instead, users deal with the network as a single system. Location transparency is provided by mechanisms and directories that map logical data items to physical locations. The mechanisms usually use information about data that's stored at all sites in the form of directories.

The distributed directory manages transparency of data location and enhances data recovery for users. The directory contains definitions dealing with the physical and logical structure for the stored data, as well as the policies and mechanisms for mapping between the two. In addition, it contains the names of all system resources and the addressing mechanisms for locating and accessing them.

Deadlock Resolution or Recovery

Deadlock detection and recovery, described in Chapter 5, are critical issues in distributed systems. The most important function is to detect and recover from a circular wait. This occurs when one process requests a resource (such as a file, disk drive, modem, or tape unit), which we call Resource B, while it keeps exclusive control over another resource, which we call Resource A. Meanwhile, a second process requests use of Resource A while it keeps exclusive control over Resource B. A directed graph for this example is shown in Figure 10.6; the solid lines represent resources allocated to processes, and the dotted lines represent resource requests by processes.

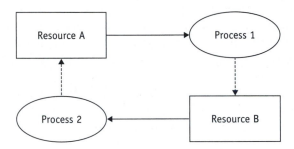

(figure 10.6)

This example of circular wait was created when Process 1 requested Resource B without releasing its exclusive control over Resource A. Likewise, Process 2 requested Resource A without releasing Resource B.

However, most real-life examples of circular wait are much more complex and difficult to detect because they involve multiple processes and multiple resources—all waiting for a resource that's held exclusively by another process.

Deadlock detection, prevention, avoidance, and recovery are all strategies used by a distributed system.

- To detect circular waits, the system uses directed resource graphs and looks for cycles.
- To prevent circular waits, the system tries to delay the start of a transaction until it has all the resources it will request during its execution.
- To avoid circular waits, the system tries to allow execution only when it knows that the transaction can run to completion.
- To recover from a deadlock caused by circular waits, the system selects the best victim—one that can be restarted without much difficulty and one that, when terminated, will free enough resources so the others can finish. Then the system kills the victim, forces that process to restart from the beginning, and reallocates its resources to other waiting processes.

Query Processing

Query processing is the function of processing requests for information. Query processing techniques try to increase the effectiveness of global query execution sequences, local site processing sequences, and device processing sequences. All of these relate directly to the network's global process scheduling problem. Therefore, to ensure consistency of the entire system's scheduling scheme, the query processing strategy must be an integral part of the processing scheduling strategy.

Network Management

The network management function is a communications function that's unique to networked systems because stand-alone operating systems don't need to communicate with other systems. For a DO/S, the Network Manager provides the policies and mechanisms necessary to provide *intra*site and *inter*site communication among concurrent processes. For intrasite processes (those within the network), the Network Manager provides process identifiers and logical paths to other processes—in a one-to-one, one-to-few, one-to-many, or one-to-all manner—while dynamically managing these paths.

The Network Manager has many diverse responsibilities. It must be able to locate processes in the network, send messages throughout the network, and track media use. In addition, it must be able to reliably transfer data, code and decode messages, retransmit errors, perform parity checking, do cyclic redundancy checks, establish redundant links, and acknowledge messages and replies, if necessary.

The Network Manager begins by registering each network process as soon as it has been assigned a unique physical designator. It then sends this identifier to all other sites in the network. From that moment, the process is logged with all sites in the network.

When processes or objects need to communicate with each other, the Network Manager links them together through a port—a logical door on one process that can be linked with a port on another process. This establishes a logical path for the two to communicate. Ports usually have physical buffers and I/O channels, and they represent physical assets that must be used wisely by the Network Manager. Ports can be assigned to one process or to many.

Processes require routing because of the underlying network topology and the processes' location. Routing can be as simple as a process-device pair address that associates one logical process with one physical site. Or it can incorporate many levels traversing multiple links in either a direct or a hop count form, as described in Chapter 9.

In addition to routing, other functions required from the Network Manager are keeping statistics on network use (for use in message scheduling, fault localizations, and rerouting) and providing mechanisms to aid process time synchronization. This standardization mechanism is commonly known as a system-wide clock, a device that allows system components at various sites to compensate for time variations because of delays caused by the distributed communication system.

Process-Based DO/S

In a process-based DO/S, interprocess communication is transparent to users. The Network Manager assumes full responsibility for allocating ports to the processes that request them, for identifying every process in the network, for controlling the flow of messages, and for guaranteeing the transmission and acceptance of messages without errors.

The Network Manager routinely acts as the interfacing mechanism for every process in the system. It handles message traffic, relieving users of the need to know where their processes are physically located in the network. As traffic operator, the Network Manager accepts and interprets each process's commands to send and receive. Then it transforms those commands into low-level actions that actually transmit the messages over network communications links.

Object-Based DO/S

A Network Manager object makes both *inter*mode and *intra*mode communications among cooperative objects easy. A process, the active code elements within objects, can begin an operation at a specific instance of an object by sending a request message. The user doesn't need to know the location of the receiver. The user needs to know only the receiver's name, and the Network Manager takes over, providing the message's proper routing to the receiver. A process can also invoke an operation that's part of its local object environment.

Generally, network communications allow some level of the following functions: send, receive, request, and reply, as described in Table 10.4.

Function	Purpose
Send	Allows objects to send a message with operations to any object in the system.
Receive	Warns objects of incoming communications from an object in the system.
Request	Provides a mechanism for objects to ask for particular services. For example, they can request that a message be sent.
Reply	Allows objects to do one of three things: • Respond to requests for communications from another object. • Respond to a send command that they aren't prepared for. • Indicate that they're ready to accept a send command; the sender can now send a message, knowing that the receiver expects it.

(table 10.4)

Communications sent by the Network Manager allow objects to perform at least one of four functions.

Network Manager services are usually provided at the kernel level to better accommodate the many objects that use them and to offer efficient service. However, depending on the system, the Network Manager may be a simple utility that handles only send

A DO/S is never dormant, while an NOS becomes dormant when no networking functions are requested.

and receive primitives. Or perhaps it's constructed using ports, or channels. A simple send-and-receive utility requires that users know the name of the objects they need to communicate with, whereas the port or channel system requires users to know only the name of the port or channel with which the object is associated. For example, if a communications facility is supported by a port-object type mechanism, then objects are grouped as senders, receivers, ports, and messages, and are linked together using capability lists.

NOS Development

An NOS typically runs on a computer, called a server, and it performs services for network workstations, called clients. Although computers can assume the role of clients most or all of the time, any given computer can assume the role of server (or client), depending on the requirements of the network. Client and server are not hardware-specific terms. Instead, they are role-specific terms.

Many modern network operating systems are true operating systems that include the four management functions: memory management, process scheduling, file management, and device management (including disk and I/O operations). In addition, they have a network management function with responsibility for network communications, protocols, and so on. In an NOS, the network management functions come into play only when the system needs to use the network, as shown in Figure 10.7. At all other times, the Network Manager is dormant and the operating system operates as if it's a stand-alone system.

(figure 10.7)

In a NOS environment, the four managers of the operating system manage all system resources at that site unless and until the node needs to communicate with another node on the network.

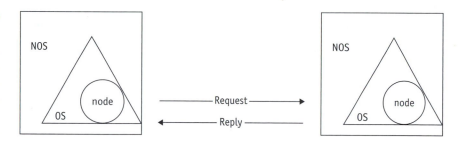

Although an NOS can run applications as well as other operating systems, its focus is on sharing resources instead of running programs. For example, a single-user operating system, such as early versions of Windows, focuses on the user's ability to run applications. On the other hand, network operating systems focus on the user's ability to share resources available on a server, including applications and data, as well as expensive shared resources.

In the following pages we describe some of the features commonly found in a network operating system, without focusing on any one in particular. The best NOS choice depends on many factors, including the applications to be run on the server, the technical support required, the user's level of training, and the compatibility of the hardware with other networking systems.

Important NOS Features

Most network operating systems provide for standard local area network technologies and client desktop operating systems. Modern networks are heterogeneous; that is, they support workstations running a wide variety of operating systems. A single network might include workstations running Windows, the Macintosh operating system (UNIX), and Linux. For an NOS to serve as the networking glue, it must provide strong support for every operating system in the larger information network, sustaining as many current standards as necessary. Therefore, it must have a robust architecture that adapts easily to new technologies.

At a minimum, an NOS should preserve the user's expectations for a desktop system. That means that the network's resources should appear as simple extensions of that user's existing system. For example, on a Windows computer, a network drive should appear as just another hard disk, just with a different volume name and a different drive letter. On a Macintosh computer, the network drive should appear as an icon for a volume on the desktop. And on a Linux or UNIX system, the drive should appear as a mountable file system.

An NOS is designed to operate a wide range of third-party software applications and hardware devices, including hard disk drives, optical disc drives, USB devices, and network interface cards. An NOS also supports software for multiuser network applications, such as electronic messaging, as well as networking expansions such as new protocol stacks.

Finally, the NOS must blend efficiency with security. Its constant goal is to provide network clients with quick and easy access to the network's data and resources without compromising network security.

Major NOS Functions

An important NOS function is to let users transfer files from one computer to another. In this case, each system controls and manages its own file system. For example, the Internet allows the use of the file transfer protocol (FTP). With FTP, students in a UNIX programming class can copy a data file from a campus computer to their laptops. To do this, each student begins by issuing something like the following command to create the FTP connection:

```
ftp unixs.cis.pitt.edu
```

This opens the FTP program, which then asks the student for a login name and password. Once this information has been verified by the UNIX operating system, each student is allowed to copy the file from the host computer.

```
get filename.ext
```

In this example, *filename.ext* is the absolute filename and extension of the required data file. That means the user must know *exactly* where the file is located—in which directory and subdirectory the file is stored. That's because the file location isn't necessarily transparent to the user.

This find-and-copy technique isn't considered true file sharing, because all users wanting access to the data file must copy the file onto their own systems, thereby duplicating the code and wasting space. This practice also adds **version control** difficulties, because when one user modifies the file in any way, those changes aren't reflected on other copies already stored in other directories (unless each user explicitly replaces the old version with the new version).

Conclusion

The first operating systems for networks were network operating systems. Although they were adequate at the time, they didn't take full advantage of the global resources available to all connected sites. The development of distributed operating systems specifically addressed that need.

Every networked system, whether an NOS or DO/S, has specific requirements. Each must be secure from unauthorized access yet accessible to authorized users. Each must monitor its available system resources, including memory, processors, devices, and files (as described in Chapters 2 through 8), as well as its communications links. In addition, because it's a networking operating system, it must perform the required networking tasks described in Chapter 9.

All of the technological advances we discussed in Chapters 1-10 have inherent security vulnerabilities. System security experts like to say that the only secure computer is one that is unplugged from its power source. In the next chapter we look at key elements of system security and ethics, and we examine the role of the system administrator in safeguarding the network's most valuable resource—its data.

Key Terms

distributed operating system (DO/S): an operating system that provides global control for a distributed computing system, allowing its resources to be managed in a unified way.

distributed processing: a method of data processing in which files are stored at many different locations and in which processing takes place at different sites.

kernel: the part of the operating system that resides in main memory and performs the most essential tasks, such as managing memory and handling input and output from secondary storage.

kernel level: in an object-based distributed operating system, it provides the basic mechanisms for dynamically building parts of the operating system by creating, managing, scheduling, synchronizing, and deleting objects.

network operating system (NOS): the software that manages network resources for a node on a network and may provide security and access control.

object: any one of the many entities that constitute a computer system, such as CPUs, terminals, disk drives, files, or databases.

object-based DO/S: a view of distributed operating systems where each hardware unit is bundled with its required operational software, forming a discrete object to be handled as an entity.

primitives: well-defined, predictable, low-level operating system mechanisms that allow higher-level operating system components to perform their functions without considering direct hardware manipulation.

process-based DO/S: a view of distributed operating systems that encompasses all the system's processes and resources.

server process: a logical unit composed of one or more device drivers, a device manager, and a network server module needed to control clusters or similar devices in a process-based, distributed operating system environment.

version control: the tracking and updating of a specific release of a piece of hardware or software.

Interesting Searches

For more background on a few of the topics discussed in this chapter, begin a search with these terms.

- Concurrency control
- Network processing
- Network process synchronization
- Operating systems kernel

Exercises

Research Topics

A. Research the concept of query processing in distributed systems. Build on the brief description provided in this chapter, and using simple terms, explain what it is and how it works in a distributed network. Is this a necessary tool? Does query processing increase network processing speed? Why or why not? What effect does the size of the network have on query processing speed? Cite your sources.

B. Identify four early operating systems for networks and explain which group each belonged to (as defined in this chapter)—NOS or DO/S. State the reasons for your answer and cite your sources.

Exercises

1. Briefly compare the advantages and disadvantages of an NOS and a DO/S, and explain which you would prefer to administer and why.

2. If your organization had an NOS with four nodes and you were the system administrator needing to apply a critical update the operating system, how many computers would need to be updated? Explain your answer.

3. If your company used a DO/S with five nodes and you were the system administrator needing to apply a critical update to the operating system, how many updates would you need to perform? Explain your reasoning.

4. Several levels of file access were discussed in this chapter, including read/write, read-only, execute-only, and no access. Assume you maintain a database containing confidential patient information and need to restrict UPDATE to only 5 individuals, allow only 15 others to view the database, and disallow any database access to all other users. Which access level would you assign to the 20 individuals in the first two groups and to the remaining users? For each of the three groups, describe every type of access granted to each one.

5. List and describe three benefits of data redundancy as described in this chapter.

6. Explain in your own words the steps a DO/S File Manager uses to open a file, read data from it, update that data, and close the file. Do those steps change if the data has not been modified? Explain the reasons for your answer.

7. Explain in your own words why process synchronization is critical in network process management.

8. Deadlocks are discussed in Chapter 5. Describe how a DO/S Processor Manager could attempt to avoid them in a real-life network. Then describe how it could try to recover gracefully if one should occur.

9. Process control blocks (PCBs) are discussed in Chapter 4 in the context of non-networked systems. In a distributed operating system, what additional information needs to be noted in the PCB in order for the Processor Manager to successfully manage processes correctly?

10. Describe in detail how a DO/S protects a file from access or modification by an unauthorized user. Compare it to NOS file protection.

11. Of the two, NOS and DO/S, which system results in the most efficient use of all resources in the system? Give your opinion and explain your reasoning.

Advanced Exercises

12. Which kind of network structure (NOS or DO/S) do you believe is less likely to crash the entire network if one node should malfunction and crash? Explain your conclusion and suggest whether or not system robustness in this instance is reason enough to choose one structure over the other.

13. Compare and contrast the advantages and disadvantages of the two varieties of distributed operating systems discussed in this chapter: a process-based DO/S and an object-based DO/S. If you were the system administrator, which would you prefer? Explain your reasoning.

14. Describe the top 10 critical duties of a network administrator for a distributed operating system. Identify which level of access would be needed by the administrator for each duty and explain why.

15. Let's say you are systems administrator for a hospital's network. Keep in mind that as system administrator, your job is to provide the correct level of accessibility to authorized users while denying access to those who lack authorization. What are the top five policies that you would implement? How would you enforce compliance with these policies? How would you educate your users to convince them to adhere to your policies?

16. Reviewing our discussion of deadlocks in Chapter 5, if you were designing a DO/S , how would you manage the threat of deadlocks in your network? Consider all of the following: prevention, detection, avoidance, and recovery.

17. Let's say you have global administration responsibility for a distributed system with multiple system administrators reporting to you. As part of your responsibility, you are required to monitor and report system administration status to your superiors. Describe in detail, in your own words, how you would manage administrative duties for your distributed network. Describe how you would divide the responsibilities, how you would decide who should be assigned which critical tasks, how you would measure compliance by your administrators, and how you would respond to both underachievers and overachievers on your team.

Chapter 11 | Security and Ethics

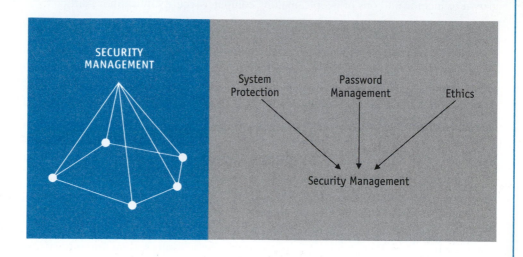

SECURITY MANAGEMENT

System Protection → Security Management
Password Management → Security Management
Ethics → Security Management

> ❝*Perfection of means and confusion of goals seem,
> in my opinion, to characterize our age.* ❞
>
> —Albert Einstein *(1879–1955)*

Learning Objectives

After completing this chapter, you should be able to describe:

- The role of the operating system with regard to system security
- The effects of system security practices on overall system performance
- The levels of system security that can be implemented and the threats posed by evolving technologies
- The differences among computer viruses, worms, and blended threats
- The role of education and ethical practices in system security

Every computing system has two conflicting needs: to share resources and to protect them. In the early days, security consisted of a secure lock and a few keys. That is, the system was physically guarded; only authorized users were allowed in its vicinity. This was sufficient when the user group was limited to several dozen individuals. However, with the advent of data communication, networking, the proliferation of personal computers, telecommunications software, Web sites, and e-mail, the user community has grown to include millions of people, making computer security much more difficult.

System security is a vast and complex subject worthy of its own text. While we cannot do justice to the subject in a single chapter, we introduce the important concepts here and encourage the reader to review current research about the subject. Keep in mind that this subject changes at lightning speed and is well worth constant monitoring by system owners, managers, and users.

Role of the Operating System in Security

Because it has access to every part of the system, the operating system plays a key role in computer system security. Any vulnerability at the operating system level opens the entire system to attack. The more complex and powerful the operating system, the more likely it is to have vulnerabilities to attack. As a result, system administrators must remain on guard to arm their operating systems with all available defenses against attack and possible failure.

System Survivability

System survivability is defined as "the capability of a system to fulfill its mission, in a timely manner, in the presence of attacks, failures, or accidents" (Linger, 2002).

An integral part of both system security and system management is the timely application of patches, detailed in the next chapter.

- The term system refers to any system. It's used here in the broadest possible sense from laptop to distributed system to supercomputer.
- A mission is a very high-level set of requirements or goals.
- In a timely manner refers to system response time, a critical factor for most systems.
- The terms attack, failure, and accident refer to any potentially damaging incident, regardless of the cause, whether intentional or not.

Before a system can be considered survivable, it must meet all of these requirements, especially with respect to services that are considered essential to the organization in the face of adverse challenges. The four key properties of survivable systems are resistance to attacks, recognition of attacks and resulting damage, recovery of essential services after an attack, and adaptation and evolution of system defense mechanisms to mitigate future attacks.

With the elevated risks in recent years of system intrusion and compromise, system designers have recognized the critical need for system survivability that's incorporated into system development. It's no longer satisfactory to add survivability factors to the system only as an afterthought. Examples of sample strategies that can be built into systems to enhance their survivability are shown in Table 11.1.

Key Property	Description	Example Strategies
Resistance to attacks	Strategies for repelling attacks	• Authentication • Access controls • Encryption • Message filtering • System diversification • Functional isolation
Recognition of attacks and damage	Strategies for detecting attacks and evaluating damage	• Intrusion detection • Integrity checking
Recovery of essential and full services after attack	Strategies for limiting damage, restoring compromised information or functionality, maintaining or restoring essential services within mission time constraints, restoring full services	• Redundant components • Data replication • System backup and restoration • Contingency planning
Adaptation and evolution to reduce effectiveness of future attacks	Strategies for improving system survivability based on knowledge gained from intrusions	• Intrusion recognition patterns

Levels of Protection

Once a system is breached, the integrity of every file on the system and the data in those files can no longer be trusted. For each computer configuration, the system administrator must evaluate the risk of intrusion, which, in turn, depends on the level of connectivity given to the system, as shown in Table 11.2.

All of the vulnerabilities shown in Table 11.2 are discussed in this chapter.

Configuration	Ease of Protection	Relative Risk	Selected Vulnerabilities
Isolated single computer (without e-mail or Internet)	High	Low	• Compromised passwords • Viruses
Local area network (without Internet)	Medium	Medium	• Sniffers • Spoofing • Compromised passwords • Viruses
Local area network (with Internet access)	Low	High	• E-mail • Web servers • Sniffers • Spoofing • Compromised passwords • Viruses

Backup and Recovery

Standard procedures for most computing systems include having sufficient **backup** and recovery policies in place and performing other archiving techniques. Many system managers use a layered backup schedule. That is, they back up the entire system once a week and only back up daily the files that were changed that day. As an extra measure of safety, copies of complete system backups are stored for three to six months in a safe off-site location.

Backups are essential when the system becomes unavailable because of a natural disaster or when a computer virus infects the system. If the problem is discovered early, the administrator can run eradication software and reload damaged files from your backup copies. Of course, any changes made since the files were backed up will need to be regenerated.

Backups, with one set stored off-site, are also crucial to disaster recovery. The disaster could come from anywhere. Here are just a few of the threats:

- water from a fire upstairs
- fire from an electrical connection
- malfunctioning server
- corrupted archival media
- intrusion from unauthorized users

Written organizational policies and procedures concerning electronic communication can help system managers enforce safe practices. Legally, these e-policies may also serve as evidence of organizational preparedness.

The importance of adequate backups is illustrated in an example from a 2005 CERT report about a system administrator who was angry about employment decisions at the defense manufacturing firm where he worked. Upon learning that he would be given a smaller role managing the computer network that he alone had developed and managed, he took the initiative to centralize the software supporting the company's manufacturing processes on a single server. Then he intimidated a coworker into giving him the only backup tapes for that software. When the system administrator was terminated, a logic bomb that he had previously planted detonated and deleted the only remaining copy of the critical software from the company's server. The cost? The company estimated that the damage exceeded $10 million, which led, in turn, to the layoff of some 80 employees. More case stories can be found at *www.cert.org*.

Written policies and procedures and regular user training are essential elements of system management. Most system failures are caused by honest mistakes made by well-intentioned users—not by malicious intruders. Written security procedures should recommend frequent password changes, reliable backup procedures, guidelines for loading new software, compliance with software licenses, network safeguards, guidelines for monitoring network activity, and rules for terminal access.

Security Breaches

A gap in system security can be malicious or not. For instance, some intrusions are the result of an uneducated user and the unauthorized access to system resources. But others stem from the purposeful disruption of the system's operation. Still others are purely accidental, such as hardware malfunctions, undetected errors in the operating system or applications, or natural disasters. Malicious or not, a breach of security severely damages the system's credibility. Following are some types of security breaks that can occur.

Unintentional Modifications

An unintentional attack is defined as any breach of security or modification of data that was not the result of a planned intrusion.

When nonsynchronized processes access data records and modify some of a record's fields, it's called accidental incomplete modification of data. An example is given in Chapter 5: the topic of a race in a database with two processes working on the same student record and writing different versions of it to the database.

Errors can also occur when data values are incorrectly stored because the field isn't large enough to hold data stored there, as shown in Figure 11.1.

(figure 11.1)

Data stored in variable length fields (top) shows all of the data in each field, but when data is stored in fixed length fields (bottom), critical data is truncated.

| Dan | Whitestone | 1243 Elementary Ave. | Harrisburg | PA | 412 683-1234 |

| Dan | | Whitesto | 1243 Elem | Harrisbur | PA | | 412 683-1 | |

Intentional Attacks

Intentional unauthorized access includes denial of service attacks, browsing, wiretapping, repeated trials, trapdoors, and trash collection. These attacks are fundamentally different from viruses and worms and the like (covered shortly), which inflict widespread damage to numerous companies and organizations—without specifying certain ones as targets.

This example comes from a 2005 CERT report on insider threats. An application developer, who lost his IT sector job as a result of company downsizing, expressed his displeasure at being laid off just prior to the Christmas holiday by launching a systematic attack on his former employer's computer network. Three weeks following his termination, the insider used the username and password of one of his former coworkers to gain remote access to the network. He modified several of the company's Web pages, changing text and inserting pornographic images. He also sent each of the company's customers an e-mail message advising that the Web site had been hacked. Each e-mail message also contained that customer's usernames and passwords for the Web site. An investigation was initiated, but it failed to identify the insider as the perpetrator. A month and a half later, he again remotely accessed the network and executed a script to reset all network passwords; he then changed 4,000 pricing records to reflect bogus information. This former employee ultimately was identified and prosecuted. He was sentenced to serve time in prison and two years on supervised probation, and ordered to pay $48,600 restitution to his former employer.

Intentional Unauthorized Access

Denial of service (DoS) attacks are synchronized attempts to deny service to authorized users by causing a computer (usually a Web server) to perform a task (often an unproductive task) over and over, thereby making the system unavailable to perform the work it is designed to do. For example, if a Web server designed to accept orders from customers over the Internet is diverted from its appointed task with repeated commands to identify itself, then the computer becomes unavailable to serve the customers online.

Browsing is when unauthorized users gain the capability to search through storage, directories, or files for information they aren't privileged to read. The term storage refers to main memory or to unallocated space on disks or tapes. Sometimes the browsing occurs after the previous job has finished. When a section of main memory is allocated to a process, the data from a previous job often remains in memory—it isn't usually erased by the system—and so it's available to a browser. The same applies to data stored in secondary storage.

Wiretapping is nothing new. Just as telephone lines can be tapped, so can most data communication lines. When wiretapping is passive, the unauthorized user listens to the transmission without changing the contents. There are two reasons for passive tapping: to copy data while bypassing any authorization procedures and to collect specific information (such as **passwords**) that will permit the tapper to enter the system at a later date. In an unsecured wireless network environment, wiretapping is not difficult.

Active wiretapping is when the data being sent is modified. Two methods of active wiretapping are "between lines transmission" and "piggyback entry." Between lines doesn't alter the messages sent by the legitimate user, but it inserts additional messages into the communication line while the legitimate user is pausing. Piggyback entry intercepts and modifies the original messages. This can be done by breaking the communication line and routing the message to another computer that acts as the host.

✔

Key logging software records every keystroke and saves it for reference later. When key logging software is installed without the knowledge and consent of the computer user, it may be a form of system intrusion. This subject is explored as a research topic at the end of this chapter.

For example, the tapper could intercept a logoff message, return the expected acknowledgment of the logoff to the user, and then continue the interactive session with all the privileges of the original user—without anyone knowing.

Repeated trials describes the method used to enter systems by guessing authentic passwords. If an intruder knows the basic scheme for creating passwords, such as length of password and symbols allowed to create it, then the system can be compromised with a program that systematically goes through all possible combinations until a valid combination is found. This isn't as long a process as one might think if the passwords are short or if the intruder learns enough about the intended victim/user, as shown in Table 11.3. Because the intruder doesn't need to break a specific password, the guessing of any user's password allows entry to the system and access to its resources.

(table 11.3)

Average time required for a human and computer to guess passwords up to 10 alphabetic characters (A–Z) using brute force.

No. of Alphabetic Characters	Possible Combinations	Average Human Attempt (time to discovery at 1 try/second)	Average Computer Attempt (time to discovery at 1 million tries/second)
1	26	13 seconds	.000013 seconds
2	$26^2 = 676$	6 minutes	.000338 seconds
3	$26^3 = 17{,}576$	2.5 hours	.008788 seconds
8	$26^8 = 208{,}827{,}064{,}576$	6,640 years	58 hours
10	$26^{10} = (1.4 \times 10)^{14}$	4.5 million years	4.5 years

Trapdoors, including backdoor passwords, are unspecified and undocumented entry points to the system. It's possible that trapdoors can be caused by a flaw in the system design, but more likely, they are installed by a system diagnostician or programmer to provide fast and easy access for debugging the system. Alternatively, they can be incorporated into the system code by a destructive virus or by a Trojan—one that's seemingly innocuous but that executes hidden instructions. Regardless of the reason for its existence, a trapdoor leaves the system vulnerable to intrusion.

Trash collection, also known as dumpster diving, is an evening pastime for those who enjoy perusing anything and everything thrown out by system users—the discarded disks, CDs, faxes, printer ribbons, as well as printouts of source code, programs, memory dumps, and notes. They all can yield important information that can be used to enter the system illegally. It's recommended that system administrators adopt a policy of routinely shredding all work that can conceivably contain data, code, passwords, access information, Web site development information, or clues to the organization's financial workings. The importance of this obvious precaution can't be overstated.

Legally, it's important to know that malicious attacks on computers may violate U.S. federal and state laws and invite penalties. Generally, those convicted in the United States have lost their computing systems and many have been sentenced to significant fines, jail terms, or both.

Viruses

A **virus** is defined as a small program written to alter the way a computer operates and is run without the permission or knowledge of the user. A virus meets two criteria:

- It must be self-executing. Often, this means placing its own code in the path of another program.
- It must be self-replicating. Usually, this is accomplished by copying itself from infected files to clean files. Viruses can infect desktop computers and network servers alike and spread each time the host file is executed, as shown in Figure 11.2.

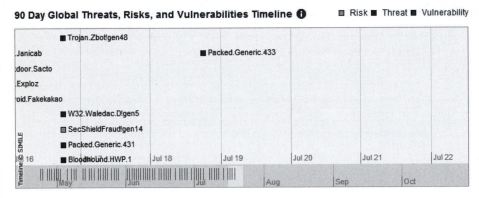

90 Day Global Threats, Risks, and Vulnerabilities Timeline ⓘ   ◻ Risk ◼ Threat ◼ Vulnerability

(figure 11.2)

Snapshot of a 90-day look at global threats, risks, and vulnerabilities. A current version of this information can be found at http://www.symantec.com/security_response.

Viruses are usually written to attack a certain operating system. Therefore, it's unusual for the same virus code to successfully attack a Linux workstation and a Windows server. Writers of virus code usually exploit a known vulnerability in the operating system software, hence the need to keep operating systems correctly updated with patches—something we discuss in Chapter 12.

Some viruses are designed to significantly damage the infected computer, such as by deleting or corrupting files or reformatting the hard disk. Others are not so malicious, but merely make their presence known by delivering unsolicited text, video, or audio messages to the computer's user. However, no virus can be considered benign, because all viruses confiscate valuable memory and storage space required by legitimate programs and often cause system failures and data loss. There are five recognized types of viruses, as shown in Table 11.4.

(table 11.4)	Type of Virus	Description
Five types of viruses.	File infector virus	Infects files on the computer, normally executable files. These viruses commonly become resident in memory and then infect any clean executable program that runs on that computer.
	Boot sector virus	Infects the boot record, the system area of secondary storage. These viruses activate whenever the user starts up (powers on) the computer.
	Master boot record virus	Infects the boot record of a disk, saving a legitimate copy of the master boot record in a different location on the volume.
	Multipartite virus	Infects both the boot record and program files, making them especially difficult to repair. Successful removal requires that all instances of the virus be removed at once—on the boot records as well as all instances of files infected with the virus. If any instance of the infection remains, the virus will infect the system again.
	Macro virus	Infects data files (such as word processing documents and spread sheets), though newer versions now infect other program files as well. Computer users are advised to disable the automatic execution of macros on files they don't completely trust.

Viruses spread via a wide variety of applications and have even been found in legitimate shrink-wrapped software. In one case, a virus was inadvertently picked up at a trade show by a developer who unknowingly allowed it to infect the finished code of a completed commercial software package just before it was marketed.

In one bizarre example, a virus was distributed to tourists in the Middle East, embedded in part of an illegally copied (and illegally bought) software package. Reportedly, the sellers told authorities that they did it to teach the buyers a lesson in ethics.

A macro virus works by attaching itself to the template which, in turn, is attached to word processing documents. Once the template file is infected, every subsequent document created on that template is infected.

Worms

A **worm** is a memory-resident program that copies itself from one system to the next without requiring the aid of an infected program file. The immediate result of a worm is slower processing time of legitimate work because the worm siphons off processing time and memory space. Worms are especially destructive on networks, where they hoard critical system resources such as main memory and processor time.

Trojans

A **Trojan** (originally called a Trojan Horse) is a destructive program that's disguised as a legitimate or harmless program that sometimes carries within itself the means to allow the program's creator to secretly access the user's system. Intruders have been known to capture user passwords by using a Trojan to replace the standard login program on the computer with an identical fake login that captures keystrokes. Once it's installed, it works like this:

1. The user sees a login prompt and types in the user ID.
2. The user sees a password prompt and types in the password.
3. The rogue program records both the user ID and password and sends a typical login failure message to the user. Then the Trojan program stops running and returns control to the legitimate program.
4. Now, the user sees the legitimate login prompt and retypes the user ID.
5. The user sees the legitimate password prompt and retypes the password.
6. Finally, the user gains access to the system, unaware that the rogue program has used the first attempt to record the user ID and password.

Later, at a convenient time, the Trojan's creator retrieves the file with its list of valid user IDs and passwords, perhaps even a root password, which would allow access to sensitive administrative functions.

Eugene H. Spafford (1956–)

Dr. Gene Spafford's current research primarily concerns information security, computer crime investigation, and information ethics, with specific focus on system reliability and the consequences of computer failures. Spafford's specific topics of interest include software debugging, intrusion detection, digital crime forensics, professional ethics, firewalls, security management, and secure architectures. He has served as a senior advisor to the National Science Foundation as well as the U.S. Air Force, and he was Purdue University's Chief

Information Security Officer for several years. Dr. Spafford's numerous honors include the NIST/NSA National Computer System Security Award (2000), the ACM President's Award (2007), and a SANS Lifetime Achievement Award (2011).

For more information, see
http://spaf.cerias.purdue.edu/

Gene Spafford received the 2005 IEEE Computer Society Technical Achievement Award for his "contributions to information security and digital forensics."

Photo by J. Underwood for Purdue University

Rogue software doesn't need to be planted by someone outside the organization. In a California case, an employee planted a Trojan in his employer's system before quitting his job. The code was designed to erase a program he'd written on the job to track the availability and prices of parts for an orbital missile program. At its conclusion, the program was instructed to erase itself. Reportedly, the programmer hoped to become a consultant, and he planned to work for his former employer reconstructing the program he had written and then erased. The plan was foiled when another technician discovered the bad code and removed it before the scheduled date of operation. The former employee was later indicted in federal court.

Logic Bombs

A **logic bomb** is a destructive program with a fuse—a certain triggering event, such as a date, a specific keystroke, or a certain connection with the Internet. A logic bomb often spreads unnoticed throughout a network until a predetermined event, when it goes off and does its damage.

A time bomb is similar to a logic bomb but is triggered by a specific time, such as a day of the year. One of the first widespread logic bombs, the Michelangelo virus in 1991, was designed to execute on the anniversary of the birth of the artist Michelangelo (March 6, 1475). The code was designed to execute when an infected computer was started up on the trigger date (March 6 of any year) and to overwrite the first 17 sectors on heads 0-3 of the first 256 tracks of the hard disk on the infected machine.

Blended Threats

A **blended threat** combines into one program the characteristics of other attacks, including a virus, a worm, a Trojan, **spyware**, key loggers, and other malicious code. That is, this single program uses a variety of tools to attack systems and spread to others. Because the threat from these programs is so diverse, the only defense against them is a comprehensive security plan that includes multiple layers of protection. A blended threat shows the following characteristics:

- Harms the affected system. For example, it might launch a denial of service attack at a target IP address, deface a Web site, or plant Trojans for later execution.
- Spreads to other systems using multiple methods. For example, it might scan for vulnerabilities to compromise a system, such as embedding code in Web page files on a server, infect the systems of visitors who visit a compromised Web site, or send unauthorized e-mail from compromised servers with a worm attachment.
- Attacks other systems from multiple points. For example: inject malicious code into the .exe files on a system, raise the privilege level of an intruder's guest account, create world-readable and world-writeable access to private files, and add bogus script code to Web page files.

- Propagates without human intervention. For example, it might continuously scan the Internet for vulnerable servers that are unpatched and open to attack.
- Exploits vulnerabilities of target systems. For example, it might take advantage of operating system problems (such as buffer overflows), Web page validation vulnerabilities on input screens, and commonly known default passwords to gain unauthorized access.

When the threat includes all or many of these characteristics, no single tool can protect a system. Only a combination of defenses in combination with regular patch management (discussed in Chapter 12) can hope to protect the system adequately.

System Protection

Threats can come from outsiders (those outside the organization) as well as from insiders (employees or others with access to the system) and can include theft of intellectual property or other confidential or sensitive information, fraud, and acts of system sabotage.

System protection is multifaceted. Four protection methods are discussed here: installing antivirus software (and running it regularly), using firewalls (and keeping them up-to-date), ensuring that only authorized individuals access the system, and taking advantage of encryption technology when the overhead required to implement it is mandated by the risk.

Antivirus Software

Antivirus software protects systems from attack by malicious software. The level of protection is usually in proportion to the importance of its data. Medical data should be highly protected. Photos and music files might not deserve the same level of security.

Software to combat viruses can be preventive or diagnostic, or both. Preventive programs may calculate a checksum for each production program, putting the values in a master file. Later, before a program is executed, its checksum is compared with the master. Generally, diagnostic software compares file sizes (checking for added code when none is expected), looks for replicating instructions, and searches for unusual file activity. Some software may look for certain specific instructions and monitor the way the programs execute. But remember: soon after these packages are marketed, system intruders start looking for ways to thwart them. Hence, only the most current software can be expected to uncover the latest viruses. In other words, old software will only find old viruses.

Information about current viruses is available from vendors and government agencies dedicated to system security, such as those listed in Table 11.5.

Web Site	Organization
www.cert.org	CERT Coordination Center
www.csrc.nist.gov	Computer Security Division, National Institute of Standards and Technology
www.mcafee.com	McAfee, Inc.
www.sans.org	SANS Institute
www.symantec.com	Symantec Corp.
www.us-cert.gov	U.S. Computer Emergency Readiness Team

While antivirus software (an example is shown in Figure 11.3) is capable of repairing files infected with a virus, it is generally unable to repair worms, Trojans, or blended threats because of the structural differences between viruses and worms or Trojans. A virus works by infecting an otherwise clean file. Therefore, antivirus software can sometimes remove the infection and leave the remainder intact. On the other hand, a worm or Trojan is malicious code in its entirety. That is, the entire body of the software code contained in a worm or Trojan is threatening and must be removed as a whole.

The only way to remove a Trojan is to remove the entire body of the malicious program. For example, if a computer game, available for free download over the Internet, is a worm that steals system IDs and passwords, there is no way to cleanse the game of the bad code and save the rest. The game must go.

(figure 11.3)

This partial list from
Symantec.com shows
a few of the recognized
threats as of July, 2013.
A current list can be found
at http://www.symantec
.com/security_response/
landing/threats.jsp.

Severity	Name	Type	Protected*
	Trojan.Zeroaccess!g50	Trojan	
	Packed.Generic.433	Trojan, Virus, Worm	07/19/2013
	Android.Fakealbums	Trojan	07/18/2013
	Android.Fakebank	Trojan	
	Trojan.Zbot!gen48	Trojan	07/17/2013
	W32.Waledac.D!gen5	Worm	07/17/2013
	SecShieldFraud!gen14		07/17/2013
	Packed.Generic.431	Trojan	07/17/2013
	Packed.Generic.432	Trojan	07/17/2013
	W32.Exploz	Virus	07/16/2013
	W32.Fypzserv!inf	Virus	07/17/2013
	W32.Fypzserv	Virus	07/17/2013
	Android.Fakekakao	Trojan	07/16/2013
	Bloodhound.HWP.1	Trojan	07/17/2013
	Bloodhound.HWP.2	Trojan	07/17/2013
	Backdoor.Sacto	Trojan	07/16/2013
	OSX.Janicab	Trojan	07/16/2013

Firewalls

Network assaults include compromised Web servers, circumvented firewalls, and FTP and Telnet sites accessed by unauthorized users, to name a few.

A **firewall** is hardware and/or software designed to protect a system by disguising its IP address from outsiders who don't have authorization to access it or ask for information about it. A firewall sits between the Internet and the network, as shown in Figure 11.4, blocking curious inquiries and potentially dangerous intrusions from outside the system.

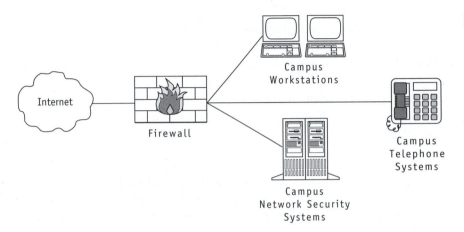

(figure 11.4)

In this example of a university system, the firewall sits between the campus networks and the Internet, filtering requests for access.

The typical tasks of the firewall are to:
- log activities that access the Internet
- maintain **access control** based on the senders' or receivers' IP addresses
- maintain access control based on the services that are requested
- hide the internal network from unauthorized users requesting network information
- verify that virus protection is installed and being enforced
- perform authentication based on the source of a request from the Internet

The two fundamental mechanisms used by the firewall to perform these tasks are packet filtering and proxy servers. Using **packet filtering**, the firewall reviews the header information for incoming and outgoing Internet packets to verify that the source address, destination address, and protocol are all correct. For example, if a packet arrives from the Internet (outside the network) with an internal source address (which should be from inside the network), the firewall would be expected to refuse its entry.

A **proxy server** hides important network information from outsiders by making the network server invisible. To do so, the proxy server intercepts the request for access to the network, decides if it is a valid request, and if so, passes the request to the appropriate server that can fulfill the request—all without revealing the makeup of the network, the servers, or other information that might reside on them. Likewise, if information is to be passed from the network to the Internet, the proxy server relays the transmission without revealing anything about the network. Proxy servers are invisible to the users but are critical to the success of the firewall.

Authentication

Authentication is verification that an individual trying to access a system is authorized to do so. One popular authentication tool is **Kerberos**, a network authentication protocol developed as part of the Athena Project at Massachusetts Institute of Technology (MIT). Kerberos is the name of the three-headed dog of Greek mythology that guarded the gates of Hades.

To answer the need for password encryption to improve network security, Kerberos was designed to provide strong authentication for client/server applications. A free open-source implementation of this protocol (under copyright permissions) is available from MIT *(http://web.mit.edu/kerberos/)* or for purchase from numerous distributors.

The Kerberos protocol uses strong **cryptography** (the science of coding messages) so that a client can prove its identity to a server, and vice versa, across an insecure network connection. Then, once authentication is completed, both client and server can encrypt all of their subsequent communications to assure privacy and data integrity.

In simplest form, here's how Kerberos works, illustrated in Figure 11.5:

1. When you (the client) want to access a server that requires a Kerberos ticket, you request authentication from the Kerberos Authentication Server, which creates a session key based on your password. This key also serves as your encryption key.

2. Next, you are sent to a Ticket Granting Server (this can be the same physical server but a different logical unit), which creates a ticket valid for access to the server.

3. Next, your ticket is sent to the server where it can be rejected or accepted. Once accepted, you are free to interact with the server for the specified period of time. The ticket is time-stamped so you can make additional requests using the same ticket within a certain time period; it must be authenticated again when the time period ends. This design feature is to limit the likelihood that someone will later use your ticket without your knowledge.

Because the user gains access using a ticket, there's no need for the user's password to pass through the network, thus improving the protection of network passwords.

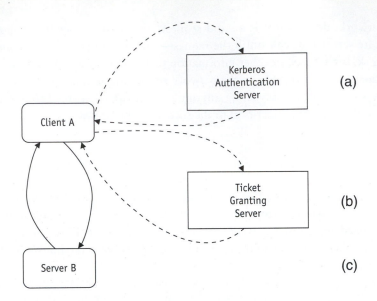

(figure 11.5)

Using Kerberos, when client A attempts to access server B, the user is authenticated (a) and receives a ticket for the session (b). Once the ticket is issued, client and server can communicate at will (c). Without the ticket, access is not granted.

An essential part of maintaining a Kerberos protocol is the systematic revocation of access rights from clients who no longer deserve to have access. For this reason, the administrators of the Kerberos Authentication Server as well as the Ticket Granting Server must keep their databases updated and accurate. By keeping records of access revocation, the administrator can spot trends and anticipate the need for user education.

For example, if the organization hires new consultants in February of each year, March and April will see numerous calls of access revocation. As shown in Figure 11.6, scheduling user education for new employees in February can be a proactive, cost effective move, thereby reducing the reason for revocation.

(figure 11.6)

Sample system administrator report. By tracking the reasons for revoking user access, the administrator can target activities to the user population, such as retraining and password management.

Encryption

The most extreme protection for sensitive data is **encryption**—putting it into a secret code. Total network encryption, also called communications encryption, is the most extreme form—that's when all communications with the system are encrypted. The system then decrypts them for processing. To communicate with another system, the data is encrypted, transmitted, decrypted, and processed.

Partial encryption is less extreme and may be used between a network's entry and exit points or other vulnerable parts of its communication system. Storage encryption means that the information is stored in encrypted form and decrypted before it's read or used.

There are two disadvantages to encryption. It increases the system's overhead and the system becomes totally dependent on the encryption process itself—if you lose the key, you've lost the data forever. But if the system must be kept secure, then this procedure might be warranted.

How Encryption Works

The way to understand cryptography is to first understand the role of a public key and a private key. The **private key** is a pair of two prime numbers (usually with 75 or more digits each) chosen by the person who wants to receive a private message. The two prime numbers are multiplied together, forming a third number with 150 or more digits. The person who creates this private key is the only one who knows which two prime numbers were used to create it.

Once the message receiver has the product, known as the **public key**, it can be posted in any public place, even an online directory, for anyone to see, because the private key can't be decoded from the public key.

Then, anyone who wants to send a confidential message to the receiver uses encryption software and inserts the public key as a variable. The software then scrambles the message before it's sent to the receiver. Once received, the receiver uses the private key in the encryption software and the confidential message is revealed. Should someone else receive the encrypted message and attempt to open it with a private key that is incorrect, the resulting message would be scrambled, unreadable code.

Sniffers and Spoofing

If sensitive data is sent over a network or the Internet in **cleartext**, without encryption, it becomes vulnerable at numerous sites across the network. **Packet sniffers**, also called sniffers, are programs that reside on computers attached to the network. They peruse data packets as they pass by, examine each one for specific information, and log copies of interesting packets for more detailed examination. Sniffing is particularly problematic in wireless networks. Anyone with a wireless device can detect a wireless network that's within range. If the network is passing cleartext packets, it's quite easy to intercept, read, modify, and resend them. The information sought ranges from passwords, Social Security numbers, and credit card numbers to industrial secrets and marketing information. This vulnerability is a fundamental shortcoming of clear text transmission over the Internet.

Wireless security is a special area of system security that is too vast to cover here. Readers are encouraged to pursue the subject in the current literature for the latest research, tools, and best practices.

Spoofing is a security threat that relies on cleartext transmission, whereby the assailant falsifies the IP addresses of an Internet server by changing the address recorded in packets it sends over the Internet. This technique is useful when unauthorized users want to disguise themselves as friendly sites. For example, to guard confidential information on an internal network (intranet), some Web servers allow access only to users from certain sites; however, by spoofing the IP address, the server could inadvertently admit unauthorized users.

Password Management

The most basic techniques used to protect hardware and software investments are good passwords and careful user training, but this is not as simple as it might appear. Many users forget their passwords, rarely change them, often share them, and consider them bothersome.

Password Construction

Passwords are one of the easiest and most effective protection schemes to implement, but only if they're used correctly. A good password is unusual, memorable to the user, not obvious, and changed often. Ideally, the password should be a combination of characters and numbers, something that's easy for the user to remember but difficult for someone else to guess. The password should be committed to memory, never written down, and not included in a script file to log on to a network.

Password files are normally stored in encrypted form so they are not readable by casual browsers. To verify a password, the system accepts the user's entry in clear text, encrypts it, and compares the new sequence to the encrypted version stored in the password file for that user, as shown in Figure 11.7.

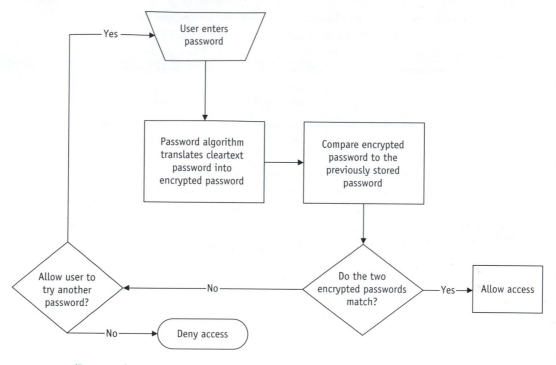

(figure 11.7)

Password verification flowchart showing how the user's password is compared to its encrypted form.

There are several reliable techniques for generating a good password:

- Use a minimum of eight characters, including numbers and symbols.
- Create a misspelled word or joining bits of phrases into a word that's easy to remember.
- Following a certain pattern on the keyboard, generate new passwords easily by starting your sequence with a different letter each time.
- Create acronyms from memorable sentences, such as MDWB4YOIA, which stands for: "My Dog Will Be 4 Years Old In April."
- If the operating system differentiates between upper- and lowercase characters (as UNIX, Linux, and Android do), users should take advantage of that feature by using both in the password: MDwb4YOia.
- Avoid words that appear in any dictionary.

The length of the password has a direct effect on the ability of the password to survive password cracking attempts. Longer passwords are more secure. For example, if the system administrator mandates that all passwords must be exactly eight characters long and contain only lowercase letters, the possible combinations number 26^8.

Likewise, if the policy mandates 10 characters of lowercase letters, the combinations total 26^{10}. However, if the rule allows eight characters from among 95 printable characters, the combinations jump to 95^8, as shown in Table 11.6. When picture passwords are allowed, the combinations increase even more, as we see in the next few pages.

	Length of Password in Characters					
	2	4	6	8	10	12
All printable characters	95^2	95^4	95^6	95^8	95^{10}	95^{12}
All alphanumeric characters	62^2	62^4	62^6	62^8	62^{10}	62^{12}
All lower (or upper) case letters and numbers	36^2	36^4	36^6	36^8	36^{10}	36^{12}
Lower case letters only or upper case letters only	26^2	26^4	26^6	26^8	26^{10}	26^{12}

(table 11.6)

Number of combinations of passwords depending on their length and available character sets.

Dictionary attack is the term used to describe a method of breaking encrypted passwords. Its requirements are simple: a copy of the encrypted password file and the algorithm used to encrypt the passwords. With these two tools, the intruder runs a software program that takes every word in the dictionary, runs it through the password encryption algorithm, and compares the encrypted result to the encrypted passwords contained in the file. If both encrypted versions match, then the intruder knows that this dictionary word was used as a legitimate password.

One technique used by some operating systems to make passwords harder to guess is to "salt" user passwords with extra random bits to make them less vulnerable to dictionary attacks. Here's how it works. The user enters the desired password, which is then encrypted. Then the system assigns the user a unique combination of bits (called the salt) that are tacked on the end of the encrypted password. That is, the stored combination of 0s and 1s contains the encrypted password combined with a unique salt. Therefore, if an intruder downloads the list of encrypted passwords, the intruder will need to guess not only the password but also the random salt. This is something that's much more difficult and time consuming to do than merely guessing obvious passwords.

Password Alternatives

As an alternative to passwords, some systems have integrated use of a smart card—a credit-card-sized calculator that requires both something you have and something you know. The smart card displays a constantly changing multi-digit number that's synchronized with an identical number generator in the system. To enter the correct password, the user must type in the number that appears at that moment on the smart card. For added protection, the user then enters a secret code. The user is admitted to the system only if both number and code are validated. Using this scheme, an intruder needs more than either the card or the code because unless both are valid, entry is denied.

Another alternative is **biometrics,** the science and technology of identifying individuals based on the unique biological characteristics of each person. Current research focuses on analysis of the human face, fingerprints, hand measurements, iris/retina, and voice prints. Biometric devices often consist of a scanner or other device to gather the necessary data about the user, software to convert the data into a form that can be compared and stored, and a database to keep the stored information from all authorized users. One of the strengths of biometrics is that it positively identifies the person being scanned.

For example, a fingerprint has about 35 discriminators—factors that set one person's fingerprint apart from someone else's. Even better, the iris has about 260 discriminators and is unique from right eye to left. Not even identical twins have the same iris pattern. A critical factor with biometrics is reducing the margin of error so authorized users are rarely turned away and those who are not authorized are caught at the door. At this writing, the technology to implement biometric authentication is expensive, but there's every indication that it will become widespread in the years to come.

Picture passwords involve the use of graphics and a pattern of clicks using a touch screen, mouse, or other pointing device, as shown in Figure 11.8. With this technology, the user establishes a certain sequence of clicks on a photo or illustration and then repeats it to gain access.

(figure 11.8)

To create a picture password in Windows 8, tap or draw three shapes over a chosen photo.

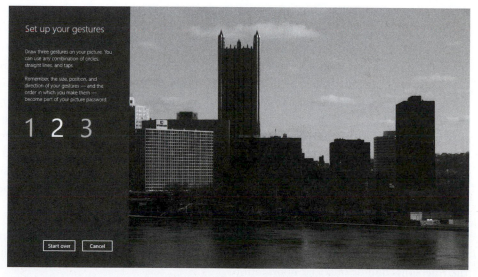

Because this system eliminates all keyboard entries, it is resistant to some techniques already described and offers many more combinations than keyboard based passwords, as shown in Table 11.7. One of the research topics at the end of this chapter allows you to explore the latest developments in this ever changing subject.

Length	10-digit PIN	Number of Combinations			
		Password from a-z character set	Password from Multi-character set	Password from picture using three gestures	
1	10	26	n/a	2,554	
2	100	676	n/a	1,581,773	
3	1,000	17,576	81,120	1,155,509,083	
4	10,000	456,976	4,218,240	612,157,353,732	
5	100,000	11,881,376	182,790,400	398,046,621,309,172	

(table 11.7)

Sample of possible combinations of alphanumeric passwords and picture passwords (adapted from Microsoft, 2013).

Social Engineering

Historically, intruders gained access to systems by using innovative techniques to crack user passwords, such as using default passwords, backdoor passwords, or trying words found in a file of dictionary terms. They also use a technique called **social engineering,** which means looking in and around the user's desk for a written reminder, trying the user logon ID as the password, searching logon scripts, and even telephoning friends and co-workers to learn the names of a user's family members, pets, vacation destinations, favorite hobbies, car model, and so on.

It even works with sophisticated targets. One such instance involved a computer system in a remote location that was reported to be exceptionally secure. To test its security, a systems consultant was hired to try to break into the system. She started by opening an unprotected document that told her where the computer was located. Then she telephoned the base and learned the names of the base commanding officer and the commander's assistant. Then she called the data center, masquerading as the assistant, informing them that the commander was having difficulty accessing the data. When the data center personnel were reluctant to help, the consultant got angry and demanded action. The data center representatives responded with enough access information so the "commander" could use the network. Soon the consultant was on the system with what appeared to be classified data.

Phishing (pronounced "fishing") is a form of social engineering whereby an intruder pretends to be a legitimate entity and contacts unwary users asking them to reconfirm their personal and/or financial information.

Default passwords pose unique vulnerabilities because they are widely known among system attackers but are a necessary tool for vendors. Default passwords are routinely shipped with hardware or software. They're convenient for the manufacturer because they give field service workers supervisor-level access to fix problem equipment on site or using a telecommunications connection. System intruders also find them useful because if they have not been changed, they allow powerful access to the system. Lists of default passwords are routinely passed from one hacker to the next, often serving as a starting point for an attack. To protect the system, managers should identify and regularly change all default passwords on their hardware and software.

Ethics

What is ethical behavior? One definition, in briefest and simplest form, it is this: Be good. Do good.

Many professional associations have addressed computer **ethics**—the rules or standards of behavior that members of the computer-using community are expected to follow, demonstrating the principles of right and wrong. In 1992, the IEEE and the Association for Computing Machinery (ACM) issued a standard of ethics for the global computing community.

The apparent lack of ethics in computing is a significant departure from other professions. For example, we take for granted that our medical doctor will keep our records private, but many of us don't have the same confidence in the individuals working for companies that keep our credit records or the intruders who break into those systems. Although ethics is a subject that's not often addressed in computer science classes, the implications are so vast they can't be ignored by system administrators or users.

At issue are the seemingly conflicting needs of users: the individual's need for privacy, the organization's need to protect its proprietary information, and the public's right to know, as illustrated in freedom of information laws.

For the system's owner, ethical lapses by authorized or unauthorized users can have severe consequences:

- Illegally copied software can result in lawsuits and fines of several times the retail price of each product for each transgression. Several industry associations publish toll-free numbers encouraging disgruntled employees to turn in their employers who use illegal software.
- Plagiarism, the unauthorized copying of copyrighted work (including but not limited to music, movies, textbooks, photographs, and databases), is illegal and punishable by law in the United States as well as in many other nations. When the original work is on paper, most users know the proper course of action, but when the original is in electronic form, some people don't recognize that ethical issues are involved.

- Eavesdropping on e-mail, data, or voice communications is sometimes illegal and usually unwarranted, except under certain circumstances. If calls or messages must be monitored, the participants usually need to be notified before the monitoring begins.

- Cracking, sometimes called hacking, is gaining access to another computer system to monitor or change data, and it's seldom an ethical activity. Although it's seen as a sport by certain people, each break-in causes the system's owner and users to question the validity of the system's data.

- Unethical use of technology, defined as unauthorized access to private or protected computer systems or electronic information, is a murky area of the law, but it's clearly the wrong thing to do. Legally, the justice system has great difficulty keeping up with each specific form of unauthorized access because the technology changes so quickly. Therefore, system owners can't rely on the law for guidance. Instead, they must aggressively teach their users about what is and is not ethical behavior.

How can users learn to behave ethically? A continuing series of security awareness and ethics communications to computer users is more effective than a single announcement. Specific activities can include the following:

- Publish policies that clearly state which actions will and will not be condoned.

- Teach regular seminars on the subject, including real-life case histories.

- Conduct open discussions of ethical questions such as: Is it okay to read someone else's e-mail? Is it right for someone else to read your e-mail? Is it ethical for a competitor to read your data? Is it okay if someone scans your bank account? Is it right for someone to change the results of your medical test? Is it acceptable for someone to copy your software program and put it on the Internet? Is it acceptable for someone to copy a government document and put it on the Internet?

For a guide to ethical behavior, see excerpts from the Association for Computing Machinery (ACM) Code of Ethics and Professional Conduct in Appendix B of this book, or visit *www.acm.org*.

Conclusion

The system is only as secure as the integrity of the data that's stored on it. A single breach of security—whether catastrophic or not, whether accidental or not—damages the system's integrity. And damaged integrity threatens the viability of the best-designed system, its managers, its designers, and its users. Therefore, vigilant security precautions are essential.

So far in this text we've discussed each manager and each operating system function in isolation, but in reality, system performance depends on the combined effort of each piece. In the next chapter, we look at the system as a whole and examine how each piece contributes to, or detracts from, overall system performance.

Key Terms

access control: the control of user access to a network or computer system.

antivirus software: software that is designed to detect and recover from attacks by viruses and worms. It is usually part of a system protection software package.

authentication: the means by which a system verifies that the individual attempting to access the system is authorized to do so.

backup: the process of making long-term archival file storage copies of files on the system.

blended threat: a system threat that combines into one program the characteristics of other attacks, including a virus, a worm, Trojans, spyware, and other malicious code.

biometrics: the science and technology of identifying authorized users based on their biological characteristics.

cleartext: in cryptography, a method of transmitting data without encryption, in text that is readable by anyone who sees it.

cryptography: the science of coding messages or text so unauthorized users cannot read them.

denial of service (DoS) attack: an attack on a network that makes the network unavailable to perform the functions it was designed to do. This can be done by flooding the server with meaningless requests or information.

dictionary attack: the technique by which an intruder attempts to guess user passwords by trying words found in a dictionary.

encryption: translation of a message or data item from its original form to an encoded form, thus hiding its meaning and making it unintelligible without the key to decode it. It's used to improve system security and data protection.

ethics: the rules or standards of behavior that individuals are expected to follow demonstrating the principles of right and wrong.

firewall: a set of hardware and software that disguises the internal network address of a computer or network to control how clients from outside can access the organization's internal servers.

Kerberos: an MIT-developed authentication system that allows network managers to administer and manage user authentication at the network level.

logic bomb: a virus with a trigger, usually an event, that causes it to execute.

packet filtering: reviewing incoming and outgoing Internet packets to verify that the source address, destination address, and protocol are correct.

packet sniffer: software that intercepts Internet data packets sent in cleartext and searches them for information, such as passwords.

password: a user access authentication method. Typically, it is a series of keystrokes that a user enters in order to be allowed to log on to a computer system.

phishing: a technique used to trick consumers into revealing personal information by appearing as a legitimate entity.

picture password: a sequence of strokes over a picture or graphic that is used to authenticate access to a computer system by an authorized user.

private key: a tool that's used to decrypt a message that was encrypted using a public key.

proxy server: a server positioned between an internal network and an external network or the Internet to screen all requests for information and prevent unauthorized access to network resources.

public key: a tool that's used to encrypt a message, to be decoded later using a private key.

social engineering: a technique whereby system intruders gain access to information about a legitimate user to learn active passwords, sometimes by calling the user and posing as a system technician.

spoofing: the creation of false IP addresses in the headers of data packets sent over the Internet, sometimes with the intent of gaining access when it would not otherwise be granted.

spyware: a blended threat that covertly collects data about system users and sends it to a designated repository.

system survivability: the capability of a system to fulfill its mission, in a timely manner, in the presence of attacks, failures, or accidents.

Trojan: a malicious computer program with unintended side effects that are not intended by the user who executes the program.

virus: a program that replicates itself by incorporating itself into other programs, including those in secondary storage, that are shared among other computer systems.

worm: a computer program that replicates itself and is self-propagating in main memory.

Interesting Searches

For more background on a few of the topics discussed in this chapter, begin a search with these terms.

- Network security tools
- Strong password security
- Encryption practices
- Kerberos
- Legal issues vs. ethical issues

Exercises

Research Topics

A. Research the practice of key logging in current literature. Describe what it is and explain why some people defend the practice while some others do not. Finally, give your own opinion and defend it. Cite your sources.

B. In current literature, research the use of graphics to replace typed passwords. Describe the historical milestones of the technology and list its significant advantages and disadvantages. Find at least two real world examples where this technology is used, citing your sources for each.

Exercises

1. Imagine that you are the manager of a small business computing center. List at least three techniques that you would use to convince a busy, reluctant night operator to perform regular backups. Explain the best and worst possible technique to assure your success.

2. Disgruntled employees can sometimes wreak havoc on a computer system because other users leave their passwords written in plain view in the space surrounding their workstations. How would you convince your users to safeguard their passwords? What specific advice would you give them?

3. Explain how you would verify the effectiveness of a new password security policy. Explain the critical elements of such a policy if it is to be successful.

4. Describe the advantages and disadvantages of password generator software. Would you recommend the use of such software for your own system? Explain why or why not.

5. Keeping the critical operating systems patches current is an important aspect of both system security and system administration. Should executive management be made aware of this or any aspect of system security? Explain why or why not.

6. U.S. legislation known as HIPAA (Health Insurance Portability and Accountability Act of 1996) protects the privacy of patient medical data. Yet in an emergency, patients know it's in their best interest if their caregivers have access to their history, medications, and so on. Acknowledging the need for privacy as well as the need for accessibility, describe several advantages and disadvantages of maintaining strict patient data confidentiality. Describe your suggestions to balance those conflicts.

7. Given multi-network access, it's not unusual for users to have multiple user identifications and passwords. How would you manage these multi-password situations? Describe both the advantages and disadvantages of your solution.

Advanced Exercises

8. Describe the unique threats to a data center posed by disgruntled employees. Describe how you would identify such people, if possible, and how you would protect your system from these threats.

9. Investigate the names and trigger events for 20 viruses discovered in the past 12 months. Research five in detail, describing which files they infect, how they spread, and their intended effects.

10. Identify three sets of security parameters (one each for good, better, and best protection) for a computer that holds a university's registration information. Consider not only the operating system, but the protection software, access controls, and the room in which the computer is located. Then make a recommendation based on the need for security vs. the cost of that security.

11. Using information from the CERT Coordination Center *(www.cert.org)*, identify the latest vulnerability for an operating system of your choice. List the threat, the criticality of the threat, the potential impact, the suggested solution, the systems that are affected, and the actions you would take as a system administrator.

12. In the U.S., HIPAA legislation imposed stringent IT security requirements on the healthcare industry. Identify the current requirements for data transmissions between two networks and the role of encryption, if any, in those transmissions. Identify any requirements for electronic communications between the patient and a health care network.

13. Wireless LANs pose unique challenges for system operators because of their accessibility. Imagine that you are the system administrator for a wireless network that is used in a scientific research setting. Identify the five biggest security challenges and discuss how you would address each of them in spite of your limited budget.

14. With identity theft becoming widespread, many organizations have moved to encode the Social Security numbers of their customers, suppliers, and employees. Imagine that you are the system administrator for a college campus where the students' Social Security numbers are used as the key field to access student records and are told that you need to extend backward protection to the records of several decades of previous students. Describe the steps you would follow to modify your system. Make sure your solution also removes the student Social Security number on transcripts, course registration forms, student-accessible data screens, student ID cards, health center records, and other record-keeping systems. Finally, identify which individuals on campus would retain access to the Social Security numbers and explain why.

Chapter 12

System Management

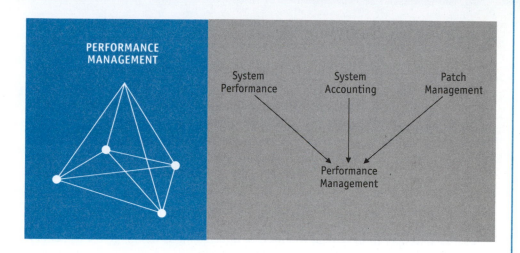

> *There is no such thing as a single problem; ... all problems are interrelated.*
>
> —Saul D. Alinsky (1909–1972)

Learning Objectives

After completing this chapter, you should be able to describe:

- The trade-offs to be considered when attempting to improve overall system performance
- The roles of system measurement tools such as positive and negative feedback loops
- Two system monitoring techniques
- The fundamentals of patch management
- The importance of sound accounting practices by system administrators

This chapter shows how of the system components work together and how the system designer has to consider trade-offs to improve the system's overall efficiency. We begin by showing how the designer can improve the performance of one component, the cost of that improvement, and how it might affect the performance of the remainder of the system. We conclude with some methods used to monitor and measure system performance, as well as the importance of keeping the operating system patched correctly.

Evaluating an Operating System

Most commercial operating systems were designed to work with a certain piece of hardware, a category of processors, or specific groups of users. Although most evolved over time to operate multiple systems, most still favor some users and some computing environments over others. For example, if the operating system was written for novice users to meet basic requirements, it might not satisfy the demands of those more knowledgeable. Conversely, if it was written for programmers, then a business office's computer operator might find it difficult to use. If it serves the needs of a multiuser computer center, it might be inappropriate for a small computing center. Or, if it's written to provide rapid response time, it might provide poor throughput.

To evaluate an operating system, you need to understand its design goals, its history, how it communicates with its users, how its resources are managed, and what trade-offs were made to achieve its goals. In other words, an operating system's strengths and weaknesses need to be weighed in relation to who will be using the operating system, on what hardware, and for what purpose.

Cooperation Among Components

The performance of any one resource depends on the performance of the other resources in the system. For example, memory management is intrinsically linked with device management when memory is used to buffer data between a very fast processor and slower secondary storage devices. Many other examples of resource interdependence have been shown throughout the preceding chapters.

How big should buffers be? If they are small, they can be filled and emptied quickly. If they're larger, they require fewer read and write commands.

If you managed an organization's computer system and were allocated money to upgrade it, where would you put the investment to best use? Your choices could include:

- more memory
- a faster CPU
- additional processors
- more disk drives
- a RAID system
- new file management software

Or, if you bought a new system, what characteristics would you look for that would make it more efficient than the old one?

Any system improvement can be made only after extensive analysis of the needs of the system's resources, requirements, managers, and users. But whenever changes are made to a system, often you're trading one set of problems for another. The key is to consider the performance of the entire system and not just the individual components.

Role of Memory Management

Memory management schemes are discussed in Chapters 2 and 3. When you consider increasing memory or changing to another memory allocation scheme, you must consider the operating environment in which the system will reside. There's a trade-off between memory use and CPU overhead.

For example, if the system will be running student programs exclusively and the average job is only three pages long, your decision to increase the size of virtual memory wouldn't speed up throughput because most jobs are too small to use virtual memory effectively. Remember, as the memory management algorithms grow more complex, the CPU overhead increases and overall performance can suffer. On the other hand, some operating systems perform remarkably better with additional memory. We explore this issue further in the exercises at the end of this chapter.

Role of Processor Management

Processor management is covered in Chapters 4, 5, and 6. Let's say you decide to implement a multiprogramming system to increase your processor's utilization. If so, you'd have to remember that multiprogramming requires a great deal of synchronization between the Memory Manager, the Processor Manager, and the I/O devices. The trade-off: better use of the CPU versus increased overhead, slower response time, and decreased throughput.

Among the several problems to watch for are:
- A system can reach a saturation point if the CPU is fully utilized but is allowed to accept additional jobs—this results in higher overhead and less time to run programs.
- Under heavy loads, the CPU time required to manage I/O queues (which under normal circumstances don't require a great deal of time) can dramatically increase the time required to run the jobs.
- With an I/O-heavy mix, long queues can form at the channels, control units, and I/O devices, leaving the CPU idle waiting as processes finish their I/O.

Likewise, increasing the number of processors necessarily increases the overhead required to manage multiple jobs among multiple processors. But under certain circumstances, the payoff can be faster turnaround time. Many operating systems offer a system monitor to display current system usage, as shown in Figure 12.1.

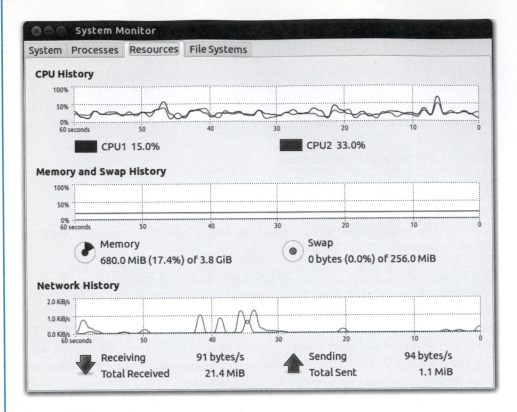

(figure 12.1)

Ubuntu Linux System Monitor showing (top) the percent usage of the two CPUs for this laptop, (middle) memory usage, and (bottom) network connection history.

Role of Device Management

Device management, covered in Chapter 7, contains several ways to improve I/O device utilization including buffering, blocking, and rescheduling I/O requests to optimize access times. But there are trade-offs: each of these options also increases CPU overhead and uses additional memory space.

Blocking reduces the number of physical I/O requests, and that's good. But it's the CPU's responsibility to block and later deblock the records, and that's overhead.

Buffering helps the CPU match the slower speed of I/O devices, and vice versa, but it requires memory space for the buffers—either dedicated space or a temporarily allocated section of main memory. This, in turn, reduces the level of processing that can take place. For example, if each buffer requires 64K of memory and the system requires two sets of double buffers, we've dedicated 256K of memory to the buffers. The trade-off is reduced multiprogramming versus better use of I/O devices.

Rescheduling requests is a technique that can help optimize I/O times; it's a queue reordering technique. But it's also an overhead function, so the speed of both the CPU and the I/O device must be weighed against the time it would take to execute the reordering algorithm. The following example illustrates this point. Figure 12.2 shows three different sample CPUs, the average time with which each can execute 1,000 instructions, and four disk drives with their average data access speeds.

(figure 12.2)

Three CPUs and the average speed with which each can perform 1,000 instructions. All CPUs have access to four drives that have different data access speeds.

CPU 1
30 ms

CPU 2
1.2 ms

CPU 3
0.2 ms

Drive B
10 ms

Drive D
50 ms

Drive A
35 ms

Drive C
5 ms

Using the data provided in Figure 12.2 and assuming that a typical reordering module consists of 1,000 instructions, which combinations of one CPU and one disk drive warrant a reordering module? To learn the answer, we need to compare disk access speeds before and after reordering.

For example, let's assume the following:

• This very simple system consists of CPU 1 and Disk Drive A.

• CPU 1 requires 30 ms to reorder the waiting requests.

• Drive A requires approximately 35 ms for each move, regardless of its location on the disk.

• The system is instructed to access Track 1, Track 9, Track 1, and then Track 9.

• The arm is already located at Track 1, as shown in Figure 12.3.

(figure 12.3)

Using a combination of CPU 1 and Drive A from Figure 12.2, data access requires 105 ms without reordering.

Tracks

| 0 | 1 | 2 | 3 | 4 | 5 | 6 | 7 | 8 | 9 | 10 |

Time 1
Time 2
Time 3
Time 4

Without reordering, the time required for this system to access all four tracks on the disk takes 105 ms (35 + 35 + 35 = 105).

Alternatively, after reordering (which on CPU 1 requires 30 ms), the arm can streamline its moves from Track 1 to Track 9 in a single move, resulting in a speed nearly twice as fast as before: 30 + 35 = 65 ms, as shown in Figure 12.4. Therefore, in this case, with this combination of CPU 1 and Drive A, reordering improves overall speed. But we cannot assume that reordering is always more efficient in this system of multiple CPUs and multiple drives.

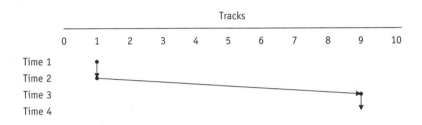

(figure 12.4)

Using CPU 1 and Drive A from Figure 12.2, data access requires only 35 ms after reordering.

For example, when the same series of actions is required by the combination of CPU 1 and the much faster Disk Drive C, we find the disk will again begin at Track 1 and make four accesses in 15 ms (5 + 5 + 5). However, if the system stops to reorder those accesses (which requires 30 ms before the first access is performed), it takes a total of 35 ms (30 + 5) to complete the task—more than twice the time required without reordering. Therefore, reordering requests isn't always warranted.

Role of File Management

The discussion of file management in Chapter 8 looks at how secondary storage allocation schemes help the user organize and access the files on the system. Almost every factor discussed in that chapter can affect overall system performance.

For example, file organization is an important consideration. If a file is stored noncontiguously and has several sections residing in widely separated cylinders of a disk pack, sequentially accessing all of its records could be time-consuming. Such a case would suggest that the files should be compacted (also called defragmented), so each section of the file resides near the others. However, recompaction takes CPU time and leaves the files unavailable to users while it's being done.

Another file management issue that could affect retrieval time is the location of a volume's directory. For instance, some systems read the directory into main memory and hold it there until the user terminates the session. If we return to our example in Figure 12.2 of the four disk drives of varying speeds, the first retrieval would take 35 ms when the system retrieves the directory for Drive A and loads it into memory.

But every subsequent access would be performed at the CPU's much faster speed without the need to access the disk. Similar results would be achieved with each of the other disk drives, as shown in Table 12.1.

(table 12.1)

A sample system with four disk drives of different speeds and a CPU speed of 1.2 ms. If the file's directory is loaded into memory, access speed affects only the initial retrieval and none of the subsequent retrievals.

Disk Drive	Access Speed for First Retrieval	Subsequent Retrievals
A	35 ms	1.2 ms
B	10 ms	1.2 ms
C	5 ms	1.2 ms
D	50 ms	1.2 ms

This poses a problem if the system abruptly loses power before any modifications have been recorded permanently in secondary storage. In such a case, the I/O time that was saved by not having to access secondary storage every time the user requested to see the directory would be negated by not having current information in the user's directory.

Similarly, the location of a volume's directory on the disk might make a significant difference in the time it takes to access it. For example, if directories are stored on the outermost or innermost track, then, on average, the disk drive arm has to travel farther to access each file than it would if the directories were kept in the center tracks.

Overall, file management is closely related to the device on which the files are stored; designers must consider both issues at the same time when evaluating or modifying computer systems. Different schemes offer different flexibility, but the trade-off for increased file flexibility is increased CPU overhead.

Role of Network Management

The discussion of network management in Chapters 9 and 10 examines the impact of adding networking capability to the operating system and the overall effect on system performance. The Network Manager routinely synchronizes the load among remote processors, determines message priorities, and tries to select the most efficient communication paths over multiple data communication lines.

For example, when an application program requires data from a disk drive at a different location, the Network Manager attempts to provide this service seamlessly. When networked devices such as printers, plotters, or disk drives are required, the Network Manager has the responsibility of allocating and deallocating the required resources correctly.

Susan L. Graham (1942–)

Susan Graham is a leading researcher in programming language implementation, software development, and high-performance computing. She led the development of the Berkeley Pascal compiler and the distribution of (and extensions of) BSD UNIX. Graham has also served as co-leader of the Titanium language and system, which is a Java-based parallel programming language, compiler, and runtime

system used for scientific applications. Among Graham's awards are the ACM Distinguished Service Award (2006), the Harvard Medal (2008), the IEEE von Neumann Medal (2009), and the Computing Research Association Distinguished Service Award (2012).

For more information:

www.cs.berkeley.edu/~graham/biography.html

In 2009, Graham was awarded the IEEE John von Neumann Medal for her "contributions to programming language design and implementation and for exemplary service to the discipline of computer science."

In addition to the routine tasks handled by stand-alone operating systems, the Network Manager allows a network administrator to monitor the use of individual computers and shared hardware, and ensures compliance with software license agreements. The Network Manager also simplifies the process of updating data files and programs on networked computers by coordinating changes through a communications server instead of making the changes on each individual computer.

Measuring System Performance

Total system performance can be defined as the efficiency with which a computer system meets its goals—that is, how well it serves its users. However, system efficiency is not easily measured because it's affected by three major components: user programs, operating system programs, and hardware. The main problem, however, is that system performance can be very subjective and difficult to quantify—how, for instance, can anyone objectively gauge ease of use? While some aspects of ease of use can be quantified—for example, time to log on—the overall concept is difficult to quantify.

Even when performance is quantifiable, such as the number of disk accesses per minute, it isn't an absolute measure but a relative one based on the interactions of the three components and the workload being handled by the system.

System performance for networks may give higher priority to certain servers, such as e-mail or Web servers, if they're critical to the operation of the organization.

Measurement Tools

Most designers and analysts rely on certain measures of system performance: throughput, capacity, response time, turnaround time, resource utilization, availability, and reliability.

Throughput is a composite measure that indicates the productivity of the system as a whole; the term is often used by system managers. Throughput is usually measured under steady-state conditions and reflects quantities such as "the number of jobs processed per day" or "the number of online transactions handled per hour." Throughput can also be a measure of the volume of work handled by one unit of the computer system, an isolation that's useful when analysts are looking for bottlenecks in the system.

Bottlenecks tend to develop when resources reach their **capacity**, or maximum throughput level; the resource becomes saturated and the processes in the system aren't being passed along. For example, thrashing is a result of a saturated disk. In this case, a bottleneck occurs when main memory has been overcommitted and the level of multiprogramming has reached a peak point. When this occurs, the working sets for the active jobs can't be kept in main memory, so the Memory Manager is continuously swapping pages between main memory and secondary storage. The CPU processes the jobs at a snail's pace because it's very busy flipping pages (or it's idle while pages are being swapped).

Essentially, bottlenecks develop when a critical resource reaches its capacity. For example, if the disk drive is the bottleneck because it is running at full capacity, then the bottleneck can be relieved by alleviating the need for it. One solution might be restricting the flow of requests to that drive or adding more disk drives.

Bottlenecks can be detected by monitoring the queues forming at each resource: when a queue starts to grow rapidly, this is an indication that the arrival rate is greater than, or close to, the service rate and the resource is soon to be saturated. These are called feedback loops; we discuss them later in this chapter. Once a bottleneck is detected, the appropriate action can be taken to resolve the problem.

To online interactive users, **response time** is an important measure of system performance. Response time is the interval required to process a user's request: it's measured from when the user presses the key to send the message until the system indicates receipt of the message. For batch jobs, this is known as **turnaround time**—the time from the submission of the job until its output is returned to the user. Whether in an online or batch context, this measure depends on both the workload being handled by the system at the time of the request and the type of job or request being submitted. Some requests, for instance, might be handled faster than others because they require fewer resources.

To be an accurate measure of the predictability of the system, measurement data showing response time and turnaround time should include not just their average values but also their variance.

Resource utilization is a measure of how much each unit is contributing to the overall operation. It's usually given as a percentage of time that a resource is actually in use. For example: Is the CPU busy 60 percent of the time? Is the printer busy 90 percent of the time? How about each of the terminals? Or the seek mechanism on a disk? This data helps the analyst determine whether there is balance among the units of a system or whether a system is I/O-bound or CPU-bound.

Availability indicates the likelihood that a resource will be ready when a user needs it. For online users, it may mean the probability that a port is free when they attempt to log on. For those already on the system, it may mean the probability that one or several specific resources, such as a plotter or a group of dedicated devices, will be ready when their programs need them. Availability in its simplest form means that a unit will be operational and not out of service when a user needs it.

Availability is influenced by two factors: **mean time between failures** (**MTBF**) and **mean time to repair** (**MTTR**). MTBF is the average time that a unit is operational before it breaks down, and MTTR is the average time needed to fix a failed unit and put it back in service. These values are calculated with simple arithmetic equations.

For example, if you buy a device with an MTBF of 4,000 hours (the number is given by the manufacturer), and you plan to use it for 4 hours a day for 20 days a month (or 80 hours per month), that means that you could expect it to fail once every 50 months (4000/80)—which might be acceptable to some administrators. The formula for this failure rate is MTBF/usage.

The MTTR is the average time it would take to have a piece of hardware repaired and would depend on several factors: the seriousness of the damage, the location of the repair shop, how quickly you need it back, how much you are willing to pay, and so on. This is usually an approximate figure. When calculating availability, make sure all your variables are in the same units (all are in hours, or all are in days, and so on).

The formula used to compute the unit's availability is:

$$\text{Availability} = \frac{\text{MTBF}}{\text{MTBF} + \text{MTTR}}$$

As indicated, availability is a ratio between the unit's MTBF and its total time (MTBF + MTTR). For our device, let's assume the MTTR is 2 hours; therefore:

$$\text{Availability} = \frac{4000}{4000 + 2} = 0.9995$$

> **Should the scheduled downtime be included or excluded in availability statistics?** Some say it shouldn't because the outage is planned. Others say it should because any outage means the system is unavailable.

So, on the average, this unit would be available 9,995 out of every 10,000 hours. In other words, you'd expect five failures out of 10,000 uses.

Reliability is similar to availability, but it measures the probability that a unit will not fail during a given time period (where t is the time period), and it's a function of MTBF. The formula used to compute the unit's reliability (where e is the mathematical constant approximately equal to 2.71828) is:

$$Reliability(t) = e^{-(1/\text{MTBF})(t)}$$

To illustrate how this equation works, let's say you absolutely need to use a certain device for the 10 minutes before your upcoming deadline. With time expressed in hours, the unit's reliability is given by:

$$Reliability(t) = e^{-(1/4000)(10/60)}$$
$$= e^{-(1/24,000)}$$
$$= 0.9999584$$

This is the probability that it will be available (won't fail) during the critical 10-minute time period—and 0.9999584 is a very high number. Therefore, if the device was ready at the beginning of the transaction, it will probably remain in working order for the entire period of time.

These measures of performance can't be taken in isolation from the workload being handled by the system unless you're simply fine-tuning a specific portion of the system. Overall system performance varies from time to time, so it's important to define the actual working environment before making generalizations.

Feedback Loops

To prevent the processor from spending more time doing overhead than executing jobs, the operating system must continuously monitor the system and feed this information to the Job Scheduler. Then the Scheduler can either allow more jobs to enter the system or prevent new jobs from entering until some of the congestion has been relieved. This is called a **feedback loop** and it can be either negative or positive.

A **negative feedback loop** mechanism monitors the system and, when it becomes too congested, signals the Job Scheduler to slow down the arrival rate of the processes, as shown in Figure 12.5.

People on vacation use negative feedback loops all the time. For example, if you're looking for a gas station and the first one you find has too many cars waiting in line, you collect the data and you react negatively. Therefore, your processor

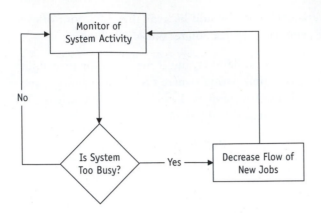

(figure 12.5)

A simple negative feedback loop. It monitors system activity and goes into action only when the system is too busy.

suggests that you drive on to another station (assuming, of course, that you haven't procrastinated too long and are about to run out of gas). As a result of using this feedback loop, long lines at some gas stations are reduced when drivers choose to look elsewhere.

In a computer system, a negative feedback loop monitoring I/O devices, for example, would inform the Device Manager that Printer 1 has too many jobs in its queue, causing the Device Manager to direct all newly arriving jobs to Printer 2, which isn't as busy. The negative feedback helps stabilize the system and keeps queue lengths close to expected mean values.

A **positive feedback loop** mechanism works in the opposite way: it monitors the system, and when the system becomes underutilized, the positive feedback loop causes the arrival rate to increase, as shown in Figure 12.6. Positive feedback loops are used in paged virtual memory systems, but they must be used cautiously because they're more difficult to implement than negative loops.

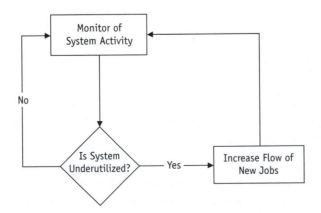

(figure 12.6)

A simple positive feedback loop. It monitors system activity and goes into action only when the system is not busy enough. System activity monitoring is critical here because the system can become unstable.

Consider this example to see how they work. The positive feedback loop monitoring the CPU informs the Job Scheduler that the CPU is underutilized, so the Scheduler allows more jobs to enter the system to give more work to the CPU. However, as more jobs enter, the amount of main memory allocated to each job decreases. If too many new jobs are allowed to enter the job stream, the result can be an increase in page faults. And this, in turn, may cause CPU utilization to deteriorate. In fact, if the operating system is poorly designed, positive feedback loops can actually put the system in an unstable mode of operation. Therefore, the monitoring mechanisms for positive feedback loops must be designed with great care.

As this example shows, an algorithm for a positive feedback loop should monitor the effect of new arrivals in two places: the Processor Manager's control of the CPU, and the Device Manager's read and write operations. That's because both areas experience dynamic changes, which can lead to unstable conditions. Such an algorithm should check to see whether the arrival produces the anticipated result and whether system performance is actually improved. If the arrival causes performance to deteriorate, then the monitoring algorithm could cause the operating system to adjust its allocation strategies until a stable mode of operation has been reached again.

Patch Management

Patch management is the systematic updating of the operating system and other system software. Typically, a **patch** is a piece of programming code that replaces or changes some of the code that makes up the software. There are three primary reasons for the emphasis on software patches for sound system administration: the need for vigilant security precautions against constantly changing system threats; the need to assure system compliance with government regulations and other policies regarding privacy and financial accountability; and the need to keep systems running at peak efficiency. An example of system patching, also called software updating, is shown in Figure 12.7.

Patches aren't new—they've been written and distributed since programming code was first created. However, the task of keeping computing systems patched correctly has become a challenge because of the complexity of the entire system (including the operating system, network, various platforms, and remote users), and because of the speed with which software vulnerabilities are exploited by worms, viruses, and other system assaults described in the last chapter.

Who has the overall responsibility of keeping an organization's software up to date? It depends on the organization. Many times, overall responsibility lies with the chief information officer or the chief security officer. For others, it falls on the shoulders

(figure 12.7)

The Update Manager for this computer running Windows shows 12 important updates waiting to be downloaded and installed.

of the network administrator or the system security officer. In still others, individual users assume that role. Regardless of which individual owns this job, it is only through rigorous patching that the system's resources can reach top performance and its information can be best protected.

Patching Fundamentals

While the installation of the patch is the most public event, there are several essential steps that take place before that happens:

1. Identify the required patch.
2. Verify the patch's source and integrity.
3. Test the patch in a safe testing environment.
4. Deploy the patch throughout the system.
5. Audit the system to gauge the success of the patch deployment.

Although this discussion is limited to managing operating system patches, all changes to the operating system or other critical system software must be undertaken in a test environment that mimics a production environment.

Patch Identification

Let's say you receive notification that a patch is available for an operating system on your network. Your first task is to identify the criticality of the patch, information that

It's generally recommended that the system be thoroughly backed up before beginning the patch process, so it can be restored if the patch software doesn't perform as expected.

is available from the vendor. To be on the forefront of patch information, many system administrators enroll in automatic announcement services offered by government and industry groups or from software vendors.

If the patch is a critical one, it should be applied as soon as possible. Remember that with every patch announcement, system attackers are also armed with this critical information, and they will move quickly to compromise your system. If the patch is not critical in nature, you might choose to delay installation until a regular patch cycle begins. Patch cycles will be discussed later in this chapter.

Patch Source and Integrity

Because software patches have authority to write over existing programming code, they can be especially damaging if they are not valid. Authentic patches will have a digital signature or validation tool. Before applying a patch, validate the digital signature used by the vendor to send the new software. This is a critical step for every computer owner.

For example, in 2011 a program called Flashback appeared to be a legitimate update to a popular software package, but that was not the case. Instead, when more than a half-million users visited its harmless-looking yet malicious Web site, the Trojan malware was loaded onto their Macintosh computers. The Flashback program posed as a simple software update, then began stealing user passwords and other personal information through Web browsers and other commonly used applications. Then the harvested data was forwarded over the Web to remote servers. Apple soon issued patching software to remove Flashback and its variants on *http://support.apple.com/kb/dl1534*. See Figure 12.8.

(figure 12.8)

This software update was made available in 2012 for users to download to remove Flashback malware from Mac computers. (Flashback Removal Security Update is registered trademarks of Apple Inc.)

The biggest complication with making this security update effort successful was that the patch had to be run on all of the half-million infected computers.

Patch Testing

Before installation on a live system, test the new patch on a sample system or an isolated machine to verify its worth. If a non-networked machine is not available, test the patch on a development system instead of the operational system.

First, test to see if the system restarts after the patch is installed. Then, check to see if the patched software performs its assigned tasks—whether it's warding off intruders or improving system performance. While it's often not feasible to test the patch on a duplicate system, the tested system should resemble the complexity of the target network as closely as possible.

This is also the time to make detailed plans for what you'll do if something goes terribly wrong during installation. Test your contingency plans to uninstall the patch and recover the old software should it become necessary to do so.

Patch Deployment

On a single-user computer, patch deployment is a simple task—install the software and restart the computer. However, on a multiplatform system with hundreds or thousands of users, the task becomes exceptionally complicated.

To be successful, the systems administrator maintains an ongoing inventory of all hardware and software on those computers that need the patch. On a large network, this information can be gleaned from network mapping software that surveys the network and takes a detailed inventory of the system. However, this assumes that all system hardware is connected to the network.

The deployment may be launched in stages so the help desk can cope with telephone calls. Often, because it's impossible to use the system during the patching process, it is scheduled for times when system use will be low, such as evenings or weekends.

Auditing the Finished System

Before announcing the deployment's success, you will need to confirm that the resulting system meets your expectations by verifying that:
• all computers are patched correctly and perform fundamental tasks as expected.
• no users had unexpected or unauthorized versions of software that may not accept the patch.
• no users are left out of the deployment.

Some systems administrators like to say that Patch Tuesday is often followed by Crash Wednesday.

The process should include documentation of the changes made to the system and the success or failure of each stage of the process. Keep a log of all system changes for future reference. Finally, get feedback from the users to verify the deployment's success.

Software to Manage Deployment

Patches can be installed manually, one at a time, or via software that's written to perform the task automatically. Organizations that choose software can decide to build their own deployment software or buy ready-made software to perform the task for them. Deployment software falls into two groups: those programs that require an agent running on the target system (called agent-based software), and those that do not (agentless software).

If the deployment software uses an agent, which is software that assists in patch installation, then the agent must be installed on every target computer system before patches can be deployed. On a very large or dynamic system, this can be a daunting task. Therefore, for administrators of large, complex networks, agentless software may offer some time-saving efficiencies.

Timing the Patch Cycle

While critical system patches must be applied immediately, less critical patches can be scheduled at the convenience of the systems group. These patch cycles can be based on calendar events or vendor events. For example, routine patches can be applied monthly or quarterly, or they can be timed to coincide with a vendor's **service pack** release. ("Service pack" is a term used by certain vendors for patches to the operating system and other software.) The advantage of having routine patch cycles is that they allow for thorough review of the patch and testing cycles before deployment.

As of this writing "Patch Tuesday," the second Tuesday of each month, is the day that Microsoft has routinely released its monthly patches. A sample summary of patches for May 2013 is shown in Table 12.2. A list of the latest patches and details about their functions can be found at *http://technet.microsoft.com/en-us/security*.

System Monitoring

As computer systems have evolved, several techniques for measuring performance have been developed, which can be implemented using either hardware or software components. Of the two, hardware monitors are more expensive, but because

Bulletin ID	Bulletin Title and Executive Summary	Maximum Severity Rating and Vulnerability Impact	Restart Requirement	Affected Software
MS13-037	Cumulative Security Update for Internet Explorer (2829530)	**Critical**. Remote Code Execution	Requires restart	Microsoft Windows, Internet Explorer
MS13-038	Security Update for Internet Explorer (2847204)	**Critical**. Remote Code Execution	May require restart	Microsoft Windows, Internet Explorer
MS13-039	Vulnerability in HTTP.sys Could Allow Denial of Service (2829254)	**Important**. Denial of Service	Requires restart	Microsoft Windows
MS13-040	Vulnerabilities in .NET Framework Could Allow Spoofing (2836440)	**Important**. Spoofing	May require restart	Microsoft Windows, Microsoft .NET Framework
MS13-041	Vulnerability in Lync Could Allow Remote Code Execution (2834695)	**Important**. Remote Code Execution	May require restart	Microsoft Lync

(table 12.2)

A summary of five security bulletins released by Microsoft on Tuesday, May 14, 2013.

they're outside of the system and attached electronically, they have the advantage of having a minimum impact on the system. They include hard-wired counters, clocks, and comparative elements.

Software monitors are relatively inexpensive, but because they become part of the computing system, they can distort the results of the analysis. After all, the monitoring software must use the resources it's trying to monitor. In addition, software tools must be developed for each specific system, so it's difficult to move them from one system to another.

In early systems, performance was measured simply by timing the processing of specific instructions. The system analysts might have calculated the number of times an ADD instruction could be done in one second. Or they might have measured the processing time of a typical set of instructions (typical in the sense that they would represent the instructions common to the system). These measurements monitored only the CPU speed because in those days the CPU was the most important resource, so the remainder of the system was ignored.

Today, system measurements must include the other hardware units as well as the operating system, compilers, and other system software. An example is shown in Figure 12.9.

Measurements are made in a variety of ways. Some are made using real programs, usually production programs that are used extensively by the users of the system,

(figure 12.9)

In Ubuntu Linux, the Disk Utility has a benchmark button (at the bottom of this screenshot) for measuring performance of the highlighted drive.

which are run with different configurations of CPUs, operating systems, and other components. The results are called **benchmarks** and are useful when comparing systems that have gone through extensive changes. Benchmarks are often used by vendors to demonstrate to prospective clients the specific advantages of a new CPU, operating system, compiler, or piece of hardware. A sample benchmark table is shown in Table 12.3.

Remember that benchmark results are highly dependent upon the system's workload, the system's design and implementation, as well as the specific requirements of the applications loaded on the system. Performance data is usually obtained in a rigorously controlled environment, so results will probably differ in real-life operation. Still, benchmarks offer valuable comparison data—a place to begin a system evaluation.

If it's not advisable or possible to experiment with the system itself, a simulation model can be used to measure performance. This is typically the case when new hardware is being developed. A simulation model is a computerized abstraction of what is represented in reality. The amount of detail built into the model is dictated by time and money—the time needed to develop the model and the cost of running it.

Designers of simulation models must be careful to avoid the extremes of too much detail, which is too expensive to run, or of too little detail, which doesn't produce enough useful information.

TPC-C-Top Ten Price/Performance Results Version 5 Results As of 30-Oct-2012 7:15 PM [GMT]

Rank	System	Performance (tpmC)	Price/ tpmC	Watts/ KtpmC	System Availability	Database	Operating System	TP Monitor	Date Submitted	Cluster
1	HP ProLiant ML350 G6	290,040	.39 USD	4.22	08/16/10	Oracle Database 11g Release 2 Standard Ed One	Oracle Enterprise Linux	Microsoft COM+	08/16/10	N
2	Cisco UCS C240 M3 Rack Server	1,609,186	.47 USD	NR	09/27/12	Oracle Database 11g Standard Edition One	Oracle Linux w/ Unbreakable Enterprise Kernel R2	Microsoft COM+	09/27/12	N
3	HP ProLiant DL580 G7	1,807,347	.49 USD	2.46	10/15/10	Microsoft SQL Server 2005 Enterprise x64 Edition SP3	Microsoft Windows Server 2008 R2 Enterprise Edition	Microsoft COM+	08/27/10	N
4	Dell PowerEdge T710	239,392	.50 USD	NR	11/18/09	Oracle Database 11g Standard Edition One	Microsoft Windows Server 2003 Enterprise x64 Edition	Microsoft COM+	11/18/09	N
5	HP ProLiant Blade BL685c G7	1,263,599	.51 USD	NR	05/23/11	Microsoft SQL Server 2005 Enterprise x64 Edition SP3	Microsoft Windows Server 2008 R2 Enterprise Ed for X64-Based Systems	Microsoft COM+	05/23/11	N
6	IBM Flex System x240	1,503,544	.53 USD	NR	08/16/12	DB2 ESE 9.7	Red Hat Enterprise Linux 6.2	Microsoft COM+	04/11/12	N
7	HP ProLiant ML350 G6	232,002	.54 USD	NR	05/21/09	Oracle Database 11g Standard Edition One	Oracle Enterprise Linux	Microsoft COM+	05/21/09	N
8	Cisco UCS C250 M2 Extended-Memory Server	1,053,100	.58 USD	NR	12/07/11	Oracle Database 11g Release 2 Standard Ed One	Oracle Linux w/ Unbreakable Enterprise Kernel R2	Microsoft COM+	12/07/11	N
9	IBM System x3850 X5	3,014,684	.59 USD	NR	09/22/11	DB2 ESE 9.7	SUSE Linux Enterprise Server 11 SP1 for X86_64	Microsoft COM+	07/11/11	N
10	IBM System x3850 X5	2,308,099	.60 USD	NR	05/20/11	DB2 ESE 9.7	SUSE Linux Enterprise Server 11 SP1 for X86_64	Microsoft COM+	11/16/10	N
11	Dell PowerEdge 2900	104,492	.60 USD	NR	02/20/09	Oracle Database 11g Standard Edition One	Microsoft Windows Server 2003 Standard Ed. x64	Microsoft COM+	02/20/09	N
12	HP ProLiant DL385G7	705,652	.60 USD	NR	09/01/10	Microsoft SQL Server 2005 Enterprise x64 Edition SP3	Microsoft Windows Server 2008 R2 Enterprise Edition	Microsoft COM+	04/08/10	N

'NR' in the Watts/Ktpmc column indicates that no energy data was reported for that benchmark.

Note: The TPC believes it is not valid to compare prices or price/performance of results in different currencies.

(table 12.3)

Benchmarking results published by the Transaction Processing Performance Council on its Web site (www .tpc.org). Current versions of this report, including benchmark results and details of the testing conditions, can be found on the TPC Web site. (Reprinted with permission of the Transaction Processing Performance Council.)

Conclusion

The operating system is more than the sum of its parts—it's the orchestrated cooperation of every piece of hardware and every piece of software. As we've shown, when one part of the system is favored, it's often at the expense of the others. If a tradeoff must be made, the system's managers must make sure they're using the appropriate measurement tools and techniques to verify the effectiveness of the system before and after modification, and then evaluate the degree of improvement.

With this chapter we conclude Part One of this book; we've seen how operating systems are alike. In Part Two, we look at individual operating systems and explore how they're different—and how each manages the components common to all operating systems. In other words, we see how close reality comes to the concepts learned so far.

Key Terms

availability: a resource measurement tool that indicates the likelihood that the resource will be ready when a user needs it. It's influenced by mean time between failures and mean time to repair.

benchmarks: a measurement tool used to objectively measure and evaluate a system's performance by running a set of jobs representative of the work normally done by a computer system.

capacity: the maximum throughput level of any one of the system's components.

feedback loop: a mechanism to monitor the system's resource utilization so adjustments can be made.

mean time between failures (MTBF): a resource measurement tool; the average time that a unit is operational before it breaks down.

mean time to repair (MTTR): a resource measurement tool; the average time needed to fix a failed unit and put it back in service.

negative feedback loop: a mechanism to monitor the system's resources and, when it becomes too congested, to signal the appropriate manager to slow down the arrival rate of the processes.

patch: executable software that repairs errors or omissions in another program or piece of software.

patch management: the timely installation of software patches to make repairs and keep the operating system software current.

positive feedback loop: a mechanism used to monitor the system. When the system becomes underutilized, the feedback causes the arrival rate to increase.

reliability: a standard that measures the probability that a unit will not fail during a given time period. It's a function of mean time between failures.

resource utilization: a measure of how much each unit contributes to the overall operation of the system.

response time: a measure of an interactive system's efficiency that tracks the speed with which the system will respond to a user's command.

service pack: a term used by some vendors to describe an update to customer software to repair existing problems and/or deliver enhancements.

throughput: a composite measure of a system's efficiency that counts the number of jobs served in a given unit of time.

turnaround time: a measure of a system's efficiency that tracks the time required to execute a job and return output to the user.

Interesting Searches

For more background on a few of the topics discussed in this chapter, begin a search with these terms.

- Patch families
- System benchmarks
- Critical OS patches
- MTBF and reliability
- Fake patches
- System optimization

Exercises

Research Topics

A. Research the current literature to find instances of malware posing as legitimate software patches. Identify the estimated number of computers affected and the availability of repairs/patches. Describe the estimated damage in time and money. Cite your sources.

B. Visit the Web site of a major operating system vendor and find the list patches that were issued in the last 12 months. For each patch, find its criticality and size. Cite your sources. Then, as if you were assigned the task of installing these patches, decide the timing for their installation. For example, how many would you install immediately and which ones could wait for the next quarterly patch cycle (assuming a four-per-year cycle)?

Exercises

1. Describe how you would use a negative feedback loop to manage your bank balance. Describe how you would do so with a positive feedback loop. Explain which you would prefer and why.

2. Describe how a supermarket manager could use a positive feedback loop to direct waiting customers to four open cash register lanes, being careful to minimize waiting time for customers and maximize the speed of customer processing. Include a description of how you would monitor the system and measure its success.

3. Revisiting the example of the gas station lines and positive feedback loops, why do you think the length of gas lines will change? Are there are other factors that could impact the length of gas lines? Explain in your own words why or why not.

4. Imagine that you are managing a university system that becomes CPU-bound at the conclusion of each school semester. If you were allowed to double the number of processors, what effect on throughput would you expect? If you could make one additional change to the system, what would it be? Explain why you'd expect your changes to improve performance.

5. Imagine that you are managing the system for a consulting company that becomes I/O-bound at the end of each fiscal year. What effect on throughput would you expect if you were allowed to double the number of processors? If you could make one additional change to the system, what would it be? Explain in your own words why you'd expect your changes to improve overall system performance.

6. Review the system with one CPU and four drives below:

   - CPU W = 4 ms (the average time to execute 1,000 instructions)
   - Drive A = 45 ms (average data access speed)
   - Drive B = 3 ms (average data access speed)
   - Drive C = 17 ms (average data access speed)
   - Drive D = 10 ms (average data access speed)

   Calculate I/O access speed using this CPU and each of the four disk drives as they evaluate the following track requests in this order: 0, 31, 20, 15, 20, 31, 15. Then, in each case, calculate the access speeds after the track requests are reordered and rank the four disk drives before and after reordering.

7. Review the system with one CPU and three drives below:

   - CPU X = 0.3 ms (the average time to execute 1,000 instructions)
   - Drive A = 0.7 ms (average data access speed)
   - Drive B = 4 ms (average data access speed)
   - Drive C = .03 ms (average data access speed)

Calculate I/O access speed using this CPU and each of the disk drives as they evaluate the following track requests in this order: 16, 4, 9, 16, 29, 31, 5. Then, in each case, calculate the access speeds after the track requests are reordered and rank the three disk drives before and after reordering.

8. Remembering that there's a trade-off between memory use and CPU overhead, give an example where increasing the size of virtual memory improves job throughput. Then give an example where doing so causes throughput to suffer, and explain why this is so.

9. Looking back over the past 12 months, let's say your computer had failed unexpectedly and catastrophically twice in that time. Identify the worst possible time for failure and the best possible time. Then compare the time and cost it would have required for you to recover from those two catastrophic failures. Describe in your own words the factors that differentiated the worst experience from the best.

10. Describe how you would convince a coworker to better manage a personal computer by performing regular backups and by keeping the system patches current.

11. Calculate the reliability of a hard disk drive with an MTBF of 2,499 hours during the last 40 hours of this month. Assume e = 2.71828 and use the formula:

$$Reliability(t) = e - (1/\text{MTBF})(t)$$

12. Calculate the reliability of a hard disk drive with an MTBF of 4,622 hours during the crucial last 16 hours of the last fiscal quarter (the three-month period beginning October 1 and ending December 31). Assume e = 2.71828 and use the reliability formula from the previous exercise.

13. Calculate the reliability of a server with an MTBF of 10,500 hours during the busy summer selling season from May 1 through September 15. Assume that the server must remain operational 24 hours/day during that entire time. *Hint*: Begin by calculating the number of hours of operation during the busy season. Assume e = 2.71828 and use the reliability formula from the previous exercises.

14. Calculate the availability of a server with an MTBF of 75 hours and an MTTR of 3 days (72 hours).

15. Calculate the availability of a hard disk drive with an MTBF of 2,040 hours and an MTTR of 8.5 hours.

16. Calculate the availability of a server with an MTBF of 50 weeks and an MTTR of 798 hours.

Advanced Exercises

17. Compare and contrast availability and reliability. In your opinion, which is more important to a system manager? Substantiate your answer in your own words.

18. In this chapter, we described the trade-offs among all the managers in the operating system. Study a system to which you have access, and assuming you have sufficient funds to upgrade only one component for the system, explain which component you would choose to upgrade to improve overall system performance. Explain why.

19. Perform a software inventory of your computer system to identify all applications resident on the computer. If you have more than a dozen applications, choose 12 of them and check each for patches that are available for your software. For each vendor, identify how many patches are available for your software, the number of critical patches, and what patch cycle you would recommend for that vendor's patches: annual, quarterly, monthly, or weekly updates.

20. As memory management algorithms grow more complex, the CPU overhead increases and overall performance can suffer. On the other hand, some operating systems perform remarkably better with additional memory. Explain in detail (using your own words) why some perform better with additional memory. Then explain in detail why some do not perform better.

21. Conduct an inventory of your computer to discover how many processes are active when it is connected to the Internet. What is the total number of processes currently running? For which processes can you identify the application? How many processes are linked to applications that you cannot identify? Discuss how the unidentifiable processes pose a challenge regarding effective system administration and explain what you would do to address this challenge.

22. Compare and contrast throughput, turnaround time, and response time. Explain what each measures and how they are monitored. Which measurement is more important in your current computing environment? Explain why.

23. Availability indicates the likelihood that a resource will be ready when a user needs it. Explain in your own words how the measurements to calculate this value are collected.

Part Two

Operating Systems in Practice

Thus far in this text, we've explored how operating system software works at the conceptual level—the roles of the Memory Manager, Processor Manager, Device Manager, File Manager, and Network Manager. To do so, we've underplayed the intricate choreography required by all managers as they work together to accomplish even the simplest tasks. We've also described operating systems in their most basic form—operating systems running relatively simple hardware configurations.

In the second part of this book, we explore operating systems in practice by exploring a few of the most popular operating systems. The following chapters each describe one operating system; they are presented in the order in which the software was released.

For each chapter in Part Two, our discourse includes the history of the operating system's development, its design goals, the unique properties of its submanagers, and its user interface, which is arguably the most unique component of any operating system.

Our discussion here cannot serve as an in-depth evaluation of any operating system, but it does present each system in a standard format to help you compare their relative strengths and weaknesses.

Chapter 13

UNIX Operating System

UNIX INTERFACE

Design Goals

Memory Management

Processor Management

Device Management

File Management

User Interface

> **"** *UNIX is simple. It just takes a genius to understand its simplicity.* **"**
>
> —Dennis Ritchie

Learning Objectives

After completing this chapter, you should be able to describe:

- The goals of UNIX designers
- The significance of using files to manipulate devices
- The strengths and weaknesses of competing versions
- The advantages of command-driven user interfaces

There are many versions of UNIX and they run on all sizes of computers using a wide range of microprocessors. This is both a strength and a weakness. If someone needs to customize a system using a robust base, this operating system can fill the bill. On the other hand, if you want to create an enhancement that will run on *all* UNIX systems, that can be a challenging assignment.

UNIX and Linux strongly resemble each other in many ways but are different operating systems. While UNIX was written several decades earlier, Linux and UNIX now compete as peers. Since 2001, when Apple introduced the Macintosh OS X operating system (which was based on the FreeBSD version of UNIX), the company has advertised that its operating system is based on a proven and powerful UNIX foundation (Apple, 2009). The continuing competition and cooperation between these two operating systems are likely to play out in the marketplace for many years to come.

Brief History

The UNIX operating system, authored by Ken Thompson, has three major advantages: it is portable from large systems to small systems; it has very powerful utilities; and it provides device independence to application programs. Its portability is attributed to the fact that most of it is written in a high-level language called C (authored by Dennis Ritchie), instead of assembly language, which is a low-level language that's specific to the architecture a particular computer. Throughout our discussion of UNIX, we'll describe AT&T's version unless otherwise specified.

UNIX utilities are brief, single-operation commands that often can be combined in a single command line to achieve almost any desired result—a feature that many programmers find endearing. And it can be configured to operate virtually any type of device. UNIX commands are case sensitive and are strongly oriented toward lowercase characters, which are faster and easier to type. Therefore, throughout this chapter, we follow the convention of showing all filenames and commands in lowercase.

The evolution of UNIX, summarized in Table 13.1, starts with a research project that began in 1965 as a joint venture between Bell Laboratories (the research and development group of AT&T), General Electric, and MIT (Massachusetts Institute of Technology).

When Bell Laboratories withdrew from the project in 1969, AT&T management decided not to undertake the development of any more operating systems—but that didn't stop two young veterans of the project, Ken Thompson and Dennis Ritchie. Some people say they needed a new operating system to support their favorite computer game. Regardless of their reasons for developing it, UNIX has grown to become one of the most widely used operating systems in history.

In this chapter, we discuss the command structures common to both UNIX and Linux. In Chapter 15, we discuss graphical user interfaces, which are similar in both operating systems.

(table 13.1)

The historical roots of UNIX. For current information about the many versions of UNIX, see www.theopengroup.org.

Year	Release	Features
1969	—	Ken Thompson wrote first version of UNIX
1975	UNIX V6	First version becomes widely available to industry and academia
1984	UNIX System V Release 2	Shared memory, more commands
1997	Single UNIX Specification 2	Support for real-time processing, threads, and 64-bit processors
2001	Mac OS X	From Apple, a UNIX-based core with Macintosh graphics and GUI
2005	FreeBSD 6.0	Multithreaded file system; expanded support for wireless technology
2009	Mac OS X 10.6 Server	A 64-bit kernel that increased the total number of simultaneous system processes, threads, and network connections for the server to use
2012	Mac OS X 10.8	New support for cloud sharing (see www.apple.com/osx).
2012	FreeBSD 9.1	Better load balancing for multithreading systems and more (see www.freebsd.org).

The Evolution of UNIX

The first official UNIX version by Thompson and Ritchie was designed to "do one thing well" and to run on a popular minicomputer. Before long, UNIX became so widely adopted that it had become a formidable competitor in the market. For Version 3, Ritchie took the innovative step of developing a new programming language, which he called C, and he wrote a compiler making it easier and faster for system designers to write code.

As UNIX grew in fame and popularity (Figure 13.1), AT&T found itself in a difficult situation. At the time, the company was a legal monopoly, and was therefore forbidden by U.S. federal government antitrust regulations to sell software. But it could, for a nominal fee, make the operating system available to universities, and it did. Between 1973 and 1975, several improved versions were developed and the most popular was written at the University of California at Berkeley, which became known as "bsd," short for Berkeley Software Distribution. Over time, its popularity with academic programmers created a demand for UNIX in business and industry.

In 1991, IBM and Hewlett-Packard were among the companies that established The Open Group, which still owns the trademark to the name UNIX.

The original philosophy of Thompson and Ritchie was soon expanded and its commands now offer many options and controls. The operating system can be

Because people can type a little bit faster by not using capital letters, standard UNIX commands use only lower case letters. They do not recognize standard commands that include "caps."

(figure 13.1)

UNIX is a registered trademark of The Open Group. Graphic supplied courtesy of The Open Group.

adapted to new situations with relative ease. In essence, the key features of the early systems have been preserved, while the potential of the commands has increased to meet new needs. The addition of graphical user interfaces, most notably with the Mac OS version of UNIX, has made it easily accessible by new generations of users.

To resolve early problems caused by multiple standards, the industry continues to establish standards to improve the portability of programs from one system to another.

Ken Thompson (1943–) & Dennis Ritchie (1941–2011)

While working together in the 1960s at the Computing Sciences Research Center (part of Bell Telephone Laboratories) Ken Thompson and Dennis Ritchie created a scaled-down version of a new operating system and called it UNIX. Soon thereafter, Ritchie created the C programming language, and after rewriting UNIX in C, it became a truly portable operating system because it could be run on many different platforms. Both C and UNIX continue to be widely used throughout the industry. As a result of their work, Thompson and Ritchie have received many joint awards, including the IEEE Computer Pioneer Award (1994), the U.S. National Medal of Technology and Innovation (1999), and the Japan Prize for Information and Communication (2011).

For more information:

http://amturing.acm.org/award_winners/thompson_4588371.cfm

The Association for Computing Machinery A.M. Turing Award in 1983 cited Thompson (left) and Ritchie (right), "for their development of generic operating systems theory and specifically for the implementation of the UNIX operating system."

Design Goals

From the beginning, Thompson and Ritchie envisioned UNIX as an operating system created by programmers, for programmers. It was built to be fast, flexible, and easy to use.

The immediate goals were twofold: to develop an operating system that would support software development and to keep its algorithms as simple as possible, without becoming rudimentary. To achieve their first goal, they included utilities in the operating system for which programmers at the time needed to write customized code. Each utility was designed for simplicity—to perform only one function but to perform it very well. These utilities were designed to be used in combination with each other so that programmers could select and combine any appropriate utilities that might be needed to carry out specific jobs. This concept of small manageable sections of code was a perfect fit with the second goal: to keep the operating system simple. To do this, Thompson and Ritchie selected the algorithms based on simplicity instead of speed or sophistication. As a result, even these early UNIX systems could be mastered by experienced programmers in a matter of weeks.

The designers' long-term goal was to make the operating system, and any application software developed for it, portable from one computer to another. The obvious advantage of portability is that it reduces conversion costs and doesn't cause application packages to become obsolete with every change in hardware. This goal was finally achieved with UNIX Version 4, the first to be **device independent**—a huge innovation at the time.

Numerous versions of UNIX meet the additional design element of conforming to the specifications for **Portable Operating System Interface for Computer Environments** (**POSIX**) (a registered trademark of the IEEE). POSIX is a family of IEEE standards that define a portable operating system interface to enhance the portability of programs from one operating system to another.

Memory Management

With POSIX, UNIX has developed into a powerful and flexible operating system for multiuser environments or single-user multiprogramming systems.

For multiprogramming systems, most UNIX operating systems use either swapping or demand paging (or both) memory management techniques. The best choice depends on the kind of applications that are running on the system: if most jobs are small, then swapping could be the best choice; but if the system will be running many large jobs, then demand paging is best.

Swapping requires that the entire program be in main memory before it can be executed, and this imposes a size restriction on programs. For example, if the system has 2GB of memory and the operating system takes up a fourth of it (0.5GB), then the size of other resident programs must be less than the remaining 1.5GB. Swapping uses a round robin policy—when a job's time slice is up, or when it generates an I/O interrupt, the entire job is swapped out to secondary storage to make room for other jobs waiting in the READY queue. That's fine when there are relatively few processes in the system, but when traffic is heavy, this swapping back and forth can slow down the system.

Demand paging requires more complicated hardware configurations; it increases the system overhead and under heavy loads might lead to thrashing. But it has the advantage of implementing the concept of virtual memory.

Figure 13.2 shows the typical internal memory layout for a single user-memory part image. An image is an abstract concept that can be defined as a computer execution environment composed of a user-memory part (all of which is depicted in Figure 13.2), general register values, status of open files, and current **directory**. This image must remain in memory during execution of a process.

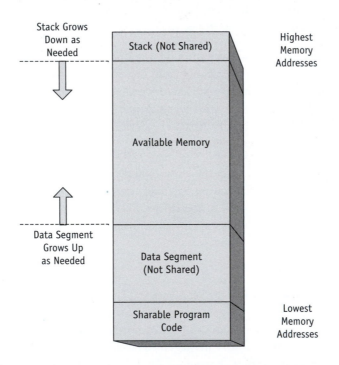

(Figure 13.2)

Illustration of the user's part of main memory and how data is stored there.

In Figure 13.2, the segment called program code is the sharable portion of the program. Because this code can be physically shared by several processes, it must be written in **reentrant code**. This means that the code is protected so that its instructions aren't modified in any way during its normal execution. In addition, all data references are made without the use of absolute physical addresses.

The Memory Manager gives the program code special treatment. Because several processes share it, the space allocated to the program code can't be released until all of the processes using it have completed their execution. UNIX uses a text table to keep track of which processes are using which program code, and the memory isn't released until the program code is no longer needed. The text table is explained in more detail in the next section on Processor Management.

The data segment shown in Figure 13.2 starts after the program code and grows toward higher memory locations as needed by the program. The stack segment starts at the highest memory address and grows downward as subroutine calls and interrupts add information to it. A stack is a section of main memory where process information is saved when a process is interrupted, or for temporary storage. The data and stack are nonsharable sections of memory, so when the original program terminates, the memory space for both is released and deallocated.

The UNIX **kernel**, which permanently resides in memory, is the part of the operating system that implements the "system calls" to set up the memory boundaries so several processes can coexist in memory at the same time. The processes also use system calls to interact with the File Manager and to request I/O services.

The kernel is the set of programs that implements the most primitive of that system's functions, and it's the only part of the operating system to permanently reside in memory. The remaining sections of the operating system are handled in the same way as any large program. That is, pages of the operating system are brought into memory on demand, only when they're needed, and their memory space is released as other pages are called. UNIX uses the least recently used (LRU) page replacement algorithm.

Although we direct this discussion to large multiuser computer systems, UNIX uses the same memory management concepts for networked computers and single-user systems. For example, a single computer with a UNIX operating system, using a demand paging scheme, can support multiple users in a true multitasking environment.

With the 64-bit addressing architecture in many current UNIX versions, including the Mac OS, the operating system can make much faster system calls, which, in turn, improves the performance of I/O applications and network response. The 64-bit addressing scheme is one shared by most operating systems as of this writing.

Process Management

The Processor Manager of a UNIX system kernel handles the allocation of the CPU, process scheduling, and the satisfaction of process requests. To perform these tasks, the kernel maintains several important tables to coordinate the execution of processes and the allocation of devices.

Using a predefined policy, the Process Scheduler selects a process from the READY queue and begins its execution for a given time slice. Remember, as we discuss in Chapter 4, the processes in a time-sharing environment can be in any of five states: HOLD, READY, WAITING, RUNNING, or FINISHED.

The process scheduling algorithm picks the process with the highest priority to run first. Because one of the values used to compute the priority is accumulated CPU time, any processes that have used a lot of CPU time will get a lower priority than those that have not. The system updates the compute-to-total-time ratio for each job every second. This ratio divides the amount of CPU time that a process has used up by the total time the same process has spent in the system. A result close to 1 would indicate that the process is CPU-bound. If several processes have the same computed priority, they're handled round-robin (low-priority processes are preempted by high-priority processes). Interactive processes typically have a low compute-to-total-time ratio, so interactive response is maintained without any special policies.

The overall effect of this negative feedback is that the system balances **I/O-bound** jobs with **CPU-bound** jobs to keep the processor busy and to minimize the overhead for waiting processes.

When the Processor Manager is deciding which process from the READY queue will be loaded into memory to be run first, it chooses the process with the longest time spent on the secondary storage.

When the Processor Manager is deciding which process (currently in memory and waiting or ready to be run) will be moved out temporarily to make room for a new arrival, it chooses the process that's either waiting for disk I/O or that's currently idle. If there are several processes to choose from, the one that has been in memory the longest is moved out first.

If a process is waiting for the completion of an I/O request and isn't ready to run when it's selected, UNIX dynamically recalculates all process priorities to determine which inactive (but ready) process will begin execution when the processor becomes available.

These policies seem to work well and don't impact the running processes. However, if a disk is used for secondary file storage as well as for a "swapping area," then heavy traffic can significantly slow disk I/O because job swapping may take precedence over file storage.

Process Table Versus User Table

UNIX uses several tables to keep the system running smoothly, as shown in Figure 13.3. Information on simple processes, those with nonsharable code, is stored in two sets of tables: the process table, which always resides in memory; and the user table, which resides in memory only while the process is active. In Figure 13.3, Process 3 and Process 4 show the same program code indicated in the text table by the number 2. Their data areas and user tables are kept separate while the code area is being shared. Process 5 is not sharing its code with another process; therefore, it's not recorded in the text table, and its data and code area are kept together as a unit.

(figure 13.3)

The process control structure showing how the process table and text table interact for processes with sharable code, as well as for those without sharable code.

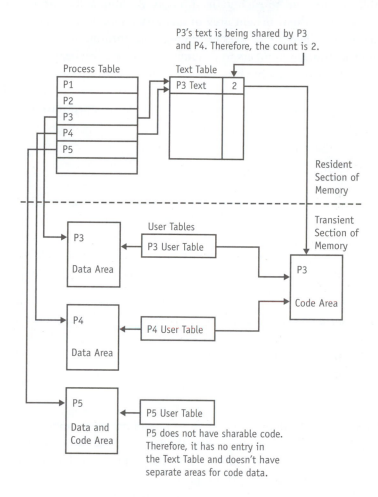

Each entry in the process table contains the following information: process identification number, user identification number, address of the process in memory or secondary storage, size of the process, and scheduling information. This table is set up when the process is created and is deleted when the process terminates.

For processes with **sharable code**, the process table maintains a subtable, called the text table, which contains the memory address or secondary storage address of the text segment (sharable code) and a count to keep track of the number of processes using this code. Every time a process starts using this code, the count is increased by 1; and every time a process stops using this code, the count is decreased by 1. When the count is equal to 0, the code is no longer needed and the table entry is released, together with any memory locations that had been allocated to the code segment.

A user table is allocated to each active process. As long as the process is active, this table is kept in the transient area of memory and contains information that must be accessible when the process is running. This information includes: the user and group identification numbers to determine file access privileges, pointers to the system's file table for every file being used by the process, a pointer to the current directory, and a list of responses for various interrupts. This table, together with the process data segment and its code segment, can be swapped into or out of main memory as needed.

Synchronization

A profound strength of UNIX is its true multitasking capabilities. It achieves process synchronization by requiring processes to wait for certain events. For example, if a process needs more memory, it's required to wait for an event associated with memory allocation. Later, when memory becomes available, the event is signaled and the process can continue. Each event is represented by integers that, by convention, are equal to the address of the table associated with the event.

A race may occur if an event happens during the process's transition between deciding to wait for the event and entering the WAIT state. In this case, the process is waiting for an event that has already occurred and may not recur.

fork

An unusual feature of UNIX is that it gives the programmer the capability of executing one program from another program using the fork command. This command gives the second program all the attributes of the first program, such as any open files it saves the first program in its original form.

The system call fork splits a program into two copies, which are both running from the statement after the fork command. When fork is executed, a "process id" (called pid for short) is generated for the new process. This is done in a way that ensures that each process has its own unique ID number. Figure 13.4 shows what happens after the fork. The original process (Process 1) is called the **parent process** and the resulting process (Process 2) is the **child process**. A child inherits the parent's open files and runs asynchronously with it unless the parent is instructed to wait for the termination of the child process.

(figure 13.4)

When the fork command is received, the parent process shown in (a) begets the child process shown in (b) and Statement 2 is executed twice.

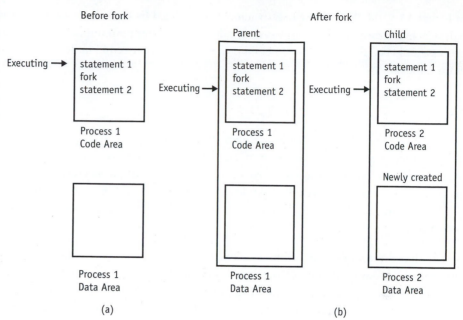

(a)   (b)

wait

A related command, `wait`, allows the programmer to synchronize process execution by suspending the parent until the child is finished, as shown in Figure 13.5.

(figure 13.5)

The wait command used in conjunction with the fork command will synchronize the parent and child processes. In (a) the parent process is shown before the fork, (b) shows the parent and child after the fork, and (c) shows the parent and child during the wait.

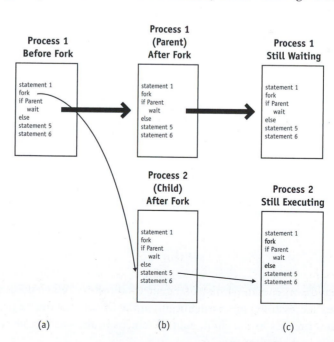

(a)   (b)   (c)

In Figure 13.5, the IF-THEN-ELSE structure is controlled by the value assigned to the pid, which is returned by the `fork` system call. A pid greater than 0 indicates a parent process; a pid equal to 0 indicates a child process; and a negative pid indicates an error in the fork call.

exec

The `exec` family of commands—`execl`, `execv`, `execle`, `execlp`, and `execvp`—is used to start execution of a new program from another program. Unlike `fork`, which results in two processes running the same program being in memory, a successful `exec` call lays the second program over the first, leaving only the second program in memory. The second program's code and data are now part of the original process, whose pid does not change.

Notice that there's no return from a successful `exec` call; therefore, the concept of parent-child doesn't hold here. However, a programmer can use the `fork`, `wait`, and `exec` commands in this order to create a parent-child relationship and then have the child be overlaid by another program that, when finished, awakens the parent so that it can continue its execution. See Figure 13.6.

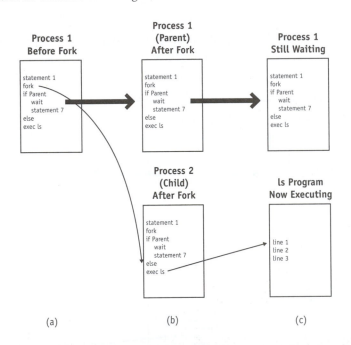

(figure 13.6)

The exec command is used after the fork and wait combination. In (a) the parent is shown before the fork, (b) shows the parent and child after the fork, and (c) shows how the child process (Process 2) is overlaid by the ls program after the exec command.

The `ls` command can generate a listing of the current directory. When the `exec ls` system call is executed successfully, processing begins at the first line of the `ls` program. Once the `ls` program finishes in the child, control returns to the executable statement following the wait in the parent process.

These system calls illustrate the flexibility of UNIX that programmers find extremely useful. For example, programmers can create a child process to execute a program by the parent process, as was done in Figure 13.6. The programmer doesn't have to write code that loads or finds memory space for a separate program (in this case, the ls program).

Device Management

An innovative feature of UNIX is the treatment of devices—the operating system is designed to provide device independence to the applications running under it. This is achieved by treating each I/O device as a special type of file. Every device that's installed in a UNIX system is assigned a name that's similar to the name given to any other file, which is given descriptors called iodes. These descriptors identify the devices, contain information about them, and are stored in the device directory. The subroutines that work with the operating system to supervise the transmission of data between main memory and a peripheral unit are called the **device drivers**.

If the computer system uses devices that are not supplied with the operating system, their device drivers must be written by an experienced programmer or obtained from a reliable source and installed on the operating system.

The actual incorporation of a device driver into the kernel is done during the system configuration. UNIX has a program called config that automatically creates a conf.c file for any given hardware configuration. This conf.c file contains the parameters that control resources such as the number of internal buffers for the kernel and the size of the swap space. In addition, the conf.c file contains two tables, bdevsw (short for block device switch) and cdevsw (short for character device switch). These allow the UNIX system kernel to adapt easily to different hardware configurations by installing different driver modules.

Device Classifications

The I/O system is divided into the block I/O system (sometimes called the structured I/O system) and the character I/O system (sometimes called the unstructured I/O system).

Each physical device is identified by a minor device number, a major device number, and a class—either block or character. See Figure 13.7.

Each class has a Configuration Table that contains an array of entry points into the device drivers. This table is the only connection between the system code and the

(figure 13.7)

When a process sends an I/O request, it goes to the UNIX kernel where the char and block device drivers reside.

device drivers, and it's an important feature of the operating system. This table allows the system programmers to create new device drivers quickly to accommodate a differently configured system. The major device number is used as an index to the array to access the appropriate code for a specific device driver.

The minor device number is passed to the device driver as an **argument** and is used to access one of several identical or similar physical devices controlled by the driver.

As its name implies, the block I/O system is used for devices that can be addressed as a sequence of identically sized blocks. This allows the Device Manager to use buffering to reduce the physical disk I/O. UNIX has from 10 to 70 buffers for I/O; information related to these buffers is kept on a list.

Every time a read command is issued, the I/O buffer list is searched. If the requested data is already in a buffer, then it's made available to the requesting process. If not, then it's physically moved from secondary storage to a buffer. If a buffer is available, the move is made. If all buffers are busy, then one must be emptied out to make room for the new block. This is done by using a least recently used (LRU) policy: the contents of frequently used buffers are left intact, which, in turn, should reduce physical disk I/O.

Devices in the character class are handled by device drivers that implement character lists. Here's how it operates: a subroutine puts a character on the list, or queue, and another subroutine retrieves the character from the list.

A terminal is a typical character device that has two input queues and one output queue. The two input queues are labeled the raw queue and the canonical queue.

Each device driver includes all the instructions necessary for UNIX to allocate, deallocate, and communicate with the device.

It works like this: As the user types in each character, it's collected in the raw input queue. When the line is completed and the Enter key is pressed, the line is copied from the raw input queue to the canonical input queue, and the CPU interprets the line. Similarly, the section of the device driver that handles characters going to the output module of a terminal stores them in the output queue until it holds the maximum number of characters.

The I/O procedure is synchronized through hardware completion interrupts. Each time there's a completion interrupt, the device driver gets the next character from the queue and sends it to the hardware. This process continues until the queue is empty. Some devices can actually belong to both the block and character classes. For instance, disk drives and tape drives can be accessed in block mode using buffers or the system can bypass the buffers when accessing the devices in character mode.

Device Drivers

Each device has a special section in the kernel, called a device driver. Device drivers for disk drives use a seek strategy to minimize the arm movement, as explained in Chapter 7.

Device drivers are kept in a set of files that can be included as needed. When upgrades are made to peripherals, small changes to the device driver file can be linked into the kernel to keep the operating system informed of the new features and capabilities. Although device files may be kept anywhere on the file system, by default and convention they are kept in the /dev directory. Keeping them in this directory marks them clearly as device files. Figure 13.8 shows the Volume screen on a Macintosh system running UNIX. It displays each volume for this system.

(Figure 13.8)

This Macintosh screen displays all three volumes for this UNIX system.

File Management

UNIX has three types of files: directories, ordinary files, and special files. Each enjoys certain privileges.

- *Directories* are files used by the system to maintain the hierarchical structure of the file system. Users are allowed to read information in directory files, but only the system is allowed to modify directory files.

- *Ordinary files* are those in which users store information. Their protection is based on a user's requests and is related to the read, write, execute, and delete functions that can be performed on a file.

- *Special files* are the device drivers that provide the interface to I/O hardware. Special files appear as entries in directories. They're part of the file system, and most of them reside in the /dev directory. The name of each special file indicates the type of device with which it's associated. Most users don't need to know much about special files, but system programmers should know where they are and how to use them.

UNIX stores files as sequences of bytes and doesn't impose any structure on them. Therefore, the structure of files is controlled by the programs that use them, not by the system. For example, text files (those written using an editor) are strings of characters with lines delimited by the line feed, or new line, character. On the other hand, binary files (those containing executable code generated by a compiler or assembler) are sequences of binary digits grouped into words as they appear in memory during execution of the program.

The UNIX file management system organizes the disk into blocks and divides the disk into four basic regions:

- The first region (starting at address 0) is reserved for booting.

- The second region, called a superblock, contains information about the disk as a whole, such as its size and the boundaries of the other regions.

- The third region includes a list of file definitions, called the *i-list*, which is a list of file descriptors—one for each file. The descriptors are called *i-nodes*. The position of an i-node on the list is called an *i-number*, and it is this i-number that uniquely identifies a file.

- The fourth region holds the free blocks available for file storage. The free blocks are kept in a linked list where each block points to the next available empty block. Then, as files grow, noncontiguous blocks are linked to the already existing chain.

Whenever possible, files are stored in contiguous empty blocks. And because all disk allocation is based on fixed-size blocks, allocation is very simple and there's no need to compact the files.

Each entry in the i-list is called an *i-node* (also spelled *inode*) and contains 13 disk addresses. The first 10 addresses point to the first 10 blocks of a file. However, if a file is larger than 10 blocks, the eleventh address points to a block that contains the addresses of the next 128 blocks of the file. For larger files, the twelfth address points to another set of 128 blocks, each one pointing to 128 blocks. For files that require even more space, there is a thirteenth address.

Each i-node contains information on a specific file, such as owner's identification, protection bits, physical address, file size, time of creation, last use and last update, number of links, and whether the file is a directory, an ordinary file, or a special file.

File Naming Conventions

Filenames are case sensitive, meaning that capital letters in filenames are considered different than the same lower case letters. For example, these are legitimate, unique names for four different files in a single directory: FIREWALL, firewall, FireWall, and fireWALL.

Most versions of UNIX allow filenames to be up to 255 characters in length, and most allow many special characters, with the exception of the colon (:). Although the operating systems don't impose any naming conventions on files, some system programs, such as compilers, expect files to have specific suffixes (which are the same as extensions described in Chapter 8). For example, prog1.bas would indicate the file is a BASIC program because of its suffix .bas, while the suffix in backup.sh would indicate the file to be a shell program.

UNIX supports a hierarchical tree directory structure. The root directory is identified by a slash (/); the names of other directories are preceded by the slash (/) symbol, which is used as a delimiter. A file is accessed by starting at a given point in the hierarchy and descending through the branches of the tree (subdirectories) until reaching the leaf (the file). This path can become very long, so it's sometimes advantageous to change directories before accessing a file. This can be done quickly by typing two periods (..) if the file needed is one level up from the working directory in the hierarchy. Typing two periods-slash-two periods (../..) moves you up two branches toward the root in the tree structure.

To access a file called april 2013 Miles in the music class directory illustrated in Figure 13.9, the user can type the following, making sure that the spelling, including capitalization, exactly matches the file and directory names:

```
/music class/Jazz 203/april 2013 Miles
/music class/to do list
```

(Figure 13.9)

File hierarchy seen as an upside-down tree with the forward slash (/) as the root, leading next to the directories and subdirectories, and then to the files shown in dashed line boxes.

The first slash indicates that this is an absolute path name that starts at the root directory. On the other hand, a relative path name is one that doesn't start at the root directory. Two examples of relative path names from Figure 13.9 are:

```
Jazz 203/april 2013 Miles
Lake Pictures/Landscaping/driveway_area
```

A few rules apply to path names:

• If the path name starts with a slash, the path starts at the root directory.

• A path name can be either one name or a list of names separated by slashes. The last name is the name of the requested file.

• Using two periods (..) in a path name moves you upward in the hierarchy (closer to the root). This is the only way to go up the hierarchy; all other path names go down the tree.

Directory Listings

As shown in Table 13.2, a "long listing" of files in a directory shows eight pieces of information for each file: the access control, the number of links, the name of the group and owner, the byte size of the file, the date and time of last modification, and, finally, the filename. Notice that the list is displayed in alphabetical order by filename.

(table 13.2)

This table shows the list of files stored in the directory journal from the system illustrated in Figure 13.9. The command `ls -l` (short for "listing-long") generates this list.

Access Control Code	No. of Links	Group	Owner	No. of Bytes	Date	Time	Filename
drwxrwxr-x	2	music class	comp	1024	Jan 10	19:32	Jazz 203
drwxrwxr-x	2	music class	comp	1024	Jan 15	09:59	Symphony 201
-rwxr--r--	1	music class	comp	54616	Jan 20	18:08	assignments
-rwxr-xr-x	1	music class	comp	51346	Jan 6	11:38	syllabus
-rwx------	1	music class	comp	35415	Jan 17	07:32	to do list

The first column shows the type of file and the access privileges for each file, as shown in Figure 13.10. The first character in the first column describes the nature of the file or directory; d indicates a directory and - indicates an ordinary file. Other codes that can be used are:

• b to indicate a block special file

• c to indicate a character special file

• p to indicate a named pipe file

(figure 13.10)

Graphical depiction of a list of file and directory permissions in UNIX.

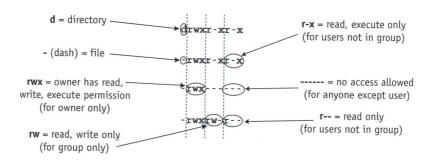

Beginning with the second column, there are three groups of three characters. The first three characters (rwx) show the access privileges granted to the owner of the file: r stands for read, w stands for write, and x stands for execute. Therefore, if the list includes rwx, the user can read, write, and/or execute that program. In Table 13.2, the user has this unlimited access to all three files.

Likewise, the following three characters describe the access privileges granted to other members of the user's group. (In UNIX, a group is defined as a set of users who have something in common: the same project, same class, same department, and so on.) Therefore, rwx for characters 5–7 means other users can also read, write, and/or execute that file. However, a hyphen indicates that access is denied for that operation. In Table 13.2, r-- means that the file called assignments can be read by other group members but can't be altered or executed.

Finally, the last three characters in the first column describe the access privileges granted to users at large, those system-wide who are not the owners or part of the owner's group. Thus, at-large users can't modify the files listed in Table 13.2, nor can they modify or execute the file named `assignments`. What's more, the file named `to do list` can't be read, modified, or executed by anyone other than the owner.

The second column in the directory listing indicates the number of links, also known as the number of *aliases*, which refer to the same physical file. Aliases are an important feature of UNIX; they support file sharing when several users work together on the same project. In this case, it's convenient for the shared files to appear in different directories belonging to different users even though only one central file descriptor (containing information on the file) exists for that file. The filename may be different from directory to directory since these names aren't kept in the file descriptor, but the numbers of links kept there is updated so the system knows how many users share this file. Often this number eventually drops to zero, indicating that the file is no longer needed and can be deleted safely.

The next three columns in Table 13.2 show, respectively, the name of the group, the name of the owner, and the file size in bytes. The sixth and seventh columns show the date and time of the last modification; the last column lists the filename.

Data Structures

The information presented in the directory doesn't all come from the same location. UNIX divides the file information into parts, some with the directory entries and some in the i-nodes. Therefore, of all the information shown in Table 13.2, only the filename and the device's physical addresses are stored with the directory. All else is kept in the i-node. All i-nodes are stored in a reserved part where the directory resides, usually in Block 1. This structure is illustrated in Figure 13.11.

Each i-node has room for 13 pointers, numbered 0 to 12. The first 10 block numbers stored in the i-node list relate to the first 10 blocks of a file. They're called direct blocks. In our example, for the file named `to do list` in Figure 13.11, only the first two entries have pointers to data blocks—all the others are zeros because this is a small file that occupies only two blocks of storage.

If a file is larger than 10 blocks, then the eleventh entry points to a block that contains a list of the next 128 blocks in the file. Because it's an extra step in the path to the data, this block is called an indirect block.

For files larger than 138 blocks, the twelfth entry points to a block that contains a list of 128 indirect blocks, each one containing pointers to 128 file blocks. Because this block introduces two extra steps in the path to the data, it's called a double indirect block. Finally, for extremely large files of more than 16,522 blocks, the thirteenth

(figure 13.11)

On the Mac OS X, the Finder uses an access control list to set permissions for file access.

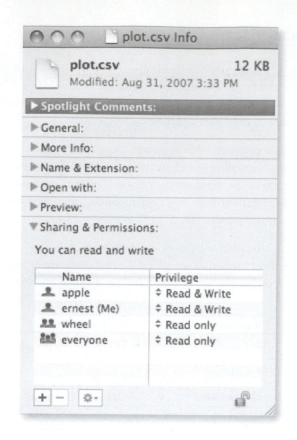

entry points to a triple indirect block. This schema allows for 2,113,674 blocks to be allocated to a single file, for a total of 1,082,201,088 bytes.

Therefore, carrying this one step further, we can see that the bytes numbered below 5120 can be retrieved with a single disk access. Those in the range between 5120 and 70,656 require two disk accesses. Those in the range between 70,656 and 8,459,264 require three disk accesses, while bytes beyond 8,459,264 require four disk accesses. This would give very slow access to large data files but, in reality, the system maintains a rather complicated buffering mechanism that considerably reduces the number of I/O operations required to access a file.

Whenever a file is created, an i-node is allocated to it and a directory entry with the filename and its i-node number is created. When a file is linked (which happens when another user begins sharing the same file), a directory entry is created with the new name and the original i-node number, and the link-count field in the i-node is incremented by 1.

When a shared file is deleted, the link-count field in the i-node is decremented by 1. When the count reaches 0, the directory entry is erased and all disk blocks allocated to the file, along with its i-node entry in the disk i-list, are deallocated.

User Interfaces

UNIX now typically supports both menu-driven systems and the traditional command-driven interfaces. Because both interfaces are nearly identical in both UNIX and Linux, we describe the command-driven interface in this chapter and the menu-driven interface in the Linux chapter.

UNIX was created as a command-driven system and its user commands (some shown in Table 13.3) are very short: either one character (usually the first letter of the command) or a group of characters (an acronym of the words that make up the command). In command mode, the system prompt is very economical, often only one character, such as a dollar sign ($) or percent sign (%).

User commands can't be abbreviated or expanded and must be in the correct case. (Remember that in most circumstances, UNIX commands are entered only in lower-case letters.) Many commands can be combined on a single line for additional power and flexibility.

Command	Stands For	Action to be Performed
(filename)	Run File	Run or execute the file with that name
cat	Concatenate	Concatenate files
cd	Change Directory	Change working directory
cp	Copy	Copy a file into another file or directory
date	Date	Show date and time
grep	Global Regular Expression/Print	Find a specified string in a file
lpr	Print	Submits a print request
ls	List Directory	Show a listing of the filenames in directory
ls -l	Long Directory List	Show a comprehensive directory list
man	Manual	Show the online manual
mkdir	Make Directory	Make a new directory
more	Show More	Type the file's contents to the screen
mv	Move	Move or rename a file or directory
rm	Remove File	Remove/delete a file or directory

(table 13.3)

Small sample of UNIX (and Linux) user commands which are entered in all lower case. Check your technical documentation for proper spelling and syntax.

The general syntax of commands is this:

```
command arguments file_name
```

The command is any legal operating system command. The arguments are required for some commands and optional for others. The filename can be a relative or absolute path name. Commands are interpreted and executed by the shell, one of the two most widely used programs. The shell is technically known as the command line interpreter because that's its function. But it isn't only an interactive command interpreter; it's also the key to the coordination and combination of system programs. In fact, it's a sophisticated programming language in itself.

Script Files

Command files, often called shell files or **script** files, can be used to automate repetitious tasks. Each line of the file is a valid command; the script file can be executed by simply typing sh and the name of the script file. Another way to execute it is to define the file as an executable command and simply type the filename at the system prompt.

Script files are used to automate repetitive tasks and to simplify complex procedures. Here is an example of a simple script file that's designed to configure the system for a certain user:

```
setenv DBPATH /u/lumber:.:/zdlf/product/central/db
setenv TERMCAP $INFODIR/etc/termcap
stty erase '^H'
set savehistory
set history=20
alias h history
alias 4gen infogen -f
setenv PATH /usr/info/bin:/etc
```

In this example, the working directory paths are set, the history is set to 20 lines, and it is given an alias of h (so the user can perform the history command simply by typing h). Similarly, 4gen is established as an alias for the command infogen -f. Finally, the path is defined as /usr/info/bin:/etc.

If this script file is included in the user's configuration file, it is automatically executed every time the user logs on. The exact name of the user configuration file varies from system to system, but two common names are .profile and .login. See the documentation for your system for specifics.

Redirection

Most of the commands used to produce output are automatically sent to your screen; the editor accepts input from the keyboard. When you want to send output to a file or to another device, this is done by using the angle bracket (>) between the command and the destination to which the output should be directed. For example, to make a copy of the files listed in your current directory and put them in the file named myfiles (instead of listing them on the screen), use this command:

```
ls > myfiles
```

Some UNIX commands may seem cryptic to those unfamiliar with the operating system because they're designed to be fast and easy to type. For example, *grep* is the command to find a specified text string in a file.

You can do this with multiple files and multiple commands. For example, the following command will copy the contents of two files:

```
cat chapter_1 chapter_2 > section_a
```

The command cat is short for "concatenate" and here's what it means:

- cat says to use the concatenate command
- chapter_1 is the name of the first file to be copied
- chapter_2 is the name of the second file to be copied
- > indicates the file to receive the new data
- section_a is the name of the resulting file

If section_a is a new file, then it's automatically created. If it already exists, the previous contents are overwritten. (When cat is used with a single file and redirection is not indicated, then it displays the contents of that file on the screen.) UNIX is very flexible. For example, another way to achieve the same result is with the wild card symbol (*) like this:

```
cat chapt* > section_a
```

When the asterisk symbol (*) is added to a filename, it indicates that the command pertains to all files that begin with "chapt"—in this case, that means the files with the names: chapter_1, chapter_2, chapter_7, and all other files that begin with the characters "chapt."

The double-angle-bracket symbol (>>) appends the new file to an existing file. Therefore, the following two commands copy the contents of chapter_1 and chapter_2 onto the end of whatever already exists in the file called section_a.

```
cat chapter_1 chapter_2 >> section_a
```

If section_a doesn't exist, then the file is created as an empty file and then filled with chapter_1 and chapter_2, in that order.

The reverse redirection is to take input for a program from an existing file instead of from the keyboard. For example, assume you have written a memo and need to mail it to several people. The following command sends the contents of the file memo to those individuals (in this case Chris, Anthony, Ida, and Roger) who are listed between the command mail and the angle bracket symbol (<):

```
mail Chris Anthony Ida Roger > memo
```

By combining the power of redirection with system commands, you can achieve results not possible otherwise. For example, the following command stores, in the file called temporary, the names of all users logged on to the system:

```
who < temporary
```

Adding the command sort puts the list in order that's stored in the file called `temporary` and displays the sorted list on the screen as it's generated.

```
who > sort > temporary
```

In each of these examples, it's important to note that the interpretation of the two angle brackets (> and >) is done by the shell and not by the individual program (such as `mail`, `who`, or `sort`). This means that input and output redirection can be used with any program because the program isn't aware that anything unusual is happening. This is one instance of the power of UNIX—the flexibility that comes from combining many operations into a single brief command.

Pipes

Pipes and filters make it possible to redirect output or input to selected files or devices based on commands given to the command interpreter. UNIX does that by manipulating I/O devices as special files.

For the example just presented, we listed the number of users online into a file called `temporary`, and we then sorted the file. There was no reason to create this file other than the fact that we needed it to complete the two-step operation required to see the list in alphabetical order on the screen. However, a pipe can do the same thing in a single step.

A pipe is the operating system's way to connect the output from one program to the input of another without the need for temporary or intermediate files. A pipe is a special type of file connecting two programs; information written to it by one program may be read immediately by the other, with synchronization, scheduling, and buffering handled automatically by the system. In other words, the programs execute concurrently, not one after the other. By using the vertical pipe symbol (|), the last example can be rewritten as:

```
who | sort
```

As a result, a sorted list of all users logged on to the system is displayed on the screen.

A pipeline is several programs simultaneously processing the same I/O stream. For example, the following command is a pipeline that takes the output from `who` (a list of all logged-on users), sorts it, and prints it out:

```
who | sort | lpr
```

Filters

UNIX has many programs that read some input, manipulate it in some way, and generate output; these programs are called filters. One example is `wc` (for word count), which counts the lines, words, and characters in a file. A word is defined as a string of characters separated by blanks. A modified version (`wc -1`) counts just the number of lines in the file.

For example, the following command would execute the word count command on the file journal and display the result:

```
wc journal
```

As a result, the system would respond with 10 140 700, meaning that the file named journal has 10 lines, 140 words, and 700 characters.

Another filter command is sort (the same command we used to demonstrate pipes). If a filename is given with the command, the contents of the file are sorted and displayed on the screen. If no filename is given with the command, sort accepts input from the keyboard and directs the output to the screen. When it's used with redirection, sort accepts input from a file and writes the output to another file. For example, here is an example of a command:

- sort wk_names > sortednames
- sort indicates the sort command.
- wk_names is the file to be sorted.
- > indicates the file to receive the new data.
- sortednames is the title of the resulting, sorted file.

If each record begins with a number, you can do a numerical sort in ascending order and send the results to the file sortednumbs by using this command:

```
sort -n wk_names > sortednumbs
```

To obtain a numerical sort in descending order, the command is this:

```
sort -nr wk_names > sortednumbs
```

- sort indicates the sort command
- -n indicates a numerical sort.
- r indicates to sort in reverse order.
- wk_names is the file to be sorted.
- > indicates the file to receive the new data.
- sortednumbs is the title of the resulting, sorted file.

In every example presented here, the sort command examines each entire line of the file to conduct the sort, so the integrity of the file is preserved—that is, each name keeps the correct address, phone, and ID number. In addition, if the structure of the data stored in the file is known, then the sort command can be used on other key fields as well.

For example, let's say a file named empl has data that follows a standard column format: the ID numbers start in column 1, phone numbers start in column 10, and last names start in column 20. To sort the file by last name (the third field), the command would be:

```
sort +2f empl > sortedempl
```

In this example, the file empl is sorted alphabetically by the third field and the output is sent to the file called sortedempl. A field is defined as a group of characters separated by at least one blank. Here's how it works:

- sort says to use the sort command.
- +2 tells the sort command to skip the first two fields of data.
- f says the list should be sorted in alphabetical order.
- empl is the name of the file to be sorted.
- > indicates the file to receive the new data.
- sortedempl is the name of the resulting sorted file.

Additional Commands

UNIX uses a vast library of commonly used commands (and many are common to Linux). Only a few are mentioned here. For a complete list, refer to valid commands for your system.

man

This command displays the online manual supplied with the operating system, shown in Figure 13.12.

(figure 13.12)

The UNIX command man will cause the online manual to be displayed. Some command arguments are shown using the Terminal screen on this Macintosh computer.

```
man, version 1.6c

usage: man [-adfhktwW] [section] [-M path] [-P pager] [-S list]
           [-m system] [-p string] name ...

a : find all matching entries
c : do not use cat file
d : print gobs of debugging information
D : as for -d, but also display the pages
f : same as whatis(1)
h : print this help message
k : same as apropos(1)
K : search for a string in all pages
t : use troff to format pages for printing
w : print location of man page(s) that would be displayed
    (if no name given: print directories that would be searched)
W : as for -w, but display filenames only

C file   : use `file' as configuration file
M path   : set search path for manual pages to `path'
P pager  : use program `pager' to display pages
S list   : colon separated section list
m system : search for alternate system's man pages
p string : string tells which preprocessors to run
            e - [n]eqn(1)   p - pic(1)    t - tbl(1)
            g - grap(1)     r - refer(1)  v - vgrind(1)
bash-3.2$
```

This command can be called with an argument that specifies which page of the online manual you are interested in seeing. For example, to display the page for the cmp (compare) command, the command to do so looks like this:

```
man cmp
```

If the cmp entry appears more than once in the manual, all the pages are displayed, one after the other. You can redirect the output to a file (in this case, named my compare help) for future reference with the command:

```
man cmp > my compare help
```

grep

An often-used command is grep—the acronym stands for global regular expression and print. This command looks for specific patterns of characters. It's one of the most helpful (and oddly named) commands. This the equivalent of the FIND and SEARCH commands used in other operating systems. When the desired pattern of characters is found, the line containing it is displayed on the screen.

Here's a simple example: If you need to retrieve the names and addresses of everyone with a Pittsburgh address from a large file called mail-list, the command would look like this:

```
grep Pittsburgh mail-list
```

As a result, you see on your screen the lines from mail-list for entries that included Pittsburgh. And if you want the output sent to a file for future use, you can add the redirection command.

This grep command can also be used to list all the lines that do not contain a certain string of characters. Using the same example, the following command displays on the screen the names and addresses of all those who don't have a Pittsburgh address:

```
grep -v Pittsburgh mail-list
```

Similarly, the following command counts all the people who live in Pittsburgh and displays that number on the screen without printing each line:

```
grep -c Pittsburgh maillist
```

As noted before, the power of this operating system comes from its ability to combine commands. Here's how the grep command can be combined with the who command. Suppose you want to see if your friend Bob is logged on. The command to display Bob's name, device, and the date and time he logged in would be:

```
who | grep bob
```

Combinations of commands, though effective, can appear confusing to the casual observer. For example, if you wanted a list of all the subdirectories (but not the files) found in the root directory, the command would be:

```
ls -l / | grep '^d'
```

This command is the combination of several simpler commands:

- ls for list directory.
- -l, which sends more detail of the listing.
- / indicates the root directory.
- | establishes a pipe.
- grep finds a text string.
- '^d', which says that d is the character we're looking for (because we want only the directories), the carat symbol (^) indicates that the d is at the beginning of each line, and the quotes are required because we used the carat symbol.

nohup

If a program's execution is expected to take a long time, you can start its execution and then log off the system without having to wait for it to finish. This is done with the command nohup, which is short for "no hangup." Let's say, for example, you want to make a copy of a very large file (old_largefile), but you can't wait around until the job is finished. The command is:

```
nohup cp old_largefile new_largefile &
```

The copy command (cp) will continue its execution copying old_largefile to new_largefile in the background even though you've logged off the system, assuming the computer is not powered off. For this example, we've indicated that execution should continue in the background by attaching the ampersand (&) symbol.

nice

If your program uses a large number of resources and you are not in a hurry for the results, you can be "nice" to other processes by lowering its priority with the command nice. This command with a trailing & frees up your terminal for different work. For example, say you want to copy old_largefile to new_largefile and want to continue working on another project at the same time. To do that, use this command:

```
nice cp old_largefile new_largefile &
```

However, you may not log off when using the nice command until the copy is finished because the program execution would be stopped prematurely.

The command nohup automatically activates nice by lowering the process's priority. It assumes that since you've logged off the system, you're not in a hurry for the output. The opposite isn't true—when nice is issued, it doesn't automatically activate nohup. Therefore, if you want to put a very long job in the background, work on some other jobs, and log out before the long job is finished, nohup with a trailing ampersand (&) is the command to use.

We've included only a few commands here. For a complete list of commands for a specific version of this operating system, command syntax, and more details about those we've discussed here, see the technical manual for your system.

Conclusion

The impact of UNIX on the computing world has been far reaching. Its power, speed, and flexibility, along with its widespread adoption on computing devices of every size, has helped it revolutionize the development of operating systems. It is no surprise that a very similar operating system, Linux, has also been met with enthusiasm. Together, they run on many millions of computers and computing devices.

One reason for the success of UNIX has been its spare, flexible, and powerful command structure. In its early years, UNIX was distributed only as a command-driven interface created by programmers for programmers, so they could quickly and easily issue commands. Recently, with the addition of several standard graphical user interfaces for users to choose from, anyone can choose from menu options to issue the powerful commands that only highly skilled users could create previously.

With its adoption by Apple as the basis for its Mac OS X operating system, UNIX has reached an even wider user base. So, what started as a minor operating system in 1969 has become one of the most popular and powerful operating systems in the world.

Key Terms

argument: in a command-driven operating system, a value or option placed in the command that modifies how the command is to be carried out.

child process: a subordinate process that is created and controlled by a parent process.

CPU-bound: a job or process that requires a great deal of nonstop processing before issuing an interrupt; a CPU-bound job can tie up the CPU for a long period of time.

device driver: a device-specific program module that controls a particular type of device.

device independent: programs that can work with a variety of computers and devices in spite of their electronic variations.

directory: a logical storage unit that may contain files.

I/O-bound: a job or process that requires a large number of input/output operations, resulting in much free time for the CPU.

kernel: the part of the operating system that resides in main memory at all times and performs the most essential tasks, such as managing memory and handling disk input and output.

parent process: a process that creates and controls one or more child processes.

Portable Operating System Interface for Computer Environments (POSIX): a set of IEEE standards that defines the standard user and programming interfaces for operating systems so developers can port programs from one operating system to another.

reentrant code: code that can be used by two or more processes at the same time; each shares the same copy of the executable code but has separate data areas.

script: a series of executable commands written in plain text that can be executed by the operating system in sequence as a single procedure.

sharable code: executable code in the operating system that can be shared by several processes.

Interesting Searches

For more background on a few of the topics discussed in this chapter, begin a search with these terms.

- POSIX Standards
- UNIX file management
- Macintosh OS X
- Embedded UNIX
- Commands for UNIX and Linux

Exercises

Research Topics

A. Research current literature to discover the current state of IEEE POSIX Standards and list several UNIX operating systems that are currently 100 percent POSIX-compliant. Explain the significance of compliance. Explain why you think a popular UNIX operating system might choose not to be compliant.

B. Explore the issues surrounding UNIX security. Specifically, identify major threats to systems running UNIX and list the steps system administrators must take to protect the system from unauthorized access. Compare the practical problems when balancing the need for accessibility with the need to restrict access. Finally, suggest the first action you would take to secure a UNIX information system if you managed one.

Exercises

1. Figure 13.13 shows a listing of files on a Macintosh computer using the Terminal window and the UNIX command ls -l.

    a. Identify by name any directories and the number of links to each directory.

    b. Identify by name any files that allow WORLD access and the type of access permitted for each file.

    c. Identify by name any files that allow access only to that file's owner and the type of access permitted for each file.

```
●○○                 Terminal — bash — 87×12
bash-3.2$ ls -l
total 464
-rw-r--r--@ 1 gumbergmusic  staff      3246 Aug 30  2010 Bookmarks.plist
-rw-r--r--@ 1 gumbergmusic  staff     11470 Aug 30  2010 Configurations.plist.signed
-rw-r--r--@ 1 gumbergmusic  staff      3078 Feb 20 16:25 Downloads.plist
-rw-r--r--@ 1 gumbergmusic  staff       425 Feb 20 16:25 History.plist
-rw-------@ 1 gumbergmusic  staff     94208 Feb 20 16:25 HistoryIndex.sk
-rw-r--r--@ 1 gumbergmusic  staff      1529 Feb 20 16:25 LastSession.plist
drwx------@ 6 gumbergmusic  staff       204 Feb 20 16:25 LocalStorage
-rw-r--r--@ 1 gumbergmusic  staff       804 Aug 30  2010 TopSites.plist
-rw-r--r--@ 1 gumbergmusic  staff    108544 Feb 20 16:25 WebpageIcons.db
bash-3.2$ ▋
```

(figure 13.13)

Screenshot from a Terminal Window on a Macintosh running UNIX.

2. Assuming that a file listing showed the following permissions: $prwxr-xr-x$. Answer the following questions.

    a. Is this a file or a directory?

    b. What permissions does the WORLD have?

    c. What permissions have been denied to the GROUP?

3. UNIX is renowned for using lower case characters in its command structure.

    a. Using your own words, explain what would happen if you issued a legal command (such as man as shown in Figure 13.12) using only upper case characters.

    b. Explain why you think Linux followed the UNIX convention of using lower case characters for its typed commands.

4. Early versions of UNIX were available only with a command-driven interface. In more recent years, graphical user interfaces have become popular. Explain in your own words why these GUIs made an impact on the popularity of this operating system.

5. Describe at least one circumstance where you would want to run commands in background mode.

6. The role of the UNIX kernel is crucial. Explain why this is so and how it is treated differently from other parts of the operating system.

7. UNIX treats all devices as files. Explain why this was an innovative feature when it was first introduced and how it adds flexibility to this operating system.

8. Create an illustration showing how an i-node would track the disk addresses for a single file that's 1GB in size.

Advanced Exercises

9. Compare and contrast block and character devices and how they are manipulated by the UNIX device manager.

10. Explain how UNIX identifies CPU- and I/O-bound jobs and uses that information to keep the system balanced.

11. Assume that you are a systems administrator. Explain why you might want to change the permissions on some of your directories to make them invisible to users.

12. Describe in your own words how a parent and child are created from the `fork` command and why you think the child process will or will not continue if the parent process is terminated.

13. Describe the importance of hardware independence to systems administrators. Explain the possible consequences if hardware was not independent.

14. Using the command `/dev`, identify which devices are available and indicate which of these devices are character-oriented and which are block-oriented. Explain your reasoning.

15. If you were using a system and a system operator deleted the list (`ls`) command accidentally, what other combination of commands could be used to list all the files in a directory?

16. Compare and contrast UNIX security in 1995 and today. Describe any significant threats to UNIX-run systems in the 1990s and how those are different than those faced now.

Chapter 14 | Windows Operating Systems

WINDOWS INTERFACE

Design Goals
Memory Management
Processor Management
Device Management
File Management
User Interface

> *Windows has this exciting central position, a position that is used by thousands and thousands of companies to build their products.*
>
> —Bill Gates

Learning Objectives

After completing this chapter, you should be able to describe:

- Design goals for Windows operating systems designers
- The role of the Memory Manager and Virtual Memory Manager in Windows
- Its use of the Device, Processor, and Network Managers
- System security challenges for Windows
- Windows user interfaces

Windows operating systems are now available for computing environments of all sizes. Windows 8, the latest release as of this writing, features a tile-like Start page, designed to work with phones and tablets with touch screens as well as with traditional computers with keyboards and cursor devices. This interface indicates a philosophy shift by Microsoft to make its operating system accommodate the market for touch screen devices.

Brief History

Before the 1995 release of the Windows 95 operating system, all Windows products (such as Windows 3) were merely graphical user interfaces that required the MS-DOS operating system to perform tasks. At that time, MS-DOS was the true operating system but took its direction from the Windows graphical user interface which allowed users to run the system. However, this layering technique had several distinct disadvantages: it couldn't perform multitasking; it had little built-in security; and it had no interprocess communication capability. In addition, it had to be customized to work with each piece of system hardware, making portability difficult when moving from one platform to another.

While Microsoft was courting the home and office environment with single-user operating systems, the company abandoned its reliance on MS-DOS and began developing more powerful networking products. Table 14.1 lists a few Windows operating systems released since 1995.

Year	Release	Features
1995	Windows 95	True operating system designed to replace MS-DOS and the Windows 3.x graphical user interfaces.
1996	Windows NT Server version 4.0	Integrated support for e-mail and Internet connectivity.
2001	Windows XP	Featured 32-bit and 64-bit versions built on the Windows NT kernel.
2008	Windows Server 2008	Reduced power requirements and increased virtualization capabilities; supported up to 64 cores.
2009	Windows 7	Six versions, most with 64-bit addressing; improved stability and response time
2012	Windows 8	Supports phones, tablets, and desktop computers.
2012	Windows Server 2012	Integrates cloud environments and distributed access.

(table 14.1)

Select Microsoft Windows operating systems. For details about these and other versions, refer to www.microsoft.com.

Each Windows product has a version number. For example, Windows XP is version 5.1, Windows 7 is version 6.1, and Windows 8 is version 6.2. To find the precise version number of a system, press the Windows logo key and the R key together. Then type winver. Alternatively, click Apps and then tap or click winver.exe. If using the tiled Start page, a screen similar to the one shown in Figure 14.1 will display, and a sample result is shown in Figure 14.2.

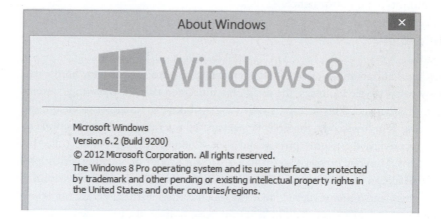

William H. Gates (1955–)

In his junior year at Harvard, Bill Gates left school to devote his energies to Microsoft, a company he had begun in 1975 with his childhood friend Paul Allen. The company's first notable operating system was MS-DOS, which they licensed to IBM to run its new line of personal computers in 1981. Allen left Microsoft in

1983 with a serious illness, and under the leadership of Gates, the Windows operating system has evolved to run computing devices of almost every size. Gates has received several honorary doctorates, including one from Harvard, and was also made an honorary Knight Commander of the Order of the British Empire (KBE) by Queen Elizabeth II (2005).

For more information, see

http://www.microsoft.com/en-us/news/exec/billg/

Time magazine named Gates one of the 100 people who most influenced the twentieth century.

Design Goals

When they were designed, Windows networking operating systems were influenced by several operating system models, using existing frameworks while introducing new features. They use an object model to manage operating system resources and to allocate them to users in a consistent manner. They use symmetric multiprocessing (often abbreviated as SMP) to achieve maximum performance from multiprocessor computers.

To accommodate the various needs of its user community and to optimize resources, the Windows team identified five design goals: extensibility, portability, reliability, compatibility, and performance.

Extensibility

Knowing that operating systems must change over time to support new hardware devices or new software technologies, the design team decided that the operating system had to be easily enhanced. This feature is called **extensibility**. In an effort to ensure the integrity of the Windows code, the designers separated operating system functions into two groups: a privileged executive process and a set of nonprivileged processes called protected subsystems. The term privileged refers to a processor's mode of operation. Most processors have a privileged mode (in which all machine instructions are allowed and system memory is accessible) and a nonprivileged mode (in which certain instructions are not allowed and system memory isn't accessible). In Windows terminology, the privileged processor mode is called **kernel mode** and the nonprivileged processor mode is called **user mode**.

Usually, operating systems execute in kernel mode only and application programs execute in user mode only, except when they call operating system services. In Windows, the protected subsystems execute in user mode as if they were applications, which allows protected subsystems to be modified or added without affecting the integrity of the executive process.

In addition to protected subsystems, Windows designers included several features to address extensibility issues:

- A modular structure allowing new components to be added to the executive process.
- A group of abstract data types called objects that are manipulated by a special set of services, allowing system resources to be managed uniformly.
- A remote procedure call that allows an application to call remote services regardless of their location on the network.

Portability

Portability refers to the operating system's ability to operate on different platforms that use different processors or configurations with a minimum amount of recoding. To address this goal, Windows system developers used a four-prong approach. First, they wrote it in a standardized, high-level language. Second, the system accommodated the hardware to which it was expected to be ported (32-bit, 64-bit, and so on). Third, code that interacted directly with the hardware was minimized to reduce incompatibility errors. Fourth, all hardware-dependent code was isolated into modules that could be modified more easily whenever the operating system was ported.

Windows is written for ease of porting to machines that use varying linear addressing schemes, and it provides virtual memory capabilities. Most Windows operating systems have shared the following features:

- The code is modular. That is, the code that must access processor-dependent data structures and registers is contained in small modules that can be replaced by similar modules for different processors.

- Much of Windows is written in C, a programming language that's standardized and readily available. The graphic component and some portions of the networking user interface are written in C++. Assembly language code (which generally is not portable) is used only for those parts of the system that must communicate directly with the hardware.

- Windows contains a hardware abstraction layer (HAL), a dynamic link library that provides isolation from hardware dependencies furnished by different vendors. The HAL abstracts hardware, such as caches, with a layer of low-level software so that higher-level code need not change when moving from one platform to another.

Reliability

Reliability refers to the robustness of a system—that is, its predictability in responding to error conditions, even those caused by hardware failures. It also refers to the operating system's ability to protect itself and its users from accidental or deliberate damage by user programs.

Structured exception handling is one way to capture error conditions and respond to them uniformly. Whenever such an event occurs, either the operating system or the processor issues an exception call, which automatically invokes the exception handling code that's appropriate to handle the condition, ensuring that no harm is done to either user programs or the system. In addition, the following features strengthen the system:

- A modular design that divides the executive process into individual system components that interact with each other through specified programming interfaces. For example, if it becomes necessary to replace the Memory Manager with a new one, the new one will use the same interfaces.

- A file system called **NTFS** (for NT File System), which can recover from all types of errors, including those that occur in critical disk sectors. To ensure recoverability, NTFS uses redundant storage and a transaction-based scheme for storing data.

✔

Like IBM before it, Microsoft uses a multitude of abbreviations as shortcuts when describing its system. Throughout this chapter, we spell them out the first time they are used.

445

- A security architecture that provides a variety of security mechanisms, such as user logon, resource quotas, and object protection.
- A virtual memory strategy that provides every program with a large set of memory addresses and prevents one user from reading or modifying memory that's occupied by another user unless the two are explicitly sharing memory.

Compatibility

Compatibility usually refers to an operating system's ability to execute programs written for other operating systems or for earlier versions of the same system. However, for Windows, compatibility is a more complicated topic.

Through the use of protected subsystems, Windows provides execution environments for applications that are different from its primary programming interface—the Win32 application programming interface (API). When running on Intel processors, the protected subsystems supply binary compatibility with existing Microsoft applications. Windows also provides source-level compatibility with POSIX applications that adhere to the POSIX operating system interfaces defined by the IEEE. (**POSIX** is short for the Portable Operating System Interface, an operating system API that defines how a service is invoked through a software package.) POSIX was developed by the IEEE to increase the portability of application software.

In addition to compatibility with programming interfaces, recent versions of Windows also support existing file systems, including the MS-DOS file allocation table (FAT), the CD-ROM file system (CDFS), and the NTFS.

Windows comes with built-in verification of important hardware and software. That is, the upgrade setup procedures include a check-only mode that examines the system's hardware and software for potential problems and produces a report that lists them. The procedure stops when it can't find drivers for critical devices, such as hard-disk controllers, bus extensions, and other items that are sometimes necessary for a successful upgrade.

Performance

The operating system should respond quickly to CPU-bound applications. To do so, Windows is built with the following features:

- System calls, page faults, and other crucial processes are designed to respond in a timely manner.
- A mechanism called the local procedure call (LPC) is incorporated into the operating system so that communication among the protected subsystems doesn't restrain performance.

• Critical elements of Windows' networking software are built into the privileged portion of the operating system to improve performance. In addition, these components can be loaded and unloaded from the system dynamically, if necessary.

That said, as of this writing, the response of some Windows operating systems can slow down as more programs or applications are installed and the computer is used over time. Even when users try to uninstall these applications, performance can remain slow and may not return to the benchmarks attained when the computer was new.

Memory Management

Every operating system uses its own view of physical memory and requires its application programs to access memory in specified ways. In the example shown in Figure 14.3, each process's virtual address space is 4GB, with 2GB each allocated to program storage and system storage. When physical memory becomes full, the Virtual Memory Manager pages some of the memory contents to disk, freeing physical memory for other processes.

(figure 14.3)

Layout of Windows memory. This is a virtual memory system based on 32-bit addresses in a linear address space. The 64-bit versions use a similar model but on a much larger scale with 8TB for the user and 8TB for the kernel.

The challenge for all Windows operating systems, especially those running in a network, is to run application programs written for Windows or POSIX without crashing into each other in memory. Each Windows environment subsystem provides a view of memory that matches what its applications expect. The executive process has its own memory structure, which the subsystems access by calling the operating system's inherent services.

In recent versions, the Windows operating system resides in high virtual memory and the user's code and data reside in low virtual memory. A user's process can't read or write to system memory directly. All user-accessible memory can be paged to disk, as can the segment of system memory labeled paged pool. However, the segment of system memory labeled nonpaged pool is never paged to disk because it's used to store critical objects, such as the code that does the paging, as well as major data structures.

User Mode Features

The Virtual Memory (VM) Manager allows user mode subsystems to share memory and provides a set of native services that a process can use to manage its virtual memory in the following ways:

- Allocate memory in two stages: first by reserving memory and then by committing memory, as needed. This two-step procedure allows a process to reserve a large section of virtual memory without being charged for it until it's actually needed.

- Provide read and/or write protection for virtual memory, allowing processes to share memory when needed.

- Lock virtual pages in physical memory. This ensures that a critical page isn't removed from memory while a process is using it. For example, a database application that uses a tree structure to update its data may lock the root of the tree in memory, thus minimizing page faults while accessing the database.

- Retrieve information about virtual pages.

- Protect virtual pages. Each virtual page has a set of flags associated with it that determines the types of access allowed in user mode. In addition, Windows provides object-based memory protection. Therefore, each time a process opens a section object, a block of memory that can be shared by two or more processes, the security reference monitor checks whether the process is allowed to access the object.

- Rewrite virtual pages to disk. If an application modifies a page, the VM Manager writes the changes back to the file during its normal paging operations.

Virtual Memory Implementation

The Virtual Memory Manager relies on address space management and paging techniques.

Address Space Management

As shown earlier in Figure 14.3, the upper half of the virtual address space is accessible only to kernel-mode processes. Code in the lower part of this section, kernel code and data, is never paged out of memory. In addition, the addresses in this range are translated by the hardware, providing exceedingly fast data access. Therefore, the lower part of the resident operating system code is used for sections of the kernel that require maximum performance, such as the code that dispatches units of execution (called threads of execution) in a processor.

When users create a new process, they can specify that the VM Manager initialize their virtual address space by duplicating the virtual address space of another process. This allows environment subsystems to present their client processes with views of memory that don't correspond to the virtual address space of a native process.

Paging

The pager is the part of the VM Manager that transfers pages between page frames in memory and disk storage. As such, it's a complex combination of both software policies and hardware mechanisms. Software policies determine *when* to bring a page into memory and *where* to put it. Hardware mechanisms include the exact manner in which the VM Manager translates virtual addresses into physical addresses.

Because the hardware features of each system directly affect the success of the VM Manager, implementation of virtual memory varies from processor to processor. Therefore, this portion of the operating system isn't portable and must be modified for each new hardware platform. To make the transition easier, Windows keeps this code small and isolated. The processor chip that handles address translation and exception handling looks at each address generated by a program and translates it into a physical address. If the page containing the address isn't in memory, then the hardware generates a page fault and issues a call to the pager. The translation look-aside buffer (TLB) is a hardware array of associative memory used by the processor to speed memory access. As pages are brought into memory by the VM Manager, it creates entries for them in the TLB. If a virtual address isn't in the TLB, it may still be in memory. In that case, virtual software rather than hardware is used to find the address, resulting in slower access times.

Paging policies in a virtual memory system dictate how and when paging is done and are composed of fetch, placement, and replacement policies:

- The **fetch policy** determines when the pager copies a page from disk to memory. The VM Manager uses a demand paging algorithm with locality of reference, called clustering, to load pages into memory. This strategy attempts to minimize the number of page faults that a process encounters.
- The **placement policy** is the set of rules that determines where the virtual page is loaded in memory. If memory isn't full, the VM Manager selects the first page frame from a list of free page frames. This list is called the page frame database and is an array of entries numbered from 0 through *n*, with *n-1* equaling the number of page frames in the system. Each entry contains information about the corresponding page frame, which at any given time can be in one of six states: valid, zeroed, free, standby, modified, or bad. Valid and modified page frames are those currently in use. Those zeroed, free, or on standby represent available page frames; bad frames are permanently disabled.

> ✔
> When pages are "removed," they are marked for deletion and then overwritten by the incoming page. These deleted pages are not normally removed from memory.

- Of the available page frames, the page frame database links together those that are in the same state, thus creating five separate homogeneous lists. Whenever the number of pages in the zeroed, free, and standby lists reaches a preset minimum, the modified page writer process is activated to write the contents of the modified pages to disk and link them to the standby list. On the other hand, if the modified page list becomes too short, the VM Manager shrinks each process's working set to its minimum working set size and adds the newly freed pages to the modified or standby lists to be reused.

- The **replacement policy** determines which virtual page must be removed from memory to make room for a new page. Of the replacement policies considered in Chapter 3, the VM Manager uses a local first-in, first out (FIFO) replacement policy and keeps track of the pages currently in memory for each process—the process's working set. The FIFO algorithm is local to each process, so that when a page fault occurs, only page frames owned by a process can be freed. When it's created, each process is assigned a minimum working-set size, which is the number of pages the process is guaranteed to have in memory while it's executing. If memory isn't very full, the VM Manager allows the process to have the pages it needs up to its working set maximum. If the process requires even more pages, the VM Manager removes one of the process's pages for each new page fault the process generates.

Certain parts of the VM Manager depend on the processor running the operating system and must be modified for each platform. These platform-specific features include page table entries, page size, page-based protection, and virtual address translation.

Processor Management

In general, a process is the combination of an executable program, a private memory area, and system resources allocated by the operating system as the program executes. However, a process requires a fourth component before it can do any work: at least one thread of execution. A thread is the entity within a process that the kernel schedules for execution; it could be roughly equated to a task. Using multiple threads (also called multithreading) allows a programmer to break up a single process into several executable segments and also to take advantage of the extra CPU power available in computers with multiple processors. Starting with Windows Server 2008 Release 2, Windows operating systems could coordinate processing among 64 cores.

Windows is a preemptive, multitasking, multithreaded operating system. By default, a process contains one thread, which is composed of the following:

- A unique identifier
- The contents of a volatile set of registers indicating the processor's state
- Two stacks used during the thread's execution
- A private storage area used by subsystems and dynamic link libraries

These components are called the thread's context; the actual data forming this context varies from one processor to another. The kernel schedules threads for execution on a processor. For example, when you use the mouse to double-click an application's icon, the operating system creates a process, and that process has one thread that runs the code. The process is like a container for the global variables, the environment strings, the heap owned by the application, and the thread. The thread is what actually executes the code. Figure 14.4 shows a diagram of a process with a single thread.

For systems with multiple processors, a process can have as many threads as there are CPUs available. The overhead incurred by a thread is minimal. In some cases, it's actually advantageous to split a single application into multiple threads because the entire program is then much easier to understand. The creation of threads isn't as complicated as it may seem. Although each thread has its own stack, all threads belonging to one process share its global variables, heap, and environment strings. See Figure 14.5.

Multiple threads can present problems because it's possible for several different threads to modify the same global variables independently of each other. To prevent this, Windows operating systems include synchronization mechanisms to give exclusive access to global variables as these multithreaded processes are executed.

For example, let's say the user is modifying a database application. When the user enters a series of records into the database, the cursor changes into a "hold" symbol that indicates a thread is writing the last record to the disk while another thread is accepting new data. Therefore, even as processing is going on, the user can perform other tasks. The concept of overlapped I/O now occurs on the user's end as well as on the computer's end.

Multithreading improves database searches because data is retrieved faster when the system has several threads of execution that search an array simultaneously, especially if each thread has its own CPU. Programs written to take advantage of these features must be designed very carefully to minimize contention, such as when two CPUs attempt to access the same memory location at the same time, or when two threads compete for single shared resources, such as a hard disk.

Client/server applications tend to be CPU-intensive for the server because, although queries on the database are received as requests from a client computer, the actual query is managed by the server's processor. A Windows multiprocessing environment can satisfy those requests by allocating additional CPU resources.

Device Management

The I/O system must accommodate the needs of existing devices—from a simple mouse and keyboard to printers, display terminals, disk drives, CD-ROM drives, multimedia devices, and networks. In addition, it must consider future storage and input technologies. The I/O system provides a uniform high-level interface for executive-level I/O operations and eliminates the need for applications to account for differences among physical devices. It shields the rest of the operating system from the details of device manipulation and thus minimizes and isolates hardware-dependent code.

The I/O system in Windows is designed to provide the following:

- Multiple installable file systems, including FAT, the CD-ROM file system, and NTFS
- Services to make device-driver development as easy as possible yet workable on multiprocessor systems
- Ability for system administrators to add or remove drivers from the system dynamically
- Fast I/O processing while allowing drivers to be written in a high-level language
- Mapped file I/O capabilities for image activation, file caching, and application use

The I/O system is packet driven. That is, every I/O request is represented by an I/O request packet (IRP) as it moves from one I/O system component to another. An IRP is a data structure that controls how the I/O operation is processed at each step. The I/O Manager creates an IRP that represents each I/O operation, passes the IRP to the appropriate driver, and disposes of the packet when the operation is complete. On the other hand, when a driver receives the IRP, it performs the specified operation and then either passes it back to the I/O Manager or passes it through the I/O Manager to another driver for further processing.

In addition to creating and disposing of IRPs, the I/O Manager supplies code, common to a variety of drivers, that it calls to carry out its I/O processing. It also manages buffers for I/O requests, provides time-out support for drivers, and records which installable file systems are loaded into the operating system. It provides flexible I/O facilities that allow subsystems such as POSIX to implement their respective I/O application programming interfaces. Finally, the I/O Manager allows device drivers and file systems, which it perceives as device drivers, to be loaded dynamically based on the needs of the user.

To make sure the operating system works with a wide range of hardware peripherals, Windows provides a device-independent model for I/O services. This model takes advantage of a concept called a multilayered device driver that's not found in operating systems, such as MS-DOS with monolithic device drivers. These multilayered drivers provide a large and complex set of services that are understood by an intermediate layer of the operating system.

Each device driver is made up of a standard set of routines, including the following:
- Initialization routine, which creates system objects used by the I/O Manager to recognize and access the driver.
- Dispatch routine, which comprises functions performed by the driver, such as READ or WRITE. This is used by the I/O Manager to communicate with the driver when it generates an IRP after an I/O request.
- Start I/O routine, used by the driver to initiate data transfer to or from a device.
- Completion routine, used to notify a driver that a lower-level driver has finished processing an IRP.
- Unload routine, which releases any system resources used by the driver so that the I/O Manager can remove them from memory.
- Error logging routine, used when unexpected hardware errors occur (such as a bad sector on a disk); the information is passed to the I/O Manager, which writes it to an error log file.

When a process needs to access a file, the I/O Manager determines from the file object's name which driver should be called to process the request, and it must be able to locate this information the next time a process uses the same file. This is accomplished by a driver object, which represents an individual driver in the system, and a device object, which represents a physical, logical, or virtual device on the system and describes its characteristics.

The I/O Manager creates a driver object when a driver is loaded into the system, and then it calls the driver's initialization routine. This routine records the driver entry points in the driver object and creates one device object for each device to be handled by this driver. An example showing how an application instruction results in disk access is shown in Table 14.2.

Event	Result
Instruction: READ "MYFILE.TXT"	READ = FUNCTION CODE 1 "MYFILE.TXT" = DISK SECTOR 10
Actions:	1. Access DRIVER OBJECT (1)
	2. Activate READ routine
	3. Access DISK SECTOR 10

(table 14.2)

Example showing how a device object is created from an instruction to read a file, illustrated in Figure 14.6.

Figure 14.6 illustrates how the last device object points back to its driver object, telling the I/O Manager which driver routine to call when it receives an I/O request. When a process requests access to a file, it uses a filename, which includes the device object where the file is stored. When the file is opened, the I/O Manager creates a file object and then returns a file handle to the process. Whenever the process uses the file handle, the I/O Manager can immediately find the device object, which points to the driver object representing the driver that services the device. Using the function code supplied in the original request, the I/O Manager indexes into the driver object and activates the appropriate routine—because each function code corresponds to a driver routine entry point.

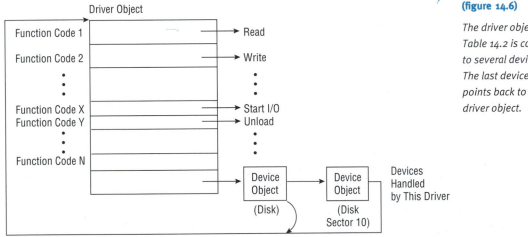

(figure 14.6)

The driver object from Table 14.2 is connected to several device objects. The last device object points back to the driver object.

A driver object may have multiple device objects connected to it. The list of device objects represents the physical, logical, and virtual devices that are controlled by the driver. For example, each sector of a hard disk has a separate device object with sector-specific information. However, the same hard disk driver is used to access all sectors. When a driver is unloaded from the system, the I/O Manager uses the queue of device objects to determine which devices will be affected by the removal of the driver.

Using objects to keep track of information about drivers frees the I/O Manager from having to know details about individual drivers—it just follows a pointer to locate a driver. This provides portability and allows new drivers to be easily loaded. Another advantage to representing devices and drivers with different objects is that if the system configuration changes, it's easier to assign drivers to control additional or different devices.

Figure 14.7 shows how the I/O Manager interacts with a layered device driver to write data to a file on a hard disk by following these steps:

1. An application issues a command to write to a disk file at a specified byte offset within the file.
2. The I/O Manager passes the file handle to the file system driver.
3. The I/O Manager translates the file-relative byte offset into a disk-relative byte offset and calls the next driver.
4. The function code and the disk-relative byte offset are passed to the disk driver.
5. The disk-relative byte offset is translated into the physical location and data is transferred.

This process parallels the discussion in Chapter 8 about levels in a file management system.

(figure 14.7)

Details of the layering of a file system driver and a disk driver. The steps shown here take place when the I/O Manager needs to access a secondary storage device to satisfy the command shown in Step 1.

Environment Subsystem
or
Dynamic-Link Library

User Mode
Kernel Mode

1. WRITE_FILE (File_handle, character_buffer)

System Services

I/O Manager

2. Write data at specified location

File System Driver

3. Translate file-relative byte offset into disk-relative byte-offset; call next driver

Disk Driver

4. Call driver to write data at disk-relative byte offset

Disk

5. Translate disk-relative byte offset into physical location; transfer data

The I/O Manager knows nothing about the file system. The process described in this example works exactly the same if an NTFS driver is replaced by a FAT driver, a UNIX or Linux file system driver, a CD-ROM driver, a Macintosh file system driver, or any other.

Keep in mind that overhead is required for the I/O Manager to pass requests back and forth for information. So for simple devices (such as serial and parallel printer ports), the operating system provides a single-layer device driver approach in which the I/O Manager can communicate with the device driver. This, in turn, returns information directly. For more complicated devices, particularly for devices such as hard drives that depend on a file system, a multilayered approach is a better choice.

Another device driver feature of recent Windows operating systems is that almost all low-level I/O operations are asynchronous. This means that when an application issues an I/O request, it doesn't have to wait for data to be transferred; it can continue to perform other work while data transfer is taking place. Asynchronous I/O must be specified by the process when it opens a file handle. During asynchronous operations, the process must be careful not to access any data from the I/O operation until the device driver has finished data transfer. Asynchronous I/O is useful for operations that take a long time to complete or for which completion time is variable.

For example, the time it takes to list the files in a directory varies according to the number of files. Because Windows is a preemptive multitasking system that may be running many tasks at the same time, it's vital that the operating system not waste time waiting for a request to be filled if it can be doing something else. The various layers in the operating system use preemptive multitasking and multithreading to get more work done in the same amount of time.

File Management

Typically, an operating system is associated with the particular file structure that it uses for mass storage devices, such as hard disks. Although there is a resident NTFS, current versions of Windows are designed to be independent of the file system on which they operate.

In recent versions of Windows, the primary file handling concept is the virtual file, introduced with UNIX. This includes any I/O source or destination—and it's treated as if it were a file. In Windows, programs perform I/O on virtual files, manipulating them by using file handles. Although not a new concept, in Windows a file handle actually refers to an executive file object that represents all sources and destinations of I/O. Processes call native file object services, such as those required to read from or write to a file. The I/O Manager directs these virtual file requests to real files, file directories, physical devices, or any other destination supported by the system. File objects have hierarchical names, are protected by object-based security, support synchronization, and are handled by object services.

When opening a file, a process supplies the file's name and the type of access required. This request moves to an environment subsystem that in turn calls a system service. The Object Manager starts an object name lookup and turns control over to the I/O Manager to find the file object. The I/O Manager checks the security subsystem to determine whether or not access can be granted. The I/O Manager also uses the file object to determine whether asynchronous I/O operations are requested.

The creation of file objects helps bridge the gap between the characteristics of physical devices and directory structures, file system structures, and data formats. File objects provide a memory-based representation of shareable physical resources. When a file is opened, the I/O Manager returns a handle to a file object. The Object Manager treats file objects like all other objects until the time comes to write to or read from a device, at which point the Object Manager calls the I/O Manager for assistance to access the device. Figure 14.8 illustrates the contents of file objects and the services that operate on them. Table 14.3 describes in detail the object body attributes.

(figure 14.8)

Illustrations of a file object, its attributes, and the services that operate on them. The attributes are explained in Table 14.3.

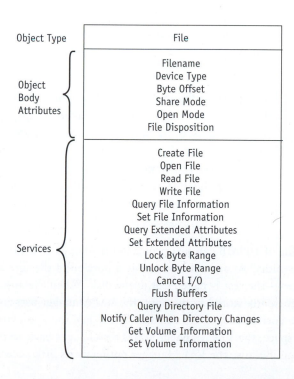

Object Type	File
Object Body Attributes	Filename Device Type Byte Offset Share Mode Open Mode File Disposition
Services	Create File Open File Read File Write File Query File Information Set File Information Query Extended Attributes Set Extended Attributes Lock Byte Range Unlock Byte Range Cancel I/O Flush Buffers Query Directory File Notify Caller When Directory Changes Get Volume Information Set Volume Information

Attribute	Purpose
Filename	Identifies the physical file to which the file object refers
Device type	Indicates the type of device on which the file resides
Byte offset	Identifies the current location in the file (valid only for synchronous I/O)
Share mode	Indicates whether other callers can open the file for read, write, or delete operations while this caller is using it
Open mode	Indicates whether I/O is synchronous or asynchronous, cached or not cached, sequential or random, and so on
File disposition	Indicates whether to delete the file after closing it

(table 14.3)

Description of the attributes shown in Figure 14.8.

Let's make a distinction between a file object, a memory-based representation of a shareable resource that contains only data unique to an object handle, and the file itself, which contains the data to be shared. Each time a process opens a handle, a new file object is created with a new set of handle-specific attributes. For example, the attribute byte offset refers to the location in the file where the next READ or WRITE operation using that handle will occur. It might help if you think of file object attributes as being specific to a single handle.

Although a file handle is unique to a process, the physical resource isn't. Therefore, processes must synchronize their access to shareable files, directories, and devices. For example, if a process is writing to a file, it should specify exclusive write access or lock portions of the file while writing to it to prevent other processes from writing to that file at the same time.

Mapped file I/O is an important feature of the I/O system and is achieved through the cooperation of the I/O system and the VM Manager. At the operating system level, file mapping is typically used for file caching, loading, and running executable programs. The VM Manager allows user processes to have mapped file I/O capabilities through native services. Memory-mapped files exploit virtual memory capabilities by allowing an application to open a file of arbitrary size and treat it as a single contiguous array of memory locations without buffering data or performing disk I/O.

For example, a file of 100MB can be opened and treated as an array in a system with only 20MB of memory. At any one time, only a portion of the file data is physically present in memory—the rest is paged out to the disk. When the application requests data that's not currently stored in memory, the VM Manager uses its paging mechanism to load the correct page from the disk file. When the application writes to its virtual memory space, the VM Manager writes the changes back to the file as part of the normal paging. Because the VM Manager optimizes its disk accesses, applications that are I/O bound can speed up their execution by using mapped I/O—writing to memory is faster than writing to a secondary storage device.

A component of the I/O system called the **cache manager** uses mapped I/O to manage its memory-based cache. The cache expands or shrinks dynamically depending on the amount of memory available. Using normal working-set strategies, the VM Manager expands the size of the cache when there is memory available to accommodate the application's needs and reduces the cache when it needs free pages. The cache manager takes advantage of the VM Manager's paging system, avoiding duplication of effort.

The file management system supports long filenames that can include spaces and special characters. Therefore, users can name a file *Spring Student Grades* instead of something cryptic like *S14STD.GRD*. Because the use of a long filename could create compatibility problems with older operating systems that might reside on the network, the file system automatically converts a long filename to the standard eight-character filename and three-character extension required by MS-DOS and 16-bit Windows applications. The File Manager does this by keeping a table that lists each long filename and relates it to the corresponding short filename.

Network Management

In Windows operating systems, networking is an integral part of the operating system executive, providing services such as user accounts, and resource security. It also provides mechanisms to implement communication between computers, such as with named pipes and mailslots. **Named pipes** provide a high-level interface for passing data between two processes regardless of their locations. **Mailslots** provide one-to-many and many-to-one communication mechanisms, useful for broadcasting messages to any number of processes.

MS-NET

Microsoft Networks, informally known as MS-NET, became the model for the NT Network Manager. Three MS-NET components—the redirector, the server message block (SMB) protocol, and the network server—were extensively refurbished and incorporated into subsequent Windows operating systems.

The redirector, coded in the C programming language, is implemented as a loadable file system driver and isn't dependent on the system's hardware architecture. Its function is to direct an I/O request from a user or application to the remote server that has the appropriate file or resource needed to satisfy the request. A network can incorporate multiple redirectors, each of which directs I/O requests to remote file systems or devices. A typical remote I/O request might result in the following progression:

1. The user-mode software issues a remote I/O request by calling local I/O services.

2. After some initial processing, the I/O Manager creates an I/O request packet (IRP) and passes the request to the Windows redirector, which forwards the IRP to the transport drivers.

3. Finally, the transport drivers process the request and place it on the network. The reverse sequence is observed when the request reaches its destination.

The SMB protocol is a high-level specification for formatting messages to be sent across the network and correlates to the application layer (Layer 7) and the presentation layer (Layer 6) of the OSI model, described in Chapter 9. An API called NetBIOS is used to pass I/O requests structured in the SMB format to a remote computer. Both the SMB protocols and the NetBIOS API were adopted in several networking products before appearing in Windows.

The Windows Server operating systems are written in C for complete compatibility with existing MS-NET and LAN Manager SMB protocols, are implemented as loadable file system drivers, and have no dependency on the hardware architecture on which the operating system is running.

Directory Services

The **Active Directory** database stores many types of information and serves as a general-purpose directory service for a heterogeneous network.

Microsoft built the Active Directory entirely around the **Domain Name Service or Domain Name System (DNS)** and **Lightweight Directory Access Protocol (LDAP)**. DNS is the hierarchical replicated naming service on which the Internet is built. However, although DNS is the backbone directory protocol for one of the largest data networks, it doesn't provide enough flexibility to act as an enterprise directory by itself. That is, DNS is primarily a service for mapping machine names to IP addresses, which is not enough for a full directory service. A full directory service must be able to map names of arbitrary objects (such as machines and applications) to any kind of information about those objects.

Active Directory groups machines into administrative units called domains, each of which gets a DNS domain name (such as pitt.edu). Each domain must have at least one domain controller that is a machine running the Active Directory server.

For improved fault tolerance and performance, a domain can have more than one domain controller, with each holding a complete copy of that domain's directory database.

To view server statistics, press the Windows logo key and the *R* key together. Type CMD to open the command window, and then type net statistics server.

Current versions of Windows network operating systems eliminate the distinction between primary domain controllers and backup domain controllers, removing the multiple hierarchies and making the network simpler to administer. Active Directory clients use standard DNS and LDAP protocols to locate objects on the network. As shown in Figure 14.9, here's how it works:

1. A client that needs to look up an Active Directory name first passes the DNS part of the name to a standard DNS server. The DNS server returns the network address of the domain controller responsible for that name.

2. Next, the client uses LDAP to query the domain controller to find the address of the system that holds the service the client needs.

3. Finally, the client establishes a direct connection with the requested service using the correct protocol required by that service.

(figure 14.9)

Active Directory clients use standard DNS and LDAP protocols to locate objects on the network.

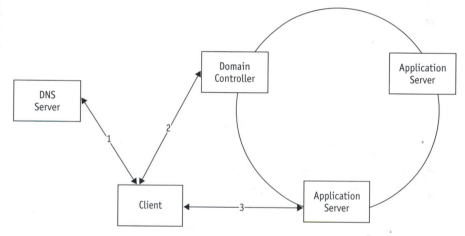

Security Management

Windows operating systems provide an object-based security model. That is, a security object can represent any resource in the system: a file, device, process, program, or user. This allows system administrators to give precise security access to specific objects in the system while allowing them to monitor and record how objects are used.

One of the biggest concerns about Windows operating systems is the need for aggressive patch management to combat the many viruses and worms that target these systems. Updates can be scheduled using the Windows Update option either automatically, as shown in Figure 14.10, or manually.

(figure 14.10)

The system can be set to automatically install updates, keeping it up to date with critical patches.

Security Concerns

The U.S. Department of Defense has identified and categorized into seven levels of security certain features that make an operating system secure. Early versions of Windows targeted Class C2 level with a plan to evolve to Class B2 level—a more stringent level of security in which each user must be assigned a specific security level clearance and is thwarted from giving lower-level users access to protected resources.

To comply with the Class C2 level of security, Windows operating systems include the following features:

- A secure logon facility requiring users to identify themselves by entering a unique logon identifier and a password before they're allowed access to the system.

- Discretionary access control allowing the owner of a resource to determine who else can access the resource and what they can do to it.

- Auditing ability to detect and record important security-related events or any attempt to create, access, or delete system resources.

- Memory protection preventing anyone from reading information written by someone else after a data structure has been released back to the operating system.

Password management is the first layer of security. Windows 8 features a built-in option to create and use a graphic password that is unlocked by drawing taps, circles, or lines on the screen.

The second layer of security deals with file access security. At this level, the user can create a file and establish various combinations of individuals to have access to it because the operating system makes distinctions between owners and groups. The creator of a file is its owner. The owner can designate a set of users as belonging to a group and allow all the members of the group to have access to that file. Conversely, the owner could prevent some of the members from accessing that file.

In addition to determining who is allowed to access a file, users can decide what type of operations a person is allowed to perform on a file. For example, one may have read-only access, while another may have read-and-write privileges. As a final measure, the operating system gives the user auditing capabilities that automatically keep track of who uses files and how the files are used.

Security Terminology

The built-in security for recent Windows network operating systems is a necessary element for managers of Web servers and networks. Its directory service lets users find what they need and a communications protocol lets users interact with it. However, because not everyone should be able to find or interact with everything in the network, controlling such access is the job of distributed security services.

Effective distributed security requires an authentication mechanism that allows a client to prove its identity to a server. Then the client needs to supply authorization information that the server uses to determine which specific access rights have been given to this client. Finally, it needs to provide data integrity using a variety of methods ranging from a cryptographic checksum for all transmitted data to completely encrypting all transmitted data.

Recent Windows operating systems provide this with **Kerberos** security, as described in Chapter 11. Kerberos provides authentication, data integrity, and data privacy. In addition, it provides mutual authentication, which means that both the client and server can verify the identity of the other. (Other security systems require only that the clients prove their identity. Servers are automatically authenticated.)

Each domain has its own Kerberos server, which shares the database used by Active Directory. This means that the Kerberos server must execute on the domain-controller machine and, like the Active Directory server, it can be replicated within a domain. Every user who wants to securely access remote services must log on to a Kerberos server. Figure 14.11 shows the path followed by a request from an application to a service provided on the network, and back again to the application.

(figure 14.11)

Requests from an application flow through these security stops on the way to and from the network.

A successful login returns a **ticket granting ticket** to the user, which can be handed back to the Kerberos server to request tickets to specific application servers.

If the Kerberos server determines that a user is presenting a valid ticket, it returns the requested ticket to the user with no questions asked. The user sends this ticket to the remote application server, which can examine it to verify the user's identity and authenticate the user. All of these tickets are encrypted in different ways, and various keys are used to perform the encryption.

Different implementations of Kerberos send different authorization information. Microsoft has implemented the standard Kerberos protocol to make the product more compatible with other Kerberos implementations.

Different security protocols can have very different APIs, creating problems for applications that might want to use more than one of them. Microsoft has addressed this problem by separating the users of distributed security services from their providers, allowing support for many options without creating unusable complexity.

User Interface

Windows 8 is designed to offer the same default screen on all devices running the operating system, from desktop computers and laptops to cell phones and tablets. When used on a laptop or desktop, users can switch from the tile-populated Start screen, shown in Figure 14.12, to the more familiar Desktop screen featured on previous versions of Windows. To switch between the two interfaces, users press the keyboard's Windows-Logo key or move (with a cursor or finger press) to the top right corner of the screen and then click or tap the windows icon.

Microsoft produced a scaled-down version of this operating system called Windows RT for use on its first Surface tablet, but as of this writing, the Microsoft Office tools available on RT are not compatible with standard Office tools.

(figure 14.12)

A typical Windows 8 Start screen featuring dynamic tiles.

This unified Start screen is a radical departure for Windows operating system. It was created in anticipation of a market-wide move to touch screen devices and, as of this writing, has met with mixed reviews. By combining powerful commands and search capabilities available from the Start screen with the traditional breadth of programs available from the Desktop screen, users have access to an array of resources.

The Windows Task Manager can be opened by pressing and holding the Ctrl, Alt, and Delete keys together or by moving to the Start screen and typing `task`. Here, users have the chance to view running applications and processes, as shown in Figure 14.13. To set the priorities of apps or processes, open the Details tab and right-click on the process you wish to change. From the other tabs, users can also view information about performance, networking, and others logged onto the system.

(figure 14.13)

Using the Task Manager, users can view the system status, assign priorities, and more.

At the bottom of the Task Manager screen, details about use of the system's hardware and software can be found using the Resource Monitor, shown in Figure 14.14. The Resource Monitor can also be opened by searching from the Start screen for the word

(figure 14.14)

The resource monitor offers running statistics for this session.

resource. Here the details of all system resources are displayed in tables and graphs; by right-clicking on items, additional operations can be performed.

A command-line interface that resembles the one used for MS-DOS is available from most Windows desktops, as shown in Figure 14.15. These interfaces include a help feature. To learn the syntax for a command, type the command help followed by the command you want to use (in this case tree). To open a command prompt window, search from the Start screen using the word command. Because Windows is not case sensitive, commands can be entered in upper or lower case; a few common ones are listed in Table 14.4.

(figure 14.15)

Exploring the syntax for the TREE command using the help option.

Command	Action to Be Performed
DIR	List what's in this directory.
CD or CHDIR	Change the working directory.
DEL or ERASE ‹filename›	Delete the listed file or files.
RENAME ‹filename›	Rename the listed file.
PRINT ‹filename›	Print the listed files.
DATE	Display and/or change the system date.
MD or MKDIR	Create a new directory or subdirectory.
FIND	Search files for a string.
CHKDSK	Check disk for disk/file/directory status.
TREE	Display relationships of files on a drive or path

Table 14.4

Selected commands that can be used in the Command Prompt Window. For a complete listing, see your technical documentation or www.microsoft.com.

One helpful Windows feature is its accommodation for users working in non-English languages. Windows has built-in input methods and fonts for many languages, including double-byte languages such as Japanese. During installation, the system administrator can select one or several languages for the system, even adding different language support for specific individuals. For example, one user can work in Chinese while another can work in Hindi. Even better, the system's own resources also become multilingual, which means that the operating system changes its dialog boxes, prompts, and menus to support many languages.

For table users or others who need enhanced accessibility options, Windows offers an on-screen keyboard, as shown in Figure 14.16, available by searching from the Start screen using the term `keyboard`. Other tools (a magnifier, a narrator, speech recognition, and more) are also available.

(figure 14.16)

Windows accommodates language-specific on-screen keyboards. This one is for users needing a French keyboard layout; notice where certain keys (such as Q, A, Z, W, and M) are located.

Conclusion

What started as a microcomputer operating system has grown to include complex multiplatform software that can run computing systems of all sizes. Windows' commercial success is unquestioned, and its products have continued to evolve in complexity and scope to cover many global markets.

With Windows 8 and its singular interface for both touch screens and traditional computers, Windows appears to be evolving into a one-size-fits-all operating system. This has been a huge step for Microsoft and threatens to alienate many millions of users. Time will tell if it is a good move for the software giant.

Windows remains a powerful operating system and significant market force. In the next two chapters we discuss two competitors that cannot be discounted.

Key Terms

Active Directory: Microsoft Windows' directory service that offers centralized administration of application serving, authentication, and user registration for distributed networking systems.

cache manager: a component of the I/O system that manages the part of virtual memory known as cache. The cache expands or shrinks dynamically depending on the amount of memory available.

compatibility: the ability of an operating system to execute programs written for other operating systems or for earlier versions of the same system.

Domain Name Service or Domain Name System (DNS): a general-purpose, distributed, replicated, data query service. Its principal function is the resolution of Internet addresses based on fully qualified domain names such as .com (for commercial entity) or .edu (for educational institution).

extensibility: one of an operating system's design goals that allows it to be easily enhanced as market requirements change.

fetch policy: the rules used by the Virtual Memory Manager to determine when a page is copied from disk to memory.

Kerberos: MIT-developed authentication system that allows network managers to administer and manage user authentication at the network level.

kernel mode: name given to indicate that processes are granted privileged access to the processor. Therefore, all machine instructions are allowed and system memory is accessible. Contrasts with the more restrictive *user mode*.

Lightweight Directory Access Protocol (LDAP): a protocol that defines a method for creating searchable directories of resources on a network. It's called "lightweight" because it is a simplified and TCP/IP-enabled version of the X.500 directory protocol.

mailslots: a high-level network software interface for passing data among processes in a one-to-many and many-to-one communication mechanism. Mailslots are useful for broadcasting messages to any number of processes.

named pipes: a high-level software interface to NetBIOS, which represents the hardware in network applications as abstract objects. Named pipes are represented as file objects in Windows NT and later, and operate under the same security mechanisms as other executive objects.

NT File System (NTFS): the file system introduced with Windows NT that offers file management services, such as permission management, compression, transaction logs, and the ability to create a single volume spanning two or more physical disks.

placement policy: the rules used by the Virtual Memory Manager to determine where the virtual page is to be loaded in memory.

portability: the ability to move an entire operating system to a machine based on a different processor or configuration with as little recoding as possible.

POSIX: Portable Operating System Interface for UNIX; an operating system application program interface developed by the IEEE to increase the portability of application software.

reliability: the ability of an operating system to respond predictably to error conditions, even those caused by hardware failures; or the ability of an operating system to actively protect itself and its users from accidental or deliberate damage by user programs.

replacement policy: the rules used by the Virtual Memory Manager to determine which virtual page must be removed from memory to make room for a new page.

ticket granting ticket: a virtual "ticket" given by a Kerberos server indicating that the user holding the ticket can be granted access to specific application servers. The user sends this encrypted ticket to the remote application server, which can then examine it to verify the user's identity and authenticate the user.

user mode: name given to indicate that processes are not granted privileged access to the processor. Therefore, certain instructions are not allowed and system memory isn't accessible. Contrasts with the less restrictive kernel mode.

Interesting Searches

For more background on a few of the topics discussed in this chapter, begin a search with these terms.

- Windows Server Essentials
- Embedded Windows operating systems
- Windows benchmarks
- Windows patch management
- POSIX standards

Exercises

Research Topics

A. Research current literature to discover the current state of IEEE POSIX Standards and find out if the version of Windows on the computer that you use is currently 100 percent POSIX-compliant. Explain the significance of this compliance and why you think some popular operating systems choose not to be compliant.

B. Some Windows products do not allow the use of international characters in the username or password. These characters may be part of an international alphabet or Asian characters. Research the characters that are allowed in recent versions of Windows and cite your sources. Describe the advantages to the operating system of limiting the character set for usernames and passwords, and whether or not you suggest an alternative.

Exercises

1. Explain in your own words the importance of monitoring system performance. Discuss how you would gather the necessary information. Also, list which elements are most important, and in your own words, explain why.

2. In a single Windows directory, you have four filenames with variations: Skiing-WP.doc, SKIing-wp.doc, Skiing-wp.docx, and Skiing-wp.doc. How many new files would be displayed: one, two, three, or four? Explain why this is so. Is the answer the same for all operating systems? Why or why not?

3. In some Windows operating systems, the paging file is a hidden file on the computer's hard disk and its virtual memory is the combination of the paging file and the system's physical memory. (This is called pagefile.sys and the default size is equal to 1.5 times the system's total RAM.) Describe in your own words how you can display the size of the pagefule.sys, and how a virtual memory size that's too small might affect system performance.

4. Some people say that if the paging file is located where fragmentation is least likely to happen, performance may be improved. Do you agree? Explain why in your own words.

5. Administrators sometimes find that when they deploy Windows in a multilingual environment, some languages require more hard-disk storage space than others. Why might that be the case? Explain your answer and give an example of one languages that could be expected to require more space.

6. The 64-bit version of Windows 7 can run all 32-bit applications with the help of an emulator, but it does not support 16-bit applications. Can you imagine a circumstance where someone might need support for a 16-bit application? Describe it.

7. Windows features Kerberos authentication. Describe the role of the ticket granting ticket to authenticate users for network access.

8. Describe in your own words the role of the Active Directory in recent Windows operating systems.

Advanced Exercises

9. The I/O system relies on an I/O request packet. Explain the role of this packet, when it is passed, and where it goes before disposal.

10. Identify at least five major types of threats to systems running Windows and the policies that system administrators must take to protect the system from unauthorized access. Compare the practical problems when balancing the need for accessibility with the need to restrict access, and suggest the first action you would take to secure a Windows computer or network if you managed one.

11. Windows Embedded is an operating system that is intended to run in real time. In your own words, describe the difference between hard real-time and soft real-time systems, and describe the benchmarks that you feel are most important in each type of system.

12–14. For these questions, refer to Table 14.5, which shows how the memory structures for a 64-bit Windows operating system using a 64-bit Intel processor compare with the 32-bit maximums on previous Windows operating systems.

(table 14.5)

Windows specifications for 32-bit and 64-bit systems (adapted from www.microsoft.com).

Component	32-bit	64-bit
Virtual Memory	4GB	16TB
Paging File Size	16TB	256TB
System Cache	1GB	1TB
Hyperspace	4MB	8GB
Paged Pool	470MB	128GB
System PTEs	660MB	128GB

12. Hyperspace is used to map the working set pages for system process, to temporarily map other physical pages, and other duties. By increasing this space from 4MB to 8GB in 64-bit system, hyperspace helps Windows run faster. In your own words, explain why this is so, and describe other improvements that increased hyperspace may have on system performance. Can you quantify the speed increase from the information shown here? Explain your answer.

13. Paged pool is the part of virtual memory created during system initialization that can be paged in and out of the working set of the system process and is used by kernel-mode components to allocate system memory. If systems with one processor have two paged pools, and those with multiprocessors have four, discuss in your own words why having more than one paged pool reduces the frequency of system code blocking on simultaneous calls to pool routines.

14. System PTEs are a pool of system page table entries that are used to map system pages such as I/O space, kernel stacks, and memory descriptor lists. The 32-bit programs use a 4GB model and allocate half (2GB) to the user and half to the kernel. The 64-bit programs use a similar model but on a much larger scale, with 8TB for the user and 8TB for the kernel. Given this structure, calculate how many exabytes a 64-bit pointer could address (one exabyte equals one billion gigabytes).

Chapter 15

Linux Operating Systems

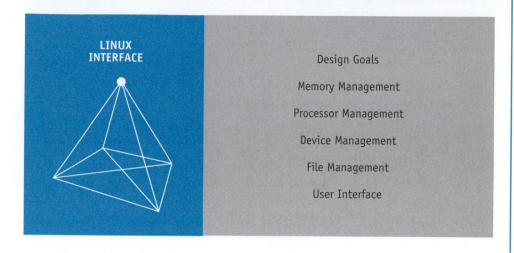

LINUX
INTERFACE

Design Goals

Memory Management

Processor Management

Device Management

File Management

User Interface

"*I'm doing a (free) operating system ...*"

—Linus Torvalds

Learning Objectives

After completing this chapter, you should be able to describe:

- The design goals for the Linux operating system
- The flexibility gained by using files to manipulate devices
- The roles of the Memory, Device, File, Processor, and Network Managers
- The impact of open source software
- Some strengths and weaknesses of Linux

Linux is not UNIX. Linux was originally based on a version of UNIX, with its designers capitalizing on the lessons learned over the previous 20 years of UNIX development to create a unique operating system. While similar in name and in appearance, Linux has features that set it apart from its predecessor. A global force in operating system development, Linux is not only powerful, but is also inexpensive or free to use.

Linux is available in versions capable of running on cell phones, supercomputers, and most computing systems in between. Unlike the other operating systems described in this book, its source code is freely available, allowing programmers to configure it to run any device and meet any specification. The frequent inclusion of several powerful desktop interfaces continues to attract users. It is also highly modular, allowing multiple modules to be loaded and unloaded on demand, making it a technically robust operating system.

Linux is an open source program, meaning that its source code is freely available to anyone for improvement. If someone sends a better program or coding sequence to Linus Torvalds, the author of Linux, and if he and his team accept it as a universal improvement to the operating system, then the new code is added to the next version made available to the computing world. Updates are scheduled every six months. In this way, Linux is under constant development by uncounted contributors around the world: people who may have never met each other and who are not paid for their work.

Brief History

Linus Torvalds wanted to create an operating system that would greatly enhance the limited capabilities of the Intel 80386 microprocessor. He started with MINIX (a miniature UNIX system developed primarily by Andrew Tanenbaum) and rewrote certain parts to add more functionality. When he had a working operating system, he announced his achievement on an Internet user group with this message:

```
"Hello everybody out there using minix. I'm doing a (free)
operating system (just a hobby, won't be big and professional like
gnu) for 386(486) AT clones."
```

It was August 1991, and Torvalds was a 21-year-old student at University of Helsinki, Finland. The name Linux is a contraction of Torvalds' first name, Linus, and UNIX. Despite the spelling, Linux rhymes with mimics, as in "Lih-nix." The operating system, originally created to run a small home computer, was built with substantial flexibility, and it featured many of the same functions found on expensive commercial operating systems. In effect, Linux brought much of the speed, efficiency, and flexibility of UNIX to small desktop computers.

The first Linux operating systems required the use of a **command-driven interface** to type UNIX-like commands that sometimes were cryptic. In recent years, several

graphical user interfaces (**GUI**) have greatly expanding the user base for the operating system. GUIs are discussed later in this chapter.

Because Linux is written and distributed under the GNU General Public License, its source code is freely distributed and available to the general public, although the name Linux remains a registered trademark of Linus Torvalds. As of this writing, the current GNU General Public License is Version 3. It can be found at: *www.gnu.org/licenses/gpl.html*.

Anyone is permitted to copy and distribute verbatim copies of the license document, but any changes to it must be submitted to Linus Torvalds for possible inclusion in the next release.

Today, a group known as the Fedora Project has responsibility for the open-source development of the Linux **kernel**. As shown in Table 15.1, the Fedora Project issues updates free to the public about every six months. There are many popular distributions of Linux, including Ubuntu, which is used in this text to illustrate this operating system.

> ✔ There are many versions of Linux that will boot from a CD or DVD, allowing potential users to test the operating system before installing it on a computer.

(table 15.1)

Selected releases of Ubuntu Linux. New releases are scheduled every 6 months. Normal Ubuntu releases are supported for 18 months; LTS releases are supported longer. (adapted from https://wiki.ubuntu.com/ Releases)

Version	Code Name	Release Date	End of Life Date
Ubuntu 13.04	Raring Ringtail	April 2013	October 2014
Ubuntu 12.10	Quantal Quetzal	October 2012	April 2014
Ubuntu 12.04 LTS	Precise Pangolin	April 2012	
Ubuntu 11.10	Oneiric Ocelot	October 2011	April 2013
Ubuntu 11.04	Natty Narwhal	April 2011	October 28, 2012
Ubuntu 10.10	Maverick Meerkat	October 2010	April 2012
Ubuntu 10.04 LTS	Lucid Lynx	April 2010	
Ubuntu 9.10	Karmic Koala	October 2009	April 2011
Ubuntu 9.04	Jaunty Jackalope	April 2009	October 2010
Ubuntu 8.10	Intrepid Ibex	October 2008	April 2010
Ubuntu 8.04	Hardy Heron	April 2008	May 2011

Design Goals

Linux has three primary design goals: modularity, simplicity, and portability. The system is personified in the mascot shown in Figure 15.1.

To achieve these goals, Linux administrators have access to numerous standard utilities, eliminating the need to write special code. Many of these utilities can be used in combination with each other so that users can select and combine appropriate utilities

(figure 15.1)

The Linux mascot evolved from discussions with Linus Torvalds, who said, "Ok, so we should be thinking of a lovable, cuddly, stuffed penguin sitting down after having gorged itself on herring." More about the penguin can be found at www.linux.org.

to carry out specific tasks. As shown in Table 15.2, Linux accommodates numerous system functions.

Function	Purpose
Multiple processes and multiple processors	Linux can run more than one program or process at a time and can manage numerous processors.
Multiple platforms	Although it was originally developed to run on Intel's processors for microcomputers, it can now operate on almost any platform.
Multiple users	Linux allows multiple users to work on the same machine at the same time.
Inter-process communications	It supports pipes, sockets, and so on.
Terminal management	Its terminal management conforms to POSIX standards, and it also supports pseudo-terminals as well as process control systems.
Peripheral devices	Linux supports a wide range of devices, including sound cards, graphics interfaces, networks, SCSI, USB, and so on.
Buffer cache	Linux supports a memory area reserved to buffer the input and output from different processes.
Demand paging memory management	Linux loads pages into memory only when they're needed.
Dynamic and shared libraries	Dynamic libraries are loaded in Linux only when they're needed, and their code is shared if several applications are using them.
Disk partitions	Linux allows file partitions and disk partitions with different file formats.
Network protocol	It supports TCP/IP and other network protocols.

(table 15.2)

Select system functions supported by Linux.

Linux conforms to the specifications for **Portable Operating System Interface** (**POSIX**), a registered trademark of the IEEE. POSIX is an IEEE standard that defines operating system interfaces to enhance the portability of programs from one operating system to another (IEEE, 2004).

Memory Management

When Linux allocates memory space, by default it allocates 1GB of high-order memory to the kernel and 3GB of memory to executing processes. This 3GB address space is divided among: process code, process data, shared library data used by the process, and the stack used by the process.

When a process begins execution, its segments have a fixed size; but there are cases when a process has to handle variables with an unknown number and size. Therefore, Linux has system calls that change the size of the process data segment, either by expanding it to accommodate extra data values or reducing it when certain values positioned at the end of the data segment are no longer needed.

Linux offers memory protection based on the type of information stored in each region belonging to the address space of a process. If a process modifies access authorization assigned to a memory region, the kernel changes the protection information assigned to the corresponding memory pages.

When a process requests pages, Linux loads them into memory. When the kernel needs the memory space, the pages are released using a least recently used (LRU) algorithm. Linux maintains a dynamically managed area in memory, a page cache, where new pages requested by processes are inserted, and from which pages are deleted when they're no longer needed. If any pages marked for deletion have been modified, they're rewritten to the disk—a page corresponding to a file mapped into memory is rewritten to the file and a page corresponding to the data is saved on a swap device. The swap device could be a partition on the disk or it could be a normal file. Linux shows added flexibility with swap devices because, if necessary, Linux can deactivate them without having to reboot the system. When this takes place, all pages saved on that device are reloaded into memory.

To keep track of free and busy pages, Linux uses a system of page tables. With certain chip architectures, memory access is carried out using segments.

Virtual memory in Linux is managed using a multiple-level table hierarchy, which accommodates both 64- and 32-bit architectures. Table 15.3 shows how each virtual address is made up of four fields, which are used by the Memory Manager to locate the instruction or data requested.

	Main Directory	Middle Directory	Page Table Directory	Page Frame
(table 15.3) *The four fields that make up the virtual address for Line 214 in Figure 15.2.*	Page 1	Table 3	Page Table 2	Location of Line 214

Each page has its own entry in the main **directory**, which has pointers to each page's middle directory. A page's middle directory contains pointers to its corresponding page table directories. In turn, each page table directory has pointers to the actual page frame, as shown in Figure 15.2. Finally, the page offset field is used to locate the instruction or data within the requested page (in this example, it is Line 214).

Page Directory   Page Middle Directories   Page Tables   Page Frames

(figure 15.2)

Virtual memory management uses three levels of tables (Main, Middle, and Page Table Directories) to locate the page frame with the requested instruction or data within a job.

Virtual memory is implemented in Linux through demand paging. Up to a total of 256MB of usable memory can be configured into equal-sized page frames, which can be grouped to give more contiguous space to a job. These groups can also be split to accommodate smaller jobs. This process of grouping and splitting is known as the **buddy algorithm,** and it works as follows.

Let's consider the case where main memory consists of 64 page frames and Job 1 requests 15 page frames. The buddy algorithm first rounds up the request to the next power of two. In this case, 15 is rounded up to 16, because 16 is 2^4. Then the group of 64 page frames is divided into two groups of 32, and the lower section is then divided in half. Now there is a group of 16 page frames that can satisfy the request, so the job's 16 pages are copied into the page frames as shown in Figure 15.3 (a).

When the next job, Job 2, requests 8 page frames, the second group of 16 page frames is divided in two, and the lower half with 8 page frames is given to Job 2, as shown in Figure 15.3 (b). Later, when Job 2 releases its page frames, they are combined with the upper 8 page frames to make a group of 16 page frames, as shown in Figure 15.3 (c).

(figure 15.3)

Main memory is divided to accommodate jobs of different sizes. In (a), the original group of 32 page frames is divided to satisfy the request of Job 1 for 16 page frames. In (b), another group of 16 page frames is divided to accommodate Job 2, which needs eight page frames. In (c), after Job 2 finishes, the two groups of eight page frames each are recombined into a group of 16, while Job 1 continues processing.

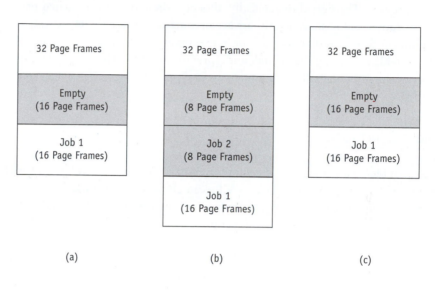

The page replacement algorithm is an expanded version of the **clock page replacement policy** discussed in Chapter 3. Instead of using a single reference bit, Linux uses an 8-bit byte to keep track of a page's activity, which is referred to as its age. Each time a page is referenced, this age variable is incremented. Behind the scenes, at specific intervals, the Memory Manager checks each of these age variables and decreases their value by 1. As a result, if a page is not referenced frequently, then its age variable will drop to 0 and the page will become a candidate for replacement if a page swap is necessary. On the other hand, a page that is frequently used will have a high age value and will not be a good choice for swapping. Therefore, we can see that Linux uses a form of the least frequently used (LFU) replacement policy.

Processor Management

Linux uses the same parent-child process management design found in UNIX and described in Chapter 13, but it also supports the concept of "personality" to allow processes coming from other operating systems to be executed. This means that each process is assigned to an execution domain specifying the way in which system calls are carried out and the way in which messages are sent to processes.

Organization of Process Table

Each process is referenced by a descriptor, which contains approximately 70 fields describing the process attributes together with the information needed to manage the process. The kernel dynamically allocates these descriptors when processes begin execution. All process descriptors are organized in a doubly linked list, and the descriptors of processes that are ready or in execution are put in another doubly linked list with fields indicating "next run" and "previously run." There are several macro instructions used by the scheduler to manage and update these process descriptor lists as needed.

Process Synchronization

Linux provides wait queues and semaphores to allow two processes to synchronize with each other. A wait queue is a linked circular list of process descriptors. Semaphores, described in Chapter 6, help solve the problems of mutual exclusion and the problems of producers and consumers. The Linux semaphore structure contains three fields: the semaphore counter, the number of waiting processes, and the list of processes waiting for the semaphore. The semaphore counter may contain only binary values, except when several units of one resource are available, and the semaphore counter then assumes the value of the number of units that are accessible concurrently.

Process Management

The Linux scheduler scans the list of processes in the READY state and chooses which process to execute using predefined criteria. The scheduler has three different scheduling types: two for real-time processes and one for normal processes. Each uses a different processor allocation scheme, as shown in Table 15.4.

Name	Scheduling Policy	Priority Level	Process Type
SCHED_FIFO	First in first out	Highest	For non-preemptible real-time processes
SCHED_RR	Round Robin and priority	Medium	For preemptible real-time processes
SCHED_OTHER	Priority only	Lowest	For normal processes

(table 15.4)

Linux has three process types, each signalling a different level of priority.

Real-time processes fall into the two highest priority levels: highest and medium priority. Those with the highest priority (those that cannot be preempted) are scheduled using only the first in, first out algorithm regardless of the urgency of any other processes in this same queue. Therefore, once execution has begun, each of these processes will run to completion unless one of the following situations occurs:

- The process goes into the WAIT state (to wait for I/O or another event to finish).
- The process relinquishes the CPU voluntarily, in which case the process is moved to a WAIT state and other processes are executed.

Only when all FIFO processes are completed does the scheduler proceed to execute processes of medium priority (real-time processes that can be preempted). When evaluating processes of this type, the scheduler first chooses those with the highest priority and uses a round robin algorithm with a small time quantum to execute first. Then, when the time quantum expires, other processes in the medium or high priority queue may be selected and executed before the first process is allowed to run to completion.

The third level of priority belongs to processes that do not belong in the urgent real-time classification. These have the lowest priority and are executed only when there are no processes with higher priority in the READY queue. From among these processes, the scheduler selects each process in order after considering their dynamic priorities (which are set by the user using system calls and by a factor computed by the system). From among these processes, the priorities of all processes that are

✔ **Numerous device drivers are available for Linux operating systems at little or no cost. More information can be found at www.linux.org.**

Linus Torvalds (1969–)

Linus Torvalds was born in Helsinki, Finland. At the age of 21, he wrote the first kernel of the operating system now known as Linux. He posted it publicly, asking for comments and suggestions to improve it. He has been quoted as saying, "open source is the only right way to do software." As of this writing, Torvalds owns the Linux trademark and continues to personally monitor all proposed updates and modifications to the Linux kernel. He has been inducted into the Internet Hall of Fame (2012) and the Computer History Museum (2008), and he received the Electronic Frontier Foundation Pioneer Award (1998).

For more information:

http://www.linuxfoundation.org

Awarded the 2012 Millennium Technology Prize by the Technology Academy Finland "in recognition of his creation of a new open source operating system for computers leading to the widely used Linux kernel."

Photo: Aki-Pekka Sinikoski/Millennium Technology Prize

CPU-bound are lowered during execution; therefore, they may earn a lower priority than processes that are not executing or than those with a priority that has not been lowered.

Device Management

Linux is **device independent,** which improves its portability from one system to another. **Device drivers** supervise the transmission of data between main memory and the peripheral unit. Devices are assigned not only a name but also descriptors that further identify each device and that are stored in the device directory, as illustrated in Figure 15.4.

(figure 15.4)

Details about each device can be accessed via the Device Manager.

Device Classifications

Linux identifies each device by a minor device number and a major device number.

- The minor device number is passed to the device driver as an argument and is used to access one of several identical physical devices.
- The major device number is used as an index to the array to access the appropriate code for a specific device driver.

Each class has a Configuration Table that contains an array of entry points into the device drivers. This table is the only connection between the system code and the device drivers. It's an important feature of the operating system because it allows the programmers to create new device drivers quickly to accommodate differently configured systems.

Standard versions of Linux often provide a comprehensive collection of common device drivers; but if the computer system should include hardware or peripherals that are not on the standard list, their device drivers can be retrieved from another source and installed separately. Alternatively, a skilled programmer can write a device driver and install it for use.

Device Drivers

Linux supports the standard classes of devices introduced by UNIX. In addition, Linux allows new device classes to support new technology. Device classes are not rigid in nature—programmers may choose to create large, complex device drivers to perform multiple functions, but such programming is discouraged for two reasons: (1) there is a wider demand for several simple drivers than for a single complex one (and such code can be shared among users), and (2) modular code is better able to support Linux's goals of system scalability and extendibility. Therefore, programmers are urged to write device drivers that maximize the system's ability to use the device effectively—no more, no less.

A notable feature of Linux is its ability to accept new device drivers on the fly, while the system is up and running. That means administrators can give the kernel additional functionality by loading and testing new drivers without having to reboot each time to reconfigure the kernel. To understand the following discussion more fully, please remember that devices are treated in Linux in the same way all files are treated.

Open and Release

Two common functions of Linux device drivers are *open* and *release*, which essentially allocate and deallocate the appropriate device. For example, the operation to open a device should perform the following functions:

- Verify that the device is available and in working order.
- Increase the usage counter for the device by 1, so the subsystem knows that the module cannot be unloaded until its file is appropriately closed.
- Initialize the device so that old data is removed and the device is ready to accept new data.
- Identify the minor number and update the appropriate pointer if necessary.
- Allocate any appropriate data structure.

Likewise, the release function (called device_close or device_release) performs these tasks:

- Deallocate any resources that were allocated with the *open* function
- Shut down the device
- Reduce the usage counter by 1 so the device can be released to another module

Modules can be closed without ever releasing the device. If this happens, the module is *not* deallocated.

Device Classes

The three standard classes of devices supported by Linux are character devices, block devices, and network devices, as shown in Figure 15.5.

Char Devices

Character devices (also known as char devices) are those that can be accessed as a stream of bytes, such as a communications port, monitor, or other byte-stream-fed device. At a minimum, drivers for these devices usually implement the *open*, *release*, *read*, and *write* system calls although additional calls are often added. Char devices are accessed by way of file system nodes, and from a functional standpoint, these devices look like an ordinary data area. Their drivers are treated the same way as ordinary files, with the exception that char device drivers are data channels that must be accessed sequentially.

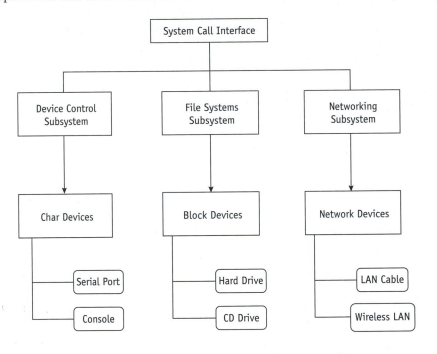

Block Devices

Block devices are similar to char devices except that they can host a file system, such as a hard disk; char devices cannot host a file system. Like char devices, block devices are accessed by file system nodes in the /dev directory, but these devices are transferred in blocks of data. Unlike most UNIX systems, data on a Linux system can be transferred in blocks of any size, from a few bytes to many. Like char device drivers, block device drivers appear as ordinary files with the exception that the block drivers can access a file system in connection with the device—something not possible with the char device.

Network Interfaces

Network interfaces are dissimilar from both char and block devices because their function is to send and receive packets of information as directed by the network subsystem of the kernel. So, instead of *read* and *write* calls, the network device functions relate to packet transmission.

Each system device is handled by a device driver that is, in turn, under the direction of a subsystem of Linux.

File Management

Linux file management is very similar to UNIX, making it easy for programmers and administrators who are familiar with one operating system to move to the other.

Data Structures

All Linux files are organized in directories that are connected to each other in a tree-like structure. Linux specifies five types of files, as shown in Table 15.5.

(table 15.5)

The file type indicates how each file is to be used.

File Type	File Functions
Directory	A file that contains lists of filenames.
Ordinary file	A file containing data or programs belonging to users.
Symbolic link	A file that contains the path name of another file that it is linking to. (This is not a direct hard link. Rather, it's information about how to locate a specific file and link it even if it's in the directories of different users. This is something that can't be done with hard links.)
Special file	A file that's assigned to a device controller located in the kernel. When this type of file is accessed, the physical device associated with it is activated and put into service.
Named pipe	A file that's used as a communication channel among several processes to exchange data. The creation of a named pipe is the same as the creation of any file.

Filename Conventions

Filenames are case sensitive, so Linux recognizes both uppercase and lowercase letters in filenames. For example, the following filenames are recognizable as four different files housed in a single directory: FIREWALL, firewall, FireWall, and fireWALL.

(figure 15.6)

A sample file hierarchy. The forward slash (/) at the top represents the root directory.

Filenames can be up to 255 characters long, and they can contain alphabetic characters, underscores, and numbers. File suffixes (similar to file extensions in Chapter 8) are optional. Filenames can include a space; however, this can cause complications if you're running programs from the command line because a program named `interview notes` would be viewed as a command to run two files: `interview` and `notes`. To avoid confusion, the two words can be enclosed in quotes: `"interview notes"`. (This is important when using Linux in terminal mode by way of its command interpretive shell. From a Linux desktop GUI, users choose names from a list, so there's seldom a need to type the filename.)

To copy the file called `checks for october`, illustrated in Figure 15.6, the user can type from any other folder:

```
cp/memo/job_expenses/checks for october
```

The first slash indicates that this is an absolute path name that starts at the root directory. If the file you are seeking is in a local directory, you can use a relative path name—one that doesn't start at the root directory. Two examples of relative path names from Figure 15.6 are:

```
Job_expenses/checks for october
memo/music 10a
```

A few rules apply to all path names:

1. If the path name starts with a slash, the path starts at the root directory.
2. A path name can be either one name or a list of names separated by slashes. The last name on the list is the name of the file requested. All names preceding the file's name must be directory names.
3. Using two periods (..) in a path name moves you upward in the hierarchy (one level closer to the root). This is the only way to go up the hierarchy; all other path names go down the tree.

Data Structures

To allow processes to access files in a consistent manner, the kernel has a layer of software that maintains an interface between system calls related to files and the file management code. This layer is known as the Virtual File System (VFS). Any process-initiated system call to files is directed to the VFS, which performs file operations independent of the format of the file system involved. The VFS then redirects the request to the module managing the file.

New Versions

All Linux operating systems are patched between version releases. These patches can be downloaded on request, or users can set up the system to check for available updates, as shown in Figure 15.7. **Patch management** is designed to replace or change parts of the operating system that need to be enhanced or replaced. Three primary reasons motivate patches to the operating system: a greater need for security precautions against constantly changing system threats; the need to assure system compliance with government regulations regarding privacy and financial accountability; and the need to keep systems running at peak efficiency.

(figure 15.7)

This Ubuntu Linux update manager displays a list of patches that are available for this computer.

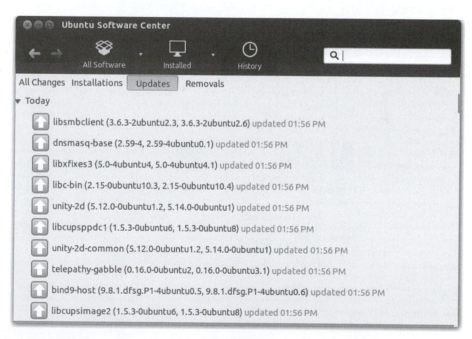

Every system manager, no matter the size of the system, should remain aware of security vulnerabilities; many can be addressed with critical patches. After all, system intruders are looking for these same vulnerabilities and are targeting computing devices that are not yet patched.

When a patch becomes available, the user's first task is to identify the criticality of the patch. If it is important, it should be applied immediately. If the patch is not critical in nature, installation might be delayed until a regular patch cycle begins. Patch cycles are detailed in Chapter 12.

User Interface

Early adopters of Linux were required to type commands requiring a thorough knowledge of valid command structure and syntax. Although most current versions include powerful and intuitive menu-driven interfaces, users can still use Terminal mode to type commands. These are often identical to those used for UNIX (described in detail in Chapter 13), which can be helpful for those migrating from an operating system that's command driven. Now there are several significant graphical user interfaces available that resemble the functionality of Windows and Macintosh interfaces, such as the one shown in Figure 15.8, an Ubuntu GUI.

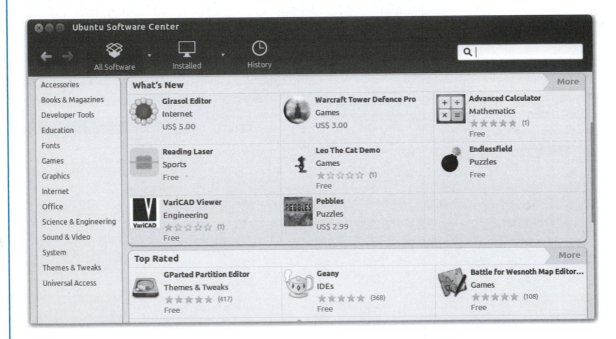

(figure 15.8)

Typical Ubuntu Linux graphical user interface (GUI).

Many Linux versions also come equipped with Windows-compatible word processors and spreadsheet and presentation applications. These software tools make it possible for Linux users to read and write documents that are generated, or read, by colleagues using proprietary software from competing operating system distributors. Because competing programs can cost hundreds of dollars, the availability of these affordable applications is one factor that has spurred the popularity of Linux.

System Monitor

Information about the moment-by-moment status of the system is available using the System Monitor window, shown in Figure 15.9. Here, one can see the immediate history of all CPUs, memory resources, and network usage. Other information available from this window includes supported file systems and information about all processes that are currently running.

(figure 15.9)

This Linux system monitor shows the recent history of both CPUs, shown in the top graph.

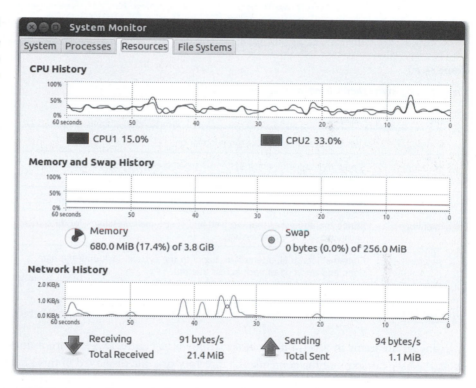

System Logs

Administrators use system logs that provide a detailed description of activity on the system. These logs are invaluable to administrators tracking the course of a system malfunction, firewall failure, disabled device, and more. Some Linux operating systems store them in the **/var/log** directory where they can be seen using a log viewer, such as the one shown in Figure 15.10.

There are numerous log files available for review (by someone with root access only). A few typical log files are shown in Table 15.6.

(figure 15.10)

The system log viewer shows details of all activity.

File	Purpose
auth.log	Lists the system authorization information.
boot.log	Stores messages of which systems have successfully started up and shut down, as well as any that have failed to do so.
dmesg	A list of messages created by the kernel when the system starts up.
mail.log	Stores the addresses that received and sent e-mail messages for detection of misuse of the e-mail system.
secure	Contains lists of all attempts to log in to the system, including the date, time, and duration of each access attempt.

(table 15.6)

A few of the many available Linux log files. See the documentation for your system for specifics.

File Listings

A listing of the items in a certain directory is shown in Figure 15.11. With a double click, the user can explore the contents of a directory or a file displayed in this kind of

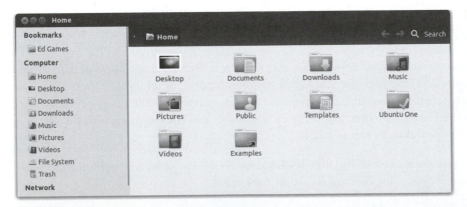

(figure 15.11)

Directories are shown in the left-most column, and the contents of the currently highlighted folder are displayed in the window on the right.

format. To establish the access control settings for any of these directories or files, the user can right click on the item's icon.

Detailed information about the system's directories and files can also be found using the Terminal window and typing the command: ls-l, which results in a listing similar to the one shown in Figure 15.12. Because the commands are almost identical to those used on UNIX systems, refer to Chapter 14 for a thorough discussion of the commands available for use in Terminal mode.

While some operating systems use a backslash (\) to separate folder names, Linux uses a forward slash (/).

(figure 15.12)

Directory details shown in Terminal mode, which is another way to explore Linux.

```
bob@ubuntu: ~
bob@ubuntu:~$ ls -l
total 18
drwxr-xr-x 7 bob bob 1024 Jun 26 15:41 Desktop
drwxr-xr-x 4 bob bob 1024 Feb 11 11:02 Documents
drwxr-xr-x 2 bob bob 1024 May 10  2012 Downloads
-rw-r--r-- 1 bob bob 8445 May 10  2012 examples.desktop
drwxr-xr-x 5 bob bob 1024 May 10  2012 Music
drwxr-xr-x 5 bob bob 1024 Jun 26 15:32 Pictures
drwxr-xr-x 2 bob bob 1024 May 10  2012 Public
drwxr-xr-x 2 bob bob 1024 May 10  2012 Templates
drwxrwxr-x 2 bob bob 1024 May 28 11:59 Ubuntu One
drwxr-xr-x 3 bob bob 1024 May 28 13:58 Videos
bob@ubuntu:~$
```

Setting Permissions

Linux offers full control for network administrators to manage access to files and directories, as shown in Figure 15.13. There are three levels of access: owner, group,

(figure 15.13)

User activity can be restricted by using document properties options.

and others; for each, the level of access can be indicated under the properties option. The types of access include create and delete files, list files only, access files, and none.

We've discussed here only a tiny sample of the many features available from a typical Linux desktop. Your system may have different windows, menus, tools, and options. For details about your Linux operating system, please see its documentation.

Conclusion

What began as one student's effort to get more power from a 1990s computer has evolved into a powerful, flexible operating system that can run supercomputers, cell phones, and numerous devices in between. Linux enjoys unparalleled popularity among programmers, who contribute enhancements and improvements to the standard code set. In addition, because there are a broad range of applications that are available at minimal cost and easy to install, Linux has found growing acceptance among those with minimal programming experience. For advocates in large organizations, commercial Linux products are available complete with extensive technical support and user help options.

Linux is characterized by its power, flexibility, and constant maintenance by legions of programmers worldwide while maintaining careful adherence to industry standards. It is proving to be a viable player in the marketplace and is expected to grow even more popular for many years to come, especially if it continues to provide the foundation for the Android operating system, as described in the next chapter.

Key Terms

argument: in a command-driven operating system, a value or option placed in the command that modifies how the command is to be carried out.

buddy algorithm: a memory allocation technique that divides memory into halves to try to give a best fit and to fill memory requests as suitably as possible.

clock page replacement policy: a variation of the LRU policy that removes from main memory the pages that show the least amount of activity during recent clock cycles.

CPU-bound: a job that will perform a great deal of nonstop processing before issuing an interrupt. A CPU-bound job can tie up the CPU for long periods of time.

device driver: a device-specific program module that handles the interrupts and controls a particular type of device.

device independent: programs that can work on a variety of computers and with a variety of devices.

directory: a logical storage unit that contains files.

graphical user interface (GUI): allows the user to activate operating system commands by clicking on icons or symbols using a pointing device such as a mouse. It is also called a menu-driven interface.

kernel: the part of the operating system that resides in main memory at all times and performs the most essential tasks, such as managing memory and handling disk input and output.

menu-driven interface: an interface that accepts instructions that users choose from a menu of valid choices. It is also called a graphical user interface and contrasts with a command-driven interface.

patch management: the installation of software patches to make repairs and keep the operating system software current.

Portable Operating System Interface (POSIX): a set of IEEE standards that defines the standard user and programming interfaces for operating systems so developers can port programs from one operating system to another.

Interesting Searches

For more background on a few of the topics discussed in this chapter, begin a search with these terms.

- Linux kernel
- Open source software
- Linux device drivers
- Linux certification
- Linux vs. UNIX
- Linux vs. Android

Exercises

Research Topics

A. Research the similarities and differences between Linux and UNIX. List at least five major differences between the two operating systems and cite your sources. Describe in your own words which operating system you prefer and explain why.

B. Research the following statement: "Open source software is not free software." Explain whether or not the statement is true and describe the common misperceptions about open source software. Cite your sources.

Exercises

1. Linux users can issue commands by choosing menu options or by issuing commands. In your opinion, which mode would be preferable for these categories of users: company executives, systems administrators, network users, and temporary data entry personnel? Explain your answer.

2. Many distributions of Linux are available free of charge to individual users. Using your own words, explain how the operating system continues to flourish in spite of the fact that it generates little income for distributors.

3. Linux is open source software. Using your own words, describe the essence of open source software and how it differs from proprietary software. Also explain which kind of software offers its users the most consistent experience.

4. Explain why Linux makes system performance monitoring available to the user. Describe how users can use this information to their advantage.

5. In Linux, devices are identified by a major and minor device number. List at least three types of devices that fall into each category. Describe in your own words the primary differences between the two categories.

6. If you wanted to add these four files (october10.doc, OCTober.doc, OCTOBER.doc, and OcTOBer.doc) to one Linux directory, how many new files would be displayed: one, two, three, or four? Explain why this is so. Do you think the answer is the same for all operating systems? Why or why not?

7. Examine the following list of permissions for four items included in a directory listing. Identify if it is a file, directory, or other. Specify the access allowed to three categories: world, user, and group. Identify any category of users who are denied any access to all of these files.

   a. `-rwx---r-x`
   b. `drwx---rwx`
   c. `d--x---r-x`
   d. `prwx-------`

8. For these five items, identify which are files and which are directories. Identify which items, if any, allow access only to the user and the group.

   a. `-rwx---r-x`
   b. `drwx---r--`
   c. `-rwxrwxr--`
   d. `dr-x---r-x`
   e. `-rwx---rwx`

9. In your own opinion, how often should a student computer user check for updates to the operating system? Is your answer different for updating applications or other installed programs? Would you recommend allowing the operating system to automatically download and install updates? Explain your answers.

10. Linux uses an LRU algorithm to manage memory. Suppose there is another page replacement algorithm called not frequently used (NFU) that gives each page its own counter that is incremented with each clock cycle. In this way, each counter tracks the frequency of page use, and the page with the lowest counter is swapped out when paging is necessary. In your opinion, how do these two algorithms (LRU and NFU) compare? Explain which one would work best under normal use, and define how you perceive "normal use."

11. Some versions of Linux place access control information among the page table entries. Explain why (or why not) this might be an efficient way to control access to files or directories.

12. Linux treats all devices as files. Explain why this feature adds flexibility to this operating system.

13. With regard to virtual memory, decide if the following statement is true or false: If the paging file is located where fragmentation is least likely to happen, performance will be improved. Explain your answer.

Advanced Exercises

14. There are many reasons why the system administrator would want to restrict access to areas of memory. Give the three reasons you believe are most important and rank them in order of importance.

15. Compare and contrast block, character, and network devices. Describe how they are manipulated by the Linux device manager.

16. There are several ways to manage devices. The traditional way recognizes system devices in the order in which they are detected by the operating system. Another is dynamic device management, which calls for the creation and deletion of device files in the order that a user adds or removes devices. Compare and contrast the two methods and indicate the one you think is most effective, and explain why.

17. Device management also includes coordination with the Hardware Abstraction Layer (HAL). Describe which devices are managed by the HAL daemon and how duties are shared with the Linux device manager.

18. Describe the circumstance whereby a module would be closed but not released. What effect does this situation have on overall system performance? Describe the steps you would take to address the situation.

19. Security Enhanced Linux (SELinux) was designed and developed by a team from the U.S. National Security Agency and private industry. The resulting operating system, which began as a series of security patches, has since been included in the Linux kernel as of Version 2.6. In your own words, explain why you think this group chose Linux as the base platform.

Chapter 16

Android Operating Systems

ANDROID INTERFACE

Design Goals

Memory Management

Processor Management

Device Management

File Management

User Interface

"*…better batteries, mobile processors, capacitive touch screens, 3G—everything fell into place and no one could have expected it.*"

—Andy Rubin

Learning Objectives

After completing this chapter, you should be able to describe:

• The design goals for the Android™ operating system

• The role of the Memory Manager and Virtual Memory Manager

• The cooperation of the Android operating system with Linux for memory, device, processor, and network management

• System security challenges

• The critical role of Android applications

Android is designed to run mobile devices, specifically smartphones and tablets. It is built on a Linux foundation and relies on Linux to perform some of the most fundamental tasks, including management of main memory, processors, device drivers, and network access.

The most customizable part of Android is its user interface, which can be arranged by each user to include almost any configuration of applications (often shortened to "apps"). Apps are programmed in **Java** using a software developer kit (SDK) that's downloadable for free. Anyone with an interest in programming can install the necessary software, learn the basics of Java, and begin creating apps for distribution through the Android marketplace to anyone using a compatible device.

Like Linux, Android is an open source operating system, publishing key elements of its source code—but not all of it. While not as open as Linux, it is much more so than the operating system that runs Apple's mobile products (Noyes, 2011).

Brief History

Andy Rubin, as co-founder of Danger Inc., formed the team that created the Android operating system to power his company's new cell phone, called the Sidekick—a precursor to today's smartphone. The team's key challenge was to create a complete computing environment that could successfully manipulate the phone despite battery power limitations, a small CPU, and reduced memory space. Using the open source Linux operating system as a base, the team was able to create a multilevel system that integrated Linux to perform user actions via unique apps from the phone's screen.

When Google purchased Android in 2005, Rubin joined the company and his operating system was soon extended to reach entire generations of mobile smartphones and tablets. In 2013, Google CEO Larry Page announced that "more than 750 million devices have been activated globally; and 25 billion apps have now been downloaded from Google Play" (Page, 2013).

Rubin had purchased the Android domain name *www.android.com* years before the operating system was complete. The logo he chose, shown in Figure 16.1, resembles a robot. It may be no coincidence that Rubin's first job after college was as a robotic engineer; it's widely reported that building robots remains one of his favorite pastimes.

In the time since Android's commercial introduction, new versions have been released about one year apart, as shown in Table 16.1. (Remember, Android is built on the Linux **kernel**, which was discussed in the previous chapter.)

Droid is a name used to identify certain smartphones that run the Android operating system. Verizon has licensed the term "Droid" from Lucasfilm Ltd., maker of the Star Wars films, which owns the trademark.

(table 16.1)

Selected releases of Android, listing the Linux kernel on which each is built. Notice that the code names (all sweet treats) are assigned in alphabetical order.

Year	Release	Code Name	Features
2008	Version 1.0		First product available to the public.
2009	Version 2.0	Eclair	Based on Linux kernel 2.6.29.
2011	Version 3.0	Honeycomb	A tablet-only version based on Linux kernel 2.6.36.
2011	Version 4.0	Ice Cream Sandwich	Based on Linux kernel 3.0.1.
2012	Version 4.1	Jelly Bean	Based on Linux kernel 3.0.31.
2013	Version 5.0	Key Lime Pie	Release scheduled for late 2013.

With each new release, Android's source code is released so that manufacturers and enthusiasts can prepare their installation and customized software. Anyone can obtain the source code by following the instructions at *http://source.android.com*.

To learn the Android version number and Linux kernel version number, device owners can look under the Systems menu, as shown in Figure 16.2 (captured using a Samsung Tablet in 2012).

(figure 16.2)

This tablet runs the Android's Jelly Bean operating system (version 4.1.1) based on the Linux kernel version 3.0.31.

Andy Rubin (1963–)

After he graduated from college, Andy Rubin's first job was as a robotic engineer; he was soon hired by Apple as a manufacturing engineer. He continued his design and engineering work at several companies, including Microsoft, before co-founding a new technology firm, Danger Inc. There, Rubin led the team effort to design mobile devices. In 2003, he started a new business to create an operating system (Android), hiring a select group of engineers and designers. From its beginning, the new operating system was designed to be open source and available to all software designers. In 2005, Android was acquired by Google and Rubin moved into that firm's executive management. He holds several engineering patents and, as of this writing, continues to be an innovation leader at Google.

For more information:

*http://www.google.com/about/company/facts/
management/*

*Rubin named his operating system "Android" after
the domain name (android.com) that he had owned
for several years.*

Design Goals

The goals of the Android system are focused on the user experience in a mobile environment, using a touch screen and connecting to networks through either telephony (using **3G** and **4G,** as of this writing) or **Wi-Fi**. The following is taken directly from the Android Web site for developers at *http://developer.android.com/design/get-started/creative-vision.html*:

> "We focused the design of Android around three overarching goals, which apply to our core apps as well as the system at large. As you design apps to work with Android, consider these goals:

> **Enchant Me**

> Beauty is more than skin deep. Android apps are sleek and aesthetically pleasing on multiple levels. Transitions are fast and clear; layout and typography are crisp and meaningful. App icons are works of art in their own right. Just like a well-made tool, your app should strive to combine beauty, simplicity, and purpose to create a magical experience that is effortless and powerful.

> **Simplify My Life**

> Android apps make life easier and are easy to understand. When people use your app for the first time, they should intuitively grasp the most

important features. The design work doesn't stop at the first use, though. Android apps remove ongoing chores like file management and syncing. Simple tasks never require complex procedures, and complex tasks are tailored to the human hand and mind. People of all ages and cultures feel firmly in control, and are never overwhelmed by too many choices or irrelevant flash.

Make Me Amazing

It's not enough to make an app that is easy to use. Android apps empower people to try new things and to use apps in inventive new ways. Android lets people combine applications into new workflows through multitasking, notifications, and sharing across apps. At the same time, your app should feel personal, giving people access to superb technology with clarity and grace." (Android Open Source Project, 2012)

Memory Management

Memory management is handled by the Linux kernel, as shown in Figure 16.3, with the help of several software modifications (including shared memory allocators) to help Android work successfully on mobile devices that are typically built with a limited amount of main memory and slower CPUs. Therefore, Android apps are explicitly designed to use resources only when they are needed, and to require minimal resources

(figure 16.3)

This simplified illustration shows that the Android software stack is built on a Linux kernel, which manages all device drivers (only a few are shown here). (Illustration is adapted from http://source.android.com/tech/security.)

when they are dormant—that is, they are built to reside in memory in a sleep-like state while consuming minimal resources.

Therefore, once an application is opened, it remains resident in main memory, even when it appears that it has been closed. By remaining in memory, an app can usually open quicker when it is called in the near future. However, this does not mean that these open apps are not monitored. Android uses a least recently used (LRU) algorithm to keep track of each resident process and when it was most recently called. Then, if memory space should become scarce, a low memory killer (called LMK) acts to free up memory by removing the processes that have remained dormant the longest. In this way, users are *not* encouraged to manually "force stop" applications that they are not currently working with; in fact, doing so will cause these apps to take longer to open.

This strategy is very different from some other operating systems that encourage users to close any programs or applications that are residing in memory to conserve system resources so they can be allocated to another program or application.

Processor Management

Processor management requires four key objects: manifest, activities, tasks, and intents.

Manifest, Activity, Task, and Intent

Each app must have one **manifest** file that holds essential information that the system must have before it can run an application. The manifest includes all of the permissions that the app must have before it can begin as well as the permissions that other apps must have to work with the application's components. It also details the app's critical components, including its activities and services. This information is held in a file called AndroidManifest.xml (using that exact name).

An **activity** is the application component that defines the user interface screen that the individual uses to interact with the application, including all the actions that can be performed. In general, an application has a collection of activities, including some that are unique to the app as well as activities from other cooperative apps.

A **task** is defined in Android as a "sequence of activities a user follows to accomplish a goal." Therefore, a task can consist of activities from just one app or from several apps. A task that runs in the background is called a service, such as a media player that continues to play even as the user moves to another app and another activity.

An **intent** is the mechanism that one app uses to signal to another app that its cooperation is requested to accomplish something. This allows apps to call on one

A manifest file is a standard part of many operating systems and is used to identify resources that are required by each program during its execution.

another as needed to meet a user's request. For example, if the user requests that an app integrate a photo, that app can call on the camera app to make itself ready to take the desired photograph. Once taken, the digital image will be sent to the referring application without the need to notify the user that one app is pausing while another executes, and then pausing so the first can be resumed.

Activity States

Each application can have one to many activities and each one is responsible for maintaining its processing state, as shown in Figure 16.4.

(figure 16.4)

The changing states of a typical activity from Created on the left to Destroyed on the right. Typically, activities can be removed from memory when they are in the Paused, Stopped, or Destroyed states.

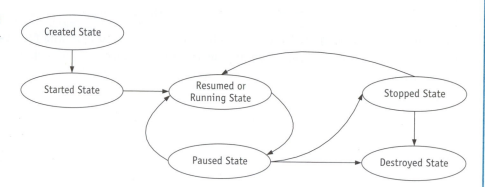

There are several states that an activity goes through from creation to destruction. (The flow of these activities is very similar to the process states described in Chapter 4.)

- *Created State*: a transient state when the activity has just begun.

- *Started State*: In this state, software initialization begins and the first screen can be drawn. This is generally considered the main screen.

- *Resumed State* (also called Running State): In this state, activities execute until they are interrupted by another activity or a user command.

- *Paused State*: This is a stop for an activity that is interrupted and ready to go into a "background" mode (such as when the user starts another application); the activity's status is typically saved. When the app returns to execution, it moves to the Resumed State. However, activities that are never recalled will never proceed to the Resumed or Stopped States and are terminated from the Pause State, so developers have to be careful to save status data when activities are paused in case that data is needed later.

- *Stopped State*: Activities in this state disappear from the user's view. From here, an activity may be terminated or it may be recalled, depending on the needs of the user and the system.

• *Destroyed State*: This is a formal indication that the activity is terminated and will be removed completely from system memory. Any background activities that could cause a **memory leak** must be properly closed. Note: it is possible for activities to be terminated without moving into this state, such as when another activity with higher priority requires a resource that is held exclusively.

Whenever a new activity begins, it replaces the activity that was previously called and its activity state is moved to a data structure called the "**back stack.**" This stack is loaded and unloaded using a last-in, first-out (LIFO) scheme. Each time that an app is replaced by another, such as when the user opens mail first and then opens the calendar, the status of the replaced app (mail) is moved into the stack so that the new app (calendar) can take over the screen. The contents of the stack are loaded in chronological order from the first one that was replaced to the last one replaced.

Later, when the user wants to backtrack to the previously viewed apps and presses the "back" button on the screen, it stops the current activity (calendar) and replaces it with the screen for the most recently opened app (mail) and restores that app's status so that it appears as it was left.

Stacks are not unique to Android. These data structures are commonly used in most, if not all, operating systems.

Let's look at the example shown in Figure 16.5. We follow an amateur photographer who opens four apps in the following order: clock (to make sure of the appointment time), maps (to verify the photo shoot location), phone (to confirm that the client is coming), and camera (to take the shots). When each app is opened, it causes the status of the previously active app to be stored in the back stack. (For example, when the phone app is opened, then the status of the maps app is moved to the back stack.)

Later, after the photo shoot is successful, it's time for the photographer to move on to the next assignment. By pressing the back button once, the camera app disappears from the screen and the next-to-last app (the phone app) is restored with the same status (same contact name and phone number) it was displaying when it was stopped.

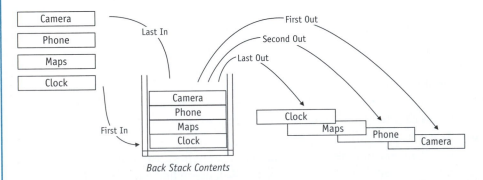

Back Stack Contents

(figure 16.5)

The last-in, first-out (LIFO) scheme moves the activity status of the current app into the back stack when that app is replaced by another one. Later, it restores each app in reverse order each time the user presses the back button.

Pressing the back button once again causes the phone app to disappear and the maps app to replace it, with its status restored. Finally, pressing the back button again causes maps to disappear and the clock to open.

As activities move through their individual lifecycles, the system relies on "callbacks" for changes in states. Examples of these callbacks are shown in Figure 16.6. For example, when the callback "onCreate()" is received, it causes the activity to be created. Then when the callback "onStart()" is received, that activity is moved from the Created state to the Started state. Likewise, the onPause() callback causes the activity to move from the Resumed state to the Paused state (this happens when the user moves from the currently displayed app to another app).

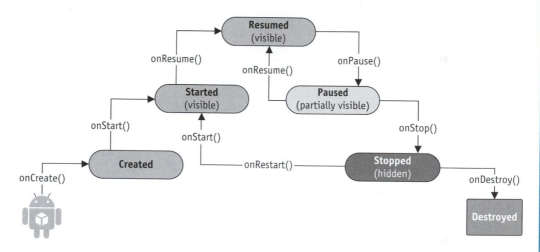

(figure 16.6)

Detailed view of the Activity Lifecycle and the system callbacks that move an activity from one state to another. (Illustration source: http://developer.android.com/training/basics/activity-lifecycle/starting.html, 2012)

To keep the Android system running smoothly, app developers need to remain aware of the many ways in which an app can be terminated because of the effect that doing so can have on resource allocation. For example, an app can be ended from any of three states: Paused, Stopped, or Destroyed. If the app is Paused after it was allocated an exclusive resource, such as a network connection or access to a critical device, these critical resources should be deallocated until it is time for the app to resume. To do otherwise is to risk the app closing prematurely (from the Paused State) still holding exclusive control of the resource. In other words, the app designer needs to make certain that each app ends gracefully whenever the user terminates it, no matter what state it happened to be in at the time.

Device Management

Because Android runs on a wide variety of mobile devices, unlike desktop computers (which can require users to explicitly change settings for each monitor size and type), apps are designed to accommodate numerous devices, often without user help.

Screen Requirements

Developers creating apps for Android must account for a wide range of screens, from the tiniest smartphone to the largest tablet. Many apps also support rotation—turning the display from portrait to landscape and back again as the user rotates the device, thus multiplying the combinations of views. Android accommodates different screen sizes and resolution, as shown in Table 16.2.

Design Factor	Sample Values	What It Means
Screen size	Phone: 3 in (5.1 cm) Tablet: 10 in (25 cm)	The screen's actual size as measured from one corner diagonally to the other.
Screen density	Phone: 164 dpi Tablet: 284 dpi	The number of pixels located within a certain area on the screen, such as a one inch line (dpi = dots per inch).
Orientation	Portrait (vertical) Landscape (horizontal)	The screen's orientation as viewed by the user.
Resolution	Phone: 240×320 Tablet: 1280×800	The number of physical pixels.

(table 16.2)

Four device display variables that directly impact the design of user interface screens.

To aid designers, Android has introduced a fifth factor, called a density-independent pixel (dp), which is the equivalent to one physical pixel on a 160 dpi screen. App designers are encouraged to create interfaces using the dp unit. In this way, device and app designers can allow the system to perform the necessary scaling for each screen based on its size, resolution, orientation, and density.

For example, if a designer is creating a simple game to run on all Android telephones, the game could end up running on screens ranging from 240 x 320 dpi to 1920 x 1030 dpi in portrait mode (and 320 x 240 to 1030 x 1920 in landscape mode). If the designer wrote a game app using dpi units, the system would require coding for every possible screen combination. But by writing the app using dp units, the same code can be used to display on every screen size. Note that using dp units does not absolve the designer from stating in the app's manifest file the types of screens that are supported.

Given the wide variation in screen configurations, designers may choose to create four different user interfaces to accommodate Android's four categories of screen sizes:

- Extra-large screens: at least 960dp x 720dp
- Large screens: at least 640dp x 480dp
- Normal screens: at least 470dp x 320dp
- Small screens: at least 426dp x 320dp

Figure 16.7 Shows Android's four size categories and how their respective densities compare.

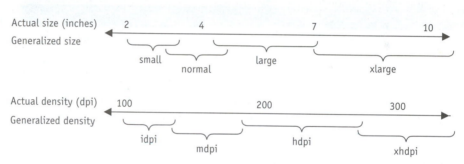

The ultimate goal of app designers is to give every user the impression that the app was designed specifically for the user's device, and not merely stretched or shrunk to accommodate various screens. Screen requirements and how to develop apps for them is a subject that's sure to change frequently. For current details about user interface screen support, see *http://developer.android.com/guide/practices/index.html*.

Battery Management

One of the key considerations for any operating system running on a mobile device is management of the power supply, especially the battery. Battery usage information for an Android device is available from the Settings tab, as shown in Figure 16.8.

To improve battery availability, users may choose to leave certain functions turned off until they are actually needed, such as **GPS**, **Bluetooth** communications, background file syncing, live wallpaper, and haptic (vibration) feedback. In addition, using Wi-Fi instead of telephony can save power.

(figure 16.8)

This device has 1 hour, 32 minutes of battery time remaining. This display also indicates that the screen is consuming 73 percent of the device's battery resources at a very bright setting and that the Android operating system is using 5 percent.

Battery management is a field of its own and, unfortunately, cannot be covered in this limited space. However, we highly recommend that readers explore this subject online to learn more about this ever-changing and fascinating subject.

File Management

Routine file control in Android operating systems is managed by Linux at the kernel level. Therefore, each application has its own User ID, the part of the operating system that is the user's own protected mode and that allows it to manage the files it creates and executes. Therefore, if the app's developer does not explicitly expose it to other applications, no other apps are allowed to read or alter its files. However, if two apps are signed with the same digital certification, then the two get the same User ID. As a result, the apps are allowed to share data, but this practice also means that the developer has to take special precautions to make sure they work correctly with each other (Burnette, 2010).

Users may need supplementary apps to perform the hands-on file manipulation one might expect from a robust operating system, but is currently not easy to do with Android devices that are right "out of the box." As of this writing, this capability can be gained by installing and using apps to move, copy, and otherwise manipulate files on the device (and the flash card if it's available).

Security Management

The Android operating system has a multiple tiered security structure designed to protect the user's data, protect the system's resources (including networking resources), and provide application isolation to prevent intentional damage or inadvertent vulnerabilities from a malicious or poorly designed app.

There are two primary classes of Android apps: those that are pre-installed (such as calendar, camera, email, contacts, browser, and so on) and those installed by the user. The greatest security vulnerabilities stem from those that are user installed.

Permissions

One critical aspect of Android security is user-defined **permissions**. Because the person who allows installation of an application is explicitly asked to grant permission for this app to access certain resources on the device, it is the individual who holds the key to device security. Before installing an app, the list of permissions is available for review, such as the display shown in Figure 16.9. This app requested access to only four permissions.

(figure 16.9)

This application requested these four permissions. The app is not installed until the user agrees to allow access.

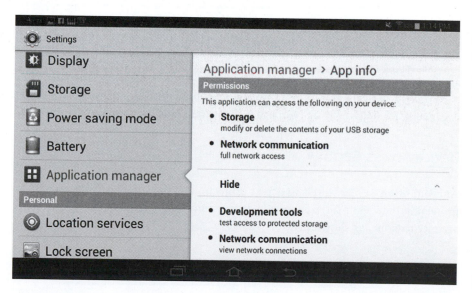

User-granted permissions, a few of which are listed in Table 16.3, are listed in the manifest.

A survey described by Sverdlove and Cilley (2012) found that the vast majority (72 percent) of the 400,000 apps that were examined, requested permissions that

Requested Permission	Application's Reason for the Request
Your location	Learn approximate user location using network information and/or precise GPS location.
Your accounts	Find accounts that have been set up for this device.
Personal Information	Read and/or modify contact lists, read and/or modify the call log, write to the dictionary.
Phone Calls	Read the status of the phone and identify callers.
Services that cost you money	Directly call phone numbers and send messages.
Network Communication	View and control network connections and/or Near Field Communication.
Storage	Modify and/or delete contents of the device's USB storage.
Hardware Controls	Record audio and activate the camera to take pictures and/or videos and/or modify haptic (vibration) controls.
System Tools	Access Bluetooth settings, connect and disconnect from Wi-Fi, modify system settings, retrieve running apps, toggle synchronization on and off, delete app cache data, disable the screen lock, close other apps, run at startup, uninstall shortcuts, write Home settings, prevent the device from sleeping.
Development Tools	Test access to protected storage.

(table 16.3)

Before installing an app, the user is presented with a list of all the permissions requested by that application. A few are listed here.

appeared to be outside of their apparent operational requirements. When that number is combined with the ability of individuals to connect their personal devices to their organization's networks, this can produce a wide range of unexpected vulnerabilities.

Device Access Security

Android offers several levels of access protection so that users can choose how much protection they want for each mobile device, and these options can range from highest security to none, as shown in Table 16.4.

Technique	Security Level
Password Matching	Highest security
PIN Matching	Medium to high security
Pattern Recognition	Medium security
Face Recognition	Low security
Finger Swipe	No security, open access

(table 16.4)

Each mobile device can be set to an appropriate level of the security.

Strong passwords are the highest built-in level of security (though even stronger security can be added through a high-security app). This assumes, of course, that the passwords chosen are not trivial and are not written down in plain sight. In a user instruction video (*http://www.google.com/goodtoknow*, as of 2012), Google recommends a two-step process to build a strong password consisting of numbers, letters, and symbols:

1. Start with a random phrase that is easy to remember.
2. Then insert random numbers, capital letters, and special characters to make it even harder to guess.

For example, the easy-to-remember phrase could be: "The Maple Tree is Shady" which is written in one word as: themapletreeisshady. Then, after making some replacements, the resulting password could be: 1heM@pleTreeZsh!dy.

The goal is to avoid words or phrases that appear in a dictionary, those that follow patterns on the keyboard (such as 123456), and anything that would be easy for someone else to guess. In general, when the password is longer, it is stronger.

An alternative to password protection is Android's pattern recognition tool, which is similar to the graphical passwords described in Chapter 11. To set one up, the user chooses Settings, opens the Lock Screen security option, chooses Pattern to reach the screen shown in Figure 16.10, and follows the instructions to connect the nine dots in a certain pattern—one that can be easily remembered. If an intruder should try to use brute force to guess the pattern, the default setting allows only a limited number of incorrect tries before locking the device and requiring an alternative mode of access.

(figure 16.10)

To establish the pattern lock security option, the device owner traces a single line to connect the dots, such as the one shown here. Later, to unlock the device, the same pattern must be retraced exactly.

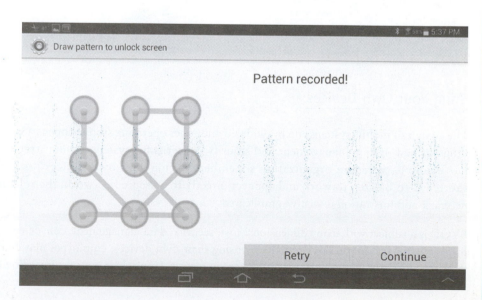

Facial recognition is not currently ranked as a strong access control tool because of several vulnerabilities: someone who looks like you could be granted access and it can be fooled by having the device evaluate a photo of the owner. This is a technology that's sure to improve in the coming years, but for now, it's wise to rely on stronger authentication tools.

Encryption Options

Android offers encrypted storage options, as shown in Figure 16.11. Once an account, setting, application, data, pictures, or other file is encrypted, the user will be required to enter a valid password with every sign-on. This option is available from the Settings/Security menu.

(figure 16.11)

For higher security, encryption is offered. It's a time-consuming option to invoke, so the device owner should have the device plugged in or at least fully charged before starting it.

Bring Your Own Devices

The advent of mobile systems run by Android and other operating systems opens a wide range of new system management and security concerns for systems administrators. For example, when an organization's members "bring your own devices" (often shortened to BYOD) to work and connect directly to a secured network, the role of network administration is vastly complicated.

BYOD is a subject with many dimensions: cost, security, data management, convenience, productivity, and more. For example, by using their own devices, employees may find they are more productive even when they are in transit. Using their own devices allows them enhanced integration of work hours and personal time. It can also be seen as a cost effective use of technology that employees have already purchased for their own use, thus significantly reducing the purchasing requirements by an organization's IT groups.

It also raises many questions. For example:

- Who decides which apps will be run on each device, and which apps can be connected to a secure system?
- How can productivity improvements attributed to BYOD be measured?
- Who should pay the usage charges when an employee's device is used for both work and personal activities?
- Is device network access limited to email or expanded to multiple database access?
- Who controls the data on the device—the personal information as well as organizational data?
- Who should pay for upgrades in device hardware and software?
- What happens if the device is misplaced or lost?
- Who else in the employee's family is allowed to use the device?
- How are the device and its data managed when the owner leaves the organization?

"Do you think phone makers focus enough on security?" When this question was asked in a small 2012 survey, 22 percent of the U.S. and Canadian respondents said "yes" and 78 percent said "no" (Sverdlove & Cilley, 2012). The report goes on to explore the vulnerability of organizational networks from unprotected devices by asking respondents to list the kinds of networked functions that personal cell devices are allowed to access. Responses are shown in Table 16.5.

(table 16.5)

Survey responses to the question, "What business services can employee-owned (personal) devices connect to via your organization's network?" (Bit9 Report, 2012).

Service	Organizations that allow connection
Company email	76%
Company calendar	67%
Company documents	34%
Mobile-specific enterprise apps	29%
Company social media accounts	19%
Company messaging and chat	18%
We do not allow personal device access	21%

Can all apps be trusted? Probably not. After all, Android apps can be authored by anyone with Java experience and downloaded by anyone with a compatible device. Therefore, this is a subject that changes daily as the work of systems administrators, software developers, and network security professionals move forward. To learn about the latest developments, we recommend that you stay current on this subject through independent Internet research.

User Interface

As of this writing, all devices running the Android operating system use a touch screen for a user interface. The touch screen consists of icons that are manipulated by the user. Along the bottom of the home screen are user-selected apps that remain in place when the user swipes the screen from side-to-side. Along the bottom row of the display screen are "soft buttons" that allow the user to perform critical tasks, such as go home, go back, or view open tasks, as shown in Figure 16.12.

(figure 16.12)

User-definable icons and buttons at the base of the display allow users to quickly access these functions.

Touch Screen Controls

Users send commands to the operating system through gestures made on a touch-screen. The standard graphical user interface recognizes seven primary gestures. See Table 16.6.

Gesture	Actions	Meaning
Touch	Press and then lift	Starts the default activity for this item. When used with a virtual on-screen keyboard, this allows typing. When used with a graphics app, it allows drawing and choosing colors.
Long press	Press, move, and then lift	Moves into the data selection mode and allows the user to select one or more items in a view and act upon the data using a contextual action bar.
Swipe	Press, move, and then lift	Moves gracefully to content located in a neighboring view, generally of the same hierarchy.
Drag	Long press, move, and then lift	Rearranges data from one place to another within this view, or moves data into a folder or another container.
Double touch	Two touches in quick succession	Zooms into content currently displayed. When used within a text selection context, it is also used as a secondary gesture.
Pinch open	Two-finger press, move outward, and then lift	Zooms into content in this view offering a closer perspective.
Pinch close	Two-finger press, move inward, and then lift	Zooms away from content to offer a wider perspective.

(table 16.6)

Seven primary gestures that users can make on their mobile devices.

When the user is immersed in a static endeavor, such as reading or watching a movie (something that would be best experienced in full screen and without distractions), Android allows the on-screen buttons to temporarily disappear. Called "lights-out mode," it allows the user to enjoy the content without any unnecessary interruption. If an important event occurs, such as a low battery warning, that message will interrupt viewing and be displayed.

Likewise, if at any time the user wants to return to active control of the system, a simple touch anywhere on the screen causes the device to exit lights-out mode and bring the controls, and the distractions, to the foreground.

User Interface Elements

A consistent navigation experience is essential to user satisfaction. To address this issue, Android developers are highly encouraged to follow the same standards regarding the placement of icons and the way in which they function. A few standards are described here, but there are many more. For details, please see: *http://developer.android.com/design/index.html*.

Along the top of each app screen is an "action bar" that generally stays in place while that app is active. This action bar, shown in Figure 16.13, provides a consistent layout so that users know where to find key elements and navigation tools in all apps: 1) app icon with the up button, 2) view control area, 3) action buttons that allow fast and easy use of the most important tools users may need for this app, and 4) action overflow area where additional tools or actions can be found. These design elements allow new apps to work well with other core Android apps.

(figure 16.13)

Sample action bar. Its four parts must be programmed according to the published standard so that users enjoy a consistent experience from one app to another.

(Figure source: http://developer.android.com/design/patterns/actionbar.html)

App Icon

The app icon is shown at the left of the action bar (shown here as the Android icon, #1 in Figure 16.13). If the screen currently shows the app's home screen, the icon stands alone. If the user moves off the home screen, the icon is shown with an arrow to the left (shown in the far left in Figure 16.13). When pressed, the apps home screen will be displayed. Repeatedly pressing the up button only moves the viewpoint to the apps top screen—it will never move to the device's home screen.

The back button, described earlier in this chapter, works slightly differently. The back button is shown at the bottom of the screen; when pressed, it moves from the current activity to the referring activity. That is, it steps in reverse. By pressing the back button repeatedly, the user moves backwards from the displayed screen to the previous screen until the home screen is reached.

View Control

If this app supports multiple views, such as tabs or alternative view, they are controlled from this part of the action bar (shown as #2 in Figure 16.13). If the app does not support such views, this space can be used for branding.

Action Buttons

This part of the action bar (shown as #3 in Figure 16.13) shows the most important actions that users will want to access when using this app. Each is represented by an icon; pressing and holding an icon will cause the action's name to be revealed.

Action Overflow

In this area, shown as #4 in Figure 16.13, users can find tasks that are not otherwise represented on the action bar, due to insufficient room in the small space available on the action bar or because these tasks are not often needed. If the app should be run on a screen that is very small, only one icon will be shown on the action bar and all other action buttons will be moved to this action overflow area, shown in Figure 16.14.

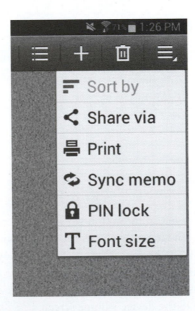

(figure 16.14)

A typical action overflow area revealing six additional actions. Any that are not currently usable are shown in light gray.

Conclusion

Android is built for mobile, multitasking, multipurpose systems that often have multiple cores. As of this writing, four years after its first release, Google claims that Android powers hundreds of millions of mobile devices in more than 190 countries. It is an open source operating system based on Linux and encourages legions of application developers to write new software for users to run on a multitude of tablets and telephones.

Android appears to have hit the market with fortuitous timing, just as touch screens became popular and mobile connectivity became widespread. Its future may depend on the ability of app developers to keep current with new emerging technologies and to use consistent design elements, so that users can enjoy a seamless experience as they meander from one app to the next. It's sure to be an intriguing journey for this operating system over the coming years.

Key Terms

3G, 4G: commercial telephony technology that allows mobile devices to make telephone calls or access the Internet without the need for wireless connectivity.

activity: a single focused thing that the user can do and, if a screen is required, the associated user screen. One app can have multiple activities.

app: an abbreviation for application.

application: a computer program, typically small, that can run on selected mobile devices.

back stack: a data structure used to hold the activity state of an app that has been interrupted so that it can be resumed if the user presses the back button.

Bluetooth®: a wireless technology that allows communication with other devices over relatively short distances.

cloud computing: in simplest terms, it is a multifaceted technology that allows computing, data storage and retrieval, and other computer functions to take place over a large network, typically the Internet.

GPS (global positioning system): a satellite-enabled navigation technology that provides ground position, velocity, direction, and time information.

intent: a mechanism that applications can send to invoke a specific Android response, such as fetching a file or sending an email.

Java: A programming language and computing platform that is often used by developers to create Android apps.

kernel: the part of the operating system that constitutes its foundation and core functionality; the kernel has complete control over everything that occurs in the system.

manifest: a list of all the installed packages in each device, including the version number of each package.

memory leak: the unintentional use of memory by an app or program that remains open even after it appears to have terminated. It can be caused when memory resources are not properly deallocated.

permissions: refers to many types of access control granted to an app.

task: a collection of activities that users interact with when performing a certain job.

Wi-Fi®: a brand name, owned by the Wi-Fi Alliance, certifying that a device or other product is compatible with a set of IEEE broadband wireless networking standards

Interesting Searches

For more background on a few of the topics discussed in this chapter, begin a search with these terms.

- Android-compatible devices
- Android development
- Open source software
- Embedded Android
- Android for servers
- Bring your own device (BYOD)

Exercises

Research Topics

A. Android limits the user's ability to move and rename files. Investigate a few apps that can help the user move files from one place to another. Give the name, cost, and effectiveness of each app and describe in your own words which apps you would prefer to install on your device, and explain why.

B. Android is open source software. Research the extent to which Android source code is available to the public and explain whether or not Android could or should be a more open system. Cite your sources and the dates of publication.

Exercises

1. Compare and contrast Android and the Linux operating systems.

2. Compare and contrast the Android and Windows operating systems.

3. Why do you think mobile devices have CPUs that are less powerful than those in a larger desktop computer?

4. Give specific examples of situations where battery performance is of crucial importance to a mobile device user. What specific recommendations would you make to battery developers to improve the user experience with mobile devices?

5. Explain in your own words why main memory is constrained in a mobile device, and compare it to main memory on a desktop computer.

6. Assume that a user opens five apps in the following order: mail, contacts, calendar, messages, and settings. Draw a picture showing the contents of the back stack before the back button is pushed.

7. Explain in your own words why a software developer might want to request from the user only a minimum number of permissions for an app. Explain why another developer might request the maximum number of permissions. Give your opinion as to which is better for the user and which for the network manager.

8. The role of the Linux kernel is crucial to the Android operating system. Explain in your own words why this is so.

9. According to Android, certain security procedures offer greater protection than others. Of these, choose the one that you would prefer, and explain the level of security it offers. Explain why you would choose that method over the alternatives.

10. In your own words, describe how you would secure an organization network if it is already well-secured but management decides to allow all employees to directly connect their own devices to it.

Advanced Exercises

11. "Android is a true operating system even though it relies heavily on Linux." Is this true? In your own words, explain why you do or do not agree with this statement.

12. Assume that you are given responsibility to create a new alarm clock app and you are limited to requesting only three permissions. A few such permissions are shown in Table 16.3. Answer the following questions.

    a. If you could choose only three, which would you choose and why? Would your app perform satisfactorily with these three permissions?

    b. If you were allowed to request a fourth permission, which would you pick and why?

    c. If there are additional permissions that you believe would be ideal to have, which would you choose and why?

13. File management in Android is not accessible to most users. Using your own words, write a brief tutorial to help someone organize pictures or data files on an Android device.

14. Research the figures for the installed base for both Android and the Apple iOS system and compare the growth rates of each.

    a. Give your opinion as to the future of both operating systems and explain your reasoning.

    b. Which do you personally prefer? Explain why.

    c. What recommendation would you give a systems administrator who had to set the policy for an organization? Would you include both, or just one? Explain.

15. Explain the advantages and disadvantages of using open source software. Describe any security implications (if any) that must be addressed when adopting an open source operating system.

Appendix A | Algorithms

The following algorithms are presented in pseudocode to describe algorithms using a program-like structure but integrating descriptive phrases to make it understandable to readers who are unfamiliar with specific language syntax. Each algorithm presents the general idea but may skip details to enhance clarity.

Algorithms from Chapter 2

Algorithm to Load a Job in a Single-User Memory System

1　Store first memory location of program into base register (for memory protection)
2　Set program counter (it keeps track of memory space used by the program) equal to address of first memory location
3　Read first instruction of program
4　Increment program counter by number of bytes in instruction
5　Has the last instruction been reached?

　if yes, then stop loading program

　if no, then continue with Step 6
6　Is program counter greater than memory size?

　if yes, then stop loading program

　if no, then continue with Step 7
7　Load instruction in memory
8　Read next instruction of program
9　Go to Step 4

Algorithm to Load a Job in Fixed Partition Memory Systems

1 Determine job's requested memory size

2 If job_size > size of largest partition

   Then reject the job

      print appropriate message to operator

      go to Step 1 to handle next job in line

   Else

   continue with Step 3

3 Set counter to 1

4 Do while counter <= number of partitions in memory

   If job_size > memory_partition_size(counter)

   Then counter = counter + 1

   Else

   If memory_partition_size(counter) = "free"

      Then load job into memory_partition(counter)

         change memory_partition_status(counter) to "busy"

         go to Step 1 to handle next job in line

      Else

      counter = counter + 1

   End do

5 No partition available at this time, put job in waiting queue

6 Go to step 1 to handle next job in line

A First-Fit Memory Allocation Algorithm

1 Set counter to 1

2 Do while counter <= number of blocks in memory

   If job_size > memory_size(counter)

      Then counter = counter + 1

   Else

      load job into memory_size(counter)

      adjust free/busy memory lists

      go to Step 4

   End do

3 Put job in waiting queue

4 Go fetch next job

A Best-Fit Memory Allocation Algorithm

1 Initialize memory_block(0) = 99999
2 Compute initial_memory_waste = memory_block(0) – job_size
3 Initialize subscript = 0
4 Set counter to 1
5 Do while counter <= number of blocks in memory
     If job_size > memory_size(counter)
       Then counter = counter + 1
      Else
        memory_waste = memory_size(counter) – job_size
     If initial_memory_waste > memory_waste
       Then subscript = counter
        initial_memory_waste = memory_waste
        counter = counter + 1
    End do
6 If subscript = 0
   Then put job in waiting queue
   Else
      load job into memory_size(subscript)
      adjust free/busy memory lists
7 Go fetch next job

An Algorithm to Deallocate Blocks of Main Memory

If job_location is adjacent to one or more free blocks
  Then
  If job_location is between two free blocks
    Then merge all three blocks into one block
    memory_size(counter-1) = memory_size(counter-1) + job_size
    + memory_size(counter+1)
    set status of memory_size(counter+1) to null entry
  Else
    merge both blocks into one
    memory_size(counter-1) = memory_size(counter-1) + job_size
Else
  search for null entry in free memory list
  enter job_size and beginning_address in the entry slot
  set its status to "free"
DONE

Algorithms from Chapter 3

The following algorithms are presented in pseudocode to demonstrate examples of the logic that can be used by the allocation schemes described in Chapter 3.

A Hardware Instruction Processing Algorithm

1 Start processing instruction
2 Generate data address
3 Compute page number
4 If page is in memory
    Then
      get data and finish instruction
      advance to next instruction
      return to Step 1
    Else
      generate page interrupt
      call page fault handler
    DONE

A Page Fault Handler Algorithm

1 If there is no free page frame
    Then
    select page to be swapped out using page removal algorithm
    update job's Page Map Table
      If content of page had been changed
      Then
      write page to disk
2 Use page number from Step 3 from the Hardware Instruction Processing Algorithm to get disk address where the requested page is stored (the File Manager uses the page number to get the disk address)
3 Read page into memory
4 Update job's Page Map Table
5 Update Memory Map Table
6 Restart interrupted instruction
   DONE

A Main Memory Transfer Algorithm

1 CPU puts the address of a memory location in the Memory Address Register and requests data or an instruction to be retrieved from that address

2 Perform a test to determine if the block containing this address is already in a cache slot:

If YES, transfer the information to the CPU register – DONE

If NO: Access main memory for the block containing the requested address

  Allocate a free cache slot to the block

  Perform these two steps in parallel:

    Transfer the information to CPU

    Load the block into slot

DONE

Algorithms from Chapter 6

The following algorithms are presented in pseudocode to demonstrate examples of the logic that can be used by the processor scheduler as described in Chapter 6.

Producers and Consumers Algorithm

```
empty:        = n
full:         = 0
mutex:        = 1
COBEGIN
    repeat until no more data PRODUCER
    repeat until buffer is empty CONSUMER
COEND
```

ACM Code of Ethics and Professional Conduct

The following passages are excerpted from the Code of Ethics and Professional Conduct adopted by the Association for Computing Machinery Council. They are reprinted here with permission. For the complete text, see *www.acm.org/about/code-of-ethics*.

Note: These imperatives are expressed in a general form to emphasize that ethical principles which apply to computer ethics are derived from more general ethical principles.

Preamble

Commitment to ethical professional conduct is expected of every member (voting members, associate members, and student members) of the Association for Computing Machinery (ACM).

This Code, consisting of 24 imperatives formulated as statements of personal responsibility, identifies the elements of such a commitment. It contains many, but not all, issues professionals are likely to face. Section 1 outlines fundamental ethical considerations, while Section 2 addresses additional, more specific considerations of professional conduct. Statements in Section 3 pertain more specifically to individuals who have a leadership role, whether in the workplace or in a volunteer capacity such as with organizations like ACM. Principles involving compliance with this Code are given in Section 4.

Section 1: GENERAL MORAL IMPERATIVES

As an ACM member I will ....

1.1 Contribute to society and human well-being.

This principle concerning the quality of life of all people affirms an obligation to protect fundamental human rights and to respect the diversity of all cultures. An essential aim of computing professionals is to minimize negative consequences of computing systems, including threats to health and safety. When designing or implementing systems, computing professionals must attempt to ensure that the products of their efforts will be used in socially responsible ways, will meet social needs, and will avoid harmful effects to health and welfare.

In addition to a safe social environment, human well-being includes a safe natural environment. Therefore, computing professionals who design and develop systems must be alert to, and make others aware of, any potential damage to the local or global environment.

1.2 Avoid harm to others.

"Harm" means injury or negative consequences, such as undesirable loss of information, loss of property, property damage, or unwanted environmental impacts. This principle prohibits use of computing technology in ways that result in harm to any of the following: users, the general public, employees, employers. Harmful actions include intentional destruction or modification of files and programs leading to serious loss of resources or unnecessary expenditure of human resources such as the time and effort required to purge systems of "computer viruses."

Well-intended actions, including those that accomplish assigned duties, may lead to harm unexpectedly. In such an event the responsible person or persons are obligated to undo or mitigate the negative consequences as much as possible. One way to avoid unintentional harm is to carefully consider potential impacts on all those affected by decisions made during design and implementation.

To minimize the possibility of indirectly harming others, computing professionals must minimize malfunctions by following generally accepted standards for system design and testing. Furthermore, it is often necessary to assess the social consequences of systems to project the likelihood of any serious harm to others. If system features are misrepresented to users, coworkers, or supervisors, the individual computing professional is responsible for any resulting injury.

In the work environment the computing professional has the additional obligation to report any signs of system dangers that might result in serious personal or social damage. If one's superiors do not act to curtail or mitigate such dangers, it may be necessary to "blow the whistle" to help correct the problem or reduce the risk. However, capricious or misguided reporting of violations can, itself, be harmful. Before reporting violations, all relevant aspects of the incident must be thoroughly assessed. In particular, the assessment of risk and responsibility must be credible. It is suggested that advice be sought from other computing professionals. See Principle 2.5 regarding thorough evaluations.

1.3 Be honest and trustworthy.

Honesty is an essential component of trust. Without trust an organization cannot function effectively. The honest computing professional will not make deliberately false or deceptive claims about a system or system design, but will instead provide full disclosure of all pertinent system limitations and problems.

A computer professional has a duty to be honest about his or her own qualifications, and about any circumstances that might lead to conflicts of interest.

1.4 Be fair and take action not to discriminate.

The values of equality, tolerance, respect for others, and the principles of equal justice govern this imperative. Discrimination on the basis of race, sex, religion, age, disability, national origin, or other such factors is an explicit violation of ACM policy and will not be tolerated.

Inequities between different groups of people may result from the use or misuse of information and technology. In a fair society, all individuals would have equal opportunity to participate in, or benefit from, the use of computer resources regardless of race, sex, religion, age, disability, national origin or other similar factors. However, these ideals do not justify unauthorized use of computer resources nor do they provide an adequate basis for violation of any other ethical imperatives of this code.

1.5 Honor property rights including copyrights and patent.

Violation of copyrights, patents, trade secrets and the terms of license agreements is prohibited by law in most circumstances. Even when software is not so protected, such violations are contrary to professional behavior. Copies of software should be made only with proper authorization. Unauthorized duplication of materials must not be condoned.

1.6 Give proper credit for intellectual property.

Computing professionals are obligated to protect the integrity of intellectual property. Specifically, one must not take credit for other's ideas or work, even in cases where the work has not been explicitly protected by copyright, patent, etc.

1.7 Respect the privacy of others.

Computing and communication technology enables the collection and exchange of personal information on a scale unprecedented in the history of civilization. Thus, there is increased potential for violating the privacy of individuals and groups. It is the responsibility of professionals to maintain the privacy and integrity of data describing individuals. This includes taking precautions to ensure the accuracy of data, as well as protecting it from unauthorized access or accidental disclosure to inappropriate individuals. Furthermore, procedures must be established to allow individuals to review their records and correct inaccuracies.

This imperative implies that only the necessary amount of personal information be collected in a system, that retention and disposal periods for that information be clearly defined and enforced, and that personal information gathered for a specific purpose not be used for other purposes without consent of the individual(s). These principles apply to electronic communications, including electronic mail, and prohibit procedures that capture or monitor electronic user data, including messages, without the permission of users or bona fide authorization related to system operation and maintenance. User data observed during the normal duties of system operation and maintenance must be treated with strictest confidentiality, except in cases where it is evidence for the violation of law, organizational regulations, or this Code. In these cases, the nature or contents of that information must be disclosed only to proper authorities.

1.8 Honor confidentiality.

The principle of honesty extends to issues of confidentiality of information whenever one has made an explicit promise to honor confidentiality or, implicitly, when private information not directly related to the performance of one's duties becomes available. The ethical concern is to respect all obligations of confidentiality to employers, clients, and users unless discharged from such obligations by requirements of the law or other principles of this Code.

Glossary

3G, 4G: telephony technology that allows mobile devices to make telephone calls or access the Internet without the need for wireless connectivity.

absolute filename: a file's name, as given by the user, preceded by the directory (or directories) where the file is found and, when necessary, the specific device label.

access control: the control of user access to a network or computer system. See also *authentication*.

access control list: an access control method that lists each file, the names of the users who are allowed to access it, and the type of access each is permitted.

access control matrix: an access control method that uses a matrix with every file (listed in rows) and every user (listed in columns) and the type of access each user is permitted on each file, recorded in the cell at the intersection of that row and column.

access control verification module: software that verifies which users are permitted to perform which operations with each file.

access time: the total time required to access data in secondary storage. For a direct access storage device with movable read/write heads, it is the sum of seek time (arm movement), search time (rotational delay), and transfer time (data transfer).

access token: an object that uniquely identifies a user who has logged on. An access token is appended to every process owned by the user. It contains the user's security identification, the names of the groups to which the user belongs, any privileges the user owns, the default owner of any objects the user's processes create, and the default access control list to be applied to any objects the user's processes create.

Active Directory: a Microsoft Windows directory service that offers centralized administration of application serving, authentication, and user registration for distributed networking systems.

active multiprogramming: a term used to indicate that the operating system has more control over interrupts; designed to fairly distribute CPU utilization over several resident programs. It contrasts with *passive multiprogramming*.

activity: an activity is a single focused thing that the user can do, and almost all activities invoke a user interface screen for this interaction. Each app can have multiple activities, and each is responsible for saving its own state when it is interrupted so it can be gracefully restored later.

address: a number that designates a particular memory location.

address resolution: the process of changing the address of an instruction or data item to the address in main memory at which it is to be loaded or relocated.

Advanced Research Projects Agency network (ARPAnet): a pioneering long-distance network. It served as the basis for early networking research, as well as a central backbone during the development of the Internet.

aging: a policy used to ensure that jobs that have been in the system for a long time in the lower level queues will eventually complete their execution.

algorithm: a set of step-by-step instructions used to solve a particular problem. It can be stated in any form, such as mathematical formulas, diagrams, or natural or programming languages.

allocation module: the section of the File Manager responsible for keeping track of unused areas in each storage device.

allocation scheme: the process of assigning specific resources to a job so it can execute.

antivirus software: software that is designed to detect and recover from attacks by viruses and worms. It is usually part of a system protection software package.

app: an abbreviation for application. An app is a computer program, typically small, that can run on selected mobile devices.

argument: in a command-driven operating system, a value or option placed in the command that modifies how the command is to be carried out.

arithmetic logic unit: The high-speed CPU circuit that is part of the processor core that performs all calculations and comparisons.

assembler: a computer program that translates programs from assembly language to machine language.

assembly language: a programming language that allows users to write programs using mnemonic instructions that can be translated by an assembler. It is considered a low-level programming language and is very computer dependent.

associative memory: the name given to several registers, allocated to each active process, whose contents associate several of the process segments and page numbers with their main memory addresses.

authentication: the means by which a system verifies that the individual attempting to access the system is authorized to do so. Password protection is an authentication technique.

availability: a resource measurement tool that indicates the likelihood that the resource will be ready when a user needs it. It is influenced by mean time between failures and mean time to repair.

avoidance: the strategy of deadlock avoidance. It is a dynamic strategy, attempting to ensure that resources are never allocated in such a way as to place a system in an unsafe state.

backup: the process of making long-term archival file storage copies of files on the system.

batch system: a type of computing system that executes programs, each of which is submitted in its entirety, can be grouped into batches, and execute without external intervention.

benchmarks: a measurement tool used to objectively measure and evaluate a system's performance by running a set of jobs representative of the work normally done by a computer system.

best-fit memory allocation: a main memory allocation scheme that considers all free blocks and selects for allocation the one that will result in the least amount of wasted space. It contrasts with the *first-fit memory allocation*.

biometrics: the science and technology of identifying authorized users based on their biological characteristics.

BIOS: an acronym for Basic Input Output System, a set of programs that are hard-coded on a chip to load into ROM at startup.

blocking: a storage-saving and I/O-saving technique that groups individual records into a block that is stored and retrieved as a unit. The size of the block is often set to take advantage of the transfer rate.

Bluetooth®: a wireless technology that allows communication with other devices over relatively short distances.

bootstrapping: the process of starting an inactive computer by using a small initialization program to load other programs.

bounds register: a register used to store the highest location in memory legally accessible by each program. It contrasts with *relocation register*.

bridge: a data-link layer device used to interconnect multiple networks using the same protocol. A bridge is used to create an extended network so that several individual networks can appear to be part of one larger network.

browsing: a system security violation in which unauthorized users are allowed to search through secondary storage directories or files for information they should not have the privilege to read.

B-tree: a special case of a binary tree structure used to locate and retrieve records stored in disk files. The qualifications imposed on a B-tree structure reduce the amount of time it takes to search through the B-tree, making it an ideal file organization for large files.

buffers: the temporary storage areas residing in main memory, channels, and control units. They are used to store data read from an input device before it is needed by the processor and to store data that will be written to an output device.

bus: (1) the physical channel that links the hardware components and allows for transfer of data and electrical signals; or (2) a shared communication link onto which multiple nodes may connect.

bus topology: a network architecture in which elements are connected together along a single link.

busy waiting: a method by which processes, waiting for an event to occur, continuously test to see if the condition has changed and remain in unproductive, resource-consuming wait loops.

cache manager: a component of the I/O system that manages the part of virtual memory known as cache. The cache expands or shrinks dynamically depending on the amount of memory available.

cache memory: a small, fast memory used to hold selected data and to provide faster access than would otherwise be possible.

capability list: an access control method that lists every user, the files to which each has access, and the type of access allowed to those files.

capacity: the maximum throughput level of any one of the system's components.

Carrier Sense Multiple Access with Collision Avoidance (CSMA/CA): a method used to avoid transmission collision on shared media such as networks. It usually prevents collisions by requiring token acquisition.

Carrier Sense Multiple Access with Collision Detection (CSMA/CD): a method used to detect transmission collision on shared media such as networks. It requires that the affected stations stop transmitting immediately and try again after delaying a random amount of time.

CD-R: a compact disc storage medium that can be read many times but can be written to once.

CD-ROM: compact disc read-only memory; a direct access optical storage medium that can store data including graphics, audio, and video. Because it is read-only, the contents of the disc can't be modified.

CD-RW: a compact disc storage medium that can be read many times and written to many times.

central processing unit (CPU): the component with the circuitry, the *chips*, to control the interpretation and execution of instructions. In essence, it controls the operation of the entire computer system. All storage references, data manipulations, and I/O operations are initiated or performed by the CPU.

channel: see *I/O channel*.

channel program: see *I/O channel program*.

Channel Status Word (CSW): a data structure that contains information indicating the condition of the channel, including three bits for the three components of the I/O subsystem—one each for the channel, control unit, and device.

child process: in UNIX and Linux operating systems, the subordinate processes that are controlled by a parent process.

circuit switching: a communication model in which a dedicated communication path is established between two hosts, and on which all messages travel. The telephone system is an example of a circuit switched network.

circular wait: one of four conditions for deadlock through which each process involved is waiting for a resource being held by another; each process is blocked and can't continue, resulting in deadlock.

cleartext: in cryptography, a method of transmitting data without encryption, in text that is readable by anyone who sees it.

client: a user node that requests and makes use of various network services. A workstation requesting the contents of a file from a file server is a client of the file server.

clock cycle: the time span between two ticks of the computer's system clock.

clock policy: a variation of the LRU policy that removes from main memory the pages that show the least amount of activity during recent clock cycles.

C-LOOK: a scheduling strategy for direct access storage devices that is an optimization of C-SCAN.

cloud computing: a multi-faceted technology that allows computing, data storage and retrieval and other computer functions to take place over a large network, typically the Internet.

COBEGIN and **COEND:** used together to indicate to a multiprocessing compiler the beginning and end of a section where instructions can be processed concurrently.

collision: when a hashing algorithm generates the same logical address for two records with unique keys.

command-driven interface: an interface that accepts typed commands, one line at a time, from the user. It contrasts with a menu-driven interface.

compaction: the process of collecting fragments of available memory space into contiguous blocks by moving programs and data in a computer's memory or secondary storage.

compatibility: the ability of an operating system to execute programs written for other operating systems or for earlier versions of the same system.

compiler: a computer program that translates programs from a high-level programming language (such as C or Ada) into machine language.

complete filename: see *absolute filename*.

compression: see *data compression*.

concurrent processing: execution by a single processor of a set of processes in such a way that they appear to be happening at the same time. It is typically achieved by interleaved execution. Also called *multiprocessing*.

concurrent programming: a programming technique that allows a single processor to simultaneously execute multiple sets of instructions. Also called *multiprogramming* or *multitasking*.

connect time: in time-sharing, the amount of time that a user is connected to a computer system. It is usually measured by the time elapsed between log on and log off.

contention: a situation that arises on shared resources in which multiple data sources compete for access to the resource.

context switching: the acts of saving a job's processing information in its PCB so the job can be swapped out of memory, and of loading the processing information from the Process Control Block (PCB) of another job into the appropriate registers so the CPU can process it. Context switching occurs in all preemptive policies.

contiguous storage: a type of file storage in which all the information is stored in adjacent locations in a storage medium.

control cards: cards that define the exact nature of each program and its requirements. They contain information that direct the operating system to perform specific functions, such as initiating the execution of a particular job. See *job control language*.

control unit: see *I/O control unit*.

control word: a password given to a file by its creator.

core: The processing part of a CPU chip made up of the control unit and the arithmetic logic unit. The core does not include the cache.

C programming language: a general-purpose programming language that combines high-level statements with low-level machine controls to generate software that is both easy to use and highly efficient.

CPU: see *central processing unit*.

CPU-bound: a job that will perform a great deal of nonstop computation before issuing an I/O request. It contrasts with *I/O-bound*.

critical region: a part of a program that must complete execution before other processes can begin.

cryptography: the science of coding a message or text so an unauthorized user cannot read it.

C-SCAN: a scheduling strategy for direct access storage devices that is used to optimize seek time. It is an abbreviation for circular-SCAN.

CSMA/CA: see *Carrier Sense Multiple Access with Collision Avoidance*.

CSMA/CD: see *Carrier Sense Multiple Access with Collision Detection*.

current byte address (CBA): the address of the last byte read. It is used by the File Manager to access records in secondary storage and must be updated every time a record is accessed, such as when the READ command is executed.

current directory: the directory or subdirectory in which the user is working.

cylinder: for a disk or disk pack, it is when two or more read/write heads are positioned at the same track, at the same relative position, on their respective surfaces.

DASD: see *direct access storage device.*

database: a group of related files that are interconnected at various levels to give users flexibility of access to the data stored.

data compression: a procedure used to reduce the amount of space required to store data by reducing encoding or abbreviating repetitive terms or characters.

data file: a file that contains only data.

deadlock: a problem occurring when the resources needed by some jobs to finish execution are held by other jobs, which, in turn, are waiting for other resources to become available. The deadlock is complete if the remainder of the system comes to a standstill as a result of the hold the processes have on the resource allocation scheme.

deallocation: the process of freeing an allocated resource, whether memory space, a device, a file, or a CPU.

dedicated device: a device that can be assigned to only one job at a time; it serves that job for the entire time the job is active.

demand paging: a memory allocation scheme that loads into memory a program's page at the time it is needed for processing.

denial of service (DoS) attack: an attack on a network that makes it unavailable to perform the functions it was designed to do. This can be done by flooding the server with meaningless requests or information.

detection: in a deadlocked system, the process of examining the state of an operating system to determine whether a deadlock exists.

device: a peripheral unit attached to a computer system including a printer, hard disk drive, optical disc drive, monitor, or flash drive.

device driver: a device-specific program module that handles the interrupts and controls a particular type of device.

device independent: a program or file that functions in the same correct way on different types of devices.

device interface module: transforms the block number supplied by the physical file system into the actual cylinder/surface/record combination needed to retrieve the information from a specific secondary storage device.

Device Manager: the section of the operating system responsible for controlling the use of devices. It monitors every device, channel, and control unit and chooses the most efficient way to allocate all of the system's devices.

dictionary attack: the technique by which an intruder attempts to guess user passwords by trying words found in a dictionary.

direct access file: see *direct record organization.*

direct access storage device (DASD): any secondary storage device that can directly read or write to a specific place. Also called a *random access storage device.* It contrasts with a *sequential access medium.*

direct memory access (DMA): an I/O technique that allows a control unit to access main memory directly and transfer data without the intervention of the CPU.

direct record organization: files stored in a direct access storage device and organized to give users the flexibility of accessing any record at random regardless of its position in the file.

directed graphs: a graphic model representing various states of resource allocations. It consists of processes and resources connected by directed lines (lines with directional arrows).

directory: a logical storage unit that contains files.

disc: an optical storage medium such as CD or DVD.

disk pack: a removable stack of disks mounted on a common central spindle with spaces between each pair of platters so read/write heads can move between them.

displacement: in a paged or segmented memory allocation environment, it's the difference between a page's relative address and the actual machine language address. It is used to locate an instruction or data value within its page frame. Also called *offset*.

distributed operating system (DO/S): an operating system that provides global control for a distributed computing system (two or more computers interconnected for a specific purpose), allowing its resources to be managed in a unified way. See also *Network Operating System*.

distributed processing: a method of data processing in which files are stored at many different locations and in which processing takes place at different sites.

DNS: see *domain name service*.

Domain Name Service (DNS): a general-purpose, distributed, replicated, data query service. Its principal function is the resolution of Internet addresses based on fully qualified domain names such as .com (for commercial entity) or .edu (for educational institution).

DO/S: see *distributed operating system*.

double buffering: a technique used to speed I/O in which two buffers are present in main memory, channels, and control units.

DVD: digital video disc; a direct access optical storage medium that can store many gigabytes, enough to store a full-length movie.

dynamic partitions: a memory allocation scheme in which jobs are given as much memory as they request when they are loaded for processing, thus creating their own partitions in main memory. It contrasts with *static partitions*, or *fixed partitions*.

earliest deadline first (EDF): a preemptive process scheduling policy (or algorithm) that selects processes based on the proximity of their deadlines (appropriate for real-time environments).

elevator algorithm: see *LOOK*.

embedded computer system: a dedicated computer system that often resides inside a larger physical system, such as jet aircraft or automobiles. Often, it must be small and fast and work with real-time constraints, fail-safe execution, and nonstandard I/O devices.

encryption: translation of a message or data item from its original form to an encoded form, thus hiding its meaning and making it unintelligible without the key to decode it. It is used to improve system security and data protection.

Ethernet: a 10-megabit, 100-megabit, 1-gigabit or more standard for LANs. All hosts are connected to a coaxial cable where they contend for network access.

ethics: the rules or standards of behavior that members of the computer-using community are expected to follow, demonstrating the principles of right and wrong.

explicit parallelism: a type of concurrent programming that requires that the programmer explicitly state which instructions can be executed in parallel. It contrasts with *implicit parallelism*.

extensibility: one of an operating system's design goals that allows it to be easily enhanced as market requirements change.

extension: in some operating systems, it is the part of the filename that indicates which compiler or software package is needed to run the files. UNIX and Linux call it a *suffix*.

extents: any remaining records, and all other additions to the file, that are stored in other sections of the disk. The extents of the file are linked together with pointers.

external fragmentation: a situation in which the dynamic allocation of memory creates unusable fragments of free memory between blocks of busy, or allocated, memory. It contrasts with *internal fragmentation*.

external interrupts: interrupts that occur outside the normal flow of a program's execution. They are used in preemptive scheduling policies to ensure a fair use of the CPU in multiprogramming environments.

FCFS: see *first come first served*.

feedback loop: a mechanism to monitor the system's resource utilization so adjustments can be made.

fetch policy: the rules used by the virtual memory manager to determine when a page is copied from disk to memory.

field: a group of related bytes that can be identified by the user with a name, type, and size. A record is made up of fields.

FIFO: see *first-in first-out*.

FIFO anomaly: an unusual circumstance through which adding more page frames causes an increase in page interrupts when using a FIFO page replacement policy.

file: a group of related records that contains information to be used by specific application programs to generate reports.

file allocation table (FAT): a table used to track noncontiguous segments of a file.

file descriptor: information kept in the directory to describe a file or file extent. It contains the file's name, location, and attributes.

File Manager: the section of the operating system responsible for controlling the use of files. It tracks every file in the system including data files, assemblers, compilers, and application programs. By using predetermined access policies, it enforces access restrictions on each file.

file server: a dedicated network node that provides mass data storage for other nodes on the network.

File Transfer Protocol (FTP): a protocol that allows a user on one host to access and transfer files to or from another host over a TCP/IP network.

filter command: a command that directs input from a device or file, changes it, and then sends the result to a printer or display.

FINISHED: a job status that means that execution of the job has been completed.

firewall: a set of hardware and software that disguises the internal network address of a computer or network to control how clients from outside can access the organization's internal servers.

firmware: the software program or set of instructions used to boot up a device or computer, generally stored on the ROM chip.

first come first served (FCFS): (1) the simplest scheduling algorithm for direct access storage devices that satisfies track requests in the order in which they are received; (2) a nonpreemptive process scheduling policy (or algorithm) that handles jobs according to their arrival time; the first job in the READY queue will be processed first by the CPU.

first-fit memory allocation: a main memory allocation scheme that searches from the beginning of the free block list and selects for allocation the first block of memory large enough to fulfill the request. It contrasts with *best-fit memory allocation*.

first generation (1940–1955): the era of the first computers, characterized by their use of vacuum tubes and their very large physical size.

first-in first-out (FIFO) policy: a page replacement policy that removes from main memory the pages that were brought in first. It is based on the assumption that these pages are the least likely to be used again in the near future.

fixed-length record: a record that always contains the same number of characters. It contrasts with *variable-length record*.

fixed partitions: a memory allocation scheme in which main memory is sectioned off, with portions assigned to each user. Also called *static partitions*. It contrasts with *dynamic partitions*.

flash memory: a type of nonvolatile memory used as a secondary storage device that can be erased and reprogrammed in blocks of data.

FLOP: a measure of processing speed meaning floating point operations per second (FLOP). See *megaflop, gigaflop, teraflop*.

floppy disk: a removable flexible disk for low-cost, direct access secondary storage.

fragmentation: a condition in main memory where wasted memory space exists within partitions, called *internal fragmentation,* or between partitions, called *external fragmentation*.

FTP: the name of the program a user invokes to execute the File Transfer Protocol.

gateway: a communications device or program that passes data between networks having similar functions but different protocols. A gateway is used to create an extended network so that several individual networks appear to be part of one larger network.

gigabit: a measurement of data transmission speed equal to 1,073,741,824 bits per second.

gigabyte (GB): a unit of memory or storage space equal to 1,073,741,824 bytes or 2^{30} bytes. One gigabyte is approximately 1 billion bytes.

gigaflop: a benchmark used to measure processing speed. One gigaflop equals 1 billion floating point operations per second.

GPS (global positioning system): a satellite-enabled navigation technology that provides ground position, velocity, direction, and time information.

graphical user interface (GUI): a user interface that allows the user to activate operating system commands by clicking on icons or symbols using a pointing device such as a mouse.

group: a property of operating systems that enables system administrators to create sets of users who share the same privileges. A group can share files or programs without allowing all system users access to those resources.

groupware: software applications that support cooperative work over a network. Groupware systems must support communications between users and information processing. For example, a system providing a shared editor must support not only the collective amendment of documents, but also discussions between the participants about what is to be amended and why.

hacker: a person who delights in having an intimate understanding of the internal workings of a system—computers and computer networks in particular. The term is often misused in a pejorative context, where *cracker* would be the correct term.

Hamming code: an error-detecting and error-correcting code that greatly improves the reliability of data, named after mathematician Richard Hamming.

hard disk: a direct access secondary storage device for personal computer systems. It is generally a high-density, nonremovable device.

hardware: the physical machine and its components, including main memory, I/O devices, I/O channels, direct access storage devices, and the central processing unit.

hashing algorithm: the set of instructions used to perform a key-to-address transformation in which a record's key field determines its location. See also *logical address*.

high-level scheduler: another term for the *Job Scheduler*.

HOLD: one of the process states. It is assigned to processes waiting to be let into the READY queue.

hop: a node network through which a packet passes on the path between the packet's source and destination nodes.

host: (1) the Internet term for a network node that is capable of communicating at the application layer. Each Internet host has a unique IP address. (2) a networked computer with centralized program or data files that makes them available to other computers on the network.

hybrid system: a computer system that supports both batch and interactive processes. It appears to be interactive because individual users can access the system directly and get fast responses, but it accepts and runs batch programs in the background when the interactive load is light.

hybrid topology: a network architecture that combines other types of network topologies, such as tree and star, to accommodate particular operating characteristics or traffic volumes.

impersonation: a term used in Windows systems for the ability of a thread in one process to take on the security identity of a thread in another process and perform operations on that thread's behalf. Used by environment subsystems and network services when accessing remote resources for client applications.

implicit parallelism: a type of concurrent programming in which the compiler automatically detects which instructions can be performed in parallel. It contrasts with *explicit parallelism*.

indefinite postponement: signifies that a job's execution is delayed indefinitely.

index block: a data structure used with indexed storage allocation. It contains the addresses of each disk sector used by that file.

indexed sequential record organization: a way of organizing data in a direct access storage device. An index is created to show where the data records are stored. Any data record can be retrieved by consulting the index first.

indexed storage: the way in which the File Manager physically allocates space to an indexed sequentially organized file.

interactive system: a system that allows each user to interact directly with the operating system.

interblock gap (IBG): an unused space between blocks of records on a sequential storage medium such as a magnetic tape.

internal fragmentation: a situation in which a fixed partition is only partially used by the program. The remaining space within the partition is unavailable to any other job and is therefore wasted. It contrasts with *external fragmentation*.

internal interrupts: also called *synchronous interrupts*, they occur as a direct result of the arithmetic operation or job instruction currently being processed. They contrast with *external interrupts*.

internal memory: see *main memory*.

International Organization for Standardization (ISO): a voluntary, non-treaty organization founded in 1946 that is responsible for creating international standards in many areas, including computers and communications. Its members are the national standards organizations of the 89 member countries, including ANSI for the United States.

Internet: the largest collection of networks interconnected with routers. The Internet is a multiprotocol internetwork.

Internet Protocol (IP): the network-layer protocol used to route data from one network to another. It was developed by the United States Department of Defense.

interrecord gap (IRG): an unused space between records on a on a sequential storage medium such as a magnetic tape. It facilitates the drive's start/stop operations.

Intent: a mechanism that applications can send to invoke certain specific Android response, such as fetching a file or send an email.

interrupt: a hardware signal that suspends execution of a program and activates the execution of a special program known as the interrupt handler. It breaks the normal flow of the program being executed.

interrupt handler: the program that controls what action should be taken by the operating system when a certain sequence of events is interrupted.

inverted file: a file generated from full document databases. Each record in an inverted file contains a key subject and the document numbers where that subject is found. A book's index is an inverted file.

I/O-bound: a job that requires a large number of input/output operations, resulting in substantial free time for the CPU. It contrasts with *CPU-bound*.

I/O channel: a specialized programmable unit placed between the CPU and the control units. Its job is to synchronize the fast speed of the CPU with the slow speed of the I/O device and vice versa, making it possible to overlap I/O operations with CPU operations. I/O channels provide a path for the transmission of data between control units and main memory, and they control that transmission.

I/O channel program: the program that controls the channels. Each channel program specifies the action to be performed by the devices and controls the transmission of data between main memory and the control units.

I/O control unit: the hardware unit containing the electronic components common to one type of I/O device, such as a disk drive. It is used to control the operation of several I/O devices of the same type.

I/O device: any peripheral unit that allows communication with the CPU by users or programs.

I/O device handler: the module that processes the I/O interrupts, handles error conditions, and provides detailed scheduling algorithms that are extremely device dependent. Each type of I/O device has its own device handler algorithm.

I/O scheduler: one of the modules of the I/O subsystem that allocates the devices, control units, and channels.

I/O subsystem: a collection of modules within the operating system that controls all I/O requests.

I/O traffic controller: one of the modules of the I/O subsystem that monitors the status of every device, control unit, and channel.

IP: see *Internet Protocol*.

ISO: see *International Organization for Standardization.*

Java: a cross-platform programming language that closely resembles C++ and runs on any computer capable of running the Java interpreter.

job: a unit of work submitted by a user to an operating system.

job control language (JCL): a command language used in several computer systems to direct the operating system in the performance of its functions by identifying the users and their jobs and specifying the resources required to execute a job. The JCL helps the operating system better coordinate and manage the system's resources.

Job Scheduler: the high-level scheduler of the Processor Manager that selects jobs from a queue of incoming jobs based on each job's characteristics. The Job Scheduler's goal is to sequence the jobs in the READY queue so that the system's resources will be used efficiently.

job status: the condition of a job as it moves through the system from the beginning to the end of its execution: HOLD, READY, RUNNING, WAITING, or FINISHED.

job step: units of work executed sequentially by the operating system to satisfy the user's total request. A common example of three job steps is the compilation, linking, and execution of a user's program.

Job Table (JT): a table in main memory that contains two entries for each active job—the size of the job and the memory location where its page map table is stored. It is used for paged memory allocation schemes.

Kerberos: an MIT-developed authentication system that allows network managers to administer and manage user authentication at the network level.

kernel: the part of the operating system that resides in main memory at all times and performs the most essential tasks, such as managing memory and handling disk input and output. It has complete control over everything that occurs in the system.

kernel level: in an object-based distributed operating system, it provides the basic mechanisms for dynamically building the operating system by creating, managing, scheduling, synchronizing, and deleting objects.

kernel mode: the name given to indicate that processes are granted privileged access to the processor. Therefore, all machine instructions are allowed and system memory is accessible. Contrasts with the more restrictive *user mode.*

key field: (1) a unique field or combination of fields in a record that uniquely identifies that record; (2) the field that determines the position of a record in a sorted sequence.

kilobyte (K): a unit of memory or storage space equal to 1,024 bytes or 2^{10} bytes.

LAN: see *local area network.*

lands: flat surface areas on the reflective layer of a CD or DVD. Each land is interpreted as a 1. Contrasts with *pits,* which are interpreted as 0s.

leased line: a dedicated telephone circuit for which a subscriber pays a monthly fee, regardless of actual use.

least-frequently-used (LFU): a page-removal algorithm that removes from memory the least-frequently-used page.

least-recently-used (LRU) policy: a page-replacement policy that removes from main memory the pages that show the least amount of recent activity. It is based on the assumption that these pages are the least likely to be used again in the immediate future.

LFU: see *least-frequently-used.*

Lightweight Directory Access Protocol (LDAP): a protocol that defines a method for creating searchable directories of resources on a network. It is called *lightweight* because it is a simplified and TCP/IP-enabled version of the X.500 directory protocol.

link: a generic term for any data communications medium to which a network node is attached.

livelock: a locked system whereby two or more processes continually block the forward progress of the others without making any forward progress itself. It is similar to a deadlock except that neither process is blocked or waiting; they are both in a continuous state of change.

local area network (LAN): a data network intended to serve an area covering only a few square kilometers or less.

local station: the network node to which a user is attached.

locality of reference: behavior observed in many executing programs in which memory locations recently referenced, and those near them, are likely to be referenced in the near future.

locking: a technique used to guarantee the integrity of the data in a database through which the user locks out all other users while working with the database.

lockword: a sequence of letters and/or numbers provided by users to prevent unauthorized tampering with their files. The lockword serves as a secret *password* in that the system will deny access to the protected file unless the user supplies the correct lockword when accessing the file.

logic bomb: a virus with a trigger, usually an event, that causes it to execute.

logical address: the result of a key-to-address transformation. See also *hashing algorithm*.

LOOK: a scheduling strategy for direct access storage devices that is used to optimize seek time. Sometimes known as the elevator algorithm.

loosely coupled configuration: a multiprocessing configuration in which each processor has a copy of the operating system and controls its own resources.

low-level scheduler: a synonym for *process scheduler*.

LRU: see *least-recently-used*.

magnetic tape: a linear secondary storage medium that was first developed for early computer systems. It allows only for sequential retrieval and storage of records.

magneto-optical (MO) disk drive: a data storage drive that uses a laser beam to read and/or write information recorded on magneto-optical disks.

mailslots: a high-level network software interface for passing data among processes in a one-to-many and many-to-one communication mechanism. Mail slots are useful for broadcasting messages to any number of processes.

main memory: the memory unit that works directly with the CPU and in which the data and instructions must reside in order to be processed. Also called *random access memory (RAM)*, *primary storage*, or *internal memory*.

mainframe: the historical name given to a large computer system characterized by its large size, high cost, and relatively fast performance.

MAN: see *metropolitan area network*.

master file directory (MFD): a file stored immediately after the volume descriptor. It lists the names and characteristics of every file contained in that volume.

master/slave configuration: an asymmetric multiprocessing configuration consisting of a single processor system connected to *slave* processors, each of which is managed by the primary *master* processor, which provides the scheduling functions and jobs.

mean time between failures (MTBF): a resource measurement tool; the average time that a unit is operational before it breaks down.

mean time to repair (MTTR): a resource measurement tool; the average time needed to fix a failed unit and put it back in service.

megabyte (MB): a unit of memory or storage space equal to 1,048,576 bytes or 2^{20} bytes.

megaflop: a benchmark used to measure processing speed. One megaflop equals 1 million floating point operations per second.

megahertz (MHz): a speed measurement used to compare the clock speed of computers. One megahertz is equal to 1 million electrical cycles per second.

memory leak: the unintentional use of memory by an app or program that remains open even after it appears to have terminated. It can be caused when memory resources are not properly deallocated.

Memory Manager: the section of the operating system responsible for controlling the use of memory. It checks the validity of each request for memory space and, if it is a legal request, allocates the amount of memory needed to execute the job.

Memory Map Table (MMT): a table in main memory that contains as many entries as there are page frames and lists the location and free/busy status for each one.

menu-driven interface: an interface that accepts instructions that users choose from a menu of valid choices. It contrasts with a *command-driven interface*.

metropolitan area network (MAN): a data network intended to serve an area approximating that of a large city.

microcomputer: a small computer equipped with all the hardware and software necessary to perform one or more tasks.

middle-level scheduler: a scheduler used by the Processor Manager to manage processes that have been interrupted because they have exceeded their allocated CPU time slice. It is used in some highly interactive environments.

midrange computer: a small to medium-sized computer system developed to meet the needs of smaller institutions. It was originally developed for sites with only a few dozen users. Also called *minicomputer*.

minicomputer: see *midrange computer*.

MIPS: a measure of processor speed that stands for a million instructions per second. A mainframe system running at 100 MIPS can execute 100,000,000 instructions per second.

module: a logical section of a program. A program may be divided into a number of logically self-contained modules that may be written and tested by a number of programmers.

most-recently-used (MRU): a page-removal algorithm that removes from memory the most-recently-used page.

MTBF: see *mean time between failures*.

MTTR: see *mean time to repair*.

multiple-level queues: a process-scheduling scheme (used with other scheduling algorithms) that groups jobs according to a common characteristic. The processor is then allocated to serve the jobs in these queues in a predetermined manner.

multiprocessing: when two or more CPUs share the same main memory, most I/O devices, and the same control program routines. They service the same job stream and execute distinct processing programs concurrently.

multiprogramming: a technique that allows a single processor to process several programs residing simultaneously in main memory and interleaving their execution by overlapping I/O requests with CPU requests. Also called *concurrent programming* or *multitasking*.

multitasking: a synonym for *multiprogramming*.

mutex: a condition that specifies that only one process may update (modify) a shared resource at a time to ensure correct operation and results.

mutual exclusion: one of four conditions for deadlock in which only one process is allowed to have access to a resource. It is typically shortened to *mutex* in algorithms describing synchronization between processes.

named pipes: a high-level software interface to NetBIOS, which represents the hardware in network applications as abstract objects. Named pipes are represented as file objects in Windows and operate under the same security mechanisms as other executive objects.

natural wait: an I/O request from a program in a multiprogramming environment that would cause a process to wait "naturally" before resuming execution.

negative feedback loop: a mechanism to monitor the system's resources and, when it becomes too congested, to signal the appropriate manager to slow down the arrival rate of the processes.

NetBIOS interface: a programming interface that allows I/O requests to be sent to and received from a remote computer. It hides networking hardware from applications.

network: a system of interconnected computer systems and peripheral devices that exchange information with one another.

Network Manager: the section of the operating system responsible for controlling the access to, and use of, networked resources.

network operating system (NOS): the software that manages network resources for a node on a network and may provide security and access control. These resources may include electronic mail, file servers, and print servers. See also *distributed operating system*.

no preemption: one of four conditions for deadlock in which a process is allowed to hold on to resources while it is waiting for other resources to finish execution.

noncontiguous storage: a type of file storage in which the information is stored in non-adjacent locations in a storage medium. Data records can be accessed directly by computing their relative addresses.

nonpreemptive scheduling policy: a job scheduling strategy that functions without external interrupts so that, once a job captures the processor and begins execution, it remains in the RUNNING state uninterrupted until it issues an I/O request or it is finished.

NOS: see *network operating system*.

N-step SCAN: a variation of the SCAN scheduling strategy for direct access storage devices that is used to optimize seek times.

NT file system (NTFS): The file system introduced with Windows NT that offers file management services, such as permission management, compression, transaction logs, and the ability to create a single volume spanning two or more physical disks.

null entry: an empty entry in a list. It assumes different meanings based on the list's application.

object: any one of the many entities that constitute a computer system, such as CPUs, disk drives, files, or databases. Each object is called by a unique name and has a set of operations that can be carried out on it.

object-based DO/S: a view of distributed operating systems where each hardware unit is bundled with its required operational software, forming a discrete object to be handled as an entity.

object-oriented: a programming philosophy whereby programs consist of self-contained, reusable modules called objects, each of which supports a specific function, but which are categorized into classes of objects that share the same function.

offset: in a paged or segmented memory allocation environment, it is the difference between a page's address and the actual machine language address. It is used to locate an instruction or data value within its page frame. Also called *displacement*.

open shortest path first (OSPF): a protocol designed for use in Internet Protocol networks, it is concerned with tracking the operational state of every network interface. Any changes to the state of an interface will trigger a routing update message.

open systems interconnection (OSI) reference model: a seven-layer structure designed to describe computer network architectures and the ways in which data passes through them. This model was developed by the ISO in 1978 to clearly define the interfaces and protocols for multi-vendor networks, and to provide users of those networks with conceptual guidelines in the construction of such networks.

operating system: the primary software on a computing system that manages its resources, controls the execution of other programs, and manages communications and data storage.

optical disc: a secondary storage device on which information is stored in the form of tiny holes called *pits* laid out in a spiral track (instead of a concentric track as for a magnetic disk). The data is read by focusing a laser beam onto the track.

optical disc drive: a drive that uses a laser beam to read and/or write information recorded on compact optical discs.

order of operations: the algebraic convention that dictates the order in which elements of a formula are calculated.

OSI reference model: see *open systems interconnection reference model*.

OSPF: see *open shortest path first*.

overlay: a technique used to increase the apparent size of main memory. This is accomplished by keeping in main memory only the programs or data that are currently active; the rest are kept in secondary storage. Overlay occurs when segments of a program are transferred from secondary storage to main memory for execution, so that two or more segments occupy the same storage locations at different times.

owner: one of the types of users allowed to access a file. The owner is the one who created the file originally. Other types are *group* and *everyone else*, also known as *world* in some systems.

P: an operation performed on a semaphore, which may cause the calling process to wait. It stands for the Dutch word *proberen*, meaning *to test*, and it is part of the P and V operations to test and increment.

packet: a generic term used to describe units of data at all layers of the protocol stack, but it is most correctly used to describe application data units.

packet filtering: reviewing incoming and outgoing Internet packets to verify that the source address, destination address, and protocol are correct.

packet sniffer: software that intercepts network data packets sent in cleartext and searches them for information, such as passwords.

packet switching: a communication model in which messages are individually routed between hosts, with no previously established communication path.

page: a fixed-size section of a user's job that corresponds to page frames in main memory.

page fault: a type of hardware interrupt caused by a reference to a page not residing in memory. The effect is to move a page out of main memory and into secondary storage so another page can be moved into memory.

page fault handler: part of the Memory Manager that determines if there are empty page frames in memory so that the requested page can immediately be copied from secondary storage, or determines which page must be swapped out if all page frames are busy.

page frame: individual sections of main memory of uniform size into which a single page may be loaded.

Page Map Table (PMT): a table in main memory with the vital information for each page including the page number and its corresponding page frame memory address.

page replacement policy: an algorithm used by virtual memory systems to decide which page or segment to remove from main memory when a page frame is needed and memory is full. Two examples are FIFO and LRU.

page swap: the process of moving a page out of main memory and into secondary storage so another page can be moved into memory in its place.

paged memory allocation: a memory allocation scheme based on the concept of dividing a user's job into sections of equal size to allow for noncontiguous program storage during execution. This was implemented to further increase the level of multiprogramming. It contrasts with *segmented memory allocation*.

parallel processing: the process of operating two or more CPUs in parallel: that is, more than one CPU executing instructions simultaneously.

parent process: In UNIX and Linux operating systems, a job that controls one or more child processes, which are subordinate to it.

parity bit: an extra bit added to a character, word, or other data unit and used for error checking.

partition: a section of hard disk storage of arbitrary size. Partitions can be static or dynamic.

passive multiprogramming: a term used to indicate that the operating system doesn't control the amount of time the CPU is allocated to each job, but waits for each job to end an execution sequence before issuing an interrupt releasing the CPU and making it available to other jobs. It contrasts with *active multiprogramming*.

password: a user access authentication method. Typically, it is a series of keystrokes that a user enters in order to be allowed to log on to a computer system.

patch: executable software that repairs errors or omissions in another program or piece of software.

patch management: the rigorous application of software patches to make repairs and keep the operating system software up to the latest standard.

path: (1) the sequence of routers and links through which a packet passes on its way from source to destination node; (2) the sequence of directories and subdirectories the operating system must follow to find a specific file.

PCB: see *process control block*.

peer (hardware): a node on a network that is at the same level as other nodes on that network. For example, all nodes on a local area network are peers.

peer (software): a process that is communicating to another process residing at the same layer in the protocol stack on another node. For example, if the processes are application processes, they are said to be application-layer peers.

performance: the ability of an operating system to give users good response times under heavy loads and when using CPU-bound applications such as graphic and financial analysis packages, both of which require rapid processing.

permissions: refers to many types of access control granted to an app or a user.

phishing: a technique used to trick consumers into revealing personal information by appearing as a legitimate entity.

picture password: a sequence of strokes over a picture or graphic that is used to authenticate access to a computer system by an authorized user.

pipe: a symbol that directs the operating system to divert the output of one command so it becomes the input of another command.

pirated software: illegally obtained software.

pits: tiny depressions on the reflective layer of a CD or DVD. Each pit is interpreted as a 0. Contrasts with *lands*, which are interpreted as 1s.

placement policy: the rules used by the virtual memory manager to determine where the virtual page is to be loaded in memory.

pointer: an address or other indicator of location.

polling: a software mechanism used to test the flag, which indicates when a device, control unit, or path is available.

portability: the ability to move an entire operating system to a machine based on a different processor or configuration with as little recoding as possible.

positive feedback loop: a mechanism used to monitor the system. When the system becomes underutilized, the feedback causes the arrival rate to increase.

POSIX: Portable Operating System Interface is a set of IEEE standards that defines the standard user and programming interfaces for operating systems so developers can port programs from one operating system to another.

preemptive scheduling policy: any process scheduling strategy that, based on predetermined policies, interrupts the processing of a job and transfers the CPU to another job. It is widely used in time-sharing environments.

prevention: a design strategy for an operating system where resources are managed in such a way that some of the necessary conditions for deadlock do not hold.

primary storage: see *main memory*.

primitives: well-defined, predictable, low-level operating system mechanisms that allow higher-level operating system components to perform their functions without considering direct hardware manipulation.

priority scheduling: a nonpreemptive process scheduling policy (or algorithm) that allows for the execution of high-priority jobs before low-priority jobs.

process: an instance of execution of a program that is identifiable and controllable by the operating system.

process control block (PCB): a data structure that contains information about the current status and characteristics of a process. Every process has a PCB.

process identification: a user-supplied unique identifier of the process and a pointer connecting it to its descriptor, which is stored in the PCB.

process scheduler: the low-level scheduler of the Processor Manager that sets up the order in which processes in the READY queue will be served by the CPU.

process scheduling algorithm: See *scheduling algorithm*.

process scheduling policy: See *scheduling policy*.

process state: information stored in the job's PCB that indicates the current condition of the process being executed.

process status: information stored in the job's PCB that indicates the current location in memory of the job and the resources responsible for that status.

Process Status Word (PSW): information stored in a special CPU register including the current instruction counter and register contents. It is saved in the job's PCB when it isn't running but is on HOLD, READY, or WAITING.

process synchronization: (1) the need for algorithms to resolve conflicts between processors in a multiprocessing environment; (2) the need to ensure that events occur in the proper order even if they are carried out by several processes.

process-based DO/S: a view of distributed operating systems that encompasses all the system's processes and resources. Process management is provided through the use of client/server processes.

processor: (1) another term for the CPU (central processing unit); (2) any component in a computing system capable of performing a sequence of activities. It controls the interpretation and execution of instructions.

Processor Manager: a composite of two submanagers, the Job Scheduler and the Process Scheduler. It decides how to allocate the CPU, monitors whether it is executing a process or waiting, and controls job entry to ensure balanced use of resources.

producers and consumers: a classic problem in which a process produces data that will be consumed, or used, by another process. It exhibits the need for process cooperation.

program: a unit of instructions.

protocol: a set of rules to control the flow of messages through a network.

proxy server: a server positioned between an internal network and an external network or the Internet to screen all requests for information and prevent unauthorized access to network resources.

PSW: see *Process Status Word*.

queue: a linked list of PCBs that indicates the order in which jobs or processes will be serviced.

QR (quick response) code: a square-like two-dimensional graphic that can be read by a QR scanner or app. Each code contains data or links that can be used by an app to access a website or data source.

race: a synchronization problem between two processes vying for the same resource. In some cases it may result in data corruption because the order in which the processes will finish executing cannot be controlled.

RAID: redundant arrays of independent disks. A group of hard disks controlled in such a way that they speed read access of data on secondary storage devices and aid data recovery.

RAM: random access memory. See *main memory*.

random access storage device: see *direct access storage device*.

read only memory (ROM): a type of primary storage in which programs and data are stored once by the manufacturer and later retrieved as many times as necessary. ROM does not allow storage of new programs or data.

readers and writers: a problem that arises when two types of processes need to access a shared resource such as a file or a database. Their access must be controlled to preserve data integrity.

read/write head: a small electromagnet used to read or write data on a magnetic storage medium.

READY: a job status that means the job is ready to run but is waiting for the CPU.

real-time system: the computing system used in time-critical environments that require guaranteed response times, such as navigation systems, rapid transit systems, and industrial control systems.

record: a group of related fields treated as a unit. A file is a group of related records.

recovery: (1) when a deadlock is detected, the steps that must be taken to break the deadlock by breaking the circle of waiting processes; (2) when a system is assaulted, the steps that must be taken to recover system operability and, in the best case, recover any lost data.

redirection: a symbol that directs the operating system to send the results of a command to or from a file or device other than a keyboard or monitor.

reentrant code: code that can be used by two or more processes at the same time; each shares the same copy of the executable code but has separate data areas.

register: a hardware storage unit used in the CPU for temporary storage of a single data item.

relative address: in a direct organization environment, it indicates the position of a record relative to the beginning of the file.

relative filename: a file's simple name and extension as given by the user. It contrasts with *absolute filename*.

reliability: (1) a standard that measures the probability that a unit will not fail during a given time period—it is a function of MTBF; (2) the ability of an operating system to respond predictably to error conditions, even those caused by hardware failures; (3) the ability of an operating system to actively protect itself and its users from accidental or deliberate damage by user programs.

relocatable dynamic partitions: a memory allocation scheme in which the system relocates programs in memory to gather together all of the empty blocks and compact them to make one block of memory that is large enough to accommodate some or all of the jobs waiting for memory.

relocation: (1) the process of moving a program from one area of memory to another; (2) the process of adjusting address references in a program, by either software or hardware means, to allow the program to execute correctly when loaded in different sections of memory.

relocation register: a register that contains the value that must be added to each address referenced in the program so that it will be able to access the correct memory addresses after relocation. If the program hasn't been relocated, the value stored in the program's relocation register is 0. It contrasts with *bounds register*.

remote login: the ability to operate on a remote computer using a protocol over a computer network as though locally attached.

remote station: the node at the distant end of a network connection.

repeated trials: repeated guessing of a user's password by an unauthorized user. It is a method used to illegally enter systems that rely on passwords.

replacement policy: the rules used by the virtual memory manager to determine which virtual page must be removed from memory to make room for a new page.

resource holding: one of four conditions for deadlock in which each process refuses to relinquish the resources it holds until its execution is completed, even though it isn't using them because it is waiting for other resources. It is the opposite of *resource sharing*.

resource sharing: the use of a resource by two or more processes either at the same time or at different times.

resource utilization: a measure of how much each unit is contributing to the overall operation of the system. It is usually given as a percentage of time that a resource is actually in use.

response time: one measure of the efficiency of an interactive system that tracks the time required for the system to respond to a user's command.

ring topology: a network topology in which each node is connected to two adjacent nodes. Ring networks have the advantage of not needing routing because all packets are simply passed to a node's upstream neighbor.

RIP: see *Routing Information Protocol*.

ROM (read-only-memory) chip: the chip that holds the software, called firmware, used to boot the device.

root directory: (1) for a disk, it is the directory accessed by default when booting up the computer; (2) for a hierarchical directory structure, it is the first directory accessed by a user.

rotational delay: a synonym for *search time*.

rotational ordering: an algorithm used to reorder record requests within tracks to optimize search time.

round robin: a preemptive process scheduling policy (or algorithm) that allocates to each job one unit of processing time per turn to ensure that the CPU is equally shared among all active processes and isn't monopolized by any one job. It is used extensively in interactive systems.

router: a device that forwards traffic between networks. The routing decision is based on network-layer information and routing tables, often constructed by routing protocols.

routing: the process of selecting the correct interface and next hop for a packet being forwarded.

Routing Information Protocol (RIP): a routing protocol used by IP. It is based on a distance-vector algorithm.

RUNNING: a job status that means that the job is executing.

safe state: the situation in which the system has enough available resources to guarantee the completion of at least one job running on the system.

SCAN: a scheduling strategy for direct access storage devices that is used to optimize seek time. The most common variations are *N-step SCAN* and *C-SCAN*.

scheduling algorithm: an algorithm used by the Job or Process Scheduler to allocate the CPU and move jobs or processes through the system.

scheduling policy: any policy used by the Processor Manager to select the order in which incoming jobs, processes, and threads will be executed.

script file: A series of executable commands written in plain text and executed by the operating system in sequence as a procedure.

search strategies: algorithms used to optimize search time in direct access storage devices. See also *rotational ordering*.

search time: the time it takes to rotate the drum or disk from the moment an I/O command is issued until the requested record is moved under the read/write head. Also called *rotational delay*.

second generation (1955–1965): the second era of technological development of computers, when the transistor replaced the vacuum tube. Computers were smaller and faster and had larger storage capacity than first-generation computers and were developed to meet the needs of the business market.

sector: a division in a disk's track. Sometimes called a *block*. The tracks are divided into sectors during the formatting process.

security descriptor: a Windows data structure appended to an object that protects the object from unauthorized access. It contains an access control list and controls auditing.

seek strategy: a predetermined policy used by the I/O device handler to optimize seek times.

seek time: the time required to position the read/write head on the proper track from the time the I/O request is issued.

segment: a variable-size section of a user's job that contains a logical grouping of code. It contrasts with *page*.

Segment Map Table (SMT): a table in main memory with the vital information for each segment including the segment number and its corresponding memory address.

segmented memory allocation: a memory allocation scheme based on the concept of dividing a user's job into logical groupings of code to allow for noncontiguous program storage during execution. It contrasts with *paged memory allocation*.

segmented/demand paged memory allocation: a memory allocation scheme based on the concept of dividing a user's job into logical groupings of code and loading them into memory as needed.

semaphore: a type of shared data item that may contain either binary or nonnegative integer values and is used to provide mutual exclusion.

sequential access medium: any medium that stores records only in a sequential manner, one after the other, such as magnetic tape. It contrasts with *direct access storage device*.

sequential record organization: the organization of records in a specific sequence. Records in a sequential file must be processed one after another.

server: a node that provides to clients various network services such as file retrieval, printing, or database access services.

server process: a logical unit composed of one or more device drivers, a device manager, and a network server module; needed to control clusters or similar devices, such as printers or disk drives, in a process-based distributed operating system environment.

service pack: a term used by some vendors to describe an update to customer software to repair existing problems and/or deliver enhancements.

sharable code: executable code in the operating system that can be shared by several processes.

shared device: a device that can be assigned to several active processes at the same time.

shortest job first (SJF): see *shortest job next*.

shortest job next (SJN): a nonpreemptive process scheduling policy (or algorithm) that selects the waiting job with the shortest CPU cycle time. Also called *shortest job first*.

shortest remaining time (SRT): a preemptive process scheduling policy (or algorithm), similar to the SJN algorithm, that allocates the processor to the job closest to completion.

shortest seek time first (SSTF): a scheduling strategy for direct access storage devices that is used to optimize seek time. The track requests are ordered so the one closest to the currently active track is satisfied first and the ones farthest away are made to wait.

site: a specific location on a network containing one or more computer systems.

SJF: see *shortest job first.*

SJN: see *shortest job next.*

smart card: a small, credit-card-sized device that uses cryptographic technology to control access to computers and computer networks. Each smart card has its own personal identifier, which is known only to the user, as well as its own stored and encrypted password.

sniffer: see *packet sniffer.*

social engineering: a technique whereby system intruders gain access to information about a legitimate user to learn active passwords, sometimes by calling the user and posing as a system technician.

socket: abstract communication interfaces that allow applications to communicate while hiding the actual communications from the applications.

software: a collection of programs used to perform certain tasks. They fall into three main categories: operating system programs, compilers and assemblers, and application programs.

spin lock: a Windows synchronization mechanism used by the kernel and parts of the executive that guarantees mutually exclusive access to a global system data structure across multiple processors.

spoofing: the creation of false IP addresses in the headers of data packets sent over the Internet, sometimes with the intent of gaining access when it would not otherwise be granted.

spooling: a technique developed to speed I/O by collecting in a disk file either input received from slow input devices or output going to slow output devices such as printers. Spooling minimizes the waiting done by the processes performing the I/O.

SRT: see *shortest remaining time.*

SSTF: see *shortest seek time first.*

stack: a sequential list kept in main memory. The items in the stack are retrieved from the top using a last-in first-out (LIFO) algorithm.

stack algorithm: an algorithm for which it can be shown that the set of pages in memory for n page frames is always a subset of the set of pages that would be in memory with $n + 1$ page frames. Therefore, increasing the number of page frames will not bring about Belady's anomaly.

star topology: a network topology in which multiple network nodes are connected through a single, central node. The central node is a device that manages the network. This topology has the disadvantage of depending on a central node, the failure of which would bring down the network.

starvation: the result of conservative allocation of resources in which a single job is prevented from execution because it is kept waiting for resources that never become available. It is an extreme case of *indefinite postponement.*

static partitions: another term for *fixed partitions.*

station: any device that can receive and transmit messages on a network.

storage: the place where data is stored in the computer system. Primary storage is main memory. Secondary storage is nonvolatile media, such as disks and flash memory.

store-and-forward: a network operational mode in which messages are received in their entirety before being transmitted to their destination, or to their next hop in the path to their destination.

stripe: a set of consecutive strips across disks; the strips contain data bits and sometimes parity bits depending on the RAID level.

subdirectory: a directory created by the user within the boundaries of an existing directory. Some operating systems call this a folder.

subroutine: also called a *subprogram*, a segment of a program that can perform a specific function. Subroutines can reduce programming time when a specific function is required at more than one point in a program.

subsystem: see *I/O subsystem.*

suffix: see *extension.*

supercomputers: extremely fast computers used for complex calculations at the fastest speed permitted by current technology.

symmetric configuration: a multiprocessing configuration in which processor scheduling is decentralized and each processor is of the same type. A single copy of the operating system and a global table listing each process and its status is stored in a common area of memory so every processor has access to it. Each processor uses the same scheduling algorithm to select which process it will run next.

synchronous interrupts: another term for *internal interrupts.*

system prompt: the signal from the operating system that it is ready to accept a user's command.

system survivability: the capability of a system to fulfill its mission, in a timely manner, in the presence of attacks, failures, or accidents.

task: (1) a term used to describe a process; (2) the basic unit of concurrent programming languages that defines a sequence of instructions that may be executed in parallel with other similar units; (3) for Android, collection of activities that users interact with when performing a certain job.

TCP/IP reference model: a common acronym for the suite of transport-layer and application-layer protocols that operate over the Internet Protocol.

terabyte (TB): a unit of memory or storage space equal to 1,099,511,627,776 bytes or 2^{40} bytes. One terabyte equals approximately 1 trillion bytes.

teraflop: a benchmark used to measure processing speed. One teraflop equals 1 trillion floating point operations per second.

test-and-set: an indivisible machine instruction known simply as *TS*, which is executed in a single machine cycle and was first introduced by IBM for its multiprocessing System 360/370 computers to determine whether the processor was available.

third generation: the era of computer development beginning in the mid-1960s that introduced integrated circuits and miniaturization of components to replace transistors, reduce costs, work faster, and increase reliability.

thrashing: a phenomenon in a virtual memory system where an excessive amount of page swapping back and forth between main memory and secondary storage results in higher overhead and little useful work.

thread: a portion of a process that can run independently. Multithreaded systems can have several threads running at one time with the same or different priorities.

Thread Control Block (TCB): a data structure that contains information about the current status and characteristics of a thread.

throughput: a composite measure of a system's efficiency that counts the number of jobs served in a given unit of time.

ticket granting ticket: a virtual *ticket* given by a Kerberos server indicating that the user holding the ticket can be granted access to specific application servers. The user sends this encrypted ticket to the remote application server, which can then examine it to verify the user's identity and authenticate the user.

time bomb: a virus with a trigger linked to a certain year, month, day, or time that causes it to execute.

time quantum: a period of time assigned to a process for execution. When it expires the resource is preempted, and the process is assigned another time quantum for use in the future.

time-sharing system: a system that allows each user to interact directly with the operating system via commands entered from a keyboard. Also called *interactive system*.

time slice: see *time quantum*.

token: a unique bit pattern that all stations on the LAN recognize as a permission to transmit indicator.

token bus: a type of local area network with nodes connected to a common cable using a CSMA/CA protocol.

token ring: a type of local area network with stations wired into a ring network. Each station constantly passes a token on to the next. Only the station with the token may send a message.

track: a path along which data is recorded on a magnetic medium such as CD, DVD, or hard disk.

transfer time: the time required for data to be transferred between secondary storage and main memory.

transport speed: the speed that a sequential storage medium, such as a magnetic tape, must reach before data is either written to or read from it.

trap door: an unspecified and nondocumented entry point to the system. It represents a significant security risk.

Trojan: a malicious computer program with side effects that are not intended by the user who executes the program. Also called a *Trojan horse*.

turnaround time: a measure of a system's efficiency that tracks the time required to execute a job and return output to the user.

universal serial bus (USB) controller: the interface between the operating system, device drivers, and applications that read and write to devices connected to the computer through the USB port. Each USB port can accommodate up to 127 different devices.

unsafe state: a situation in which the system has too few available resources to guarantee the completion of at least one job running on the system. It can lead to deadlock.

user: anyone who requires the services of a computer system.

user mode: name given to indicate that processes are not granted privileged access to the processor. Therefore, certain instructions are not allowed and system memory isn't accessible. Contrasts with the less restrictive *kernel mode*.

V: an operation performed on a semaphore that may cause a waiting process to continue. It stands for the Dutch word *verhogen,* meaning *to increment*, and it is part of the P and V operations to test and increment.

variable-length record: a record that isn't of uniform length, doesn't leave empty storage space, and doesn't truncate any characters, thus eliminating the two disadvantages of fixed-length records. It contrasts with a *fixed-length record*.

verification: the process of making sure that an access request is valid.

version control: the tracking and updating of a specific release of a piece of hardware or software.

victim: an expendable job that is selected for removal from a deadlocked system to provide more resources to the waiting jobs and resolve the deadlock.

virtual device: a dedicated device that has been transformed into a shared device through the use of spooling techniques.

virtual memory: a technique that allows programs to be executed even though they are not stored entirely in memory. It gives the user the illusion that a large amount of main memory is available when, in fact, it is not.

virtualization: the creation of a virtual version of hardware or software. Operating system virtualization allows a single CPU to run multiple operating system images at the same time.

virus: a program that replicates itself on a computer system by incorporating itself into other programs, including those in secondary storage, that are shared among other computer systems.

volume: any secondary storage unit, such as hard disks, disk packs, CDs, DVDs, or removable media. When a volume contains several files it is called a *multi-file volume*. When a file is extremely large and contained in several volumes it is called a *multi-volume file*.

WAIT and SIGNAL: a modification of the test-and-set synchronization mechanism that is designed to remove busy waiting.

WAITING: a job status that means that the job can't continue until a specific resource is allocated or an I/O operation has finished.

waiting time: the amount of time a process spends waiting for resources, primarily I/O devices. It affects throughput and utilization.

warm boot: a feature that allows the I/O system to recover I/O operations that were in progress when a power failure occurred.

wide area network (WAN): a network usually constructed with long-distance, point-to-point lines, covering a large geographic area.

widget: a program that smaller than an app designed to provide an "at-a-glance" view of an app's post important data to run on the device's home screen.

Wi-Fi®: a brand name, owned by the Wi-Fi Alliance, certifying that a device or other product is compatible with a set of IEEE broadband wireless networking standards.

working directory: the directory or subdirectory in which the user is currently working.

working set: a collection of pages to be kept in main memory for each active process in a virtual memory environment.

workstation: a desktop computer attached to a local area network that serves as an access point to that network.

worm: a computer program that replicates itself and is self-propagating in main memory.

Bibliography

Amdahl, G. (1967). "Validity of the Single Processor Approach to Achieving Large-Scale Computing Capabilities" (PDF). *AFIPS Conference Proceedings* (30): 483–485.

Anderson, R. E. (1991). ACM code of ethics and professional conduct: *Communications of the ACM. 35* (5), 94–99.

Apple (2012). *OS X Mountain Lion.* http://movies.apple.com/media/us/osx/2012/docs/OSX_MountainLion_Core_Technologies_Overview.pdf Accessed 8/17/2012.

Apple (2012). *OS X Server.* http://movies.apple.com/media/us/osx/2012/server/docs/OSXServer_Product_Overview.pdf. Accessed 8/17/2012.

Barnes, J. G. P. (1980). An overview of Ada. *Software Practice and Experience*, vol. 10, pp. 851–887.

Bays, C. (1977, March). A comparison of next-fit, first-fit, and best-fit. *CACM,* 20, 3, 191-192. http://doi.acm.org/10.1145/359436.359453. Accessed 8-17-2012.

Belady, L. A., Nelson, R. A., & Shelder, G. S. (1969, June). An anomaly in space-time characteristics of certain programs running in a paging environment. *CACM, 12*(6), 349–353.

Ben-Ari, M. (1982). *Principles of concurrent programming.* Englewood Cliffs, NJ: Prentice-Hall.

Bhargava, R. (1995). *Open VMS: architecture, use, and migration.* New York: McGraw-Hill.

Bic, L. & Shaw, A. C. (1988). *The logical design of operating systems* (2nd ed.). Englewood Cliffs, NJ: Prentice-Hall.

Bic, L. & Shaw, A. C. (2003). *Operating systems principles.* Upper Saddle River, NJ: Pearson Education, Inc.

Brain, M. (1994). *Win32 system services. The heart of Windows NT.* Englewood Cliffs, NJ: Prentice-Hall.

Bourne, S. R. (1987). *The UNIX system V environment.* Reading, MA: Addison-Wesley.

Burnette, E. (2010). Hello, Android: Introducing Google's Mobile Development Platform, third edition. Pragmatic Programmers.

Calingaert, P. (1982). *Operating system elements: A user perspective.* Englewood Cliffs, NJ: Prentice-Hall.

Christian, K. (1983). *The UNIX operating system.* New York: Wiley.

Cisco (2012) 802.11ac: The Fifth Generation of Wi-Fi, technical white paper, http://www.cisco.com/en/US/prod/collateral/wireless/ps5678/ps11983/white_paper_c11-713103.pdf , Accessed 11/27/12.

Columbus, L. & Simpson, N. (1995). *Windows NT for the technical professional.* Santa Fe: OnWord Press.

Courtois, P. J., Heymans, F. & Parnas, D. L. (1971, October). Concurrent control with readers and writers. *CACM, 14*(10), 667–668.

CSO Online (2011). 2011 CyberSecurity Watch Survey Results., www.csoonline.com, Accessed 8-17-2012.

Custer, H. (1993). *Inside Windows NT*. Redmond, WA: Microsoft Press.

Deitel, H., Deitel, P., & Choffnes, D. (2004). *Operating systems* (3rd ed.). Upper Saddle River, NJ: Pearson Education, Inc.

Denning, D.E. (1999). *Information warfare and security*. Reading, MA: Addison-Wesley.

Dijkstra, E. W. (1965). *Cooperating sequential processes*. Technical Report EWD-123, Technological University, Eindhoven, The Netherlands. Reprinted in Genuys (1968), 43–112.

Dijkstra, E. W. (1968, May). The structure of the T.H.E. multiprogramming system. *CACM, 11*(5), 341–346.

Dougherty, E.R. & Laplante, P.S. (1995). *Introduction to real-time imaging, Understanding Science & Technology Series*. New York: IEEE Press.

Dukkipati, N., Ganjali, Y., & Zhang-Shen, R. (2005). *Typical versus Worst Case Design in Networking*, Fourth Workshop on Hot Topics in Networks (HotNets-IV), College Park.

Fitzgerald, J. (1993). *Business data communications. Basic concepts, security, and design* (4th ed.). New York: Wiley.

Frank, L. R. (Ed.). (2001). *Quotationary*. New York: Random House.

Gal, E. & Toledo, S. (2005). *Algorithms and data structures for flash memories.* (Author Abstract). In ACM Computing Surveys, 37, 138(26).

Gollmann, D. (1999). *Computer security*. Chichester, England: Wiley.

Gosling, J. & McGilton, H. (1996). *The Java language environment: Contents*. Sun Microsystems, Inc., http://java.sun.com/docs/white/langenv/. Accessed 8-17-2012.

Harvey, M.S. & Szubowicz, L.S. (1996). Extending OpenVMS for 64-bit addressable virtual memory. *Digital Technical Journal, 8*(2), 57–70.

Havender, J. W. (1968). Avoiding deadlocks in multitasking systems. *IBMSJ, 7*(2), 74–84.

Haviland, K. & Salama, B. (1987). *UNIX system programming*. Reading, MA: Addison-Wesley.

Holt, R. C. (1972). Some deadlock properties of computer systems. ACM Computing Surveys, 4(3), 179–196.

Horvath, D. B. (1998). *UNIX for the mainframer* (2nd ed.). Upper Saddle River, NJ: Prentice-Hall PTR.

Howell, M.A. & Palmer, J.M. (1996). Integrating the Spiralog file system into the OpenVMS operating system. *Digital Technical Journal, 8*(2), 46–56.

Hugo, I. (1993). *Practical open systems. A guide for managers* (2nd ed.). Oxford, England: NCC Blackwell Ltd.

IEEE. (2004). *Standard for Information Technology — Portable Operating System Interface (POSIX) 1003.1-2001/Cor 2-2004*. IEEE Computer Society.

Intel. *What is Moore's Law?*, http://www.intel.com/about/companyinfo/museum/exhibits/moore.htm. Accessed 8-17-2012.

Johnson, J.E. & Laing, W.A. (1996). Overview of the Spiralog file system. *Digital Technical Journal, 8*(2), 5–14.

Laffan, L., (2011) "Open Governance Index, Measuring the true openness of open source projects from Android to WebKit" http://www.visionmobile.com/rsc/researchreports/Open%20Governance%20Index%20%28VisionMobile%29.pdf. Accessed Aug 17, 2012.

Lai, S.K. (2008). Flash memories: successes and challenges, IBM Journal Research & Development. 52(4/5), 529–535.

Lewis, T. (1999). Mainframes are dead, long live mainframes. *Computer, 32*(8), 102–104.

Ling, Y., Chen S., and Chiang C.-Y.J. 2006. On Optimal Deadlock Detection Scheduling. *IEEE Trans. Comput.* 55, 9 (September 2006), 1178-1187. DOI=10.1109/TC.2006.151 http://dx.doi.org/10.1109/TC.2006.151. Accessed 8/17/2012.

Linger, R.C. et al. (2002). Life-cycle models for survivable systems. (CMU/SEI-2002-TR-026). Pittsburgh, PA: Software Engineering Institute, Carnegie Mellon University.

Markoff, J., (2007, Nov 4) I, Robot: The Man Behind the Google Phone, The New York Times. http://www.nytimes.com/2007/11/04/technology. Accessed 1/16/13.

Merritt, R., (2012). Andy Rubin: After rough start, Android goes viral, eetimes.com. http://www.eetimes.com/electronics-news/4402119/Andy-Rubin–After-rough-start–Android-goes-viral. Accessed 2/11/13.

Microsoft (2012). Microsoft, Security Bulletin Summary for November 2012. http://technet.microsoft.com/en-us/security/bulletin/ms12-nov. Accessed 11/14/12.

Microsoft (2012). Windows Server 2012 Essentials Datasheet. http://www.microsoft.com/en-us/server-cloud/windows-server-essentials/default.aspx. Accessed 2/8/13.

Microsoft (2013). Signing in with a picture password. http://blogs.msdn.com/b/b8/archive/2011/12/16/signing-in-with-a-picture-password.aspx Accessed 5/20/13.

Moore, G. (1965, April 19). Cramming more components onto integrated circuits. *Electronics*, 38 (8), 114–117.

Negus, C. et al. (2007). *Linux Bible 2007 Edition*. Indianapolis, IN: Wiley Publishing.

NIST (2012). Guide to Enterprise Patch Management Technologies (Draft): Recommendations of the National Institute of Standards and Technology. NIST Special Publication 800-40, Revision 3 (Draft). http://csrc.nist.gov/publications/drafts/800-40/draft-sp800-40rev3.pdf. Accessed 10/30/2012.

Noyes, K. (2011, December 13) Is Android Open? Not so Much, Study Finds. PCWorld. http://www.pcworld.com/article/246140/is_android_open_not_so_much_study_finds.html. Accessed 4/24/13.

Open Group (2008), Base Specifications Issue 7, IEEE Std 1003.1-2008 http://pubs.opengroup.org/onlinepubs/9699919799/ Accessed 2/7/13.

Otellini, P. (2006). Paul Otellini CES Keynote. http://www.intel.com/pressroom/kits/events/ces2006/transcript-pso-keynote-ces2006.pdf. Accessed 8/17/2012.

Page, L. (2013) Update from the CEO. http://googleblog.blogspot.com/2013/03/update-from-ceo.html. Accessed April 25, 2013.

Pase, D.M. & Eckl, M.A. (2005). *A comparison of single-core and dual-core Opteron processor performance for HPC.* ftp://ftp.support.lotus.com/eserver/benchmarks/wp_Dual_Core_072505.pdf, Accessed 8-17-2012.

Petersen, R. (1998). *Linux: the complete reference* (2nd ed.). Berkeley, CA: Osborne/McGraw-Hill.

Pfaffenberger, B. (Ed.). (2001). *Webster's new world computer dictionary (9th ed.).* New York: Hungry Minds.

Pinkert, J. R. & Wear, L. L. (1989). *Operating systems: concepts, policies, and mechanisms.* Englewood Cliffs, NJ: Prentice-Hall.

Ritchie, D. M. & Thompson, K. (1978, July–August). The UNIX time-sharing system. *The Bell Systems Technical Journal, 57*(6), 1905–1929.

Root Uninstaller Team (2012). Battery Statistic on Android-powered Device Report (update 18 December 2012). http://www.rootuninstaller.com/2012/12/battery-statistic-on-android-powered.html. Accessed 2-12-13.

Rubini, A. & Corbet, J. (2001). *Linux Device Drivers* (2nd ed.). Sebastopol, CA: O'Reilly.

Ruley, J. D., et al. (1994). *Networking Windows NT.* New York: Wiley.

Shoch, J. F. & Hupp, J. A. (1982, March). The "worm" programs—early experience with a distributed computation. *Communications of the ACM, 25*(3), 172–180.

Stair, R.M. & Reynolds, G.W. (1999). *Principles of Information Systems* (4th ed.). Cambridge, MA: Course Technology-ITP.

Stuart, Brian L., (2009). *Principles of Operating Systems.* Course Technology, Boston.

Sverdlove, H. & Cilley, J. (2012). Pausing Google Play: more than 100,000 Android apps may pose security risks. www.bit9.com/download/reports/Pausing-Google-Play-October2012.pdf. Accessed 4-17-13.

Swabey, M., Beeby, S., Brown, A., & Chad, J. (2004). "Using Otoacoustic Emissions as a Biometric," *Proceedings of the First International Conference on Biometric Authentication, Hong Kong, China*, July 2004, 600–606.

The Open Group, (2012). The History of the Single UNIX® Specification Poster. www.unix.org/Posters/. Accessed 8-17-2012.

Thompson, K. (1978, July–August). UNIX implementation. *The Bell Systems Technical Journal, 57*(6), 1905–1929.

United States House of Representatives Committee on Energy and Commerce Subcommittee on Telecommunications and the Internet, March 2007. "The Future of the World Wide Web", Hearing on the "Digital Future of the United States: Part I. Washington, D.C.

Wall, K., Watson, M., & Whitis, M. (1999). *Linux programming unleashed.* Indianapolis, IN: Sams Publishing.